EXAMPLES & EXPLANATIONS

Sales and Leases

Ninth Edition

Scott J. Burnham
Professor Emeritus
Gonzaga University School of Law

James Brook
Professor Emeritus
New York Law School

ASPEN PUBLISHING

To contact Customer Service, e-mail customer.service@aspenpublishing.com, call 1-800-950-5259, or mail correspondence to:

Aspen Publishing
Attn: Order Department
1 Wall Street
Burlington, MA 01803

Printed in the United States of America.

1 2 3 4 5 6 7 8 9 0

ISBN 979-8-8920-7386-8

Library of Congress Cataloging-in-Publication Data application is in process.

SUSTAINABLE FORESTRY INITIATIVE Certified Sourcing
www.forests.org
SFI-00756

About Aspen Publishing

Aspen Publishing is a leading provider of educational content and digital learning solutions to law schools in the U.S. and around the world. Aspen provides best-in-class solutions for legal education through authoritative textbooks, written by renowned authors, and breakthrough products such as Connected eBooks, Connected Quizzing, and PracticePerfect.

The Aspen Casebook Series (famously known among law faculty and students as the "red and black" casebooks) encompasses hundreds of highly regarded textbooks in more than eighty disciplines, from large enrollment courses, such as Torts and Contracts to emerging electives such as Sustainability and the Law of Policing. Study aids such as the *Examples & Explanations* and the *Emanuel Law Outlines* series, both highly popular collections, help law students master complex subject matter.

Major products, programs, and initiatives include:

- **Connected eBooks** are enhanced digital textbooks and study aids that come with a suite of online content and learning tools designed to maximize student success. Designed in collaboration with hundreds of faculty and students, the Connected eBook is a significant leap forward in the legal education learning tools available to students.
- **Connected Quizzing** is an easy-to-use formative assessment tool that tests law students' understanding and provides timely feedback to improve learning outcomes. Delivered through CasebookConnect.com, the learning platform already used by students to access their Aspen casebooks, Connected Quizzing is simple to implement and integrates seamlessly with law school course curricula.
- **PracticePerfect** is a visually engaging, interactive study aid to explain commonly encountered legal doctrines through easy-to-understand animated videos, illustrative examples, and numerous practice questions. Developed by a team of experts, PracticePerfect is the ideal study companion for today's law students.
- The **Aspen Learning Library** enables law schools to provide their students with access to the most popular study aids on the market across all of their courses. Available through an annual subscription, the online library consists of study aids in e-book, audio, and video formats with full text search, note-taking, and highlighting capabilities.
- Aspen's **Digital Bookshelf** is an institutional-level online education bookshelf, consolidating everything students and professors need to ensure success. This program ensures that every student has access to affordable course materials from day one.
- **Leading Edge** is a community centered on thinking differently about legal education and putting those thoughts into actionable strategies. At the core of the program is the Leading Edge Conference, an annual gathering of legal education thought leaders looking to pool ideas and identify promising directions of exploration.

For Trevor, Grace, and Lenny
S.J.B.

For Isabelle
J.B.

Contents

Preface

I start with a simple assumption. You come to this book because for one reason or another you want to learn the basic law relating to sales and leases of goods as such transactions are governed by Articles 2 and 2A of the Uniform Commercial Code. You may be trying to pick this knowledge up on your own, but more likely you are in a course—a course devoted distinctly to these topics, a more expansive survey course in Commercial Law, or even a course in Contracts that covers these topics. The book may have been assigned or recommended as additional reading by the professor teaching the course, or you may have come upon it on your own as a means of review. Whatever the circumstances, I hope this book is of help. If it is, it will not be simply because you bought it, or even because of the considerable energy I put into writing it, but because of the time, energy, and the thought you put into using it. Here are a few basic points you should understand from the outset if you are to make the best use of what I have written and what you have bought.

- You can use it as a review text, but you may find it more helpful to think of it as a kind of workbook, giving you an organized way of working through the various sections, definitions, concepts, and controversies that make up the modern law of sale and lease of goods as rendered in Articles 2 and 2A of the Uniform Commercial Code.
- This volume is not a substitute for your own copy of the Uniform Commercial Code (including Official Comments). I will be quoting the Code from time to time. At other points, I may simply suggest that you consult or refresh yourself on the Code rule. What you have here should not distract you, however, from the fundamental proposition that the law you are learning is found in, not merely suggested by or illustrated through, the exact language of the Code as it has been enacted into law in the several states. I assume throughout that as you work through the material, you will always have at your side the primary text for the study of the sale and lease of goods, the Code itself.
- The general organization and sequence of chapters follows what is a fairly standard order in which the various topics are taken up in courses on Sales. If this book has been assigned or recommended by your professor, you will of course follow his or her instructions as to which chapters to look to and which examples to prepare. If you

are working through the book on your own and trying to coordinate it with your course, you should be able to determine fairly easily which chapters to take up just by the chapter headings, but if you are having any trouble finding where to turn, there is help available in the index and the table of U.C.C. sections at the back of the book.

- Each chapter is structured in the same way: an introductory text, a set of examples for you to ponder, followed finally by my own explanations of the questions asked and issues raised by the examples. The introductory text does not purport to outline or give a full account of the chapter's topic. In some chapters, the introductory text can be very brief. In others, it goes on for a while. But in any event the introductory text is meant only to set the stage; its purpose is to put you on the best possible course for learning through the examples by applying the Code rules to the facts given. To get the most out of this method, you should try to determine on your own how you expect the Code would deal with the example before you look at the explanation.

One final note on the examples. You might think of them as sample exam questions. If you do, it will not surprise you that analysis sometimes concludes with a "maybe" rather than with a simple yes or no. I am, after all, a law professor, and this subject, like any other you have already studied, has its unresolvable questions, places where the statute seems to be of little or no help, and "subtle" difficulties. On the other hand, don't think just because this is the study of law that the answer to even the simplest question must necessarily be open to argument or subject to competing analyses. Sometimes, perhaps most of the time, a question can and should be answered in a word or two, directly and without any hedging. Beyond that, of course, you should go on to say why—citing the Code, chapter and verse—you respond as you do. Here is some advice that applies both to analyzing the examples and to writing examination answers:

- Where an answer is given or suggested by a specific section of the Code, make reference to that section.
- Where a particular subsection is relevant, cite the subsection.
- Where a particular word or phrase in the section or subsection is of importance to your answer, identify exactly what that word or phrase is.
- Where an Official Comment answers—or seems to answer—the question, refer to it, reporting as you do whether you have any qualms or questions about the position taken in the Comment.
- Where the answer appears to be dictated by a single fact or a set of facts, make clear which facts are relevant.

If, as will sometimes be the case, the answer has to be "that depends," say on what you see the outcome depending. If you need to know other facts to better analyze the situation, say what you would want to know. If the answer seems to depend on how a court would interpret a particular provision or how it would settle a seeming conflict between two provisions, explain the various possible interpretations or resolutions and state what argues for one resolution over the other.

As I have said, I hope and expect this book will be helpful. If at the same time you find it stimulating and even mildly entertaining, then so much the better.

James Brook
October 2014

As this book has transitioned to a new principal author, you will find that most of Professor Brook's content remains, but there has been some significant reorganization.

The book now begins with a new chapter on Article 1. That chapter is part of a revised Part I that includes other introductory material; material on Formation is now in Part II. The book now ends with a new Part VII on Leases that consolidates the material on leases that was previously distributed throughout the book. Finally, the former Part VI, on Documentary Transactions, has been cut. If you are a faculty member who uses those chapters, you can find them at the Professor's Resources link on the product page of the Aspen Publishing website.

The Ninth Edition incorporates the changes made to the U.C.C. by the 2022 Amendments, primarily to address hybrid transactions and electronic commerce.

I am grateful to Professor Brook and to Aspen Publishing for the opportunity to contribute to this excellent book.

Scott J. Burnham
October 2023

Acknowledgments

I would like to thank Dean Anthony Crowell and former Dean Rick Matasar as well as Associate Deans Deborah Archer, Jethro Lieberman, and Carol Bucker, who have shown their support for this project in a variety of ways. I would also like to acknowledge the continuing contribution of my staff assistant, Silvy Singh, without whom my workdays would be far more difficult and a lot less pleasant. Thanks as well to my colleagues on the faculty at New York Law School and to the vast numbers of students at that school who have given me the opportunity to practice my teaching methods (and madness) on them over the years. The feedback that I've been given on my classroom work, as well as on various parts of these materials, in ways subtle and not so subtle, has been of enormous help even if I have not always recognized it at the time.

There is no question that this book would never have been brought to any kind of conclusion without the enthusiastic support and encouragement of a number of good people at Wolters Kluwer Publishers. I would particularly like to thank Carol McGeehan and Susan McClung. I also have to single out for special mention Joe Glannon, who was a friend long before either of us even dreamt of going to law school, much less making a career out of teaching law. His initial work on the Examples and Explanations series was the genesis for all that followed, including this effort.

James Brook

I would like to thank Joseph Wagner, a student at Gonzaga University School of Law, Nick Jordan, a student at University of Baltimore School of Law, and Jay Baker, a student at The University of Montana School of Law, for their assistance. I am grateful to the people at Aspen Publishing, including in particular Elaine Page, for their work on this Ninth Edition.

Scott J. Burnham

Introduction — A Brief History of Sales Law

People have been buying and selling stuff for a long time, and so it should come as no surprise that the law governing such activity has a long and varied history. In this book, we will be concerned with the rules governing the buying, selling, and leasing of goods as they now stand under Articles 1, 2, and 2A of the Uniform Commercial Code. A bit of history, however, will help to put our studies into perspective.

For our purposes, we pick up the story of the sale of goods in medieval England. By the 1300s and 1400s, the system of common law courts acting in the name of the King had already taken shape and their far-reaching powers had been recognized. Disputes involving sales of goods, however, did not, for the most part, find their way into this national court system. Such disputes were the province of a separate set of more narrowly focused courts operating at the local level. Such courts were usually to be found in one of the principal market towns or occurring in conjunction with the regional trading fairs that were held on a regular basis at various places in England. Such courts became the specialists in dealing with disagreements between merchants, applying a set of rules that came to be thought of as, to some degree, a coherent body of rules and principles comprising the law merchant or mercantile law.

It was only later, during the seventeenth century, that the national system of common law courts began to expand its competence and jurisdiction to include commercial disputes. Eventually, the common law of sales, which often but not always adopted the reasoning and results of the mercantile law, replaced the older system. Eventually, the distinct set of mercantile courts died out.

What we characterize as the modern law of sales is a relatively recent phenomenon. It was only in the middle of the 1800s that there appeared the first general treatises attempting to set out a systematic view of the common law as it related to the purchase and sale of goods. At the same time, however, one of the grandest features of the common law — its very commonality, the supposed uniformity and predictability that it offered to the country as a whole — was being sorely tested in the United States of America, which is after all one big patchwork quilt of jurisdictions. No doubt each of the states applied what it saw as the principles of the common law of sales to purchase-and-sale transactions. Similarly, each state applied common law principles to other areas of commercial life. The problem, however, was that as each state's common law jurisprudence in a given field of commercial endeavor was advanced, refined, and further explicated by a steady stream of decisions, it was perhaps inevitable that there would develop a growing disparity among the common law renderings of the several states.

At the same time, there was a "codification" movement in Anglo-American law that called for the law to be reduced to codes that were intended to supplant the common law. Louisiana had its French civil code from the beginning—and is the only state that has not enacted Article 2 of the U.C.C. to govern sales law. The most famous American code, the Field Code written by David Dudley Field, was largely enacted in California after that state obtained statehood in 1849, providing California with a code for contracts and sales. Other states followed suit, and codes modeled on the California Code were enacted in states that included Montana, the Dakotas, and Oklahoma. So, in the United States, lawyers (and, not incidentally, ordinary folks going about their daily business) were subject to different variants of the same commercial law principles in each of the states, some found in the common law and others found in codes.

In many fields, the steadily increasing divergence, both stylistic and substantive, in the law of the states was troubling, and not just in a theoretical sense; it made life more difficult. It was perhaps in the arena of commercial endeavor that this lack of uniformity and predictability was felt most keenly. As more and more individuals and firms reached out to enter into contracts and do business in places farther and farther from their home base, it became increasingly apparent that the lack of uniformity of basic commercial law was more than a minor nuisance. It might be noted that until it decided *Erie Railroad Co. v. Tompkins*, 304 U.S. 64, in 1938, the U.S. Supreme Court weighed in on commercial law matters, but its rulings were piecemeal and did not provide a cohesive body of federal common law.

Throughout the nineteenth century, pressure was building for a change and some way out of this predicament. One response was the advancement of what is referred to as the "uniform law movement," which also tapped into the growing sentiment in favor of a codification or statutory treatment of difficult areas of the law. At the end of the nineteenth century, a group was formed by the name of the National Conference of Commissioners on Uniform State Laws (NCCUSL, or as it has chosen to refer to itself in more recent years, the Uniform Law Commission, or ULC). The Uniform Law Commission, a kind of quasi-government group, is made up of representatives of each of the states. These representatives are chosen by different methods in different states, usually by the governor acting alone or in conjunction with the state legislature. The Commission itself can make no law. Its role is to investigate, argue over, and eventually formulate and adopt recommended legislation. The "Official Versions" of its recommended Uniform Acts are then forwarded to each of the states for consideration. The fate of any of the recommended Uniform Acts is up to the legislative processes in each of the states. The idea is that if each of the states adopts the suggested legislation in exactly the Official Version form, then blessed uniformity and predictability has been achieved. Of course, in reality it doesn't work that way. An adopting state more often than not enacts a variation of the Official Version.

Among the earliest of the Uniform Acts was the Uniform Sales Act, drafted for the Uniform Law Commission by the eminent Professor Samuel Williston of Harvard. Promulgated in 1906 and later amended in 1922, the Uniform Sales Act was eventually adopted in more than 30 states. By the late 1930s and into the 1940s, the feeling began to grow, however, that this Uniform Sales Act, along with several other uniform acts covering other aspects of commercial law, were in need of revision and updating. Teamed up by this time with the American Law Institute (ALI) (whose work you are no doubt familiar with in connection with the various Restatements of common law topics), the Uniform Law Commission determined that the various pieces of recommended uniform commercial legislation would be reconfigured into a single Uniform Commercial Code. The Uniform Commercial Code (U.C.C.) would bring together, in substantially revised form, a number of previous uniform acts as well as some topics not previously subjected to the uniform law approach. The noted Professor Karl Llewellyn of Columbia University was appointed Chief Reporter (a kind of editor-in-chief) of the project.

The history of the drafting and redrafting, politicking, name-calling, and eventual set of compromises that led up to the adoption of the Uniform Commercial Code in its 1962 Official Version is a story unto itself. See Allen Kamp, *Between-the-Wars Social Thought: Karl Llewellyn, Legal Realism, and the Uniform Commercial Code in Context*, 59 Alb. L. Rev. 325 (1995); *Uptown Act: A History of the Uniform Commercial Code: 1940-49*; 51 S.M.U. L. Rev. 275 (1998); *Downtown Code: A History of the Uniform Commercial Code 1949-1954*, 49 Buff. L. Rev. 359 (2001). Suffice it to say that by 1968, the U.C.C. had been adopted by all 50 states (although Louisiana did not enact Article 2), the District of Columbia, and the Virgin Islands. Guam came aboard in 1977. Although §1-101 tells us that "This [Act] may be cited as the Uniform Commercial Code," in fact, because of the local variations, it would be more accurate to say that there is a New York U.C.C., an Idaho U.C.C., etc. Article 2 of this Uniform Commercial Code was the successor of the Uniform Sales Act, dealing with the sale of goods. In 1990, a new and distinct Article 2A, dealing with the lease of goods, made its way into the Official Version of the U.C.C. and was quickly adopted by the states. See Amy Boss, *The History of Article 2A: A Lesson for Practitioner and Scholar Alike*, 39 Ala. L. Rev. 575 (1988).

Article 2 was promulgated when a substantial part of the U.S. economy involved the sale of goods. While that is still the case, information transactions are now a significant and growing part of the economy. To meet the demand for a body of law to govern information transactions, after exploring the idea of adding a Code section on point, the ULC drafted UCITA, the

Uniform Computer Information Transactions Act. After UCITA was enacted in only two states—Maryland and Virginia—the ULC withdrew it and it is unlikely to have any further enactments. So what law governs information transactions? In the absence of a specifically applicable body of law, many courts have applied Article 2 to them. Furthermore, many drafters of software licenses have modeled their agreements (often called EULAs, or End User License Agreements) after contracts for the sale of goods. Therefore, while it makes sense to apply Article 2 to information transactions, always remember that you are applying the provisions of Article 2 by analogy rather than directly, since the transaction does not involve the sale of goods.

International trade has grown exponentially since Article 2 was first adopted. The need for law to govern international sales of goods has been satisfied in many ways, including the promulgation of a treaty called the United Nations Convention on the International Sale of Goods, often called the UNCISG or CISG. It governs goods transactions between businesses (but not individuals) located in countries that have signed the treaty, including the United States and most of its trading partners. The CISG has many similarities to Article 2, though it also has significant differences, including the absence of a Statute of Frauds and a Parol Evidence Rule. In spite of these similarities, many U.S. businesses use their freedom of contract to opt out of the applicability of the CISG. They often provide instead that the U.C.C. of a particular state governs the transaction. Therefore, you will find that Article 2 often applies to international transactions for the sale of goods because of the parties' choice of law.

For the most part, the original version of Article 2 has stood the test of time fairly well. Inevitably, however, difficulties were soon encountered, as courts and commentators discovered gaps and ambiguous or simply infelicitous statutory language. Concern was also expressed that the original version of Article 2 was not adequate to address certain issues that had arisen in connection with the newer commercial practices that had evolved since the 1960s, such as electronic commerce. In early 1988, the bodies responsible for the upkeep of the Code, the ULC and the ALI, appointed a study committee to make a recommendation on whether Articles 2 and 2A as they then stood should be revised. This study group eventually reported its belief that a significant revision was necessary. By 1991, a drafting committee was appointed to take on the task.

The process from this point forward was decidedly rough going. The original drafting committee's labors eventually resulted in a 1999 draft for proposed revision, but its proposal encountered significant opposition from several powerful and well-placed groups. The 1999 draft was withdrawn from consideration at the last minute during the ULC Annual Meeting held that year. See *Symposium, Perspectives on the Uniform Laws Revision Process*, 52 Hastings L.J. 603 (2001). The drafting committee, finding its ambitious proposal for revision rejected (or perhaps merely misunderstood), felt honor-bound to resign. Soon thereafter, a new drafting committee was appointed and given a much more modest charge. It was to craft a less sweeping set of revisions to the original Articles 2 and 2A and report its proposals back to the appropriate governing bodies quickly. The product of this new drafting committee was eventually approved by both the ULC and the ALI in the summer of 2003. What resulted was referred to as the "new" or "revised" 2003 Official Version of Articles 2 and 2A of the Uniform Commercial Code.

However, there were still powerful forces opposed to the revision and no particular significant groups with that much interest in lobbying for its adoption. Many knowledgeable Code observers quickly concluded that the proposed revision would be for all intents and purposes "dead on arrival" when it was forwarded to the state legislatures for their consideration. As things proceeded, such predictions proved to be spot on. Not a single state adopted or even evinced any great interest in the revision proposals. Finally, in the late spring of 2011, both the ALI and the ULC decided to bow to the realities of the situation. The 2003 proposed revision of Articles 2 and 2A were formally withdrawn from those organizations' Official Text of the Uniform Commercial Code.

There were revisions to Article 1 in 2001 that resulted in the tweaking of a few sections of Article 2. In 2022, Amendments to the Code were adopted that facilitated electronic commerce and that clarified the applicability of Article 2 to "hybrid transactions"—transactions that involve goods and something else. The states have been slow to adopt the 2022 Amendments, however, largely because of controversial changes to Article 9. This book discusses the changes the 2022 Amendments made to Articles 1, 2, and 2A, but because they have not been widely adopted, it also continues the discussion of the prior version. The challenge to adapt a code written for an earlier time to our modern needs continues.

Sales and Leases

PART I

Introduction to Articles 1 and 2

CHAPTER 1

Article 1

ARTICLE 1

Our study of Article 2 begins with Article 1. That is because the provisions in Article 1 apply to all the Articles in the Code. So the provisions of Article 1 are just as much a part of Articles 2 and 2A as anything else in those Articles. In case there is any doubt, §1-102 tells us that. You would think this was so obvious that the Code would not have to spell it out, but in fact there have been some court decisions that applied the rules of Article 1 to non-Code cases. So when Article 1 was revised, the drafters added this provision to prevent that from happening again. They also included a snarky Official Comment, telling us that this provision adds nothing new but merely "makes clear what has always been the case."

Article 1 contains definitions of terms that apply throughout the Code. When the Code uses a term, you don't want to use the dictionary definition if the term is defined in the Code, so you will frequently refer back to Article 1 as you read other Code sections. For example, here's §2-204(1), which we will examine shortly. The italicized words are all defined in Article 1.

> (1) A *contract for sale* of *goods* may be made in any manner sufficient to show *agreement*, including conduct by both parties which recognizes the existence of such a *contract*.

If you use a statutory supplement that contains the Code, at the end of the Official Comment, you will find a list of "Definitional Cross References."

This guide is not always accurate, however, and the section may well include other defined terms, but it is a good place to start to determine which words in the section are defined in the Code.

Section 1-201 is captioned "General Definitions." However, Article 1 defines some terms in other sections. See §§1-202 to 1-205. Furthermore, each Article has its own definition section, and sometimes the same word has a different definition in a different Article. For example, in Article 2, §2-105(1) defines "goods." But "goods" is also defined in §9-102(a)(44), so when you are working with Article 2, you should use the definition of "goods" in §2-105, and when you are working with Article 9, you should use the definition of "goods" in §9-102.

When you are faced with a contracts question, either on an exam or in real life, the first issue you will have to resolve is usually: What law applies to this transaction? If it involves the sale of goods, you will search for applicable rules in Article 2 because that body of law is the subset of contract law that applies to transactions in goods. But frequently you will find an issue in a goods transaction for which Article 2 does not supply a rule. In that case, you will go to other statutes or the common law to find the rule. In fact, §1-103(b) tells you to do this:

> (b) Unless displaced by the particular provisions of the Uniform Commercial Code, the principles of law and equity, including the law merchant and the law relative to capacity to contract, principal and agent, estoppel, fraud, misrepresentation, duress, coercion, mistake, bankruptcy, and other validating or invalidating cause supplement its provisions.

Note that this provision tells you that the rules outside the Code apply only if the Code has not "displaced" the other rule. That is, if there is an Article 2 rule on point, then it has expressly displaced the other rule, so you apply the Code rule. But if there is no Article 2 rule on point, then you apply the other rule. You will find, for example, that Article 2 has a rule on unanticipated events in §2-615, so when that is the issue, you would apply the Article 2 rule. On the other hand, Article 2 has nothing to say about frustration of purpose, so if that is the issue, then you would apply the common law rule on frustration.

For transactional lawyers, probably the most important provision in Article 1 is §1-302(a), which I call the "freedom of contract" provision. It tells us that many of the Code rules are default rules, and the parties are free to change them. There are some rules that are specifically immutable, however; that is, the parties cannot draft around them. For example, parties cannot agree that a provision that is unconscionable under §2-302 is nevertheless enforceable. Some Code sections are prefaced by language such as "unless otherwise agreed," signaling that what follows is a default rule. Unfortunately, however, the rules don't always make clear which are default rules and which are immutable rules. The confusion is not ameliorated by §1-302(c), which tells us that just because a section is not prefaced by the "unless otherwise agreed" language, that does not mean it is not a default rule. Figuring that out will be part of our study.

The Code uses a lot of weasel words like "reasonable." Section 1-302(b) tells us that although the parties may not disclaim the obligations of good faith, reasonableness, diligence, and care, they may "determine the standards by which the performance of those obligations is to be measured." This language invites the drafter to replace the flexible term with a more precise one. For example, the buyer has a reasonable time to inspect the goods before they are deemed accepted. See §2-513. The parties have freedom of contract to change this default rule by providing that the buyer has a certain amount of time to complete the inspection. This freedom is not unlimited, however. Although §1-302(b) provides that the parties have the freedom to define what they mean by "reasonable," the provision cannot be "manifestly unreasonable."

Another important provision is the admonition in §1-103(a) to "liberally construe" the Code in order to carry out its purposes:

> The Uniform Commercial Code must be liberally construed and applied to promote its underlying purposes and policies, which are: (1) to simplify, clarify, and modernize the law governing commercial transactions; (2) to permit the continued expansion of commercial practices through custom, usage, and agreement of the parties; and (3) to make uniform the law among the various jurisdictions.

This provision takes on greater weight because of the inability of the Uniform Law Commission (ULC) and the American Law Institute (ALI) to substantially revise Article 2 in the more than 50 years since its initial enactments. To continue to modernize the law, courts need to be flexible in applying Code provisions.

The purpose of honoring custom, usage, and agreement of the parties, brings to mind the practicality of Lord Mansfield, who was the Lord Chief Justice of England in the late eighteenth century. Rather than dictating the rules from on high for the merchants of England to follow, he instead formed juries of merchants to determine what their practices were, and he would adopt that practice as the law. The Code wants the tradition of incorporating practices into the law to continue.

Section 1-201(b)(3) defines the "agreement" of the parties as including course of performance, course of conduct, and trade usage even though they did not expressly agree to do so:

> **"Agreement"**, as distinguished from "contract", means the bargain of the parties in fact, as found in their language or inferred from other circumstances, including course of performance, course of dealing, or usage of trade as provided in Section 1-303.

Because these principles are so important, we will devote an entire chapter to them. See Chapter 7.

Another goal of the Code is to make the law uniform, so there are not 51 laws of Sales in the various U.S. jurisdictions, but ideally only one. That ideal is rarely attained, however. Although the ULC frowns on the practice, every jurisdiction has gone its own way by adopting nonuniform Code provisions. You can find useful secondary sources that enumerate the nonuniform provisions by Code section and by state. See, for example, Uniform Laws Annotated and the U.C.C. Digest.

The Code also becomes nonuniform because there are many areas where it does not speak and courts have to fill in the gap in the law. Ideally, courts should fill those gaps in uniform ways. For example, there was a case in which the Seventh Circuit was asked to fill in a gap in a Code provision by applying the law of Illinois even though Illinois had not decided the question. Judge Posner had a clear view on what he thought the applicable rule should be. However, he noted that his role as a federal judge in a diversity case that applied state law was not to determine the best rule, but to determine what rule the Illinois Supreme Court would apply. He found that Illinois often followed the rule that most other courts had chosen. Therefore, instead of applying the better rule, he chose the rule that had been adopted by most other states, thus helping to further the Code goal of uniformity. See *Northrop Corp. v. Litronic Industries*, 29 F.3d 1173 (7th Cir. 1994).

My reference to that Seventh Circuit case should serve as a reminder that Code law is state law. If a federal court has jurisdiction of a Code case, usually because of diversity jurisdiction, it will apply the law of a particular state. Which state law a court applies is a matter of applying the body of law known as "choice of law." There are choice of law rules to determine which state's law governs, but these are default rules. As stated in §1-301, the parties generally have freedom to choose the applicable law as long as the transaction bears a "reasonable relation" to the law that is chosen. As you read Code cases, make it a habit to determine which state's law is being applied and how that choice of law was made.

The nonuniform Code provisions will be important in your practice, when you will need to work with the Code as enacted in a particular jurisdiction. But for purposes of your law school class and the uniform bar exam, you will need to be familiar only with the uniform version.

EXAMPLES

Examples

1. The parties to a contract for the sale of goods provide that the buyer has ten days from delivery to complete an inspection. Is that provision enforceable? What if they provide that the buyer has ten minutes to complete the inspection?

2. The Seventh Circuit Court of Appeals is asked to determine whether a provision in a contract for the sale of goods is enforceable when it gives the buyer two days to inspect the goods. The court finds that Indiana law governs the case, but it finds no Indiana cases on point. The court decides that under the facts, two days is manifestly unreasonable, so the provision is not enforceable. Shortly after that decision came down, a state court in Illinois (which is in the Seventh Circuit) is asked to decide a case on the same facts. Is the Seventh Circuit decision mandatory authority for that court? What if it was a state court in Indiana?

3. A contract for the sale of goods between a California corporation and a China corporation provides, "California law applies to this transaction." What law governs?

4. You are an attorney in Montana and your client wants to buy a horse from a horse dealer in Montana. You check the copy of the Uniform Commercial Code that you used for class, and you see that §2-314(1) provides that "a warranty that the goods shall be merchantable is implied in a contract for their sale if the seller is a merchant with respect to goods of that kind." Because your client is purchasing from a seller who is a horse merchant, are you sure that your client is getting a warranty of merchantability?

5. A man agrees in writing to sell his car to his neighbor for $2,000. He then tries to avoid the transaction on the grounds that he suffered from a lack of capacity at the time he entered the contract. Is this transaction governed by Article 2?

6. You are researching the Montana law of good faith in a Code transaction. "Good faith" is defined in §1-201(b)(20). You find a 1990 case from Montana and a case that just came down from New York that seem right on point. Before you cite either of these cases as authority, what do you need to find out?

7. ABC Corporation, which is incorporated in Delaware, agrees to sell widgets to DEF Corporation, which is incorporated in California. The contract is first signed by ABC at its headquarters in Chicago, Illinois, and then signed by DEF at its headquarters in Seattle, Washington. The

widgets will be manufactured in Nevada, where ABC will ship them by carrier to DEF's plant in Texas. The contract provides that Montana law applies to the transaction. A dispute arises that is heard in federal court in Delaware. What state's U.C.C. governs this transaction?

Explanations

EXPLANATIONS

1. The default rule of §2-513 provides that the buyer has a reasonable time to inspect the goods before they are deemed accepted. Using the freedom of contract rule of §1-302(b), the parties would be free to vary the default rule by replacing "reasonable time" with ten days. However, they would probably not be free to provide that the buyer has ten minutes. That would be "manifestly unreasonable" because it would in effect vitiate the buyer's right of inspection.

2. Sales law is state law. Therefore, when the Seventh Circuit decides the case using Indiana law, it is merely deciding how it thinks the Supreme Court of Indiana would rule on the question. Even though it is in the Seventh Circuit, the ruling is not mandatory authority for an Illinois court; it is merely persuasive. In fact, it is not mandatory authority for an Indiana court either. That court is perfectly free to prove the Seventh Circuit wrong about how it thought an Indiana court would rule. See, e.g., *Kinesoft Development Corp. v. Softbank Holdings, Inc.*, 139 F. Supp. 2d 869, 889 (N.D. Ill. 2001) (pointing out that in *Air Safety, Inc. v. Teachers Realty Corp.*, 706 N.E.2d 882 (Ill. 1999), the Illinois Supreme Court had rejected the view of the Seventh Circuit in *AM International, Inc. v. Graphic Management Assoc., Inc.*, 44 F.3d 572 (7th Cir. 1995)).

3. Since the United States and China have both signed the United Nations Convention for the International Sale of Goods (UNCISG or CISG), the default rule is that the CISG applies. However, the parties have attempted to use their freedom of contract to change that default rule. Several cases have found, however, that this language is not sufficient to change the default rule. See, e.g., *Assante Technologies, Inc. v. PMC-Sierra, Inc.*, 164 F. Supp. 2d 1142 (N.D. Cal. 2001). While I don't agree, their reasoning goes like this: *You chose California law. California is a state in the U.S. and must honor all treaties entered into by the U.S. The U.S. is a signatory to the CISG. Therefore, California law includes the CISG. Therefore, the CISG applies to this transaction.* To avoid this problem, a more careful drafter would provide "The California U.C.C. applies to this transaction" or "California law applies to this transaction except that the parties expressly do not want the UNCISG to apply to this transaction."

4. The copy of the U.C.C. you use in class is the uniform version, but no state has adopted that version without changes. Each state is free to enact nonuniform provisions. Therefore, in an actual transaction, you need to

check the Code enacted by the state whose law is applicable. If Montana law applies, you will find that Montana has enacted a nonuniform provision in this area. Montana Code Annotated §30-2-316(d) provides: "in sales of cattle, hogs, sheep, or horses, there are no implied warranties, as defined in this chapter, that the cattle, hogs, sheep, or horses are free from sickness or disease." The lesson—make sure you research the law of the particular jurisdiction in case that jurisdiction has enacted a nonuniform provision.

5. Trick question! Because a car is a good, the transaction involves the sale of goods, so it is governed by Article 2. However, there is no rule in Article 2 on capacity to contract. Therefore, we would use §1-103(b) to supplement the Code with the state's rule on capacity to contract in order to answer this question.

6. The language of the Code is not the same in every jurisdiction, and even within a jurisdiction, it is sometimes revised. Article 1 was substantially revised in 2001, and among the significant changes was a change in the definition of "good faith." See Chapter 9. Therefore, the Montana case may no longer be relevant since the definition has changed. While cases from other jurisdictions may be persuasive authority, again you have to check whether the statute is the same in each jurisdiction. In fact, Montana enacted the definition of "good faith" in Revised Article 1, but New York did not—it retained the old definition. Therefore, the New York case may not be relevant since the definition is different.

7. According to §1-301, the parties are free to choose the governing law as long as it bears a reasonable relation to the transaction. Here, the parties chose Montana law, but the facts do not indicate that Montana has any relation to the transaction. Therefore, the court is unlikely to enforce this provision and instead will choose the law of the jurisdiction that would have applied if the parties had not chosen the law.

   Solving this problem is complicated by the fact that there are two competing choice of law rules, and which one is applied will depend on which is the law of the forum state, which is Delaware. One rule, known as the old rule, is that you choose the law of the jurisdiction where the last act took place that resulted in the formation of a contract. Here, when ABC signed the contract, it made an offer; when DEF signed the contract, it signified acceptance. Because acceptance is the last act that took place that resulted in contract formation, that act took place in Washington, so that state would provide the law if Delaware applies the old rule.

   The other choice of law rule, known as the new rule, is that you choose the law of the jurisdiction that has the most significant contacts with the transaction. Here, there are many states that have contacts with the transaction. Restatement (Second) of Conflict of Laws §191 states that with the sale of goods, the most significant contact is the place of delivery. You might think that is Texas, where the goods will be delivered. But as you will learn in Chapter 24, when goods are shipped by carrier, they are usually considered delivered when they are put in the hands of the carrier. Here, that happened in Nevada, so Nevada law would apply if Delaware applies the new rule.

Unfortunately, although the Code is largely uniform, there are many variations, so the jurisdiction that supplies the law may make a significant difference. Fortunately, you will not encounter these problems until you are in practice.

CHAPTER 2

The Scope of Article 2

BY WAY OF INTRODUCTION

Let's start at the very beginning. Look at §2-101. I often joke that even though it is called a Uniform Commercial Code, it is not uniform, it is not commercial, and it is not a code. Although this is a bit of an exaggeration, here's what I mean. As discussed in the Introduction, each adopting jurisdiction has its own version of Article 2, so it isn't really uniform. And while we often think of "commerce" or "commercial" as involving big business, that is not true of Article 2. It applies to any sale of goods, including my selling you a pen for 25 cents, your buying a box of pens from a store, or a large corporation buying thousands of pens from a distributor or manufacturer. Think of "commerce" in Article 2 as meaning buying and selling. Finally, while it is in the form of a code, Article 2 is hardly self-contained. Frequently, it incorporates concepts from the common law, and some of its provisions are not meaningful without the common law to put meat on the bones. As Grant Gilmore famously said, it is a "common law code."

Now move on to §2-102. Necessarily, this section is of prime importance. If there is a reason for studying Article 2 of the Uniform Commercial Code—and as a user of this book you had better believe there is—it is because Article 2 is the *source of law* covering a large number of claims and controversies. Section 2-102 is the obvious starting point for our discussion because it states which situations are governed by the law as laid down in Article 2. As a practical matter, when a bar exam or a client asks you a question about contracts, you must immediately decide which fork in the road to take—if it is a situation not "within the scope" of Article 2 (or Article 2A, the subject of Part VII), you will have to look elsewhere for the rules and for a book to guide you. If it is a situation governed by either Article 2 or Article 2A, you've come to the right place.

To the lawyers and parties to actual controversies, it can be vitally important which body of law governs their individual situation. If neither Article 2 nor 2A governs, there should be some law out there waiting to be applied to the dispute. Often enough, the results under varying bodies of law will differ, and the success or failure of a party's case will ride on which rules apply. That's the way the law works.

This is not the place to recite all of the particular results generated by Article 2 and how its workings differ from other possibly applicable legal regimens. That is, in effect, what this entire book is about. By way of introduction, however, and to offer some context for the issues of scope that this chapter will explore, a few examples may be helpful. First, there is the Statute of Limitations. If a dispute is governed by the law laid down in Article 2, then the applicable Statute of Limitations is found in §2-725 (which may vary from one jurisdiction to another). If the dispute is governed by other law, then the applicable Statute of Limitations is to be found in the law of the jurisdiction that governs the transaction. It may provide for a longer limitation period, or the period could be shorter. It is almost assuredly going to be different in at least some respect. Sometimes you will see a claim for personal injuries brought as an Article 2 claim. This is often because the plaintiff missed the Statute of Limitations for a tort claim and brought the claim as consequential damages resulting from a breach. See §2-715(2). Especially given the all-or-nothing consequences that attach to the application of the Statute of Limitations, it is not surprising that many cases in which the scope of Article 2 is made an issue have dealt with the problem of which Statute of Limitation governs.

A second important aspect of Article 2 for which many litigants find it important to fight is the wide range of warranty protection granted to buyers under §§2-312 through 2-315. The details of warranty law under Article 2 will take us a number of chapters to master (see Part III). Suffice it to say for the present that being allowed to proceed on a warranty theory can be very powerful for a claimant. Liability on a warranty is a matter of strict liability. The warranty claims can be asserted against the seller even though it was not the seller's fault that the goods are defective. Obviously, that fact alone can easily spell the difference between success and defeat for a plaintiff. For many an aggrieved individual, the most important part of his or her case may be establishing the right to go by the name of "buyer" under Article 2 of the U.C.C. and to assert the buyer's rights.

As an example, a few years ago I bought a candy bar from a big box retailer. When I bit into it, I broke a tooth. I wrote to the manufacturer of the candy bar but got no relief other than a coupon for a free candy bar, which is not exactly what I was looking for. Finally, more than three years later, I sent a demand letter to the retailer I had purchased it from. I got a letter in response that said, in effect, "You call yourself a law professor? Don't you know that the statute of limitations for a negligence claim is three years?" I had the exquisite pleasure of responding that I was not bringing a negligence claim. I was bringing a claim for breach of the implied warranty of merchantability under §2-314 of the U.C.C. According to that statute, I could bring the claim against the seller, even though the seller had done nothing wrong. I did not have to prove negligence—I only had to prove that the candy bar was not merchantable. And I had four years to bring the claim instead of three. I ended up with a nice settlement.

SO WHAT'S THE SCOPE?

Now we return to §2-102. We immediately encounter a thorny problem. This section was substantially revised by the 2022 Amendments to the U.C.C. in order to address the issue of what law applies to a "hybrid transaction"—a transaction that involves goods and something else—a matter that had previously been left to the courts. The problem is that as of this writing in mid-2023, few jurisdictions have adopted the Amendments and the process may be slow. (You can see which jurisdictions have enacted the 2022 Amendments by going to the ULC website at uniformlaws.org. Click on "Search Acts" and enter "2022 U.C.C. Amendments.") I have therefore decided to discuss both the outcome of this issue in court decisions, which will still be relevant in jurisdictions that have not enacted the 2022 Amendments, and the outcome under the Amendments. We will proceed in this fashion: We will first discuss the provisions of §2-201 that were not changed by the Amendments; we will then discuss the meaning of "goods" in Article 2; finally, we will explore what a "hybrid transaction" is, how courts have dealt with them under the prior law, and how they are supposed to deal with them when applying the 2022 Amendments.

The parts of §2-102 that were not changed by the Amendments state what Article 2 applies to and what it doesn't apply to, so let's look at those first. Stripped of some language around the edges, the core of the section is the pronouncement that Article 2 applies to "transactions in goods." The first problem we encounter is that the drafters of the Code nowhere define the word *transactions*, nor do they leave a clear trail on exactly what it covers. In fact, it is fairly curious that they used the word here. Life would be easier if they had said in this section that Article 2 covers "sales of goods." There certainly is a good argument to be made that this is all they meant and that the only transactions with which we need be concerned are those that we would term *sales*. By the way, this is a good time to emphasize that when the

Code uses a term, you should pay attention to how it is defined in the Code, and not in a dictionary. As you can see in the Definitional Cross References following §2-101, *sale* is defined in §2-106(1). We saw that §2-101 invited us to call Article 2 the "Sales" Article. The Official Comment to that section informs us that the entire Article is arranged "in terms of contract for sale and the various steps of its performance." As you will see as you move through its sections, Article 2 always refers to the parties under its sway as the "buyer" and the "seller."

For all practical purposes, then, it seems legitimate simply to conclude that Article 2 covers the sale of goods and move on from there. This understanding does at least eliminate some kinds of dealings in goods that everyone seems to agree are not covered by Article 2. One example is the *gift*. Suppose Susan makes a gift of a brand new Cadillac to Peter. Should some problem come up, whatever it is, Article 2 does not govern. Similarly, if Susan *lent* her car to Peter for a few days, Article 2 would not come into play. For the legal principles governing their situation, they'd have to look to the law of bailment and particularly the rules pertaining to what is termed a *gratuitous bailment*.

For most of the history of Article 2, since its initial promulgation in 1962, one type of transaction in goods about which there was a good deal of controversy was the *lease* of goods. In a significant number of cases, courts were asked to apply all or a particular piece of Article 2 to a lease transaction, and not all of them declined. Various theories developed about when, if ever, and on what justification Article 2 could be applied to the lease situation—and if so, what provisions of Article 2 governed when. The results of the cases were anything but consistent. Fortunately, this is one issue that has now been laid to rest with the drafting and adoption by the states within the past few decades of a distinct Article covering the lease of goods, Article 2A. It is easiest to understand Article 2A after you have familiarity with Article 2, so we will postpone our study of it to Part VII. In any event, the answer is now clear: Article 2 does not apply to the true lease of goods. That "transaction in goods" is covered by Article 2A.

THE LANGUAGE AROUND THE EDGES

Our reading of §2-102 necessarily focused on the core language and the meaning to be given to the term *transactions in goods*. That phrase is, however, found amid some other bits of language, and we consider them here. The entire section is introduced with the warning that Article 2 will not apply where "the context otherwise requires." Perhaps because the word *transactions* built sufficient (or more than sufficient) play into the scope section, little has been made of this introductory phrase. Perhaps it is just the drafters' way of hedging their bets a bit and at least suggesting that a practical and not a literal approach to this section is to be preferred.

Next, consider the injunction that the Article does not apply to a security transaction (the Amendments use the more accurate "security interest"). We must first be aware of what a "security interest" is, for which the Comment refers us to Article 9 of the Code. The topic of secured transactions under Article 9 is an entire book in itself. Do not worry about it here. For a glimmer of what is meant, read the first sentence *only* of §1-201(b)(35). Suppose that Sheldon, a car dealer, sells Betty a car on credit. Betty will owe him money, to be paid over time. To secure payment of the loan, Sheldon may require that Betty grant him a security interest in the car itself; she will have used it as *collateral*. If she does not repay, Sheldon can repossess the car—the right to do that is the *security interest*. If it were all as simple as this, we wouldn't need a whole separate Article and a distinct book just on secured transactions. But for the present, this example will do. As the Comment says, the *sales aspects* of this transaction are governed by Article 2; the *secured transaction* part of the deal is governed by Article 9. In some instances, a party will give a security interest in goods to another even when there is no underlying sale. The forms and terminology they use may make it appear that a sale is involved, but the language in §2-102 itself makes clear that the form does not control. If the transaction is intended "to operate *only* as a security transaction," then Article 2 has no part to play.

The final phrase of the section is a recognition that various states and the federal government have passed specialized legislation for the purposes of consumer protection, regulation of farming, and so on. Article 2 applies to those transactions, of course, but it does not "impair or repeal" any such specific legislation. As a rule, "the specific governs over the general," so it works in tandem with them. Article 2 has only one provision that refers to consumers. However, any time a sale is a consumer transaction (that is, an individual enters into it for personal, family, or household purposes, according to §1-201(b)(11)), a plethora of state and federal consumer protection legislation kicks in that also applies to the transaction. In Chapter 15, we will look at one such statute, the Magnuson-Moss Warranty Act, but everything else is beyond our scope.

ON "GOODS"

We return to the central proposition that Article 2 covers "transactions in goods," but now focusing on the meaning to be given the word *goods*. Look at the definition in §2-105(1):

> (1) "Goods" means all things (including specially manufactured goods) which are movable at the time of identification to the contract for sale other than the

> money in which the price is to be paid, investment securities (Article 8) and things in action. "Goods" also includes the unborn young of animals and growing crops and other identified things attached to realty as described in the section on goods to be severed from realty (Section 2-107).

Don't worry about the meaning of "identification" — it will be explained later. Note that you are also led to some special rules for special types of property to be found in §2-107. The examples and explanations that follow will lead you through the application of these sections. Problems and subtleties there will be, but as you go through the questions, don't lose sight of the big (and comforting) picture — goods are "things" that are "movable." As you yourself have experienced, the study of law tends to focus on the so-called "grey areas" — the matters on the fringes. Don't take from this that nothing is ever certain and that everything is always up for grabs. In most real-life situations, whether you are dealing with a sale of goods or not, will be entirely clear-cut. Rarely will you (or your adversary) find something to argue about here. But the grey areas are interesting for any number of reasons and deserve our attention. And, as is always true in the law, once an issue is legitimately in doubt, its resolution is anything but academic to the parties involved. The grey areas can make a great difference to those particular people.

Examples

The question in each instance is the same: Does the transaction involve the sale of goods and is therefore governed by Article 2?

1. On the advice of a number of her friends, Annie visits her local bookstore where she buys a copy of a book, *Sales and Leases: Examples and Explanations.*
   (a) Because of an amazing demand, the bookstore runs out of the book and must contract to buy a large number of copies from the publisher. Is your answer changed by the fact that the publisher informs the store that all previous printings of the book have been completely sold out and that it will fill this order only when a later printing is completed sometime in the next month?
   (b) In light of his success with the book, the author is hired to give a series of lectures on the law of sales (and leases) by a group representing all of the commercial-law students in the Metropolitan New York area.
   (c) The author decides to move out of his rental apartment and move into a larger home. He enters into an agreement to buy a house at 789 Widget Lane.
   (d) Assume the author holds the copyright to the book in his own name. He enters into an agreement with Megalith Pictures Incorporated, giving that company the right to produce a television miniseries based on the book.

(e) With just a small part of his accumulated fortune, the author buys some stocks and bonds through a newly acquired stockbroker.
(f) Before he leaves on a triumphal around-the-world tour, the author contacts a dealer in foreign currency and arranges to buy 10,000 euros.

2. Bob contracts to buy a cocker spaniel from Sally's Pooch Emporium. Would it matter if the contract was for a puppy not yet born? Or not yet conceived?

3. Mrs. Carroll needs a pair of dentures. She orders a set of teeth out of a mail order catalog from a firm called Dentures-R-Us, sending that firm some measurements of her mouth as they request.

4. Wimpy goes into a local diner and orders a hamburger, some fries, and a soda. See particularly §2-314(1).

5. Jones owns some land on which there is a lot of gravel. He enters into an agreement with Grady under which Grady may enter onto the land and with her equipment take as much gravel as she wishes paying a stated amount per ton. Would your answer be the same if Jones was expected to dig and bag the gravel, so that Grady could just come and pick it up as needed? You'll want to check out §2-107 for this and the next question.

6. There is also a stand of timber on Jones's land. He enters into an agreement with Woody under which Woody can enter onto the land, fell some trees, and remove them.

7. Beth just finished law school and is now working in elder care. While business is going pretty well, Beth has an idea to create an app for her clients to communicate with her using extra-large text and loud, interactive sounds. Beth makes an arrangement with her 18-year-old-cousin, Jeff, who has always been a computer whiz. He agrees to program the app and launch it on the SmartPhone App Store. Lydia agrees to pay Jeff for his efforts on a per-hour basis.

8. Several years after graduating from law school, Lydia has a successful law practice. Several years ago, she went to an office supply store and bought a shrink-wrapped box that contained "Bill 'em" accounting software on CDs that she installed on her computer. One day, the software crashed due to a programming error. No longer able to get such CDs from stores, Lydia went online, paid for the updated "Bill 'em" software on a website, then downloaded the product to her computer.

9. Yanni has always liked the traditional word-processing software on his computer, but he realized he needed a more reliable solution when his computer crashed and he lost his outlines just before his Contracts exam. Yanni started using CloudWordz, a web app that stored his data and files

in the cloud. While working on page 92 of his outline, the site suddenly crashed. All of his files were gone when he logged back in.

Explanations

1. Yes. This is a sale of goods governed by Article 2. The book contains copyright-protected material, but you are not buying that. You are buying the paper on which that material is found and the binding that holds it together. Under the definition of goods in §2-105(1), the book is a "thing" that is "moveable at the time of identification to the contract for sale." You don't know what "identification" means in this context, and you won't have to know until Chapter 16, but that's no problem here. By the way, you'll just have to get used to the awkwardness of *goods* seeming to function as a singular as well as a plural noun. You can say "the book is goods" or "the book is a good" for the purposes of Article 2. You can also say "the book is good," but that statement has nothing to do with Article 2.
   a. Yes. The large order of books is a contract for the sale of goods. Notice that Article 2 covers any sale, no matter how small or how large, as long as the subject is goods.

      It should make no difference to your answer if the books which were to be sold didn't even exist at the time of the contract. By the time they are to be "identified to the contract," that is, we know which particular books are involved, they will exist, and at that time they will be moveable. Look at subsection (2) of §2-105. "Goods which are not both existing and identified are 'future' goods." The important thing here is that *future goods are goods*, and it makes no difference for the applicability of Article 2.
   b. No. The author's contract is for the provision of services, not for the sale of goods. His lectures are not "moveable" simply because they don't have a physical nature, a tangible form which goods must have. (The notes that the author uses to give the lectures are, of course, goods. So if many years hence these notes were sold to a collector of valuable memorabilia, that transaction *would* be covered by Article 2. However, the buyer would not own the copyright to the notes unless specifically agreed—the buyer would only own the physical object.) Contracts for services are a major category of contract not covered by the U.C.C., but still left to the common law of the states.
   c. No. This is a sale of real property. Real property isn't moveable and thus can't be considered goods. Contracts dealing with the purchase and sale of real property are another big chunk of legal activity outside the scope of the U.C.C. It would be easier to remember this in Spanish—real estate is *las propiedades inmobiliarias*—property that is not moveable.

d. No. The author's deal involves what is usually referred to as a *chose in action*, but which §2-105(1) anglicizes to a *thing in action* and which is directly read out of the definition of goods. A traditional definition of a chose in action is something like "an incorporeal right, a right not reduced to possession but recoverable by bringing and maintaining an action." The author's right to prevent others from trading on the success of this book is just such a right. It has no tangible form. An interesting case along these lines is *Collins v. Kentucky Lottery Corp.*, 399 S.W.3d 449 (Ky. App. 2012), in which the Court of Appeals of Kentucky confirmed a lower court's determination that the sale of lottery tickets was not an Article 2 sale of goods, noting that "a lottery ticket represents a chance to win an unknown amount of money. . . . A chance to win money is intangible and cannot be physically moved at the time that it is purchased. The definition of *goods* does not include intangible property."

e. No. "Investment securities" are expressly excluded from the scope of Article 2 by language in §2-105(1). Transactions in such things are governed by Article 8 of the Code and not by Article 2. You can look at §8-102(a)(15) for an idea of what these include, but your basic instincts probably are on target on this one.

f. Yes. The sale of foreign currency is covered by Article 2. See Comment 1 to §2-105. The dollars with which the author will pay for the euros cannot be goods, but the euros themselves are. Compare the situation if the author agrees to buy some dollars, taking delivery in the present, in exchange for his agreement to repay a greater number of dollars in the future. This is what we call a "loan" of money, not a sale of goods, and is perforce not covered by Article 2.

2. Yes. Bob's transaction with Sally is governed by Article 2. The fact that the object of the sale is a living thing makes no difference, and in fact we'll see many cases decided under Article 2 dealing with animals as goods. If the contract was for a puppy not yet born or even conceived, Article 2 still governs. This is specifically provided for in the second sentence of §2-105(1). The puppy is *future goods*, but we remind ourselves that's just one type of goods. Under Article 2 (as indeed under the common law) one can legally bind oneself to sell something that one does not yet possess or which doesn't even exist yet. All that this means is that the seller assumes the risk of getting his or her hands on the thing in order to meet a contract obligation.

3. Yes. It is not for us to comment on the wisdom of Mrs. Carroll's move, only on the law governing it. The answer should be clear: the teeth are movable things, so this is a sale of goods directly within the scope of Article 2. Note that even if the dentures are specially made for her, §2-105 explicitly includes "specially manufactured goods" in its definition of "goods."

4. Yes. The last sentence of §2-314(1) leaves no question that at least *that* section applies to Wimpy's purchase. Since a dinner at a diner or a restaurant is such a medley of sales and service, the prior law was not consistent as to whether sales law applied. The drafters of the Code gave us this answer in §2-314. But are we to take the placement of this sentence in §2-314 as meaning that the rest of Article 2 does *not* apply to such a situation or that there is some doubt whether it does? This question isn't particularly troubling, since it is hard to think of a real situation where a suit would be brought other than when the warranties of quality are involved. And I know of no court questioning the application of the other two warranty sections (§§2-313 and 2-315) to the sale of food.

5. No. Under §2-107(1) Grady's purchase is not governed by Article 2 if she is to sever it from the land. If Jones, the seller, is to do the severing, Article 2 does cover. This all follows from the fact that gravel constitutes "minerals or the like."

6. Yes. Sale of standing timber is governed by §2-107(2). It is covered by Article 2 "whether or not the subject matter is to be severed by the buyer or by the seller." Notice this rule applies not only to timber, but also to "growing crops or other things attached to realty and capable of severance without material harm thereto but not described in subsection (1)" of the section. What is the distinction between the items sold in §§2-107(1) and 2-107(2)? I think the idea is that the items in subsection (1) are not replenished after removal, but the items in subsection (2) are renewable.

7. No. Beth and Jeff's contract is likely not governed by Article 2. This would pretty clearly be a contract for the provision of services by Jeff and, as such, is not governed by Article 2. See *Pearl Investments, LLC v. Standard I/O, Inc.*, 257 F. Supp. 2d 326 (D. Me. 2003), where the court held that a contract under which one party agreed to create for the other "software from scratch (concept to realization)" was not governed by Article 2. The same result can be found in *Systems America, Inc. v. Rockwell Software, Inc.*, 2007 WL 218242 (N.D. Cal.). Courts additionally may look to the nature of the billing as evidence of whether the sale of the system or the services dominate. See *Springbrook Software, Inc. v. Douglas County*, 2015 WL 2248449 (W.D. Wis.). Beth paying Jeff on an hourly basis lends support to the services aspect dominating over the sale of the software itself.

8. Opinions vary. Some courts have held that an end user's purchase of a standardized, "off-the-rack," shrink-wrapped CD would be a sale of goods governed by Article 2. See *Advent Systems Ltd. v. Unisys Corp.*, 925 F.2d 670 (3d Cir. 1991). The court in *Advent* reasoned that where the information and intellectual property can be reduced to a tangible form and sold, the thing being sold—the CD—is like any other good in many respects—that is, it is moveable—and thus falls under the definition

of goods. Despite the lack of a physical medium on which the software is contained, some courts have continued to extend this view to downloaded software. See *Rottner v. AVG Technologies USA, Inc.*, 943 F. Supp. 2d 222 (D. Mass. 2013) (software obtained through one-stop payment and download was goods governed by Article 2); *Gross v. Symantec Corp.*, 2012 WL 3116158 (N.D. Cal.) (anti-virus software download without rendition of additional services was goods). But other courts do not go so far as to find that software is goods. Instead, they find that software is not goods, but that Article 2 should nonetheless be applied by analogy. Other courts, however, hold that software is not goods and outright reject the application of Article 2 and instead apply the common law.

Many scholars and courts analogize software to a book—a book is a physical moveable good that contains information. Opponents counter that the analogy breaks down because it is unlikely that the purchaser of a book would bring a claim for breach of the warranty of merchantability when the book contains a defective story. See Holly K. Towle, *Enough Already: It Is Time to Acknowledge that UCC Article 2 Does Not Apply to Software and Other Information*, 52 S. Tex. L. Rev. 531, 556 (2011) (citing *Winter v. G.P. Putnam's Sons*, 938 F.2d 1033, 1034–36 (9th Cir. 1991)). Does the analogy to the printed book work very well or even make much sense in this situation? The buyer of a book might feel aggrieved if the ink immediately starts to run or if pages are missing. That's just the kind of thing the law regarding the "sale of goods" is meant to address. But would the book buyer be looking to Article 2 for relief if the *information* contained in the book was wrong? Many authorities further contend that software transactions should not be governed by Article 2 because they are not actually "sales" but rather "licenses." Under §2-106, a sale involves "a passing of title from buyer to seller." While a buyer may own the physical disk that contains the software, the buyer does not own the copyright in the software and is entitled to use it only under certain terms and conditions. The issue of licensing versus sale has gone multiple ways as well. Some courts have held that software licenses are not true licenses since possession is never returned to the licensor. See *Softman Products Co. v. Adobe Systems, Inc.*, 171 F. Supp. 2d 1075 (C.D. Cal. 2001). But other courts have found that there was a license rather than a sale where the user did not retain all rights, such as copying rights, to the software. *Adobe Systems v. Stargate Software*, 216 F. Supp. 2d 1051 (N.D. Cal. 2002). There are few bright-line rules as to whether standalone software, unaccompanied by services or other hardware, is goods under Article 2, so the safe rule is to always check your local jurisdiction.

When the ULC and ALI revised Article 2 around the turn of the century, the draft provided that goods did not include "information." The revision nevertheless provided in a Comment that "the sale of 'smart goods' such as an automobile is a transaction in goods fully within this article even though the automobile contains many computer programs. On the other hand, an architect's provision of architectural plans on a computer disk would not be a transaction in goods." Revised Article 2, §2-103(1)(k) Comment 7. As you recall from the Introduction, the revision failed to gain any traction, but it could still be cited as persuasive authority.

9. Probably not. The methods for distributing software have changed drastically over time. Where once the software was primarily sold and distributed via tangible means and had to be physically installed on computers, now most software can be acquired or used online without the user ever encountering a physical object. The question remains whether courts will find such "software as a service," or SaaS, to be goods under Article 2. In *Kentwool Co. v. NetSuite Inc.*, 2015 WL 693552 (N.D. Cal.), the court found access to a cloud platform not to be goods when the user didn't install a copy of the pre-existing software but instead purchased access to the platform for a year. The court's reasoning additionally considered that services provided by the software provider may have been the predominant factor. If the court in this example followed *Kentwool*, it would likely find that Yanni would be out of luck and that the web app is not goods under Article 2. But some courts have extended the application of Article 2 to downloads, so it would be of little surprise if some extended Article 2 coverage to cloud-based applications that are not embedded in a tangible medium and that do not convey title to the purchaser. Still, this remains an area of much controversy. For further discussion, see Michael L. Rustad and Elif Kavusturan, *A Commercial Law for Software Contracting*, 76 Wash. & Lee L. Rev. 775 (2019); Holly K. Towle, *Enough Already: It Is Time to Acknowledge that UCC Article 2 Does Not Apply to Software and Other Information*, 52 S. Tex. L. Rev. 531, 556 (2011). Finally, it is often the warranty aspect of the transaction that is in issue. We will look at Article 2 warranties in Chapters 10 through 14. Frequently, the contract for a software transaction contains the same language of warranty—and warranty disclaimer—that is found in contracts for the sale of goods, so software providers seem to be creating a situation where application of Article 2, at least by analogy, is appropriate. It would doubtless be helpful if we had a distinct body of law that governed this transaction, but the ULC's efforts to promulgate UCITA, the Uniform Computer Information Transactions Act, were not successful.

ON "HYBRID TRANSACTIONS"

Things become more complicated when we have to decide not only whether a transaction involves the sale of goods, but whether it also involves something else. The "something else" could be services, leased goods, or an interest in other property, such as land or intellectual property. We call such a transaction a "hybrid transaction," a term that was introduced into the Code by the 2022 Amendments. Amended §2-106(5) provides:

> "Hybrid transaction" means a single transaction involving a sale of goods and:
> (a) the provision of services;
> (b) a lease of other goods; or
> (c) a sale, lease, or license of property other than goods.

We know that Article 2 governs if we have a transaction in goods. What law governs a hybrid transaction? That was a gap in the Code that was first filled in by the courts and is now addressed in §2-102(2), which was added by the 2022 Amendments. Let's first look at what courts have done, since that is still good law in many jurisdictions and the precedents may influence the interpretation of the new statute.

The great majority of decisions rely on the so-called *predominant factor test* (often called the "predominant purpose" test) to characterize the hybrid transaction. The question is whether, when all factors are considered, it is more like a sales contract with a little something else on the side or more like something else with some sales thrown in. One aspect will dominate, and that will determine whether Article 2 governs or not. A well-known case putting forth this test is *Bonebrake v. Cox*, 499 F.2d 951 (8th Cir. 1974), where the court stated:

> The test for inclusion or exclusion is not whether [the sales and service aspects of a contract] are mixed, but granting they are mixed, whether their predominant factor, their thrust, their purpose reasonably stated, is the rendition of service with goods incidentally involved (e.g., contract with artist for painting) or is it a transaction of sale, with labor incidentally involved (e.g., installation of a water heater in a bathroom).

Utilizing this distinction, the court in *Bonebrake* held Article 2 applicable to a contract for the sale and installation of some used bowling-alley equipment. The fact that the contract involved a significant amount of labor did not prevent its being found to be within the scope of Article 2 in its entirety.

In *Kaitz v. Landscape Creations, Inc.*, 2000 Mass. App. Div. 140, the plaintiff brought suit against the landscaping company for breach of contract and for negligence when some locust trees that had been planted on his property as part of the overall landscaping design done by the defendant were damaged or destroyed in a storm several years after the work had been done. The plaintiff's claim based on negligence had been dismissed as barred by the Statute of Limitations. Could the plaintiff proceed on a breach of warranty, an Article 2 theory? The Massachusetts Appellate Division said no: The original transaction between the parties had been a contract for the provision of landscaping services in which goods (the various plants, shrubs, and trees) were "incidentally provided," and not a sale of these goods. The court noted that the "scope of the project was extensive," taking several months to complete. Beyond this, the project entailed the development of a landscaping design, grading of the soil, mulching, planting, and so on. "This made the project labor intensive rather than mere provision of goods." Similar is the case of *Openaire, Inc. v. L.K. Rossi Corp.*, 940 A.2d 724 (Vt. 2007), in which the contract in question called for the contractor to design and build a free-standing enclosure for an outdoor, in-ground swimming pool for a total price of $239,000. The Vermont Supreme Court concluded that "the contract included much more than simply the production of a specially manufactured good and the attachment of that good to the premises," and hence was to be characterized as a service contract, not one for the sale of goods.

One of the most straightforward and easiest-to-appreciate examples of the predominant factor test in application is the construction-contract situation. The owner of some land arranges for a building contractor to come onto the land and construct a barn according to a set of specifications. As the barn is being built, the landowner will, of course, be receiving both goods and services from the building contractor, yet there is rarely any dispute that the predominant factor here is the service aspect of the arrangement and that, hence, Article 2 will not govern the transaction. Contrast this to the situation which gave rise to the decision in *Generation Ranch, LLC v. Zarbock*, 2012 WL 161814 (Ariz. App.). The seller was a manufacturer of prefabricated modular steel barns. The buyers contracted to purchase such a barn, which was to be delivered to their land in a number of component pieces, fabricated at the seller's factory, which were then to be assembled on the land on a concrete pad that would serve as a floor and foundation for the completed structure. The Arizona Court of Appeals affirmed a lower court's decision to apply Article 2 to the transaction. This was a sale of goods, a prefabricated barn, with some services, erection and assembly of the structure, incidental to the sale.

Contracts for repair are also usually viewed as not covered by Article 2, even if the cost of parts is significant. See, e.g., *Northwestern Equipment, Inc. v. Cudmore*, 312 N.W.2d 347 (N.D. 1981), where the repair of a bulldozer by a sales agency was held not to be within Article 2 even though the cost of the repair parts was almost three times what was charged for labor. The court concluded that "the primary purpose" of the contract in the minds of the parties was the repair of the bulldozer, the sale of parts being incidental to this purpose. "The essence of the contract between the parties was the skill and judgment to be employed by Northwestern's employees in repairing the transmission, torque converter, and hydraulic control box." To the same effect, see *Bamcor LLC v. Jupiter Aluminum Corp.*, 767 F. Supp. 2d 959 (N.D. Ind. 2011) and *Accessory Overhaul Group v. Mesa Airlines*, 994 F. Supp. 2d 1296 (N.D. Ga. 2014).

In *Heart of Texas Dodge, Inc. v. Star Coach, L.L.C.*, S.E.2d 61 (Ga. App. 2002), the controversy centered on an agreement under which Star Coach, in the business of converting sports utility vehicles and pickup trucks into "custom vehicles" by the incorporation of parts obtained by it from other sources into factory-fresh vehicles owned by dealers, was to customize one Dodge Durango at the request of Heart of Texas Dodge, a dealership. At trial the instructions given to the jury were based partly on Article 2 precepts. The Georgia Court of Appeals, noting that the situation was "closely analogous to repair cases," held that Article 2 did not apply to the contract in question and that the complained-of instructions had therefore been given in error. Furthermore, since the rules under Article 2 were not the same as they would be under the common law appropriate to this service contract, the error could not be considered to be harmless. The judgment of the trial court, under which the conversion specialist had been awarded damages, was therefore reversed. See also *Janke v. Brooks*, 2012 WL 1229891 (D. Colo.). As the court related:

> Plaintiffs are the owners of a classic, 1957, Chevrolet Nomad. After seeing a feature on the ESPN program, *On The Block*, plaintiffs contacted defendants, Donald and Normandy Brooks, about restoring their car. Plaintiffs traveled to defendants' shop in Sparks, Nevada, to discuss the project. After receiving an estimate for the work and forwarding a deposit, plaintiffs shipped the Nomad to defendants in September 2008.

The district court judge who had to sort things out when matters did not all go according to plan determined that while the defendants, in agreeing to restore the classic car to its original condition, were expected to both round up and supply needed parts as well as to install those parts and buff the whole thing up, they were predominantly engaged for the services they were to provide and not for the sale of any goods. As the judge explained, after consideration of all of the facts of the case, and of the various authorities cited to him by each side in the dispute, "what the contract primarily contemplated was that defendants would bring their specialized knowledge and experience to bear in selecting and installing appropriate parts, repairing existing components, and generally refurbishing the car in such a way as to restore it to a show-worthy condition."

A court applying the predominant factor test is basically making an all-or-nothing decision. The entire transaction is reviewed and judged to be either a sales contract or a service contract. Which is it? With good reason, courts often thought this binary approach did not make sense, and sometimes used approaches that apply different law to different parts of the transaction. One approach is the "gravamen test." Under this test, if the issue relates to the goods aspect of the transaction, the court applies Article 2, and if the issue relates to something else, it applies other law to those aspects. For example, assume a transaction involving installation of a good. If the problem was with the good itself, the court would apply Article 2, but if the problem was with the installation, it would apply other law. Under another approach, known as "bifurcation," the approach would split the transaction into parts and apply the appropriate law to each part. For example, if a farmer bought a field with a sprinkler system, the court would apply real estate law to the purchase of the field and Article 2 to the purchase of the sprinkler.

Now let's look at the approach in the 2022 Amendments. Section 2-102(2) provides:

> (2) In a hybrid transaction:
>
> (a) If the sale-of-goods aspects do not predominate, only the provisions of this Article which relate primarily to the sale-of-goods aspects of the transaction apply, and the provisions that relate primarily to the transaction as a whole do not apply.
>
> (b) If the sale-of-goods aspects predominate, this Article applies to the transaction but does not preclude application in appropriate circumstances of other law to aspects of the transaction which do not relate to the sale of goods.

Notice that to apply this test, we still have to determine which aspect of the transaction predominates. However, in making this determination, the drafters wanted to steer us away from relying on the "predominant purpose" test. Instead, Official Comment 3 provides some guidance in determining which aspects of the transaction predominate (I have added the tabulation):

> Factors that may be relevant to that determination include, but are not limited to:
>
> 1. the language of the agreement,
> 2. the portion of the total price that is attributable to the sale of goods (as to which an agreed-upon allocation will ordinarily be binding on the parties),
> 3. the purposes of the parties in entering into the transaction (when that is ascertainable), and
> 4. the nature of the businesses of the parties (such as whether the seller is in the business of selling goods of that kind).

The third factor asks us to consider the purpose of the parties, so the common law "predominant purpose" may well continue to have influence.

Let's assume we have done our analysis and concluded that the sale of goods aspects do not predominate. Under the "predominant purpose" test, other law would have applied to the entire transaction. But subsection (2)(a) tells us—let's go to the last clause first—"the provisions [of Article 2] that relate primarily to the transaction as a whole do not apply." What are the provisions that "relate to the transaction as a whole?" Official Comment 5 is helpful in telling us it includes provisions having to do with formation of contract and the statute of frauds—provisions that address issues that concern the entire transaction rather than issues that arise from the goods themselves. So if the issue involved areas that relate to the transaction as a whole, we would look to other law. But if the issue involved the goods aspect of the transaction, we would apply the provisions of Article 2 that relate primarily to the sale-of-goods aspects to those aspects.

Let's take the example of a construction contract, which has both goods and services aspects. Under both the pre-Amendment rule and the Amended rule, we would likely decide that the services aspects of the transaction predominate. But then there is a split. Under the pre-Amendment rules, we would apply other law to the entire transaction. Under the Amendments, we would not apply the provisions of Article 2 that relate to the transaction as a whole to the entire transaction. But we would apply certain Article 2 provisions to the goods aspects. Among the provisions of Article 2 that relate to the sale-of-goods aspect of a transaction are the warranty provisions, as we will see in Part III. So those provisions would apply to the goods aspects of the transaction. This would mean that for the goods part of the transaction—like the materials used in construction—the buyer would presumptively get Article 2 warranties. As we will see, this can be a benefit to buyers. It is a major change in the Amendments to have those aspects of the transaction governed by Article 2.

Now let's assume we have conducted our analysis of which aspects predominate, and we have concluded that the sale-of-goods aspects predominate. Under the pre-Amendment rule, Article 2 would apply to the entire transaction. Amended §2-102(2)(b) also tells us that Article 2 applies to the transaction. This may appear to be the same result as we would get under the former rule, but subsection (2)(b) says there is an exception—we would apply other law "in appropriate circumstances." For example, assume we concluded in a contract that involved goods and services that the goods aspects predominate. The issue involves whether the provider of the services had done a reasonable job. Article 2 does not have anything to say that would help us evaluate the quality of services, but if there is a coherent body of other law that has dealt with this issue, it might be appropriate to apply it.

Examples

The following are examples of hybrid transactions. What law would be applied to resolve the issue under the pre-Amendment "predominant factor" approach? Under the approach in Amended §2-102?

1. Suppose in our earlier Example 3 that instead of ordering mail-order dentures, Mrs. Carroll went to a dentist to fill her need. Over a series of visits, the dentist prepares a set of false teeth for her and fits them to her

mouth. At the end of the final visit, she takes the new teeth home and discovers a problem.

2. Bigelow decides to fix up the kitchen in his bungalow. He enters into an agreement with Hammer for the construction and installation of a new set of kitchen cabinets. The specifications call for a particular type of knotty pine and designated brass handles and hinges. The agreed price is $3,000, which covers all materials and labor.

3. Bigelow goes to a local carpet store and picks out a style of "100% wool" wall-to-wall carpeting for his living room. He buys it from the store for a price that includes installation by the store's personnel. He later finds that the carpet is not all wool as described. What if he has problems with the carpeting not because of its makeup but because it was installed improperly?

4. Taylor bought a new "smart" car equipped with a back-up camera, integrated wireless calling, GPS, and other apps. One day, Taylor's defective GPS told him to drive into a lake, thereby destroying the vehicle.

Explanations

EXPLANATIONS

1. If Carroll's purchase from the mail order house was covered by Article 2, is there any question that the same is true when she gets her dentures from a dentist? As a matter of fact, in the actual case on which this part of the example is based, *Carroll v. Grabavoy*, 396 N.E.2d 836 (Ill. App. 1979), the court held that Article 2 did not govern. What is the difference? The argument is that the dentist is not primarily engaged in selling the dentures but is really rendering a professional service, of which only one part is the handing over of the finished product. The reason she went to a dentist was to get the benefit of such services, which presumably included examining her teeth, taking impressions, making professional judgments about how to proceed, and fitting the dentures. In *Carroll* the court, relying on an earlier pre-Code case, held that "the dentist was not engaged in selling false teeth to the patient but rather that his charges were for his skill and knowledge for his personal work in the examination and in the making of the dentures in question." In another case involving dentures, this holding was followed, the court concluding, "Without a doubt, plaintiff paid for and received a course of health care treatment and services, not merely a piece of merchandise." *Preston v. Thompson*, 280 S.E.2d 780, 785 (N.C. App. 1981).

   You see the same reasoning and the same result where a patient tried to rely on Article 2 protection in a suit against her ophthalmologist following problems with a pair of contact lenses prescribed and fitted to the patient during the course of several office visits. In *Lamb v. Newark Emergency Room, Inc.*, 1983 Del. Super. LEXIS 753, the court stated:

> Here, the plaintiff was purchasing a product but in the context of medical care and treatment for her vision deficiency. She consulted Dr. Hall in his capacity of a medical doctor trained in ophthalmology. The acceptability of the product he dispensed depended on the degree of skill and acumen he applied to the examination of the eyes, the prescription he developed and the fitting and care of the patient after insertion. If a breach of care occurred in any of these areas the remedy is through an action for negligence, not breach of warranty.

A question that has come up with some frequency is whether the insertion of a medical device into a patient during the course of surgery should be considered a sale of the device by the individual doctor or hospital to the patient. The majority of courts faced with this issue have concluded that the doctor or hospital is not an Article 2 "seller" in such a situation but rather a provider of specialized services under a common law contract for provision of those services. See, for example, *Brandt v. Boston Scientific Corp.*, 792 N.E.2d 296 (Ill. 2003), or *Reid v. Albizem, M.D.*, 2014 WL 2915883 (E.D. Pa.). A few courts have, however, declared Article 2 to be applicable to the matter. For a good discussion and roundup of the cases on point, see *Phillips v. Medtronics, Inc.*, 754 F. Supp. 2d 211 (D. Mass. 2010). It's important to note in such a case that the court following the majority approach, as in *Brandt*, is not saying that there has never been any sale of the offending product, but only that the doctor or hospital who delivered over the product to the ultimate user was not making such a sale, even if the cost of the product was a big factor in the doctor's or hospital's bill fee. There was presumably a sale by the manufacturer of its product somewhere up the line, and as we will see (in Chapter 14), the patient may be able to sue the manufacturer or distributor of the device based on Article 2 principles (or may be barred from doing so by the problem of "lack of privity" as we will later consider it). See, for example, *Jones v. Ram Medical, Inc.*, 807 F. Supp. 2d 501 (D.S.C. 2011). But the doctor or hospital, in providing the product as part of a package of professional services, is not making a sale to the patient. He, she, or it is primarily providing a service, and any action by the patient presumably will be governed by the local law of medical malpractice. Again, it is perfectly good law — just not part of the Uniform Commercial Code.

Returning to the provision of contact lens, should the result be the same if a patient, having once been fitted with a pair of prescription lenses but having lost them, orders a replacement pair through the ophthalmologist and they are found to be improperly made or contaminated? Should the doctor in that situation be treated any differently from the typical retail seller, who *does* warrant whatever he sells to his buyer, even if he is in no way responsible for the problem but only passing on what he bought from the manufacturer or wholesaler? Would it matter if the doctor made some profit from supplying replacement lenses or if it were done only as a convenience for patients? Certainly if an individual orders a pair of contacts from an independent supply house, that seller's liability is grounded in Article 2 and the law of sales.

So the bottom line is this is a hybrid transaction, and the services aspects probably predominate. This would likely be the case even if the cost of the dentures was greater than the cost of the services. Even if the Amended Comments downplay it, I think the predominant purpose test is helpful here. Carroll did not buy dentures from the dentist and incidentally have them installed; she bought dental services, which included the purchase of the goods. Having concluded that the services aspects predominate, under the old rule, other law would apply to the entire transaction. This result does not make a lot of sense if the problem is with the dentures. Under Amended §2-102(2)(a), we would apply other law to issues involving the entire transaction, but we would apply Article 2 to the goods aspect of the transaction—the dentures. This might mean, for example, that Carroll received express warranties and received the implied warranty of merchantability with respect to the dentures.

2. In this hybrid transaction, Bigelow has purchased cabinets and hardware and installation services. Many courts looking at situations like this have concluded that the transaction was not for a sale of goods but was for service of the type typically performed by a workman. Such is usually found to be the case when a construction contractor is performing services, even if a good deal of what he or she charges for is the cost of materials. The relative "cost" or "value" of the sales versus the service component is not necessarily the decisive factor. If the crafting of the materials is the primary reason—that is, the thrust of why the agreement has been made by the buyer—then it is services he or she is after and not a sale of goods. But it could go the other way, especially if there was a substantial quantity of goods and insubstantial services, like an agreement for the installation of premade cabinets.

   Let's see how it plays out both ways. If other aspects predominate, under the old rule, other law would apply to the entire transaction, whether the problem was with the goods or with the services. Under Amended §2-102(2)(a), we would apply other law to issues involving the entire transaction, but we would apply Article 2 to the goods aspect of the transaction—the cabinets and hardware. This would likely mean, for example, that Bigelow received the implied warranty of merchantability with respect to the goods.

If we conclude that the goods aspects predominate, then under Amended §2-102(2)(b), we would apply Article 2 to the entire transaction unless it was appropriate to apply other law to the non-goods aspects of the transaction. So whichever we decided predominates, Article 2 would apply to the goods under the Amendments.

3. In this hybrid transaction, Bigelow has purchased both goods—the rug—and services—the installation of the rug. We must first determine which is the predominant factor. A court would probably find this was predominantly a sale of goods. This was the result in *Snyder v. Herbert Greenbaum & Assocs. Inc.*, 380 A.2d 618 (Md. App. 1977), *Colorado Carpet Installation, Inc. v. Palermo*, 668 P.2d 1384 (Colo. 1983), and *Pittsley v. Houser*, 875 P.2d 232 (Idaho App. 1994). Even if the goods that the seller agrees to provide will have to be custom-made to fit the buyer's specific order, and hence some labor will have to go into their fabrication as well as their installation, this does not necessarily mean that the contract won't be judged to be for the sale of goods under the predominant factor test. Section 2-105 explicitly includes in its definition of "goods" what it refers to as "specially manufactured goods." See, for example, *Propulsion Technologies, Inc. v. Attwood Corp.*, 369 F.3d 896 (5th Cir. 2004), and *Erin Printing and Promotional Marketing, Inc. v. Convum, LLC*, 2005 WL 366895 (Tenn. App.).

   Under the old rule, once the transaction is found to be governed by Article 2, Article 2 would apply to the entire transaction and it would not matter whether the gist of Bigelow's complaint was about the quality of the carpet itself or the manner of its installation. However, under Amended §2-102(2)(b), we would presumptively apply Article 2 to the entire transaction, but we would apply other law where appropriate. For example, if the complaint involved the manner of its installation, there might be a coherent body of law in the jurisdiction addressing what constitutes "workmanlike performance" that could better address that issue than Article 2.

4. Let's put aside Taylor's poor decision making and focus on the call of the question—what law applies? This is a hybrid transaction, involving information technology embedded in the goods. Which factor predominates? As we have seen above in Examples 8 and 9, courts have gone many different directions when deciding whether software standing by itself is goods. Smart goods are one area of clarity. Typically, courts have held that with "turn-key" systems, the goods aspects predominate. See *AudioVisual Artistry v. Tanzer*, 403 S.W.3d 789 (Tenn. Ct. App. 2012) (smart home system was goods when actual goods cost $56,000 versus $10,000 programming cost); *Neilson Business Equipment Center, Inc. v. Italo V. Monteleone, M.D., P.A.*, 524 A.2d 1172 (Del. 1987) (defective billing and other malfunctions in computer for doctor's office consisting of hardware, software, and actual computer was goods); *Triangle Underwriters, Inc.*

> v. Honeywell, Inc., 604 F.2d 737 (2d Cir. 1979) (turn-key computer system with pre-installed software that malfunctioned was goods). Thus, where a good comes "fully-loaded" with software and the cost of programming is low compared to the cost of the goods, it is likely that courts will find that the goods aspects predominate.

Therefore, under the old rule, we would apply Article 2 to the entire transaction. This can be easily done in most cases, as courts have often applied Article 2 to software transactions by analogy. Under Amended §2-102(2)(b), we would also presumptively apply Article 2 to the entire transaction, but we would apply other law where appropriate. For example, if that jurisdiction has adopted UCITA, the Uniform Computer Information Transactions Act (Maryland and Virginia have), then it might be appropriate to apply that body of law to the software aspects of this transaction.

PART II

Formation and Basic Terms

CHAPTER 3

Who Is a "Merchant" and Why It Matters

WHY DOES IT MATTER WHO'S A MERCHANT?

Article 2 of the Uniform Commercial Code rules over all of us. Each and every person selling or buying goods in a jurisdiction that has adopted Article 2 of the Uniform Commercial Code is subject to the provisions of that Article. Buyers and sellers of goods are governed by the Code's provisions simply because of who they are: buyers and sellers of goods. It makes no difference that people might not think of themselves as engaging in a "business" or "commercial" transaction when, for example, they buy a burger at a fast food restaurant or pick up a pair of shoes at the local shoe store. Anyone who is a participant in a transaction within the scope of Article 2 (a subject on which Chapter 2 had plenty to say) is governed by the provisions of that Article.

Article 2 lays out some special rules for a unique set of players, however: those it defines and refers to very carefully as "merchants." The important point initially is just that—there need be no guesswork involved in deciding when a distinct rule or standard of Article 2 law applies to a merchant. You need only look for the word *merchant*, and it is found in only 13 rules. If a rule or part of a rule applies to merchants, it is because the Code language clearly states that this is so. In those cases, it is not for you or me to decide whether in a particular situation someone we think of as a merchant has any different responsibility than a mere mortal nonmerchant. Those decisions have already been made by the drafters of the Code.

This chapter is not intended as a full discussion of the special rules governing merchants under Article 2. That discussion must necessarily be woven into the following chapters and our coverage of individual topics. I will not even attempt here a full listing of all 13 places in Article 2 where merchant status can make a difference. Obviously, the general idea is that that party is a professional, and the Code imputes to them greater knowledge and experience than a nonmerchant has. The purpose of this chapter is simply to alert you to the significance placed on this definition by the drafters. This is as good a place as any to study the definition set out in §2-104. You may well find yourself referring back to this chapter when particular rules for merchants are invoked in later material.

For the purposes of this discussion, however, a few examples may be in order. In Chapter 4, we look briefly at the §2-205 firm offer rule, which applies only to "an offer by a merchant." On the other hand, §2-314 (which gets the full treatment in Chapter 12) tells you that a buyer only benefits from the "implied warranty of merchantability" when "the seller is a merchant with respect to goods of that kind." Note that while §2-205 applied to "a merchant," this rule applies to the narrower class of "a merchant with respect to goods of that kind." You have to read carefully to see the difference. In Chapter 6 we will go into the details of the Statute of Frauds in §2-201. There, we will see an important exception in subsection (2), which applies only in the case of agreements made "between merchants." The term *between merchants*, as you see in §2-104(3), is defined as meaning "any transaction with respect to which both parties are chargeable with the knowledge or skill of merchants." Which leads us to the definition of *merchant* itself.

THE MERCHANT CLASS

The definition of *merchant* in §2-104(1) is sufficiently important that it deserves to be quoted in full. Unfortunately, the definition, while only a single sentence, may seem on first reading a particularly dense and tangled bit of statutory prose, including a full eight instances of the word "or." Perhaps it will help if I reproduce it here in a somewhat reformatted fashion, along with some language I added in brackets:

> "Merchant" means:
>
> [1] a person who deals in goods of the kind, or
>
> [2] [a person who] otherwise [that is, other than by dealing in goods of the kind] by his occupation holds himself out as having knowledge or skill peculiar to the practices or goods involved in the transaction, or

> [3] [a person] to whom such knowledge or skill may be attributed by his employment of an agent or broker or other intermediary who by his [that is, the agent's] occupation holds himself out as having such knowledge or skill.

So a party to a transaction gets to be a merchant in three different ways—as a goods merchant, a practices merchant, or a merchant by agency. A goods merchant has experience with the goods in the transaction, while a practices merchant has experience with business practices generally. A party can become a practices merchant because they use an agent who is familiar with practices. For example, a purchasing department buys goods for a university, or I hire a professional to negotiate the purchase of a new car for me. See Comment 2 for further explanation. Note that it says that a party is not a merchant when they are not acting in that capacity—a car dealer buying a fishing rod for her own use is not a merchant. The important takeaway is (1) identify when a particular Code section uses the term *merchant* or *merchants*, and (2) note whether the section refers to a *merchant* generally, which would be any of the three types of merchant, or more specifically as *a merchant who deals in goods of the kind*, which would be only a goods merchant. Taking this all together, you have plenty to think about in analyzing the examples that follow.

Examples

1. Ned, a lawyer, is the proud owner of a purebred female cocker spaniel that he arranges to have mated with a purebred male owned by a neighbor. When the puppies are born, he posts a handwritten "Puppies For Sale" notice on bulletin boards around town and posts a short notice describing the puppies in the "items for sale" section of a website devoted to information about what's happening in his local community. Would a buyer of one of the puppies get the §2-314 warranty of merchantability along with the puppy?

2. It later turns out that Ned, while keeping his lawyering job, expands his dog breeding activities considerably. He now owns several females that he regularly breeds, advertising and selling the offspring under the name of "Spaniels of Springfield." Would your answer to the previous question be any different?

3. The Wauwatosa High School Band Mothers Association organized a fundraising luncheon at which they served turkey salad and a dessert. Pearl Samson attended the lunch, ate some of the food (for which she paid $1.25), and by the next day was seriously ill. Eventually she was diagnosed as having contracted salmonella food poisoning. There was evidence that the turkey salad was to blame. Can Pearl bring an action

against the Mothers Association based on §2-314 and the warranty of merchantability?

4. Dr. Newbolt had been a dentist for many years when she decided to give it all up and try something else. She opens a furniture store. During the "Grand Opening Sale" on her first day in business, she sells a sofa to one Sophie. Does Sophie get a warranty of merchantability along with the sofa? Would it make any difference if Sophie had long known Dr. Newbolt and had, in fact, discussed with her the whole idea of her going into the furniture business?

5. In the process of building a vacation home on some land that he owned in Maine, Joe heard about some new "super efficient" insulation manufactured by a California company called NewTech. Joe contacted his local building supply store, Sarah's Supply of Portland. Sarah said she had never heard of the product but that she would contact NewTech and try to order some for Joe. Eventually just enough insulation to fill Joe's order is shipped to Sarah, who duly delivers it to Joe's building location and bills Joe for the price, which she calculates as the cost of the material to her plus a customary markup. Later it turns out that the insulation is defective. If Joe sues Sarah, can she defend on the basis that she had never ordered the new product before or since and had not held herself out as having any special knowledge or expertise about it?

6. Flora owns a flower shop. Whenever she sells any flowers, her buyer would, of course, be getting a warranty that they were merchantable. Suppose that in remodeling her store, Flora decides to get rid of her old refrigeration unit and buy a new one. She sells the old unit to a dealer in used refrigeration equipment. Does *this* buyer get the warranty of merchantability from Flora?

7. Flora of the previous example enters into an oral agreement with a salesperson from Chillers, Inc., under which she will buy an expensive new refrigerated display case. She later tries to get out of the deal using an argument based on the Statute of Frauds, which requires certain contracts to be evidenced by a signed record, as we will explore in Chapter 6. Chillers argues that there is an exception that applies only "between merchants." Does the exception apply?

8. Michael Jones, M.D., delivers $50,000 to Wide World of Cars, Inc., as a deposit on a Ferrari F40. When a dispute arises as to how much Jones is obligated to pay for the car—the seller argues for a stipulated price of $800,000 while Jones argues for a mere $400,000—the deal falls through. In the course of the resulting litigation, Wide World argued that Jones should be classified as a merchant buyer. Jones replied that the only other car he has ever purchased for more than $80,000 was a

348 Ferrari, "which he continues to own and utilize for personal enjoyment." Wide World countered that whether Jones had purchased "one, or fifty automobiles" was not dispositive and that his ability to purchase an $800,000 automobile was sufficient to confer merchant status. Who has the better argument here?

9. Farmer Brown is, as you might expect, a farmer. During the summer, he harvests a large crop of summer squash, a small portion of which he sells to the public at a roadside stand. The rest of the harvest is claimed by a large company, Agribuyer, Inc., on the basis of an agreement it entered into with Brown earlier in the year. Brown would like to get out of the deal with Agribuyer, relying on the Statute of Frauds.
   (a) When a few squash are purchased by Dan Urban, a city-dweller out for a drive in the country, does Urban get a warranty of merchantability?
   (b) Will Agribuyer have any success invoking the "between merchants" exception to the Statute of Frauds?

Explanations

1. No, Ned would not be considered a merchant on these facts. The buyer would not get the warranty of merchantability. (As you'll see in later chapters, this doesn't mean the buyer doesn't get any warranty protection, only that the particular warranty of merchantability isn't available to him or her.) In the language of the section, Ned does not "deal in goods of the kind" or "hold himself out" as having any "special knowledge or skill." As Comment 1 sets out, the definition of the term "merchant" is supposed to distinguish between the "professional" on the one hand and the "casual or inexperienced seller or buyer" on the other. See also Comment 3 to §2-314, which states that "[a] person making an isolated sale of goods is not a 'merchant' within the meaning of the full scope of the section, and, thus, no warranty of merchantability would apply." In *Nuijens v. Novy*, 543 N.Y.S.2d 887 (Justice Ct. Wayne Co. 1989), a town justice in New York faced with a disgruntled puppy buyer held that the warranty of merchantability did not apply when there was no evidence that the seller, a self-employed farrier, had engaged in the sale of more than one litter in the course of the year. In *Bev Smith, Inc. v. Atwell*, 836 N.W.2d 872 (Mich. App. 2013), the Court of Appeals of Michigan held that a "hobbyist" was not to be deemed a merchant for the purposes of Article 2, even if his hobby involved the collection of classic racecars of great value, including the one at the center of the dispute before the court, which had been appraised at more than $2 million and was on "semi-permanent" display at the Chrysler Museum. In coming to this conclusion, the court explained:

> It is true that Nicholas Smith described himself as a serious collector of classic cars. However, plaintiff did not purchase the Dodge [the subject of the dispute] in furtherance of its trade and did not specifically hold itself out as possessing specialized knowledge or skill concerning classic automobiles. Nor does the success of plaintiff's business depend on collecting classic racecars. Plaintiff is akin to a hobbyist and purchased the Dodge merely for pleasure.

2. Under these facts, buyers would get the warranty of merchantability. It is not necessarily the larger scale of Ned's venture that makes the difference. It becomes relevant, however, that he is in fact running it as an ongoing business and holding it out to the public as such by his use of the name "Spaniels of Springfield" and, presumably, such indicia of a professional business venture as letterhead using this name and a telephone listing under it.

   It should be obvious that drawing the line between the "professional" dealer and the "casual or inexperienced" individual who is making only an "isolated" sale is not always so easy to draw. In some situations it will seem something like a toss-up. Then it's got to be a judgment call. What we can say is that the more "professional" the party appears to be, the more likely it is that he or she will fall within the merchant class. The more "casual or inexperienced," the less likely.

3. The Wisconsin Supreme Court held that the Mothers Association was not a merchant in *Samson v. Riesing*, 215 N.W.2d 662 (Wis. 1974). The court distinguished between folks like the Mothers Association and the "commercial restauranteur." But does this make a difference to Pearl? It's best to reserve judgment until we study the merchantability idea in Chapter 12.

   Of course the result might well have been different if it had been shown that the Association sponsored meals on some kind of regular or continuing basis.

4. Newbolt is a merchant of furniture from the moment she opens up the store. Even as a new entrant in the business world, she "holds herself out" as having the kind of knowledge and skill that others in the field have. If Newbolt doesn't have this degree of expertise, it's her problem, and she can't shift the risk to her buyers. Under the language of §2-104(1), it shouldn't make any difference that the particular buyer might know she is new to the field or that she doesn't have the requisite knowledge or skill. In *Golden Needles Knitting & Glove Co., Inc. v. Dynamic Marketing Enterprises, Inc.*, 766 F. Supp. 421 (W.D.N.C. 1991), the defendant, which had entered into an agreement to be the exclusive distributor of plaintiff's surgical gloves, claimed not to be a merchant since the company was new in the business. The court noted:

> Such an argument is undermined in light of a letter by [the defendant's] President, Victor Ragucci, to Plaintiff's marketing manager, Roger Sutton, on December 20, 1989. In that letter, Ragucci states, "Dynamic Medical (the predecessor of defendant) has presently dealers in Massachusetts, Michigan, and California, promoting our quality latex glove lines." . . . The letter demonstrates that Victor Ragucci, the alter-ego of defendant, had extensive experience distributing goods similar to the ones manufactured by plaintiff. Therefore, the court finds that defendant, through Ragucci, was a merchant for the purposes of the UCC.

The important point, of course, is not that Ragucci did in fact actually have a measure of expertise, but that he "held himself out" as having it in his business dealings.

5. Sarah would probably be liable on the warranty of merchantability. Her argument against liability is based on the language in §2-314 that requires that the seller be a merchant "with respect to goods of that kind." She argues she does not normally deal in nor did she hold herself out as having any special expertise with respect to this type of insulating material. But a court would most likely read the "goods of that kind" requirement more broadly. Sarah does regularly deal in building materials, and that should be enough. After all, her supply company is in business to make money; Joe contacted her because of her general experience in the area, and she was willing to deal with him and make money off of this sale. The question is based on *Ashley Square, Ltd. v. Contractors Supply of Orlando, Inc.*, 532 So. 2d 710 (Fla. Dist. Ct. App. 1988), which held the supply company to be "a merchant with respect to goods of that kind" in a similar situation having to do with some special stucco it ordered at the request of a buyer. For another case that comes to essentially the same conclusion, see *Gared Holdings, LLC v. Best Bolt Products, Inc.*, 991 N.E.2d 1005 (Ind. App. 2013).

6. The buyer of the refrigerator would presumably not get the warranty of merchantability because Flora is not a "merchant with respect to goods" of the refrigerator kind. As far as the trade in refrigerators goes, this seems to be a particularly good example of the "isolated sale" that in and of itself does not make the seller a merchant who gives the warranty of merchantability.

   The distinction between flowers and refrigeration equipment is pretty clear. In other situations, sellers have tried, often with success, to draw a very fine line with the "goods of that kind" language in §2-314. In *Fear Ranches, Inc. v. Berry*, 470 F.2d 905 (10th Cir. 1972), the defendant ranchers had previously sold all of the cattle they raised to packers. Because of financial difficulties they were forced to sell some of the animals to the plaintiff buyer who, allegedly unknown to the sellers, was to use them for breeding. The court held that the sellers had not given any warranty of merchantability that would protect the plaintiff when the cattle sold turned out to be unfit for breeding. Contrast this to the case of *Alpert v. Thomas*, 643 F. Supp. 1406 (D. Vt. 1986). The sellers, operating under the name Georgian Hill Arabians, were engaged in the business of training, breeding, and selling Arabian horses. They sold one such horse, a 20-month-old Russian-Arabian stallion named Raxx, to the buyer for a price of $175,000. The sellers understood that the buyer was buying Raxx for breeding purposes. Over time, and after many examinations by a series of expert veterinarians, Raxx was found (while having "excellent libido") to fall under guidelines established by the Society of Theriogenology in the category of "unsatisfactory prospective breeder." So much for Raxx, at least in the eyes of the buyers, who sought relief under the doctrine of the warranty of merchantability. The sellers argued that, under the *Fear Ranches* case, they could not be held to have given the warranty of merchantability as they had never before sold a stallion for this purpose. However, the cases were easily distinguishable on the facts. Here the sellers had known of the buyer's intention to try to breed Raxx. They had previously been involved in the sale of seven or eight mares for breeding purposes, and they had sold shares in a breeding stallion. The court had no difficulty in finding that these sellers, unlike the ranchers in *Fear Ranches*, were merchants for the purposes of §2-314.

While Flora the florist is almost assuredly not a merchant with respect to the refrigerator, it would not be right to conclude that a seller will never be held to have given the warranty of merchantability unless it makes a sale of exactly the stuff it is in business to sell. The Massachusetts Supreme Judicial Court has held that the Massachusetts Bay Transportation Authority, which is presumably in the business of providing mass transit services, was a merchant and gave the warranty of merchantability in connection with its sale of eight used trolly cars to a dealer in scrap metals. *Ferragamo v. Massachusetts Bay Transportation Authority*, 481 N.E.2d 477 (Mass. 1985). The suit was brought in the name of a worker who died following his work dismantling the cars, allegedly because of the level of certain materials in them that gave off deadly fumes when exposed to the worker's acetylene torch. The MBTA had argued that the sale was "incidental" to its primary business and, hence, was not made by it as a merchant. The Supreme Judicial Court, however, noted:

> The MBTA was highly "experienced and knowledgeable" with respect to the goods involved. The MBTA had, through its employees, a long-term and thorough acquaintance with the cars sold to the plaintiff: MBTA employees had contributed to the manufacture of the cars, had operated, repaired, refurbished, and maintained them for twenty-five years. [W]hile the MBTA may not be a merchant of scrap, there was sufficient evidence to conclude that it was a merchant of used trolly cars.

Nor did the MBTA's sale of these used trollies fall within the category of an "isolated sale." The court found that the jury could have rightly concluded that the MBTA routinely sold off its used and discarded cars.

7. After analyzing the previous question, we concluded that Flora was not a merchant, so what's the problem here? Comment 2 to §2-104, which is widely quoted and respected, informs us (even if the actual language of the section does not) that a person can be a merchant for one purpose and not for another:

    > The professional status under the definition may be based upon specialized knowledge as to the goods, specialized knowledge as to business practices, or specialized knowledge as to both and which kind of specialized knowledge may be sufficient to establish merchant status is indicated by the nature of the provision.

    Read the rest of this Comment if you have not already done so. The question of whether Flora sold the old refrigerator as a merchant for the purposes of §2-314 was, we are told, a much narrower question than whether she should be classified a merchant for the purposes of the Statute of Frauds of §2-201. For purposes of that section, "almost every person in business" would be deemed to be a merchant. Flora is in business; she owns and operates a flower shop. The transaction was undertaken by her in that business capacity. Chiller should win on its argument that this deal took place "between merchants."

8. Being filthy rich does not in and of itself make you a merchant. In *Jones v. WideWorld of Cars, Inc.*, 820 F. Supp. 132 (S.D.N.Y. 1993), the district court held Doctor Jones not to be a merchant under the circumstances, stating, "Financial status alone is insufficient to impart a consumer with the specialized knowledge and skill that merchants are deemed to possess." Jones is, at least as far as §2-104(1) of the U.C.C. is concerned, a simple consumer no different from you or me.

9. Here again we face the possibility that the question whether Brown fits under the Code definition of merchant will be answered differently depending on what section of Article 2 is being invoked. In (a) the question is one for §2-314, and the answer is fairly straightforward: Brown is a merchant selling his squash to Dan Urban at the roadside stand. Urban gets the warranty of merchantability. The issue in (b) is trickier and has no easy answer. There are an amazing number of cases dealing with just this issue, that is, whether a farmer is to be considered a merchant for the purposes of §2-201(2). The results are split just about down the middle. For a look at this problem, see *Brooks Cotton Co., Inc. v. Williams*, 381 S.W.3d 414 (Tenn. App. 2012). Some courts hold that a farmer's once-a-year sale of his or her entire crop is to be thought of as an "isolated sale" by a nonprofessional. Others see the modern farmer as more than a simple

hayseed. He or she must be as sophisticated in business as other actors on the commercial scene. Those states that have held that a farmer can be a merchant for the purposes of this section typically say that whether a *particular* farmer is a merchant is a question of fact and that the court has to look into the degree of business acumen he or she has shown, length of time in the trade, and so on. For all their talk of "the intention of the drafters," the cases seem to turn on the individual court's attitude toward farmers and farming as much as on anything else. There is no reason to think that there will be any agreement in the foreseeable future on whether a farmer is a merchant under Article 2. See David B. Harrison, *Farmers as "merchants" within provisions of UCC article 2, dealing with sales*, 95 A.L.R.3d 484 (1979).

CHAPTER 4

Offer and Acceptance: The Basics

CONTRACT FORMATION UNDER ARTICLE 2

In the basic Contracts course, much time and energy is invariably spent on what are generically referred to by Contracts teachers as "problems of contract formation." Students more regularly refer to this material as simply "the offer and acceptance stuff." Here the totally innocent student can be excused for feeling that he or she is being hit by a veritable blizzard of rules, subrules, generalizations, and exceptions not just about offers and acceptances but all manner of revocations, rejections, counteroffers, "deviant acceptances," and what-not. And any or all of these can come in the form of different media, not to mention a phone conversation, a nod, or a shrug, or the intriguing possibility of communication by silence. The whole topic can easily begin to seem like a grotesque dance of innumerable intricate (and dizzying) steps.

You might therefore initially be surprised at how *few* sections Article 2 devotes to contract formation issues. To a large measure, this is because of the overall approach the drafters took—and wished us to take—to such problems. Look at §2-204 on Formation in General and particularly at the first subsection. "A contract for sale of goods may be made in any manner sufficient to show agreement, including conduct by both parties which recognizes the existence of such a contract." We are encouraged to conceive of the necessary "mutual assent" in a much more flexible way than was true in the traditional or classical common law of contract, where formal structure and a myriad of technicalities took center stage. As a matter of fact, this more laissez-faire attitude of the Code is not so far from more recent thinking about contract law in general. As I hope you saw in studying this material, many of the more recent common law contracts cases (and certainly recent commentators) tend to downplay the technicalities and, like the Code, instead focus on the fact of agreement, using the notions of offer, acceptance, and so on not as ends in themselves, but as means to delve into the (reasonable) reality of the situation in which the two communicating parties find themselves. This so-called modern law of contract had its influence on the drafting of Article 2 and has in turn itself been influenced by that Article's overall success.

There is a second related reason why Article 2 does not go into all the details of offer and acceptance law as you might have expected. It cannot ignore these problems entirely, but, to the extent that the sections we are discussing in this and the next chapter don't answer a particular question, there will always be the general common law of offer and acceptance on which to fall back. Note the effect of §1-103(b). The drafters of Article 2 did not purport to be codifying all the minutiae of the law of contract formation. What was left uncodified remains governed by the general principles of contract law. As an example, you will find no mention in the Code of that old standby, the mailbox rule. But that's just the point. You really can think of it as a standby. In the unlikely event you are ever called upon to deal with a potential sale of goods in which an unambiguous revocation of an offer and an equally unambiguous acceptance of that offer cross in the mails, then by all means refer to your notes on the common law's way of sorting out the mess. Otherwise, be glad that the Code drafters did not clutter up their work with each and every detail. Focus your thoughts, as they would have you do in §2-204 and the following sections, on *why* such communications matter. The question is whether the parties have as a practical matter reached sufficient agreement for contract liability to arise. If they have in fact reached agreement, *how* they did so is of secondary or no importance. In this regard, note also §2-204(2). However, as we will see in the next chapter, there is a major exception to this generalization in §2-207.

The third subsection of §2-204 deserves a bit more comment. *Indefiniteness* has always been itself a particularly indefinite and troublesome term for the common law of contracts, but if anything, the drafters seem to be saying that some greater degree of indefiniteness may be possible in the negotiations for the sale of goods without putting the formation of a legally binding contract into jeopardy. Read by itself, this statement may seem like so much handwaving and, in that respect, not particularly helpful. But §2-204(3) is not left to work on its own. See the last two paragraphs of the Comment to this section. As we will discuss in later chapters, Article 2 takes particular note of how often negotiations that would seem hopelessly indefinite or merely bizarre to the observing layperson will be perfectly clear to the parties themselves. (The crucial role of so-called trade terms is left to

Chapter 7. A set of particular sections, the so-called gap fillers of Article 2, are dealt with in Chapter 9.) For the moment, it is enough to take to heart the Comment's message that *commercial* standards of indefiniteness, not the standards of an uninformed layperson and certainly not the standards of a pettifogging lawyer, are what are relevant to the question of contract formation.

AGREEMENT SEEN IN CONDUCT

Section §2-204(1) specifies that an agreement can be established by "conduct by both parties which recognizes the existence of such a contract." This provision can be of particular importance when the parties never quite get all the record completed and one is later trying to rely on this fact alone to establish that a contract never existed. The drafters recognized that all too often contracting parties, either through lack of diligence or because they continue to squabble over minor details none of which would be a "deal breaker," fail to produce a nice, neat package of terms all in a signed record. At the same time, both parties may be well into performance of their obligations, speaking and acting for all the world as if there was a binding agreement. The law of the Code is that if this is the case (and if there is "a reasonably certain basis for giving an appropriate remedy" in the event of a breach), then there actually *is* a binding agreement. No one gets out of his or her deal on this particular technicality.

In *Nebraska Builders Products Co. v. The Industrial Erectors, Inc.*, 478 N.W.2d 257 (Neb. 1992), for example, the parties entered into an agreement for the purchase and sale of some industrial cranes, which were to be prepared according to detailed specifications. The parties never executed a formal writing. Industrial, the seller, claimed that as a result it was not bound by any contract. The trial court agreed, ruling that no contract had been formed, but the Supreme Court of Nebraska held this to be error. The key was §2-204. While the buyer may or may not have accepted the seller's written sales proposal over the telephone soon after it was made, the court noted that for several months after it sent its proposal the seller acted *as if* a contract existed, preparing shop drawings and corresponding with the buyer about obtaining approval for minor variances in the specifications. In addition, a representative of Industrial had visited the buyer's offices almost five months "after the alleged agreement was made," in the words of the court, "to answer questions on the crane system that Industrial would supply." On behalf of Industrial, of course, it could be argued that all this activity was carried out not in accordance with an obligation already undertaken but in pursuit of a possible deal. But that is exactly the point. Under §2-204 the question is to be decided as one of fact—did sufficient agreement exist?—and the facts are to be viewed in their own unique commercial context. Similarly, see *Crest Ridge Construction Group, Inc. v. Newcourt Inc.*, 78 F.3d 146 (5th Cir. 1996). In another case, *American Plastic Equipment, Inc. v. CBS Inc.*, 886 F.2d 521 (2d Cir. 1989), the court stressed, among other facts, that at the conclusion of a negotiation session between representatives of the two parties, the buyer's negotiator "asserted that a deal had been made and the two thereupon shook hands—a formality indicating intent to be bound." Needless to say, not every handshake concludes a legally binding contract, but this court rightly took note of the fact that in such a situation, parties do not take an offered handshake lightly. Along with other activities on the part of the seller, it constituted "conduct which recognize[d]" the existence of a contract. Of course, it will not have to be true in all instances that conduct does lead to the conclusion that a contract has been formed. For an example of a case in which the court found that a contract had *not* been formed by the conduct of the parties, who had continued to trade in large quantities of chemicals used in the production of fertilizer all the while bickering over what would be the specific terms of a written agreement they were both determined eventually to sign on their terms and their terms only, see *PCS Sales (USA), Inc. v. Nitrochem Distribution Ltd.*, 2004 WL 944541 (S.D.N.Y. 2004), *aff'd*, 128 F. App'x 817 (2d Cir. 2005).

Two final points about contracts established in this way by conduct. First of all, note that the "conduct" called for in this section presumably need not rise to the level of what is studied in Contracts courses as *detrimental reliance*. The point of finding the conduct relevant here is really informational or evidentiary—not as is the case with true detrimental reliance that it significantly alters the balance of equities between the parties because of one's conduct influenced by the fact of the contract. For example, imagine that after a period of negotiation between a prospective Buyer and Seller, Buyer contacts the head of his purchasing department and directs that a computer file be initiated "to handle this account" including information such as where payments are to be sent and so on. Meanwhile, Seller tells her billing and shipping departments to put Buyer in their computer files. Further assume that she tells these departments to get all pertinent information from the sales department, which will be putting in deep computer storage its own relevant file on Buyer, as its practice is to keep current files only on "active prospects." Here I have posited a whole mess of conduct consistent with a contract having been entered into on both parties' parts. And yet it would take a very watered-down view of "detrimental reliance" to find it on either Seller's or Buyer's part here, at least if their computer systems come equipped with the delete function.

A second point is that, while behavior of the type we have been discussing may be sufficient to establish a contract under §2-204, it is not necessary. This section (and Article 2 in general) does not preclude finding a contract in the more old-fashioned way, by identifying an offer and an acceptance and leaving it at that. If one party can establish the existence of a contract by the mechanism of offer and acceptance, further conduct evidencing the existence of the contract is icing on the cake, but it is not required. Certainly no reliance on the deal need be shown to make it enforceable. The parties having agreed to a purchase and sale, that is enough.

MATTERS OF OFFER AND ACCEPTANCE

While the drafters of Article 2 did not think it necessary to restate all of the law of offer and acceptance, they did apparently find some tinkering in order. The three sections beginning with §2-205 are the result. Section 2-205 concerns what the Code refers to as *firm offers*. As you know, traditional contract law held as sacred the principle that an offer could be revoked by the offeror at any time before its acceptance. At the same time, this result could create a dilemma for even the most honest, diligent, and cooperative offeror and offeree. How could the offeree be given sufficient confidence that the offer would be held open for a length of time necessary for the offeree to explore the advisability of taking up the offer or to put in place other related plans? The common law approach was that the offeror and offeree could enter into an option contract in which the offeree would promise the offeror a consideration in return for keeping the offer open. The Code's approach, as set forth in §2-205 is explored in the first example that follows.

Other "fixes" to the common law are found in §2-206. One of the problems addressed by that section has been called the "unilateral contract trick." At common law, a buyer asks a seller, a beer distributor, to deliver five cases of Brand A beer for his party on Sunday. This is a unilateral contract—an offer to be accepted by performance. The seller responds by delivering five cases of inferior Brand X beer. Is the seller in breach? No. Under the common law "mirror image" rule, a purported acceptance that does not match the offer is not an acceptance, but a counteroffer. The buyer is free to reject the beer, but there are no consequences to the seller for shipping the wrong goods. We will see how this outcome has been changed in the remaining examples.

You may have seen how the common law approach—at least in its most traditional mechanistic mood—can actually thwart the intentions of the parties. Since the adoption of Article 2, the common law of contracts has been "modernized" partly through the Code's influence. The results of §2-206 will probably not strike you as unusual or remarkable as they would someone who had studied Contracts prior to the 1960s and to Article 2's widespread acceptance. That is partly because Article 2 has had a tremendous influence on the common law, as can be seen in many sections of the Restatement (Second) of Contracts.

The final of the Code's three special sections on offer and acceptance, §2-207, is sufficiently tricky to warrant its own chapter, that being the one that follows.

Examples

1. Sam, a used car dealer, offers to sell a certain 2010 Chevy to Beth for $1,000. She tells him that she can't make up her mind right away. Sam says to her, "Don't worry. I'll keep the offer open for the next week. You can accept any time until then." The very next day Beth decides to buy the car, but before she can get over to Sam's, she receives a message from him on her telephone answering machine in which he says that he has decided not to sell the car to her at this price. His message concludes, "I would sell at $1,200."
   (a) Can Beth still get the car for $1,000?
   (b) Suppose that at their initial meeting Sam had scribbled on a memo pad bearing his company's logo the following: "Offer to sell 2010 Chevy to Beth for $1,000. Good for one week as of today." The only other marking on the piece of paper was the day's date. Does this change your answer to the question?
   (c) Bonnie, a bank president, drives her car into Sam's looking to sell it. She is asking $2,400. Sam says he'll consider this deal, but only if she signs a record he prepared that says, "Bonnie offers to sell her car to Sam for $2,400, this offer to remain open and irrevocable for a period of one month from this date." Sam dates the record and Bonnie signs it. Is Bonnie bound to keep this offer open for the full month? Would your answer be any different if Bonnie were herself a dealer in automobiles and not a banker?

2. Seller sends a fax to Buyer making a definite offer to sell. Buyer immediately sends back a letter clearly stating that she accepts the offer. It arrives in the normal course of post. Has a contract been formed?

3. After some preliminary and inconclusive negotiations over the telephone, Buyer sends Seller a record setting forth the terms of a proposed deal. The record ends with the statement, "This offer may be accepted by Seller only by his returning to Buyer a copy of this record signed and dated by him." At the bottom of the record is a line for the Seller's signature under the heading "Accepted on by Seller." Seller never returns this record, but instead calls and leaves a message with Buyer's secretary that he accepts the offer mailed to him. Has a contract been formed?

4. Betrand, a maker of appliances, needs some electrical switches. He reviews a catalog and price list that he had received from Switches International,

a major vendor of such things, and concludes that he wants their switch XR7, which is listed at a price of $5 per unit. He sends Switches a Purchase Order form he has filled out that calls for 2,000 of the XR7 switches. Under "Date of Delivery" on the form, he puts "Immediate Delivery."

(a) When Switches receives this order, what may it do in order to accept this offer?

(b) Suppose that Switches accidentally ships 2,000 of its XR9 switches. Betrand cannot use this model, does not accept the shipment, and is hurt by the delay. If Betrand sues Switches for breach, can that firm argue that there never was a contract for the XR7 switches as it never accepted the order?

(c) Suppose instead that the shipment of the XR9s was not a mistake. When it received Betrand's order it found itself temporarily low on the XR7 switch. Believing that the buyer could use the more advanced XR9 in its place, and being willing to accept the same price for them, it shipped the newer switches in response to this order. Is Switches in breach of contract?

5. Mr. and Mrs. Hill ordered a computer over the telephone by speaking directly with a sales representative of the manufacturer, using a credit card to make payment. When the box arrived, it contained the computer and a listing of terms said by the manufacturer to govern the transaction unless the customer returned the computer within 30 days. Among the terms listed was an arbitration clause. The Hills kept the computer for more than the 30 days, after which they began to experience difficulties with it. When they filed suit, the manufacturer argued that the Hills were bound by the terms that had been sent to them along with the computer, including the arbitration clause, and that hence their suit had to be dismissed and the matter sent to arbitration.

(a) Does the manufacturer win with this argument?

(b) Suppose instead the Hills had ordered and paid for their new computer by visiting a web site set up by the manufacturer for just this purpose, so that purchases could be made directly through use of the web site and without the purchaser having to speak with any real live person representing the manufacturer. The web site prominently displayed a link to the "Terms and Conditions" governing the transaction. Had the Hills clicked on this link, they could have seen the arbitration clause conspicuously displayed amidst a host of other terms. Should the manufacturer's contention that the purchasers are thus bound to arbitrate any dispute be more or less convincing under these circumstances?

EXPLANATIONS

Explanations

1. a. No. Sam has effectively revoked the original offer. Beth would want to argue that his promise to keep the offer open was binding on him under §2-205, but she loses because it was not in a record. Reading this section you find a number of criteria that must be met in order for an ordinary, revocable offer to be made into a firm offer: The offeror must be a merchant, the offer must be made in a signed record, and the record must "by its terms give assurances that it will be held open" for some time. Note that if no exact period of time is stated, the offer will be firm for "a reasonable time." If a time limit is stated, it must be no longer than three months.

   What happens if an offer is made meeting all of these criteria but purporting to be irrevocable for a longer period, say six months? Does this failed attempt to take advantage of §2-205 mean that the offer is revocable from its inception? Comment 3 says no. "A promise made for a longer period will operate under this section to bind the offeror only for the first three months of the period but may of course be renewed." See, e.g., *Norca Corp. v. Tokheim Corp.*, 643 N.Y.S.2d 139 (App. Div. 1996). Is there any way under Article 2 that an offeror can bind him or herself to a longer period of irrevocability? The Comment goes on to remind us that an offer "supported by consideration" may continue for a longer period. This is just the old common law option, the possibility of which presumably survives the passage of Article 2—at least if the consideration is real and of some value and not merely a token amount or the recitation of a purported consideration like "one dollar in hand paid." So a seller is perfectly free to agree to hold an offer open for six months in consideration of the offeree paying $5. That transaction is outside the scope of §2-205, which applies only to options that lack consideration.

   b. Here all the criteria appear to be met, and the offer would be irrevocable for the week. The language on the memo sheet is a bit vague, but it should be enough to constitute an "assurance" that the offer would be held open for that period of time. Note that if Sam had stated instead something like, "Offer will lapse one week from today," this would probably not constitute a firm offer. That language would be taken as meaning only that the offer would lapse naturally of its own accord after a week, not as a promise that the buyer couldn't make it lapse earlier by a revocation effectively communicated.

   The one problem Beth might have here is establishing that this was a *signed* record, as Sam never did add his personal signature to the paper. But look at the definition of "sign" in §1-201(b)(37) and the Comment to that subsection. The fact that the paper had Sam's logo on it and was given by him to record something to do with his business should be enough. See also Comment 2 to §2-205, which supports this conclusion.

c. Bonnie cannot be held to her promise not to revoke the offer. Her case is easy because she is not a merchant. On who is and who is not a "merchant" under Article 2, see §2-104 as discussed in Chapter 3. Note in Comment 2 to that section that for the purposes of §2-205 almost every person in business would be a merchant. But the Comment goes on to say that even if Bonnie is president of a bank, if she is here dealing in a personal capacity, she need not worry about making a firm offer.

   If Bonnie deals in cars, she would be a merchant and could presumably make a firm offer to sell one under §2-205. In that case, the final language of that section becomes crucial, though it has rarely arisen in the cases. Read it. The idea here, as noted in Comment 4, is to prevent any offeror, even a merchant, from "inadvertently" giving up the precious right to revoke by too casually signing a record put in front of him or her. This is a good example of the concept of "reasonable expectations" found in many Code provisions. The Code knows that Bonnie will not read the contract carefully, so the burden is on the other party to call an unusual provision to her attention.

2. Yes, if responding with a letter was a medium "reasonable in the circumstances" under §2-206(1)(a). Of course if in the particular situation the buyer should have recognized that the seller would expect a speedier response, then the ordinary post might not be a reasonable medium. Presumably a fax, an email, or a telephone call would be. Maybe even a letter sent by special overnight delivery. It all depends on the particular circumstances. As Comment 1 suggests, this language in §2-206(1)(a) was included to do away with any lingering adherence to an older set of highly technical (and often "unreasonable") rules about offer and acceptance. (This Comment's reference to the possibility of new media of communication developing is particularly interesting in light of the explosive rise in electronic communications quite beyond what would have been anticipated even a few years ago. People who before led perfectly productive lives are now wondering how they ever got along without such gadgets.) I hope that in your study of the modern law of contract formation you saw this more flexible and realistic approach as it has been adopted more generally, thanks in part to the influence of Article 2's drafters.

   It will not surprise you to learn that most courts have found a contract to have been formed by the exchange of emails. See, for example, *Republic Bank, Inc. v. West Penn Allegheny Health Systems, Inc.*, 475 F. App'x 692 (8th Cir. 2012).

3. No. This section does not do away with the old idea that the offeror is "master of his or her offer." Here the offer unambiguously indicates a particular mode of acceptance, and §2-206(1) allows this to control. Courts have upheld this result. In fact, in an interesting set of circumstances, this provision can work to the advantage of an *offeree* who later changes his or her mind. Sales made by travelling and door-to-door salespeople often are written up by the seller's representative filling out a Purchase Order on the spot and getting the buyer to sign it. The buyer will be given the impression that he or she is committed from that moment on. Somewhere on the Purchase Order form, however, is language to the effect that a contract will be entered into only when the form is accepted or signed by a higher official of the seller at its home office. This is put there by the company, of course, to be sure that an overeager sales representative hasn't committed his or her employer to a deal that he or she shouldn't have. It may also be in there because under the choice-of-law rules in some jurisdictions, the applicable law is the law of the state where the last act took place that resulted in the formation of the contract. But notice the result. Until the form is transmitted back to the home office and until it is actually signed there, the record is merely an offer made by the buyer. So the buyer has the right to get out of the deal by revoking the offer before it has been accepted at the home office. Sellers sometimes are sloppy with their own internal procedures and have to take the consequences. See, for example, *Beard Implement Co., Inc. v. Krusa*, 567 N.E.2d 345 (Ill. App. 1991), and *InfoComp, Inc. v. Electra Products, Inc.*, 109 F.3d 902 (3d Cir. 1997).

4. a. Switches has several options on how to accept. Read §2-206(1)(b) and §2-206(2). It can promptly reply with a promissory acceptance in any reasonable medium. It can promptly ship the switches off to Betrand. It may even be able to accept by "the beginning of [the] requested performance," although what that might be in this instance is unclear. If, for example, Switches ran its business not with a large inventory on hand but began to fabricate switches only when they were ordered, it might be deemed to have accepted once it starts making up the XR7s needed to fill this order. Would it be enough if Switches had itself ordered from its own suppliers the component parts it would need to make up these units? What if Switches did sell from inventory and had already begun to "make up" Betrand's order by pulling the switches from the shelves, packaging them, and labelling the packages? This would not be an acceptance by shipment under §2-206(1)(b), at least according to Comment 2, but could it constitute the beginning of performance under subsection (2)? Betrand, if he tried to revoke before actual shipment, would argue that this was not the beginning of performance but only preparation

for performance. After all, Switches would have felt free to unpack the goods or change the address on the packages if a more lucrative deal came along. Comment 3 suggests that in such a situation the court should look to the developing common law in this area. In any event, if a seller later wants to claim under §2-206 that the beginning of performance made for its acceptance, note that it must have notified the buyer of its acceptance within a reasonable time. Good advice, of course, would be to notify the buyer as soon as possible and take no chances.

For an interesting example of a contract offer deemed accepted by performance, see *In re Wegener*, 186 B.R. 692 (D. Neb. 1995). In the course of a bankruptcy proceeding, the debtor argued that he was never legally bound to pay for $12,500 worth of (what turned out to be losing) lottery tickets because he had never written a check to pay for them—unlike the other $12,280 worth of tickets for which he had at least given the vendor a check, even if it had bounced. The court ruled that a contract to pay for the $12,500 batch of tickets was valid and enforceable. "The debtor made an offer to purchase the tickets. The offer was accepted by performance of the [ticket vendor] by the preparation and issuance of the tickets at debtor's request, and the physical delivery of the tickets to debtor."

b. Switches will be bound to the contract for the XR7 switches. Note in §2-206(1)(b) that prompt shipment of *nonconforming goods* can act as an acceptance of the original offer. So Switches has accepted and breached the contract both at the same time! This result may seem odd, but look at it from Betrand's point of view. Should Switches be able to get out of all obligation to him because it made this mistake? Even worse, what if the seller *intentionally* shipped nonconforming goods? The common law would have it that this constituted a counteroffer. The buyer, faced with having to make a quick decision when this shipment arrived at the door, might be under pressure to accept the shipment. The consequence would be that he ended up buying some things he never ordered and never really intended to buy. An argument in favor of the Code result is that it takes away from the seller this possibility of what is called *strategic behavior*.

   Notice that, while in this hypothetical situation the nonconformity involves the actual type of good ordered, the result would be the same if the shipment was nonconforming in some other way. For example, suppose Switches had indeed shipped the XR7 chip, but only 1,850 of them. This too would be an acceptance and a breach.

c. Again, by shipping nonconforming goods Switches would be both accepting and breaching a contract for the goods ordered by Betrand. Under §2-206(1)(b) Switches could avoid this result if it "seasonably notifies the buyer that the shipment is offered only as an accommodation to the buyer." Betrand, of course, would not then have to accept the shipment—it would be merely in the nature of a counteroffer—but if he did there would be a contract for the XR9 switches. For a case involving the accommodation notion, which the court itself acknowledges to be, despite its lengthy recitation of facts, "a straightforward sale of goods problem resembling those found in a contracts or sale of goods casebook," see *Corinthian Pharmaceutical Systems, Inc. v. Lederle Laboratories*, 724 F. Supp. 605 (S.D. Ind. 1989).

5. a. In the notorious case of *Hill v. Gateway 2000, Inc.*, 105 F.3d 1147 (7th Cir.), *cert. denied*, 522 U.S. 808 (1997), the Seventh Circuit Court of Appeals vacated a district court opinion favorable to the Hills and remanded the case with instructions that it be sent to arbitration. The circuit court found that the manufacturer had in effect made an offer to sell the computer on the terms to be found in the box along with the item itself and that, "[b]y keeping the computer beyond 30 days, the Hills accepted Gateway's offer, including the arbitration clause." Does the result strike you as obviously right? Consider the following language from Judge Easterbrook's opinion:

> Payment preceding the revelation of full terms is common for air transportation, insurance and many other endeavors. Practical considerations support allowing vendors to enclose the full legal terms with their products. Cashiers cannot be expected to read legal documents to customers before ringing up sales. If the staff at the other end of the phone for direct-sales operations such as Gateway's had to read the four-page statement of terms before taking the buyer's credit card number, the droning voice would anesthetize rather than enlighten many potential buyers. Others would hang up in a rage over the waste of time. And oral recitation would not avoid customer's assertions (whether true or feigned) that the clerk did not read term X to them, or that they did not remember or understand it. Writing provides benefits for both sides of commercial transactions. Customers as a group are better off when vendors skip costly and ineffective steps such as telephonic recitation, and use instead a simple approve-or-return device. Competent adults are bound by such documents, read or unread.

Do you think this explanation would satisfy the Hills? Does it sit right with you?

As you might expect, the decision in *Hill v. Gateway* generated a good deal of controversy among courts and commentators. Not all courts immediately followed its reasoning or result. In a relatively short time, however, the result in *Hill* seems to have become the predominant view. See, for instance, *Sherr v. Dell, Inc.*, 2006 WL 2109436 (S.D.N.Y. 2006), in which the district judge simply stated, without acknowledging any contrary argument or authority, that:

> [a]pprove-or-return contracts have been found to be enforceable in consumer transactions. [citations omitted]. In this case, the arbitration provision at issue appears in a "standard 'approve-or-return' contract." See Provencher v. Dell, Inc., 409 F. Supp. 2d 1196 (C.D. Cal. 2006) (a standard approve-or-return contract is enforceable). In order to avoid ineffectual, costly steps, it is not practical to expect salespeople to read legal documents to customers before ringing up sales [citing Hill v. Gateway 2000]. Due to this reality, some clauses received even after the initial transactions are enforceable.

See also the decision of the Supreme Court of Rhode Island in *DeFontes v. Dell, Inc.*, 984 A.2d 1061 (R.I. 2009).

b. In *Hubbert v. Dell Corporation*, 835 N.E.2d 113 (Ill. App. 2005), the arbitration clause was found by the Appellate Court of Illinois to be binding upon the purchasers under circumstances such as I have posited:

> We find that the online contract included the "Terms and Conditions of Sale." The blue hyperlink entitled "Terms and Conditions of Sale" appeared on numerous Web pages the plaintiffs completed in the ordering process. The blue hyperlinks for the "Terms and Conditions of Sale" also appeared on the defendant's marketing Web pages, copies of which the plaintiffs attached to their complaint. The blue hyperlinks on the defendant's Web pages, constituting the five-step process for ordering the computers, should be treated the same as a multipage written paper contract. The blue hyperlink simply takes a person to another page of the contract, similar to turning the page of a written paper contract. Although there is no conspicuousness requirement, the hyperlink's contrasting blue type makes it conspicuous. Common sense dictates that because the plaintiffs were purchasing computers online, they were not novices when using computers. A person using a computer quickly learns that more information is available by clicking on a blue hyperlink.
>
> Additionally, on three of the defendant's Web pages that the plaintiffs completed to make their purchases, the following statement appeared: "All sales are subject to Dell's Terms and Conditions of Sale." This statement would place a reasonable person on notice that there were terms and conditions attached to the purchase and that it would be wise to find out what the terms and conditions were before making a purchase. The statement that the sales were subject to the defendant's "Terms and Conditions of Sale," combined with making the "Terms and Conditions of Sale" accessible online by blue hyperlinks, was sufficient notice to the plaintiffs that purchasing the computers online would make the "Terms and Conditions of Sale" binding on them. Because the "Terms and Conditions of Sale" were a part of the online contract and because the plaintiffs did not argue that their claims were not within the scope of the arbitration agreement, they were bound by the "Terms and Conditions of Sale," including the arbitration clause.

Do you agree with this result? If you disagree, would your mind be changed if it were to be true—as it was not in *Hubbert*—that the purchaser also had to click an "I Agree to the Terms and Conditions" button on the manufacturer's web site before being allowed to place its order?

Several cases have come to the same result as the *Hubbert* case, but others have not. For example, in *Hines v. Overstock.Com, Inc.*, 668 F. Supp. 2d 362 (E.D.N.Y. 2009), *aff'd*, 380 F. App'x 22 (2d 2010), the United States District Court found that the plaintiff had not agreed to an arbitration provision contained in the defendant's web site's "Terms and Conditions of Use" given the facts of the case. "In the instant case," the court concluded:

> [I]t is clear that Plaintiff had no actual notice of the Terms and Conditions of Use. Defendant has also failed to show that Plaintiff had constructive notice. The Hawkins Affidavit, upon which Defendant relies, conclusorily states that by accessing Overstock's website, an individual accepts Overstock's Terms and Conditions—but, crucially, does not explain how a site-user such as Plaintiff is made aware of the Terms and Conditions. Despite Defendant's assertion that "all customers to Overstock's website are advised of the company's terms and conditions prior to their entry onto the site," neither the Hawkins Affidavit nor any other evidence submitted by Defendant refute Plaintiff's sworn statement that she was never advised of the Terms and Conditions and could not even see the link to them without scrolling down to the bottom of the screen—an action that was not required to effectuate her purchase. Notably, unlike in other cases where courts have upheld browsewrap agreements, the notice that "Entering this Site will constitute your acceptance of these Terms and Conditions," was only available within the Terms and Conditions [citing, and distinguishing, *Hubbert*]. Hines therefore lacked notice of the Terms and Conditions because the website did not prompt her to review the Terms and Conditions and because the link to the Terms and Conditions was not prominently displayed so as to provide reasonable notice of the Terms and Conditions. Very little is required to form a contract nowadays—but this alone does not suffice.

See also *In re Zappos.com, Inc.*, 893 F. Supp. 2d 1058 (D. Nev. 2012).

CHAPTER 5

Offer and Acceptance Advanced: The Battle of the Forms

THE BATTLE JOINED

As we saw in the previous chapter, the drafters of Article 2 did not mean to codify, much less to revamp, all of the common law of offer and acceptance. They did hope to push it along a bit in a more modern, less mechanistic direction, and they did that in §2-204. There was also some minor tinkering in §§2-205 and 2-206, but nothing terribly radical or difficult.

Some changes were not so uncomplicated nor so neat. This chapter concerns what is universally referred to as *the Battle of the Forms*. The considerable problems that we will encounter come about because actual contracting parties tend not to order their affairs just to make things easy for their lawyers or for law students. They don't conveniently label their documents "Offer" and "Acceptance" and follow the rules of the offer and acceptance game, whatever version is in operation. Instead people in business tend to rely heavily on form documents that they have had preprinted for their use, detailing all manner of terms and conditions that not surprisingly suit them just fine. They will title their forms in whatever manner they choose. But it takes two to tango and two to make a deal. If each party relies upon or insists upon its own form, and the two forms differ as they almost invariably will, what have we? From the time of the drafting of Article 2, the answer was pretty clear: We have a situation that does not lend itself well to traditional analysis. The drafters, as we will see, get credit for facing the problem squarely. How successful their end product, the revolutionary §2-207, has turned out to be is another matter altogether.

Our first order of business must be to review how the common law dealt with the battle of the forms. Only then can we turn to the questions on the workings of §2-207. As you work through the examples and explanations, you may come to your own conclusion about why the later drafters of Article 2A chose not to include anything like §2-207 in their work. It may be worth noting that §2-207 is declining in significance as many sellers do not exchange forms with buyers but have the buyers go to the seller's website to enter a contract on the seller's terms.

A COMMON LAW NUTSHELL

Imagine that Buyer sends one of his standard forms captioned "PURCHASE ORDER" to Seller. The form is mostly boilerplate of terms and conditions drafted to Buyer's liking. It does have a few blank spaces on it, which Buyer fills in with the item number and description of the goods he is ordering, the price per unit, and the requested time of delivery. He gets the information about the item from a catalog and price list that Seller had previously sent him. Seller receives this purchase order. Under the common law, would a contract for purchase and sale have been formed as of this point? The answer was almost certainly no. You may remember the old saw about how a catalog or a price list generally does not constitute an offer, but only an invitation to the recipient to make an offer. So Buyer's sending of the form is the making of an offer. That's as far as they've gotten.

Suppose now that Seller responds in a timely fashion by sending Buyer its own form, headed with "ACKNOWLEDGMENT." This form was printed up for Seller's use and, as you by now expect, has its own boilerplate, here tailored to Seller's interests. The few places on the Acknowledgment that call for insertion of particularized information have been filled in with the item number, description, price, and so on. All of these bits of information specific to this deal—what we will end up referring to as the "dickered terms"—are consistent with what Buyer put into the Purchase Order. Once Seller sends off this Acknowledgment form and Buyer has received it, has a contract been formed?

The short answer is that under the common law it was very unlikely that such an exchange of forms would result in a binding contract. This was true even though Buyer and Seller, being perfectly reasonable types, would probably think that they were bound, they had a done deal, or however you want to phrase it. The common law of offer and acceptance took a very rigid approach to a lot of things that ordinary business people, having to make their way in the hustle and bustle of commerce and not the idealized realm of classical theory, reacted to very differently. In particular the common law rule was that for an acceptance to be an acceptance (that is, for it to conclude a binding agreement) it had to be the "mirror image" of the offer. Any additional or different terms in the response, even if seemingly trivial to the parties involved, made that response into a counteroffer. There could be no contract unless that counteroffer was itself accepted by a perfectly conforming mirror image acceptance. It's a pretty fair assumption that the boilerplate on Seller's Acknowledgment contains some provision that isn't found on Buyer's form. It's also likely that neither party noticed this and even more likely that if they did notice they didn't care. Buyer wanted to buy. Seller wanted to sell. They might have thought they had a done deal, but under the common law they did not.

The upshot of this was that if later, before the time for performance, one of them wanted to back out of the deal, even if the reason had nothing to do with anything printed on the forms, his or her lawyer would be able to make a perfectly good legal argument that there never was a contract. The Acknowledgment not being the mirror image of the Purchase Order, that offer was never accepted. The Acknowledgment was itself a counteroffer, but *that* offer was never accepted, the buyer never having responded to it. Neither could legally be held to the deal. Not to put too fine a point on it, the result of the common law rule was to allow a party who had for all practical purposes committed itself to later wriggle out of the deal on what can most charitably be called a technicality. This hardly seems fair. More than that, it's not what Buyer and Seller themselves would have expected.

To continue with our review, imagine that neither Buyer nor Seller tries to welsh on the deal. Seller ships the goods and Buyer accepts them. Now is there a contract? If so, what are its terms? Obviously, if controversy later develops about the goods or payment of the price, the precise terms of the contract can be vitally important. The common law answer was, again, fairly consistent: Now there is a contract. Seller's shipment of the goods arrived at the Buyer's door following on the heels of Seller's offer to sell subject to the terms and conditions on which Seller had, through its Acknowledgment, previously expressed its willingness to sell. Buyer could, of course, have summarily rejected this offer, but if, as we posited, he accepted the goods, he accepted the offer. There is a contract between the two, and its terms are to be found in Seller's Acknowledgment form. What of the special terms Buyer placed in the Purchase Order? They go for naught. As we saw, that form was just an offer that was never accepted. That's past history; it has no legal effect.

So Seller's later form gets to lay out the terms of the deal. This result is an example of what was characterized as the *last shot rule* (or perhaps we should say the "last shot" result) of the common law. It does not always work to the benefit of the seller, as it did in this hypothetical; in some situations it was the buyer whose form document was the last to travel between the parties before performance actually began. In such a situation, the analysis was that this buyer's form constituted an offer to buy on a strict set of terms laid out therein and the seller's shipment was an acceptance of all those terms. That's the way the last shot rule worked. One party, the one whose purely self-interested form was the last in the series, won the grand prize. The other party was out of luck.

A FIRST LOOK AT §2-207

Even a quick glance at §2-207 makes clear that the drafters of Article 2 were trying to make some changes from the common law approach. What they were trying to do and what in fact they wound up doing is the matter that can no longer be avoided. Let's look at what they came up with. In its entirety, §2-207 has been referred to by one court as "a murky bit of prose," and I know of no one who would violently disagree. Still, a bit of creative typography might help. First look at §2-207(1) as it appears in your copy of the Code. Try to parse it if you can. The result should be something like this:

> [A COMMUNICATION that is either]
>
> (i) a definite and seasonable expression of acceptance
>
> or
>
> (ii) a written confirmation which is sent within a reasonable time
>
> OPERATES AS AN ACCEPTANCE
>
> *even though* [that communication] states terms additional to or different from those offered or agreed upon
>
> UNLESS . . .

I have left the concluding "unless" part out for the moment, because my experience has shown that students are always rushing to worry over that language and not paying attention to what comes before. The concluding language is after all only an exception to the general rule first expressed. That general rule will give you enough to think about for the moment as you look at the first example. I'll point you to other parts of the section as they become important for later questions.

Curiously, at this point in the Code the drafters of the 2022 Amendments seem to have run out of steam and stopped changing "written" to "record," the definition of which in §1-201(b) includes electronically stored information as well as information in tangible form. We explain in Chapter 6 that a uniform law called UETA fills this gap, providing in §7(c) that "[i]f a law requires a record to be in writing, an electronic record satisfies the law." Official Comment 8 to §2-207 makes explicit the connection between Article 2 and UETA. So when you see references in this chapter to "written" or "writing," you can assume that the communication could be electronic.

EXAMPLES

Examples

1. Boston Universal Yoyos ("BUY") is a major manufacturer of the popular children's toy. Finding the firm in need of a quantity of string, BUY's Purchasing Director reviewed the catalogs and price lists she always keeps on hand from various string suppliers. She decided to order from a company called String Emporium of Lexington ("SEL") and instructed a clerk to place the order. That clerk found on his computer BUY's standard purchase order form. This form, which BUY had been using for a number of years, came with a lot of legal-looking material (what the clerk always thought of as "our terms") as well as blank spaces calling for the item, amount, and so on. In the spaces provided he filled in SEL's item number for the kind of string he was told to order, the amount required, and the price listed in SEL's most recent price list, and indicated "For Immediate Delivery." He emailed this off to the address given on SEL's materials. A week later he received back from SEL a copy of that firm's Acknowledgment form. He checked that this form had been filled in with the same item number and description, amount, price, and delivery terms as he had put into the Purchase Order. He did not bother to read all of the other stuff on the Acknowledgment (what he always discounted as simply the seller's "boilerplate"). He stored this Acknowledgment along with a copy of his Purchase Order in the files, told the Purchasing Director that the order had been placed, and notified the head of manufacturing that the string would be arriving shortly. If SEL never delivers the string (for example, because it realizes the price it stated was too low), will it be in breach of contract? If SEL does deliver the string but BUY no longer wants it, can that firm simply refuse the shipment without being in breach of contract?

2. Would the result be any different if it were shown that SEL's Acknowledgment form contained on the reverse the following language in print no different from all the rest of the terms?

   > SEL hereby agrees to sell only on the terms and conditions expressly stated herein. No other terms apply. SEL's agreement to this order is made conditional on purchaser's acceptance of all of the terms and conditions of this Acknowledgment form.

   What if in addition the front of the Acknowledgment had printed on it in big bold letters "SEE REVERSE FOR TERMS AND CONDITIONS"? You should now look at the concluding language of §2-207(1), beginning with the word "unless."

3. Imagine that SEL came to you asking for advice. There was a particular term on its Acknowledgment that it really did care deeply about. It was willing to sacrifice a sale rather than enter into a contract without this particular provision. What advice would you give?

4. Assume you conclude that BUY and SEL have entered into a contract for the purchase and sale of string. What are the terms of that contract? In particular, imagine that the string is delivered and used by BUY in its manufacturing process. Many yoyos are returned to BUY because of defective strings that keep snapping.
   (a) BUY wants to sue SEL for damages, but that firm points to a provision on its Acknowledgment stating:

   > Buyer's rights in the event any product delivered pursuant to this agreement proves defective are limited to the replacement of any defective goods. Buyer agrees that SEL is not responsible for any consequential damages.

   Is this clause binding upon BUY? For this question and the two that follow, you'll have to move on to §2-207(2).
   (b) Suppose that the Acknowledgment had no language relating to a disgruntled buyer's remedies. Instead the clause of concern is one found in BUY's Purchase Order form. It states:

   > Seller agrees that BUY may return any product found defective for a full cash refund, and that such right to return shall continue in BUY for no less than two years from date of delivery.

   Is this enforceable against SEL?
   (c) Would your answer to the previous question be any different if the following language had appeared in SEL's Acknowledgment?

   > Purchaser agrees that it shall have no remedy for a claimed defect in the goods provided pursuant to this agreement unless demand and proof of defect has been made to SEL no later than one year from the date of delivery of said product.

5. We now change the hypothetical fundamentally. Assume that the various differences on the two forms are in fact spotted by employees of the parties when the forms are first exchanged. Someone from BUY calls someone at SEL and says that her firm wants the string but can't agree to several terms, including the one-year limitation. The man from SEL says he is happy to take BUY's order, but "under company policy" has to insist on this term and indeed must object to certain others in the Purchase Order. This bickering continues over a period of months. Maybe some higher-ups from the two companies get involved. Meanwhile, life goes on. The string is shipped by SEL. The shipment is accepted by BUY's manufacturing unit without any comment. The string is used to make yoyos. Then some problem develops. Is there a contract at all? If so, what are the terms of that contract that will be referred to in settling the dispute? Look at §2-207(3).

EXPLANATIONS

Explanations

1. As noted in the introductory text, under the common law and its mirror image rule, neither party would have been bound at this point, and either could get out of the deal if it chose. It did not matter whether either or both of the parties believed that the purchase and sale had been finalized or whether that belief was justified in the circumstances; a nice technical argument allowed for slipping out from under what was probably considered by both a done deal. The drafters of Article 2, in accordance with their general principle that the law of sales should comport with and support what people involved in doing the buying and selling would think their obligations to be, had in mind changing this result via their drafting of §2-207(1).

   This subsection determines when a communication in response to an offer operates as an acceptance as a matter of Article 2 law. To "operate as an acceptance" is to *bind both parties*. As we know, the common law had it that the only thing that operated as an acceptance was an *actual acceptance*, by which it meant a response that mirrored the offer in each and every detail and provided for nothing new. Section 2-207(1) changes this. Now something called a "definite and seasonable expression of acceptance" will do the trick, and this is so "even though it states terms additional to or different from" those in the offer. So our first question is how to recognize a "definite and seasonable expression of acceptance" when we see one. The key is to be found at the beginning of Comment 2: "Under this Article a proposed deal which in commercial understanding has in fact been closed is recognized as a contract." Courts in making this determination must necessarily look to the real commercial world of the parties and how they themselves treated the communication. In our hypothetical the people at BUY took the Acknowledgment as the conclusion of a deal. We know that from their actions. No one was saying, "Well, maybe we have a deal with SEL for some string if we can work it out." We don't know firsthand how the people at SEL were viewing the situation and what they were doing, but certainly they gave BUY no reason to think that there was something iffy in the situation or that they expected negotiations to continue. In the commercial world a deal had been struck, and in the law of sales under Article 2, an effective acceptance had bound both parties.

   In *Idaho Power Co. v. Westinghouse Electric Corp.*, 596 F.2d 924 (9th Cir. 1979), it was the seller, Westinghouse, that made the offer, on a form designated a Price Quotation. Idaho Power, the buyer, replied with a Purchase Order that the court found to operate as an acceptance:

   > Here, Idaho Power referred to and accepted the price quoted in Westinghouse's offer. It requested shipment within the time limits specified

> by Westinghouse. No other correspondence ensued and the [machinery] was shipped and installed accordingly. In commercial transactions such an order, especially when followed by performance, would normally be understood to have closed the deal between the parties. Consequently, it was a "definite and seasonable expression of acceptance," even though it contained the additional terms.

The fact that in our situation the parties have not yet actually begun to perform as if they had a contract should not make a difference. What the courts will look to in making the determination is, in effect, what the clerk in the BUY office looked at. Did the response he received give any hint that SEL wasn't willing to sell to them the particular stuff at the particular price on the particular delivery terms? What matters most is that the fill-in-the-blank items—the "dickered terms" unique to this specific transaction—have been approved and repeated in the return form.

Compare the situation if SEL's Acknowledgment had stated a higher figure under "Price Per Unit." Then the parties should know that the deal was not yet finalized and that more negotiation would have to occur if there were ever to be agreement; there would be no acceptance, either in commercial understanding or under this section. Apparently in the battle of the forms, nobody expects the boilerplate to match up, and now under Article 2 neither must the courts.

There are two other things to note about the language of §2-207(1) with which we are working. The first is nothing difficult nor new. To act as an acceptance a return communication, be it an expression of acceptance or a confirmation, must be "seasonable" or "sent within a reasonable time." Obviously an offeree cannot sit on an offer forever and then send something back in the mails expecting it to land the deal. The offeror may expressly set a time limit on his or her offer. If not, the offer will naturally lapse of its own accord after a reasonable time. On *reasonable time* generally see §1-205, which not surprisingly emphasizes both the principles of freedom of contract and the desirability of making judgments based on the circumstances of an individual transaction.

The second matter is not so simple. Though we have so far discussed acceptances arising out of the "definite and seasonable expression of acceptance," there is a second part to what we've seen. Under §2-207(1) a "written confirmation" may also "act as an acceptance even though . . . ." The first Comment indicates this refers to situations where a written confirmation is sent by one party after an agreement has already been reached. Suppose, for example, the buyer and seller effectively conclude, under the type of analysis we saw in the previous chapter, a contract of sale through their exclusively oral communications. One of the parties then sends a "confirmation" of its understanding of the agreement—either a purchase order sent by the buyer or an invoice sent by the seller. Or imagine the situation where one party sends a record containing an effective offer and the other party accepts by taking some definitive action—either the seller's delivery of the goods or the buyer's acceptance of them. Suppose furthermore that the single record in either such situation contains terms additional to or different from those previously agreed to. Does §2-207(1) apply? If so, then this single document "operates as an acceptance" under that provision. But if an agreement had already been reached, this means that an acceptance had already been rendered in some form or another. So is the confirmation an acceptance piled on top of an already valid acceptance? The Comment even suggests the possibility of both parties sending their own confirmatory memoranda. How many acceptances have we now? This is only one example of the clumsy way §2-207 has been put together, but perhaps it doesn't matter that much, at least as far as the first subsection is concerned. Once there is an acceptance there is a deal, and confirmatory records, no matter what they say, certainly aren't going to undo this result. The real problem with confirmations that state additional or different terms is whether those terms can possibly become part of the contractual relationship and, if so, how. But that's a problem for subsection (2), which we haven't even begun to tackle yet. For a couple of cases that have wrestled with the conundrum posed by the "confirmation" language in §2-207(1), you may want to look at and puzzle over, *Tacoma Fixture Co., Inc. v. Rudd Co., Inc.*, 174 P.3d 721 (Wash. App. 2008), and *Rocheux International of New Jersey, Inc. v. U.S. Merchants Financial Group, Inc.*, 741 F. Supp. 2d 651 (D.N.J. 2010). Do not be surprised, however, if you find the discussion by these courts—and indeed all that follows on §2-207—often difficult and downright frustrating. After all, as the court in the *Tacoma Fixture* case noted, this section has been described as "a defiant, lurking demon patiently waiting to condemn its interpreters to the depths of despair." [citing *Reaction Molding Techs., Inc. v. Gen. Elec. Co.*, 585 F. Supp. 1097, 1104, 588 F. Supp. 1280 (E.D. Pa. 1984)]. With that cheery remark in mind, we continue.

2. SEL here would be arguing that by virtue of this language on its Acknowledgment form, its acceptance was "expressly made conditional on assent to the additional or different terms." Therefore, it claims, its Acknowledgment never operated as an acceptance, only as a counteroffer. SEL never heard back from BUY acceding to these terms, and hence SEL was never legally obligated to make the delivery. (Of course in the abstract this argument could backfire on SEL since it would also imply that had SEL wanted to go through with the deal, BUY could have gotten out of it without any problem. But under the circumstances SEL couldn't care less. Is it too cynical to suggest that an argument like this only comes to light when one party has later decided to pull the plug on a deal to which it had, in all commercial reality, committed itself?)

Is SEL correct in its reliance on this language, which is often referred to as "the proviso to §2-207(1)" or "the language after the comma"? That depends on whom you ask, although the overwhelming trend of decisions is not in its favor. The earliest decision interpreting this language was *Roto-Lith, Ltd. v. F. P. Bartlett & Co., Inc.*, 297 F.2d 497 (1st Cir. 1962), which is now universally referred to as the "infamous" *Roto-Lith* case and credited with setting back a correct appreciation of this proviso language by at least a decade. In *Roto-Lith* the court held that any response that "states a condition materially altering the obligation solely to the disadvantage of the offeror" would trigger the proviso. But this broad a reading is clearly wrong. Virtually every form response will have something in the boilerplate that would fit this description, with the result that just about any form response would not operate as an acceptance under this view. In practice, this reading resurrects quite nicely the result if not the exact language of the old common law mirror image rule. And everyone recognizes that the whole idea of §2-207(1) was to do away with that outcome.

The *Roto-Lith* result is today pretty much dead and laid to rest in most jurisdictions—even if generations of Sales professors insist on bringing it up if only as an example of horrid Code methodology. Even the First Circuit, which came up with *Roto-Lith* to begin with, eventually concluded that the rule has "outlived its usefulness as circuit precedent" and overruled that decision. *Ionics, Inc. v. Elmwood Sensors, Inc.*, 110 F.3d 184 (1st Cir. 1997). Clearly it should take more than differing terms in the return form to bring the proviso into play. What constitutes more? Some courts focus on the word *expressly* and find it enough that there is language on the form that states that the offeree intends his or her form to be taken as a counteroffer. A clear statement is said to suffice. If SEL is held to this standard, it should be able to make its argument stick. Read again the language it has put in its form.

But should this be enough? True, this language is very clear when you read it, but the whole point about boilerplate is that no one *does* read it. And more than that, no one truly expects that the recipient of the form will read it. A somewhat more realistic standard would at least require that any expression of the conditional nature of the acceptance be made somehow glaringly conspicuous so there is a better chance that it will come to the recipient's attention. If that is what is called for, then perhaps the bold legend on the front of the form would make a difference. But probably more is required than even this.

The trend for courts looking at this question is to take a fairly narrow view of the proviso, seeing this as essential if the overall philosophy of §2-207(1) is not to be undermined. One articulation that has gained a considerable following is that found in *Dorton v. Collins & Aikman Corp.*, 453 F.2d 1161 (6th Cir. 1972). There the court held that the proviso was intended to apply "only to an acceptance which clearly reveals that the offeree is unwilling to proceed with the transaction unless he is assured of the offeror's assent to the additional or different terms therein." For a purported acceptance to operate as a counteroffer under the proviso, it must actually be a counteroffer, not just in words but in effect. It should be worded and presented in such a manner as is calculated to bring a reasonable recipient to the understanding that no deal has yet been concluded and none will be concluded unless and until either it responds favorably to the new terms being presented or even more negotiation hammers out a compromise. Under the *Dorton* type of test, the question whether BUY and SEL have been bound to a contract is not merely a matter of what language appears somewhere in SEL's boilerplate. Was BUY put on some kind of reasonable notice that all was not well with this string deal, that it could not count on receiving string from SEL unless the final terms were settled? Even if upon consideration BUY may decide it can live with the terms SEL is pushing, the "Acknowledgment" should be such that BUY would have to realize that nothing more is going to happen until it in turn communicates its willingness to go along with those terms to SEL.

3. There is no doubt that the offeree in the battle of the forms (SEL in our hypothetical) can if it truly wishes refuse to deal except on its own terms. But to do so it must make a true counteroffer and get an actual knowing acceptance of that counteroffer by the other party. It cannot count on this result simply because of some fancy language its lawyers have drafted up to include in its Acknowledgment form. If you were advising SEL, which was willing to insist on its own terms even if it meant losing a customer, you would tell it not merely to make perfectly clear that its response is a counteroffer (perhaps by a personalized letter attached to the Acknowledgment making clear you need to hear from BUY) but also by *acting* like an offeror. Above all, do not ship the stuff off on the assumption that you do have a deal on your terms. What an offeror does is sit and wait. It cannot assume that its offer will be taken up. Some, perhaps most, offers are turned down.

   Of course, don't be too surprised if the people at SEL are not terribly happy with this advice. How, they will ask you, can they run a business this way? You will have to respond (or perhaps more tactfully, only think to yourself), why do they expect they can have their cake and eat it too?

   Finally, notice what is likely to happen if SEL immediately sends out the Acknowledgment and the order of string, figuring that it can insist on its understanding of the contract later on. Under the common law's "last shot" rule, we know SEL would have been in a position to argue that the differing provisions in its Acknowledgment made for a counteroffer that BUY accepted by performance the minute it took delivery of the goods. Thus the common law could have found for SEL a contract, and on its terms. It got to eat the cake and keep it too. Section 2-207, of course, does not allow for this analysis. Even if SEL had some gobbledygook in its Acknowledgment of the type suggested in the previous question, should it ship off the stuff without getting an actually acquiescing response to its Acknowledgment, it will be hard for it later to argue that it had made an effective counteroffer under the proviso that was thereafter accepted. So a deal would have been struck before performance. But on what terms? We now turn to that issue in the questions that follow.

4. a. The first subsection of §2-207 has to be deemed fairly successful measured against its principal objective, which was getting past the old and easily criticized common law mirror image rule. It is now clear that a contract for sale may be created by the parties' having exchanged forms that contain different terms as long as the differences are not of the type that in the commercial environment usually make or break a deal. But now the obvious question presents itself: What are the terms of the contract formed in this fashion? This is much trickier. We can no longer say, as we could in the good old days of the common law rule, that the terms must necessarily be those that were offered and which were then perfectly mirrored by the offeree in response. Almost everyone who has had anything to say on the matter (and just about everyone remotely interested in the Code seems to have taken a whack at it) agrees that §2-207 is far less successful in laying out the answer to this question. But it is a question that will not go away.

   As a starting point, of course, there is nothing for it but to look at the words of §2-207 itself, now focusing on both the first and second subsections. At the outset the conclusion seems unavoidable (although some courts and commentators have gone to great length to talk their way out of it) that all of the terms present in the form that constituted the offer, if that offer is found to have been accepted via subsection (1), are then binding terms of the contract. Section 2-207(1) says the acceptance "acts as an acceptance," and it's hard to understand what that could mean except that a deal has been formed on the terms offered. It has been suggested that the responding communication only accepts "those terms which it intends to accept" or some such idea, but there really is no statutory support for such an analysis beyond a generalized belief that the Code drafters must have intended to do what is in the particular commentator's opinion the obviously correct thing.

   So the terms of the offer are the terms of the contract. Beyond that, §2-207(2) indicates that *some* "additional terms," which were in the "definite and seasonable expression of acceptance," or which are to be found in a later confirmation sent by one party to the other, may also become terms of the contract. But the passage of any such additional term through the tangle of §2-207(2) and into the heart of the contract is pretty tricky, as we will see.

Under §2-207(2) there seem to be two ways that an additional term in the acceptance can become part of the contract. The first is implicit in the statement that such additional terms are to be "construed as proposals for additions to the contract." There's always the chance, even if it is slim, that such a proposal will be accepted. So, for example, if BUY had somehow become aware of the limitation of remedy clause that SEL put in its Acknowledgment and beyond that had communicated to SEL that this limitation was acceptable to it as a buyer, the term would become binding between the two. Of course there would be no obligation on BUY's part to acquiesce to this term (and we might wonder why on earth a buyer would), but you have to allow for the possibility. So an "additional term" can become part of the contract by its express acceptance by the original offeror.

The second mechanism for such a term to make its way into the contract is given by the second sentence of §2-207(2). Such a term may *automatically* become part of the contract if a series of conditions are met. The first condition is that such automatic inclusion is possible only in dealings "between merchants." Once we establish that we are dealing only with two parties each of which would be classified as a merchant for Article 2 purposes, it is further necessary that (a) the offeror not have expressly limited acceptance to the terms of the offer, (b) the new term not be a "material alteration" of the contract already formed, and (c) notice of objection to the new terms has not already been given by the offeree nor is it seasonably given after the offeror becomes aware of them. Take each of these requirements in turn.

In one sense every offer could be said to expressly limit acceptance to the terms contained therein. But reading clause (a) this way would effectively make the whole possibility of automatic inclusion meaningless. By analogy to the better reading of the proviso of sub section (1), this language in (2)(a) should probably be taken to refer only to those situations where the offeror has given the offeree clear reason to believe that it will under no circumstances consider even the most trivial addition to its terms and truly *won't proceed* with the deal as long as the offeree is even suggesting any. Again analogizing to the better understanding of the proviso, this condition will presumably not be met by the inclusion of some generalized boilerplate in the offer to the effect that the offeree deals on its terms and its terms only. The offeror will have to bring home to the offeree that it really would rather lose business than enter into a contract on any terms other than its own. The fact is, of course, that plenty of firms will say this is their position, but how many really can consistently take this high ground, act on it, and still stay in business?

In practical application, clause (b) is more important. There is no way a suggested additional term can be incorporated into the contract automatically (even between merchants) if it would work a "material alteration" to the contract as it stands without that term. This question of materiality has been heavily litigated, and the results are not easily characterized. For the drafters' attempt at drawing the line, see Comments 4 and 5. Language at the end of Comment 5 suggests that the clause SEL is trying to insist upon need not be considered material. (As we will see in Chapter 13, it is a kind of provision expressly allowed for as part of a sales agreement under §2-719.) The courts are not so sure. In *Burbic Contracting Co., IAC v. Cement Asbestos Prods. Co.*, 409 So. 2d 1 (Ala. 1982), the Alabama Supreme Court found that such a limitation of remedy clause was not material and hence could become part of the contract while conceding that "the courts are split on this issue." Moreover it held for Alabama that no blanket answer could be given for all such limitation provisions; the question had to be addressed on the facts of each case. Perhaps the determination should turn on how common such terms are in the particular industry involved, the extent to which its inclusion could work a hardship on the other party, and other such factors. But if the materiality question is to be determined on anything like a case-by-case basis, how are contracting parties ever to know with reasonable certainty what terms they have bound themselves to? In a later case, *Glyptal, Inc. v. Engelhard Corp.*, 801 F. Supp. 887 (D. Mass. 1992), the federal district court applying Massachusetts law decided to follow what it characterized as a "recent trend . . . to find that such [remedy-limiting] provisions are material alterations" for the purposes of §2-207(2)(b). For two more cases that explore how courts determine whether a proffered term would work a "material alteration" for §2-207(2)(b) purposes, see *Vulcan Automotive Equipment, Ltd. v. Global Marine Engine & Parts, Inc.*, 240 F. Supp. 2d 156 (D.R.I. 2003), and *Polytop Corp. v. Chipsco, Inc.*, 826 A.2d 945 (R.I. 2003).

Finally, under §2-207(2)(c), it is possible for the offeror to block the automatic inclusion of even the most immaterial and innocuous term by objecting to it. What constitutes an "objection" in this situation? Again, for this clause (2)(c) to make any real sense, it has to be referring to something more than a boilerplate or prepackaged response. Would it be enough if BUY's clerk had a routine of sending out in response to any form Acknowledgment a preprinted letter that said in effect, "Thank you for your order and we object to any and all terms in your form that are in addition to any in our form"? I think not. If, however, the management of BUY did think it worth the time and expense for this clerk to go over SEL's Acknowledgment form in detail and then send out to that firm an individualized letter painstakingly objecting to each and every additional term, it seems clear BUY could keep out any and everything it didn't like.

b. Yes. By the analysis given above, any term in the communication that makes up the offer is a term of the contract. The long and the short of it seems to be that BUY can get all its idiosyncratic boilerplate terms into the contract and SEL will have a devil of a time getting any of its terms in.

Some commentators are exceedingly troubled by this result. They question how in doing away with the common law's much criticized "last shot" rule, the drafters could have in effect replaced it with an equally unbalanced and arbitrary "first shot" principle. Ideally, they argue, neither party should get an advantage simply because of the order in which the two standard forms were sent. They point to §2-207(3), which makes binding only "those terms on which the writings of the parties agree" as an example of a more principled approach. But the important point here is that subsection (3) does not, as written, apply to a situation where the parties receive and make no objection to each other's forms and only later are arguing terms. By its language, that subsection relates only to cases where "the writings [read as "records" under UETA] of the parties do not otherwise establish a contract," and writings that contain different terms most assuredly *can* establish a contract. That's what subsection (1) is all about; that is what has happened to BUY and SEL here. Strict impartiality between the combatants in the battle of the forms may, indeed, be an ideal worth striving for—although others are not so sure—but unfortunately for its proponents the language of §2-207 doesn't leave much room for argument. Unless and until §2-207 is substantially revised, something like a "modified first shot" is the rule of the day.

c. This would appear to be the toughest case yet. The two documents have distinctly *differing* terms on the same topic, herein the length of time the buyer has to complain of a problem with the goods. The courts have been all over the place on what to do with such differing terms under §2-207. At least three modes of analysis have been adopted. The first is simply to ignore differing terms found in the communication operating as an acceptance. The reasoning is very direct. There is simply no language in subsection (1) or (2) that even suggests that such differing terms could ever become part of the contract. Subsection (2) does make allowance for some terms of the acceptance being incorporated into the final contract, but it speaks only to "additional" terms. Since we know from (1) that the drafters considered additional and different terms to be two separate and distinct things—why else would they have mentioned both?—we have to read (2) as implicitly ruling out the possibility that "differing" terms can ever find their way into the agreement or even affect its contents. Under this analysis BUY's provision is enforceable and SEL's is simply ignored.

A second approach to the problem of differing terms argues that not so much should be made of the nitpicking distinction between "additional" and "different" terms in reading §2-207. After all, in many cases this will probably be as much a matter of degree as of kind. Note also that Comment 3 refers to subsection (2) as relating to "additional or different" terms. Several courts have adopted the position that subsection (2) does apply to so-called differing terms as well as to additional ones. But does this really help the offeree, SEL in this instance? It would seem that any term in the acceptance that differs from an explicit term of the offer would by its nature be an attempt to "materially alter" the terms of the contract. As such it could never automatically make its way into the agreement. BUY still wins and gets its term, only under a different technical analysis.

A third view does, at least, potentially come up with another result. It even has a colorful name. Under the so-called *knock-out approach*, conflicting terms in the offer and the acceptance in effect cancel each other out. Neither term becomes part of the contract. What's left are the terms on which the two records do not conflict, presumably the dickered terms among them. These terms of agreement, as supplemented by various provisions of Article 2 itself, make up the terms of the contract.

This knock-out analysis has been receiving increasing adherence in the courts. A noted example is *Daitom, Inc. v. Pennwalt Corp.*, 741 F.2d 1569 (10th Cir. 1984), the case that inspired this question. Seller submitted a proposal for the sale of some industrial machinery on September 7, 1976. Its typewritten proposal specified the equipment to be sold, the price term, and delivery and payment terms. Attached was a preprinted sheet containing a list of conditions of the sale and a statement that the conditions were to be considered an integral part of the proposal. Buyer responded with its own preprinted Purchase Order, containing plenty of its own boilerplate, on October 5, 1976. The machinery was delivered in May of the following year, but because of delay in the construction of buyer's plant, was not installed until June of 1978. Buyer soon notified seller of serious troubles with the machines. Seller responded by pointing to a condition in its printed list that gave the buyer a period of one year in which to bring any breach of warranty action. The district court granted summary judgment to the seller based on this clause in its offer, applying in effect a first-shot analysis. The circuit court reversed. It noted that in its responsive Purchase Order the buyer had its own boilerplate clause, this one expressly reserving all warranties and remedies available in law. The circuit court first held that this clause "impliedly reserves the statutory period of limitations," which under §2-725 would be four years, not one. The court then went on to apply the "knock-out" rule to what it now took to be conflicting express provisions of the offer and the acceptance:

> [T]he conflicting terms in Pennwalt's offer and Daitom's acceptance regarding the period of limitations and applicable warranties cancel one another out. Consequently, the other provisions of the U.C.C. must be used to provide the missing terms.

The relevant other provision of the Code in this case was of course the standard statute of limitations found in §2-725. Victory for the buyer As you will note, use of the knock-out approach was particularly creative in *Daitom* since one of the "differing terms" with which the court claimed to be unavoidably confronted was at least partially of its own making. The buyer's reservation of a longer period in which to bring a warranty claim was nowhere near as explicit as I have made it in my hypothetical. It was found "impliedly" in a very general boilerplate reservation of right. One judge in dissent opined that whatever the value of the knock-out rule in dealing with differing terms in the offer and acceptance, its application should not extend to cases where there are no clear-cut conflicts between explicit provisions. In the particular situation, he noted, "there was no term in [the buyer's] purchase order in conflict with the express one-year limitation within which to bring warranty actions." Indeed, it's far from clear that the majority's result works a fair compromise. Certainly Article 2 does not take away from sellers the right to sell on the precise terms they wish. Setting shorter limitation periods, as the seller attempted to do in this instance, is specifically allowed for in §2-725. Should the buyer be able to block any limitation or modification of the seller's warranties merely by the inclusion of a generalized reservation of any and all rights stuck into the middle of its boilerplate?

The majority in *Daitom* believed its whole-hearted adoption of the knock-out principle to be "supported persuasively by the underlying rationale and purpose behind the adoption of §2-207 . . . . To refuse to adopt the 'knock-out' approach and instead adopt one of the remaining two approaches would serve to re-enshrine the undue advantages derived solely from the fortuitous positions of when a party sent a form." Indeed, formal adoption of the knock-out approach does seem to be the trend. See *Flender Corp. v. Tippins International, Inc.*, 830 A.2d 1279 (Pa. Super. 2003) (stating that the knock-out approach has been adopted by "a strong majority of U.S. jurisdictions that have considered the issue"), and *General Steel Corp. v. Collins*, 196 S.W.3d 18 (Ky. App. 2006). Perhaps §2-207 should have been drafted to get this result. But was it? There is precious little support, if any, in the text or comments for the knock-out way of doing things. At least one court has relied on §2-207(3) for authority, but this clearly won't work. As we have already noted, by its terms that subsection deals only with cases where the records passing between the parties do not effectively create an agreement. That's not the case when one form responds to another so as to be "a definite and seasonable expression of acceptance." Knock-out proponents have taken some comfort in Comment 6, but even they must acknowledge that this Comment seems to be speaking exclusively to conflicting terms in later records that confirm a prior oral agreement, not to terms in records that constitute an offer and an acceptance.

The receptivity by some courts to the knock-out approach seems to be a reflection more of the increasing frustration with §2-207 in general than of any new, brilliant flash of insight. In *Richardson v. Union Carbide Industrial Gases, Inc.*, 790 A.2d 962 (N.J. Super. 2002), which adopted the knock-out approach for New Jersey, the Superior Court quoted the trial judge, who had initially settled on this way of handling the mess with which he had been presented and whose decision the court was to affirm, to the following effect:

> The truth is, and this really is the truth, what's happening is some little person some place writing these little—trying to plan it out, trying to conflict these things out, but the business people are out there delivering and taking money. And if the people really want to really get into all of this, then they should have taken their stuff away and they should have said, ooh, you know, we—you know, this is real here and, sorry, I'm not going to be able to take your check and, sorry, you're not going to be able to keep the stuff, but, they're not doing that. They're just playing a little game with forms.

All of this, needless to say, leaves the litigants and judges left to deal with the outcomes through the decidedly imperfect tool of §2-207 to play *their* games as best they know how. For a thorough (and highly opinionated) review of the various approaches taken by the courts to this problem—how the current Article 2 treats provisions in the offeree's form, which serves as an acceptance, that are different from, and not just in addition to, the terms of the offer, see Chief Judge Posner's opinion for the Seventh Circuit in *Northrop Corp. v. Litronic Industries*, 29 F.3d 1173 (7th Cir. 1994). Note that because he is a federal judge deciding a state-law matter, Judge Posner must determine not what is the best rule, but what rule he thinks the state would likely apply. Even though he thinks it is a stupid rule, he holds his nose and properly finds that the knock-out rule is the applicable rule in the case.

5. There is a contract under §2-207(3) and the terms are as stated there. Here, finally, is an unarguably appropriate use of that subsection. The two parties' disagreement over terms is out in the open and it is never resolved. The records cannot be said to establish a contract for sale, but the conduct of both parties clearly does. In such a case, the terms of the contract are "those terms on which the writings of the parties agree, together with any supplementary terms incorporated under any other provisions of this Act." Where are such other provisions to be found? Patience. As you progress through the book, you'll get a chance to explore terms incorporated by custom and usage (Chapter 7), the so-called "gap-filler" provisions (Chapter 9), the Code's elaborate warranty regime (Part III), and other default terms that apply in the absence of the parties' agreement otherwise.

CHAPTER 6

The Statute of Frauds and UETA

AND THERE SHALL BE "SOME WRITING"

Anyone who has ever studied basic contract law—at least anyone who has done so since the English Parliamentary session of 1677—can be expected to have an acquaintance with the Statute of Frauds. The basic idea behind the Statute is relatively straightforward. Sometimes you have to produce some written evidence of a contract if you expect to enforce that contract in a court of law. The problems come when we try to firm up just when these "sometimes" are and what kind of writing will be sufficient.

Contrary to what the uninformed layperson might think, there is no general requirement in the law that for a contract to be valid it must be put down in writing. *As a general proposition*, a contract that arises solely from oral communications and is in no way evidenced or memorialized by a writing is perfectly enforceable. Certainly, getting the other party to sign on the dotted line is a good idea, and no one would advise against it, but *generally* it is not a legal requirement. Even in those cases that defy this generalization—i.e., those classes of contracts that are said to "fall within the Statute of Frauds"—there has never been a requirement that the contract *in and of itself* be in writing. In the words of the original enactment, what will be needed is only "some note or memorandum of the said bargain to be made and signed by the parties to be charged by such contract, or their agents thereunto lawfully authorized."

The long course of history has not been kind to the Statute of Frauds. Its enactment was originally intended to deter the "fraude and perjurie" to be feared from those rascals bold enough to sue on a totally trumped up (and what they will be maintaining just happened to be a totally oral) agreement. The fear was of course that the rascal might actually win, once he or she got this fabrication in front of an easily deceived or overly sympathetic jury. Undoubtedly the Statute does stand in the way of such knavery, but this result is not without a price. The Statute of Frauds can be, and often is, criticized as a totally mindless mechanistic response to a problem that, at least in the present day, could be handled more effectively by other means. It cannot be denied that in many instances the Statute does provide a purely "technical" but highly effective defense to what would otherwise be a perfectly appropriate and meritorious contract action based on a valid and easily proven oral agreement.

In Great Britain such criticisms resulted in the 1954 repeal by Parliament of the Statute of Frauds in all instances covering the sale of goods. Meanwhile in the USA, during the course of drafting and eventual adoption of Article 2, there was substantial argument that the better course would be for the American law of sales to likewise say good riddance to what was to many simply an anachronism whose time had long passed. This, however, was not to be. As we will see in this chapter, the drafters of the Code retained the basic Statute of Frauds for sales at a price of $500 or more. It's found in §2-201. The core language is right there in the first sentence of subsection (1), as you should now check.

The drafters did, however, make some important changes to the Statute. Their attempt at a compromise solution was to concoct for Article 2 what they apparently hoped would be regarded as a less rigid, more pragmatic Statute of Frauds. Its positive effect would be to protect parties and the courts from even being bothered with contract claims that were too flimsy to be countenanced, if not to be believed. At the same time, they codified in §2-201 a series of exceptions to the writing requirement which, they believed, would ameliorate some of the more egregious side-effects of that writing requirement. As electronic commerce grew, another question arose: Does an electronic record satisfy the requirement of a signed writing? How well the drafters succeeded in crafting a workable and beneficial "modern" version of the Statute of Frauds is a question that necessarily runs throughout this chapter.

THE HEART OF THE MATTER

A preliminary bit of business goes to the very heart of the Statute of Frauds and is crucial to understanding the Statute no matter where we find it or what the version. All too often students, and maybe just as often the courts, fail to make the distinction between two very different analytic issues. Quite apart from any Statute of Frauds concerns must be the elemental question, first in our hearts and minds, of *whether a contract exists at all*. This has to do with the whole notion of agreement, with all those matters of offer and acceptance with which we dealt in the previous two chapters. Whether a contract exists, and of course what its provisions are if it is found to exist, are questions to be answered on their own terms. These things are *not* what the Statute of Frauds is about.

Parties do not invoke a Statute of Frauds defense as a way of arguing that no contract was ever agreed to. Their contention is rather that *even* if a contract was entered into, that contract is not enforceable against them in this court at this time. They escape enforcement, they contend, because of the lack of a sufficient writing or the lack of the right signature. Their position is not necessarily that they did not enter into the agreement the breach of which is being argued against them, but rather that the court lacks the power, under a rule of law, to do anything about it even if they did.

As a practical matter, of course, a Statute of Frauds defense if one is available is often among the very first arguments a defendant will advance. If you can get a complaint against you thrown out on a technicality quickly and easily, well, then you do. Why go to all the bother of arguing and trying to prove that the alleged agreement never took place when you can get the whole thing resolved in your favor so very neatly? This is especially true when you consider how hard it can be to prove a negative, that is, to prove that an agreement never was. It is of course just this difficulty of making such proof—and the prospect that a clever claimant could somehow make what never was appear to a jury to be all too believable—that has been the rationale for the Statute of Frauds from the seventeenth century through today.

To make sure you can distinguish between the issue of contract formation and the Statute of Frauds defense, consider the following two hypotheticals. In the first, two law students, Andy and Betty, are asked by their Sales professor to engage in a simulation of contract negotiation. The subject is to be the supposed sale by Andy of his used car to Betty. Their negotiations result in a "sale price" of $750. To complete their assignment, the two draft up a Contract of Sale for the car. Each signs this document. Let's assume they both get A's not only for effort but because the document is well-drafted in all respects. Now assume further that Andy then brings suit against Betty *in a real court of law* charging her with failing to live up to this agreement. A copy of the Contract of Sale is appended to his complaint. Betty is going to have to defend herself. If there is any justice in this world, she should be able to win, but it won't be through a Statute of Frauds defense. If she relies only on the Statute, the court (with a signed document right before it) must give a decision for Andy. She will have to plead and prove (with no small help from the unimpeachable testimony of her professor) that no actual legal agreement for purchase and sale ever existed between her and Andy.

Now consider this situation: Carl and Donna are also two law students. Carl really does want to sell his old car to Donna, and Donna is really interested in buying it. In front of their Sales professor and a number of other witnesses, they conclude an oral agreement for the purchase and sale of the car for $950. They shake hands on it. Later, Carl refuses to go through with the sale. Donna brings suit, again in *a real court of law*. If the facts are as simple as I've made them here, Carl can prove that the §2-201 Statute of Frauds defense applies. Was there an agreement? Yes. There are all kinds of witnesses. Carl will forever be known as someone who doesn't stick to his bargains. Was it a contract under the Code? Yes, again. The agreement resulted in a contract governed by Article 2. To convince yourself that there is a contract here, look at Comment 4 to §2-201. Can Donna enforce this contract against Carl? No, not without some writing signed by him that will satisfy the Article 2 Statute of Frauds. Does that make sense, given that multiple credible witnesses can testify that the transaction in fact took place? No. That is one reason courts are hostile to the Statute of Frauds, and tend to find it easily satisfied.

Thus far we have been discussing satisfying the Statute of Frauds with a "signed writing." You may imagine a piece of paper with a signature on it. But today many exchanges are made electronically. Federal and state legislation has been enacted to address the question of whether those electronic exchanges satisfy the requirement of a signed writing. We will look at those statutes before exploring the details of §2-201.

INTRODUCTION TO THE UNIFORM ELECTRONIC TRANSACTIONS ACT

The surge of technology since the U.C.C.'s adoption has created a flurry of legal issues relating to electronic documents and electronic signatures. In response, the Uniform Law Commission promulgated UETA, the Uniform Electronic Transactions Act. While UETA was being adopted by the states, Congress in 2000 adopted ESIGN, the Electronic Signatures in Global and National Commerce Act, to solve the problem. ESIGN provided that it was not effective in a state that had enacted UETA, so the bottom line is that there is similar legislation affecting all states, either directly through UETA or indirectly through ESIGN. The primary objective of UETA is "to establish the legal equivalence of electronic records and signatures with paper writings and manually-signed signatures, [and] remov[e] barriers to electronic commerce." The primary mechanisms UETA uses to accomplish this are articulated in §7:

(a) A record or signature may not be denied legal effect or enforceability solely because it is in electronic form.
(b) A contract may not be denied legal effect or enforceability solely because an electronic record was used in its formation.
(c) If a law requires a record to be in writing, an electronic record satisfies the law.
(d) If a law requires a signature, an electronic signature satisfies the law.

UETA applies to both merchants and nonmerchants alike. Where enacted, UETA complements both the common law and U.C.C. Articles 2 and 2A. It is important to note that UETA is not intended to be a source of substantive law regarding contracts—it relies upon other applicable laws for matters such as contract formation and enforceability. Additionally, it does not force the parties to use electronic records, electronic signatures, or other electronic processes.

INTENT TO CONDUCT TRANSACTIONS ELECTRONICALLY

For UETA to apply, both parties must agree to conduct the transaction electronically. Thus, a few guiding principles should be kept in mind in determining whether UETA applies:

- Both parties must have the intent to conduct the transaction electronically, although this does not necessarily mean a formal agreement is required. UETA §5(b).
- If any dispute arises regarding intent, the parties' actions and words should be construed broadly from all circumstances to determine whether the required intent exists. UETA §5 Comment 4.
- The parties may refuse to conduct the transaction electronically despite having conducted prior transactions electronically. UETA §5(c).

UETA does not require the parties to formally agree upon UETA's application—it only requires that both parties had the intent to conduct the transaction electronically. UETA §5 Comment 4. Courts have found intent by looking at a broad range of circumstances; some factors analyzed were the completion of legally mandatory forms in an employment contract, *Rosas v. Macy's, Inc.*, 2012 WL 3656274 (C.D. Cal.), expressing availability only through email and complaining of the speed of non-electronic methods, *Crestwood Shops, L.L.C. v. Hilkene*, 197 S.W.3d 641 (Mo. Ct. App. 2006), and the interval between electronic communications, *International Casings Group, Inc. v. Premium Standard Farms, Inc.*, 358 F. Supp. 2d 863 (W.D. Mo. 2005). See also Jay M. Zitter, *Construction and Application of Uniform Electronic Transactions Act*, 4 A.L.R. 7th 2 (2015).

Section 5 Comment 4 of UETA also provides guidance for determining intent in a number of situations. For example, a businessperson handing out a business card with an email address on it may indicate a willingness to conduct transactions electronically; but where someone has several email addresses, intent to conduct transactions electronically might only be imputed based on the purpose of the account. For example, if Joanna gives out her business card with her business email address on it but is contacted by a client on her personal email, then there likely is not the intent to conduct transactions electronically because use of the personal email does not necessarily imply an agreement to conduct the transaction electronically.

ELECTRONIC SIGNATURES AND ELECTRONIC RECORDS

We now have to discuss the changes the 2022 Amendments made to §2-201 as well as to other sections of the Code. Prior to the Amendments, §2-201(1) required "some writing . . . signed by the party against whom enforcement is sought." "Writing" is defined in §1-201(b)(43) as follows: "'Writing' includes printing, typewriting or any other intentional reduction to tangible form." Prior to the enactment of UETA, the "tangible form" requirement raised an issue as to whether an email constituted a writing for purposes of the statute. Most cases held that it did. See John E. Theuman, *Satisfaction of Statute of Frauds by E-Mail*, 110 A.L.R. 5th 277 (2003). As noted above, the issue was resolved by UETA, which states in §7(c) that "If a law requires a record to be in writing, an electronic record satisfies the law." The Amendments did not change the definition of "writing" but revised the text of §2-201(1), so now it reads that what is required is not "some writing" but "a record." And "record" is defined in §1-201(b)(31) as follows: "'Record' means information that is inscribed on a tangible medium or that is stored in an electronic or other medium and is retrievable in perceivable form." So a record can be either tangible or electronic.

Turning to the definition of "signed," prior to the Amendments, §1-201(b)(37) defined it as follows: "'Signed' includes using any symbol executed or adopted with present intention to adopt or accept a writing." Note that this definition seems limited to the signing of writings. But again UETA comes to the rescue. In §7(d) it states, "If a law requires a signature, an electronic signature satisfies the law." The Code definition was completely rewritten in the Amendments to state:

> "Sign" means, with present intent to authenticate or adopt a record:
> (A) execute or adopt a tangible symbol; or
> (B) attach to or logically associate with the record an electronic symbol, sound, or process.

The Official Comments to §1-201(b)(37) make clear that it is very easy to satisfy this requirement —"the question is always whether the symbol, sound, or process was executed or adopted by the party with present intention to authenticate or adopt the record." A letterhead, for example, is a symbol that was adopted with intent to authenticate or adopt a record because it evidences that it comes from that party. If you scribble your name on an electronic pad, that is an electronic symbol that is attached to the record to indicate that it came from you. When a website asks you to "click here" to indicate your assent, you have signed the record because there was an electronic process associated with the record.

Issues have arisen as to whether there was intent to adopt an electronic signature by the mere sending of an email. Courts have broadly construed UETA's intent-to-adopt requirement; some courts have ruled that the mere clicking of the send button was the adoption of the process, others that the email header data was a symbol executed with an intent to adopt, and that a name at the bottom of an email was sufficient. See *International Casings Group, Inc. v. Premium Standard Farms, Inc.*, 358 F. Supp. 2d 863 (W.D. Mo. 2005); *Whinfield v. Capitas Distributors, Inc.*, 2015 WL 3505642 (D. Conn.). A Canadian court, relying on that country's similar statutes, held that a thumbs-up emoji in an email constituted a signature for purposes of the Statute of Frauds! 👍 See *South West Terminal Ltd. v. Achter Land & Cattle Ltd.*, 2023 CarswellSask 300 (K.B.).

Thus, in a jurisdiction that has not enacted the 2022 Amendments, UETA will work in concert with §2-201 so that a transaction that requires a signed writing, such as a sale of goods for $500 or more, can be evidenced with an electronic record with an electronic signature. In a jurisdiction that has enacted the 2022 Amendments, the revised definitions in the Code will do the job. By accommodating emerging technologies, all of these changes have doubtless helped bring the Code into the world of twenty-first century commerce.

Examples

1. The "King Leopold Ferrari" was custom designed and built in 1954 for King Leopold III of Belgium, who had by that time abdicated his throne and was living in exile in Switzerland. Through a series of perfectly lawful transactions the car ended up in the hands of one Wayne Golumb, a resident of Illinois, where he, his brother Larry, his parents, and his girlfriend Graceia Voyles spent more than a decade restoring it to its original

condition. Robert M. Lee, a big-game hunter and exotic car fancier, took a shine to the Ferrari and desperately wanted to add it to his collection. Several times Golumb rebuffed his steadily increasing offers. Finally one day Lee said he would be willing to give $275,000 for the car. Golumb said, "OK, you've got yourself a deal," and the two shook hands on it. Several people, friends of both of the parties and just the types who would make excellent witnesses, were present at this exchange.

(a) Two days later Golumb signed and sent a letter to Lee that stated, "I'm sorry that I cannot sell you the Ferrari for the price you offered." If Lee brings suit against Golumb, what results?

(b) Would your answer to the previous question be any different if the letter sent by Golumb had contained the following language: "I don't know what I was thinking of agreeing to sell you the car at that price"?

(c) What would your answer be if Golumb had sent no letter to Lee, but at the time of the oral agreement had written "K.L. Ferr.—R.M.L.—$275,000" on a piece of paper on which was printed "From the Desk of Wayne Golumb"? Would it matter whether Golumb had given this paper to Lee or if he had kept it himself in his desk?

2. Samantha, a manufacturer of gaskets, enters into an oral agreement to sell 100,000 of her Number 2 gaskets at a price of $0.50 each to Buddy, who will use them in his widget assembly plant. They shake hands on the deal. The next day, Buddy sends a letter to Samantha that reads:

> This is to confirm our agreement entered into yesterday for the purchase and sale of 100,000 of your Number 2 gaskets for immediate delivery at 50 cents per as discussed. Glad to be doing business with you.

(a) Samantha receives this letter and files it away. If she later tries to go back on the deal, could she successfully defend in a suit brought by Buddy based on the fact that she never signed anything relating to this sale? Would your answer be any different if she could show to the satisfaction of the court that she had never received Buddy's letter?

(b) What would be your answer to the previous question if Samantha had received Buddy's letter but had immediately written back:

> Wait one minute, Buddy! We never agreed on immediate delivery. We'll have to work out a timetable or I can't do it. You'd better give me a call if you want those gaskets.

3. Lydia is a lawyer. She is visited in her office by Hal, a representative of Atomic Office Systems, the maker of a line of computerized office equipment. Lydia agrees to give Hal a few minutes of her time. He gives

her a very detailed proposal for a complicated computer setup that he "recommends" to her. After a few minutes, Lydia shows him out of her office with the statement that she'll "think about" the proposal. The pesky salesman having been dealt with, she gets back to work. Several days later she receives a letter signed by Hal that states that "I am happy to confirm your order of the system as proposed and as detailed on the attached memorandum. I will call soon to arrange for payment and installation." Attached to this letter is a detailed description of a system that is if anything even more complicated (and more expensive) than what Hal had pitched to her in her office. Uttering a mild expletive, Lydia tosses this letter into the garbage. Six months later Lydia is served with papers in a suit bought by Atomic Office Systems, charging her with breach of contract. You can imagine what she says now. What is she to do? Can she get the suit dismissed on summary judgment based on the Statute of Frauds? Would it have helped her situation any if she had called Hal when she got his letter and given him a piece of her mind?

4. Lydia, the lawyer from the previous example, decides to add an email address to the letterhead she uses in her business. She calls up Pam the printer who has done work for her before and, over the phone, orders 25 boxes of letterhead identical to her previous orders (a copy of which Pam has on file) but with one addition: Pam tells her that the cost will be $30 a box, to which Lydia agrees. Pam creates the printing plate necessary for doing the work and runs off the first box. Before she does any more, she receives a call from Lydia, who says that she has changed her mind and will not require any new letterhead. If Pam decides to sue Lydia for breach of contract, will she have any Statute of Frauds problem?

5. Sam and Dave are both model railroad enthusiasts. At a convention held for such types, they discuss a particular antique caboose that Sam owns and Dave craves. No paper changes hands. Dave is willing to swear that they did agree to a sale at $1,250 and believes he can find some witnesses who would confirm that the two parted with a hearty handshake. Sam refuses to sell. When confronted by Dave he does not deny their deal but says, "Oh yeah, let's see you prove it in court." When Dave does sue, Sam moves for summary judgment based on the Statute of Frauds. Is that the end of it? Or can you see an argument for Dave that the case should proceed at least long enough for him to take Sam's deposition? What result?

6. Tidwell enters into an oral agreement with Anthony to purchase 100 head of cattle for $500 each. He delivers a check for $1,000, which Anthony holds on to but does not immediately put into his bank account. There are no special markings on the check.

(a) The value of the cattle starts to climb to at least $570 a head. Anthony returns the check, refusing to go through with the deal. Will Tidwell have an action for damages and be able to overcome Anthony's defense of the Statute of Frauds? How much can he claim as damages

(b) Suppose instead that the market value of the cattle drops to $480. Anthony has already delivered 12 head of cattle, which have been taken onto Tidwell's ranch where they reside. No payments have been made by Tidwell. Can Tidwell demand Anthony take the return of these 12? If Anthony sues for damages, will he have a Statute of Frauds problem?

7. Robert X. Lee, a relative of Robert M. Lee from Example 1, is a collector of antique salt and pepper shakers. The shakers are, needless to say, worth much more when they are in their matched sets. One day Lee spots in Saul's antique shop the salt half of a famous set, the "King Leopold Salt and Pepper," which had long been thought lost. As a connoisseur of such things he is aware that the matching pepper is owned by one Paul. Saying something about how he intends to buy the pepper now that he's found the salt, he enters into an oral agreement with Saul to buy the saltshaker for $550. They shake hands on the deal. Lee is to bring in the money and to pick up the shaker within the week. As soon as he leaves Saul's store, Lee contacts Paul and offers to buy the pepper from him. Paul, figuring that Lee must have some good reason to buy it, drives a hard bargain and eventually gets Lee to agree to a price of $3,800. Lee and Paul sign a contract for sale. Lee returns to Saul's shop only to find that Saul is refusing to sell the salt at the $550 price. Will Lee be able to enforce his agreement with Saul in a court of law? What argument will he make? Will he succeed? Should he?

8. Summer, the owner of Summer's Restaurant, frequently buys her restaurant supplies from Lindsay's Wholesale. Summer typically calls Lindsay and leaves a voicemail detailing her order. One day, Summer tried calling Lindsay to place an order but the phone was disconnected. Summer had never emailed Lindsay before but urgently needed 140 cases of Blue Beer for an upcoming basketball game. Summer found Lindsay's personal email address and sent her an email describing the order. Lindsay quickly replied, "Okay. I'll call you in a minute." Lindsay called Summer shortly thereafter and confirmed an order for 140 cases. Lindsay then wrote an order out to the stock room on a notepad with the company logo, "Please deliver 120 cases to Summer.—Lindsay." Lindsay delivered only 120 cases and Summer sued, claiming they had a contract for 140 cases. Lindsay raised the Statute of Frauds defense. What result? Would the result differ in a jurisdiction that has enacted the 2022 U.C.C. Amendments?

9. Lindsay frequently emailed Casey from Casey's Microbrews to order beer. Lindsay heard that Casey was holding a 30-day fire-sale of his most recent batch for half price, so she emailed him, asking "Will you make me a firm offer to sell me 100 cases of Blue Beer for $55 per case for thirty days?" Casey emailed back "I agree to do that, but I only make such offers through the snail mail." Casey didn't write his name at the bottom of the email and did not follow up with an offer in the mail. Lindsay tried to accept the offer several days later, but Casey claimed he had never made the offer. What result? Would the result differ in a jurisdiction that has enacted the 2022 U.C.C. Amendments?

10. Dlovan is starting a new wholesale business to supply businesses like Lindsay's with "America's new favorite food—doner kebabs." Dlovan is always on the run and frequently sends emails and text messages to product suppliers. What advice would you give Dlovan when contracting with merchants and with nonmerchants? Does it matter whether she is in a jurisdiction that has enacted the 2022 U.C.C. Amendments?

Explanations

EXPLANATIONS

1. a. Golumb should be able to get the action dismissed under §2-201. As you might have suspected, this question is based on an actual case. In *Lee v. Voyles*, 898 F.2d 76 (7th Cir. 1990), the circumstances were only a little more complex than I've related here. As Judge Easterbrook noted, "Sometimes fascinating facts bring with them exciting legal issues. This is not such an occasion." There being no writing signed by Golumb evidencing the agreement and no exception to §2-201 being available, the contract was held to be "not enforceable by way of action or defense" against Golumb.

   Note that Lee does in fact have a writing signed by Golumb, but it does not fit the bill as it is not "sufficient to indicate that a contract for sale has been made between the parties." The letter in and of itself indicates that an offer had been made by Lee, but not that it had ever been accepted. Does Lee have a right to introduce other evidence to show that the letter meant something else, that there had in fact been an agreement and that it was now being repudiated? It depends on what the other evidence is. Several courts have held that two or more documents taken together can satisfy the Statute even if no one of them would on its own. For example, suppose Seller sends a written offer replete with terms, including a quantity term, to Buyer. Buyer sends back a signed note saying only, "I accept." Neither piece by itself satisfies the requirements of §2-201(1). Taken together they do. See, for example, *Simplex Supplies, Inc. v. Abhe & Svoboda, Inc.*, 586 N.W.2d 797 (Minn. App. 1998).

Of course, not all collections of communications back and forth between two parties make up a packet satisfying the Statute of Frauds. See, for example, *Central Illinois Light Co. v. Consolidated Coal Co.*, 349 F.3d 488 (7th Cir. 2003), in which the parties had without question engaged in lengthy negotiations involving the exchange of many documents. As the Seventh Circuit pointed out, however, "documents that *merely* evidence negotiations do not satisfy the statute of frauds" (emphasis in original). The critical point, it noted, "is that the documentation presented by the party seeking to demonstrate compliance with the Statute of Frauds must 'indicate' or 'confirm' the existence of a contract." Referring to one particular document on which the plaintiff was heavily relying to demonstrate that the demands of the Statute had been met, the court concluded that all that document showed is that the plaintiff "prepared an invoice consistent with what it *hoped* would be a contract," and that it was apparent "that the invoice was *wishful thinking* rather than evidence of an oral contract" (emphasis added).

b. If this were the language in Golumb's letter, Lee should be able to get past the Statute of Frauds. It is important to focus on the fact that the writing need not set out all details of the agreement but can be something far less formal. It need not be what a layperson thinks of as "a written contract" that the other side has signed. In *Rosenfeld v. Basquiat*, 78 F.3d 84 (2d Cir. 1996), the Second Circuit held that a document created impromptu—done in crayon on a large piece of paper laid on the floor—signed by both an art dealer and the precociously talented, profligate, and eccentric (in the words of the court) modern artist Jean-Michel Basquiat satisfied the requirements of the Statute.

Read Comment 1 to §2-201. The last paragraph sets forth three definite and invariable requirements that the writing must meet. First of all it must "evidence a contract for the sale of goods." Earlier the Comment says that in this regard all that is required "is that the writing afford *a basis for believing* that the offered oral evidence rests on a real transaction." Professor Karl Llewellyn, draftsman of §2-201, is often quoted for his statement, "What the section does . . . is require some objective guaranty, other than word of mouth that there really has been some deal." Here the letter surely meets the test. How likely is it that there would exist such a letter signed by Golumb saying what this one says if he had not in fact ever entered into an agreement with Lee about selling the car?

Remember, the issue here is not whether the offered writing is conclusive proof that an agreement was made or what its terms were. It is enough if there is some writing that backs up the claim. That will satisfy the Statute and get the litigation into a further stage. Lee still needs to prove that there was a contract for the sale of this Ferrari and at this price; Golumb will still have the opportunity to dispute this claim, but he will have to do so based on the facts of the situation, that is, on what transpired between them on the car lot, not on the lack of a writing.

We should check that the other two requirements mentioned in the Comment are met here. The writing must be "signed," and that's been given. It also must specify a quantity. Here it says, "the car," which should make clear that the quantity is one automobile.

A question arises as to why the drafters made the quantity term and not, say, the price term crucial to the writing. See, for example, *Simmons Foods, Inc. v. Hill's Pet Nutrition, Inc.*, 270 F.3d 723 (8th Cir. 2001), upholding a lower court's ruling that a fax setting forth a three-year deal for the purchase of pet food poultry meal satisfied the Statute of Frauds only for the first of the three years since, while it did set forth the quantity to be delivered in the first year ("36.6 million pounds"), it did not contain any mention of the quantities to be delivered for the second or third year of the agreement. Apparently the drafters of §2-201(1) thought that there was less of a problem that someone would assert a wholly fraudulent contract at a wholly fraudulent price designed to give him or her a huge advantage simply because there usually is some external "reality check" on what price could have been agreed upon. No amount of documentation is going to make believable my claim that you agreed to sell me something at one-tenth your usual price or your claim that I agreed to pay ten times market value. Contrast this to the question of quantity. There is no way of ferreting out even an approximately normal, usual, or reasonable amount that might be bought and sold in any given situation. One party may purchase ten widgets and another may want 10,000. See the second paragraph of Comment 1.

c. This writing may well satisfy the Statute. Initially it may seem the signature requirement has not been met, but look at §1-201(b)(37), the Comment to that definition, and then return to Comment 1 of §2-201. The writing and the signature requirements have obviously been loosened up considerably by Article 2. But query whether the language is "sufficient to indicate that a contract for sale has been made between the parties." Golumb would argue that a note like this is just as easily understood as his way of recording an offer made to him that he was going to consider. But again, the measure is whether the writing affords "some basis," not "an overwhelming basis," for believing an agreement had been entered into. This note should suffice. For a case holding that scribblings such as this on a personalized memo pad *could* as a matter of law satisfy the statutory requirement of a signed writing even if it would be up to the jury to determine whether in the particular case the preparer actually *had* "intended to authenticate the memoes by using the pre-printed memopad sheets" and hence signed in this way, see *Owen v. Kroger Co.*, 936 F. Supp. 579 (S.D. Ind. 1996). On the other hand, a preprinted form bearing the party's name will not be held a "signed" document where in addition the form contains the legend "Not Valid Unless Signed and Accepted by an Officer of the Company" and a space for an authenticating signature that was never filled in. *Toppings v. Rainbow Homes, Inc.*, 490 S.E.2d 817 (W. Va. 1997).

On the question of whether the note had to have been delivered to Lee, see Comment 6. It is sufficient that some writing exists. As another example, suppose the only writing Golumb signs is a note to a friend saying, "I have gotten myself into terrible trouble by selling the King Leopold to a guy named Lee." It's the creation of this note that is his real trouble. If Lee becomes aware of it, he does not have to worry about Golumb's raising a Statute of Frauds defense.

2\. a. Samantha has never signed anything, but she won't be able to assert the Statute of Frauds due to the so-called *merchants' exception* found in §2-201(2). You should check for yourself and for Buddy that all of the criteria of that exception are met. If you have any doubt that this is a transaction "between merchants," you might want to review Chapter 3.

Incidentally, as was pointed out in that chapter, a major dispute in applying the Article 2 definition of "merchant" is whether a farmer falls within its scope. The issue has come up often and in fact usually in the context of the §2-201(2) exception. A farmer allegedly enters into an oral agreement to sell his or her crop with the travelling representative of some large buyer of agricultural produce. On return to the home office, the agent sends out a "Confirmation Letter" to which the farmer never responds. The farmer has signed nothing, but has he or she lost the right to rely on the Statute of Frauds should a dispute arise? Obviously the drafter didn't think this was an unduly harsh result against a merchant, as opposed to your ordinary Joe or Jane consumer, as someone who is in business should know enough to read—and promptly give an appropriate response to—his or her mail. As we noted in Chapter 3, the courts have come to no agreement whether a farmer should be held to this level of professionalism and responsibility. For a case that offers a particularly thorough review of the issue of whether a farmer is always, never, or sometimes (to be determined on a case-by-case basis) to be deemed a "merchant" for the purposes of §2-201(2), see *Brooks Cotton Co., Inc. v. Williams*, 381 S.W.3d 414 (Tenn. App. 2012).

In going through the numerous criteria of this merchants' exception, you notice first that it is necessary that the confirmatory memorandum be sent out "within a reasonable time" of the contract being entered into. For a good discussion of what factors are to be considered in determining whether the confirmation had in fact been sent out within a reasonable time (as well as a helpful mini-history of the Statute of Frauds in general), see *St. Ansgar Mills, Inc. v. Streit*, 613 N.W.2d 289 (Iowa 2000). The Iowa Supreme Court there concludes that "all relevant circumstances, including the custom and practices of the parties," must be considered in determining what constitutes a reasonable time for these purposes and furthermore that the question is normally one for the trier of fact. See also *Irvington Elevator Co., Inc. v. Heser*, 982 N.E.2d 824 (Ill. App. 2012).

Since in our example Buddy sent out the confirmatory letter the very next day, there seems to be no question that he met the "reasonable time" requirement. The next questions to ask are whether the letter was actually "received" by Samantha and if so *when* it was received. For a working definition of *received*, see §1-202. The contrast between receipt and the giving of *notice* or *notification* is important in the Code, and you should be sure to work through §1-202 carefully now if you have not done so before. (On the question of when a notification such as a confirmation would be considered received by a complex organization, see §1-202(f).) Note that in §2-201(2) the objection must be in writing but that it is sufficient that it be "given." Receipt of the objection is not necessary.

One issue that has divided the courts is the standard for determining whether a writing sent by one party to another can be considered "a writing in confirmation of the contract." The subsection goes on to require that the writing be one "sufficient against the seller" under §2-201(1). As we've seen, this can be a very loose standard requiring only that it offer "some basis" for believing a contract exists. Must a confirmation say anything more? A number of courts, troubled by the possibility of a party's being bound by a writing it did not itself sign, have held that there must be some clear language of confirmation in the writing and that it must explicitly alert the recipient it is intended to confirm a previous agreement. In the *Bazak* case (cited in Example 1a), the New York Court of Appeals rejected this approach, placing itself in line with what it maintained to be a majority of courts and commentators:

> [I]n determining whether writings are confirmatory documents within UCC §2-201(2), neither explicit words of confirmation nor express references to the prior agreement are required, and the writings are sufficient as long as they afford a basis for believing that they reflect a real transaction between the parties.

In justification of its position, the court stressed that:

> as additional protection against abuse and inequity . . . the consequence of a failure to give timely written notice . . . is only to remove the bar of

> the Statute of Frauds. The burden of proving that a contract was indeed made remains with [the party alleging one], as does the burden of proving the terms of the contract.

Look at Comment 3 to §2-201. Of course not all communications claimed to be "confirmatory of the contract and sufficient against the sender" will meet even the somewhat looser standard enunciated in *Barzak*. In *Vision Systems, Inc. v. EMC Corporation*, 19 Mass. L. Rep. 139 (Mass. Super. 2005), the court found that an email argued by the plaintiff to trigger the merchants' exception failed to serve as a "confirmation" for two reasons:

> First, the cover memorandum part of the e-mail states: "As promised see the attached document. Please run it up the flagpole and let me know what you think. I will call you to discuss." This is not language indicating that a contract for sale has been made. Rather, it is, at best, an invitation to [make an offer, which is then to be] considered and accepted, modified or rejected. The "run it up the flag pole and let me know what you think" language can have no other meaning. Second, the document attached with the e-mail is full of tentative and qualifying language. It speaks of "projections," "forecasts" and "elections" by [the defendant].

In our particular example, of course, there is no doubt that Buddy's letter is a confirmation and sets the merchants' exception in motion.

Another issue that has troubled the courts regarding the merchants' exception of §2-201(2) is what to make of a document sent by one party to the other that is headed something like an "ORDER CONFIRMATION" and is written in terms suggesting a deal has been finalized but that also asks for the recipient to "sign and return" a copy of the form? If the recipient does sign and return this form there is, of course, no Statute of Frauds problem. If he or she does not, however, can the sender invoke the merchants' exception, saying this was indeed a "writing in confirmation of the contract and sufficient against the sender" and that its request for the return of a signed copy was just for bookkeeping or accounting purposes? In *GPL Treatment, Ltd. v. Louisiana-Pacific Corp.*, 914 P.2d 682 (Or. 1996), the Oregon Supreme Court concluded, over the vigorous dissent of three members of the court, that "there is no single correct answer to the question of the effect of a 'sign and return' clause. Each writing must be examined independently and in the light of its own contents and context," then going on to find as a matter of law that the forms there in question were "confirmations" sufficient to trigger the merchants' exception. The dissenters argued and found support in other cases for holding that forms that ask for the signature and return of the recipient are by their nature offers to be accepted and nothing more. Agreeing with the position taken by the dissenters is *International Meat Traders, Inc. v. H & M Foods Systems Co., Inc.*, 70 F.3d 836 (5th Cir. 1995). For a decision more in harmony with the majority in *GPL Treatment*, see that of the Seventh Circuit in *ReMapp International Corp. v. Comfort Keyboard Co., Inc.*, 560 F.3d 628 (7th Cir. 2009). Incidentally, one judge in *GPL Treatment* woke up and said in effect, "Wait a minute — why are we even discussing this issue? This is a contract between a U.S. company and a Canadian company. It is therefore governed by the United Nations Convention on the International Sale of Goods, and the CISG does not have a Statute of Frauds."

b. Samantha will claim that her timely response effectively countered Buddy's reliance upon his confirmation. But is what she wrote "objection to its contents"? The courts and commentators have taken this language to mean that the writing must state an objection to the principal thrust of a confirmation, that is, that a contract in fact exists between the parties. Here Samantha's response in effect acknowledges a contract and is only contesting a term. The kind of objection contemplated in §2-201(2) is a response that does not merely quibble about terms or dispute who's to do what under the agreement, but a clear disavowal that any agreement was ever finalized. In order to preserve her Statute of Frauds defense, Samantha would have to reply not only in a timely fashion but object in no uncertain terms to the very idea that a contract had been concluded.

3. You understand why I put this example in: A word to the wise. If there is any justice in this world, Lydia should eventually win this suit, but she won't be able to do it that easily with a summary judgment based on the Statute of Frauds. She's going to have to establish that she and Hal never came to an agreement during their earlier meeting, which is a question of fact and looks like it will be her word against his. If you have any doubt that Lydia is a merchant for these purposes, see the second paragraph of Comment 2 to §2-104. Here a lawyer is alleged to be buying not fishing tackle for her own use but office equipment for her place of business. A phone call to Hal might have done Lydia some good psychologically, but it would not have helped her legal position. The objection must be in writing. It is worth noting that this exception is found only in the Code and does not apply to other Statutes of Frauds.

4. Pam will rely on the exception found in §2-201(3)(a) for contracts involving *specially manufactured goods*. The general idea behind this exception should be fairly obvious. As one court has said, "in these cases the very nature of the goods serves as a reliable indication that the contract had been formed." Furthermore, not only is the likelihood of a perjured claim significantly diminished, but "denying enforcement to such a contract would impose substantial hardship on the aggrieved party." *Impossible*

Electronic Techniques, Inc. v. Wackenhut Protective Systems, Inc., 669 F.2d 1026 806 (5th Cir. 1982). What's Pam going to do with all this stuff if she can't sell it to Lydia?

There are a number of distinct criteria in (3)(a), but it appears Pam meets most of them with no question. Her only problem would be in showing that she had made "a substantial beginning" of the manufacture of the letterhead. Is one box out of 25 substantial enough? It would seem so, especially since a large part of the cost must be tied up in the preparation of the plate that had also been completed. What if she had only made the plate but not put any ink to paper? She should get past the Statute. This does seem a significant part of the printing job and a particularly good basis for believing a contract had been previously formed. Making the plate also seems analogous, if not exactly the same thing, as "making commitments for . . . procurement" as mentioned in (3)(a).

Not all courts have given such an expansive reading to this language. In one noted case, *Epprecht v. IBM Corp.*, 1983 WL 160571 (E.D. Pa.), the plaintiff alleged that IBM had ordered 50,000 print-head assemblies to be made to that company's specifications, but there was no written instrument to that effect. Seven thousand were delivered. IBM accepted 4,000 of them but rejected the rest and refused to take any more, claiming quality problems. Epprecht's suit to make IBM pay for the rejected units and acknowledge the full extent of the deal was dismissed on Statute of Fraud grounds. The court ruled that manufacture of the 7,000 was not a substantial beginning on the alleged 50,000. (Apparently no work whatsoever had been done toward making the other 43,000. The result may well have been different if those units were all in production at the plaintiff's plant at the time IBM told them the deal was off.) The *Epprecht* court seems to have been concerned that to read this exception too broadly would open up a buyer of a small or reasonably sized purchase of specifically manufactured goods to potential perjured claims that the orders were for much, much larger amounts.

Later, in *EMSG Systems Division, Inc. v. Miltope Corp.*, 1998 WL 1095078 (E.D.N.C.), the court, following *Epprecht*, held:

> [t]he special manufacture [by the seller] of 1,000 [circuit board] sets would remove an oral contract for 1,000 sets out of the statute of frauds. However, those 1,000 sets are not sufficient to except an additional 5,000 sets [alleged to have been ordered] which were never actually produced, from the writing requirement of [§2-201(1)]. . . . Otherwise, the actual manufacture of 1,000 sets could potentially support an alleged oral contract for any number of additional sets, be it 5,000 or 50,000 or 500,000.

The Supreme Court of Virginia, in *Delta Star, Inc. v. Michael's Carpet World*, 666 S.E.2d 331 (Va. 2008), decreed the courts could not enforce an alleged oral contact for the purchase and installation of floor covering in two offices on the defendant's premises—given the plaintiff's attempted reliance on the "specially manufactured goods" exception of §2-201(3)(a)—even though the particular type and style of tile alleged to have been chosen from a set of samples shown to defendant's representative had been ordered by the plaintiff and received by it. As of the time of trial, these tiles remained in plaintiff's warehouse. Central to the court's holding was its finding that "[t]he flooring materials chosen by Delta Star were selected from the samples displayed, were not altered in any way to suit only Delta Star, and were suitable for sale to others in Michael's ordinary course of business."

It is certainly arguable that the reading of the specially manufactured goods exception by these three courts is unnecessarily narrow. Remember, once again, that in either case had the seller's case survived the Statute, it would still have had to prove as a matter of fact that a contract for the exact larger amount it was alleging had been agreed to by the buyer.

5. Dave seeks to rely on the exception to the writing requirement found in §2-201(3)(b), the *admissions exception*. See also Comment 7. This provision has caused a good deal of concern and controversy. Note that not just any subsequent statement will do: The "admission" must be made in a particular legal setting where it is made under oath. Voluntary admissions are not a big problem, although there is some question about exactly what constitutes an "admission." See, for example, *Essco Geometric v. Harvard Industries*, 46 F.3d 718 (8th Cir. 1995), in which it was held that the admissions exception was not satisfied by the testimony of a retired employee of the defendant that he had while still in the company's employ entered into an oral agreement on its behalf with the plaintiff. The admission, if it is one, must be by the "party" to be charged, and the former employee's statement could not bind his former employer as at the time of the statement he was not acting as its agent even if he may have been at the time of the purported oral agreement. Compare this case to *Saga Solutions, LLC v. Sherwin Williams Co.*, 2002 WL 1145373 (Conn. Super.), in which the court found the admissions exception to apply when its existence was admitted by someone who was still at the time of trial an employee of the defendant company about what a former employee had in fact done, acting at the time on behalf of the defendant company.

Returning to our hypothetical about Sam and Dave, suppose that Dave were to be deposed or testify in court that, yes, he and Sam did have the conversation Sam alleges and that, yes, they did shake hands. He further states under oath that he did not and does not see this as a completed deal. He claims they just had a productive and friendly negotiation session. Could the court look at what admittedly happened and conclude that by admitting the details he had in effect admitted the existence of a contract, whether he admits to having so admitted it or not? The courts are not clear on this, although some have said yes. See, for example, *Wehry v. Daniels*, 784 N.E.2d 532 (Ind. Ct. App. 2003).

The real problem, however, is whether an *involuntary* admission can sink a Statute of Frauds defense, and in particular how much leeway and time the complainant should be given to try to force such an admission—under penalty of perjury—out of the defendant. In our hypothetical, can Sam resist the motion for summary judgment, arguing that Dave should at least be made to file a complete answer to the complaint? The idea is that it may be hard for Dave to frame a truthful answer that doesn't admit the existence of the deal. Even if Dave can frame such an answer and *then* moves for summary judgment based on the Statute, does Sam have the right to insist on at least some time for discovery and the chance to depose Dave? At the deposition, of course, he would ask the pointed questions intended to put Dave between the proverbial rock and a hard place.

I think most authorities would say that the defendant should have the right to use and succeed with the Statute of Frauds defense in a summary fashion, at least if he has somewhere been willing to have recorded under oath his denial that a contract existed. Otherwise, if involuntary admissions can fit the bill and if the complainant is given full court backing in trying to wring a confession out of the defendant no matter how long it takes, this exception might swallow up the whole Statute of Frauds idea. This has been the conclusion of several cases, most notably *DF Activities Corp. v. Brown*, 851 F.2d 920 (7th Cir. 1988), in which Judge Posner opined the following:

> When there is a bare motion to dismiss, or an answer with no evidentiary materials, the possibility remains a live one that, if asked under oath whether a contract had been made, the defendant would admit it had been. The only way to test the proposition is for the plaintiff to take the defendant's deposition, or, if there is no discovery to call the defendant as an adverse witness at trial. But where . . . the defendant swears in an affidavit that there was no contract, we see no point in keeping the lawsuit alive. Of course the defendant may blurt out an admission in a deposition, but this is hardly likely, especially since by doing so he may be admitting to having perjured himself in his affidavit. Stranger things have happened, but remote possibilities do not warrant subjecting the parties and the judiciary to proceedings almost certain to be futile.

When the defendant counters the complaint with only a "bare motion to dismiss," however, and does not offer even an affidavit denying the existence of a contract, the case will probably be allowed to continue. See *Theta Products, Inc. v. Zippo Mfg. Co.*, 81 F. Supp. 2d 346 (D.R.I. 1999), *aff'd* 8 F. App'x 3 (1st Cir. 2001), holding that dismissal prior to the plaintiff's "opportunity to use the discovery process to probe the [§2-201(3)(b)] exception would be wholly inappropriate." To grant the defendant's motion to dismiss prior to discovery would, the court stated, allow it to "defeat a cause of action on an oral contract before the plaintiff had any opportunity to seek an admission that the contract existed." For a discussion of this issue, see *Carbon Processing & Reclamation, LLC v. Valero Marketing & Supply Co.*, 2010 WL 3925261 (W.D. Tenn. 2010), in which a United States District Court, called upon to determine how the courts of Tennessee would view the admission's exception, concluded that the plaintiff-buyer should be granted a greater amount of time to a judicial admission from the defendant-seller that an enforceable contact for sale of goods had existed between the parties. While noting that this was not a matter that the courts of Tennessee had directly addressed and that contrary authority from other jurisdictions did exist, the district court held:

> Plaintiffs are entitled to an opportunity to obtain a judicial admission from Defendants about the existence of the oral contract. The Court finds no evidence that the Tennessee courts have dismissed claims for breach of an oral contract at the pleadings stage where the plaintiff has sought an opportunity to obtain the judicial admission. On the contrary, the Tennessee courts have applied the exception to testimonial admissions made at trial long-after the pleadings were closed. Based on this limited case law, the Court finds no basis to conclude that the Tennessee courts would dismiss on the pleadings a breach of oral contract claim based on the judicial admission exception found at Tenn. Code Ann. §47-2-201(3)(b). The Court notes that Defendants have filed their Answer as to the breach of contract claim (Count V) and denied Plaintiffs' allegations about the existence of the alleged December 2007 agreement. Nevertheless, the Court concludes that Plaintiffs should have an additional opportunity to obtain the judicial admission in this case and argue for the application of this exception to Tennessee's Statute of Frauds. [citations omitted]

Even if a party does "blurt out" an admission in the course of a deposition, should this be the end of the story? Note the decision of the New York Appellate Division that a single statement by a party that an agreement had been reached made in response to "excessive badgering on this issue" during the course of an extensive (and apparently intensive) deposition was insufficient to invoke the admissions exception in light of the party's otherwise steadfast insistence that negotiations had never been finalized. *Gaultney-Klineman Art v. Hughes*, 642 N.Y.S.2d 265 (App. Div. 1996). To the same effect is *Conagra, Inc. v. Nierenberg*, 7 P.3d 369 (Mont. 2000), holding that an effective "admission" of the existence of a contract made during the course of a trial must be "deliberate, clear, and unequivocal." Such an admission could not be pieced together by the opposing party from his adversary's answers to "carefully worded questions" posed by opposing counsel that used the word "contract," to the use of which the party testifying did not object. It remained clear from the totality of his testimony that the alleged seller never thought that a legally binding agreement had ever been concluded between himself and the hopeful buyer.

What if Dave is willing to sign an affidavit that he and Sam never entered into a contract? Sam just *knows* this is not so and thinks he has great evidence that Dave has just perjured himself. What can he do? Perhaps he can get Dave ostracized by all right-thinking members of the community, but the Statute of Frauds seems to make clear this is the end of it as far as the courts and the law of sales are concerned. It is worth noting that the admission exception, like the confirmation exception, is found only in the Code and does not apply to other Statutes of Frauds.

6. a. Tidwell has an action good against the Statute of Frauds based on the *payment exception* found in §2-201(3)(c): "A contract which does not satisfy the requirements of subsection (1) but which is valid in all other respects is enforceable . . . with respect to goods for which payment has been made and accepted. . . ." The idea here is pretty well spelled out in Comment 2. Tidwell's delivery of the check and Anthony's holding on to it are both acts that give some basis for believing Tidwell's claim that a contract had been made. Tidwell's problem is that under the Code he will be able to enforce the contract only to the extent that goods have been paid for. This is a change from the prior law under which partial payment took the whole contract outside the Statute of Frauds. Under the Code's provision, with its particular passion for preventing fraudulent assertions of excessive quantities, a partial payment will in effect support only a partial contract. Tidwell paid $1,000, which will allow him a suit for two of the cattle but no more, as the court in fact held in *Anthony v. Tidwell*, 560 S.W.2d 908 (Tenn. 1977). The idea is that this amount of payment does support a conclusion that at least two head were contracted for at this price, but doesn't give any basis for believing that there was an agreement for 100 head any more than that they contracted for 200 or for 2,000 of the beasts.

What if Tidwell had given a check for only $400 in down payment? Would he be entitled to sue for only 80 percent of a cow? No, the courts have held that such a down payment would support the assertion that *at least one* animal was agreed to and Tidwell could sue for that one. In a situation that has come up many times, someone enters into an agreement to buy a car from an auto dealer but the dealer never signs any papers. The buyer gives a check in down payment. When the dealer later tries to renege on the deal, the delivery and acceptance of the down payment will serve to take the buyer's case out of the Statute of Frauds. While partial payment will normally only support a partial contract, when partial payment has been made on a single indivisible item the contract for that one unapportionable whole is supported. We don't usually think of a person's buying some percentage of an automobile, so a suit for the car is not blocked by the Statute of Frauds. See, for instance, *Sedmak v. Charlie's Chevrolet, Inc.*, 622 S.W.2d 694 (Mo. Ct. App. 1981).

If Tidwell's argument here is based on the idea that his payment had been "accepted" by Anthony, does it make a difference that the latter had never negotiated the check but just held on to it? Probably not. Comment 2 says that "part payment may be made by money or check, accepted by the seller." Here Anthony did accept the check even if he did not immediately cash or deposit it. This was held to be sufficient in *Buffaloe v. Hart*, 441 S.E.2d 172 (N.C. App. 1994). If, however, Anthony could show that the check had been delivered to him for some other reason entirely, such as another deal, then that presumably would make a difference.

b. Now it's Anthony who would take advantage of subsection (3)(c) since the Statute cannot block enforcement of a contract "with respect to goods . . . which have been received and accepted." Again, he can sue only on a contract for the amount delivered—12 head of cattle and no more. Here there should be no problem in establishing that Tidwell accepted these 12. Sometimes, however, there will be a real question whether the delivered goods have been accepted. While the Code has no special provision relating to when a payment has been "accepted," it does go into considerable detail on when there has been an "acceptance of goods." This is all found in §2-602, which we will go over in scrupulous detail in Chapter 17. Don't worry about it for now.

7. This set of facts I *did* make up, but you can see they make for a particularly troubling situation. If Lee does bring suit against Saul, he will run smack dab into the Statute of Frauds. The price is over $500. There is no writing signed by anybody, no specially manufactured goods, and no partial payment or delivery. If Saul is careful in his response to the suit, he'll admit nothing. Section 2-201 is fully in force, and there is no exception provided for in that section that would help Lee. It seems that in spite of the fact that he had an oral contract with Saul he won't be able to enforce it.

Lee's argument, of course, is that he so obviously and earnestly relied upon this contract, a possibility that Saul had good reason to expect, that it would be wrong for him to be left with no relief simply because of a technicality like the Statute of Frauds. You'll recall from your Contracts study the notion of a suit based on the doctrine of *promissory estoppel* (you'll recall it from that course because we can't and won't rehearse the whole idea here). The present problem is a relatively narrow one, but one which has given the courts and commentators a good deal of grief and over which there is no agreement whatsoever. Assuming for the moment that a plaintiff could make out a good cause of action under the doctrine of promissory estoppel, may that action be barred for lack of a writing under §2-201? If so, the result may seem very harsh against Lee. If not, then there must be a further exception to the §2-201(1) writing requirement that is not found in any language in Article 2 but is inherent in the estoppel notion. Lee could sue and could win getting some relief (his loss incurred in reliance, if not the full value of the contract promise to him) based on his handshake agreement with Saul even though no writing was ever signed by anybody.

As I've suggested, numerous academic writers have written on the question and several courts have had to address the issue head-on. There is no agreement on whether the Statute acts as a bar, or indeed is in any way relevant, to an action once promissory estoppel is the claimant's theme. At one extreme is the position that the Statute of Frauds is no bar whatsoever. Adherents of this view point out the language of §1-103(b), which specifically preserves the law relative to estoppel among other things. The Statute of Frauds bars *contract* actions, they would argue, but a suit brought on the reliance theory is something else altogether. At the other extreme are those of the opinion that there can be no exceptions to the §2-201 Statute of Frauds not explicitly provided for in that section. Note the introductory language of subsection (1): "Except as otherwise provided *in this section*. . . ." Those taking this position argue in effect that the Article 2 Statute of Frauds has been drafted with enough care and operates with sufficient sensitivity to any potential hardship it may cause through its various carefully crafted exceptions that the potential harshness of mechanical application of a writing requirement has been sufficiently ameliorated. For the courts to start finding other exceptions not provided for by the drafters is just an invitation to judicial circumvention of the rule as adopted by the legislature. See, for example, *International Products & Technologies, Inc. v. Iomega Corp.*, 1989 WL 138866 (E.D. Pa.), *aff'd mem.*, 908 F.2d 962 (3d Cir. 1990), where the federal district court, called upon to determine whether the courts of Pennsylvania would allow for an estoppel exception to §2-201, concluded that they would not:

> Since the statute allows three limited and express exceptions, other exceptions should not be allowed. These exceptions are sufficient to protect against unequitable results. If estoppel claims were not barred by the application of the statute of frauds, every promise satisfying §90 of the Restatement [of Contracts], but which was otherwise invalid under the statute of frauds, would be actionable under an estoppel claim. Such a reading would strip the statute of its purpose.

See also *Architectural Metal Sys., Inc. v. Consolidated Sys., Inc.*, 58 F.3d 1227 (7th Cir. 1995), and *Control Solutions LLC v. Oshkosh Corp.*, 2012 WL 3096678

(N.D. Ill.), each coming to the same conclusion as to how Illinois law responds to this argument. But compare *Byl v. Van Beek*, 810 N.W.2d 896 (Iowa App. 2012), in which the Court of Appeals of Iowa declared, "In *Warder & Lee Elevator, Inc. v. Britten*, 274 N.W.2d 339, 342 (Iowa 1979), the court stated, '[W]e have long recognized promissory estoppel as a means of defeating [that state's general statute of frauds].' The court also stated that [the state's Article 2 Statute of Frauds] should not be read as requiring a different result."

Some courts have tried to find some middle ground, such as: requiring that the potential injury to the claimant whose action would otherwise be barred be "particularly inequitable or harsh;" requiring a showing that the defendant had deceitfully promised; or looking for a distinct promise made, if never kept, to later reduce the agreement to writing. See, for example, the case of *Packgen v. BP Exploration & Production Co.*, 754 F.3d 61 (1st Cir 2014), in which the First Circuit Court of Appeals did what it could to anticipate how the state courts of Maine would respond to the assertion of a promissory estoppel exception to the Article 2 Statute of Frauds.

Clearly, the jury is still out on the interplay between promissory estoppel and the Statute of Frauds. For Mr. Robert X. Lee of our example the lesson is now painfully clear. He may win on such a theory, but think of how much easier it would be for him had he taken the time and effort to get something in writing and not relied solely on an oral agreement before he went off and spent all that money on the King Leopold Pepper. There's a moral here.

8. For UETA to apply, Summer must first prove that both parties had the intent to conduct their transactions electronically. Lindsay may likely claim that she never expressly consented to conduct business via email because Summer sent the email to her personal address. See UETA §5 Comment 4. Further, their agreement over the phone does not constitute an electronic record under UETA because an oral electronic record must actually be stored or preserved. UETA §2 Comment 10. The signed note that Lindsay wrote on the company notepad will likely suffice to evidence a transaction for 120 cases, but recall that a writing satisfying the Statute of Frauds is effective only up to the quantity stated on the writing. U.C.C. §2-201(1). A voicemail may be sufficient as an electronic signature, as UETA allows a sound to be adopted as a signature if there is an intent to so adopt it and there is storage or preservation. UETA §2 Comments 7, 10. But for Summer to enforce the contract against Lindsay would require Lindsay to have left a voicemail, which she did not. It therefore appears that there is no electronic transaction and Summer can enforce the agreement only to the extent of the 120 cases found in Lindsay's writing. The definitions of "record" and "sign" in the U.C.C. are virtually the same as those in UETA, so the result would be the same.

9. Under the "firm offer" rule of U.C.C. §2-205, an offer by a merchant to hold an offer open is effective if there is a signed writing to that effect. Here, the parties had conducted business by email in the past and Casey said "I agree to do that" in his email. But a party is free to retract consent to conduct transactions electronically despite having conducted transactions electronically in the past. UETA §5(c). Thus, despite whatever prior dealings the parties may have had, Casey clearly stated he would only conduct this transaction by mail, so his email will not constitute a signed writing. Thus, under this scenario, Casey likely has not made a firm offer. In addition, there is an issue as to whether Casey "signed" the email. Many courts, although not all, will hold that by pressing the "send" button he was adopting that process as his signature, or alternatively, that the email header was an adopted symbol. The result under the 2022 U.C.C. Amendments would be the same. Under the definition of "sign" in the Amendments, a court is likely to conclude that an email is signed.

10. It is important in conducting transactions electronically that Dlovan ensure that the parties she is working with have the intent to conduct transactions electronically as well as the intent to adopt an electronic signature. This might look like Dlovan confirming that the other party agrees to conduct the transaction electronically, and making sure to channel communications appropriately, such as by ordering from business email addresses and not personal email addresses. Dlovan may draft a standard form agreement that states that the other party agrees to conduct transactions electronically and that emails sent from the party's email address are signed with the requisite intent under UETA. Dlovan should also be aware that the party may retract its consent under UETA §5(c), and if this is done then Dlovan must ensure that the transaction is properly completed in written form if required. Lastly, while it is important to remember that UETA applies both to merchants and nonmerchants, Article 2 contains a number of merchant rules that contain writing and signature requirements, such as the firm offer rule, and the Statute of Frauds confirmation rule, Thus, Dlovan should pay special attention when these circumstances arise. The 2022 U.C.C. Amendments have changed most of the provisions of Article 2 to require a record rather than a writing. Where a provision requires a writing, which is a tangible document even under the Amendments, UETA would supplement the Code to permit a record to satisfy the statute. See UETA §7(c) and Official Comment 8 to Amended U.C.C. §2-207.

CHAPTER 7

Usage of Trade, Course of Dealing, and Course of Performance

THE TERMS OF THE CONTRACT

The three previous chapters dealt with the fundamental issue of whether the parties had ever entered into a contract that could be enforced against either or both of them. But that is in general the easy question. We now turn to the often more troubling problem of exactly *what* the contracting parties have obliged themselves to do. Given that they have bound themselves by their actions and by the law of the Code into a contract, what are the precise terms of that contract to which they will be held? Believe it or not, the Code actually defines the term "term." According to §1-201(b)(40), when used in the Code, it means "that portion of an agreement which relates to a particular matter." Admittedly this is, in itself, not very helpful, but it does remind us that any contractual relationship has to be thought of as a compendium of any number of individual terms covering all sorts of things, large and small. Where do these various contract terms come from? Or, putting it only slightly more legalistically, where does an advocate or a court go for authority that such-and-such is a term of the parties' contract?

Article 2 of the Code incorporates a scheme, often referred to as the *hierarchy of terms*, for testing and determining what ultimately are the enforceable aspects of the contract between the buyer and seller. It is worth the effort to review this scheme in broad outline before getting too involved in any of the details.

We start, naturally, with the agreement between the parties. First and foremost, of course, terms of a contract will be found in the explicit arrangement entered into by the parties. This express agreement is found in the specific language used by the parties, in their negotiations, and in their final words of commitment. The various bits of the negotiation may of course be in writing, or they may be oral. Just a reminder that when you see the word *writing* in connection with Article 2, you should automatically think *record*, the word is used in the 2022 U.C.C. Amendments to include both physical documents and electronic documents, like those negotiated and signed in cyberspace. In addition the parties often, but not always, will in the end adopt a common writing or writings as setting forth their agreement. As you will no doubt remember from your study of the common law of contracts, the exact contours of a contract, even one memorialized (or *integrated*) in this formal written manner, are not always perfectly distinct. For one thing, not even the most meticulous use of language will eliminate all questions of interpretation. Beyond this, the common law saw fit to adopt the *parol evidence rule*, a particularly vexing doctrine (if not exactly a succinct rule) that adds greatly to the complexity of the task. The parol evidence rule makes it possible for a party to argue that something to which he or she expressly *did in fact agree* has ultimately been rendered unenforceable because it was not later set forth in the writing adopted by the parties.

We reserve the intricacies of (and the frustration engendered by) the parol evidence rule for the next chapter. This chapter concentrates on something else. It introduces an integrated set of three concepts—trade usage, course of dealing, and course of performance—carefully laid out in Article 1, which together make possible terms of the agreement *in addition to* those explicitly agreed to. Such *trade terms*, as they are sometimes collectively called, may be used by a party to argue for a better or more sophisticated understanding of the agreement (and hence the contract) by which he or she is bound. They help in interpretation. But beyond that, it is clear that authority for actual substantive terms of an agreement can be found not merely in the express overt conduct of the parties themselves, but in what we might think of as the underlying context in which their acts are to be judged. The Code makes the importance of these terms clear in its definition of *agreement* found in §1-201(b)(3): "'Agreement' means the bargain of the parties in fact as found in their language or by implication from other circumstances including course of dealing or usage of trade or course of performance. . . ." Under the Code, trade terms are *part of* the agreement as much as are those provisions explicitly dickered over by the buyer and seller.

Determining the dimensions of the agreement between the parties is, of course, not the end of the quest for the terms of the contract. *Contract*, in the language of the Code, means "the total legal obligation which results from the parties' agreement as affected by this Act and any other applicable rules of law." §1-201(b)(12). The terms of the contract are the terms of the agreement (which we now know includes trade terms), subtracting those that the Code renders unenforceable for one reason or another and adding those for which the Code is itself authority irrespective of the parties' agreement. In later chapters we'll see examples of each of these. For instance, the operation of the parol evidence rule (of §2-202 and the next chapter) can in the right instance render unenforceable a term of the agreement. It reads a term of the agreement-in-fact out of the contract. The prime examples of those provisions of Article 2 that may actually add contract terms not found in the agreement as broadly understood are the so-called "gap-filler provisions" (which we will discuss in Chapter 9) and the whole structure of the Code's warranty provisions (to which all of Part III is devoted).

Let's conclude this section by putting the various sources of terms of the parties' contract in a hierarchy, so that it is clear which source governs over another:

1. Mandatory U.C.C. provisions
2. Express terms of the contract
3. Course of performance
4. Course of dealing
5. Usage of trade
6. Default U.C.C. provisions

Thus ends our outline of the Code's hierarchy of terms. We will leave the additions and subtractions for the moment. This chapter is dedicated to a better understanding of the agreement of the parties, as that term is used in Article 1, and in particular the part that commercial usage and prior dealings play in marking and delineating the extent of that agreement.

THE WAYS OF (THE PARTIES') WORLD

From your introductory study of the common law governing the interpretation and construction of contracts, you will recall how often you were tempted (or cajoled by your instructor) to ask what was "always done" or "usually done" by experienced commercial actors in situations similar to the particular one before you. You may have heard this invocation of business practice referred to under the classic rubric of *custom*, a common law notion that some ways of doing things in a particular trade were so well-recognized, so certain, so unvarying, and above all so ancient that by these facts alone they became part of the contractual relationship between the parties. The doctrine of custom, as you may have seen, has always been ringed in by a number of technicalities, qualifications, and limitations. Traditionally, it played a limited and uneasy part in classical contract theory. In more recent times, customary commercial practices have begun to take a more important role in much of the workings of contract law simply because so much of the standard formulation of general principles is now laced with references to "reasonable" expectations and "reasonable" ways of behaving. To a large measure, if such "reasonable" language means anything, it serves as an invitation to look at the larger social and commercial context in which the parties acted out their story and to take that context into account in judging the legal consequences of their behavior.

The trend toward greater receptivity of such real-world-based material in evaluating contracting behavior is everywhere in evidence in Article 2, and in fact the adoption of the entire Code has in itself been seen as giving additional momentum to development along these lines. Among the bedrock "underlying purposes and policies" of the Code, as set forth in §1-103(a)(2), is that of "permit[ting] the continued expansion of commercial practices through custom, usage and agreement of the parties." Comment 1 to §1-303 declares that the Code:

> rejects both the "lay-dictionary" and the "conveyancer's" reading of a commercial agreement. Instead the meaning of the agreement of the parties is to be determined by the language used by them and by their action, read and interpreted in the light of commercial practices and other surrounding circumstances. The measure and background for interpretation are set by the commercial context, which may explain and supplement even the language of a formal or final writing.

In actual operation, the drafters of the Code carried forward these goals by articulation of three distinct concepts. Look at subsections (a) through (c) of §1-303, in which you will find the definitions of *course of performance*, *course of dealing*, and *usage of trade*. As you will appreciate, since these terms and other statutory directives that make up the remainder of §1-303 are to be found in Article 1, they are applicable to any transaction governed by any other Article of the Code, and in particular to any sale of goods governed by Article 2 or lease of goods governed by Article 2A.

Note initially that the power of these concepts extends to two related, but at least analytically distinct, tasks. First, trade terms will have a part to play in how the parties argue about the correct interpretation of the express agreement entered into, whether in a record or orally. Beyond this, however, you should recognize that adequate proof of this type of commercial background may under the Code actually *create* terms entirely supplemental to those of the express agreement. You see this in the expansive definition of "agreement" quoted in the previous section, as well as in the seemingly innumerable times the phrase "unless otherwise agreed" pops up in the various sections of Article 2. Finally we note that the drafters included in the general provisions of the Code a statement that "The presence in certain provisions of this Act of the words 'unless otherwise agreed' or words of similar import does not imply that the effect of other provisions may not be varied by agreement. . . ." §1-302. The importance of usage of trade, course of dealing, and course of performance to the real working of Article 2 in the real world in which sales transactions take place cannot be overstated.

This chapter's examples and explanations are not intended to be a full and complete survey of how these concepts play their parts in Article 2. That would be impossible in such a limited space and not very helpful in any event. In everything you study and in every problem involving the sale of goods, the possibility of trade terms coming into play must be borne in mind. The following questions and analyses are offered only as a way of introducing the broad outlines of each of the three concepts and discussing some of the principal issues their use brings forward. Fortunately, there are not many difficult issues of law involved in §1-303. Each offered instance of a usage or a course of dealing or performance may, of course, generate some very heated debate: Does such a usage actually exist? Has it been sufficiently proven? What exactly is the extent of and effect of the usage? Is it rightly applied in this situation or against this particular party? But such questions point to issues of fact important to resolution of the particular case, not intrinsic disagreement on what the law relevant to commercial practices is. The significance of trade terms as provided for in the Code was intended by the drafters not to engender complex discussion of legal norms or abstract jurisprudential theory. The idea was to a great extent to get beyond all that and actually to facilitate the resolution of factual issues of real importance to the parties involved. All in all, the results seem to work well to this end.

If you have not done so yet, you should read over §1-303 carefully before going on to the examples.

Examples

1. The Knits Corporation is a manufacturer of knitwear located in Capitol City. Through one of its salesmen it enters into a contract to deliver 1,200 sweaters to Mazie's Department Store, also located in Capitol City. The written agreement contains specifications for the various numbers of sweaters to be delivered, by size and color, but no language pertaining to how the sweaters are to be packaged for delivery to Mazie's. When the sweaters are delivered, Mazie is angered to find that they are boxed according to size, with the colors all mixed together. She has expected them to be presorted by color, which is much more in line with how she stores merchandise in her stockroom.

   (a) If she were to complain and to sue over this, would it be a sufficient defense on Knits' part if its distribution manager were to testify that The Knits Corporation always packaged and shipped its products sorted by size? That is, the manager insists (we will assume truthfully), "That's the way we always do it." If this testimony alone would not vindicate Knits, what additional information would allow it to argue successfully that packing by size became a term of its contract with Mazie as an applicable trade usage?

(b) Imagine that Knits is not able or chooses not to establish a trade usage to support its position. Would it still win if it could show that in the previous year it had entered into a similar contract for sale of scarves and mittens to Mazie's and furthermore that Mazie had accepted delivery of these—sorted by size—without complaint?

(c) Suppose that Knits is able to establish a course of dealing between the parties that knitwear it sells to Mazie is to be sorted by size. Mazie, however, claims that she was legitimately surprised because there is a general usage of trade that when manufacturers sell clothes to retail stores the items are delivered presorted by color. Who wins?

(d) Finally, suppose that the contract between Knits and Mazie called for delivery of 1,000 sweaters during each month for a year starting in May. Knits made deliveries in May and April, which remained unopened in Mazie's storehouse. When the June shipment arrived, Mazie decided it was time to break out all the sweaters in anticipation of the winter sales season. Only then did she discover that the goods are not packed in the way she expected. Is it too late for her to complain?

(e) Would your answer to the previous question change if the written agreement between the parties contained a clause that read, "Items to be presorted by color"?

2. Sunny Toy Manufacturers and Bunny, the owner of a toy store, sign a contract for the purchase by Bunny of a specified number of talking dolls manufactured by Sunny. Sunny delivers the dolls on June 1. On June 17 Bunny attempts to return some of them to Sunny because there is something wrong with them. They will not talk. There is no language in the record regarding how long after delivery the buyer has to return defective goods. Sunny is able to show that virtually all contracts for the sale of toys by manufacturers to retail stores in the area contain language stating something to the effect that "All returns must be made no later than two weeks from the date of delivery." Sunny argues that this creates a trade usage that is binding on Bunny. Should Sunny win on this argument?

3. Williams, a Georgia farmer, contracted to sell all of the "slaw cabbage" to be grown on his land to one Curtin, a dealer working out of New York who intended to resell it to various cole slaw manufacturers. Because of poor growing conditions, most of the cabbages grown on Williams's land turned out to be fairly small. Meanwhile the value of all cabbage has risen. Curtin demands the delivery of all the cabbages grown by Williams. Williams offers to prove that in Georgia "slaw cabbage" refers particularly to larger cabbages that are generally used for making cole

slaw. Curtin objects to the introduction of any such evidence claiming that it is not applicable to their deal. What is the result?

4. Assume instead that Williams in the previous example had sold his "slaw cabbage" to one Tyro. Tyro is a former New York City law professor who, tired of the pace and pressure of the academic life, recently moved to rural Georgia and opened up a plant to make homemade cole slaw based on his mother's secret recipe. He entered into the contract with Williams and now wants all the cabbages, including the smaller ones, which would work perfectly fine in his slaw-making process. Williams asserts that he is obligated to deliver only the larger cabbages, based on the trade usage for the Georgia area, which he again offers to prove. Should Tyro be allowed to prove that he never knew of the existence of this usage? Even if he does prove this, should it make any difference in the contract between him and Williams?

Explanations

1. a. The fact that Knits itself "always does it this way" would presumably not be enough to establish a trade usage. Section 1-303(c) requires that the practice have "such regularity of observance in a place, vocation or trade as to justify an expectation that it will be observed with respect to the transaction in question." To make their point crystal clear, the drafters go on to state specifically, "The existence and scope of such a usage are to be proved as facts." A mere assertion that such-and-such is a valid trade usage will not make it so. See, for example, the case of *Trumm v. Feeder's Supply, Inc.*, 2002 WL 31640755 (Iowa Ct. App.). The Trumms entered into a contract with FSI for the sale of a given number of "high-quality" segregated early-weaned ("SEW") pigs. Eventually, FSI, the buyer, began to complain that the pigs delivered were not of the quality contracted for, arguing that when they were marketed six months after FSI's acquisition of them they "were not cutting out at fifty-one percent lean." Litigation ensued. After an initial ruling in the sellers' favor, the buyer appealed, but to no avail:

> FSI first contends the term "high-quality SEW pigs" is defined by trade usage as pigs that cut out at fifty-one percent lean or better as market pigs. The evidence presented at trial indicates that the term "high-quality" as defined by Farmland Foods, FSI's buyer, [has this meaning]. However, trial testimony also revealed that different hog buyers used different standards as to the percentage lean considered acceptable and the method by which lean was measured. Leroy Trumm testified he had had buyers accept anywhere from forty-nine to fifty-four percent lean. Trumm also testified that, although he had raised pigs his entire life, he had never heard there was a fifty-one percent lean industry standard.

The Court of Appeals of Iowa affirmed the trial court's determination that FSI had failed to establish what it claimed to be a trade usage of 51 percent lean.

Contrast this case with *Panike & Sons Farms, Inc. v. Smith*, 212 P.3d 992 (Idaho 2009). The defendant farmers contracted prior to the beginning of the growing season to sell to the plaintiff, a packing company, a given quantity of onions to be grown during the season. The written agreement provided for onions of a certain size and quality and furthermore that "buyer was to designate fields," meaning which of the seller's fields were to be the source of the onions the plaintiff was buying. During the growing season the seller did, indeed, designate those of the seller's fields from which the onions it was purchasing were to come. When the seller eventually delivered onions from other fields, the buyer rejected the delivery. The seller argued that it understood the field selection clause meant that the buyer could have designated the desired field only at the time the parties entered into the preseason contract. The district court found that the buyer had established through the combined testimony of five separate witnesses, each knowledgeable about the ways of the onion trade in the vicinity, that the designation of fields in mid to late summer is the normal practice in the industry. The Idaho Supreme Court concluded:

> The district court based its determination that designating fields during the growing season was the usage of the onion trade on substantial and competent evidence. Therefore, [the buyer] had a contractual right to designate the fields from which [the seller] was to tender the onions.

The buyer was, therefore, within its rights to reject the tendered onions.

Returning to our hypothetical, what would Knits have to show to establish a trade usage, and how could they show it? First of all, of course, counsel for Knits would have to make clear in his or her own mind exactly *what* usage was to be established and, particularly, to what "place, vocation or trade" it was meant to apply. Knits could argue that packing goods sorted by size is a usage within the sweater trade, or the trade of knitwear sellers, or indeed the whole clothing manufacturing industry. It could argue that it was an established usage within the realm of Capitol City, or the whole country, or some other identifiable area of commerce. Assuming, for example, that counsel sought to establish that Knits had followed a usage well established in the knitwear industry within the entire United States, what evidence will it need to present? What witnesses should it be prepared to call and what should it hope these witnesses will say? The last sentence of §1-303(c) makes clear that Knits would do well if it were able to provide the court with something like a "Knitwear Manufacturers of

America Code of Uniform and Fair Dealing." See, for example, *Foxco Industries, Ltd. v. Fabric World, Inc.*, 595 F.2d 976 (5th Cir. 1979), where the court found admissible an industry group's standard definition of "first quality goods." If no such trade code exists, they'll try to find others who regularly deal within this industry who can testify, in effect, that sorting by size is "how it is always done," but they might have to be satisfied with statements that are a little less global. Would Knits' evidence have to establish that it *always* is done this way? No, but how close to always is a matter of fact and not easily quantified. Note the language in Comment 4 to §1-303 giving support to usages "currently observed by the great majority of decent dealers, even though dissidents ready to cut corners do not agree."

I find it interesting to think about exactly what it takes for some practice, even if it is clearly one regularly observed in an area, to "justify an expectation" that it will be observed in a given transaction. The language of the Code seems to say that regularity of observance is enough in and of itself to create such a justification, but I think there is a subtle (or maybe not so subtle) further requirement. There are after all practices or rituals that we regularly go through that are so common as to justify an expectation that they'll be followed, but that do not seem to justify an expectation or an argument that another party has a *right* to their observance each and every time. I give you the following example. I enter a fashionable restaurant and order and enjoy a truly fine meal. The service has been more than adequate. I am presented with the bill. Legally, it's clear I owe this amount. Surely the waiter and the establishment owner as well have a reasonable expectation that I'm going to leave a tip. Almost certainly I will. But if I don't, would they have any legal right to insist on one? I argue that leaving a tip is something that is virtually always done, especially by those "decent dealers" that the Comment talks about, but it isn't a trade usage because there is no justifiable expectation that "it will be observed" *as a matter of law* "with respect to the transaction in question."

One final point is worth mentioning here. Notice that nothing in the definition of usage of trade or in the operative language in §1-303(d) makes it necessary that Knits prove that any usage of trade it is able to establish was actually known by Mazie, either at the time of contracting or the time of delivery. Look again at §1-303 and notice how many times *or* is used. We'll return to the problems this can create for a party new to the industry, and how the courts have responded, in explaining Example 4.

b. Here Knits would be trying to establish a course of dealing between itself and Mazie. Check out the definition in §1-303(b). Knits would apparently lose because one prior incident would not be "a sequence of previous conduct," and it has been so held. See *Remco Equipment Sales, Inc. v. Manz*, 952 S.W.2d 437 (Tenn. App. 1997), and *Guidance Endodontics, LLC v. Dentsply International, Inc.*, 2009 WL 3672452 (D.N.M.). Neither the Code nor the Comments give us any help on how many prior incidents are necessary to make up a sequence, but presumably it would be at least two. Note also that even if some specified conduct had occurred more than once in the performance of prior contracts between the parties, this does not necessarily prove a valid course of dealing if that conduct has taken place only sporadically and infrequently. In *Shell Trading (US) Co. v. Lion Oil Trading & Transportation, Inc.*, 2012 WL 3958029 (Tex. App.), the court declined to find that a course of dealing had been established between two parties when the conduct in question had occurred in only two instances, "out of hundreds of contracts over several years," and that in fact each of these two instances had arisen out of unusual circumstances following Hurricane Katrina in 2005.

Even if in our example Knits could show that it entered into two or more previous contracts for scarves and mittens, and that in each case deliveries had been packaged by size, you can see Mazie might still have an argument that this did not establish a course of dealing relevant to this transaction. All this evidence could do would be to establish a course of dealing in scarves and mittens, Mazie would argue, and now we're talking sweaters. Could a course of dealing in those other knit products "fairly be regarded as establishing a common basis of understanding" for interpreting their contract for the purchase and sale of sweaters? Here it would be helpful to know if practices and customs are generally the same across the whole larger knitwear industry. If so, then Knits would have established a course of dealing covering this transaction as well. If for some reason, or if only by tradition, scarves and mittens are sold, packaged, and delivered in ways quite distinct from how sweaters are dealt with, Knits would not have a course of dealing to go on.

Note that the definition of "course of dealing" makes it clear that, unlike a usage of trade, which at least theoretically could bind a party who was never even aware of it, a course of dealing depends on prior dealings of these particular parties—things of which they are themselves presumably intimately aware.

c. Knits wins. Its course of dealing controls over the usage of trade established by Mazie. See §1-303(e) and the hierarchy set forth therein.
d. Mazie may have trouble complaining now. Knits will claim that the May and June deliveries established a course of performance for this particular contract under §1-303(a). Mazie could argue here that she did not have "knowledge of" the nature of the earlier deliveries and hence had no "opportunity for objection" to how the sweaters were

packaged, but I doubt that would be successful. If Knits has been making its monthly deliveries for some time and Mazie has not made any mention of the shape they were in, doesn't Knits have the right to claim Mazie "accepted or acquiesced without objection"? The language of knowledge and the opportunity to object obviously adds something to the definition of "course of performance," but whereas here Knits would be reasonable to assume that its having heard no objection to the earlier shipments meant that Mazie was at least "acquiescing," I'd think Knits would win. Perhaps the answer would be otherwise if Mazie could show that Knits would have or should have been aware that a buyer of its sweaters would not unpack any shipments made in the spring immediately, but would rather open them up only when several shipments had arrived. But then, what was the point of the earlier deliveries?

e. If express language of the written agreement calls for packaging by color, that should give Mazie what she wants. Neither a usage of trade, a course of dealing, nor a course of performance will overcome the express agreement. See, for example, *Indian Harbor Citrus, Inc. v. Poppell*, 658 So. 2d 605 (Fla. App. 1995), and *William M. Hendrickson, Inc. v. National Railroad Passenger Corp.*, 2002 WL 398641 (E.D. Pa.), *aff'd*, 63 F. App'x 61 (3d Cir. 2003). Review §1-303(e). This seems pretty clear-cut, and in most situations it will be. Remember the significance the Code gives to the parties' ability to vary "by agreement" just about any result and to tailor their contract as they see fit.

2. No. Sunny has not established a trade usage by showing that virtually all contracts of the type he and Bunny entered into contain specific language like that quoted. What he'd have to show is that similarly situated parties usually consider themselves bound to this time limitation *even though* it is nowhere expressly agreed to. In fact, dealers in this market apparently think it sufficiently important to get it expressly and explicitly in the record. If anything, this should *hurt* Sunny's case. A court could (and I think should) make a negative inference from the fact that Sunny and Bunny did not include it. This reminds us that a usage of trade is "what people usually do" in addition to or in elaboration of their explicit agreement. That's quite different from what people usually actually agree to in so many words. The express terms are just the stuff they implicitly don't want to leave to trade usage or course of dealing.

3. This example, raising the interesting issue of the geographical scope of a trade usage, is based on the case of *Williams v. Curtin*, 807 F.2d 1046 (D.C. Cir. 1986). It is easy enough to say that a trade usage is good for the entire area for which the usage holds true, but that doesn't help here. We can assume that if both the buyer and the seller of the "slaw cabbages" were doing business in Georgia they would be bound by the Georgia

usage of this term. But if it's a usage only good in Georgia, what weight does it carry when the seller is in Georgia and the buyer is not? The Code does not make clear the answer, nor do we have a batch of cases to help out. As to the particular cabbage involved in *Williams v. Curtin*, Williams, the seller, argued that "because the planting, nurturing, cutting, sizing, and bagging of the cabbage" all took place in Georgia, that state was the "focus of performance" and that hence the usage governed. This argument got nowhere with the court, which held that even if such a usage did exist in Georgia it was not applicable between these parties as "the relevant aspect of the performance is delivery" and delivery had been called for and taken place in "the interstate market." "Since the transaction is an interstate transaction," concluded the court, "it cannot fairly be expected that the parties contracted only with reference to the Georgia market." But is it all that simple? In the actual case the seller was not a farmer, but a dealer in cabbage, who the court notes did business with out-of-state buyers on a regular basis. Is this what made the difference? And did the court give sufficient attention to the fact that this was not simply a transaction made at long distance over the phone or by mail? The buyer had initially visited the Georgia cabbage fields before entering into the sales agreement and visited the cabbages as they grew on at least one occasion. Perhaps the court was most impressed in reality with the fact that the seller's reliance on the Georgia usage at this point if successful would have allowed it to make a killing off of the dramatic rise in the value of cabbage during 1982 and the large loss it would have imposed on the buyer who had had to cover on the open market.

4. Tyro would probably be stuck with the usage even if he truly had not known of it when he made the deal. Note again the language of §1-303(d). Parties are affected by any usage of trade "in the vocation or trade in which they are engaged *or* of which they are *or* should be aware." That is very expansive language, and presumably the drafters meant us to take it just that way. Recall also the articulation of general purposes of the Code in §1-103(a)(2). Here we could simply say that Tyro is engaged in the cabbage-buying trade in Georgia and that would be that. The language of §1-303(d), with all those *or*'s, makes clear that if anything people who are not themselves in the trade but who for other reasons are or should be aware of how the trade operates will be held to the usages in their own dealings outside the trade. So, for example, if Williams entered into a contract with one Baggott, who was in the business of manufacturing packaging material, for some bags to hold his "slaw cabbage," Baggott might be held to this usage even though he is not in the cabbage trade. A court could determine he actually knew what "slaw cabbage" meant in that trade or that he "should have been aware" for some reason or another.

Returning to the original example, we see that a literal reading of the Code puts a very heavy burden on anyone just starting out in a highly specialized business. (And what businesses nowadays are not highly specialized?) Should there be any leeway given to the new entrant? That argument was made in *Heggblade-Marguleas-Tenneco, Inc. v. Sunshine Biscuit, Inc.*, 131 Cal. Rptr. 183 (Ct. App. 1976), but to no avail. The court answered:

> [P]ersons carrying on a particular trade are deemed to be aware of prominent trade customs applicable to their industry. The knowledge may be actual or constructive, and it is constructive if the custom is of such general and universal application that the party must be presumed to know of it.

The lesson would seem to be that the new entrant into any field should bone up thoroughly on exactly how things are done in the industry or at least acknowledge that he or she is taking the risk of not learning of all the customs and usages. But should this always be so? In our example, would it make any difference if Williams actually knew that Tyro was innocently ignorant of the usage? Would this be enough to be some burden on Williams to straighten him out or, failing that, forego later to reliance on the usage? What if Williams knew only that Tyro was a first-time buyer and that most outsiders did not know and had no reason to know what people in the cabbage trade meant by "slaw cabbage"? Perhaps these difficulties are what justify a fairly rigid notion that once you hang out your shingle as being part of a trade you must necessarily be held to live by all of its most arcane mysteries.

CHAPTER 8

The Parol Evidence Rule

THE AGREEMENT, THE RECORD, AND THE RESULT

In studying contracts under the common law, you almost certainly spent some time and a good deal of energy on a doctrine going under the name *the parol evidence rule*. Briefly put, the one thing that became clear was that this so-called rule could not be put briefly and still make much sense to the uninitiated reader. Learning how the law deals with parol evidence is a whole course of study and not the memorization of any short and tidy formula. Still, the drafters of Article 2 did about as good a job as anyone has in setting forth the rule in the English language, so we might as well start with a look at the Code's version of the "rule" in its entirety. It's found in §2-202, which I've "reformatted" below:

> Terms
>
> with respect to which the confirmatory memoranda of the parties agree
>
> or
>
> which are otherwise set forth in a record intended by the parties as a final expression of their agreement with respect to such terms as are included therein
>
> *may not be contradicted* by evidence of any prior agreement or of a contemporaneous oral agreement
>
> *but [such terms] may be explained or supplemented*
>
> (a) by course of performance, course of dealing, or usage of trade (Section 1-303);

and

(b) by evidence of consistent additional terms *unless* the court finds the record to have been intended also as a complete and exclusive statement of the terms of the agreement.

Now the question is what to make of all this. Section 2-202 is one of those parts of Article 2 that has to be read and appreciated with an eye to history and pre-Code law. The authors of §2-202 did not pull this one out of thin air. (Who would?)

The drafters did give us considerable help in thinking about this material, however, with their clear definition of the word *agreement* as used in the Code. Look at §1-201(b)(3). The *agreement* of parties is "the bargain of the parties in fact as found in their language or by implication from other circumstances" including any applicable course of dealing, usage of trade, or course of performance. Because these latter three concepts are particularly important in this chapter as exceptions to evidence excluded under the parol evidence rule, you might want to review them at this time. See Chapter 7. The agreement is what really happened between the parties in the real world. How they came to this agreement is the kind of thing we talked about in Chapters 4 and 5. It may have been at the moment the two signed a carefully negotiated and minutely detailed record littered with numerous instances of *whereas, herein agreed,* and the like, but that certainly is not required. Probably the great majority of agreements for purchase and sale of goods are concluded simply through an oral understanding or even through nods, shrugs, or other body language.

The agreement is simply what it is. It has an existence in fact, but not a corporeal existence in our three-dimensional physical universe. The parties' *agreement* could never be lost or stolen or burned up in a house fire. To borrow from the world of the detective story, the parties' agreement is the "what happened" to be deduced from the various clues found lying about, but it itself is not something that the detective can trip over or waggle in the face of a suspect. Yet many clues to the nature and content of the agreement, of which we naturally want to take advantage, *are* in the tangible form of a written record or in the intangible form of an electronic record. People in these situations will often leave a trail, either on purpose or otherwise. Note, by the way, the definition of *writing* in §1-201(b)(43), which we discussed in Chapter 6 in connection with the Statute of Frauds. Recall that while that definition embraces only an "intentional reduction to tangible form," UETA provides that "[i]f a law requires a record to be in writing, an electronic record satisfies the law."

If the parties to a contract for sale are arguing about the terms of their agreement, pretty much any evidence they can bring to bear on the question of fact—what did they agree to do?—is fair game and will be thrown into the mix. The history of the common law parol evidence rule, however, and its inclusion in pretty much the traditional form in Article 2 are premised on the idea that once some piece or pieces of evidence have this particular tangible form, once they are in a record, they have a specially privileged part to play. Today, an electronic record should share the same privilege as a tangible document. Even without a parol evidence rule, of course, evidence in a record presumably would have a powerful effect on the trier of fact. Our fictional detective would, we assume, be delighted to find that extraordinarily incriminating note in a suspect's handwriting or the will that has been so mysteriously missing. But then any detective worth his or her salt would also be aware how easily such records can mislead, or at least how often they tell only part of the story. The detective, as he or she is always sure to explain to the somewhat slow-witted sidekick, is not constrained to take any one piece or any one kind of evidence at face value. All evidence is considered and valued for its own unique explanatory power whatever its form, size, or shape.

In ferreting out to what the parties to a contract of sale actually committed themselves—that is, what the Code refers to as their *contract* (§1-201(b)(12))—however, the legal detective finds a strange constraint on his or her methods. The rules of the game have been changed. Evidence in a record *must* be given a special credence. In this endeavor, records—or at least records of a certain kind—get special pride of place and will perforce have special explanatory power *as a matter of law* beyond what nature might have provided them. It is this special rule of law that is the parol evidence rule. At its most powerful, the rule can actually delete from the enforceable contract a term or terms undoubtedly included in the agreement and on which one or the other party might have heavily relied. On my assumption that you have already studied the rule in the common-law context, I will not here rehearse the numerous objections that have been raised to it over the years and that are heard probably even more loudly today. The parol evidence idea is not without its critics, to say the least. Nor will I here recount the various justifications for it that have been advanced in the past and in the modern setting. The nature of this debate will soon be apparent as it appears in the particulars of application. It is these particulars that we explore in this chapter's examples. Before the examples, though, a couple of preliminary issues should be considered: On what records does the parol evidence rule bestow its special favors, and who makes the decisions that make the rule run?

WHAT RECORDS COUNT?

As you know, there is no absolute requirement under Article 2 that a contract for sale be in a record. In general, an oral agreement is perfectly fine and enforceable. Should the price of the goods equal or exceed $500, of course, the Article 2 Statute of Frauds may require that a party, in order to hold a contract enforceable against another, produce "a record sufficient to indicate that a contract for sale has been made" signed by that other party. The full workings of this Statute of Frauds provision were explored in Chapter 6, and we will not repeat them here. Suffice it to recall for our present purposes that the record requirement of §2-201 applies only in a specific subset of all sales situations. Beyond that, to "satisfy" the Statute of Frauds a record need not be a document setting forth the contract itself. It may be, and often is, a record prepared by only one of the parties and not a joint production. It need not state all of the material terms of the agreement, nor even recount those that it does state correctly. In the words of a Comment to §2-201, the record made necessary in some cases by the Statute must serve only as some "basis for believing" that the proffered agreement (the substance of which may be proven by entirely oral evidence) "rests on a real transaction."

The parol evidence rule is like the Statute of Frauds in that it deals in and with records, but there the two part company. The parol evidence rule makes no demand on the parties that they produce any record whatsoever in order to enter into an enforceable contract. The parties are free to have a record of their transaction or not. They may choose to enter into a record because of Statute of Frauds concerns, or because it is convenient, or out of mere force of habit. Once, however, the parties *have* together brought into existence a record memorializing all or some of the terms of the agreement, then the parol evidence rule comes into play.

Just because a proffered piece of evidence is in a record does not mean, however, that it triggers application of the rule. The rule traditionally takes special cognizance only of those records that are so-called *integrations* of the agreement. In the words of §2-202, the record must have been "intended by the parties as a final expression of their agreement with respect to such terms as are included therein." The important thing here is that records that qualify as integrations are those that are produced or at least accepted by *both parties* as setting forth what they mean to put in the record about their agreement. Records that are the exclusive work of one or the other of the parties usually will not do unless there is strong evidence of the other party's adoption of that record as correct in some sense. So, for example, an internal memorandum produced by a seller for her own files that details what she took away from a final negotiating session would not constitute an integration. If the seller wanted her document to have that special status, she would have to show it to the buyer and get the buyer to literally or figuratively "sign on" to the memo as correctly setting forth what has been agreed to. Similarly, early tentative drafts of proposed contract language of the type that are regularly exchanged by parties (often ad nauseam) in the course of negotiations cannot be seen as integrations.

Just because an offered record is the only recorded evidence of the agreement, it will not necessarily be an integration. So, for example, in *General Matters, Inc. v. Penny Products, Inc.*, 651 F.2d 1017 (5th Cir. 1981), the buyer introduced a copy of its purchase order, which was acknowledged by all to be the only writing generated in the course of the transaction and argued that testimony of an oral statement by the seller should therefore be barred under §2-202. The court rightly held that the purchase order had no such effect, as there was no evidence that the two parties together intended the particular piece of paper to be a joint memorial of their understanding. At the same time, for a record to constitute an integration, it is unnecessary for it to have any precise heading or format or for it to carry any particular language of integration. It need not look like dozens of lawyers slaved over it in every detail. In *Intershoe, Inc. v. Bankers Trust Co.*, 571 N.E.2d 641 (N.Y. 1991), for example, a confirmation sent by the bank to the Intershoe Corporation, which was then signed by that corporation's Treasurer and returned, was held to be an integration for the purposes of §2-202. The facts here, though interesting, are not easily related in terms of a "Seller" and a "Buyer," for the question of exactly who was doing the selling and who was buying lay at the very heart of the case. Both parties agreed that Intershoe had placed a telephone order with the foreign currency department of the bank for the purchase and sale of a stated quantity of Italian lira. Following the conversation the Bank sent Intershoe a confirmation slip including, among others, the following terms: "WE HAVE BOUGHT FROM YOU ITL 537,750" and "WE HAVE SOLD TO YOU USD 250,000.00." Apparently other parts of the slip made it clear that the "We" was the Bank and the "You" was Intershoe. Intershoe's Treasurer signed the slip and returned it to the Bank. Later Intershoe claimed that the confirmation was a mistake, that it had intended to *buy* the lira from the Bank, and that such a deal was in fact what had been agreed to over the phone. It offered in support of this position an affidavit of its Treasurer stating in effect that, while he couldn't recall the particular conversation, he just *knew* he never had placed an order to sell lira to the Bank any time during that year. Obviously, if the confirmation slip was seen to be an integration, this offered statement was about as contradictory to the writing as you can get, so Intershoe was forced into the claim that the confirmation slip never was "a writing intended by the parties as a final expression of their agreement." They pointed out that no language in the slip said in so many words that it was intended as such. The Court of Appeals of New York showed little patience with this argument, saying:

> We reject [Intershoe's] contentions that UCC §2-202 requires that there be some express indication in the writing itself or some other evidence that the parties intended it to be the final expression of their agreement. A holding that

> the writing must include express language that it represents the parties' final expression would introduce a technical, formal requirement not contemplated by the Code and one that would frustrate the Code's purpose of facilitating sales transactions by easing the process of contract formation. . . .

Section 2-202 potentially adds a little something to the traditional parol evidence rule with its introductory language referring to "terms with respect to which the confirmatory memoranda of the parties agree." Unfortunately, we are hampered here by the drafters' failure to define "confirmatory memoranda" or "confirmation." Taken on its face, however, this language can be given meaning that is of some help. Suppose the buyer and seller make an agreement over the telephone. The buyer sends a confirmation email to the seller, saying something like, "This will confirm the agreement entered into this day with you to buy 5,000 covered widgets at $5.62 per piece." He does not ask the seller to respond in any way. He just sends it. Simultaneously, the seller sends an email to the buyer reading in part, "This confirms our sale to you of 5,000 widgets (with covers) at $5.64 each." Neither of these emails would constitute an integration in the classical sense, nor would either be a "record intended by the parties" in the words of §2-202. Should a dispute arise about the terms of the agreement, however, §2-202 will make it impossible for either side to contest the amount of 5,000 or the fact that the widgets were to be of the covered variety. Argument over what price had been agreed on is still open to proof by the two parties, of course, but neither email will have a special role to play in resolving that dispute, at least not by virtue of §2-202.

One final problem: What if the buyer and the seller, egged on perhaps by overeager lawyers, simultaneously sign two or more records to finalize their agreement? So, for example, at some kind of elaborate closing they both sign one document captioned "SALES AGREEMENT," another "DISTRIBUTION AGREEMENT," and a third denoted a "SERVICE AGREEMENT." All relate to the same purchase and sales transaction of a single set of goods. They all bear the same date, the date of the closing. Is there an integration? If so, what is it? Here the answer is straightforward. The parties have indeed prepared an integration. It is found in a single record consisting of the three documents taken as one three-part exposition. Staple them together and you have an integration. There is the potential, of course, that language in one of the three documents will conflict with what is said in one of the others. But then it is always perfectly possible for even the most careful negotiators (and even the most careful attorneys) unintentionally to throw contradictory language into a *single* document. Should problems arise, whether the integration is crafted as one compact document or as several meant to be read as a package, these are problems of interpretation. They do not defeat the basic conclusion that an integration was intended and hence created. Incidentally, the prudent attorney might include a provision stating that in the event of a conflict among the documents, there is a hierarchy, and A will govern over B, which will govern over C.

WHO'S IN CHARGE HERE?

One question that is easy to answer with regard to the parol evidence rule is who, judge or jury, makes the key decisions under the rule. Throughout its long pre-Code history, it had always been clear that the application of the rule was within the special province of the judge. To many commentators (especially those who would argue for what we will end up calling a very liberal application of the rule), this may be the most important feature of the rule in actual operation. It serves as a tool for the judge to keep from the jury certain arguments thought by him or her to contradict a record intended by the signatories to settle those arguments once and for all.

This special role for the court in the application of the rule was clearly intended to continue under §2-202. Note that subpart (b) hinges on "the court" making a finding about the completeness of the record. Also, although it is nowhere specifically stated in the section, it seems to be assumed by everyone that the crucial determination of whether a record was "intended by the parties as a final expression" of at least "such terms as are included therein" is for the judge alone. Of course, once the judge determines that certain evidence can be admitted over any parol evidence objection, it is for the jury as the trier of fact to decide whether that evidence is to be believed and whether it proves what the offering party claims it does about the nature of the parties' agreement.

Because of this special role for the court in the day-to-day operation of the parol evidence rule, it is no surprise that when such decisions are brought up on appeal, the appellate courts show little hesitancy to weigh in with their own determinations, almost as if they were making judgments de novo. The questions that follow explore a number of easy decisions—and some close calls—that have to be made in applying the rule. You be the judge.

Examples

EXAMPLES

1. Bernice, who runs a clothing store, enters into a record for the purchase of a large quantity of men's dress shirts from Shirtmakers of Boston. The record says nothing about how the shirts are to be packaged. When they are delivered to Bernice, she finds they are all simply jammed into the crates. They are wrinkled and will need to be ironed, folded, pinned up, and labelled before she can put them out on her shelves.

(a) In an action against Shirtmakers, Bernice seeks to prove a usage in the apparel industry that shirts such as these are to be delivered properly folded, individually wrapped, and marked as to size. Is she barred from making such a presentation by the parol evidence rule?

(b) Will it make any difference if Bernice is seeking to show that the type of packaging she expected—and claims she had a right to expect—is based on a course of dealing established between herself and Shirtmakers?

(c) Assume that the packaging causes no problems between them; the shipment is just fine. The problem comes when Bernice receives the invoice. It calls for her to pay $10 per shirt. The record, in the space provided for "Price," had been filled in with the figure "$10," but Bernice claims there is a well-established usage of the trade—which she assumed would apply—that gives buyers a 10-percent discount off of the stated price if they take delivery immediately, which is what she did. Will she be allowed to prove this usage?

2. Buyer and Seller enter into an agreement for the purchase and sale of some lumber. The number of feet of lumber is specified. The type of lumber is identified in the record as "standard two-by-four pine." When the lumber arrives, Buyer inspects it. He has received lumber of the lowest grade of pine, which is usually not used to make two-by-fours as they are known in the industry.

   (a) In a lawsuit against Seller, would Buyer be allowed to show a general trade usage that so-called two-by-four lumber is actually supposed to be made out of a better grade of pine? If he complained that the lumber was not in fact "two-by-four," would the Seller be allowed to show a general trade usage that the size of a "two-by-four" is actually smaller? What if Buyer is not familiar with such a usage?

   (b) Suppose the record signed by Buyer and Seller specified a price of 50 cents per foot for "10,000 board feet of White Pine of Grade B." Prior to his signing, Buyer seemed hesitant to enter into the agreement, and Seller said to him, "Tell you what—I'll make that the better Grade A stuff at no extra charge." With this Buyer signs the agreement, although no change is made in its wording. Does Buyer have the right to insist on Grade A lumber?

   (c) What if Seller in the previous problem had instead said, "I'll let you upgrade that to Grade A stuff for only one cent more a foot." This is, in fact, practically a giveaway of the upgrade. Buyer eagerly signs the document. Again, no change is made in its wording; it still speaks only of Grade B lumber at a stated price. Does Buyer have the legal right to buy the Grade A lumber at 51 cents a foot?

3. The remaining examples all involve sales made by Smiling Sol of Smiling Sol's Used-Car-O-Rama. Barry, visiting one Saturday, takes a fancy to a

particular 2005 Cadillac. Sol sees his interest and offers to sell him the car for the price written on the windshield ($8,999) and prepares a standard Sales Agreement putting "$8,999" in the blank provided for "Purchase Price." Barry is wavering on whether or not to sign the agreement. Trying to wrap up the sale, Sol makes the following statements:

(a) "If you buy it, I'll throw in a new set of tires."
(b) "If you buy it, I'll take the cost of your first tank of gas off the price."
(c) "I'm so sure you'll love it that, if you don't, you can return it and get your money back."

Barry then signs the agreement with no changes having been made in its language. Can Barry enforce any of these statements (a) through (c) against Sol?

4. Suppose you discover that the Sales Agreement signed by Sol and Barry contains the following language:

> THIS SALES AGREEMENT IS INTENDED BY THE PARTIES HERETO AS A FINAL EXPRESSION OF ALL TERMS AGREED TO BY THE PARTIES AND IS A COMPLETE AND EXCLUSIVE STATEMENT OF THOSE TERMS.

Does your analysis of the previous question change?

5. On Monday, Andy enters into a written Sales Agreement with Sol to buy a used Chevy. When Andy picks up the car on Tuesday, Sol tells him, "That's the original paint job, you know." Sol had previously said nothing about the paint on the car, and the Sales Agreement makes no mention of it. It turns out that, unknown to Sol, the Chevy had been repainted prior to its having arrived on his lot. Does Andy have rights against Sol based on the statement made on Tuesday?

6. On Wednesday, Betty sees a used Lexus on Sol's lot that she likes very much. She tells him she will not be able to commit herself on buying the car until she knows whether she is getting a raise, which she won't know for about a week. Sol suggests to her that "to hold the car" she sign a Sales Agreement, telling her that "it won't mean a thing unless you do get that raise." Betty signs on that understanding. She does not get the raise. Sol comes against her relying on the Sales Agreement that she had signed. The agreement reads as an absolute obligation on her part to buy and contains no mention of their oral understanding. Is Betty stuck with a contract to buy the car?

7. Charles enters into a Sales Agreement with Sol to buy a used Toyota Corolla. Prior to Charles's signing the agreement, Sol told him that the car had been driven by "a little old gentleman who used it only on Sundays." Charles later finds out that this statement is patently untrue—it was previously owned by a teenage rock musician who spent a lot of time on the road—and *furthermore* that Sol knew what he was saying was false when

he made the statement. Can Charles use the statement against Sol or is it barred by the parol evidence rule?

EXPLANATIONS

Explanations

1. a. No. Bernice's argument based on a usage of trade (if she can successfully establish that such a usage exists and can be used against Shirtmakers) is not barred by the rule. From the hypothetical, we know there is nothing in the record about the method of packaging. She is not seeking to "contradict" the record. Rather this is a case of her "supplementing" its terms by a usage of trade. Clause (a) of §2-202 specifically authorizes this.

   b. The result is no different if what Bernice is arguing is a course of dealing. Same result if this were an installment contract calling for several deliveries over time and the first deliveries had established a course of performance. An important point to be made here is that trade terms such as these are, according to the drafters, to be allowed in to "explain or supplement" *whether or not* the language of the record appears on its face to need explanation or supplementation. Prior to the Code, many courts held that trade custom would be allowed to vary or explain the terms of a written agreement only if that agreement was first found by the court to be "ambiguous." This condition is rejected by §2-202. See Comment 1 and particularly its subpart (c). The courts have been generally good in following the intention of the drafters as set forth in this Comment. See, for example, *C-Thru Container Corp. v. Midland Mfg. Co.*, 533 N.W.2d 542 (Iowa 1995), *Campbell Farms v. Wald*, 578 N.W.2d 96 (N.D. 1998), and *Anadarko Petroleum Corp. v. Williams Alaska Petroleum, Inc.*, 737 F.3d 966 (5th Cir. 2013).

      Of course, while a trade term can "explain or supplement" the record, it cannot flat-out contradict it. But, as we'll see in what follows, you have to have a pretty flexible idea of what constitutes "contradiction" when it comes to the modern parol evidence rule.

   c. Now it appears that Bernice has gone too far. Shirtmakers will argue that in this instance she isn't just trying to explain or to supplement the record, but to directly contradict it. If there is any point to the parol evidence rule, they will contend, it is to prevent just such arguments from getting anywhere.

      But maybe Shirtmakers' case isn't as clear-cut as all that. If Bernice can show there is a well-established practice in the trade of giving such a discount (that is, that knowledgeable traders treat it as a matter of buyers' rights and not just a friendly gesture on the part of sellers, and that this is so *even when* the price is as seemingly clear and unambiguous as it is here), then she might have a right to insist upon it. The extent to which many courts are disposed in favor of supplementation through trade usage, even where an initial reading appears to render the usage improperly contradictory, is often demonstrated by the well-known case of *Columbia Nitrogen Corp. v. Royster Co.*, 451 F.2d 3 (4th Cir. 1971). Both parties were in the fertilizer business. Royster was a producer of so-called mixed fertilizers, the primary components of which are nitrogen, phosphate, and potash. Columbia Nitrogen was, as you might expect, primarily a producer and seller of nitrogen. In fact, in past dealings Royster had itself purchased nitrogen from Columbia. The contract in question, however, involved a sale *by* Royster of some of its excess phosphate *to* Columbia, which needed some of this other stuff. The contract document recited "Products Supplied Under Contract—Minimum Tonnage Per Year" totaling 31,000 tons over a three-year period. A price per ton was specified, subject to an escalator clause based on the seller's production costs. After the contract was made, the market price of phosphate plunged. Columbia, the buyer, ordered only a small fraction (under 10 percent) of the amount specified as a "minimum" for the first year. Royster brought suit for Columbia's failure to take the minimum.

At trial Columbia sought to introduce evidence of a usage of trade that, because of uncertain crop and weather conditions, farming practices, and government agricultural programs, quantity terms in contracts for materials in the fertilizer industry were regarded by the parties thereto as "mere projections to be adjusted according to market forces." Furthermore, Columbia offered to prove that in their past dealings with Royster, where Royster was the buyer and it, Columbia, was the seller, they had actually operated in keeping with this usage. In at least four instances, Columbia claimed, Royster took none of the goods for which it had contracted as buyer (presumably under language substantially the same as in the instant agreement) and had not been held in breach by Columbia.

The District Court had held the proffered evidence of a trade usage inadmissible, reasoning that it was being offered to contradict, not merely supplement or explain, the writing. The Court of Appeals reversed on this issue, remanding the case for a retrial in which Columbia would be allowed to show "a practice of mutual adjustments so prevalent in the industry and in prior dealings between the parties that it formed a part of the agreement governing this transaction." This certainly is an expansive reading of the Code and the deference to be paid to trade terms. In defense of the result, note that one knowledgeable insider, addressing the unique characteristics of the fertilizer industry that would explain this seemingly bizarre contracting behavior, offered this testimony:

> the contract is considered binding to the extent, on [the buyer] morally that if he uses the tonnage that he will execute the contract in good

> faith as the buyer. . . . I have never heard of a contract of this type being enforced legally. . . . Well, it undoubtedly sounds ridiculous to people from other industries, but there is a very definite, several very definite reasons why the fertilizer business is always operated under what we call gentlemen's agreements [sic].

But if evidence such as this were offered at the retrial, would it necessarily give the day to the buyer? Does the Uniform Commercial Code make every "gentlemen's agreement" enforceable? Consider the following language from a decision that declined to follow the *Royster* result. The case involved a sale of concrete to be used in construction of a building:

> The type of evidence which the Royster decision might allow and which the defendant here undoubtedly wishes to introduce would probably show that a very few contracts specifying quantity and price in a particular industry have been strictly enforced. . . . While in some industries it may be virtually impossible to predict future needs under a contract, in other industries, such contracts may not be strictly adhered to for entirely different reasons. Lawsuits are costly and they do not facilitate good business relations with customers. A party to a contract may very much prefer to work out a renegotiation of a contract rather than rest on its strict legal rights. Yet the supplier or purchaser knows that he may resort to those enforceable contract rights if necessary. If the courts were to conclude that this reluctance to enforce legal rights resulted in an industry-wide waiver of such rights, then contracts would lose their utility as a means of assigning the risks of the market.

Southern Concrete Services, Inc. v. Mableton Contractors, Inc., 407 F. Supp. 581 (N.D. Ga. 1975). So no easy conclusion can be based on *Royster* read alone. Remember, it is one thing to say that because of trade practice, some party has no legal right under a contract; it's something else to observe that a party in that position has such-and-such a right but rarely if ever chooses to pursue it.

2. a. Buyer and Seller should not have any difficulty establishing these usages and their relevance to the contract here. Nothing in §2-202 would bar proof of such trade usages and their relevance to correct understanding of the contract in such a situation. If Buyer claimed he was not in the trade, most courts will say a common usage is binding on you if a reasonable person would have been familiar with it.

   This is as good a place as any to consider the relationship between this part of the parol evidence rule in §2-202 and the specific language of §1-303 that deals with the hierarchy of terms when express provisions meet trade terms. You should reread these subsections and convince yourself that they are consistent with what we've been seeing in §2-202. Express terms are to dominate, yes, but only when a construction that finds those terms "consistent" with the trade terms is patently "unreasonable." If cases like *Royster* and hypotheticals like the one in this question are to be believed, a court can correctly be very liberal in finding consistency between express and trade terms. One question that remains is why, if these subsections are consistent with §2-202, they were needed at all. At least two explanations can be given. First note that §1-303 refers to *express terms*. Express terms need not be in a record, but can be part of an oral agreement. If the express terms are all oral, the parol evidence rule doesn't come into play at all, and these subsections are then needed to instruct us on how to reconcile those express oral terms with the various trade terms offered by the litigants. Second, even when the express terms are in a record, the subsections are still useful as a guide to interpretation once a whole variety of terms—in a record, oral, trade usage, course of dealing, and course of performance—are all on the table. Section 2-202 speaks more to the question of what evidence should be allowed into the contract interpretation mix by the court. If, once all the evidence is collected, there still remains any question about how it is all to be reconciled and the contract interpreted, these subsections are intended as guides on interpretation in general.

b. No. Buyer has no contract right to Grade A lumber. The result is really mandated by the introductory language of §2-202. That the subject of the contract was to be Grade B lumber is found in a term that is "set forth in a record intended by the parties as a final agreement with respect to such terms as are included therein." Hence this term may not be "contradicted by evidence of any prior agreement or of a contemporaneous oral agreement." Later we'll have to deal with exactly how to read the word "contradicted" in this context, but there doesn't seem to be any doubt that a claim for Grade A contradicts a record that calls for "Grade B." If the parol evidence rule means anything (and there are those who wish it didn't, but for now it does) it would have to bar proof of the kind Buyer wants to make here.

c. In this example, Buyer will argue he is not trying to contradict the record with his claim of an upgrade term, but only to supplement it. At least, as he has articulated it, the upgrade is to be for an additional consideration of one cent per foot, so he'll claim this isn't trying to contradict either the price term or the quality term. If he clears that hurdle, does Buyer necessarily get to introduce evidence of a contemporaneous oral agreement that would only supplement what was in the record? Not necessarily. The court must in addition find that the record involved was not "intended also as a *complete and exclusive* statement of the terms of the agreement" (emphasis added). How does the court make such a determination? It can be a tough call. Comment 3 is often quoted:

> Under paragraph (b) consistent additional terms, not reduced to a record, may be proved unless the court finds that the record was intended as a complete and exclusive statement of all the terms. If the additional terms would certainly have been included in the record in the view of the court, then evidence of their alleged making must be kept from the trier of fact.

A reading of this Comment suggests that just about the only time a court could rule out of order an "alleged" oral term is when the court just doesn't believe the allegation. This reading doesn't make much of the parol evidence rule, of course, although it does give a judge some additional control over what a jury can hear and decide. Such a reading, however, goes against the long history of the parol evidence rule, which rests on the idea that something more is going on even if it isn't clear exactly what. Presumably the court will look not just to what it actually believes these parties did, but also to what it thinks other "reasonable" parties similarly situated (going back to an idea from the common law parol evidence rule) "would certainly have done" in like circumstances. A pretty flaccid notion, granted, but there must be something to it.

When such a question arises, the court will presumably take into account the situation in which the parties found themselves. Was it what we would call a formal setting or something fairly casual? Beyond that, the court will look at the record itself. Was it the product of a long, laborious negotiation process, during which every clause, every word was fought over? Were lawyers involved, working their tedious way through numerous drafts and innumerable details? If so, and if the argued supplemental term is anything of significance, it seems likely that parties such as these "would certainly" have put their energies into including this in the document along with everything else. Compare this to the situation where the record being relied upon is merely a blanket form prepared in advance of the transaction with some details of the particular deal dropped into the few blank spaces. In such a situation, a court will much more easily find that the argued supplemental term could have been reasonably left out by parties such as these.

3. Here, as in the previous question, the buyer will be arguing that the oral terms were merely "consistent" additions to the written agreement and should be considered part of their enforceable deal. If the Sales Agreement used by Sol is a fairly standard one and if the two just signed it in Sol's office without much fuss and without making any variations to its printed language, it would seem pretty easy for Barry to argue that the writing can be supplemented by a wide range of terms not included in it.

The language that ends subpart (b), "unless the court finds the record to have been intended also as a complete and exclusive statement of the terms of the agreement," might suggest that the matter of so-called *complete* versus *partial integration* is an all-or-nothing kind of game. Either the record is found to be a complete integration, in which case nothing can possibly supplement it, or it is found not to be complete, in which case maybe just about anything can be added. But the parol evidence rule doesn't work that way. A record may in fact be found to be complete as to some aspects of the agreement, yet not complete as to others. Imagine, for example, if Sol had eventually promised Barry a lower price but had not changed it in the writing. Sol could argue that the writing was clearly complete as to the purchase price. Even if this is so, that doesn't mean it is necessarily complete as to how the car will be equipped when it is delivered. The real issue is whether the offered terms can be thought of as consistent with the writing. In effect, a totally one hundred percent "complete integration" is merely one that is found to be so thorough and detailed that absolutely no term not included in it could possibly be thought consistent with the very existence of such a long, drawn-out document. Anything less is only a partial integration, which may be supplemented by (but only by) consistent terms. The question still centers on the notion of *consistency*; unfortunately this is a concept that, at least at the edges, will have to remain fairly nebulous.

Barry would probably win on the issue of the tires. He'd have a harder time with the promise in (b). Sol would argue that saying that the price would be anything but $8,999 is by its nature not consistent and is in fact downright contradictory. Barry will answer that this is not a change in the purchase price, just a little supplemental perk thrown into the bargain. It's not clear who would win on this one. Barry would presumably have a much harder time still when it comes to the alleged buy-back provision. This is, after all, a fairly unusual term for a used car dealer to agree to, and it's of no small significance if it were ever to be invoked. Even if it believes Barry as to what transpired, I think a court would probably conclude that such a term "would certainly" have been included if the parties meant it to be effective and rule it not an enforceable part of their contract.

In terms of the language of §2-202 itself, Sol's argument must be that the alleged buy-back provision was not consistent with the other terms of the writing. True, there is no language in the document that says that Sol *won't* buy back the car on these terms, but isn't the whole idea that "a seller sells and a buyer buys for keeps" in a sense inconsistent with an understanding that one party can reverse the deal whenever he wants with no ramifications? This question of exactly how to determine when an alleged term is a consistent addition is one that has troubled the courts from the inception of the Code. Dealing as each will with a unique fact situation, it is unlikely that the cases will ever be terribly consistent on what exactly counts for consistency. An early case, *Hunt Foods & Industries, Inc. v. Doliner*, 270 N.Y.S.2d 937 (App. Div. 1966), took what was later to be criticized as a very narrow view on this issue. The court there held that, to be inconsistent, an offered term had to "contradict or negate a term of the writing." In other words, there had to be some particular language in the writing itself that was just flatly at odds with the offered term. If that standard were used, Barry would presumably be able to prove his unusual, but not flatly and expressly contradicted, buy-back provision.

Most commentators and courts have rejected the *Hunt Foods* test. Among other reasons is that this would make the consistency requirement in part (b) merely duplicative of the earlier language in §2-202 that rules out any contradictions generally. Most courts today use instead a standard under which an offered term is found inconsistent in "the absence of reasonable harmony in terms of the language *and* respective obligations of the parties." *Snyder v. Herbert Greenbaum & Associates, Inc.*, 380 A.2d 618 (Md. App. 1977) (emphasis in original). In *Snyder*, the Maryland Court of Appeals held that parol evidence of a contractual right to unilateral rescission was inconsistent with a written agreement for the sale and installation of carpeting. Following this line of reasoning, Barry's claim for enforcement of the offered buy-back provision would presumably fail.

Note, in comparison, that even if a court were to find a record a "complete and exclusive statement of the terms," this would *not* bar the introduction of trade terms as set forth in subpart (a) unless they were found to be "contradictory" to the record itself. The language of complete versus partial integration, for what it's worth, is found only in subpart (b) of the section.

4. The presence of such language in the Sales Agreement might make a difference, but this result may not be as clear-cut as Sol (who wants us to read only that language and throw the case out of court) would have us believe. *Merger clauses* are common in records, and in general it should be said that they are as enforceable as any other term agreed to by the parties. They serve a very useful function when the record truly *is* what the merger clause says that it is—a detailed and well-drafted final version of a record over which the parties have been laboring. There is in such a situation every reason to think that the parties *did* intend to wrap every single thing up in the document and tie it with a bow, and the merger clause just makes this official. An important case revealing of how at least some courts will look at the effect of the presence of a merger clause in a written agreement is *Betaco, Inc. v. Cessna Aircraft Co.*, 103 F.3d 1281 (7th Cir. 1996). While acknowledging that the inclusion of such a clause does

not in and of itself preclude a court's determination in any given circumstance that the writing under consideration is not a complete integration, the Seventh Circuit stressed that such a provision is to be considered "strong evidence" that the written contract "represented the entirety of the agreement between the parties" and hence bars proof of terms outside of the writing's four corners. It should be noted that the transaction involved was the purchase at a price of $2,495,000 of a six-passenger jet aircraft and that the buyer against whom the merger clause was held to operate had "extensive experience as a pilot, airline executive, and purchaser of aircraft," even if he later seemed to be arguing that he had treated the transaction "more like the purchase of a family car than the purchase of a multi-million dollar jet."

It is a very different matter, however, when we have a consumer buyer signing a standard agreement provided by the seller without any dickering over the language. There a court will usually not be as impressed by the merger language. In such cases the clause is often viewed by the court as mere boilerplate with no independent legal effect just because it has been thrown in among the mass of verbiage. The intention of the parties is still the key. If the court is not favorably disposed toward the integration and to such a standard merger clause in a standard agreement, it can easily hold that even though the buyer signed a record having such language in it he or she did not actually intend the record to have the effect argued for. The court can determine, in effect, that the alleged merger clause was no more actually "agreed to" than was anything else.

In any situation, a party wishing to secure a valid and enforceable merger clause in a record would do well to follow a few simple guidelines: (1) make the language as conspicuous as possible (don't bury it); (2) provide evidence that the other party gave his or her considered assent to that clause in particular by having it separately signed or initialed; (3) draft the clause as carefully as possible to cover the specific concerns of the parties involved and tailor it to the particular situation. Faced with a clause meeting these criteria, a court will find it difficult (although still not impossible) to set it aside in order to allow supplementation to the terms of the record.

(Note that when language such as is suggested here is being argued to have disclaimed a warranty or to have limited the seller's liability in the event of a breach, Article 2 provides a set of special rules that must be applied. Disclaimers and limitations are special cases. We deal with them directly in Chapter 13.)

5. The parol evidence rule would not bar this statement. This was a statement made *subsequent to* the parties entering into an integration of their agreement, so §2-202 is simply inapplicable. Andy may have a problem taking advantage of this statement, but there isn't a parol evidence issue.

For one thing, Sol may claim that as a later modification of their agreement, it is unenforceable as lacking "consideration," although this argument shouldn't go far because of §2-209(1). Also, as a claimed express warranty, Andy may have to worry about the timing and the "part of the basis of the bargain language" of §2-313 (see Chapter 11). The point here is simply that there is no parol evidence problem at all once Andy is relying on a later statement.

6. Betty's argument is that, whatever may appear to someone viewing the record, no final agreement of any kind was ever entered into between her and Sol because a condition to her acceptance of his offer never came to pass. This is often referred to as the *conditional delivery exception* to the parol evidence rule, but it is not really an exception at all. The concept is more rudimentary: There is simply no reason to invoke the rule whatsoever, because the parties never created an integration of an enforceable agreement; in fact, there never was an agreement in the first place. This argument is accepted by the courts. For example, in *King v. Fordice*, 776 S.W.2d 608, (Tex. Ct. App. 1989), the seller presented an exchange of mailgrams that he claimed set forth the agreement between himself and the buyer for the sale of a Cessna 414 aircraft. The alleged buyer presented a different view of the events. He claimed that he had agreed to an exchange of mailgrams solely for the purpose of the seller's getting the airplane to Dallas for his inspection and that he had no intention at the time of entering into a binding agreement to buy the plane for $400,000. The buyer pointed out that "in accordance with the understanding that the exchange of mailgrams was an inspection ticket and not a binding contract he did not send the $25,000.00 deposit as mentioned in the mailgrams." Prior to trial the seller filed a motion to suppress all evidence that would vary or expand the terms as they appeared in the pair of mailgrams. The Texas Court of Appeals upheld the trial court's decision to deny this motion and to allow into evidence the buyer's testimony about his oral understanding with the seller. The appellate court considered both the general common law notion of conditional delivery and how it was affected by the adoption of Article 2, concluding:

> that parol evidence is always competent to show the nonexistence of a contract, or the invalidity of a contract even if there is a writing purporting to be an integration, and that such matters are outside the scope of the common law parol evidence rule and the ambit of §2-202, with regard to the sale of goods. These matters are admissible on their own merit and not as an exception to the parol evidence rule or §2-202. . . . The trial judge did not err in admitting the complained of testimony on a "no contract" or non-formation theory. Such oral testimony did not vary the terms of the mailgrams as contended by [the seller] but showed that the mailgrams were never intended to be a contract or of binding force between the parties.

Determining that this evidence was admissible and not barred by the parol evidence rule did not, of course, completely decide the case. The trial court's attention had to be directed toward whether it believed the characterization of events as related by the buyer. It did, and the buyer was found never to have entered into an agreement to buy the plane. The result thus turned not on the mechanics of the parol evidence rule but on a factual determination of what had actually transpired between the parties.

7. Charles has a good case of fraudulent inducement. Such claims are generally not held to be barred by the parol evidence rule. Again, as in the last example, the issue is not over identifying the terms of an agreement acknowledged to be enforceable between the parties, but rather whether the agreement is in fact enforceable at all, here in light of the fraud committed by one of the players. Section 2-202 is simply not applicable if for some reason recognized in law there is no enforceable agreement between the parties. Where does Charles find authority for his argument on the theory of fraud? See §1-303(b). Charles's case, if he can prove it, seems perfectly clear. The courts will be wary, of course, to be sure that claimants don't circumvent the effect of the parol evidence rule merely by framing their arguments in terms of fraud. Key here is that Charles will show that Sol intentionally misled him with a statement he knew to be untrue.

CHAPTER 9

Good Faith, Unconscionability, and Gap Fillers

THE AGREEMENT "AS AFFECTED BY THIS ACT"

A brief review is in order. The starting point for determining the terms of the sales contract is the agreement of the parties. As noted in the introduction to Chapter 7, the Code uses the word *agreement* to refer to the "bargain of the parties in fact" (§1-201(b)(3)). So first we have to piece together just what the operative agreement is. Chapters 4 and 5 focused on the parties' express agreement as it arises out of their direct communications one with the other. Chapter 7 added to the mix (and to the agreement) terms arising from trade usage, course of dealing, and course of performance.

But delineating the agreement is not the end of the story. The sales *contract* under the U.C.C. is "the total legal obligation which arises from the parties' agreement as affected by this Act and any other applicable rules of law" (§1-201(b)(12)). To find the terms of the contract, we start with the terms agreed to—but then the Code giveth and the Code taketh away. Chapter 8 was all about one particular way in which an agreed term or terms might be taken out of the eventual contract by operation of law. In certain circumstances, Article 2's parol evidence rule (§2-202) makes unenforceable a "prior agreement" or "contemporaneous oral agreement" reached by the parties. The parties' *agreement* may include many a term that, given §2-202 and the fact that the term hasn't been included in a final and complete record, will not make it into their *contract* — their total legal obligation.

This chapter is concerned with a further set of provisions in Article 2 that can work to add or subtract terms from the contract. They are variously referred to as the *gap fillers* of Article 2 or the sections allowing for and regulating *open terms*. Two other provisions—*good faith* and the doctrine of *unconscionability*—get a separate treatment.

GOOD FAITH

Section 1-304 provides:

> **Obligation of Good Faith.**
> Every contract or duty within the Uniform Commercial Code imposes an obligation of good faith in its performance and enforcement.

Knowing that the obligation of good faith is found in every contract is not helpful without knowing what good faith means. Let's examine how good faith is defined. Prior to the 2001 revision of Article 1, the definition provided that good faith was only honesty in fact. The honesty standard is often referred to as "subjective" good faith because it goes to a party's motive, which requires a determination of their state of mind. However, Article 2 provided in §2-103(1)(b) that merchants (recall the discussion of Article 2's special rules for merchants in Chapter 3) also had an obligation to observe reasonable commercial standards of fair dealing. The reasonable standard is often referred to as "objective" good faith because it can be measured according to proven standards. So prior to the revision, the bottom line was that in all Articles of the U.C.C., all parties had to observe subjective good faith, while in Article 2, only merchants had to also observe objective good faith. Revised Article 1 then moved the definition that was formerly reserved for merchants under Article 2 to the Article 1 definitions section, where it is now found in §1-201(b)(20):

> "Good faith," except as otherwise provided in Article 5, means honesty in fact and the observance of reasonable commercial standards of fair dealing.

Therefore, because Article 1 now provides that throughout the Code (except in Article 5) all parties have to observe both objective and subjective good faith, jurisdictions enacting Revised Article 1 repealed §2-103(1)(b) as superfluous. Is it possible for a party who is not a merchant to be know what "reasonable commercial standards" are? I think so, if you think of "commercial" meaning buying and selling. For example, in Chapter 10 we will talk about the "good faith purchaser for value." If you buy something for a low price from a seller who is selling it out of the trunk of their car in a parking lot, you may honestly think you are entering into an ordinary business transaction, but even one who is not in business ought to know that this sale does not satisfy reasonable standards of buying and selling. One wrinkle: A number of jurisdictions did not go along with this part of the revision and retained the old definition of good faith and the exception for merchants in Article 2. In that case, the ordinary person would not be subject to "reasonable commercial standards."

Since the obligation of good faith is found in every contract, we can think of it as an implied term. Note that because there are two kinds of good faith in most transactions, the duty can be breached by failing to observe either one of them. However, don't make the mistake of taking the duty of good faith too far. For one thing, it probably does not apply to the negotiation of a contract. For example, suppose I am discussing the sale of my car to you, and I say, "I won't take a penny less than $10,000 for it." This is an outright lie, for I would be happy to take $8,000. It certainly looks like I lacked "honesty in fact." Nevertheless, while honesty is a requirement of good faith, it is not a requirement of negotiation, so this behavior is not a breach of the duty of good faith.

Perhaps more importantly, "breach of the duty of good faith" is not a stand-alone claim. A party breaches the duty of good faith in connection with their performance or enforcement of the contract; that is, some particular provision is not carried out in good faith. For example, in the case of *Neumiller Farms, Inc. v. Cornett*, 368 So. 2d 272 (Ala. 1979), a merchant buyer agreed to buy potatoes at a stipulated price only if, in his judgment, they were satisfactory for making potato chips. The market price of potatoes went down and the buyer refused to buy them.

Was he in breach? Note that this happened prior to the adoption of Revised Article 1, so the buyer was subject to both requirements of good faith—subjective and objective—because he was a merchant in an Article 2 transaction. If it happened today, he would also be subject to both requirements because of the definition in Article 1. It turned out he did not act in subjective good faith because it was proven by his own admissions that he had a dishonest motive—the real reason he rejected the potatoes was because the market price went down, not because they would not make good potato chips. Furthermore, the seller had the potatoes tested by an independent laboratory, which found that they made good potato chips, so he did not act in objective good faith either—a potato buyer observing reasonable commercial standards would have accepted them. So while good faith supplies the means to interpret his performance, his breach was a breach of his duty to accept goods that conform to the contract.

It also follows that breach of the duty of good faith is just a breach and the remedy is the same as the remedy for any other breach of contract. There are no punitive damages for this breach. Some jurisdictions have found an exception when the parties are in a "special relationship," but the only special relationship that courts have regularly found is that of insured and insurer. So in some jurisdictions, bad faith denial of an insurance claim can give rise to a claim for punitive damages. See, e.g., *Neal v. Farmers Insurance Exchange*, 582 P.2d 980 (Cal. 1978).

THE UNCONSCIONABILITY POLICE

People are not necessarily fair. Certainly they may not be when they are out to make the best deal possible for themselves. People going into a bargain can reasonably be expected to look out for themselves and do what they can to get the best deal available. Furthermore, a contracting party will normally expect that the opposing party will likewise be ruled by self-interest and take appropriate care. If some people drive hard bargains, well, more power to them: That's what freedom of contract is all about, and Comment 1 to §1-302 reminds us (if we needed any reminding) that "freedom of contract is a principle of the Code." There was no general rule in the common law of contracts, and there is certainly nothing in Article 2 that requires parties to a sales agreement be fair to each other, or reasonable in what they ask for, or anything like that. As a general rule, it's "every man or woman for him or herself," and we have to assume the drafters would have had it no other way.

But sometimes things get out of hand. Even under the common law, extracting a bargain by duress, coercion, or fraud is impermissible. These doctrines still apply to sales contracts governed by Article 2 by virtue of §1-103(b). Beyond this, will there be any limit to what parties may agree to? Does the law "police" the substance of the bargain itself? The traditional doctrinal response was no, even though the courts often found ways to accomplish what was not technically allowed. See the first two sentences of Comment 1 to §2-302. As the Comment goes on to state, this section was intended to allow courts to do a bit of policing directly and out in the open. Under §2-302 an agreement that as a whole is *unconscionable* or contains an unconscionable provision need not necessarily be enforced by the court. Unconscionability is a defense. In §2-302 the Code empowers a court to eliminate from the enforceable contract any unconscionable term or terms of the agreement or even to refuse to enforce the agreement entirely.

You should read §2-302(1) now if you have not already done so. Clearly the court is given great leeway in dealing with unconscionability. Unfortunately what this section doesn't tell us is the one thing we most would like to know: What exactly does it mean for a clause or for an entire contract to be unconscionable? The word is never defined in the Code. Indeed most everyone seems to agree that a simple one-line definition is not possible (and probably not even desirable). Unconscionability is a doctrine, a thesis, a concept. Still we need to get some handle on what it's all about. Comment 1 is of limited help:

> The basic test is whether, in the light of the general commercial background and the commercial needs of the particular trade or case, the clauses involved are so one-sided as to be unconscionable under the circumstances existing at the time of the making of the contract.

This language is important in that it makes clear that unconscionability is to be measured at the time a contract is entered into and not in the light of later events. Beyond that, it cautions that any determination must be made in light of the overall commercial setting. We are dealing with the real world here, not some utopian community.

But we are still left with a "basic test" that seems to define unconscionability in terms of "that which is unconscionable." Not much help. Later language in this Comment is often cited:

> The principle is one of prevention of oppression and unfair surprise . . . and not of disturbance of allocation of risks because of superior bargaining power.

Is this any clearer? The Comment concludes with a recitation of some illustrations. You may look at them if you wish, but don't be surprised if you come away with the idea that for unconscionability, like some other things, the only test is that you are supposed to know it when you see it. Indeed not a few commentators, including many who heartily support the whole §2-302 agenda, have concluded that there's not much more that can be said on the matter and certainly no definition or precise set of criteria that separates the unconscionable from the merely naughty.

Perhaps more can be said about the substance of the doctrine of unconscionability, of what it is, and of how we spot it. Before venturing into those waters, however, there are some points to be made of a more procedural nature. At least here we can make some statements with confidence. Note first that under §2-302(1) and Comments 2 and 3, the unconscionability doctrine is firmly in the hands of the court; it will be up to the judge to apply its provisions. Decisions about unconscionability are not for a jury to make. This is, of course, of no small significance. Whatever the doctrine of unconscionability is about, §2-302 is not meant to be a means for the jury to roam freely over an agreement, striking those provisions it views as unfair or inappropriate, especially as those terms may affect a party who has gained its sympathy. Judges, we are to believe, are made of sterner stuff and are not so easily swayed. Beyond that, judges will not so readily be distracted from the underlying virtues and benefits of freedom of contract. The power to police via the notion of unconscionability is heady stuff, which is firmly in the control of the judiciary.

A second point of importance is found in the dictate of §2-302(2). Look at that subsection. Whether a particular contract or clause is unconscionable is not solely a matter of judicial instinct. The court in making the determination must be guided not just by first impressions but by *evidence*—evidence of the commercial setting, as well as the purpose and effect of the accused clause. Both parties must be given a reasonable opportunity to present such evidence. It would be a serious mistake to dismiss this statutory language as merely a vague incantation that in trying a case, a court should really try the case. In fact, subsection (2) may be the most important part of §2-302 from the perspective of a party trying to defend a challenged clause. "Hear me out," he or she will be heard to say. "There is a legitimate and quite comprehensible reason for what I bargained for given the circumstances." In any number of cases, clauses that initially might seem like clear unconscionability (whatever that may be) will upon closer inspection take on a very different character. Depending on your overall view of the unconscionability doctrine, in fact, you may be among those who conclude that few if any challenged clauses will fail to stand up to scrutiny once the full facts are revealed and the commercial justification for the particular provision understood. Perhaps bargainers who later fall victim to the unconscionability doctrine are not doing such bad things after all; perhaps they are just having trouble helping a court appreciate the commercial realities under which they necessarily must carry on business.

Of course you may well conclude that there is much more to unconscionability than this. Virtually all the commentators seem to acknowledge that there is *some* substance here, even if they can't exactly put their finger on what it is. An age-old rubric has it that conduct is unconscionable if it "shocks the conscience." This language isn't very helpful and isn't heard that often anymore. Among other problems, it begs the question of whose conscience we are talking about. What is shocking to your run-of-the-mill professor of ethics might look very different to a hardened businessman or woman who spends each and every day out in the real world.

The modern discussion of unconscionability usually starts out with some language from Judge Skelly Wright in the oft-discussed case of *Williams v. Walker-Thomas Furniture Co.*, 350 F.2d 445 (D.C. Cir. 1965):

> Unconscionability has generally been recognized to include an absence of meaningful choice on the part of one of the parties together with contract terms which are unreasonably favorable to the other party.

Following up on this, Professor Arthur Leff, writing soon after the adoption of the Code, suggested an analysis that distinguished between two types or flavors of unconscionability. See Leff, *Unconscionability and the Code—The Emperor's New Clause*, 115 U. Pa. L. Rev. 485 (1967). He offered the term *procedural unconscionability* for what he saw as "bargaining naughtiness," that is, some significant taint in the process by which the agreement was extracted out of the innocent party. This ties in to Judge Wright's reference to "an absence of meaningful choice" on that party's part and the *means* by which the overreaching party put the other in this pickle. What Leff termed *substantive unconscionability*, on the other hand, calls for a focus on the *ends* that are achieved by the bargaining process. How one-sided or unfair did the contract turn out to be? Substantive unconscionability relates to Wright's requirement of "terms which are unreasonably favorable" to the one party at the expense of the other. The Leff analysis has stuck, partly because of its genuine usefulness and partly because nothing better has come along. Courts and commentators regularly make reference to it. We can pursue it a bit more here.

Procedural unconscionability can be found—and has been found—where one party knowingly takes advantage of the other's lack of education or unfamiliarity with the English language. It is found in too-fine print or in contractual gobbledygook that, however large on the printed page, is virtually impossible for any mere mortal to make sense out of. A court looking for signs of procedural unconscionability can usually find some high-pressure salesmanship thrown in as well. Procedural unconscionability is the sin of preying on the guileless and vulnerable consumer.

This raises an immediate question. Does the particular individual's economic position, that is, his or her clout in the marketplace, bear on the defense of unconscionability? Certainly courts often take pains to justify a determination of unconscionability with a showing of the lack of bargaining power by the injured party. Lack of bargaining power alone would presumably not be enough to call for an invocation of §2-302. Note the language previously quoted from Comment 1 that the principle is *not* "the disturbance of allocation of risk because of superior bargaining power." There is no reason to think the drafters meant to turn their backs on the basic assumption underlying the free-market economy and everything that is dear to capitalism. But unequal bargaining power does seem to play a part. How else could you explain the complaining party's having entered into such a grossly unfair and shocking deal? And yet we know that even a fairly sophisticated and intelligent consumer may later feel he or she was unfairly roped into a deal. Can that consumer call upon the principle of unconscionability? Possibly, but the instances where unconscionability would be found in favor of a sophisticated consumer will presumably be rare. For people such as this it will be hard to say there has been an "absence of meaningful choice." Your typical middle-class consumer always has the option of saying no to a deal and taking his or her business elsewhere—and would be wise to do so.

I have been writing so far as if questions of unconscionability can only come up in what we would think of as the "consumer protection situation." Could a party who has entered into an agreement as part of his or her business (a commercial actor) ever be successful in claiming unconscionability? Again the answer is that this is possible. Nothing in the language of or Comments to §2-302 limits its applicability, and there have been cases where business entities have been successful with this defense. But the instances of unconscionability in a commercial setting should be few. Certainly once both parties to a business arrangement have had legal counsel advising them during the negotiation and conclusion of an agreement, the doctrine of unconscionability would seem inappropriate to the situation. Unconscionability is largely, albeit not exclusively, a doctrine intended to give some measure of protection to the poor and disadvantaged consumer who suffers unduly from the harsh realities of the marketplace. In *Northrop Corp. v. Litronic Industries*, 29 F.3d 1173 (7th Cir. 1994), Chief Judge Posner of the Seventh Circuit found himself called upon to "remind Northrop and companies like it that the defense of unconscionability was not invented to protect multi-billion dollar corporations against mistakes committed by their employees [in entering into contracts on terms later found to be unfavorable], and indeed has rarely succeeded outside the area of consumer contracts." (Citations omitted.) Similarly, Judge Newman of the Federal Circuit found that the doctrine of unconscionability could not be used in favor of a company which, while it was much smaller than its adversary, Intel, was still "one of the Fortune 1000, and does not plead inadequate legal advice in its commercial dealings." *Intergraph Corp. v. Intel Corp.*, 195 F.3d 1346 (Fed. Cir. 1999).

So far, we have been concentrating on so-called procedural unconscionability. Don't forget that both elements are required. It is not enough to show that one party had no bargaining power—that party must also show that the party with all the bargaining power used that power to impose unfair terms. This is the notion of *substantive unconscionability*—the question becomes whether the results of bargaining (the terms that are agreed to) are so one-sided as to call into question their very enforceability. Note the various examples set forth in Comment 1, most of which we will discuss in connection with §§2-316 and 2-719 in Chapter 13. It's hard to define or delineate substantively unconscionable terms in the abstract, and no one ever tries. Presumably the taint of substantive unconscionability lies in a term's (or an entire contract's) being not just a hard bargain nor a losing one, but something beyond that. Recall the use of the term *oppression* in Comment 1 and the old *shocks the conscience* language.

In following Leff's popular and helpful two-branch analysis, we naturally ask, what is the relationship between procedural and substantive unconscionability? Will one alone do to state a defense under §2-302? Here we have an issue on which the commentators disagree and the courts have not been all that clear. Certainly the typical case of unconscionability (at least the typically strong one) will exhibit both procedural and substantive problems. Furthermore, everyone seems to agree that the more of one you have, the less of the other is necessary to make out a case. As we've highlighted, unconscionability is to be addressed solely by the judge, and courts invariably look to the totality of the situation and the "mix" of factors in making such determinations. Rarely if ever does a court think it necessary or wise to parse too closely all of the considerations involved.

A particularly troubling question on which there is no agreement is whether the §2-302 power can be exercised by a court when there is no showing whatsoever of procedural unconscionability, but only what appears to be a substantively unconscionable *result*. The issue is seen in its most pristine form when it is reduced to the question of so-called *price unconscionability*. Imagine that a buyer has agreed to a price far in excess of what "should be" or "normally would be" charged for the product in question. Can this fact alone support a court's nullification of the agreement—or adjustment of the price—under §2-302?

The courts and the commentators are decidedly split on how they would handle such a situation. In several cases, courts have explicitly stated that an excessive price in and of itself may render the deal unenforceable. In reality, of course, one suspects that the courts in many if not all of these cases could easily have pointed to a questionable bargaining technique or two had it found the need to do so. Other courts and some commentators have stated just as confidently that an excessive price or other substantively unconscionable term can be excised by the court under §2-302 only if some discernable element of procedural unconscionability is also present. Notice that the previously quoted language of Judge Wright, which started out this whole line of analysis, speaks of unconscionability being found in an absence of meaningful choice on one party's part *together with* a term or terms unreasonably favorable to the other party. Of course it may not be that hard for a court following this approach to find some procedural taint. How else to explain the buyer's agreement to such an "excessive" price or "outrageous" provision?

In point of fact it has been noted how relatively few claims of unconscionability based primarily on excessive pricing, at least as reflected in the published cases, have been brought in recent years. One possible reason for this relates back to an initial point made about §2-302(2). If the buyer asserts an unconscionably high price, the seller has to be given an opportunity to present evidence "as to its commercial setting, purpose and effect." Perhaps sellers are just getting wiser in their use of this provision. There may be perfectly legitimate reasons why the price charged to poor or disadvantaged consumers, the least powerful members of the community, ends up being significantly higher than what is charged for the same merchandise in a trendy suburban store or a rustic enclave. Once challenged by a buyer claiming price unconscionability, the seller may be able to justify this price based on the increased costs of doing business in the particular area. This would not, of course, justify sharp practices, "oppression," or the "unfair surprise" such as that which fits within our notion of procedural unconscionability. But a higher price alone may eventually have to be understood as a reflection of the prevailing conditions in certain segments of the economy and of forces quite beyond the power of the seller to influence even if he or she wanted to. And on this, an argument of unconscionability would presumably have to fail.

It remains to be seen whether the courts will ever come up with a single, consistent answer to the question of the pure case of so-called price unconscionability. But then price unconscionability is only the most dramatic and perhaps the most troubling aspect of that more general mystery—the doctrine of unconscionability and its uneasy place in a law of sales fundamentally premised on traditional notions of freedom of contract.

INTRODUCTION TO THE GAP FILLERS

As we saw in Chapter 4, Article 2 takes a more liberal (the drafters would say a more realistic) view of when a contract has been entered into than does the traditional common law of contract. The question is always that of intent. In particular, recall §2-204(3), which states:

> Even though one or more terms are left open a contract for sale does not fail for indefiniteness if the parties have intended to make a contract and there is a reasonably certain basis for giving an appropriate remedy.

If a contract can exist in this way, who or what sets the terms "left open" by the parties? For one thing, the Code's rich scheme for identifying any applicable trade usage or course of dealing and incorporating it into the agreement will fill in many of the holes. (See Chapter 7.) Beyond this the drafters of Article 2 included an extensive set of rules (usually referred to as the *gap fillers*) to set the terms of the contract of sale that the parties themselves have otherwise left open. Please review §§2-304 through 2-311. You may recall that in Chapter 5, in the context of the Battle of the Forms, these provisions played an important role when either subsection 2-207(3) or the judicially incorporated "knockout rule" eliminated conflicting provisions from both parties' forms and substituted "other provisions of this act." Please examine §§2-304 through 2-311, which contain these gap-fillers.

Examples

EXAMPLES

1. Hector has an exercise bicycle that he never uses. Cleo has been given an expensive hammock that she doesn't want at all. They agree to a trade. Is this transaction covered by Article 2? If so, who is the "seller" and who the "buyer"?
2. Arnold Moneybucks, the noted art patron, goes into Stella's gallery, where he looks over the various paintings on display. Every artwork in

the gallery is up for sale, but in keeping with the classy nature of the establishment, no price tags are visible. A price list is kept discreetly in Stella's office. Arnold spots a painting he particularly admires and tells Stella, "I simply must have that one." Stella invites him to step into her office, to which he responds, "That won't be necessary. I'll send my assistant around for it tomorrow. Have it ready." Stella is barely able to utter, "Anything you want, Mr. Moneybucks," before her flamboyant visitor is out the door. Is there a contract for the sale of the painting? If so, what is the contract price?

3. On his lunch hour, the office clerk Benny is looking over the paintings in Stella's gallery. She approaches him as he is staring intently at a particular work and identifies herself. He tells her, "I'd really like to own this one." She grabs his hand, gives it a good shake, and says, "You've got yourself a deal. You're not going to be sorry." Is there a contract for sale here?

4. We are still at Stella's gallery. A third individual, one Constance, is sitting with the owner in her private office discussing art. She points to a small statue on Stella's desk. "Now that," says Constance, "is something I'd love to have." Stella says that the statue was a gift from the artist, who was at the time just starting out but who has since become very popular, and that the piece is now undoubtedly worth a good deal of money. She had not intended to sell it, but if Constance is really interested, she is willing to let her have it. The two sign a purchase and sale agreement. Where the agreement calls for a "Price," they fill in "As fixed by Ken Clark." Ken is a noted authority on modern art who often acts as an appraiser in the local art market.
   (a) Under these circumstances is there a contract for sale, and if so at what price?
   (b) What if Stella and Constance find out the next day that Ken has left the country, saying he will have no more to do with the art market?
   (c) What result if instead Ken is available but Stella, regretting her agreement, tells Constance to forget about their deal and that she is not going to let Ken have a look at the statue?

5. Buyer goes into Seller's bookstore and asks for a particular book. Seller says that he does not have the book in stock, that it is in fact out of print, but that he is sure he can find a used copy for Buyer. He says, "I'd get one if you are going to buy it. I don't know exactly how much a used copy will cost. I'd have to see what to charge you for it." Buyer says, "That's OK. I'll take it." Seller later contacts Buyer to tell him that he's obtained a copy of the book and that the price will be $125. Is Buyer obligated to buy the book at this price? What if Buyer could show that the original manufacturer's suggested price marked on the book had been $49.95?

6. Candy is a candy manufacturer. One of the several candies she produces is the Pecan Supreme, for which she quite understandably needs pecans. She contacts Shelly, a major nut supplier. They enter into an agreement under which Candy will purchase "all of her pecan requirements" from Shelly for a period of three years at a stated price. Under the agreement, Candy will notify Shelly by the 15th of any month how many nuts to deliver by the beginning of the following month. During the course of their negotiations, Candy has told Shelly that she anticipates a need for something like 1,000 to 1,200 pounds of pecans per month.
   (a) Is there a contract here? Would your answer be the same if the record had not referred to "all" of Candy's pecan requirements?
   (b) Thanks to a very successful marketing campaign, sales of Pecan Supremes rise dramatically. Candy's orders to Shelly begin to range around 2,000 pounds a month. Shelly is concerned because he finds he has made a bad deal with Candy and is losing money on every pound he delivers to her. Is he obligated to fill these larger orders?
   (c) Assume that the reason Candy's orders to Shelly had jumped was that Candy, realizing that (due to a worldwide pecan shortage) she had a particularly good deal on pecans, decided to add a new product to her line of treats. She plans to put together and distribute little packets of pecans under the name of Candy's Fresh Pecan Packets. Is Shelly obligated to fill these larger orders?
   (d) Suppose instead that during the second year of their agreement, Candy looks at her sales figures and concludes that the Pecan Supreme is not a big seller. It is just barely breaking even. She decides to discontinue making it in favor of a new product, the Walnut Delight, which she anticipates will sell better. She notifies Shelly that she no longer needs any pecans from him. Does Shelly have any rights against Candy? Would it make a difference if Candy could show she was actually losing money on the pecan product? What if she were losing money just because her pecan costs under the deal with Shelly were higher than those of her competitors?
   (e) Looking again at the basic question of enforceability in Example 6(a), would the agreement between Candy and Shelly still be binding if the record they signed had not been for a definite term of years and in fact had left its duration totally up in the air? See §2-309.

7. Babs is building her own house and has almost completed the job. She agrees to buy three truckloads of topsoil from Sol's garden supply firm. The record states that the price is $600 and calls for delivery "the week of May 15." Payment is to be made "On Delivery." On Monday, May 15, Sol arrives at Babs's, his truck loaded with topsoil. He says he is ready

to dump the dirt wherever Babs tells him to and that he expects $200 right away. He plans to bring another truckload on Wednesday and the final one on Friday. Babs refuses to take the single truckload on Monday. At the most, she tells Sol, she would be willing to let Sam dump the dirt but will not pay him anything until the final load has been delivered on Friday. Is Babs within her rights to take this stand?

8. Bert contracts to buy a dinette set consisting of a table and four matching chairs from Selma's Table City, which is to make delivery the following week. When the truck from Selma's shows up at Bert's, the driver starts to unload the table but has only three chairs. He asks Bert to take and "sign for" these items, saying that he'll bring the last chair the following day. Would Bert be within his rights to refuse the partial delivery?

9. Over the telephone Sam and Dave enter into an agreement for the sale of Sam's used car to Dave for $450. They agree that Dave "can have the car next week" but say nothing more about delivery. When the following week comes around, Sam calls Dave and tells him to come and pick up the car. Dave insists that Sam should bring it over to his house.
   (a) Who's got the better legal argument?
   (b) Suppose instead that when Sam and Dave concluded their used car deal, it was specifically agreed that Sam would deliver the car to Dave's house. There was no mention, however, of *when* he was to do so. A week passes and Sam has not shown up at Dave's. Is he in breach?
   (c) Finally, assume that Sam does drive the car over to Dave's. He offers to hand over the registration certificate and the keys to the car in exchange for $450 cash from Dave. Dave tells him that he's waiting to get some money owed him in order to pay for the car, but that he will definitely mail Sam a check within a week. Does Sam have to accept this method of payment? What if Dave offers to give him a personal check for $450 then and there?

10. Ms. Blandings is in the process of organizing a new company, which will manufacture and sell widget holders. She realizes that she will need to have cardboard cartons to use in shipping the goods. She enters into an agreement with Shipshape's Cartons Unlimited for the purchase of 10,000 cartons to be delivered on or about April 1. Shipshape makes cartons in three standard sizes. The agreement states that Shipshape will deliver the cartons "in an assortment of sizes to be specified by Blandings no later than March 10." Under place of delivery, the parties put in "Per Buyer's instructions." Is there a contract here? What result if Blandings contacts Shipshape on March 5 and asks for a shipment of all large boxes to be delivered to Mexico? See §2-311. What would be the

consequences if Shipshape has not heard from Blandings by the end of the day on March 10?

EXPLANATIONS

Explanations

1. The answer is clear from §2-304(1). This transaction is covered by Article 2. Hector is the seller of the exercise bicycle and the buyer of the hammock. Cleo sells the hammock and buys the bike. A typical situation where this result is relevant is the purchase by a consumer of a new car where he or she gives a trade-in as part of the deal. The buyer of the new car is a seller of the trade-in. As we'll discuss in Part III, as a seller he or she will almost certainly be giving some warranties about the trade-in along with turning over the used car itself.

   Note also the provision in §2-304(2) that makes clear that even if an interest in realty is part of the overall deal, Article 2 governs the transfer of the goods.

2. There should be a contract here, and the price will be whatever was noted on Stella's list. We can harken back to §2-204(3) and the fundamental test of whether "the parties have intended to make a contract" as long as there is a "reasonably certain basis for giving a remedy." Perfectly in tune with this idea and more directly to the point, §2-305(1) provides, "The parties if they so intend can conclude a contract for sale even though the price is not settled." You could argue here that although the price was never mentioned, it was in fact "settled," at least if Arnold knew that galleries set prices in the way Stella does. Or you might conclude that the price hadn't been "settled" here, in which case the second sentence of this subsection holds that the price is to be "a reasonable price at the time of delivery." You could then maintain that this would be the price Stella listed it for, at least if that's the way sales of such artworks usually operate.

   Suppose Arnold could show that buyers from such galleries, or from Stella's in particular, customarily paid some lower price (say, 10 percent less) than what was actually listed in the seller's catalogue. First of all, would this defeat the existence of a contract? I think not. The question is still whether the parties intended to be bound, and there's no suggestion here that either had any reservations about that. Could Arnold argue that if he is so bound, he should only have to pay 90 percent of the listed price? That's trickier. It would presumably depend on how the "customary 10-percent discount" was arrived at. If it was because buyers typically do go into the gallery owner's office and haggle, even if only in a perfunctory way, then it seems Arnold by not even making this gesture can't argue for any reduction in this instance. If Arnold were to show that the discount had in the past automatically been given, then it could be a usage of trade or a course of dealing between him and Stella and presumably would be part of this deal.

3. Benny should not have to worry about being bound to a contract with Stella. Again, what is crucial is a question of fact. Do you find here that Benny and Stella both intended to be so bound? Section 2-305(4) just states the obvious. If "the parties intend not to be bound unless the price be fixed or agreed and it is not fixed or agreed there is no contract."

   Notice also the treatment in §2-305 of the so-called "agreement to agree." The common law questioned whether such an agreement can ever be enforceable. This section makes clear that the central issue is whether the parties themselves intend to be bound in such a situation. There is no rule of law barring them from being held to a contract if that is in fact what they wanted. What is the price? If the parties do later agree on a price, that is presumably that. If they fail to agree then §2-305(1) sets the price at a "reasonable price at the time [and, one would assume, the place] for delivery."

4. a. There is a contract for sale since the parties clearly so intend. The price will be whatever Ken fixes it at.
   b. Under §2-305(1)(c) there would still be a contract, and the price would be "a reasonable price at the time for delivery." If the parties cannot now agree on a price, perhaps they can agree on a substitute appraiser. If not, then somewhere down the road a court would have to determine the statue's "reasonable price" taking into account whatever evidence the parties want to muster. An important point here is that under this section neither party could simply call the deal off because of Ken's unavailability.
   c. Look at §2-305(3). Constance now has an option. She can treat the contract as canceled or herself fix "a reasonable price." Of course this doesn't mean she can just pick a number out of the air. But look at Comment 5 and its reference to a "reasonable leeway."

5. There is a contract and under §2-305(2) the price will be as set by the Seller, as long as he acts in good faith. Note that good faith requires not merely honesty in fact but "the observance of reasonable commercial standards of fair dealing in the trade." Seller should be able to get the $125 if this is the kind of price he would have placed on the book had he simply put it out on his shelves in the hope of attracting a buyer. Look at Comment 3. Notice that while we normally think of used goods as being cheaper than new, this would not necessarily be true when it comes to a copy of an out-of-print book. So the original list price is only part of the story.

   For a case dealing with the possibility of a contract being formed for the purchase and sale of large quantities of fuel oil over a ten-year period in spite of an open price term, with the price to be set according to the §2-305 gap filler, you can look to *Stern Oil Co., Inc. v. Brown*, 817 N.W.2d 395 (S.D. 2012).

Finally, and to bring things closer to home, has something like this ever happened to you?

> [A Mr. Ted Pauly] visited a Houlihan's restaurant in Brick, New Jersey. While there, he purchased "several beers . . . and several mixed drinks" offered on the menu. The prices for the beverages Mr. Pauly ordered and consumed were not listed on the menu. Mr. Pauly did not learn of the Brick Houlihan's beverage prices until he received a check for these drinks after he had consumed them. After Pauly received the check, he proceeded to pay his bill in full.

Mr. Pauly may have paid the amount he was billed, but he apparently was not happy about it. He subsequently sought to bring an action against the restaurant chain alleging among other things that the amount he was billed was greater than "a good faith reasonable price" for what he had consumed (and furthermore that his paying of his tab could not be construed as his acquiescence to the fact that the price was appropriate because under New Jersey law, a bar or restaurant patron is considered guilty of theft if he or she purposefully walks out of the establishment without paying). The district court judge declined to grant the defendant's summary judgment motion, noting that §2-305 of the Code was relevant and that Mr. Pauly should have the opportunity to show as the litigation progressed that he had been charged an excessive, unreasonable price for what he had consumed.

6. a. Even though the quantity of nuts to be sold under this agreement has been left indefinite, there is a binding contract. This is a *requirements contract*, and it is dealt with in §2-306(1). What is important here is that Candy's situation is such that it makes sense to talk of a "stated estimate" or a "normal or otherwise comparable prior . . . requirement." The parties can each have in contemplation at least some idea of roughly how many nuts they are talking about over the next three years. Assume that Candy was not a manufacturer with some kind of "pecan requirement" and could make no estimate of how many she might want over time. For instance, she could herself be a speculator and a dealer in nuts. She waits until the price is right and then buys as many as she can. If the price is not right, she simply leaves them be. She never really *needs* any kind of nut at any time, although she may really *want* them. Comment 1 seems to say that there would still be a contract to bind Shelly for three years, but is that correct? How can you speak of a nut speculator's "requirements" for pecans? How can you measure what she needs in "good faith"?

In this example you were also asked about how your answer might change if Candy had not agreed to buy her pecans exclusively from Shelly over the three years. It would at first appear that *exclusivity* is necessary to the very idea of a requirements contract. How can you say I will buy my "requirements" from you but also be free to buy the same stuff from others? The Sixth Circuit found no binding requirements contract in *Orchard Group, Inc. v. Konica Medical Corp.*, 135 F.3d 421 (6th Cir. 1998), where the factual background disclosed no promise of exclusivity on the buyer's part and where, furthermore, the dealing between the parties gave no identifiable quantity term as an estimate or one that could be implied from prior course of dealing. To the same effect is *Brooklyn Bagel Boys, Inc. v. Earthgrains Refrigerated Dough Products, Inc.*, 212 F.3d 373 (7th Cir. 2000), where the court found the agreement between the parties not to be a requirements contract, "as it does not explicitly obligate Earthgrains to purchase all, or any specified quantity, of its requirements of bagels for [its] Fort Payne facility from Brooklyn Bagel."

At least two courts confronted with contracts that did not have any language of exclusivity, however, salvaged the agreements by concluding that exclusivity could be implied from the particular circumstances. *Cyril Bath Co. v. Winters Industries*, 892 F.2d 465 (6th Cir. 1989), and *PMC Corp. v. Houston Wire & Cable Co.*, 797 A.2d 125 (N.H. 2002).

A third case went further. *Hoover's Hatchery, Inc. v. Utgaard*, 447 N.W.2d 684 (Iowa App. 1989), involved baby chicks—hundreds of thousands of them. Hoover alleged a contract under which his hatchery, which took such chicks and raised them, would supply substantially all of Utgaard's chick requirements for 1985. An initial estimate was that 400,000 chicks would be required. Utgaard took far fewer. Hoover ended up with hundreds of thousands of chicks on his hands that he could not easily resell. He sued for his damages. Utgaard argued that no contract for any number of chicks had ever arisen. Specifically he claimed that there could not be a requirements contract under §2-306(1) since he had nowhere agreed to use chicks only from Hoover. He pointed to the fact that Hoover would have been aware that he, Utgaard, would be raising some chicks that had been hatched in his own hatchery.

The Iowa Court of Appeals concluded that exclusivity was not an absolute prerequisite to the establishment of a requirements contract. How then could it ever be determined whether the buyer had kept to its end of the §2-306(1) bargain? The court concluded that "the inclusion of [the buyer's] expected requirements set forth in the correspondence which constitutes the agreement, is a sufficient standard by which the good faith of the parties may be measured." Under this type of analysis, if Candy did not promise to buy *all* of the pecans she required from Shelly, perhaps we could conclude that she did commit herself to buy something like 1,000 to 1,200 pounds a month from him, at least if she used that many in her ongoing business. Once she started needing many more, she would presumably be free to go to someone else and ask for a lower price on the rest of the nuts. Is that fair to Shelly? If he has committed himself to her, shouldn't she at least give him first crack at any larger orders? Cases like *Hoover's Hatchery* make for interesting discussion, but in practice the parties almost invariably will carefully express the exclusivity of a requirements deal if that is what is contemplated, and the issue should never arise.

b. Shelly will probably be bound to deliver this larger amount of nuts. Section 2-306, having established that agreements with vague "requirements" quantity terms are enforceable, then sets forth two separate criteria as to how much can be or must be taken by the buyer. The first test is that of "good faith." Once again we recall that in Article 2, good faith requires not only honesty in fact but commercially reasonable behavior. Certainly Candy has not been dishonest here. She's telling no lies or anything like that. Is her behavior reasonable in light of her situation and commercial practices? It would help if we knew more about the commercial setting and what type of elasticity could have been anticipated here. I'd think it hard to find Candy guilty of bad faith just because her business was booming.

A second criterion enunciated in §2-306(1) is that "no quantity unreasonably disproportionate" to the stated estimates (if there were such estimates) may be demanded by the buyer. Here Candy is asking for something like twice as much as was estimated. Is that disproportionate? If so, is it *unreasonably disproportionate?* Look at Comment 2:

> [A] sudden expansion of the plant by which requirements are to be measured would not be included within the scope of the contract as made but normal expansion undertaken in good faith would be within the scope of this section.

Candy's recent success with the Pecan Supreme seems to me more a normal expansion than a sudden one, but you have to admit the difference is not all that obvious.

The courts have not come up with any single test to determine whether a request is unreasonably disproportionate so as to fail under §2-306(1). Indeed it would be unreasonable of us to expect that they could. One court enumerated the factors to be considered thusly:

> A number of factors should be taken into account in the event that a buyer's requirements greatly exceed the contract estimate. These include the following: (1) the amount by which the requirements exceed the contract estimate; (2) whether the seller had any reasonable basis on which

> to forecast or anticipate the requested increase . . . ; (3) the amount, if any, by which the market price of the goods in question exceeded the contract price; (4) whether such an increase in market price was itself fortuitous; and (5) the reason for the increase in requirements.

Orange & Rockland Utilities, Inc. v. Amerada Hess Corp., 397 N.Y.S.2d 814 (App. Div. 1977). In Candy's case the reason for the increase seems perfectly benign. And as far as we know, Shelly is not claiming that his financial distress is the result of any increase in market value of the nuts, fortuitous or otherwise. It seems Candy is within her rights here to insist on the 2,000 pounds.

c. Under this set of facts, Shelly probably would not be obligated to deliver the larger amount of nuts. Look again at the factors given by the court in the *Amerada Hess* case. Elsewhere in its opinion that court noted:

> It is well settled that a buyer in a rising market cannot use a fixed price in a requirements contract for speculation. . . . Nor can a buyer arbitrarily and unilaterally change certain conditions prevailing at the time of the contract so as to take advantage of market conditions at the seller's expense.

Note also the concern about the fact of a rising market price in Comment 2.

You might have a question about whether Candy's request, if it is found to be out-of-bounds here, fails because it is made in bad faith or because of its being "unreasonably disproportionate" to the estimate. In truth, while the subsection lays these out as two distinct concepts, they quickly blend one into each other—at least when the buyer's good faith is subject to a test of commercial reasonableness. You can see that the two are not easily kept distinct in Comment 2. This is presumably nothing to worry about. The two concepts certainly don't conflict.

d. The problem here is whether the buyer can in effect scale its requirements back to zero without being liable to its supplier under a requirements contract. There is no easy answer to this. Scaling back to zero is certainly possible. Comment 2 says, "A shut-down by a requirements buyer for lack of orders might be permissible when a shut-down merely to curtail losses would not." One court, dealing with the analogous situation of whether an outputs seller could stop making the single product involved even as it continued in business generally, set the test as whether "its losses from continuance would be more than trivial." *Feld v. Henry S. Levy & Sons, Inc.*, 335 N.E.2d 320 (N.Y. 1975). The court contrasted such a "trivial" loss or the "yield of less profit" with something like "a bankruptcy or genuine imperiling of the very existence of [the output producer's] entire business," which would presumably allow cessation of production without liability. If *Feld* is to be believed, it would be very hard for Candy to avoid liability should she stop making the pecan candies for any of the reasons given.

There are situations, of course, where the requirements buyer may actually end up buying nothing and still not be in breach of the contract. In *R.A. Weaver and Assocs., Inc. v. Asphalt Construction, Inc.*, 587 F.2d 1315 (D.C. Cir. 1978), the court determined that the parties had entered into a requirements contract under which the buyer, a construction company, had agreed to buy from the seller all of the limestone it would need on a particular project. When it later turned out that no limestone whatsoever was called for in the revised construction specifications, buyer notified seller that it would not need any of the stone. The buyer was held not to be in breach. It had acted in good faith. Furthermore, the circuit court held, while zero would seem to be "the quintessentially" disproportionate amount, §2-306(1) does not preclude reductions all the way to nothing if they are made in good faith.

A later case, *Empire Gas Corp. v. American Bakeries Co.*, 840 F.2d 1333 (7th Cir. 1988), went somewhat further. Judge Posner, writing for the majority, declared that the concluding language in §2-306(1) about disproportionality had been intended by the drafters to apply only where the requirements buyer was demanding *more than* had been estimated or anticipated. In the case of a *lowering* of the demand, even to the point of demanding nothing, the only test is that of good faith. This does not mean that the subsection has no bite when the buyer makes drastically reduced demands. In *Empire Gas* itself the buyer was found to be in bad faith for taking nothing under the contract, where throughout the lengthy litigation it offered no reason for its actions that would justify a conclusion other than that it had simply had "second thoughts" about the terms of the agreement. For a buyer's request for less than was anticipated to be in good faith "requires at a minimum that the reduction of requirements not have been motivated solely by a reassessment of the balance of advantages and disadvantages under the contract to the buyer."

The *Empire Gas* analysis was followed in both *Sea Link Int'l, Inc. v. Osram Sylvania, Inc.*, 969 F. Supp. 781 (S.D. Ga. 1997), and *Schawk v. Donruss Trading Cards, Inc.*, 746 N.E.2d 18 (Ill. App. 2001), and in both instances the buyer was not found to have been lacking in good faith even though its requirements under the circumstances ended up being zero. The district court in *Sea Link* confessed itself particularly "confused" as to how the supplier could have argued itself to have been caught off-guard, with an excess inventory of almost one-half million of the component parts that it had been supplying under the requirements contract, when in fact the buyer had been signaling the supplier for some time that its need for the particular part was soon to come to an end due to a change in the needs of its own buyers. "It appears, from the evidence presented, that Sea Link [the supplier] simply 'over-ordered' jack screws [the part in question] beyond its customer's needs, leaving excess inventory for which Sea Link, not [the customer], remains liable."

Two more decisions both consider the basic result in *Empire Gas*—that when a buyer takes less than originally estimated in a requirements contract, its actions are to be tested by the good faith test only—as the majority view. See *Dienes Corp. v. Long Island R.R. Co.*, 2002 WL 603043 (E.D.N.Y.), and *MDC Corp., Inc. v. John H. Harland Co.*, 228 F. Supp. 2d 387 (S.D.N.Y. 2002). The Supreme Court of Alabama, however, while conceding the wide support for the *Empire Gas* analysis, has chosen to differ. In *Simcala, Inc. v. American Coal Trade, Inc.*, 821 So. 2d 197 (Ala. 2001), the court held that, under what it took as the "plain meaning" of §2-306(1), "unreasonably disproportionate" decreases in requirements can be impermissible even if the buyer has acted in good faith. As to *Empire Gas* and its progeny, the court concluded, "If adverse effects on market conditions warrant a different result, it is for the Legislature, not this Court, to amend the statute."

In deciding the *Empire Gas* case, Judge Posner commented, as others have before and since, on how relatively few reported cases there are on the problem of scaled-back requirements. His observation is worth quoting (even if obviously not persuasive to the Alabama Supreme Court):

> This is a good sign; it suggests that, while we might think it unsatisfactory for the law to be unclear on so fundamental a question, the people affected by the law are able to live with the lack of certainty. The reason may be that parties linked in an ongoing relationship—the usual situation under a requirements contract—have a strong incentive to work out their disagreements amicably rather than see the relationship destroyed by litigation.

As a student of Article 2, are you as sanguine about the lack of certainty here? But then if the parties involved can learn to live with it, shouldn't we? In *Keyes Helium Co. v. Regency Gas Services, L.P.*, 393 S.W.3d 858 (Tex. App. 2012), in which the Court of Appeals of Texas, following a lengthy review of the controversy, decided to take the path charted by *Empire Gas* and the line of cases following it. "In reaching this conclusion," the court wrote, "we reject [the plaintiff's] reliance on [the Alabama Supreme Court's decision in] *Simcala, Inc. v. American Coal Trade, Inc.*... Since its publication, no other court has followed its holding."

e. The problem now is not lack of certainty over quantity but the lack of a definite term. Under §2-309(2) the agreement is valid "for a reasonable time but unless otherwise agreed may be terminated at any time by either party." On the need for "reasonable notification" on the part of either Candy or Shelly to terminate, see subsection (3). So either party could end the agreement at any time but would have to give the other some reasonable warning. After several years of operation Candy could not, presumably, call Shelly on the 15th of a month and announce she wasn't taking any pecans the following month. Nor could Shelly take Candy's order in the regular manner and then on the 16th inform her that he wasn't filling that order.

7. Under §2-307 it is a question of fact whether "the circumstances give [Sol] the right to make . . . delivery in lots" apportioning the price among the lots. A *lot* is defined in §2-105(5). As you might remember from your Contracts course, under the common law it was regularly held that all of the goods had to be delivered or tendered before any money was due on any of them. This was the result, for example, in *Kelly Construction Co. v. Hackensack Brick Co.*, 103 A. 417 (N.J. 1918). As you can see from Comment 3, the drafters' intention was to reject this result and to substitute a rule based on the facts of the particular situation. From the earlier part of that Comment, it appears that Sol has a good argument here that Babs should take the single load and pay for it. Dirt is, after all, dirt.

8. Bert shouldn't have to take the partial shipment. A dinette set is not the kind of thing that can be delivered in lots. The value of sets like this is that they match, and the buyer shouldn't have to accept any part until he or she can look at all of the pieces together to be sure they do in fact make up a good set. Nothing in §2-307 is to the contrary; the general rule is still tender of a single delivery, and there is nothing in "the circumstances" here that would change that result.

9. a. Under §2-308(a), the place of delivery is Sam's place of business, or if he has none, his residence. Dave will have to come over and pick up the car. In reality it is probably the very rare situation where this tie-breaking provision comes into play. Note that §2-308 sets forth the place of delivery only where the parties have not "otherwise agreed." Remember that agreement on this point could be found in a trade usage, a course of dealing, or a course of performance. The responsibility for delivery may also arise from reference to one of the so-called delivery terms, such as F.O.B. or the Incoterms, which will be discussed in Chapter 24.

   b. Under §2-309(1) Sam must deliver within "a reasonable time." Is a week too late? You can make the call. If Dave plans to rely later on Sam's failure to deliver on time, wouldn't it be prudent for him to make some kind of demand for action before he uses Sam's lateness as an excuse to call the whole deal off? In *Lundy v. Low*, 408 S.E.2d 144

(Ga. App. 1991), no time for delivery had been set and the buyer of some Christmas trees argued that those delivered on December 5 had come too late. The court had little patience with this argument, especially in light of the fact that the buyers had "expressed their gratitude for the trees on December 27" and had told the seller that they planned to purchase trees again from him in the following year. If timing is that important to the buyer, of course, he or she is best off setting a particular date for delivery in the agreement and insisting upon delivery by that date.

c. Under §2-310(a) the assumption is that payment is due on delivery. Credit in favor of either the seller or the buyer must be mutually agreed upon. Of course in many situations, such agreement can be found in trade terms, but that wouldn't seem to be the case here. The sale is for cash. Dave must pay cash to get the car. This is also found in §§2-507 and 2-511. Will giving a personal check be enough? See §2-511(2) and (3) and Comment 4 to that section. We are told payment by check is "commercially normal and proper," at least where the party giving the check is "seemingly solvent." It would have made sense for Sam to get Dave's express agreement that payment was to be made in cash or by an equivalent, say a certified check. If he did not, §2-511(2) does give him the right to demand payment in legal tender, but he's going to have to allow Dave a reasonable extension of time to produce the cash.

For a very interesting, if somewhat unusual, example of §2-310 in operation, see *State of Oregon v. Alexander*, 64 P.3d 1148 (Or. App. 2003). The agreement was for the purchase and sale of hay. The buyer left his truck and trailer at the sellers' farm with the keys in it. As agreed, the sellers' son and an employee loaded the truck and trailer with hay and drove it to the front gate of the sellers' farm. When the buyer returned to take the hay, he got into a "dispute" about the quantity that the sellers had provided. (The evidence was unclear as to whether a gun was brandished by the buyer during the incident.) The buyer got into his truck and drove it and the loaded trailer away. He did not pay for the hay prior to his driving off with it. As a matter of fact, he had still not paid anything for the hay as of the date of his trial—and conviction on criminal charges of second-degree theft. The Oregon Court of Appeals affirmed his conviction based on §2-310, from which it deduced that, in the absence of contrary agreement, "the seller is entitled to retain possession of the goods until the buyer pays for them" and that the evidence at trial supported the jury's determination that the sellers still had the right to possession of their hay at the time the buyer drove off with it.

10. Under §2-311(1) there is a contract here even though the agreement leaves "particulars of performance" to be specified by Blandings. Here both the assortment and the place of delivery were left to her as buyer. She is then allowed to set the specifications "in good faith and within limits set by commercial reasonableness." It all depends on the facts. Is she being commercially reasonable in asking for shipment to Mexico? It isn't clear. If Shipshape is to pay for the shipping and if international shipment is much more expensive, maybe she is not within her rights. If Shipshape is in Texas, of course, shipment to Mexico might be cheaper than to New England. Is it commercially reasonable to ask for all large boxes? Again, we'd have to know more about the situation.

    If Blandings does not set the specifications in time, §2-311(3) gives Shipshape an excuse if his delivery is late because of this. In addition, after a time, he may be able to treat the failure on her part as a breach.

PART III

Warranty Terms

CHAPTER 10

The Warranties of Title and Against Infringement

This chapter deals with two related topics that are sometimes dealt with at different points in the Sales course. The first is the concept of title and how title in goods passes from one party to another. The second topic is the warranty of title under §2-312. If you are now only dealing with preliminary title issues, you can skip the last section of text and work through only the first three examples. When you later hit the warranty of title material, you can revisit this chapter, concentrating on that last bit of text and the later examples.

THAT "INTANGIBLE SOMETHING" AND PRACTICAL PEOPLE

Prior to the adoption of the Uniform Commercial Code, a whole host of issues in the law of sales were dominated by the concept of title. Title is basically a property notion. In a society where private ownership of property is not only possible but on the order of something sacred, the concept of title has come to sum up the whole complex relationship that a person has with the things he or she owns. Make that he, she, or it owns, for we know that under our law title to property can be held by "persons," nonhuman legal constructs such as a corporation or a trust. Indeed, the very idea of "legal personality" in the common law can be seen as a question of what manner of individual, organization, or collective can legally hold title to property in its own name.

That to which you hold title is the stuff that is yours—yours to possess, use, or dispose of as you please, and which you can protect against the claims of the rest of the world. If you have title to it, you can take it where you want and do with it what you will. You can give it to a friend, recover it from a thief, or toss it into a ravine. The word *title* encompasses a lot. Unfortunately, words that carry so much weight do not serve so well when precision is required. The drafters of the Code thought this was definitely true of "title." Whatever may have been its history or its value in property law, it never served with distinction in the law of sales. Cases on title were legion, concerning just about every issue in sales law. Even if one was able to work through and make sense of any particular line of cases, trying to apply this learning to a different question (even if it also hinged on "title") tended only to result in additional confusion, rarely insight or any measure of clarity. And it was said that the resourceful lawyer could always find authoritative statements about "title" to support just about any side of a proposition, no matter how tangentially related to the case at hand.

In the single Comment to §2-101, the very first section of Article 2, the drafters make their position known in no uncertain terms:

> The arrangement of the present Article is in terms of contract for sale and the various steps of its performance. The legal consequences are stated as following directly from the contract and action taken under it without resorting to the idea of when property or title passed or was to pass as being the determining factor. The purpose is to avoid making practical issues between practical men turn upon the location of an intangible something, the passing of which no man can prove by evidence and to substitute for such abstractions proof of words and actions of a tangible nature.

The drafters meant to accomplish their goal by making the concept of title and even the use of the word irrelevant to a large number of important issues where previously, including under the predecessor Uniform Sales Act, title had been determinative. Note, most specifically, the preamble to §2-401:

> Each provision of this Article with regard to the rights, obligations and remedies of the seller, the buyer, purchasers or other third parties applies *irrespective of title to the goods* except where the provision refers to title.

The emphasis is mine, but it might as well be that of the drafters. As examples of issues that were once mired in the world of title but which the Code now deals with directly and without reference to that concept, we can point to the problem of risk of loss (which will be dealt with in Part V) and the seller's action for the price under §2-709 (to be considered along with other remedies in Chapter 26).

PASSING TITLE AROUND

Having observed the significant degree to which the Code downplays the abstraction of title, we now turn to the situations in which it *does* matter. Article 2 does not, indeed could not, avoid the notion altogether. In fact, the very definition of a *sale* in §2-106(1) provides that it "consists in the passing of title from the seller to the buyer for a price" and points us to §2-401, which deals with "Passing of Title" among other things. For various purposes, the problem of who has title, whether it passes, and when it passes must be determined. The question of *when* title passes from the seller to the buyer is dealt with in §2-401, which you may want to read now. The basic idea is that the purchaser and seller may agree as they please regarding when title will pass, but in the absence of such an agreement, the time of delivery of the goods or of a document of title covering the goods will be key. Fortunately, the time when title passes rarely causes much problem, as the issues in the law of sales to which it had once been so central (primarily risk of loss) are now resolved under Article 2 with no reference to title whatsoever.

The issues still remaining, and to which we must give some attention, have to do with not when but *whether* title passes at all. Did the seller have title? Does the buyer get title? This last question will obviously be crucial if the warranty of title is to mean anything. The initial questions of this chapter explore these fundamental concerns. In particular they explore the workings of §2-403, which you should read in conjunction with these questions.

Discussion of these issues seems inevitably (and unfortunately) to revolve around three phrases: *good title*, *void title*, and *voidable title*. A word of warning is in order. *Good title* (also called *real title* or *clear title*) is not defined in the Code, but it can mean only one thing—just plain title. It is the legal position of ownership that we've been talking about. In theory at least, either you have title or you don't. It is unencumbered and uncontested.

On the other hand, what is sometimes referred to as *void title* isn't title at all. In fact it is the very absence of title. A person may claim whatever he or she wants, but whether the person making the claim knows it or not, if that person doesn't have title, then he or she just doesn't have title. As you'll see in the analysis of the examples to follow, we tend to use the term *void title* when referring to an item in the hands of a thief or someone who has taken from a thief, but it would be just as correct to say that I, your author, have *void title* to the Chrysler Building. Believe me, I don't own it. I do not have title to it. Not even a bit. My guess is that you have *void title* to the Chrysler Building along with me.

The third phrase, *voidable title*, is most troublesome of all, not least because §2-403 uses the term without ever defining it, though it does give some examples of how it can be created. The wording suggests it is title that is presumptively valid, but subject to being invalidated. Best of all is to avoid worrying about *voidable title* in the abstract altogether. What will matter are the particulars, and the questions will run through the various possibilities to be considered. "Voidable title" is as "voidable title" does, and it shouldn't end up being too mysterious if you allow yourself to think about it on a case-by-case basis.

THE WARRANTY OF TITLE AND AGAINST INFRINGEMENT

Whatever this strange thing title is, it is something that the buyer wants and expects to get from the seller as an integral part of the deal. If the seller cannot or does not provide title, the buyer obviously will be hurt and will deserve some legal right to relief. The buyer gets this protection as part of the contract of sale by virtue of §2-312. Basically the idea is pretty clear-cut. In a typical contract of sale, the seller warrants that "the title conveyed shall be good, and its transfer rightful" and furthermore that title to the goods sold is delivered free of any encumbrances of which the buyer is unaware. Buyers are to get what they expect—more precisely, what any reasonable person in their situation would expect they would be getting. The later examples in this chapter deal with the operation of §2-312 and the warranty protection it provides.

Examples

EXAMPLES

1. Alice is the owner of a necklace. It has been in her family for years, and you may assume that she has title. She gives the necklace as a gift to her niece Betty. Betty wears it for some time before selling it to Clara.
   (a) Did Betty have title? Does Clara?
   (b) Suppose that instead of giving Betty the necklace as a gift, Alice only lent it to her to wear to a party. After the party Betty, who lost heavily at the gaming tables, sells it to Clara to raise money to pay her debts. In this situation, does Clara get title to the necklace?

2. Among the several valuable paintings in his collection, Dan is the proud owner of a beautiful portrait called "Young Man with a Horn." One day he discovers the painting missing. It turns out it has been stolen by one Earl. Earl sold it to Felice, who had no reason to question how it came into Earl's possession. Felice in turn sold it to Gayle. Gayle happens to show her new acquisition to her friend Dan, who recognizes it as the piece missing from his collection.
   (a) Can Dan recover the painting from Gayle?
   (b) Suppose that Earl did not actually steal the painting. Instead he arranges to buy it from Dan at a very hefty but perfectly reasonable

price. Earl picks up the painting, giving Dan in exchange a personal check for the entire purchase price. The check bounces. Dan tries to get in touch with Earl, but the rascal has disappeared. When he later sees the painting in Gayle's possession, will Dan be able legally to get it back? Would it make any difference to your analysis if Dan could show that the only reason he took a personal check from Earl was that Dan thought him to be another person, also named Earl, who was known to be one of the wealthiest and most upstanding people in the community? Finally, suppose that instead of taking a check, Dan had insisted on cash on delivery. At the time of sale, Earl had picked up the rather bulky canvas and then said he was taking it out to his car to stow safely in the trunk. He said he'd be right back with the cash. Earl, of course, disappears. Now what result? There must be a lesson in all of this. What is it?

(c) In all of the situations considered above, would it make any difference if Felice could be shown to have been aware that Earl had obtained the painting in the way that he did and had used this information to buy it at a "steal" from Earl? What if Felice had no direct knowledge of Earl's way of doing business, but the price for which he sold it to her was very much below what such a painting would normally be worth?

3. Rick has a rare and expensive electric guitar, which he values highly. The story is that it had once been played by Elvis. But it is on the blink. He takes it in for repair to Cathy's Music City, a retail store selling various musical instruments which also has a service department. When he goes to pick it up, an embarrassed Cathy tells him that one of her clerks mistakenly sold it to Chris. Can Rick just go to Chris's house and insist that he get the guitar back? What more do you need to know to advise Rick?

4. Recall the situation in Example 2, the case of the purloined painting. If Gayle is made to give the painting back to Dan, what rights does she have against Felice? Should Felice be found liable, does she in turn have rights against anyone?

5. Recall the situation in Example 3, where the "Elvis" guitar ended up in Chris's hands. When Rick comes calling, Chris might understandably decide to put up a fight to keep such a precious object. She engages a high powered attorney in an effort to retain the instrument, but eventually loses the case and has to give it back to Rick.

(a) What amount can she now collect from her seller, Cathy's Music City? See §§2-714 and 2-715. Assume that Chris had originally paid $12,400 for the instrument but that she had soon thereafter been offered upwards of $16,000 for it. Assume further that she had to pay her attorney $2,560 for her unsuccessful defense.

(b) Assume instead that in the previous question Chris ultimately prevails and is allowed to keep the guitar. She wins! Of course, she is still out $2,560 in attorney's fees and maybe more as a result of all the hassle. Should she have any right to recover from Cathy for the costs of her *successful* defense?

6. I buy an Alpha smartphone from Smartphones, Inc, a retailer of electronic goods. Months later, Beta sues Alpha for patent infringement for using its technology. Beta gets an injunction against Alpha's use of its technology in its phones, and my phone stops working. Do I have a claim against Smartphones? What if my contract with Smartphones stated that the phone was sold "AS IS"?

7. Pacific Swimwear, a clothing retailer, purchased from a supplier, Olaes Enterprises, a large number of "Hot Sauce Monkey" tee-shirts depicting, on the front, a monkey drinking a bottle of hot sauce and, on the back, the same monkey in apparent pain, expelling fire. Centered underneath each of the images is a two-word caption: on the front, the phrase "Smile Now"; on the back, the phrase "Cry Later." A third-party clothing maker, Smile Now Cry Later Inc., filed a complaint in the federal district court against Pacific Swimwear for trademark infringement. Its complaint alleged that Olaes had manufactured shirts that infringed on SNCL's trademark, and Pacific Swimwear had sold the shirts in its retail stores. SNCL included in its complaint a copy of its registered trademark, which depicted two masks in the style of ancient Greek theater masks. One of the masks is smiling and the other is crying. Underneath the corresponding masks are the words "Smile Now" and "Cry Later." In the ensuing litigation, Pacific Swimwear, with cooperation from Olaes, defended itself, denying that the "Hot Sauce Monkey" tee-shirts infringed SNCL's trademark. SNCL filed a motion for a preliminary injunction barring further sales of the "Hot Sauce Monkey" tee-shirts, which was denied by the district court. All parties then entered into a settlement agreement. Pacific Swimwear then brought an action against Olaes under §2-312(3) seeking to recover the costs it had incurred in having to defend itself and then settle SNCL's action. Is Pacific Swimwear entitled to recovery?

8. Harry buys an Oriental rug from his friend Marv for a cost of $12,000. The rug is old and is worn in spots. The parties agree that the sale will be "as is," and a provision to this effect is included in the contract of sale. It later turns out that the rug, unbeknownst to Marv, had once been stolen from a mansion in the community. Its true owner shows up to recover it from Harry.
   (a) Can Marv use the "as is" provision in defense against a breach of warranty claim by Harry?
   (b) Suppose instead that Harry bought the rug from Marv at a foreclosure sale. The rug had been the property of Joan, who had borrowed

money from Marv putting up the valuable rug as collateral. When Joan did not repay Marv, he as a secured creditor was entitled to take possession of the rug and could sell it off to get at least part of his money back. It is under these circumstances that Marv made the sale. When it turns out the rug had been stolen by Joan and is reclaimed by its rightful owner, can Harry go against Marv on the warranty of good title?

(c) Finally, imagine that Marv is a stranger to Harry. In fact he's a bit of a mysterious stranger. He shows up at Harry's home one evening claiming that he's heard Harry is "the kind of man who appreciates fine oriental rugs." He offers to sell Harry the rug at a price that seems, to Harry, to be incredibly low. Marv explains that he has "low overhead," which does seem true since he appears to be operating out of the back of a pick-up truck. Harry buys the rug. Has he gotten any warranty protection if he should end up without good title?

Explanations

1. a. Alice has title to the necklace originally; at least, that's what I asked you to assume. (Of the goods to which you would claim title, how many of these could you actually *prove* were truly yours? For the most part, we tend to assume title in goods just because there's no reason to doubt it.) When Alice gives the bauble as a gift, the effect is to vest title in Betty. This has nothing to do with the law of sales. It comes from property law and the legal rules pertaining to gifts, so we needn't get into any detail here. Suffice it to say that the real essence of a gift of personal property is not simply transferring possession (that isn't even absolutely necessary), but rather bestowing title on someone else. Once Betty has title, she can sell the thing and, by doing so, transfer the title to Clara. This last bit is just the direct application of the first sentence in §2-403(1): "A purchaser of goods acquires all title which [her] transferor had or had power to transfer. . . ." As a matter of fact, this language can be made to justify the first result we needed, that Betty had acquired title, because the Code's idea of a "purchaser" is pretty broad. See §1-201(b)(30), which leads us to §1-201(b)(29) and the notion that *purchase* under the Code includes taking by "gift or other voluntary transaction creating an interest in property."

   b. Under these facts, Betty never got title to the necklace. Since her aunt let her have possession, at least temporarily, she would be a *bailee* but that's all, and we presume that this does not create "an interest in property" in Betty. This being so, and because a seller with void title cannot pass good title on to her buyer, Clara does not have title. Where does this leave Clara? Holding Alice's property, that's where.

Jumping ahead just a bit, we recognize that in this situation if Alice becomes aware that Clara has the necklace, she can get it back from her. Where does *that* leave Clara? It certainly isn't hard to see that Clara should have rights against Betty here. And, as we'll see, that's just what §2-312 will give her.

It isn't hard to see just from these first two simple examples that the question of who has title to a piece of personal property, even if in theory nice and neat, can be made very messy by the facts of a situation. The result in the second question, when the necklace is only loaned temporarily to Betty, does not depend on Betty's believing she does or does not have title to the piece of jewelry. The conversation between Alice and Betty may have been ambiguous, and Betty could have honestly thought that her aunt was giving it to her forever. We can assume that she never would have sold it to Clara if she had realized that eventually a court would determine that she hadn't been given an outright gift in the situation. But Betty's belief as to her status at the time she sells means nothing to Clara's interest. As you'll see from the following questions, law professors love to seize on the case of property that was at one time in its history the subject of an out-and-out theft when discussing problems of title. In truth, many of the actual cases that come up do have this intriguing element in them, but as the story of Alice, Betty, and Clara shows, there can be genuine questions as to title, and an innocent person can try to pass on title that he or she does not legally have to give, even when there's been no skullduggery in the past.

An interesting case is *Kenyon v. Abel*, 36 P.3d 1161 (Wyo. 2001). Rick Kenyon, the defendant, purchased a painting for $25 from the Salvation Army. It turned out that the thrift store had mistakenly taken the box in which the painting had been stored when it made a pickup from the Abel household of other boxes that were in fact intended for donation. It further turned out that the painting was the work of a noted Western artist and was valued at somewhere between $8,000 and $15,000. Beyond that, the work had special sentimental value to the plaintiff because it had been given by the artist himself to a beloved aunt who had expressed to her nephew her desire that it always remain in the family. The trial court found that Abel had no intent to give the painting to the Salvation Army and that, hence, the thrift shop never gained title through gift. It followed that it had void title, which could never legitimately be transferred to Kenyon even though he qualified as a good faith purchaser for value. The work went back to Abel.

2. a. Dan can get the painting back from Gayle. In fact he can get it back from anyone who has it, whenever and wherever he finds it. Well, not

exactly whenever. If enough time has passed, Dan may have a problem with the Statute of Limitations in making his claim against Gayle. This has been a problematic issue with the recovery of art looted by the Nazis. A movie called *Woman in Gold* deals with these legal issues. But leaving that issue aside, in this example we have a chain of possession involving theft. Earl never had title. He didn't take by anything that the Code, or any other rule of law, would see as "creating an interest" (by which is presumably meant creating some legally enforceable interest) in the painting. When Earl sells it to Felice, she cannot and does not get good title. Because Felice does not have good title, Gayle cannot get good title by purchase. It is as straightforward as that. As a practical matter, we don't have to worry about how Dan goes about getting actual possession. Once he proves it's his painting that had been stolen, there shouldn't be any difficulty. His right to get it need not be found in the Code—it's a classic property action (*replevin*) to recover one's property wrongfully held by another. Notice again that this is so in spite of our assumption that neither Gayle nor Felice had any bad motive or any reason to know they were dealing in hot property. For two cases applying the principle that valid title can never be claimed in goods that have once been stolen, see *Alamo Rent-A-Car, Inc. v. Mendenhall*, 937 P.2d 69 (Nev. 1997) and *Depetris v. Warnock*, 2000 LEXIS 428 (N.Y. Sup. Ct.).

You might think the result given here is hard on Gayle, who will be left with nothing of value and out the amount she paid to Felice. The answer, as we will see, is that she'll be able to sue Felice for her damages. Felice will have the right to go against Earl for *her* damages. To be sure, the right to go against a thief may not be all that comforting. People like Earl tend to disappear into the night after they have carried out their wicked deeds and are rarely amenable to suit. So Felice may be left holding the bag. Again, this may not seem terribly fair to poor Felice. But remember that the alternative would be to conclude that Dan, whose property was stolen, could not recover it. What would we say to him? True, he could go after Earl and make him return the stolen property or pay the consequences. But why should Dan have to bear this terrible burden of tracking Earl down and suing him for every last penny? The real question in such cases, of course, is which of two innocent people (in our hypo, Dan or Felice) should have to bear the theft loss. The conventional wisdom, and the answer that the common law and the U.C.C. supply, is that the person who purchases from the thief should bear this risk. The conventional explanation, for what it is worth, of this allocation of risk is that the purchaser in such a situation could presumably guard against buying stolen property by checking into the Article's past history, asking the right questions, and asking to see proof of her seller's ownership. The person from whom the item is filched has presumably already done what could reasonably be done to prevent his or her stuff from being stolen. He or she would be unlikely to behave cavalierly with regard to possible thefts on the strength of a legal principle which says that the owner can get it back from whomever eventually has it. That all depends on the goods making an appearance again. Most stolen property just vanishes, and we expect owners will protect to the appropriate extent against this possibility. When it comes to dealing with thieves, at least, it definitely still is the case that the buyer must be wary.

b. First the case of the bounced check. We note that the use of checks is dying out, but the same principle would apply to any means of payment. This may seem awfully similar to what we just saw, but in fact the result will be different. Gayle has good title in the painting. How could this be? Earl's behavior is perhaps a bit less monstrous, but why should that make such a difference? The answer is to be found in the concept of voidable title and its consequences as laid out in §2-403(1) in the material that follows the first sentence. Note the second sentence: "A person with voidable title has power to transfer a good title to a good faith purchaser for value." The final part of the subsection gives four instances of when a person can get this thing called "voidable title." Here we're relying on clause (b). The painting was delivered "in exchange for a check which was later dishonored." Because this was so, Earl himself did *not* gain title; he did not have the *right* to sell what wasn't properly his to sell. What he did get was the *power* to transfer a good title to Felice, provided she is what the Code calls a *good faith purchaser for value*. We'll assume that in this situation she is such a person. But if she had purchased it at a fraction of its value from a seller who offered it out of the back of his car in a parking lot, she probably did not act in good faith, as we will shortly see. So, upon purchase, Felice had good title. Felice sells it to Gayle, who thereby gets good title. See the discussions in *Brinkley v. Haluska*, 982 N.E.2d 1019 (Ind. Ct. App. 2012) and *Hodges Wholesale Cars v. Auto Dealer's Exchange of Birmingham*, 628 So. 2d 608 (Ala. 1993).

An obvious question is why the outcome of this problem should be so different, in fact the exact opposite of the prior one. Remember the justification that was suggested there. It is at least arguable that someone who buys from a thief should have been able to avoid doing so by using a little more care and circumspection. We do not say the same thing about someone who "allows" a thief to get at this property. But here Dan did not take all the precautions he could have to avoid losing the painting to Earl in this way. He took a personal check. In the real world, that's got to be understood as taking a big risk. Personal checks can and sometimes do bounce. If Dan had wanted to further protect himself, he could have asked for cash, or for a certified check, or something of the sort. And it's also very possible in this situation that Dan allowed Earl to get his hands on the kind of documentation of ownership (for instance, a Bill of Sale signed by Dan and to all appearances perfectly valid) that Felice would expect to rely on to guard against buying something of doubtful pedigree. The equities between the two innocents, Dan and Felice, work out quite differently in this situation. See the discussion in the case of *West v. Roberts*, 143 P.3d 1037 (Colo. 2006).

The same argument explains the parallel result when we find that Dan sold to Earl believing him to be someone else. Read §2-403(1)(a). The case where Earl is supposedly buying for cash but somehow manages to drive off with the goods without having paid the money is dealt with in §2-403(1)(c). Again, Dan will suffer the consequences of not protecting himself more successfully against this kind of behavior. And finally look at §2-403(1)(d), which states that the transferee gets voidable title whenever "the delivery was procured through fraud punishable as larcenous under the criminal law." The four instances given in this section where a transferee gets voidable title are not meant by the drafters of the Code to be exhaustive. There are other situations that in the common law would give rise to such voidable title, and by virtue of the second sentence of §2-403(1), the holder in such an instance has the power to create good title in his or her purchaser. You can think of some from your knowledge of Contracts. For example, you take voidable title from a minor (a person under 18) since that person has the power to avoid the transaction.

It's worth pointing out once more that none of this business about voidable title is saying that the person whose behavior is the direct cause of all the trouble—the person who gives the bum check, who somehow forgets to deliver the cash, and so on—can rightfully benefit or get any interest in the property by this type of behavior. Our concern is with the innocent third party who deals with and buys from the person with voidable title. This leads us to the following question and the issue of just exactly who counts as a good faith purchaser for value.

c. If Felice knows how Earl came to have the painting, she cannot get good title from him. A person with voidable title can transfer good title only to a *good faith purchaser for value*. This creature plays an important role in the law of commercial transactions. He, she, or it is featured in several sections of the U.C.C. (mostly in other Articles with which we are not concerned). We will not go here into all the details and all the controversy about how someone qualifies for this favored status. Note, however, that one must first be a *purchaser*, as defined in §1-201(b)(30), and have given *value*, as defined in §1-204. Neither of these are a problem for Felice. The more difficult question here, and in most actual situations, is whether the purchaser had been acting in good faith in taking the goods. Buying property that you actually know the seller does not rightfully own would not qualify as good faith behavior.

A more difficult question is raised when we assume Felice has no direct knowledge of Earl's way of doing business, but does buy the painting at a price far below its worth. If she was well aware that the price was less than she would normally have to pay for such an item, it's probable that she wouldn't be able to qualify as a good faith purchaser. She would have a much better chance of qualifying if it were shown that she did not know she was getting such an unusual (and presumably suspicious) bargain. In such situations, the courts and commentators have in the past gotten all wrapped up in questions of whether the issue is exclusively one of the buyer's subjective knowledge and intent (the "pure-heart-and-empty-head" test) or a supposedly objective consideration of what a "reasonable person" would have or should have known under the circumstances. Prior to the introduction of the revised version of Article 1, Felice would have had to show only "honesty in fact" to prove she had acted in good faith, unless she could legitimately be considered a merchant for Article 2 purposes, in which case she would have also had to have acted in accordance with the more demanding requirement of "reasonable commercial standards of fair dealing." Since the adoption of the revised version of Article 1, however, all actors—whether they are Article 2 merchants or not—will have their good faith judged by requiring that they have behaved with "honesty in fact *and* the observance of reasonable commercial standards of fair dealing." (Except, that is, in a handful of states that, in adopting the new version of Article 1, elected to stick with the less demanding requirement of only "honesty in fact" as the definition of "good faith.") An interesting corollary to what has gone before is that *if* Felice does qualify as a good faith purchaser for value, hence actually herself getting good title, she will pass on good title to anyone who buys from her (in our case Gayle) even if *that* person does know of the improper way it got into her seller's hands. This *shelter principle* is a straightforward application of the first sentence of §2-403(1). So Gayle could get good title from Felice even if Gayle knew all about Earl's larcenous behavior. Can you think of an explanation, apart from mere contrariness of the drafters, why this should work out the way it does?

3. If Rick has trouble recovering the guitar from Chris, it will be because of the doctrine of *entrustment* as set forth in subsections (2) and (3) of §2-403. Clearly Cathy did not get title from Rick, nor is there any way for Chris to argue that Cathy had obtained voidable title. But under

subsection (2), "Any entrusting of possession of goods to a merchant who deals in goods of that kind gives him power to transfer all rights of the entruster to a buyer in ordinary course of business." Since Rick presumably had all the rights of a title holder, if this section applies to the situation, Chris now has good title. Rick could not get the guitar back from Chris and would only have an action against Cathy for conversion for what she did.

There are several subsidiary questions apparent from these subsections, but none is especially tricky. First of all, did Rick actually "entrust" the goods to Cathy? It seems clear he did. The fact that he delivered the guitar to her only for the limited purpose of repair would not, by virtue of the language in subsection (3), make any difference. See *Bank of New Hampshire v. Schreiber*, 219 B.R. 938 (D.N.H. 1998), where the requisite "entrustment" was found of a pickup truck left for repair at an auto dealership that was later sold. In our hypothetical, Cathy seems clearly to be an Article 2 merchant, but is she a merchant "who deals in goods of this kind"? This is a factual question, and the answer is not obvious from the facts given. True, she runs a retail store that sells musical instruments, but would every such mom-and-pop store deal in rare memorabilia like this piece? Does Cathy's Music City normally deal in such precious objects? Presumably the question should be addressed from the point of view of the person buying the goods. Would they think it unusual to find a rare guitar for sale in such a store?

The final question is whether Chris can qualify as a buyer in ordinary course of business from Cathy. Such a person is, like the good faith purchaser for value, a type very important to commercial law. The two are not identical. Look at the definition of the *buyer in ordinary course of business* in §1-201(b)(9). The party must be buying in good faith and "without knowledge that the sale violates the rights of another person in the goods." So Chris could not have title to the goods if she were somehow acting in bad faith or if she had reason to know that the guitar was Rick's and he wasn't interested in giving it up. Beyond that, the purchase must be from a person "in the business of selling goods of that kind." So again we come to the question of whether Cathy deals in goods "of the kind," but here more from the buyer's perspective. Was there any reason for Chris to doubt that this retail store would normally sell an item like this?

The definition of buyer in ordinary course of business also requires, in its second sentence, that "[a] person buys goods in the ordinary course if the sale to the person comports with the usual or customary practices in the kind of business in which the seller is engaged or with the seller's own usual or customary practices." In other words, a buyer in ordinary course of business generally buys from inventory. In the case of *Donovan v. Mario D'Addario Buick, Inc.*, 2009 WL 765702 (Conn. Super.), the 19-year-old Katelyn Donovan bought a used car with a car loan she was able to obtain with the help of her mother, Kathleen Donovan. All of Katelyn's dealings were with one Donald Scinto, a licensed automobile wholesaler who had been entrusted with the car by its owner, the D'Addario Buick dealership. Katelyn first saw the car when she, along with her boyfriend, met with Scinto in a Walmart parking lot where she and her boyfriend viewed and test-drove the vehicle. At this time, Katelyn signed an agreement to purchase the car. After obtaining a check under a car loan agreement facilitated by her mother's signature from a credit union, Katelyn and her boyfriend arranged to meet Scinto in a Burger King parking lot in a nearby town. There Katelyn signed the check over to Scinto and received possession of the car. At that time, however, she did not receive a temporary registration or title to the car. The car was delivered with dealer plates of unknown origin. The court found that Scinto was a merchant who dealt in used cars and further that the car in question had indeed been "entrusted" to him by its owner, the dealership. Katelyn did not, however, get good title to the car as she could not qualify as a buyer in ordinary course. The court explained as follows:

> [T]he evidence shows that the only prior information the plaintiffs had about Scinto was that he had previously sold an automobile to Katelyn's boyfriend's grandmother. Although Scinto apparently had a business address, neither plaintiff testified that they ever looked for him at that address. Indeed, all of the plaintiffs' attempts to contact Scinto were by the telephone. Additionally, Scinto initially showed Katelyn the car in a Walmart parking lot and sold it to her in a Burger King parking lot. There was no evidence presented that it was Scinto's customary practice to meet prospective buyers in random parking lots to sell cars. Furthermore, when the vehicle was sold, no temporary registration, bill of sale or title for the vehicle was furnished to the plaintiffs. The fact that the car was turned over with dealer plates should have been a red flag to anyone that there was a problem with the sale and that it was not in the ordinary course of business. Even if the 19-year-old Katelyn might not have realized it, her mother, an attorney, should have realized there was a problem. It is incomprehensible to this court that Kathleen would allow her daughter to buy this automobile in a Burger King parking lot without having met the seller or seeing the car before it was purchased. Based on these facts alone, the court finds that this transaction did not occur in the ordinary course of business.

The Court of Appeals of the State of Washington has summarized the underlying justification for the commercial law's "entrustment" doctrine, as now codified in §2-403, as follows:

> Three general policies support . . . the UCC provision placing the risk of loss on the entruster. First, it protects the innocent buyer who, based on his observation of the goods in the possession of a merchant of those goods, believes that the merchant has legal title to the goods and can, therefore, pass title in the goods to another. . . . Secondly, the entrustment clause

> reflects the idea that the entruster is in a better position than the innocent buyer to protect against the risk that an intermediary merchant will not pay for or not deliver the goods. . . . Thirdly, the entrustment clause facilitates the flow of commerce by allowing purchasers to rely on a merchant's apparent legal right to sell the goods. . . . Without the safeguards of the entrustment provision, a prudent buyer would have to delay the finalization of any sizeable sales transaction for the time necessary to research the merchant's ownership rights to the goods.

Heinrich v. Titus-Will Sales, Inc., 868 P.2d 169 (Wash. Ct. App. 1994) (citations omitted). See also *Spainerman Gallery v. Merritt*, 2003 WL 289704 (S.D.N.Y.), and *Jones v. Mitchell*, 816 So. 2d 68 (Ala. Civ. App. 2001).

A typical, if not very momentous, case that touches upon both the voidable title and entrustment concepts is *Atlas Auto Rental Corp. v. Weisberg*, 281 N.Y.S.2d 400 (N.Y. City Ct. 1967). Atlas Auto Rental would, from time to time, sell off its used autos. Herbert Schwartzman offered to purchase a two-year-old Chevrolet station wagon, which Atlas was offering for sale at $1,250. His offer of a personal check for this amount was, according to the testimony of Atlas's manager, rejected. Nevertheless, the manager allowed Schwartzman to take the car out for a test run. Schwartzman got in the car, drove off, and was never seen again, at least not by anyone at Atlas. Atlas's manager found that he still had Schwartzman's check around, but when he tried to cash it, it was returned marked "No Funds." A week later the car was traced to an establishment in the Bronx run by the defendant Weisberg, who was licensed to do business there as an auto wrecker and junk dealer. But the car was no longer there. Weisberg claimed that he had purchased it from Schwartzman for a price of $900, paying $300 down, the rest to be paid at a later time. Schwartzman had never been heard from again and never collected the rest of the $900. Weisberg had not received from him either a bill of sale or a registration certificate for the car. Where was the car? Weisberg had immediately resold it, for $1,200, to a dealer. That's the story.

Atlas brought suit against Weisberg for conversion, seeking to recover the value of the station wagon. Weisberg's defense was that he had acquired good title to the car. He made two arguments to support his claim. The first was based on §2-403(1) and the notion of voidable title. After all, the reason Atlas was aggrieved could be said to be the bounced check. But, the court reasoned, when Atlas actually delivered the car to Schwartzman it was "solely for the purpose of permitting a test run, not with any idea of conferring title upon him." Admittedly, the fact of the bounced check raised "troublesome questions as to whether or not plaintiff had in fact intended to convey a voidable title dependent on whether the check cleared," but at least if the manager's statements were to be believed, this intention did not exist when he gave Schwartzman the keys and allowed him to drive it away.

The defendant also made a claim that the auto had been entrusted to Schwartzman and that he, Weisberg, got good title under §2-403(2). But this would all depend on Schwartzman's being a merchant who deals in goods of the kind of a used Chevy. The defendant was able to offer into evidence an invoice headed "Herbert Schwartzman, Wholesale Automobiles," which he later found in his files. But it did not appear that he was relying on this when he bought from Schwartzman. Beyond this, it in no way showed that *Atlas* would have believed Schwartzman to be such a merchant. "Since the 'entrusting' provisions of UCC §2-403 are an extension of the principle of estoppel," the court concluded, "it would appear to be essential that the actual vocational status of the merchant be established, but also that the original owner and the ultimate purchaser must be shown to have been aware of that status."

If there had been any hope for Weisberg at this point, it was dashed by the court's conclusion that, under the circumstances, he could qualify as neither a good faith purchaser for value (which would have been necessary to prevail on the voidable title idea) nor a buyer in the ordinary course of business (which was crucial to the entrustment claim). After all, he was licensed in the Bronx only to do business in "junk." He had in effect paid only $300 in cash for an automobile which he was immediately able to sell for $1,200. He had apparently not been troubled that his seller could show him neither a bill of sale nor a certificate of registration. The court concluded the following:

> It was [Weisberg] who had prior dealings with Schwartzman. Certainly if he was not working with him, he had every reason to be skeptical of Schwartzman's claim of ownership. The Uniform Commercial Code protects the innocent purchaser, but it is not a shield for the sly conniver, the blindly naive, or the hopelessly gullible.

For a successful invocation of the entrustment doctrine, we can look to *Prenger v. Baker*, 542 N.W.2d 805 (Iowa 1995). *Prenger* involved a number of Iowa farmers engaged in buying and selling ostriches, emus, and other flightless birds (known as ratites). Baker sold two ostriches to Rasmus, but left them in his care. Richards then purchased them from Rasmus and sold them to Pregner. An effective entrustment of the ostriches was held to have occurred to a party who could be classed as a merchant dealing in goods of the kind and the purchaser was found to qualify as a buyer in the ordinary course, giving him clear title as against Baker. You may also want to take a look at the decision by the Supreme Court of Connecticut in *Lindholm v. Brant*, 925 A.2d 1048 (Conn. 2007), in which the defendant was found to have obtained good title under the entrustment doctrine of a painting by Andy Warhol entitled "Red Elvis" once owned by the plaintiff and her former husband. The court upheld a finding that the defendant, who had purchased the painting from one

Malmberg who "enjoyed a reputation as a well respected art dealer" located in Switzerland, was a buyer in ordinary course of the painting, having observed the idiosyncratic customary ways of doing business in the fine art market.

For a couple of cases considering what does and what does not amount to good faith purchase in the sometimes questionable dealings surrounding the purchase and sale of pieces of high-end fine art, see *Davis v. Carroll*, 937 F. Supp. 2d 390 (S.D.N.Y. 2013) and *Dorothy G. Bender Foundation, Inc. v. Carroll*, 975 N.Y.S.2d 708 (Sup. Ct. N.Y. 2013). If your interest runs more to things like livestock, 190 heifers to be exact, which were the subject of an entrustment, see *Nordhues v. Maulsby*, 815 N.W.2d 175 (Neb. 2012).

4. Gayle can sue Felice for breach of warranty and should have no trouble winning. This is the heart of §2-312, and it is perfectly direct. There is nothing in the question to suggest that Felice in selling to Gayle attempted to exclude or modify the warranty of title, so subsection (2) doesn't come into play. Under subsection (1), therefore, the contract for sale between Felice and Gayle included a warranty by Felice that "the title conveyed shall be good, and its transfer rightful." Our assumption in this question is that Dan could get the painting back, which means that the title conveyed to Gayle was not good. Felice has breached the warranty of title. Note that this result does not depend on a finding that Felice knew she could not give good title, or even that she should have known this. It's simply a matter that she didn't give what she contracted to give. What can Felice do now? Since she bought from Earl, she'll be able to go against him on the warranty of title herself. So the responsibility under the Code is ultimately Earl's, as it should be. The problem, of course, will be finding him and getting him to live up to this responsibility. The risk that he can't be forced to make amends for what he's done thus falls on Felice, the person who directly took from him.

In the question as I've set it up, Gayle had already taken the painting and paid for it. When she has to give it back, the only sensible remedy for this breach of warranty will be an action for damages. In other situations, the breach (or an arguable breach) of the warranty of title plays out in different ways. If, for example, Gayle had purchased the painting from Felice on credit, the breach of warranty would be a good defense for her when Felice tries to collect on the contract.

Suppose instead that the two had simply contracted for the purchase and sale of the painting, delivery, and payment to take place at a later date. When Felice delivers the painting, Gayle—maybe because she's sensible and cautious—is worried about whether she'll get good title. She asks Felice for some form of proof that the painting is Felice's to sell. Felice cannot show her anything of the type that would normally be available for a valuable artwork with a good pedigree. Gayle would want to argue that the delivery, lacking as it does assurances of good title, fails to conform to what was required under the contract. As we will see in Chapter 17, if the seller's delivery fails to conform, the buyer will ordinarily not have to accept the goods. Gayle may not have to take the painting. Beyond that, if Felice is never able to perform under the contract, Gayle would have an action for damages.

Note that the warranty of title will be breached not only where the buyer gets no interest in the goods whatsoever, but also where the buyer gets an interest diminished by a lien. The statute provides that "the goods shall be delivered free from any security interest or other lien or encumbrance of which [he or she] at the time of contracting has no knowledge." Thus, if the goods are later found to be worth less because there is unknown to the buyer some security interest in the goods held by a third party and that third party must be paid off, the buyer will have an action for damages against the seller.

5. a. Section 2-312 itself says nothing about the measure of damages for a breach of the warranty of title. We have to look at the general provision for damages in a breach of warranty action, which is found in §2-714. This in turn leads us to §2-715 on the buyer's incidental and consequential damages. These sections will be discussed fully in Chapter 27. We do not want to go into all the details now. Still, breach of the warranty of title is sufficiently distinct from the more typical breach of warranty action where a warranty of quality is involved, so it's worth some consideration here.

In the question as posed, clearly Chris can recover from Cathy for the loss of the guitar, but for what amount? Over the years the courts have not been terribly consistent in answering this question, first under the common law, then under the Uniform Sales Act, and now under the Code. Should Chris simply be entitled to the return of her purchase price plus any interest from the time of the sale? Or should she be able to prove that even at the time of the sale the guitar was worth more than the purchase price, say $13,400, and that she is entitled at least to "the benefit of her bargain"? Or is Chris right if she argues that the only way *now* to fully compensate her for the fact that she is left without the guitar is for her to be allowed to recover the full market value of the guitar as of the date it is taken away from her? Recently the courts seem to be moving in the direction of giving this last measure of value, at least where the goods are of the type that could have been expected to significantly appreciate in value and in fact have done so. In so ruling, they often refer with approval to the noted case of *Menzel v. List*, 246 N.E.2d 742 (N.Y. 1969), which because of the date on which the contract was entered into, was actually decided under the New York counterpart to the Uniform Sales Act. In *Menzel*, a valuable Chagall painting had been purchased by Albert List in 1955 from the Perls, proprietors of a New York art gallery, for a price of $4,000. The painting, it later turned out, was the rightful property of Mrs. Erna Menzel and her husband, who had purchased it in Belgium in 1932. When the Menzels fled Belgium at the time of the Nazi invasion in 1940, they left the picture behind. When they returned to their home six years later the picture was gone. Only a receipt had been left by the German authorities. What happened to the painting between the time of the Menzels' flight and early 1955, when the Perls purchased it from a Parisian art gallery, was unknown. Only in 1962 did Mrs. Menzel become aware that the painting was in the hands of Mr. List. She sued for its recovery and won. In the same action, List brought a third-party complaint against the Perls for breach of the warranty of title. Even though the Perls were apparently unaware of the painting's history, having relied upon the reputation of the Paris gallery, they clearly were in breach of the seller's warranty. The jury assessed damages at $22,500, the value of the painting at the time of the trial. On appeal to the Appellate Division this amount was reduced to $4,000, the purchase price List had paid, plus interest from the date of the sale to List. On further appeal, the New York Court of Appeals reinstated the judgment for the higher amount. Mr. List was entitled to damages from the Perls for the full value of the painting as of the time of trial, when the painting was taken from his possession.

A second issue in the question is whether our claimant Chris can recover from Cathy her attorney's fees spent in her unsuccessful bid to retain possession. As a matter of fact, in *Menzel v. List* the party who had to give up possession (Mr. List) was awarded attorney's fees by the jury, although the award of this amount was apparently never appealed and the court had little to say on it. A case that does consider the question in some detail, and which allows an award of the buyer's attorney's fees as legitimate consequential damages in a similar situation, is *Universal C.I.T. Credit Corp. v. State Farm Mutual Automobile Ins. Co.*, 493 S.W.2d 385 (Mo. Ct. App. 1973). Note that the Code does not provide for the prevailing party to recover attorney's fees as such; here, the claim was that the attorney's fees were a form of consequential damages.

A novel case worth noting is *De La Hoya v. Slim's Gun Shop*, 146 Cal. Rptr. 68 (Cal. Ct. App. 1978). The plaintiff had purchased what turned out to be a stolen handgun from the defendant, a licensed gun dealer, for $140. De La Hoya apparently did nothing illegal or untoward with the gun, but in any event the police became aware that he was in possession of a stolen gun and arrested him. It ultimately cost him

$800 in legal fees to have the criminal charges against him dropped. In his suit for breach of the warranty of title, the gun shop was made to pay not only the $140 value of the gun but the $800 expense it had caused the plaintiff as well.

One way a buyer can avoid having to deal with the question of attorney's fees in such a situation is to take advantage of the so-called "vouching in" provision of Article 2, which provides a process for a seller sued for breach of warranty to seek recourse against *his* seller. See §2-607(5).

b. Chris should be able to recover the costs involved in a successful defense, although the authority for this is not that easy to find in the Code. In earlier law, and in the Uniform Sales Act, there was found a direct expression of a *warranty of quiet possession* to deal with cases such as this. There is no such language in §2-312 and, in fact, Comment 1 to the section states that "[t]he warranty of quiet possession is abolished." However, the Comment goes on to say, "Disturbance of quiet possession, although not mentioned specifically, is one way, among many, in which the breach of warranty of title may be established." It's hard to read this in any other way than that something pretty close to the historical warranty of quiet possession is still available to aggrieved buyers, even if they aren't allowed to call it exactly that. The courts support this understanding, the most famous language being from *American Container Corp. v. Hanley Trucking Corp.*, 268 A.2d 313 (N.J. Super. 1970):

> The purchaser of goods warranted as to title has a right to rely on the fact that he will not be required, at some later time, to enter into a contest over the validity of his ownership. The mere casting of a substantial shadow over his title, regardless of the ultimate outcome, is sufficient to violate the warranty of good title.

The Code does not answer the question of exactly how substantial a shadow must be in order to put the burden of defending against it on the seller under this theory. In one case, the court commented:

> [A] purchaser can recover for breach of warranty of title when he demonstrates the existence of a substantial cloud or shadow on his title, regardless of whether it eventually develops that any third party's title is superior. Whether a substantial cloud or shadow exists in relation to a purchaser's title is a mixed question of law and fact and must be determined on a case-by-case basis. Surely the cloud on the title must be predicated on some objective factor and the baseless anxiety of the hypersensitive purchaser regarding the validity of his title will not result in a breach of warranty.

Maroone Chevrolet, Inc. v. Nordstrom, 587 So. 2d 514 (Fla. Dist. Ct. App. 1991). So much for the question of how dark the shadow or how gloomy the clouds. Nor is it clear under §2-312 whether the buyer must show some way in which his seller's behavior helped create the difficulty. In other words, suppose that some stranger came to me with the allegation that the computer on which I'm writing this had in fact been stolen from him one year before I bought it from the retail dealer. Sounds pretty flimsy, but I'd still have to defend against this stranger's account if he persisted in his claim. (You can't just lay this off on my hypersensitivity. A suit has been filed against me.) We can assume that I would win eventually, but not without incurring some expense and a good deal of aggravation. If the claim were no stronger than appears from what I've just laid out, and if there were no reason to suspect that anything the dealer did or failed to do helped give rise to the claim or encourage this stranger's strange behavior, would I have any rights against the dealer? It's very unlikely. I do, indeed, have the right to the quiet possession of my computer, but not all disruptions of that quietude should be the responsibility of the dealer.

For another case where the notion of quiet possession was involved, see *Jefferson v. Jones*, 408 A.2d 1036 (Md. 1979), which arose out of the sale of a motorcycle. As part of the transaction, the seller delivered to the buyer a certificate of title covering the machine. Unfortunately, and due only to an innocent mistake on the seller's part, the serial number on the certificate was wrong. It didn't match that of the motorcycle. When a policeman became aware of this mismatch (some two years after the sale), the motorcycle was impounded. The buyer was ultimately successful in establishing title, but it took him a significant amount of time and money to prove the property was his and actually get it back. The court held that a breach of the warranty of title had occurred and that the buyer was to be compensated for his losses. Presumably this could include some measure of damages for the loss of use of the machine for a period of time. Such was the case in *Colton v. Decker*, 540 N.W.2d 172 (S.D. 1995). See also *Saber v. Dan Angelone Chevrolet*, Inc., 811 A.2d 644 (R.I. 2002).

6. It may not seem intuitive, but I do have a claim. Section 2-312(3) provides that "a seller who is a merchant regularly dealing in goods of the kind warrants that the goods shall be delivered free of the rightful claim of any third person by way of infringement or the like." This warranty will doubtless prove more important in the future, as more "smart goods" containing intellectual property appear on the market. Note that it is not given by all sellers, but only by those who regularly deal in goods of the kind. It does not matter that Smartphones is an innocent party. A warranty claim under the Code is a matter of strict liability, not fault. The Code says that the claim is against the *seller*, so Smartphones is liable to me. Do they have any recourse? Sure. Their seller gave them the

same warranty, so they have a claim against that party. Like a claim for breach of the warranty of title, this claim will work its way up the chain to the responsible party. Can Smartphones avoid liability by selling the phone with the "AS IS" disclaimer? Curiously, this is a gap in the Code. While §2-312(2) makes clear that the disclaimer of the implied warranty of title can be disclaimed "only by specific language or circumstances," there is no such provision regarding the warranty against infringement. I suspect, however, that a court would apply the same standard. In any event, as we will see, the "AS IS" language disclaims only "implied warranties" and the Code does not call this warranty an implied warranty.

7. This example is based on the case of *Pacific Sunwear of California, Inc. v. Olaes Enterprises, Inc.*, 84 Cal. Rptr. 3d 182 (Cal. Ct. App. 2008). The trial court had ruled that SCNL had never had a "rightful claim" against Pacific Sunwear so as to bring into play the warranty against infringement of §2-312(3). On appeal, the principal dispute was what was a "rightful claim" under this subsection. Olaes contended that a rightful claim is a valid claim—that is, one that has proven, or will likely prove, meritorious in litigation. Pacific Sunwear argued that any claim "in the form of litigation" constituted a rightful claim regardless of its underlying merits. After a lengthy consideration, the appellate court determined that the correct interpretation lay somewhere between these two extremes. It concluded that "as used in §2-312(3) the term 'rightful claim' is intended to broadly encompass any nonfrivolous claim of infringement that significantly interferes with the buyer's use of a purchased good." On this basis, the trial court's summary judgment in favor of Olaes was reversed with a new trial to proceed under the proper standard.

8. a. It is doubtful here that Marv has any defense based on the "as is" clause. Any argument by a seller that the warranty of title has been effectively "excluded or modified" is governed by §2-312(2). (Later, in Chapter 13, we will take an extended look at warranty disclaimers as they are governed by other sections, but the point here is that those sections deal only with the warranties that are called an "implied warranty" in Article 2. While Article 2 says that the warranty of title "is in a contract for sale," it is never called an implied warranty. See Comment 6 to §2-312.) The question then is whether the "as is" provision is the kind of "specific language" that will satisfy §2-312(2). As you can imagine, getting title and the warranty of title are of major importance to just about any buyer. It's rare that a buyer will pay good money for something that may or may not turn out to be his or hers at the end of the day. The courts respond to this by holding any language argued to disclaim the warranty of title up to a particularly high standard. "As is" was found not to be sufficiently specific in *Eccher v. Small Business Administration*, 643 F.2d 1388 (10th Cir. 1981). In

Jones v. Linebaugh, 191 N.W.2d 142 (Mich. Ct. App. 1971), the bill of sale given to the buyer by the seller of two Bugatti automobiles said that the seller was transferring all of his "right, title and interest" in the autos and that to the "best of [his] knowledge there [was] no title in existence by way of registration with the State of Michigan or with any other State or Nation." In the course of the earlier negotiations, the seller had acknowledged to the buyer that he didn't have title, but the buyer had asked him to get title, and the seller had said that his attorney was working on it. Under the situation, the court held that the warranty of title had not been disclaimed by the language in the bill of sale.

b. Harry will not have an action based on the warranty of title. Marv can argue that any such warranty was excluded in this instance because the sale was made under "circumstances which [gave] the buyer reason to know that the person selling does not claim title in himself or that he is purporting to sell only such right or title as he or a third person may have." The strength of Marv's position may not be obvious from this language, but he will point to Comment 5, which makes clear what kinds of "circumstances" the drafters were thinking of here. This result, of course, depends on Harry's having been aware, or having had reason to know, that Marv was selling only in the capacity of a foreclosing lienholder. See *Landmark Motors, Inc. v. Chrysler Credit Corp.*, 662 N.E.2d 971 (Ind. App. 1996).

c. The question here is whether the mysterious Marv can make the argument that the sale was made under "circumstances" that gave Harry reason to know that he, Marv, wasn't purporting that he could legitimately transfer good title. This is probably only an academic question, of course, since it's hard to imagine that Harry would ever be able to find Marv (if that is his real name) now and get an effective suit going against him. Not surprisingly, I know of no reported cases on point.

CHAPTER 11

Express Warranties of Quality

A BIT OF HISTORY

Buyers buying particular goods expect to get something. They expect to get the tangible object itself, of course, and beyond that to be blessed with title to the property as we discussed in the previous chapter. It is important to recognize, however, the whole host of other expectations buyers will normally have. A buyer is not, we assume, buying a mysterious object hidden in a black box. He or she is making the purchase because of what the thing is, or at least because of what the buyer believes the thing is (what it is made out of, what it can do, etc.). The buyer wants the thing itself, but beyond that wants it for the *qualities* he or she understands it to have. If it does live up to these expectations (or if it is even more desirable), all well and good; if the goods are not as the buyer presumed them to be, he or she might expect to have some rights against the seller. If such rights are available, it is because he or she has, as an Article 2 buyer of goods, received certain *warranties of quality* along with actual delivery of and title to the goods. As the Code drafters say in Comment 4 to §2-313, the whole idea behind the law of warranty is "to determine what it is that the seller has in essence agreed to sell."

This and the following chapters will explore the law relating to warranties of quality as it pertains to sales of goods under Article 2. We live, study, and practice law in the present. To make sense of the Article 2 approach, however, it is worthwhile to spend some time on a bit of history, going back to seventeenth-century England and the heyday of the doctrine of *caveat emptor*. As a matter of fact, there is plenty of historical evidence that in even earlier times the English legal system afforded more protection to the buyer, albeit in forms that we would not easily recognize today as warranty law, than it would in the common law courts of the 1600s. But discussion of warranty law always seems to start then and there with the well-known case of *Chandelor v. Lopus*, 79 Eng. Rep. 3 (1625), and in this we can follow tradition.

In *Chandelor*, the plaintiff had sold the defendant something that he had described as a "bezoar [or bezar] stone." A bezoar stone was apparently a hard object recovered from the internal organs of a goat believed at least by some at the time to have remarkable healing powers. The seller never received payment for this distinctive bit of goods. When he brought suit for the purchase price, the buyer defended on the ground that what he had received was not what he thought he was getting. He claimed it wasn't a bezoar stone at all. Whether by this the buyer meant that he believed it hadn't come from a goat's innards or that even if it had, it didn't work like a real bezoar stone should, we do not know. In any event, such subtleties would not have mattered to the Exchequer Chamber, which ruled that the seller had given no warranty of any kind that it was such a stone. Why? The seller may have referred to the item as a "bezoar stone." He may have affirmed that it was just such a thing. But, the court noted, he had never expressly and explicitly *promised* that it was a bezoar stone. That being the case, there could be no warranty. In the words of the court:

> [T]he bare affirmation that it was a bezar-stone, without warranting it to be so, is no cause of action; and although he knew it to be no bezar-stone, it is not material; for everyone in selling his wares will affirm that his wares are good, or the wares which he sells is sound; and yet if he does not warrant them to be so, it is no cause of action.

We should be careful in reading this. The law in seventeenth-century England was not that a buyer had no hope of receiving warranty protection from his seller. The concept of warranty was around. If the buyer expected to get a warranty, however, he had to have elicited for his benefit a direct and explicit promise to that effect from the seller. A "mere description" of the goods as being such-and-such would not suffice. Use by the seller of the explicit language of promise was all-important.

Moving forward in time and across the pond, we find the highest court of New York following essentially the same line in *Seixas v. Woods*, 2 Caines 48 (1804). The defendant sold some wood to the plaintiff that had been advertised as "brazilletto," a particular kind of expensive wood. The bill of sale delivered to the buyer called it "brazilletto." The invoice the seller had received from the person who sold it to him, a paper that he showed to the buyer, referred to it as "brazilletto." There was apparently no reason to doubt that the seller himself thought it was indeed the stuff. "In fact," said the court, "neither party knew it to be other than brazilletto, nor was any fraud imputed." It turned out of course that the wood was nothing of the kind but was instead peachum, an inferior type of wood "worth hardly anything." The buyer sued the seller to get his money back but recovered nothing. Again, the fact that the entire sale was made with reference to a particular description of the goods was of no avail for the buyer. It was, said the court, "a clear case for the defendant." As of 1804 a buyer could, we are told, protect himself and make sure he is getting exactly what he expects by his own vigilance. He can inspect the goods and make sure of what he is getting. "And even against his own want of vigilance, the purchaser may provide, by requiring the vendor *expressly* to warranty the article." The emphasis in this quotation is mine, not the court's, but the point is unmistakable. "The mentioning the wood, as brazilletto wood in the bill of parcels, and in advertisement some days previous to the sale, did not amount to a warranty to the plaintiffs." Even in 1804 the evidence must show that the seller *intended* to create a warranty. Otherwise, let the buyer beware.

The common law doctrine of *caveat emptor* began to wear away with the passage of time. The process, however, was anything but rapid. Only in 1872 did an authoritative court in New York recognize that the doctrine of *Chandelor v. Lopus* "has long since been exploded, and the case itself is no longer regarded as good law in this country or England." *Hawkins v. Pemberton*, 51 N.Y. 198 (1872). The court went on to remark that "the rule" of *Seixas v. Wood* "has been thoroughly overturned since the courts hold that any positive affirmation or representation as to the character or quality of an article sold may constitute a warranty."

This movement in the direction of greater warranty protection for buyers was furthered by the adoption of the Uniform Sales Act in the early years of the twentieth century. Section 12 of that Act provided in one subsection that, "Any affirmation of fact or any promise by the seller relating to the goods is an express warranty if the natural tendency of such affirmation or promise is to induce the buyer to purchase the goods, and if the buyer purchases the goods relying thereon." Meanwhile, in other parts of the forest, the notion was developing that even where there was no express language—not an affirmation of fact much less a promise—that the buyer could point to as having influenced his or her purchase, warranty protection might be appropriate. The idea that a seller might warrant the goods' qualities in other ways (what would come to be known by the awkward terms *merchantability* and *fitness for a particular purpose*) was beginning to take hold. Our interest, of course, is in the shape these ideas were eventually to take in Article 2.

THE ARTICLE 2 SCHEME FOR WARRANTIES OF QUALITY

Warranties of quality under Article 2 come in two flavors, *express* and *implied*. This chapter deals with the creation and extent of the express warranties as provided for under §2-313. The following chapter will deal with both the implied warranty of merchantability and the implied warranty of fitness for a particular purpose. As we will see in later parts of the book, if the goods are not as warranted, the buyer has a variety of possible responses. He or she may decline to accept the faulty goods, may in some instances revoke an acceptance already made, or may seek money damages for breach of warranty. These default rules may be altered by the seller. But all that will come later. For the moment, we are concerned only with *when* and *how* buyers can claim that the goods they have purchased are warranted as to quality and beyond that *exactly what* that warranty covers.

It needs to be emphasized at the outset that any time a buyer wants to make an argument that the goods are not as warranted, it is imperative that his or her argument be made with precision and in detail. I can't stress this enough. It is not sufficient just to wave one's hands about and say that there surely is some warranty of some sort or another floating out there somewhere. The buyer will be expected to state as precisely as possible *what type* of warranty he or she is claiming as part of the contract, *what qualities* it covers, and *how* it was created. What are the *specific facts* in the instant situation that brought *this particular warranty* into being?

Once you have finished this and the following chapter, it will be apparent to you how often warranties can overlap. That is, it will often be possible for the buyer in even the simplest fact pattern to claim that more than one warranty or warranties of more than one type were breached. It is tempting for the law student and also for the practitioner in such situations to end the analysis as soon as one idea pops up that seems to work. This, however, would be a mistake. If a situation allows for the argument that a set of cumulative warranties were created, it is important to at least note each and every one. See §2-317. Why this piling on? For one thing, of course, the skillful advocate is usually well advised to keep as many arrows in the quiver as possible. But there's more to it than this. As you will learn in Chapter 13, the warranties of quality may be (and often are) excluded or modified by the seller in a variety of ways, but the means by which these warranties may be so disclaimed, and the effectiveness of these means, are different for different types of warranties. In particular, it will be much more difficult for a seller effectively to disclaim any warranty that can be successfully characterized as an express warranty, as opposed to an implied warranty. The type of warranty established can make a big difference to the ultimate result. As you work your way through the next couple of chapters, keep alert to all possibilities.

EXPRESS WARRANTIES UNDER ARTICLE 2

Section 2-313 is the one place we need look in Article 2 for the rules regarding when and how "express warranties by the seller are created." You should read through that section now. The overall intention of the drafters seems fairly clear. Still, even in a first rough reading you undoubtedly noted some phrases that suggest the kinds of problems we are in for when we actually try to apply the language. The questions that follow will lead you through the issues that have come up under §2-313. There are, as you might expect, a large number of cases decided under this section. Also as you might expect, the results do not quickly (or perhaps ever) give way to any easy generalities. Each decision (even those we may admire) seems so grounded in the facts of the particular case that it will be hard to say much more with assurance than that the questions of when and how an express warranty arises under this section tend to be resolved by the facts as they are presented. This doesn't mean, of course, that there is not plenty to be gained by carefully working through the questions. Section 2-313 is typical of the sort of Code provision that is best studied with a mind toward picking up an approach to and an appreciation of the issues that come up and the facts that tend toward one result as opposed to the other, rather than any hard and fast rules. With that said, we proceed.

Examples

EXAMPLES

1. Sal, a dealer in industrial chemicals, receives 20 barrels from a chemical manufacturing company in response to her order for this much of a chemical called blue vitriol. Each barrel is marked "B. Vitriol." Bernard, who uses this chemical in his business, arranges to buy a barrel of it from Sal. His purchase order and the confirmation sent back to him by Sal both refer to "Blue Vitriol." Sal delivers to him one of the 20 barrels, which it turns out actually contains a compound called red vitriol, similar in composition to blue vitriol but inferior in quality.
   (a) Has Sal breached an express warranty?
   (b) Could Sal successfully defend herself by showing she never explicitly said she "guaranteed" or "warranted" that the delivery would be of blue vitriol?
   (c) Could she defend herself by showing she had no intention of assuming responsibility for its being blue vitriol?
   (d) Could she defend herself by showing she had every reason to believe there was blue vitriol in the barrel? That is, she can show that she had never had trouble with mislabeling or misdelivery from this manufacturer before, and that it is not customary for a dealer in her position to open and independently check what is in the barrels it sells to buyers such as Bernard.

(e) Would your answers be any different if what was delivered was actually *purple* vitriol, a product much more valuable than standard blue vitriol?

2. Buyer contracts to purchase a stated quantity of "#2 milling wheat" from the seller. Is an express warranty part of the deal? If so, for what?

3. Betty goes to Carmen's Used Auto Emporium, where she sees a used car that appeals to her. It is marked "2018 Honda Civic" on the windshield. She agrees to buy the car from Carmen, and the bill of sale states that the sale is of a "2018 Honda Civic." Betty drives off in the car. Based on each of the following additional facts, determine what express warranties, if any, Betty got from Carmen.
   (a) First, the baseline: *no* additional facts.
   (b) Prior to entering into the sales agreement, Carmen told Betty that "it has power steering and power brakes."
   (c) When first examining the car, Betty looked at the odometer and saw that it read 131,257 miles.
   (d) In the car's glove compartment Betty found the various papers that had been issued to its original owner. Among these were a "Maintenance Log," which indicated that the car had been regularly serviced.
   (e) The car's windshield bore a sticker indicating that it had passed the state's mandatory safety and pollution control inspection for the current year.
   (f) In the course of negotiations Carmen had said to her, "This is the finest car I've ever had on my lot!"

4. The Royal Business Machine Corporation sold some 128 plain paper copiers to Boohler, a dealer in copying machines. In a suit brought by Boohler, the trial court found that the manufacturer had made and breached the following express warranties:
   (a) that the models purchased and their components were of high quality;
   (b) that experience and testing had shown that the frequency of repairs was very low on such machines and would remain so;
   (c) that replacement parts were readily available;
   (d) that the cost of maintenance for each machine and cost of supplies was and would remain low, no more than ½ cent per copy;
   (e) that the machines had been extensively tested and were ready to be marketed;
   (f) that experience and reasonable projections had shown that the purchase of these machines by the buyer for lease to his customers would return substantial profits to him;
   (g) that the machines were safe and could not cause fires; and
   (h) that service calls would be required for the machines on the average of every 7,000 to 9,000 copies, including preventative maintenance calls.

The trial court awarded the buyer $1,171,216.16 in damages along with substantial attorney's fees. On appeal Royal Business Machine argued that, contrary to what the lower court had found, none of the statements attributed to it were the type of language that created express warranties. As the appellate judge, which of these findings by the trial judge, if any, would you reverse?

5. Alan, a suburban homeowner, was having trouble with crabgrass on his property. He went to Chuck's Lawn and Garden Supply shop. As he looked over the vast assortment of lawn care products and weedkillers, he confided his problem to Chuck. Chuck pointed to a product called "Miracle Kill" and said to Alan, "This will do you just fine." When Alan buys the stuff, has he gotten any express warranties from Chuck?

6. Janine Sugawara bought a box of "Cap'n Crunch with Crunchberries" cereal. In addition to the use of the word *berries* in the product's name, the box prominently featured the product's namesake, "Cap'n Crunch," thrusting a spoonful of "Crunchberries" at the prospective buyer. Sugawara eventually discovered that the Crunchberries were not really berries, but rather round, brightly colored cereal balls. The cereal, in fact, contained no fruit whatsoever. Sugawara brought suit, on behalf of herself and other consumers similarly situated, against the maker of the cereal, contending that the colorful Crunchberries, combined with use of the word *berry* in the product name and reinforced by additional marketing representing that "Crunch Berries is a combination of Crunch biscuits and colorful red, purple, teal and green berries," created an express warranty that the cereal would not consist only of processed sugar and starch, but contain at least some fruit. Do you expect her argument will be successful? Should it be?

7. Nuts Incorporated is in the business of selling fresh nuts to processors. It sent a small sample of fresh Malawi peanuts to Snacks International along with an offer to sell such nuts at stated prices. Snacks had the sample fried, oil-roasted, and tested. The results were satisfactory, and Snacks entered into a contract to buy a large amount of these nuts. When the first delivery was put through Snacks' production process, the outcome was a large batch of processed nuts that had a terrible taste and gave off an awful odor. It becomes clear that the nuts are the problem. Unlike those originally sent to the processor, those delivered do not respond favorably to Snacks' process (to put it mildly). Has Nuts breached an express warranty?

8. Karl goes into Sam's jewelry store intent on buying a watch. Among those out on display is a Chrono SX. Beside it is a display card listing various features. Included on the list is the line "Stop-Watch Feature." Karl looks over the display carefully and then buys the watch. Later he discovers that, despite all its dials, read-outs, and buttons, there is no

way it can operate as a stopwatch. Karl brings the watch back in to Sam demanding satisfaction.

(a) Karl would seem to have a clear breach of express warranty argument. Would it make any difference if it turned out that when Sam was trying to make the sale, he had made a special point of the Stop-Watch Feature to Karl, who had said something like, "Oh, I don't care about that. Who needs a stopwatch anyway?"

(b) What would be the result if there had been no discussion at all about this feature at the time of sale, and while the display did mention it, Karl has to admit he never took a look at the card?

(c) Annie comes into Sam's shop. She has been lured in by an advertisement in that day's newspaper that features another watch, the Timola LT, listing among its attributes a "Glow-In-The-Dark Dial." This feature is important to Annie, but it never comes up in her direct discussions with Sam. She buys the watch. Does she have an express warranty for a dial that glows in the dark?

(d) Another potential customer, Barbara, comes into the store and is shown the Timola LT. She has not seen the ad in the paper, nor does the glowing feature come up in conversation with Sam. She agrees to buy the watch. After he has written up the sale and taken her credit card for payment, and while he is handing over her purchase, she asks him, "By the way, is this one of those watches you can read in the dark?" He answers, "Yes, it has a glow-in-the-dark dial." Barbara takes the watch and walks out of the store. She walks out with the watch, but does she also take with her any express warranty regarding the dial?

(e) That same day a third customer, Carol, buys a Timola LT from Sam. When she makes the purchase, she has not yet seen the ad in the newspaper, nor does any mention of this feature come up while she is in the store. That evening at home she finally gets around to reading the paper. She sees the ad. Later that night she finds that the dial on her watch does not in fact glow in the dark. Does she have any claim against Sam?

Explanations

EXPLANATIONS

1. This question is inspired by the famous pre-Code case of *Hawkins v. Pemberton*, 51 N.Y. 198 (1872), but you should consider it under §2-313. It should be clear from reading that section that Sal has indeed breached an express warranty created when she sold Bernard the chemical blue vitriol. This is a classic warranty by description now dealt with under §2-313(1)(b). The description of the goods as "Blue Vitriol" was made "part of the basis of the bargain" between Sal and Bernard and hence "creates an express warranty that the goods shall conform to the description." (The "basis of the bargain" criterion will cause no end of difficulty

in some cases, as we'll discuss later on, but there can be no question it is met here.)

None of the factors offered up by Sal makes any difference. The first part of §2-313(2)—the language up to the comma—expressly states that the fact that Sal did not use the exact language of warranty does not matter, nor is it relevant whether or not she had the intention to make such a warranty. She is responsible under the warranty because she made the sale with reference to this description. The fact that she did not, or could not, or customarily would not check before sending a barrel out is irrelevant as well. It is a matter of strict liability. *She breaches the warranty when the stuff isn't what it is supposed to be.* How or why the mix-up occurred is, of course, something she may want to worry about. The point is, however, that it is *her* problem and not one she has shifted in these circumstances onto Bernard.

Regarding Example 1c, nothing in the analysis would change if what was delivered was the much more valuable purple variety. True, Bernard might in this situation not want to make a stink about the improper delivery, but Sal has still breached an express warranty. This serves to remind us that what is injurious about a seller's breaching a warranty of quality is not that he or she has intentionally tried to mislead or defraud the buyer or even that he or she has tendered to the buyer something decidedly worse than what was expected. The tender of something *different* from what was contracted for, even if done in total innocence, is the nature of the wrong.

2. Clearly a warranty has been made by description just as in the previous example. It is a warranty that what is delivered will in fact be "#2 milling wheat." The question, of course, is what exactly that is. How do we determine precisely what is covered by a given description? Presumably the test in such a situation is something like what a reasonable person in the buyer's position, buying in that particular market, would expect to be delivered when a contract is made under this description. In the case of *W.A. Davis Realty, Inc. v. Wakelon Agri-Products, Inc.*, 351 S.E.2d 816 (N.C. Ct. App. 1987), the buyer, a milling company that produced self-rising flour, bought wheat of this description. The court held that, under the circumstances, among its other protections, the buyer had received an express warranty that it would receive wheat that was "grade Number 2 according to U.S. Department of Agriculture standards."

   Sometimes the issues involved in a sale by description are trickier than you might expect, as the next example makes all too clear.

3. a. This is easy, at least initially. Carmen warrants to Betty that the item she is purchasing is a 2018 Honda Civic. In most cases I think we know what that means, or more specifically, what that would mean to "a reasonable used car buyer." The car is a Honda Civic, meaning

that it was made by the company that makes Hondas and was made by that company to be the Civic model. Further we take it that the car was made as a Civic during the 2018 model year. This seems straightforward enough, but consider the following cases.

The easiest cases are ones of simple erroneous description. In *Best Buick, Inc. v. Welcome*, 18 U.C.C. 75 (Mass. Ct. App. 1975), the defendant traded in his old Mercedes Benz when he purchased a new car from the plaintiff dealership. The agreement between the parties referred to the trade-in as a "1970 Mercedes," which is what the defendant believed it to be. He had earlier bought it as a 1970 model. When it turned out that it was actually a 1968 Mercedes, the dealership sued for the difference in the trade-in value of the two models. The defendant was considered to be the seller of the car he traded in, and hence to have given an express warranty that the trade-in was as described. As the court pointed out, the fact that this consumer was innocent of any intent to deceive and had in fact himself been deceived earlier was no defense. "When a seller makes an express warranty which is not true, it is no defense that the seller had acted in good faith without knowledge of the defect." A similar result was reached in *Goodwin v. Durant Bank & Trust Co.*, 952 P.2d 41 (Okla. 1998), where the seller was held to have breached an express warranty when a used backhoe it sold as a 1990 model turned out to be in fact a 1987 model, even though there was no dispute that the seller itself had been honestly mistaken about the equipment's model year and had had no intention of deceiving or taking advantage of the buyer.

In *Curry Motor Co., Inc. v. Hasty*, 505 So. 2d 347 (Ala. 1987), it was the consumer buyer who was able to take advantage of the concept of express warranty. In 1983 he purchased from the seller a truck that was described in the sales pitch and identified in the bill of sale as a "1979 Ford" pickup. It was, indeed, a Ford pickup truck and was in large part a 1979 model, but evidence showed that the engine had been replaced with an engine model that was vintage 1970 to 1973. Apparently it is common for dealers in used automobiles to put different components in used cars and trucks to get them in shape for resale. Here the evidence was that this substitution was not made by the seller himself, nor had he any knowledge that the 1979 truck he sold the buyer had an early 1970s engine in it. Nevertheless, the court held that it was proper for the jury to conclude that the buyer had received an express warranty that the engine, and not just the body of the truck, was manufactured in the 1979 model year.

Would the result in the *Curry* case have been the same if the evidence had been that the engine was of a 1979 vintage, even if it hadn't been the original engine installed in that particular chassis? That is, could the 1983 buyer of a used "1979 Ford" pickup argue that he had received an express warranty—based on the model year and name alone—that the vehicle was still basically the same set of pieces that were put together to make up one truck back in 1979? A reasonable buyer would presumably know that over time cars and trucks are repaired and new and replacement parts incorporated into them, but would replacement of the whole engine be too much? If at any time the seller had said that the car "has the original engine," then there would be no problem for the buyer. This would be an express warranty created by the affirmation of fact. The question I pose is whether the buyer could argue this warranty from the year and make description alone.

In *Currier v. Spencer*, 772 S.W.2d 309 (Ark. 1989), Spencer had been sold what was described as a "one-owner 1984 Datsun 300ZX." Before his check had cleared, Spencer experienced troubles with the car and "discovered that the rear one-third had previously been replaced with that of another vehicle and the entire car had been repainted." The court found Currier, the seller, to be in breach of an express warranty. "Currier warranted the car to be a one-owner 1984 Datsun. What Spencer purchased was two-thirds of one car and one-third of another." Compare this case to *Zappanti v. Berge Service Center*, 549 P.2d 178 (Ariz. App. 1976). Zappanti, a man with some experience in auto mechanics, had prior to his purchase considered constructing for himself a "dune buggy." Instead he and his wife decided to purchase the vehicle in dispute from the defendant. The window sticker identified it as a 1969 model, and the bill of sale referred to a "1969 Volkswagen Dunebuggy." After purchase, Zappanti discovered, according to his allegations, that all the parts of the special reconstructed vehicle were from Volkswagen models of years earlier than 1969. It was not disputed that the major components were from models of 1967 and earlier. The defendant–seller had identified the dune buggy as a 1969 model because that is how it was described to him when he took it as a trade-in from someone who had registered it in another state, Michigan. It turned out that under Michigan law, since such a vehicle has no model year, it is registered for title purposes as being of the model year in which it was cobbled together out of pieces of other vehicles. Apparently, the same rule would have applied in Arizona, the site of the sale to Zappanti, for registration purposes. Referring to the great deference played in the Code to trade usage and the commercial context of agreements, the court concluded:

> While plaintiffs contend that the affidavits with respect to vehicle title practices are not conclusive as to contractual dealings, plaintiffs have not offered any controverting affidavits reflecting a contrary trade usage, nor have they presented any sound legal or practical basis for holding as a matter of law that the defendant warranted that the components of

> the vehicle were 1969 components. In view of the material differences between specially constructed vehicles and conventional vehicle models, the absence of any express statements relating to the model year of the components of this vehicle, and in the further absence of any showing of trade usage supporting the position of the plaintiffs, there is no disputed issue of material fact. The summary judgment for defendant must be affirmed.

At least it's not going to be difficult to know what's a Pontiac and what's not. Or so you would think. In *Szajna v. General Motors Corp.*, 503 N.E.2d 760 (Ill. 1986), the Illinois Supreme Court held that the designation of a new automobile as a "1976 Pontiac Ventura" did not in and of itself create an express warranty "of the kind or nature of the car's components." Thus, the purchaser of such a car could not recover under a breach of express warranty theory despite the fact that the car he bought had been equipped at the factory with a transmission engineered for a Chevette and not the transmission specifically designed and intended for the 1976 Ventura.

b. This clearly creates an express warranty that the car has power steering and power brakes. Betty's authority for this is found in §2-313(1)(a). Carmen's statement was "an affirmation of fact" that "relates to the goods." For the moment we'll assume that it also became "part of the basis of the bargain," even if that phrase will later be shown to be anything but easy to apply (see Example 7).

c. There are several cases to serve as authority that the odometer reading creates an express warranty that the car has been driven that number of miles and no more, at least where the odometer reading is written into the sales agreement. Once in the bill of sale, it is easy to see this number as "an affirmation of fact or promise" as the section calls for. Would it be enough that Carmen should realize that a potential buyer would look at the car's dashboard itself and take some information from what she sees there? See *Rogers v. Crest Motors, Inc.*, 516 P.2d 445 (Colo. Ct. App. 1973), which suggests this would suffice.

d. Logbooks relating to airplanes were found to create express warranties in *Miles v. Kavanaugh*, 350 So. 2d 1090 (Fla. Dist. App. 1977), and *Limited Flying Club, Inc. v. Wood*, 632 F.2d 51 (8th Cir. 1980). In each case, however, the buyer had been shown the records by the seller. If not an "affirmation of fact," doesn't this constitute a "description of the goods" that will create an express warranty? Should the situation be any different because the buyer found and looked at the maintenance records on her own?

e. Even if the sticker is never distinctly referred to by the seller, it would seem to be part of the description of or an allegation about the car. After all, the seller may never directly point to the seats as part of the car, but isn't she warranting that they'll be there when it is delivered?

In the one case that dealt with an inspection sticker, the court had no trouble finding that it did create an express warranty. The problem for the buyer was how far the warranty extended. The court concluded that "the sticker warrants only that on the date of inspection the car complied with the safety criteria designated by the Department of Revenue. . . . And, since an accident or other circumstance might alter the condition of the vehicle, the sticker could not serve to guarantee that the car would continue to meet those criteria after the date the sticker was issued." *Hummel v. Skyline Dodge, Inc.*, 589 P.2d 73 (Colo. App. 1978).

f. Betty would try to argue that this created an express warranty as "an affirmation of fact or promise" under subsection (1)(a). Carmen, however, would point to the concluding language in subsection (2): "[A]n affirmation merely of the value of the goods or a statement purporting to be merely the seller's opinion or commendation of the goods does not create a warranty." This language was meant by the drafters to continue the doctrine that what is sometimes called mere "seller's language" or "puffing" of the product does not in and of itself create any warranty protection for the buyer. Such language, which a reasonable buyer will presumably understand to mean no more than that the seller is very much in favor of making the sale, is in effect nothing on which the buyer should rely or even take particularly seriously.

In the instant case, the expression that the car is "the finest" ever is just about as good an example of pure puffery as you're likely to find. Or is it? Couldn't Betty make the argument that this is an affirmation or promise that the car is better than others she's been looking over at Carmen's? But the word "finest" is so nebulous that this argument would be hard to sustain. Would you, or anyone you know, make anything out of such a statement uttered by a used car dealer in the course of trying to close a sale?

Of course, making the distinction between language that does create an express warranty of quality and mere puffery is not always this easy, and in some cases it is as much a matter of guesswork as anything in Article 2. Anyone who suggests he or she has a sure-fire method of regularly sorting out mere puffing language from true warranties is, one might suggest, in training for the used car business. Often the question, if it is at all close, is simply left up to the trier of fact, and little can be said except that appellate courts usually give great deference to any decision that gets them off the hook. As a sampling involving statements by used car dealers, consider the following typical cases. In *Crothers v. Cohen*, 384 N.W.2d 562 (Minn. Ct. App. 1986), the Minnesota Court of Appeals ruled that the trial court had not erred in submitting to the jury the question of whether an express warranty was created by the statement that a certain 1970 Dodge was a "good runner" made by the salesman to the 16-year-old plaintiff and his friend as they were all looking at the engine and listening to it run. The jury, in a suit to recover for the serious injuries sustained by the buyer when the Dodge went out of control and crashed into a tree on the day after the sale, apparently had no trouble in finding that a warranty had been created by the salesman's words. The Minnesota court let this stand, noting, "Statements using the word 'good' in referring to the condition of personal property have been found to create express warranties in a number of cases." Similarly, in *Felley v. Singleton*, 705 N.E.2d 930 (Ill. App. 1999), the Illinois Appellate Court upheld a verdict for a disgruntled buyer of a six-year-old Ford Taurus based on a statement at the time of sale by the seller that the car was "in good mechanical condition." Contrast these results to that in *Web Press Services Corp. v. New London Motors, Inc.*, 525 A.2d 57 (Conn. 1987). There the Supreme Court of Connecticut held that it was not error for the lower court to conclude that oral statements that a used 1980 Ford Bronco was "excellent," in "mint" and "very good" condition and that it was an "unusual" vehicle all constituted no more than puffery and did not rise to the level of warranty language. Supporting its conclusion, the Connecticut court was able to point to cases in which "[s]tatements to the effect that a truck was in 'good condition' and that a motor was in 'perfect running order' have been held not to create express warranties." For a thoroughgoing discussion of how a court is to go about determining what is and what is not puffery, you might want to consult either of two cases: *Avola v. Louisiana-Pacific Corp.*, 991 F. Supp. 2d 381 (E.D.N.Y. 2013) or *Lester v. Wow Car Co., Ltd.*, 2014 WL 2567087 (S.D. Ohio 2014), *aff'd*, 675 F. App'x 588 (6th Cir. 2017). In the latter case, the court determined that the representative of the Wow Car Company was merely puffing when he described the used car that the Lesters eventually bought as "reliable," "good on gas," and a "good car."

As a final note on the subject of puffery, consider the case of *Anderson v. Bungee Intern. Mfg. Corp.*, 44 F. Supp. 2d 534 (S.D.N.Y. 1999). The District Court held that the statements "Premium Quality" and "Made in the USA," appearing on the packaging of a 23-piece assortment of Bungee cords, did not rise to the level of express warranties:

> The statements that the Bungee cords are of premium or superior quality [and presumably the statement that they were American-made, even though they were, we are told in a short dismissive footnote, manufactured in Taiwan and only "assembled" in the United States] are generalized statements of salesmanship and are indistinguishable from statements that this court and others have held to be puffery under New York law.

4. The question is based on *Royal Business Machines, Inc. v. Lorraine Corp.*, 633 F.2d 34 (7th Cir. 1980). The Seventh Circuit held that substantial evidence supported the district court's findings as to items *e, g, h,* and "the maintenance aspect" of *d,* but that as a matter of law *a, b, c, f,* and "the cost of supplies portion" of *d* could not be considered express warranties. Some of these seem fairly easy to categorize. Items *a* and *f* are good examples of puffery in its most classic form. The court also found *b* to be a puff, because the imprecise nature of the term *very low* "lacked the specificity of an affirmation of fact upon which a warranty could be predicated." The result is probably correct, but couldn't the buyer have argued that this assurance gave at least some kind of warranty that the frequency of repairs on such machines was lower than for many (most?) plain paper copiers? If the buyer's experience with this brand of copier had been particularly poor, might not assertion *b* stand for something?

The court's explanation for why item *c* and the portion of *d* that asserts that the future cost of supplies would remain low did not create express warranties is worth considering. It held that neither was an assertion "relating to the goods" as is required by §2-313(1)(a). Doesn't the availability of replacement parts for a complicated bit of machinery relate to that machine in just the kind of way that buyers care about and indeed ask about? The relationship criterion of §2-313 must have some purpose, but I'm not sure it's meant to eliminate assertions like that in item *c*. What would be a clear example of something where the lack of relationship would rule out the finding of an express warranty? What about an assertion by the seller that "new government regulations will be issued soon that will mean many more small businesses will need to do copying"? If true, this could make the deal much more attractive to the buyer, and it certainly is a statement of fact, not mere puffery. But it doesn't seem the kind of information that the buyer would or should rely upon the seller for, nor would the buyer expect the seller to be warranting that it is true. I don't find the allegations in the actual case, at least as to replacement parts, to be in this league. The language "relates to the goods," seems to me sufficiently encompassing to include such a statement about replacement parts.

The court in *Royal Business Machines*, by the way, expressed the test it was applying as follows:

> The decisive test for whether a given representation is a warranty or merely an expression of the seller's opinion is whether the seller asserts a fact of which the buyer is ignorant or merely states an opinion or judgment on a matter of which the seller has no special knowledge and on which the buyer may be expected also to have an opinion and to exercise his judgment.

Does this clarify matters? Was the court clearly following its own rule in the actual decisions rendered?

5. Alan could argue that Chuck has given him an express warranty that the "Miracle Kill" does indeed kill crabgrass, or at least that it destroys it as well as anything else Alan could have bought in the store (or elsewhere?). As you will see in the following chapter, the situation will also give rise to the implied warranty of fitness for a particular purpose, and you might be tempted to wonder why we even bother with it here under the rubric of express warranties. (The answer to *that* question will be apparent in the second chapter to follow, which covers warranty disclaimers.) The implied warranties are much easier to disclaim, so if the stuff fails to have any effect on the crabgrass, Alan's ability to establish an express warranty based on the language used here may be crucial to his fate. See also *Triple E, Inc. v. Hendrix & Dail, Inc.*, 543 S.E.2d 245 (S.C. App. 2001), holding that advertisement for a crop fungicide created express warranties with its statements of "proven control" and "season long control."

6. You may think what you like, but be aware that United States District Judge Morrison C. England, Jr. concluded that Sugawara had not presented a good claim for a breach of an express warranty. *Sugawara v. Pepsico, Inc.*, 2009 WL 1439115 (E.D. Cal.). The judge explained:

   > [W]hile the challenged packaging contains the word "berries" it does so only in conjunction with the descriptive term "crunch." This Court is not aware of, nor has Plaintiff alleged the existence of, any actual fruit referred to as a "crunchberry." Furthermore, the "Crunchberries" depicted on the [box] are round, crunchy, brightly-colored cereal balls, and the [principal display on the box] clearly states both that the Product contains "sweetened corn & oat cereal" and that the cereal is "enlarged to show texture." Thus, a reasonable consumer would not be deceived into believing that the Product in the instant case contained a fruit that does not exist. . . . Additionally . . . the instant packaging makes no claim to be particularly nutritious or to be designed specifically to meet the nutritional needs of toddlers or children, nor does it contain any images of actual fruit that would convince this Court the instant packaging was even potentially deceptive. In this case, there is no reference to fruit on the [box] unless one believes that a "Crunchberry" is some form of produce. Indeed, even though Plaintiff claims that the brightly-colored cereal balls are shaped to resemble berries, she acknowledges that "[c]lose inspection reveals that Crunchberries on the [box] are not really berries." Accordingly, it is entirely unlikely that members of the public would be deceived in the manner described by Plaintiff.

   For a case decided by another California district court that had previously rejected similar claims directed against the makers of "Froot Loops" cereal, and brought by the same plaintiff's attorneys, see *McKinniss v. Kellogg USA*, 2007 WL 4762172 (C.D. Cal.). Carrying on in this vein, if you are interested in what you have a right to expect when you purchase a beverage named "Premium Diet Soda" said to contain "all natural flavor," you may want to consult *Viggiano v. Hansen Natural Corp.*, 944

F. Supp. 2d 877 (C.D. Cal. 2013). See also *Bohac v. General Mills, Inc.*, 2014 WL 1266848 (N.D. Cal.).

7. Yes. Nuts Incorporated created an express warranty by sample. See §2-313(1)(c) and *Alimenta (U.S.A.), Inc. v. Anheuser-Busch Cos., Inc.*, 803 F.2d 1160 (11th Cir. 1986), on which this question is based. Of course there is always the problem of exactly what the warranty was for. Here, presumably, the warranty is that the peanuts delivered would be *like those in the sample,* in that they would fry and roast up in the same way that the sample nuts did. The Court of Appeals quoted with approval a statement by the district court that there was an express warranty "that the peanuts supplied under the contract would conform to the size, appearance, and flavor of the sample peanuts." But assume the sample was handpicked to contain only nice, plump nuts—the kind you'd want to show off to a potential buyer. Does this mean the seller warranted that in the tons that were to be eventually delivered, there'd not be a single dried-out dud? I doubt it. On that question, I think it would be better to look at any other express warranties about overall uniformity and quality. Or trade usage could come into play. Failing that, we would have to turn to the implied warranty of merchantability, a concern for the next chapter. For a case involving an express warranty created by a sample, you might want to look at *Artistic Carton Co. v. Thelamco, Inc.*, 2009 WL 3060205 (N.D. Ind. 2009). The plaintiff's primary customer was a "high-end retailer" for whose packaging plaintiff required a specific kind of paperboard that was capable of being laminated. A sample of the paperboard the defendant offered to provide for the job was tested, successfully, when run through the anticipated lamination process. A supply contract was entered into, but the entire project was "foiled, or perhaps unfoiled" (in the words of the court), when the paperboard eventually delivered would not take to the laminate process. Continuing problems with the defendant's paperboard caused the plaintiff's production schedule to become "unglued" (again, the words of the court), and the plaintiff was eventually forced to hire a temporary summer workforce of 125 college students to complete the order for its primary customer.

   As you may have noted, §2-313(1)(c) refers to *models* as well as *samples.* What's the difference? Comment 6 explains that a sample is "actually drawn from the bulk of the goods which is the subject matter of the sale," while a model is "offered for inspection when the subject matter is not at hand and has not been drawn from the bulk of the goods." In *Logan Equipment Corp. v. Simon Aerials, Inc.*, 736 F. Supp. 1188 (D. Mass. 1990), the buyer of eight specially manufactured, 80-foot boomlifts argued that an express warranty that the lifts would not tip over under certain circumstances had been created by a demonstration of some 42-foot lifts constructed by the seller for another company. The plaintiff buyer apparently characterized its argument as one based on a sample, but this would seem to be a good case for a model, if anything. If, for example, the lifts delivered to the buyer had been only 42 feet long, it surely could have been expected to complain. Unfortunately for the plaintiff, it ultimately wasn't a good case on any terms. The court held that differences between the machines demonstrated and those ordered, "as well as [the buyer's] own knowledge that a boomlift's design varies greatly with such characteristics as its boom length and weight," precluded any finding that the demonstration of the 42-foot cranes had in and of itself created any express warranty on the 80-foot units.

If the distinction between samples and models isn't all that clear, we are fortunate in that it rarely seems to matter in any individual case. Either can create an express warranty, provided it "is made part of the basis of the bargain." As a full reading of Comment 6 makes clear, it is that last phrase that can cause the problem here, as it does generally for §2-313(1). The remaining questions finally take it on.

8. a. If Karl saw the display before he made the purchase, there should be no problem in his claiming an express warranty. Would he have to prove, or even make some affirmative allegation, that he would not have bought the watch if he had not been led to believe it had this feature? That's doubtful under the Code. Why should there even be any doubt about this? The answer lies in the cryptic phrase *part of the basis of the bargain* and its history. Prior to adoption of Article 2, the governing law was laid out in the Uniform Sales Act. Section 12 of that Act required that for an affirmation of fact or a promise to create an express warranty, it had to be shown that "the natural tendency of such affirmation or promise is to induce the buyer to purchase the goods," and further that "the buyer purchased the goods relying thereon. . . ." This was the classic language of a strict *reliance* requirement, and the courts in applying §12 took it seriously. The language of reliance was left out (purposefully, we are told) of the express warranty provision of Article 2. In its place is the requirement in each of the parts of §2-313(1) that the affirmation, or description, or sample, or whatever it is that is argued to give rise to an express warranty, must become or be made a part of "the basis of the bargain." This unquestionably creates a statutory criterion of some sort, but of exactly what sort is anything but clear. The language, and particularly that nebulous word "basis," came with no history attached. Over the years since its adoption, it is fair to say that neither the courts nor the commentators have come to any agreement exactly what it means.

   Is the part-of-the-basis-of-the-bargain test just the reliance criterion in another guise? The drafters apparently thought (or hoped) not. Notice the language in Comment 3:

> No specific intention to make a warranty is necessary if any of these factors is made part of the basis of the bargain. In actual practice affirmations of fact made by a seller about the goods during a bargain are regarded as part of the description of those goods; hence no particular reliance on such statements need be shown in order to weave them into the fabric of the agreement.

Whatever the drafters might have meant by this Comment, some writers have concluded that in actual practice the courts are left with little choice in applying the language of the statute itself other than to interpret it as virtually indistinguishable from the fairly strict reliance test of old. Others have found some room for a difference. At the very least, it may be that under §2-313 the obligation of the plaintiff buyer to plead and prove actual reliance in a very concrete way has been eliminated, or very much watered down. Once the particular affirmation or model or what-have-you has been in some way brought into the picture during the sales process, the intention of the drafters at least seems to be that it can be assumed that it has become part of the basis of the bargain. I don't think Karl in our question would have much trouble, if any, with this requirement as long as he alleged in some general way that the display card was out and he was aware of it. I doubt he would have to swear that he had been looking for a watch with this feature, or that he would have bought something else if the Chrono SX didn't have it. He would probably still be OK if in a deposition he said something like, "Yeah, I probably would have bought it with or without the stopwatch, but I saw the display and it sure did have a lot of nifty features. For that kind of money, and with all those buttons and dials, I certainly figured I'd get a lot of gadgets."

The basis-of-the-bargain test must have some bite to it, however, and we see this when we ask what would happen if at the time of sale Karl made the statement suggested in the example—that is, that he just couldn't care less about having a stopwatch. One suggestion is that what the basis of the bargain criterion does at the very least is shift the burden of proof on the issue of reliance to the seller. See *Weng v. Allison*, 678 N.E.2d 1254 (Ill. App. 1997). In our present example, Sam seems to have the evidence in hand to actually meet, at least initially, a burden of showing that Karl put *no reliance* on this line in the display card. A court would be hard pressed at this point to find for Karl. Perhaps Karl could show that, while he did indeed make this statement, by the time he left the store he had in fact been taken with this feature, or at least had been more impressed with the watch simply because it did have all of these doodads in the one package. Would it be fair to Sam to say that to prevail on this criterion he'd have to show that the stopwatch feature was actually a detriment or of absolutely no consequence in making the sale to Karl? I tend to think how such a case would come out would depend as much on how a particular court looked on the whole controversy and on other aspects of the parties' behavior as on anything else. If Karl's position were otherwise sympathetic, the basis-of-the-bargain criterion might well not stand in his way. If it appeared to the court that Karl for entirely other reasons wanted to get out of his deal and was simply latching onto the lack of stopwatch as a convenient excuse, the phrase could be found to have much more vitality.

b. We now consider how a court would handle the case if Karl had made no such disparaging comment about stopwatches but did have to admit that he never really looked over the display card. Again, there is no easy—or at least no consistent—answer from the cases. There are indeed cases that declare in no uncertain terms that for a buyer to make a claim of express warranty, he or she must have at least been *aware* of the affirmation on which it is based prior to entering into the agreement. This does seem a minimal requirement, and even if adopted does not automatically bring into play all of the prior fussiness about full-blown reliance from the earlier law. It could be argued to be a minimal kind of reading of the "part of the basis of the bargain" language. But even this is in doubt. Some courts have found instances in which a warranty existed even where the buyer couldn't make a showing of knowledge at the time of purchase. Once again, all is up for grabs, and I tend to think that a lot would depend on the court's general disposition toward Karl's claim. A sympathetic court might take very seriously an argument by Karl that while at the time of purchase he wasn't cognizant of the particular assertion about the stopwatch feature, he had been induced to buy the expensive Chrono SX by the whole aura surrounding it, which certainly included the display card listing lots of impressive features. In this way perhaps the whole card, and all that it said, had become a part of the basis of the bargain and could now be used by Karl to his advantage.

c. Annie should have the protection of an express warranty. As a matter of fact she does rely on an affirmation in the ad, but I doubt a court would make her prove it in any real way. The basis-of-the-bargain test, whatever it is, has been met here. There are a number of cases finding an express warranty based on statements, or even fair implications from pictures or other material, found in advertisements or sales brochures that were seen by the buyer. This is in keeping with the intention of the drafters. See the language from Comment 3 quoted above. Of course not all inferences that might possibly be made from advertising material will necessarily result in enforceable express warranties. In *Hubbard v. General Motors Corp.*, 1996 WL 274018 (S.D.N.Y.), for instance, the court found that GM's "advertising proclamations that [its Chevy] Suburbans are 'like a rock,' 'popular,' and 'the most dependable long-lasting trucks on the planet,' . . . are generalized and exaggerated claims which a reasonable consumer would not rely upon as statements of fact." Such verbiage was, in effect, mere puffery and did not create any express warranties as to the condition of the brakes on the new Suburbans. And in *Maneely v. General Motors Corp.*, 108 F.3d 1176 (9th Cir. 1997), the Ninth Circuit ruled that print and television advertising by GM, some of which showed young people standing or sitting in the cargo beds of pickup trucks, would not in itself give rise to any reasonable expectation that riding in the back of a moving pickup was warranted to be safe, especially since in most of the ads upon which the plaintiffs relied the trucks appeared to be stationary and driverless.

d. Barbara will have a problem showing that Sam's statement to her became "part of the basis of the bargain" as required by §2-313(1)(a). The requirement must mean something, and it will be hard for her to argue that, whatever it means, it is satisfied in a situation where she did not even hear the statement until after the bargain was struck. But consider Comment 7:

> The precise time when words of description or affirmation are made or samples are shown is not material. The sole question is whether the language or samples or models are fairly to be regarded as part of the contract. If the language is used after the closing of the deal (as when the buyer when taking delivery asks and receives an additional assurance) the warranty becomes a modification, and need not be supported by consideration if it is otherwise reasonable and in order (Section 2-209).

The directive of this Comment is far from indisputable given the statutory language and far from clear in its own right. If the affirmation comes after the bargain is struck, do the writers assert it is directly available to the buyer even given the basis-of-the-bargain test, which seems to be the import of the first sentence, or only because it is a later modification otherwise valid—that is, a distinct addition to the contract? In many situations, it might not make any difference, but in others it could. For example, if there is an arguably valid warranty disclaimer made part of the initial agreement, such a disclaimer would presumably operate on any term that was itself "a part of the basis of the bargain." It might not have the same effect on a term that was added later. The closing sentences in this Comment seem to try to duck the inevitable issue under the statutory criterion, while the first sentence states "precise timing" to be "not material" without explanation.

I think that Barbara can make a good argument that the glow-in-the-dark feature is "part of the basis of the bargain" and hence creates a warranty to her. Of course it assumes that the §2-313(1) criterion and reliance, as conventionally understood, are not identical. Imagine, if you will, what might have happened if Sam's answer to her question had been different. That is, he tells her that the watch she has picked out has no such feature. There is then some likelihood that she might want to call the deal off, explaining the importance to her of being able to read her watch in the dark. Suppose she says that she's going to wait to buy a watch that makes this possible. What would Sam's response be? It's always possible, I guess, that Sam would adamantly refuse to let her change her mind now, giving her a lecture on the sanctity of contract, with its traditional notions of a completed acceptance and all that. In the real world, however, it seems to me at least as likely that Sam will think something like, "That's one deal that got away," take the watch back and rip up the credit card slip. If he does do this, his thinking might be that, while he is sure she has already bought the watch and has no legal right to return it, it is simply good business for him to allow her to get away with this. But it's also possible that Sam's attitude is that he really hasn't made a sale until the (at least momentarily) satisfied customer leaves the shop with the item in hand. If that is so, then it doesn't seem to me incorrect to consider his *affirmative* answer to her question as part of the selling language he's put into the mix to nail down the sale and hence as "part of the basis of the bargain."

This argument does at least suggest some meaning for the basis-of-the-bargain test that isn't simply classical reliance in another guise and might actually work for Barbara before a court, although there is no real authority for it as of yet. We look not at the "precise timing" of the contract in the traditional sense of when the formal offer was formally accepted, but rather at when such a deal would "reasonably" seem set and inviolate as parties actually behave in commerce. But see what a slender reed it is. Suppose instead that Barbara had not asked Sam this question. Rather, as he was wrapping up her purchase, he said something like, "You're really going to be happy you chose this watch. It has all kinds of features I didn't even mention. Did I tell you about the glow-in-the-dark dial?" Barbara hears him, thanks him, and leaves the store with her purchase. Does the fact that the seller offered this information gratis mean that she cannot later use it to her advantage? Note that the language of Comment 7 suggests that this would indeed make a difference, as the case I'm now posing is not one in which the buyer "asks and receives an additional assurance."

e. Here's a case where there has clearly been no reliance, and it would be hard to argue there is anything even close to it. I think Carol would be out of luck. The argument we crafted for Barbara in the previous question might work here as well, but it seems to be stretching things beyond the breaking point. What if Carol sees the ad two or three weeks later? Would she then be able to act as if she had never purchased the watch? There are a number of cases that contain clear statements to the effect that while an advertisement or a seller's brochure may indeed create an express warranty for the buyer, he or she must at least have seen or been aware of its existence at the time of purchase, and it seems hard to argue with this conclusion. See, for example, *Schmaltz v. Nissen*, 431 N.W.2d 657 (S.D. 1988), in which the Supreme Court of South Dakota reasoned that a farmer buying seed could not have received an express warranty based on language found on the bags containing that seed as the language had not been read until delivery, after the sale was completed. "Without having read or even known of this language," the court said, "it is impossible to say this language was part of the basis of the bargain." So much for Comment 7's assertion that timing in such matters is "not material," although to be fair the Comment does say that *precise* timing doesn't matter, and maybe that's all we need.

One final puzzler before we leave the topic of express warranties. Imagine that Sam makes one more sale of the Timola, this time to someone named Darla. Several months later, Darla is in his store on an unrelated matter. He says to her, "I see you are wearing that Timola I sold you. I hope you're happy with it. It really is an amazing deal. Did you realize that it's totally waterproof on top of everything else?" The next weekend, Darla wears the watch while swimming and it is ruined. The Timola, whatever its other merits, is not waterproof. We presume that if a friend had innocently misled her in this way, she wouldn't have any legal cause of action against the friend. Does she have any rights against Sam, the jeweler who sold it to her initially, because he was the one to make the statement, albeit much later in time and unrelated to the transaction? Your guess is as good as mine.

CHAPTER 12

Implied Warranties of Quality

INTRODUCTION TO THE IMPLIED WARRANTIES

As we saw in the preceding chapter, express warranties become part of the sales contract through some overt behavior on the part of the seller. In arriving at a deal, the seller makes some statement of fact, adopts a particular description of the goods, or makes reference to a model or a sample. In other words, the seller takes some *action* that gives rise in the buyer to some manner of expectation as to the quality of the goods. The implied warranties, on the other hand, arise more out of the seller's *inaction*. Beyond what flows from the seller's explicit words and deeds, other expectations on the part of the buyer about the character of the goods seem to spring naturally from the overall circumstances of the sale coupled with the seller's doing nothing in the circumstances to disabuse the buyer from these perfectly reasonable beliefs. In the following chapter, we will discuss the tools a seller will have at hand to *escape* giving any type of implied warranty if that is his or her intention. Before we go into that, however, we will explore how and when implied warranties arise and become enforceable aspects of a contract for the sale of goods. In essence, we are concerned with how the seller's *failure to act* can result in warranty protection for the buyer.

Under Article 2, implied warranties of quality are of two types. Note that the §2-312 warranties—the warranty of title and the warranty against infringement—are not described in Article 2 as implied warranties. We will see why in the next chapter. The initial challenge is to see what circumstances give rise to either or both implied warranties. Look at §2-314(1).

Barring an effective disclaimer or modification (which we've put off for a chapter), a *warranty of merchantability* is implied as long as two factual criteria are met. First of all, the transaction must be a contract of sale. As to this requirement, you can refer back to Chapter 2. The second criterion is that the sale of goods must have been made by "a merchant with respect to goods of that kind." We dealt with Article 2's definition and special treatment of the *merchant* in Chapter 3, which you should review now if you haven't already done so.

That's it. If these two criteria are met, then there is a warranty that the goods will be merchantable. Notice the various factors that need *not* be demonstrated in order to bring §2-314 into play. Just as in §2-313, there is no requirement that the seller intended to make any warranty or used any particular language of promise, nor is it relevant whether the seller knew or even could have known of the shortcomings of the goods. Unlike warranties arising under §2-313, however, there is no necessity that the seller use *any* language, samples, or models, or express anything in any way to the buyer. Nor is there any need for the buyer to show reliance on the seller, that anything became "part of the basis of the bargain" between the two, or even that the seller's merchant status played any part in the buyer's decision to purchase the product.

The issues of greatest concern under this section are by and large not whether a warranty of merchantability was made part of the contract. It's usually fairly obvious when this is so. In the examples that follow, you can assume that there was a sale and that the seller was a merchant who deals with goods of the kind. The puzzle will be to figure out as best we can exactly *what* the warranty of merchantability covers. The buyer is promised something, but what exactly is far from self-evident. The drafters made no effort to define *merchantability* or the word *merchantable* in the Code. What help they give is to be found in §2-314(2), which you will want to read in connection with the examples. This subsection provides not a definition but what is more like a listing of the least, the very minimum, that is and can be expected when purchasing from a merchant. It is not meant to be exhaustive. See Comment 6. As you'll soon discover, the heart of this provision is the right the buyer has to insist that anything bought from a merchant will be at least "fit for the ordinary purposes" for which such stuff is normally used. But what does this mean in actual day-to-day affairs?

The later examples of this chapter also ask you to examine the second type of implied warranty provided for in Article 2. The implied *warranty of fitness for a particular purpose* arises under §2-315. Here the substance of the warranty is at least initially much easier to characterize. If the buyer has a "particular purpose" for which he or she purchases the goods, and if a series of other criteria are met by the facts in the particular case, there is as part of the contract a warranty that the goods will be fit *for that particular purpose*. As to what is a "particular" versus an "ordinary purpose," you should read Comment 2 to this section. But is it all that clear? You should review now the various criteria that §2-315 sets up for anyone wanting to plead and prove this warranty. Notice in particular that it is not a requirement of §2-315 that the seller be a merchant. A casual seller can give this warranty as well as a merchant.

We explore the *when* and the *what*, and even a bit of the *wherefore*, of these implied warranties in the examples. I think you'll find them particularly interesting. Moreover, if my years of experience with students are any indication, you may well be inspired by this material to think more than you ever have before about the purchases you make each day, what you expect will be true when things go right, and what horrible fate awaits you if things go even slightly wrong.

Examples

1. Lisa goes into the Springfield Stationery Store, where she finds a display of regular wooden pencils on the front counter. She removes three from the display and places them before the clerk who says, "That'll be $1.50." Lisa pays that amount, takes the pencils, and makes her way home.
   (a) Lisa sharpens one of the pencils to a nice point. When she starts to do her homework, she discovers that no matter how hard she tries, she can't make any marks on her paper with the pencil. Was this pencil merchantable at the time of sale?
   (b) Lisa takes the second pencil and sharpens that one. She writes with it for a time, but then the point breaks. Has she a claim that *this* pencil was unmerchantable?
   (c) In frustration, Lisa decides to do her homework in ink. Writing with a ballpoint pen is fine for a while, but eventually she makes a mistake. She tries to erase her error using the rubber tip on the end of the third of her pencils. It doesn't work. Was this pencil, unmerchantable because the eraser doesn't erase?
   (d) Lisa drops the idea of working in pen. She sharpens the third pencil, which writes perfectly well and without any breakage. She gets her homework done with no problem. She continues to use this pencil to do her schoolwork. Later in the week when she is resharpening the pencil, she is surprised to discover that the lead in the pencil runs out about halfway down its original length, leaving her with only a solid stick of wood painted yellow. Does she have a breach of warranty claim against the seller? Would your answer be the same if the lead had disappeared only as she was trying to get use out of the very last bit, say the last one-half inch of the pencil? In other words, how much lead should there be in an ordinary lead pencil?

2. At the Springfield Kwik-E-Mart, Marge takes from the shelf a can marked "Peas" and buys the can along with other groceries. At home when she opens the can, she discovers it contains nothing but canned corn. It's perfectly safe, nutritious, and tasty corn, but it's just that—corn. Was this can merchantable? If she chose to, could Marge successfully sue the Kwik-E-Mart for this grave infraction? If so, what options would Apu, the owner of the Kwik-E-Mart, have?

3. Bart, a ten-year-old boy, goes into a local variety store. From the candy selection, he picks out a package of cinnamon flavored, wooden toothpicks marketed under the name "Hot Cinnamon Fire Pix." Later on the playground, he is sucking on one of the picks when he falls from the jungle gym, landing face-down on the surface below. The toothpick breaks and punctures his lower lip, leaving him with a scar. Bart sues the owner of the variety store claiming that the toothpick sold to him was unmerchantable. What result?

4. Homer decides to repaint the living room of his home. He goes to the local hardware store where, after looking over the color charts, he buys three cans of No Problemo brand paint, each of which is marked "Interior Egg-Shell White." He paints his walls. When the paint is dry, he is distressed to find that the area painted with two of the cans is slightly but noticeably darker than the area painted with the third. Either color comes close to that shown on the color chart, and either would satisfy Homer, but they are not the same: The overall effect is just not right. Does Homer have a claim against the store for breach of warranty?

5. Holiday Products Incorporated puts together baskets of fruits, candies, and other goodies, which it buys from various suppliers. It contracts to buy a large number of grapefruit "of size from 6 to 7 inches in diameter" from farmer Jones. When the grapefruits are delivered, Holiday discovers that they are virtually all from six to six and one-quarter inches in size. None is smaller than six inches, but very few are anywhere near seven inches. Has Jones breached the warranty of merchantability?

6. Maria buys a bright red tee-shirt in a local discount store for $5. After several washings, she is unhappy because the color of the shirt has faded considerably and has begun to shrink and lose its shape.
   (a) Was the shirt unmerchantable at the time of sale?
   (b) Suppose Maria had purchased the tee-shirt for $50 from a classy store ("The Gorge") located in a trendy upscale mall she visited when she went to the big city on her vacation. Was the shirt unmerchantable at the time of sale?

7. In 2023, Mr. Ireland bought a used 2012 Ford automobile with 82,364 miles on it from Jane's Auto Sales. During the sale, Jane was careful not to make any express warranties about the car's quality. Within weeks of his purchase, the car's engine began to repeatedly stall, knock, and wheeze. Would Ireland have a claim against Jane for breach of the implied warranty of merchantability?

8. Mrs. Webster, who had been born and brought up in New England, entered the Blue Ship Tea Room, a quaint Boston restaurant located on a wharf overlooking the ocean. She ordered a cup of fish chowder. After taking several spoonfuls, she could feel something lodged in her throat. Later, at Massachusetts General Hospital, a fish bone was found in her throat and removed. Was the chowder unmerchantable?

9. Tommy Phillips suffered injury when a chunk of turkey bone got caught in his throat. The bone had been hidden in a bite-sized cube of white turkey meat ladled, along with gravy and peas, onto a mound of mashed potatoes in his high school cafeteria in West Springfield, Massachusetts. Does Tommy have a case against the cafeteria?

10. Harold buys a new aftershave lotion. He liberally splashes it on his face. Within a few minutes, his face is covered with a rash and has swollen up considerably. He discovers that the medical term for his condition is *contact dermatitis* and that it was brought on by an allergic reaction to the aftershave. On the basis of this information, can you conclude whether the aftershave was merchantable?

11. During her vacation in the country, Bella goes into a photographic supply store owned by Steve. Showing Steve her camera, she says, "It's supposed to be a beautiful cloudless night tonight, and I'd love to take some pictures of the sky. I'll need some film. What have you got?" Steve takes a roll of Supermax 200 from a shelf and sells it to Bella. Using this film, Bella takes a series of pictures, mostly of the night sky, which she has developed when she returns home. The pictures taken during daylight hours come out fine, but none of the nighttime pictures comes out. She then discovers that while Supermax 200 is a perfectly good film for general picture taking, it is not suitable for nighttime photography and certainly not for taking pictures of the stars.
    (a) Has Steve breached the warranty of merchantability here? What about an implied warranty of fitness for a particular purpose?
    (b) Suppose instead that Bella, after commenting on her interest in taking pictures of the stars, had concluded, "I hear that Supermax 200 is a good film. Give me some of that." Does this affect your answer to the previous question?

EXPLANATIONS

Explanations

1. a. Lisa's pencil is not merchantable. To be merchantable, goods must be "at least . . . fit for the ordinary purposes for which such goods are used." This language from §2-314(2)(c), while it can't be held up as a code definition of merchantability or even the exclusive criterion, is obviously key to the concept. A pencil that won't make a mark on a piece of regular homework-type paper doesn't meet the standard. It would be different, of course, if Lisa were trying to write on wax paper or on a piece of plastic. Crucial, of course, is what we consider the "ordinary purposes for which such goods are to be used." In a case decided by the Supreme Court of Pennsylvania, *Phillips v. Cricket Lighters*, 883 A.2d 439 (Pa. 2005), a two-year-old child had gotten hold of a Cricket disposable butane cigarette lighter that belonged to his mother and started a fire that left the child, his mother, and one other child dead. In a suit against the manufacturer of the lighter, one argument was that the lighter was unmerchantable because it lacked any "child-resistant" feature. The court concluded that the claim based on a warranty of merchantability theory should have been dismissed:

   > The word "ordinary" is readily understood to mean "common" or "average." See American Heritage Dictionary of the English Language 925 (1981). In the context of this matter, it is apparent that the ordinary purpose of the Cricket lighter was to allow an adult user to produce a flame. Its ordinary purpose certainly was not to be a two year old child's plaything. The fact that the product was tragically misused in such a way does not alter the ordinary purpose of the product. As the lighter was fit for its ordinary purpose, it was merchantable.

   b. Pencil number two would seem to be merchantable. For goods to be merchantable, they need not be perfect or all that the buyer would hope. Of course the pencil would not be merchantable if Lisa could demonstrate that the point repeatedly broke when no more than "ordinary" pencil-pushing force was applied.

   While it never appears in §2-314, the phrase or notion of *reasonable expectations* is useful, if admittedly fuzzy, in considering questions of merchantability. (We'll see later that it actually has become a term of art in one particular situation, when foodstuffs are involved.) In the field of express warranties, we could ask what reasonable expectations were created by the overt actions and words of the seller; now we concentrate on what the buyer can reasonably expect from the goods based solely on the fact that they were purchased from a merchant who deals in goods of that kind. The goods should be what the buyer assumes them to be, what merchants sell when they sell goods of this kind. Pencils are expected to make marks on paper, but pencil points do break now and then. Let's be reasonable. Pencils are pencils.

We expect them to do certain things, but they have their limitations, and we have learned to live in this less than perfect world. Lisa is learning the same lesson.

A case that I like in this regard, even if the court managed to decide it without any citation to the Code, is *Fanning v. Lemay,* 230 N.E.2d 182 (Ill. 1967). It was a rainy day. Ruth Fanning entered a laundromat intending to do some laundry, wearing a pair of shoes made by the U.S. Rubber Company that she had bought at Montgomery Ward. The asphalt tile floor of the laundromat was wet and slippery. Ms. Fanning slipped and fell to the floor, sustaining serious injuries. She sued, along with other defendants, the manufacturer of her sneakers and the store that sold them to her. Among the counts was one claiming that the shoes were not fit for the ordinary purposes for which they were purchased because the soles became "slippery and dangerous when wet and used upon asphalt tile." The Illinois Supreme Court approved the dismissal of this part of her claim:

> No facts are alleged setting forth any specific defect in the shoes, nor are there facts to show that in the respect alleged they were any different from shoes ordinarily worn by millions of other people. It is a matter of common knowledge that shoes are more likely to slip when wet than dry, but this provides no basis for the conclusion that a particular pair of shoes is dangerous or unsafe.

The court concluded, "The law does not require that common articles such as shoes be accident-proof, or that a manufacturer warn and protect against mishaps in their use." Reason and reasonableness triumphant.

Another case you may find of more than passing interest is *Hubbs v. Joseph Enterprises,* 604 N.Y.S.2d 292 (App. Div. 1993), in which the plaintiff, an 80-year-old woman suffering from arthritis and osteoporosis, brought suit for injuries to her hand and wrist against the retailer of a device known as "The Clapper," designed to turn electrical appliances on and off by responding to sound. The Appellate Division determined that the complaint should have been dismissed as her injuries were not the result of any defect in the device, "but were, rather, the sole result of the plaintiff's deliberate act of attempting one last 'extra hard' clap after repeated prior efforts to activate the device had failed."

c. It doesn't seem reasonable to think that the eraser at the end of a pencil will erase a mark made in ink. It should, of course, erase pencil marks. But even here we can't push things too far. Suppose Lisa, using a pencil, makes a mistake in her work and tries to erase it. The eraser at the pencil's end does lift most of the markings from the paper, but it doesn't do so perfectly. There are still faint traces of what she had written, or perhaps more likely an indistinct smudge.

The first few times this happens she may be surprised and even upset that the paper is not brought back to its pristine condition, but she's going to have to learn to live with it. Lisa continues to learn her lessons so she can grow up to be a better, more "reasonable" person. As the Texas Supreme Court has observed, "A product which performs its ordinary function adequately does not breach the implied warranty of merchantability merely because it does not function as well as the buyer would like, or even as well as it could." *General Motors Corp. v. Brewer*, 966 S.W.2d 56 (Tex. 1998).

d. This is a trick question. There should not be any lead in a lead pencil, if by "lead" we mean the heavy bluish-gray metallic chemical element with atomic weight of 207.21. Even the yellow paint we commonly see on pencils is now expected to be lead-free for health and safety reasons. According to a definitive (and highly entertaining) study, the blackish substance that's inside an American-made pencil of the twentieth century "might be a proprietary mixture of two kinds of graphite, from Sri Lanka and Mexico, clay from Missouri, gums from the Orient, and water from Pennsylvania." Henry Petroski, The Pencil: A History of Design and Circumstance (1992).

So we'll change the question to read how much of what we might call "pencil lead" should there be in your standard variety yellow wooden pencil? My guess is that most people assume the lead goes the whole way through the pencil's seven inches. I know I do. Where this assumption comes from and why I tend to think it a "reasonable" one, I'm not sure. I've never sharpened a pencil down that far. As a matter of fact, as Professor Petroski demonstrates (citing Jane Austen's *Emma*, among other authorities), even well into the nineteenth century the lead of a pencil didn't necessarily extend through its entire length. It was a matter of economy. Graphite was not cheap. Once the pencil got so short, it would be difficult to handle, no one would use it anyway. They would, as I do today, move on to a new pencil.

Would it make sense to go back to these good old days when pencils had less lead in them but were presumably cheaper to some degree? As one who would benefit by spending less on pencils and suffer no countervailing loss, I'd be all for it. Why should I pay for some pencil lead I never choose to use? Others who presently work their way through the last little bit of the pencil, and who may even positively enjoy doing so, would object. You begin to see how much is subsumed in this notion of "reasonable" expectations and "ordinary" use. Notice that the issue need not be characterized as some titanic struggle between righteous and demanding buyers and the penny-pinching sellers who will always try to get away with giving the consumer as little as possible. What we are really talking about is a balance, an implicit set of trade-offs, between various sets of consumers.

When we're dealing with standard off-the-shelf products (the kind that merchants sell day in and day out), some consumers are going to be paying for features or a higher level of quality than they actually want or need. These people in effect subsidize their neighbors who do take advantage of the added features or appreciate the greater quality. Meanwhile others in the community would be willing to pay *even more* for a product that was distinctly better but may not be able to find anything like it in the stores. As you continue on, you should keep in mind this notion of balance and trade-offs, not between naturally antagonistic buyers and sellers, but *among various groups of consumers*. It's always in the background, but starts to come to the fore in the food cases and is to be seen most dramatically in the case of atypical reactions or allergies with which we deal in Example 10.

2. The can was not merchantable. Even if you assume that canned corn is fit for the ordinary purpose for which people buy other canned vegetables, including peas, its contents did not "conform to the promise or affirmations of fact made on the container," which is another thing to look for under §2-314(2)(f). The Kwik-E-Mart operator is responsible for the breach of warranty. There would be no need for Marge to show that Apu knew the can was mistakenly labelled nor that there was any reason he "should have known" or was negligent in any way. Remember, breach of warranty liability is strict liability. The seller's intentions and state of mind are irrelevant. The thing sold was not what it was supposed to be. End of story, at least as far as Marge is concerned. Of course, if the Kwik-E-Mart is made to pay Marge for this breach, it should itself have a warranty action against whatever seller supplied it with the mismarked can. Eventually the claim will work its way back to the wrongdoer. See *Sparks v. Total Body Essential Nutrition, Inc.*, 27 So. 3d 489 (Ala. 2009).

   Note also from this example that, while many claims of breach of the warranty of merchantability involve products that end up harmful or downright dangerous to the buyer, this need not be the case. We can assume that canned corn is perfectly good for Marge and her family. The character of the breach is in her surprise or disappointment; what she got wasn't what she reasonably believed she was buying.

3. No, I didn't make this one up. See *Killeen v. Harmon Grain Products, Inc.*, 413 N.E.2d 767 (Mass. App. 1980). In addition to the store, the other defendants in the case were the manufacturer of the Hot Pix, the manager of the variety store, the manager's minor child (who had actually delivered the Pix to the injured child right there on the playground), and a teacher at the school. The appellate court upheld directed verdicts in favor of all defendants. Of interest to us is its holding that there was nothing unmerchantable about a toothpick just because it could splinter in this fashion or because it had a pointy end or two. In fact, as the trial judge pointed

out, a consumer would presumably regard a toothpick with no pointed ends as defective rather than the other way around.

Here we see that just as a product doesn't have to be unsafe or harmful to be unmerchantable, a product that does offer the possibility of injury—that is "dangerous" in some fashion—isn't necessarily unmerchantable. In fact some things *must* have sharp edges or dangerous curves if they are to meet the buyer's expectations. A hunting knife would not be merchantable if it didn't come with a pretty sharp blade. A stick of dynamite that couldn't be made to explode under any condition whatsoever might be harmless, but it wouldn't be merchantable.

Neither is a product rendered unmerchantable just because it might cause some harm if used in other than an "ordinary" fashion. In *Birdsong v. Apple, Inc.*, 590 F.3d 955 (9th Cir. 2009), the plaintiffs filed a class action suit against Apple arguing that an iPod was defective and unmerchantable because its use with the earphones provided and the sound level pushed to its highest "posed an unreasonable risk of noise-induced hearing loss to its users." The plaintiffs had argued that the iPod was unmerchantable in that it "(1) comes with 'stock ear buds . . . designed to be placed deep into the ear canal rather than over the ears, which increases the danger of hearing damage,' (2) lacks 'noise isolating or cancelling properties,' and (3) lacks any volume meter that will inform users they are listening at dangerous levels." The district court concluded that the danger of hearing loss did not exist unless the consumer decided to use the iPod "in an extreme way." The appellate court affirmed the district court's decision, noting that the plaintiff's complaint itself included statements that:

> (1) the iPod is *capable* of playing 115 decibels of sound; (2) consumers may listen at unsafe levels; and (3) iPod batteries can last 12 to 14 hours and are rechargeable, giving users the *opportunity* to listen for long periods of time. (Emphasis by the court.)

"Taken as true," the Ninth Circuit concluded, "such statements suggest only that users have the option of using an iPod in a risky manner, not that the product lacks any minimum level of quality."

4. The three cans of paint sold together were not merchantable. See §2-314(2)(d), requiring that the goods "run, within the variations permitted by the agreement, of even kind, quality and quantity within each unit and among all units involved." I know of no case focusing on this particular language in the section, although it would seem to be important. Would Homer's case still be good if he had originally bought only two cans of paint and then, finding that he needed more, returned to the hardware store for the third a day or two later? What if he had dawdled so long that a month separated the two purchases?

5. It appears Jones has breached. See §2-314(2)(b) and Comment 7.

6. a. Just because the shirt eventually looks less than brand-new doesn't mean it was unmerchantable when sold. But how long should goods wear and how well? How do you react to this—as a reasonable person?

We might take note of the case of *Suminski v. Maine Appliance Warehouse, Inc.*, 602 A.2d 1173 (Me. 1992). Paul Suminski bought a brand new television set from the defendant seller for $713.97 in May of 1988. Sometime in June 1989, the set began to turn off by itself, although it would come back on when Suminski clicked it off and then on again. About two months later, it would not turn on at all. He contacted the seller, whose representative told him that the period of express warranty had run and that the store's only obligation was to give him the name of a repair technician. It did not help matters any that the seller's manager stated that he had been in the appliance business a long time and had never heard of any implied warranty of merchantability. (When Suminski's attorney suggested to the manager that he contact his own attorney to confirm the existence of such a warranty, he promptly hung up.) Be that as it may, the Supreme Judicial Court of Maine held that the buyer had failed to establish a breach of the warranty of merchantability:

> No evidence was presented concerning the specific defect in the product. In some circumstances a breach of the implied warranty of merchantability under the U.C.C. may be established by circumstantial evidence. . . . In the case at bar, however, the television set was in all respects satisfactory during approximately thirteen months after it was purchased. For all that appears in the record, the malfunction at the time may have resulted from a defective switch, repairable at a small cost. We conclude that the sale of a major appliance with a switch that fails more than a year later, cannot support a finding that the entire appliance was unmerchantable when sold.

Was the key fact here that a switch is only a small part of the package? In later language, the court suggests this underlies its result. But if the switch had not worked on delivery of the set, so that it could not have been turned on from day one, this would clearly have made the whole set unmerchantable. Isn't it of importance that the problem only cropped up after some time? But then if the picture tube had blown after thirteen months, what should be the result? If you think this would render a TV set unmerchantable, how long do you think a picture tube must last?

How long and how well a product can be expected to last must also be considered in light of the use to which it is put and how it is treated. Consider the case of *Hollingsworth v. Queen Carpet, Inc.*, 827 S.W.2d 306 (Tenn. Ct. App. 1991). The plaintiff bought a large quantity of carpeting from the defendant for installation in an apartment complex he was constructing. It was concluded that the carpeting was installed properly, but after something like 18 to 24 months, the top part of the carpeting began to unravel and separate from the backing. Technically this is known as *delamination*. In the words of one witness, it began to "look like an ol' wrinkly dog." The plaintiff testified that carpeting in his other apartment projects usually had a life expectancy of 10 to 12 years. Other evidence suggested the normal life span of such carpeting to be in the range of at least five to seven years. It did seem something had gone wrong. The defendant seller offered evidence to back up its assertion that the bedraggled state of the carpet was a result of moisture left in it when it had been cleaned by tenants with the Rinse-n-Vac system that could be rented at the local grocery store. As the court sharply noted, the plaintiff offered no expert evidence on the cleaning matter. He rested his case solely on the short length of time the carpet had been useable. A trial court judgment for the plaintiff was reversed. The court of appeals held that the buyer had not met its burden of proof "that it was more probable that the carpet was not fit for its ordinary purpose at the time it was installed rather than that the delamination was caused by excessive moisture." Had you represented the buyer here, what would you have included in your evidentiary case? How hard do you think it would be to meet the burden imposed on the plaintiff here? (Or can you answer that question without knowing more about carpeting in general, carpet cleaning as it is usually carried out in Tennessee, and the Rinse-n-Vac system in particular?) On the interesting, if somewhat macabre, question of how long and in what condition a wooden casket should remain in good shape following its being placed in the ground, I point you to the decision of the Supreme Court of Mississippi in *Moss v. Batesville Casket Company, Inc.*, 935 So. 2d 393 (Miss. 2006).

One additional hypothetical that is certainly worth thinking about is easy enough to state, if slightly unsettling. You buy a pet from a pet store. You give it a name, you give it a home. Later that pet dies. Does this mean it was unmerchantable at the time of sale? See *Bazzini v. Garrant*, 455 N.Y.S.2d 77 (Dist. Ct. Suffolk Co. 1982), the case of the expiring toucan. Unfortunately, the opinion doesn't have a particularly good discussion of the merchantability issue, but it does contain a whole series of truly outrageous puns and some suggestion of what to do if your exotic pet bird suddenly is taken with a seizure. (Hint: Have some Gatorade on hand.) For a later New York case, not nearly so entertaining but, to its credit, directly on point, see *Saxton v. Pets Warehouse, Inc.*, 691 N.Y.S.2d 872 (App. Div. 1999).

We return finally to where we began. Did Maria have the right—the *legal* right under the U.C.C.—to expect better of this tee-shirt? Certainly if it had lost all of its color on the very first washing, she would have had a right to complain, but she can't expect it to remain in a like-new condition indefinitely. What would you expect, or rather what *do* you expect, of a $5 tee-shirt?

b. What you pay for an item surely influences what you expect of it. It seems the notion of merchantability would have to take this into account. Comment 7 says that "[i]n cases of doubt as to what quality is intended, the price at which a merchant closes a contract is an excellent index of the nature and scope of his obligation under this section." So the question now is what Maria could and would reasonably expect *of a $50 tee-shirt?* Why do (we have to assume reasonable) people sometimes pay more when they could get away with paying less? If you posit that more expensive tee-shirts are desired only because of the added status they afford the owner, then perhaps this shirt doesn't have to wear any better than a cheap one. If, however, you believe that certain shirts can be successfully marketed at higher prices because they are of better materials, made with more care, or made to last longer (or if potential buyers are expected to believe something of the sort), then the amount of wear Maria has a right to expect is that much higher.

7. The warranty of merchantability applies to the sale of used goods. See Comment 3, which notes however that the seller's obligation is only such as is "appropriate to such goods." How fit must used goods be? As numerous courts have noted, that depends. One court stated:

> A late model, low mileage car, sold at a premium price, is expected to be in far better condition and to last longer than an old, high mileage, 'rough' car that is sold for little above scrap value.

Dale v. King Lincoln-Mercury, Inc., 676 P.2d 744 (Kan. 1984).

For a review of used car cases in Kansas following *Dale*, you might want to take a look at *Hodges v. Johnson*, 199 P.3d 1251 (Kan. 2009).

For an affirmative statement of what the buyer can rightfully expect of a used car, different courts have come up with a variety of formulations, although there doesn't seem to be any real disagreement in substance. The car should be "in reasonably safe condition and substantially free of defects that would render it inoperable." It should "perform up to the level reasonably expected of a car of the same age, mileage, and price." The defects should not be so serious as to "deprive the buyer of the beneficial use of the automobile." In *Faulkingham v. Seacoast Subaru, Inc.*, 577 A.2d 772 (Me. 1990), the Supreme Judicial Court of Maine refused to overturn a judgment against a seller where the trial judge had found that the car "proved to be unreliable transportation as a commuter vehicle or for the other travel use of the [buyer]." In a later case, the North Dakota Supreme Court upheld a finding that a used tractor that kept stalling and therefore could not be depended on to pull an implement across the buyer's land was not fit for the ordinary purposes for which it was to be used. After all, as the Supreme Court quoted the trial judge as observing, "I mean, within a couple hundred hours it stopped in the middle of the field. That's not what a tractor is supposed to do." *Eggl v. Letvin Equipment Co.*, 632 N.W.2d 435 (N.D. 2001).

At the same time, a used car or tractor is just that—used—and can't be expected to be in the same shape as a brand-new model. As the court noted in *Ireland v. J.L.'s Auto Sales, Inc.*, 574 N.Y.S.2d 262 (Justice Ct. Town of Acadia 1991), *rev'd*, 582 N.Y.S.2d 603 (Co. Ct. Wayne Co. 1992) (the case on which this question is based), "no eleven-year-old motor vehicle, having in excess of 82,000 miles, could reasonably be expected to perform without continuous repairs being required." So what do you do with a car that starts to stall and knock? There's no obvious answer. Once again, you are in as good a position as any reasonable person to make the call. The court in *Ireland* did not have to decide. In addition to its other problems, Mr. Ireland's car turned out to have a thoroughly rotten frame, which he was informed would not pass state inspection and could never be repaired well enough to do so. The court based its decision on this fact, concluding:

> As to the frame, in considering the extent of merchantability in an eleven year old motor vehicle driven in excess of 82,000 miles, on which [the seller] declared no guarantee was being given, it would be reasonable to expect some rust, but not to such a degree that the vehicle would not survive beyond four months.

See also, *Soto v. CarMax Auto Superstores, Inc.*, 611 S.E.2d 108 (Ga. App. 2005), and *Patches Farms, Inc. v. Thompson Machinery Commerce Corp.*, 2008 WL 5244458 (N.D. Miss.).

8. This is the well-known case of *Webster v. Blue Ship Tea Room, Inc.*, 198 N.E.2d 309 (Mass. 1964). The cases concerning unwelcome contaminants in food are legion, and don't always make for the most pleasant reading. Prior to the adoption of the Code, a principal question was whether the warranty concept applied to such cases at all. Many states held that, at least when the adulterated dish had been served up in a restaurant, liability was to be based not on a "sale" but on the law pertaining to the rendition of services. Section 2-314 settled at least this question for once and for all. See the concluding sentence of §2-314(1) and Comment 5.

   So under the Code, any food served up must be merchantable. It must be "fit for the ordinary purposes" for which such food is used, and we know what that means. But we also know that in order for any product to be merchantable, it need not be perfect. Even with the adoption of the Code, there continues to be legitimate dispute as to what the result should be when faced with a case like that of Mrs. Webster and her fish chowder.

The courts are not even in agreement as to what the *test* should be in such situations.

Earlier cases often relied upon a distinction and an analysis that came to be referred to as the *natural substance–foreign substance test*. In principle, under this approach, there is no warranty liability as a matter of law if the injury-causing substance is "natural" to the food, but there is liability and it is indeed automatic if the offending item is something "foreign" or "alien" to the particular foodstuff. This view was most forcefully presented and adopted by California in the case of *Mix v. Ingersoll Candy Co.*, 59 P.2d 144 (Cal. 1936), in which the plaintiff had swallowed a fragment of a chicken bone lurking in a restaurant's chicken pot pie. The Supreme Court of California concluded that "[b]ones which are natural to the type of meat served cannot legitimately be called a foreign substance, and a consumer who eats meat dishes ought to anticipate and be on his guard against the presence of such bones." Under *Mix*, foreign substances that would give rise to liability are such things as nails, wires, or ground glass (also presumably beef bones in a chicken pot pie). Coincident with deciding *Mix*, the court held in favor of a plaintiff who swallowed some glass while eating chow mein at a lunch counter. *Goetten v. Owl Drug Co.*, 59 P.2d 142 (Cal. 1936).

So no relief for Mr. Mix, and none for Mrs. Webster had the Massachusetts Supreme Judicial Court in 1964 chosen to follow this approach. But by that time, the *Mix* case and the natural-foreign test had come under a good deal of criticism for reasons that you can imagine. After all, there are all kinds of natural things that one would never expect to find in one's soup, just as there may be foreign matter that would come as no great surprise (a grain of sand in the spinach, for example). The court in *Webster* chose not to deny relief to Mrs. Webster solely on the quite obvious fact that a fish bone is naturally part of a fish. Instead it engaged in a different analysis and concerned itself with the nature of fish chowder and, more specifically, fish chowder as it is traditionally served in New England and in eateries of the kind where Mrs. Webster sat down to dine. The court asked the question: What would and could reasonably be anticipated of the chowder served to such a consumer in just such a place? Following an extended review of the received definition and history of chowders, complete with a number of traditional recipes including one offered up by Daniel Webster himself, the highest court for the Commonwealth of Massachusetts concluded:

> It is not too much to say that a person sitting down in New England to consume a good New England fish chowder embarks on a gustatory adventure which may entail the removal of some fish bones from his bowl as he proceeds. We are not inclined to tamper with age old recipes by any amendment reflecting the plaintiff's view of the effect of the Uniform Commercial Code.

Thus Mrs. Webster lost her case, but not because of any blanket rule of law about "natural" versus "foreign" substances. As the court remarked:

> [W]e consider that the joys of life in New England include the ready availability of fresh fish chowder. We should be prepared to cope with the hazards of fish bones, the occasional presence of which in chowders is, it seems to us, to be anticipated, and which, in the light of a hallowed tradition, do not impair their fitness or merchantability.

This type of reasoning, if not always so heavily reliant on actual recipes and regional chauvinism, has over the past years increasingly come into the cases. Almost all courts that have had to consider the question recently have implicitly or explicitly declined to follow the rigid natural substance–foreign substance distinction, preferring instead the *reasonable expectations test* for adulterated foods. This test calls for application on a case-by-case basis. It depends on no blanket rules of law, but instead provides that, whether or not the substance causing harm is natural to a food product, liability for a breach of the warranty of merchantability lies whenever the consumer would not reasonably have expected to find the substance in the product.

Slowly but surely this approach has been adopted by virtually every state. See for example *Jackson v. Nestle-Beich, Inc.*, 589 N.E.2d 547 (Ill. 1992), in which the reasonable expectations test was expressly adopted for Illinois and any lingering support for the Mix decision in that state abandoned. Jackson filed suit alleging a breach of warranty when he broke his tooth on a pecan shell embedded in a Katydid (a chocolate-covered pecan and caramel candy manufactured by Nestle). The Supreme Court of Illinois found he was entitled to a trial on the issue of merchantability even though pecan shells are perfectly "natural" to pecans. The manufacturer's argument that a lower court's dismissal of the action was proper under the Mix rationale or that at least some distinction should be recognized between natural and foreign impurities was dismissed as not "salutary to our jurisprudence."

The older natural substance–foreign substance test has generally gotten a pretty thorough thumbs-down in recent cases and by virtually all the commentators. Is there any life left to this distinction? That depends where you look. In a series of cases through the early 1990s, the Louisiana appellate courts tried to preserve the test in a fashion, or at least to find a middle ground. More importantly, the Supreme Court of California (by a 4 to 3 vote) adopted what it referred to as the *Louisiana approach* in *Mexicali Rose v. Superior Court*, 822 P.2d 1292 (Cal. 1992). (Just to make things that much more confusing, the Louisiana Supreme Court had by the end of the 1990s rejected this approach to the problem, substituting for it a purely negligence-based analysis. See *Porteous v. St. Ann's Cafe & Deli*, 713 So. 2d 454 (La. 1999).)

California's important *Mexicali Rose* case involved a one-inch chicken bone that turned up in a chicken enchilada. Under California's Mix rule, of course, the plaintiff would have had no relief as a matter of law. The California Supreme Court overturned Mix, but only partially. What we must now call the *California approach* involves a two-step analysis under which the natural–foreign substance distinction still plays a part. If the substance causing injury was foreign to the food product, then the injured party can state a cause of action in warranty and a reasonable expectations test applies. If, however, the substance was "natural to the preparation of the food served," then the court held, "it can be said that it was reasonably expected by its very nature and the food cannot be determined unfit or defective. A plaintiff in such a case has no cause of action in strict products liability or implied warranty." So, for example, in *Ford v. Miller Meat Co.*, 33 Cal. Rptr. 2d 899 (Cal. App. 1994), one Grace Joyce Ford was barred from bringing a breach of warranty action when she broke a tooth on a small fragment of (presumably beef) bone that she encountered when taking a sample taste of some prepackaged ground beef she was browning for tacos. "Clearly," the court concluded, "under *Mexicali Rose*, a bone fragment remains a natural substance under the foreign-natural distinction." In such a case, under this California approach, the plaintiff could prevail only by establishing that negligence in the preparation of the ground beef was to blame for her injury.

I think it very doubtful that many other states will follow this California line, much less insist on holding to the unadulterated natural substance–foreign substance distinction. Most commentators appear to agree that a straight reasonable expectations approach is not only the current rule in a majority of jurisdictions, but is also the wave of the future and a good thing, too.

In what follows, we continue to explore the workings of the reasonable expectations test. Perhaps there's not much more to say than that, as a reasonable person, you should be able to apply it as well as anyone else. We can, however, pick up on an earlier point—a suggested way of contemplating the ramifications of merchantability doctrine. Like any test in which the word "reasonable" takes center stage, what we are talking about is some kind of balancing act. You could think of the balance that must be struck between the seller of the food product and its customers, but there is another way to look at it. As you can see from reviewing the *Webster* language quoted above, the court is in essence striking a balance between the rights of the particular plaintiff and the rights of the community as a whole. Apparently many people like a good hearty fish chowder. Their interests would not be served by a decision that could result in New England fish chowder, even when served in the quaintest of oceanside restaurants, in the words of the defendant's brief, "degenerating into an insipid broth containing the mere essence of its former stature as a culinary masterpiece."

We should not make light of the fact that Mrs. Webster was really hurt by that bone in the throat, nor did the Massachusetts Supreme Judicial Court do so. The court was willing to concede that her injury was "not insubstantial" and to sympathize with what it termed her "peculiarly New England injury." Still, think of the consequences if they had ruled in her favor. We can assume that one of three things would have eventually happened. The Blue Ship Tea Room and other places of like kind might have had to charge more for each bowl or cup, to reflect the increased cost of doing business (a kind of built-in fish-bone insurance). That affects each and every one or us, including those who are perfectly capable of working around some bones in the chowder. A second possibility is that restaurants would be greatly pressured to change how they prepared fish chowders, endeavoring to make sure that not even the smallest bone or minimally chunky chunk of any other ingredient made its way into the final mix. The result could be survival not of the fittest or the tastiest, but of the blandest. You just have to think about what airline food is like to appreciate what this would mean. If that's going to be the case, we might all be better off if the Tea Room and every other eatery followed a third alternative strategy and simply dropped fish chowders from their menus altogether.

The reasonable expectations test for adulterated foods represents, like all of the law of merchantability when you get down to it, a kind of compromise that lies somewhere between the shoddy and the perfect. It's a compromise between each of us as individuals and where we stand as part of the larger community in which we live—that mass of humanity looking for a life that is reasonably safe but also reasonably varied and reasonably exciting.

9. This problem is taken from *Phillips v. Town of West Springfield*, 540 N.E.2d 1331 (Mass. 1989), decided by the Supreme Judicial Court of Massachusetts as something of a twenty-fifth anniversary celebration of *Webster*. In *Phillips*, the court firmly and unequivocally adopted the reasonable expectations test for Massachusetts. The injured schoolboy, it held, was entitled to a trial on "what the reasonable expectations of an ordinary high school student would be concerning the likely presence of a bone in this meal." Putting aside the court's assumption that there is such a thing as a reasonable and ordinary high school student, notice that the court refers to that character's expectations about *this meal*, meaning one slopped over mashed potatoes in a school cafeteria. There seems little doubt that a jury could determine that expectations of any food, even fish chowder, served in a school cafeteria could be different than they would be about a dish nominally the same when served in the Blue Ship Tea Room. The facts of each case will control. Elsewhere in a footnote the court says, "In particular circumstances, the

special knowledge and experience of a plaintiff may have a bearing on the reasonableness of his expectations and his right to recover."

There's fish chowder and then there's fish chowder, and a jury applying the reasonable expectations test is expected to be able to tell the difference. In some extreme cases, of course, a judge may conclude that there is really no issue for a jury. Imagine, for example, the case of even a small bit of bone in a jar of "Baby's First Fish Chowder" marketed for the toddler set.

At the same time, there can be instances in which even the most dangerous contaminants will not render a food unmerchantable. See, for instance, *Hohn v. South Shore Service, Inc.*, 529 N.Y.S.2d 129 (App. Div. 1988), in which it was held that a supplier of raw pork contaminated with the bacterium causing trichinosis could not be held liable for a breach of warranty. While a distributor impliedly warrants that foods sold are fit for human consumption and merchantable, this warranty does not apply to the wholesomeness of raw pork when it is anticipated the pork will undergo ordinary cooking. Does this result surprise you?

10. We would have to know more about the situation, and even then, the answer would be far from clear. The issue over an otherwise harmless product that causes an allergic or idiosyncratic reaction in only some people obviously sets up the merchantability balancing act in its most delicate form. In the cases on the issue a number of factors come into play, but not one of them is decisive. First of all is the question of how many people may be affected. One bit of language that reappears throughout the decisions is the requirement that for a product to be unfit, it need not cause harm to every user, but that there must be a "reasonably foreseeable harm to an appreciable number of consumers." What makes up an "appreciable number"? As you would expect, there is no clear line on this. In one early case, the likelihood of a reaction in something like 4 to 5 percent of the population was deemed to be enough. *Zirpola v. Adam Hat Stores, Inc.*, 4 A.2d 73 (N.J. 1939). The distinction is sometimes drawn between this type of situation and a "one-in a million" chance of harm that is not likely to compromise merchantability.

    The courts will also be concerned with what the manufacturer or seller knew or should have known about the possible allergic reaction. Some allergies are well-known or at least should be known by people incorporating these ingredients into their products. What did the manufacturer put into the aftershave that gave Harold such a problem? Was it a chemical that was generally known to cause this reaction in an appreciable number of people? In some instances, it can even be shown that the manufacturer was perfectly aware, or in fact had been periodically informed, of adverse reactions. But even if this is so, if such reactions are only reported rarely out of the millions of bottles of aftershave sold, should the product automatically be deemed unmerchantable? Harold might argue that in this case, the manufacturer's failure was in not putting any warning on the product, and indeed this might make a difference. There is, however, an obvious downside to requiring a warning on every product sold of each and every conceivable harm that could possibly be associated with its use. A bottle of aftershave loaded down with a detailed listing of possible adverse effects no matter how rare or bizarre—or worse yet, accompanied by a lengthy legalistic warning insert—could scare just about anybody off of the product. And those who did take fate into their hands and used the stuff would be so burdened down with information that the number of psychosomatic reactions could well outnumber those that arise from the allergy itself. Warnings of possible known adverse reactions are relevant but cannot be the exclusive factor considered in the allergic reaction situation.

At the other extreme, consider the situation where the manufacturer has no advance warning or even reason to suspect that this particular ingredient would cause such a reaction in anybody. After all, every allergy was once unknown until it was first discovered by someone's getting a rash, feeling queasy, or dropping down dead. Harold's case might just be the first such reaction to surface. Could the manufacturer be made to pay when it had no way of anticipating this problem? Or should we say that the manufacturer was responsible because it incorporated a certain chemical into its product without first testing and proving to its own satisfaction that it was harmless?

Add to the mix the question whether the complaining consumer knew of his or her allergy prior to the problem with the particular product. The courts are clear that, at least for people who do know of their own allergies, some of the burden of avoiding injury lies with them. A person who knows herself to be allergic to strawberries, for example, would not be heard to complain if she suffers an adverse reaction to some strawberry sherbet. But what should be the result if some strawberry syrup had been snuck in as the secret ingredient of a dish that didn't proclaim itself as having strawberries in it and that would normally not be expected to have anything like berries in it whatsoever? The allergic person could always protect herself by specifically asking if there were any berries in even the most seemingly innocuous dish, thereby either being warned off of the item or gaining protection of an express warranty (or the warranty of fitness for a particular purpose to be discussed below). But can we really expect such diligence of each and every allergy sufferer even when there is nothing to bring the potential problem to light? ("Can you assure me no strawberries were used in making this fish chowder?") On the other hand, if the dish is found to be unfit and the restauranteur liable, the result could well be fewer secret ingredients in restaurant food and less exotic cuisine altogether. Which brings us back to the problem of airline food, and the less said about that the better.

In *Pai v. Spring Industries, Inc.*, 795 N.Y.S.2d 98 (App. Div. 2005), the plaintiff, Rose Pai, suffered an allergic reaction to some sheets manufactured by the defendants apparently because of the formaldehyde used in their manufacture. The appellate court upheld the trial court's dismissal of the plaintiff's claim based on a breach of warranty theory, stating:

> The defendants demonstrated, prima facie, that the sheets in the instant case were fit for the ordinary purposes for which they are used. The plaintiff is the only person to date that has complained about an allergic reaction to the sheets. When a product is widely sold and easily purchased, "the mere fact that an infinitesimal number experienced a discomforting reaction is not sufficient to establish that the product was not fit for the purpose intended." The plaintiffs failed to raise a triable issue of fact in opposition. [Citations omitted.]

The court also pointed out in its opinion that the manufacturer had "further established that it had attempted, but failed, to create a design for the same type of sheets that did not include the use of formaldehyde."

11. a. Because the other pictures turned out all right, it appears that the roll of film wasn't defective. It just wasn't a type of film that could capture pictures of the night sky. It's doubtful there has been a breach of the warranty of merchantability. Steve would say that the film was fit for the ordinary purposes, though there's always a question, of course, about what the ordinary purposes are for any particular goods. Maybe the best we can do is revert to our "reasonable expectations" notion. Would you assume that any run-of-the-mill type of photographic film would be serviceable for taking snapshots of the heavens in the deep of night? If someone did make and act on this assumption, would he or she be acting "reasonably"?

It's a very different matter when we are talking about the particular buyer's *particular purpose*. Read Comment 2 to §2-315. For a buyer's purpose to be "particular," take note, it need not be freakish or even especially idiosyncratic. It just has to be particular. On the other hand, just because the purchase was made by the particular buyer with a particular use in mind doesn't make it a situation that can rightfully be deemed a "particular purpose." In *Duffee v. Murray Ohio Mfg. Co.*, 866 F. Supp. 1321 (D. Kan. 1994), a children's bicycle was bought, apparently with a particular child in mind—one who was later hurt when it was alleged the brakes failed at a critical moment.

Among the claims made on behalf of the injured child was one based on the implied warranty of fitness for a particular purpose, which was dismissed. As the court explained, "A child riding and braking his bicycle are not unusual, but customary uses of a children's bicycle." In another case, the feeding of dogs was found to be an ordinary, not particular, use of dog food and hence the buyer's claim based on a particular fitness warranty failed as a matter of law. *Stover v. Eagle Products, Inc.*, 896 F. Supp. 1085 (D. Kan. 1995). And a federal district court felt secure in its determination that the particular circumstances under which a buyer had agreed to purchase a large quantity of pantyhose from a Mexican supplier—that is, that the pantyhose were destined for ultimate sale in Lithuania to *Lithuanian women* in particular—did not suffice to define a "particular purpose" allowing the buyer to invoke §2-315. That section, the court opined:

> does not contemplate the imposition of any additional liability on [the seller's] part for allegedly knowing of the allegedly idiosyncratic attributes of some of [the buyer's] Lithuanian customers. If the Mexican pantyhose failed to allow Lithuanian women to engage in their normal activities without having the pantyhose fall down, wear out, or bleed color, these are failings which are encompassed by the implied warranty of merchantability and do not trigger the protection of §2-315.

Lithuanian Commerce Corp., Ltd. v. Sara Lee Hosiery, 219 F. Supp. 2d 600 (D.N.J. 2002).

There are, of course, situations where it does seem right to conclude that the buyer did have a particular purpose, and not just some conventional ordinary purpose, in mind for the goods he or she has contracted to purchase. I can think of no better example of this than the situation that gave rise to the decision in *E & B Giftware, LLC v. Fungoplay, LLC*, 2014 WL 2451355 (Sup. Ct. N.Y.). The buyer in the case had contracted to purchase a large number of "electronic soccer balls and frisbees." The buyer claimed that the balls and frisbees furnished to it were defective; there were problems with the batteries in both products and faulty circuitry in the frisbees. If you are wondering why some particular soccer balls or frisbees had to come with batteries and proper wiring, you can take a look at the case. In any event, the court decided that the buyer was correct in framing its claim that the goods delivered to it were defective in terms of an argued breach of the implied warranty of fitness for a particular purpose of §2-315.

Returning to Bella's case, taking pictures of the stars does seem more like mountain climbing than just walking around on "ordinary ground," to use the Comment's example. Bella will argue here that under the circumstances sale of this roll of film created a warranty of fitness for a particular purpose—that is, a warranty that it was fit for photography of the night sky in that part of the world and when used with her camera. To make her case, she has to show that Steve had "reason to know" her particular purpose in buying the film and that she was "relying on [Steve's] skill or judgment" to select the right stuff. From the facts I've given you, it seems like Bella will be able to show a warranty arising under §2-315.

As I noted in the introduction to this chapter, in order to find a warranty of fitness for a particular purpose, there is no requirement that the seller be a merchant. Of course in most instances the kinds of sellers whose "skill or judgment" can be called into play in making the choice of goods are in fact professional sellers of some sort.

A case that illustrates application of §2-315 well is *Klein v. Sears Roebuck & Co.*, 773 F.2d 1421 (4th Cir. 1985). Soon after their marriage, Steven and Claudia Klein moved into a new home in the suburbs. Claudia's parents came for a visit and offered to buy the newlyweds a riding power lawn mower as a housewarming gift. Steven went to the local Sears with his in-laws, where the trio informed the salesman that they had no experience with lawnmowers and that the Kleins' new property was a tract of almost an acre containing numerous hills. The salesman recommended a model in the Sears Craftsman series. A sale was concluded, conditioned however on an inspection of the property at the time of delivery. A few days later, the mower was delivered. The salesman inspected the property and pronounced the mower suitable, although he did warn that the mower was to be driven vertically up and down the hills. The next summer, as Steven was driving the mower vertically up a 19 degree slope, it tipped over backwards. His right hand was cut and seriously injured, which was all the more unfortunate because his injuries made it impossible for him to continue in his profession as a jeweler. He sued Sears. The court of appeals concluded that he had a good cause of action based on the implied warranty of fitness for a particular purpose (here the purpose of mowing his particular hilly bit of land). Compare this result to the earlier case of *Myers v. Montgomery Ward & Co., Inc.*, 252 A.2d 855 (Md. 1969). Mr. Myers was hurt when the rotary power mower he had purchased from Montgomery Ward slipped on a sloping part of his property. The court found that this fact alone did not establish any breach of warranty. There was, of course, a warranty of merchantability. However, observed the court, this did not extend to a warranty "that it was fit to cut grass *safely* under all circumstances." And there was nothing in the situation to suggest that anyone connected with the seller had been aware of the slope on Myers' land or any special use to which he would put the mower.

b. Once Bella herself makes the choice of which film to buy, she presumably has no warranty claim against Steve. Note the last line in Comment 1 to §2-315, which says, "The buyer, of course, must actually be relying on the seller." In the following two cases, a buyer alleging the seller's failure to provide goods that were fit for the buyer's particular purpose was held not to have satisfied the reliance criterion of §2-315, as the buyer had engaged in their own testing of what the seller had on offer and the ultimate selection of the specific goods the seller was to deliver. See *Viggiano v. Hansen Natural Corporation*, 944 F. Supp. 2d 877 (C.D. Cal. 2013), and *Gared Holdings, LLC v. Best Bolt Products, Inc.*, 991 N.E.2d 1005 (Ind. App. 2013).

What if Bella had mistakenly asked for the Supermax 200 because of some poor advice she had been given by a friend called Frank? She would not, as far as I can tell, have any legal claim against Frank for her loss. If you take free advice from a friend, I guess, you get what you pay for. If Frank had given the advice in a professional capacity, for example, as a highly paid photographic consultant, then he presumably could be liable. But because his liability would have to arise from breach of a service contract, it's most likely that Bella would have to show negligence on his part, not just that the advice for which she paid turned out to be wrong. Compare this to the seller's potential exposure under §2-315, which is, like all warranty obligation, a matter of strict liability. There is no need on the buyer's part to show that the seller was negligent or "should have known" that the goods involved were not fit for the particular purpose intended.

So if Bella herself specified the type of film, it seems she's out of luck. Can't she make an argument that Steve, as someone who specializes in this type of goods and who was after all perfectly aware of what she wanted to do with the film, was under some type of *affirmative obligation* to warn her off of the Supermax 200 if it was so clearly unsuitable? Is there nothing wrong with his making this sale even when he knows she's making a big mistake and will be disappointed with her purchase? Would it make any difference to your response if it were to turn out that Steve did not have on hand any film that would have met her needs, so that by wising her up he would have lost a sale?

Based on the language of the statute and Comment 1, it seems unlikely that a seller would ever have a duty to stand in the way of a purchase the buyer seems intent on making. At least one case, however, suggests that it may not be so simple. And the stakes were high. See *Addis v. Bernardin, Inc.*, 597 P.2d 250 (Kan. 1979). Addis was engaged in the production, bottling, and distribution of salad dressing to the wholesale market. Bernardin manufactured jar lids. At a meeting in

1974, Addis advised Hooper, Bernardin's sales representative, that his salad dressing contained both vinegar and salt and that any lids he purchased would have to be compatible with those ingredients. He showed the representative a sample of a lid he was now using, saying he needed a similar product with a "plastisol" lining and a gold lacquer interior. Later Addis called to place an order for lids of this description. Hooper advised him that he would not recommend this type of lid for products containing vinegar and salt. Addis, in the court's words, "insisted that he wanted lids exactly like those he had purchased" from his previous supplier. "In spite of Bernardin's recommendations," Addis ordered 350,000 lids of the type he had described (apparently he was hung up on the plastisol part of it.) What Hooper had not explained was that the problem would be the gold lacquer interior—something that was in fact apparently never made clear to Addis until the lawsuit was almost over. As you might expect, there followed a saga of spoiled salad dressing and disgruntled customers. Eventually Addis paid various of his buyers for the spoilage, for an amount claimed by him to be $115,000. The Supreme Court of Kansas held that there was sufficient competent evidence to support the trial court's finding of a breach by Bernardin of a warranty of fitness for a particular purpose:

> Here, although Addis insisted upon ordering white plastisol-lined lids with gold interiors that looked like the lids he had ordered from [his previous supplier], he did not realize he was ordering lids that would be incompatible with his product. . . . Hooper, on the other hand, knew the type of highly acidic product the lids would be used with and failed to explain the difference between the type of lid Addis ordered and the type he thought he was ordering. He allowed Addis to place an order for a lid that was not suitable for his product with only a recommendation against the order. It is clear the seller in this instance had superior knowledge and failed to properly caution the buyer.

Should this case be confined to its facts, or does it stand for a more general principle? If so, how is that principle to be articulated? Is it something compelled by §2-315 or at least consistent with that section? Does it help Bella in the hypothetical I've posed?

CHAPTER 13

Disclaimer of Warranties and Limitation of Remedies

FREEDOM OF CONTRACT REVISITED

As we saw in the prior chapters, Article 2 goes into some detail about how warranties of quality arise in a contract for the sale of goods. It's important to appreciate, however, that the drafters expressed no opinion as to whether any precise warranty or degree of warranty protection was appropriate to a specific transaction. That is up to the parties. A very paltry set of warranties, or none at all, might be just what is called forin a given situation. Look again at the general Code deference to freedom of contract as articulated in §1-302 and its Comment 1. While "obligations of good faith, diligence, reasonableness and care prescribed by" the Code may not be disclaimed by agreement, the warranty obligation is in general open to bargaining by the parties just as are the price term and the delivery date.

There is nothing inherently evil, or unreasonable, or lacking in good faith, about the seller's disclaiming responsibility for the goods having any special characteristics or meeting a given level of quality. In fact, Article 2 (in §2-316) instructs the seller on just how to go about doing this. Likewise, there is nothing intrinsically wrong with the parties' concluding at the time of contracting that the buyer's remedies in the event of a breach will be different from or less than what they otherwise would have been if the matter hadn't been taken up and a different agreement concluded beforehand. Contractual modification or limitation of remedy was specifically anticipated and provided for by the drafters in §2-719.

Did the drafters take away with these provisions all they provided the buyer in §§2-313, 2-314, and 2-315? Have we gone back to the days of *caveat emptor* ("let the buyer beware")? Far from it. The buyer is now if not entirely in the driver's seat at least assured of a role in navigating the way toward the enforceable agreement. Recall that even in the days of *caveat emptor* it was never the case that a buyer was unalterably barred from securing warranty protection for the goods that he or she purchased. What was true was that there would be no protection *unless* and *until* the buyer made a point of getting it by successfully eliciting special language of promise from the seller. The buyer had to beware, but the wary buyer could (at least in theory) have insisted on warranty protection without which he or she would walk away from the deal. Under the more modern law of warranty and today under Article 2, the seller who carefully follows the rules can choose to lower or virtually eliminate warranty protection in any individual transaction. But the burden will be on the seller to take the initiative and get the buyer's considered agreement (again, at least in theory) if warranty protection is going to fall below the mark set in general by Article 2's provisions. The drafters' only assurance to buyers under this Article's scheme is that they are not to be subject to "unexpected or unbargained language of disclaimer" or limitations that come as a "surprise." See Comment 1 to §2-316. See also the introductory paragraph of Comment 1 to §2-719.

It is important to acknowledge that this motif of "freedom of contract" in the Code's treatment of warranties is not just mindless political blather, nor is it a craven surrender to the awesome power that we tend to think of sellers as having in our society (probably because most of us do more buying than selling). Freedom of contract is freedom, and opportunity, for the buyer as well as for the seller. Allowing the parties to agree to a limitation or modification of warranty protection is merely (again, and finally, we say in theory) allowing them to bargain free and uninhibited over one of the terms of the contract. Buyers whose individual circumstances allow them comfortably to take a product with a lesser degree of warranty protection or who are willing to take greater risks to get what they want are able to bargain for the lower price or other positive features that they desire even more. They are not forced to pay for warranty protection that they do not want or need. As one example, consider the individual who is extremely good at automotive repair. He or she may even relish buying a clunker for the challenge it represents. There is no sense in making such an accomplished and energetic person pay for a car that is warranted to be like new or close to it. Other buyers may be less energetic, but they are as keenly aware of their own best interests. If I have no intention of ever going scuba diving with my watch on, I would just as soon not pay extra because any watch I might buy is necessarily made so that the manufacturer can warranty it for use down to any number of fathoms. A conscientious buyer should neither be surprised by a lack of warranty protection nor barred from agreeing to such a state of affairs knowingly and in furtherance of his or her own interests. Just one more cheer for freedom of contract.

FREEDOM OF CONTRACT RESTRAINED

Having paid appropriate homage to the principle of freedom of contract, it must be said that in reality as the law now stands, no seller should feel confident that he or she has been freed from any and all potential warranty obligation just because the buyer signed a record containing something to this effect somewhere along the line. First of all, Article 2 in §§2-316 and 2-719 does put *some* restrictions on how, when, and whether the buyer can get out from under the significant warranty obligations imposed by other sections of that Article. (Otherwise why this chapter?) As you can imagine, the limitations laid down in these sections can be enforced quite rigorously by a court unsympathetic to the particular seller's way of doing business, especially when a consumer buyer is involved. Furthermore, §1-103(b) makes clear that other "supplemental" principles of common law such as the doctrines monitoring capacity to contract, fraud, misrepresentation, duress, and so on are still available to limit sellers' behavior. Nor should we forget §2-302 setting forth the general Article 2 precept on unconscionability, which may or may not (depending on whom you ask) play a part in constraining the seller's ability to disclaim warranties or limit remedies under the Code. (We'll come to this in the examples and explanations.)

One overriding issue that you will want to consider as you work your way through the examples and explanations is whether the compromise between freedom of contract and what we might loosely label "buyer protection" that the drafters of Article 2 crafted is a workable one. If so, is the balance that has been struck the right one in your view or does it favor the crafty seller over the unsuspecting and unprotected buyer? You should be aware that in many states and localities the legislative judgment has been that a consumer buyer needs and is entitled to a greater measure of protection. Many states have adopted nonuniform amendments to Article 2's warranty provisions that provide greater protection to consumers. In addition, every state has adopted consumer protection statutes that go beyond what the Code drafters provided. Note the concluding language to §2-102. The federal government has weighed in as well with consumer protection legislation such as the Federal Trade Commission Act. The only one of these federal laws we will study is the Magnuson-Moss Warranty–Federal Trade Commission Improvement Act, the subject of Chapter 15. If you are later confronted with a situation of attempted warranty disclaimer or limitation of remedy in the consumer context, you will I trust check out the effect of your local laws and the Magnuson-Moss act as well as the Article 2 provisions on which we focus here. That being said, let's move on to a brief review of these sections before we get into the examples.

EXCLUSION OR MODIFICATION OF WARRANTY UNDER §2-316

To determine whether a particular warranty can be excluded or modified—or as is usually said, *disclaimed*—by the seller, and if so how, it is first of all crucial to have clearly in mind what kind of warranty we are talking about. (I've been warning you about this for a few chapters now.) Is it an express warranty or an implied warranty? If an implied warranty, is it the implied warranty of merchantability or an implied warranty of fitness for a particular purpose? It's going to make a difference.

Any attempt by the seller to out-and-out disclaim an *express* warranty is for all practical purposes ruled out by §2-316(1). Why should the seller be permitted to take away with one hand what was given with the other? If the seller does not want to create an express warranty, he or she has only to be careful to avoid doing so by keeping silent, by refraining from using models or samples, or by making clear that something is not "an affirmation of fact or promise." As you'll see from the first few questions, however, it isn't always this straightforward. For one thing, language in the agreement or conduct that purports to negate or limit a warranty may legitimately have the effect of influencing how broadly an express warranty urged by the buyer will be interpreted. After all, §2-316(1) begins with the injunction that "[w]ords or conduct relevant to the creation of an express warranty and words or conduct tending to negate or limit warranty shall be construed wherever reasonable as consistent with each other." Furthermore, even where the words offered as creating the warranty and the limitation cannot possibly be reconciled, the limitation, if part of an integrated record, can take its toll by virtue of the parol evidence rule. Note the explicit reference in §2-316(1) to §2-202.

Unlike the case of express warranties, there is nothing in §2-316 that would prohibit or limit the degree to which the *implied warranties* may be disclaimed. Disclaiming implied warranties is perfectly legitimate, as long as it's done properly. And §2-316 tells the seller just how to go about it! Subsection 2-316(2) gives the method for disclaiming implied warranties by particular language made part of the parties' agreement. Subsection 2-316(3) sets forth other circumstances in which the implied warranties may be found to have been excluded or modified. We saw in the earlier chapters that while an express warranty has to be created by some overt act by the seller, the implied warranties arise from the surrounding circumstances and in light of the seller's failure to act in such a way as to counter the buyer's reasonable expectations. The implied warranties arise, in effect, from *omissions* on the seller's part. The drafters in §2-316 were more than happy, it would seem, to give the seller instructions on how to turn the situation around with some carefully chosen words or deeds.

Finally, you will note in §2-316(4) that this section is intended to link in with the provisions of Article 2 on liquidation of damages and on contractual modification of remedy in §§2-718 and 2-719. That is because often a seller will not exclude warranties but will limit the remedies available for breach of the given warranties. The first of these, liquidation, we will leave to the separate chapters on remedies. The second, §2-719, is part of a package with §2-316 and must be dealt with here.

MODIFICATION OR LIMITATION OF REMEDY UNDER §2-719

Before looking at how the parties may by agreement modify or limit the remedies available under their contract, we have to at least note what remedies would be available if the particular buyer and seller do *not* take advantage of this invitation to "shape their remedies to their particular requirements" (Comment 1 to §2-719). What are the standard, off-the-shelf remedies available (here, to the buyer for a breach of warranty) under Article 2? For one thing, of course, if the buyer catches the breach in time he or she may be able to reject the goods on delivery. We deal with the so-called "goods-oriented remedies" of *rejection* and *revocation of acceptance* in the next part of the book. If the goods are accepted, then the same remedies apply that apply to any breach of contract—the non-breaching party is entitled to money damages measured by the expectancy, which is the amount that will put them where they would have been had the contract been performed. See §2-714. In the appropriate case, the aggrieved buyer is entitled to "incidental and consequential damages." We'll examine these provisions in much more detail in Chapter 27. For the time being, it is sufficient to recognize that the buyer who suffers a breach of warranty is fairly well protected by the provisions of Article 2.

Again, it must be emphasized that there is nothing necessarily evil or underhanded about a seller's concluding that he or she would rather not, or cannot afford to, sell at a given price if the full measure of potential liability remains looming over the transaction. If parties can bargain over price and other terms until they arrive at something that suits both of them, they should also be allowed to bargain over the extent of liability and reach their own, individualized, workable solution on that bit of business as well. While in the examples and explanations we will necessarily focus on the restrictions placed on the agreement by subsections (2) and (3) of §2-719, this should not distract you from the main force of the section, which comes earlier on in subsection (1)(a):

> the agreement *may* provide for remedies in addition to or in substitution for those provided in this Article and *may* limit or alter the measure of damages recoverable under this Article, as by limiting the buyer's remedies to return of the goods and repayment of the price or to repair and replacement of nonconforming goods and parts.

The emphasis has been added. But that is exactly my point. The restrictions that follow in this section are meant in the words of Comment 1 to insure some baseline of protection for the buyer, but no more:

> [I]t is the very essence of a sales contract that at least minimum adequate remedies be available. If the parties conclude a contract for sale within this Article they must accept the legal consequence that there be at least a fair quantum of remedy for the obligations or duties outlined in the contract.

As we will see, §2-719 attempts to meet this goal in two ways. Subsection (2) introduces the concept of *failure of essential purpose*. Subsection (3) invokes the principle of *unconscionability* in this special context. There will be plenty of issues to explore under each provision. Keep in mind, however, that remedies only kick in when there has been a breach; if a seller has not promised anything, then there can be no breach and no remedy.

SOME QUESTIONS REMAINING

As even this brief introduction should have made clear, the drafters anticipated that sellers will try to protect themselves from an unwanted warranty burden either by disclaimer, which effectively eliminates the warranty altogether, or by extending the warranty but limiting the remedies available for a breach to some level acceptable to the seller. The scheme presupposes that the two types of clauses can be distinguished one from the other and calls for different analysis depending on which it is. Attempted disclaimers of warranty are governed by §2-316. If a disclaimer is effective then the fact that the goods are not of a given type or fail to meet a given measure of quality is simply not a breach. If a gem is warranted only to be a zircon, that it is not a diamond should surprise no one and certainly is no grounds for complaint against the seller. If, however, the seller *has* given a warranty but has sought to modify or limit the remedies available to the buyer, then a breach of contract by the seller can occur. It's just that the *remedies* available to the aggrieved buyer may not be all he or she would hope. And such a provision we know to be governed by §2-719.

While the two concepts—disclaimer of warranty and limitation of remedy—are meant in theory to be analytically distinct, I doubt it will shock you to learn that in practice the difference often is hard to make out. The effect of either type of provision on a disappointed, perhaps even a severely injured, buyer can be for all practical purposes the same: It will not matter to the buyer who loses out on all meaningful recovery whether §2-316 or §2-719 did the job.

There is another point as well. Sellers are always inventing new language for incorporation into their sales forms, and it has never been hard to come up with a clause that intentionally or otherwise reads as a bit of both disclaimer and limitation of remedy. In which case, what rule or rules do we apply in judging the effectiveness of the provision? This is of particular importance because, as you no doubt already have noticed, the two sections we consider go about their business of policing in such divergent ways. Section 2-316 speaks in the language of procedure. It is a matter of by what *means* disclaimer may be accomplished. The seller may disclaim a large measure of the warranties (indeed, all of the implied warranties) rather simply as long as it is done in the correct form. Section 2-719, on the other hand, is all substance. The governing principles there focus on what outcomes, what *ends*, are to be tolerated as reasonable limitations on the buyer's right to a remedy.

You can immediately appreciate, therefore, some of the unanswered questions that this Code scheme necessarily puts into play. Is there any way for a buyer to argue with any chance of success that a clause in the form of a disclaimer should be invalidated because of the overall effect it would have, even if all of the procedural niceties of §2-316 have been observed? On the other hand, do the §2-316 criteria or any other mechanistic constraints play any part in consideration of a provision clearly worded as a limitation of remedy? Add to the mix the issue whether the general provision on unconscionability (§2-302) is relevant to these matters at all. We will not want in this chapter for complexity. Nor shall we be astounded to find a number of seemingly fundamental questions on which the commentators and courts have and continue to disagree.

By now you are understandably anxious to get into the examples and explanations. We will in just one moment. First, however, there is one preliminary matter that we want to acknowledge, explore, and then put to one side.

A MATTER OF TIMING

Both §2-316 and §2-719 deal with the effect to be given terms incorporated by the parties into their agreement of sale. As such, it is important that the particular clause or language at issue actually *be* a part of that agreement. One of the most forceful arguments—in fact the most forceful—that can be made by a buyer whose warranty action seems at worst doomed and at best significantly hampered by language that the seller can point to in one document or the other is that this language, however it might normally be treated by these provisions, was simply not a part of the bargain in the particular case. Most typically the buyer will argue (many times with success) that the language was introduced into the relationship *after* the contract had been entered into. As such, it is at best an attempted modification on the seller's part and would be binding on the buyer only if it can be shown that there was assent to the modification. Not surprisingly courts rarely find an agreement to modify by the buyer in such circumstances. (Lack of consideration cannot be used as an argument against the modification because of §2-209(1).) Courts are often predisposed to find against such limitations anyway, and will find very appealing any argument that the clause can simply be disregarded because it is not part of the operative contract between the parties. See, e.g., *Terrell v. R & A Manufacturing Partners, Ltd.*, 835 So. 2d 216 (Ala. Civ. App. 2002).

This type of argument—the attempted disclaimer was what is sometimes referred to as a *post-contract disclaimer* and hence of no effect whatsoever—often comes up in the consumer context. The language on which the seller relies is found somewhere in the packet of materials, including for example an "Owner's Manual," which came to the buyer only with the actual delivery of the goods. Sometimes it appears for the first time on an invoice that accompanies the goods or as part of a label affixed directly to them. In any case, if the court can rightly conclude that the contract for sale was made at an earlier date and that this language could have been seen by the buyer at or after the time of delivery at the earliest, the seller's argument based on the language can be made simply to disappear. See, for example, the discussion in *Hartford Fire Insurance Co. v. Roadtec, Inc.*, 2010 WL 4967979 (S.D.N.Y.). Of course, to be a part of the agreement, it is only necessary that the seller show the buyer could have been aware of this language at the time the contract was entered into, not that the buyer actually was aware of it. The buyer who chooses to enter into a contract of sale without reading what he or she is signing does not later have the luxury of arguing his or her own willful ignorance. As we will see, the drafters' "conspicuousness" requirement seeks to minimize the chances of a buyer's being caught by "surprise," but it can only do so much. The buyer still has to act reasonably, and with reasonable care, to protect his or her own interests.

In the larger commercial context, language on a seller's standard form that purports to disclaim warranties or limit liability may, in the appropriate circumstances, fall victim to the Code's treatment of the battle of the forms. It all depends on whose papers initiated the transaction, on what each of the various forms actually said, and on what the parties actually did. But an argument based on §2-207 can, given the right facts, eliminate the language from the parties' agreement altogether—a result devoutly to be wished by the buyer. In particular, the courts have pretty consistently held that if the buyer's purchase order constituted the offer of contract, then any language in the seller's form that raises for the first time a disclaimer or limitation of liability will be a "material alteration" under §2-207(2)(b) and hence cannot work its way into the contract by that route. And if the seller's disclaimer language is a "different" term under §2-207, then the knock-out rule applied by most jurisdictions will eliminate that language and insert the default liability rules that favor the buyer.

In the examples that follow we will assume that the language of exclusion, modification, disclaimer, or limitation on which the seller seeks to rely is part of the parties' agreement in fact. The issues before us focus on the effect to be given such language or other circumstances, which the seller can argue gives him or her some degree of protection from full-blown warranty obligation under the Code.

Examples

EXAMPLES

1. Billows, a manufacturer of women's blouses, contracts to buy a large order of brightly colored silk from Silky Unlimited. Billows receives the silk and makes it into blouses. After manufacture they are sent through a standard washing process during which the color on all of them fades significantly. Billows wants to sue Silky.
   (a) Billows points to the written contract, which refers to the goods as "Colorfast, Washable Silk." Silky can point to a prominent provision in the same document which reads, "SELLER MAKES NO WARRANTY THAT PRODUCTS SOLD PURSUANT TO THIS CONTRACT WILL RETAIN ORIGINAL COLOR IN PROCESSING, CLEANING OR WASHING." Will Billows' rights against Silky be affected by this language?
   (b) Suppose instead that the provision in the agreement (which, recall, described the goods as "Colorfast, Washable Silk") had read as follows: "WASH IN COOL WATER ONLY. SELLER MAKES NO WARRANTY THAT PRODUCTS SOLD PURSUANT TO THIS AGREEMENT WILL RETAIN ORIGINAL COLOR IF WASHED AT TEMPERATURES ABOVE 70 DEGREES FAHRENHEIT." Billows' process exposed the material to temperatures of at least 80 degrees. What is your evaluation of Billows' claim under these circumstances?
   (c) Imagine that, in addition to the circumstances given in Example 1b, Billows could prove that, prior to his signing the agreement, Silky's salesperson said, "This new stuff is terrific. Even a warm or hot water wash doesn't make it fade one bit." Does this help Billows' case?

2. Worldwide Jars Unlimited produces plastic jars and other containers to order for industry. One of Jars' representatives visits the plant of Peter Piper (a pickle-packing potential plaintiff) in an attempt to get new business. Piper asks her to suggest a kind of plastic jar that would be suitable for a new kind of extra-dill pickle he plans to produce. She tells Piper that jars made of her company's "#3 mid-grade" plastic should work well for these purposes. Piper and the representative of Jars sign a contract. The document itself is a standard form of Purchase Memorandum used by Jars for taking orders. The number of jars, their size, the type of plastic from which they are to be made ("#3 mid-grade"), and other relevant terms are all filled into the appropriate blanks on the form. The back of the form contains among a variety of terms the following language in type no larger or darker than that which surrounds it:

> EXCEPT AS EXPRESSLY PROVIDED IN THIS PURCHASE MEMORANDUM, SELLER MAKES IN CONNECTION WITH THIS TRANSACTION NO WARRANTIES, EXPRESS OR IMPLIED, INCLUDING BUT NOT LIMITED TO THE IMPLIED WARRANTY OF MERCHANTABILITY.

When the jars arrive Piper packs them with the new extra dills. He soon discovers that many of the jars are cracked or split and that they leak as soon as anything is put into them. Other jars hold tight, but within a couple of days the plastic begins to discolor. Apparently because of its high acid content, this particular pickle must be packed in plastic jars of a higher grade plastic than #3 mid-grade (which would be suitable for most foodstuffs including most pickled products).

(a) Does Piper have any recourse against Jars because of the leakage problem? Because of the discoloration problem?
(b) What if the quoted language was on the front of the form and was printed in red ink?
(c) The language was in red ink, but was on the back of the form?
(d) The language was in black ink and was on the back of the form, but the front of the form carried a legend in bold red type, "SUBJECT TO TERMS, CONDITIONS AND LIMITATIONS ON THE REVERSE" just above where Peter Piper signed?
(e) Assuming that the language of disclaimer was in big, bold, and bright letters right smack on the front of the form, would it influence the outcome if Piper could convincingly demonstrate that he personally did not take notice of the attempted disclaimer until after he had entered into the contract, had received the delivery, and had packed the pickles?
(f) What about the converse situation? That is, assume that the disclaimer language was in type no different from any of the other printing on the back of the form but that Piper, a very picky person, had insisted on reading every line of the form before signing it. He noticed the

language on the back of the form and objected to the Jars representative. She told him, "Sorry, but I'm not authorized to sell with any change of the form. They insist on this." Piper tells her that he is upset with the idea that they could limit their responsibility this way, but he signs the form anyway as he is in need of the jars. What result here?

3. Piper's pickle-packing business is booming and he decides to expand his plant. He sees an ad placed in an industry newsletter by Simon, who is selling a used labelling machine of a kind with which Piper is familiar and which he believes would meet his needs. Piper journeys to Simon's factory where the machine sits idle in a corner. He agrees to buy it for $12,000. The contract of sale that he signs bears a bold legend on the front stating "MACHINE IS SOLD AS IS." When the machine is delivered to Piper's plant, he plugs it in and flips the "On" switch, but nothing happens. It turns out that the machine's electrical system is shot and that it will need $1,000 worth of repairs before it can be made operable.
   (a) Does Piper have any recourse against Simon for breach of warranty?
   (b) Suppose instead that the contract of sale Piper signed with Simon bore no language of disclaimer, but that prior to their signing the document Simon had said to Piper, "Do you want to turn it on and see how it runs?" Piper had replied, "No thanks, I've seen this type before." Does Simon have any warranty liability under these facts?

4. Betty goes into Selma's Appliance City where she buys a new television set, signing a contract of sale that bears in fine print on the back the following legend:

   > In the event that the merchandise sold pursuant to this agreement shall prove defective in any way, seller agrees to repair or replace the product for up to one year at no charge to the buyer.

   Betty takes the TV home and plugs it in. A picture appears but she is unable to make it hold steady. Something is seriously wrong with the vertical hold. She takes the set back and says she wants to return it and get her money back. Selma, citing the language on the sales form, says that she will not take the set back, but will agree to take it into her shop for repair. If the vertical hold cannot be repaired, she will replace the set with another of identical make and model.
   (a) Betty would prefer to have her money back so that she could go and shop elsewhere. Is she entitled to this as a matter of law?
   (b) Would your answer be any different if, instead of being buried in the fine print, the quoted language had been in large bold capital letters on the front of the sales form?
   (c) How would you answer the previous question if in addition to being prominently displayed on the front of the form, the provision had included the following sentences:

> IT IS AGREED THAT REPAIR OR REPLACEMENT UNDER THIS PROVISION IS TO BE THE SOLE REMEDY AVAILABLE TO BUYER. UNDER NO CIRCUMSTANCES IS SELLER LIABLE FOR ANY OTHER INJURY OR LOSS SUFFERED BY THE BUYER, INCLUDING BUT NOT LIMITED TO ANY INCIDENTAL OR CONSEQUENTIAL DAMAGES OR DAMAGES RELATING TO INJURY TO PERSON OR PROPERTY SUFFERED BY BUYER AS A RESULT OF ANY DEFECT.

(d) Assume that Selma's limitation language is as prominent and as complete as in 4c above. Once the language is pointed out to her, Betty bends to Selma's will and agrees to leave the TV set for repair. She picks up the repaired set the following week. When she turns it on at home, she finds that the problem with the vertical hold has apparently not been fixed, only slightly slowed down. Again, she takes it in to Selma's for repair. When she next gets it back, she finds that while the vertical hold appears to be fine, now the horizontal hold no longer works. This time when she takes it back to Selma's she insists on getting her money back. Selma once again points to the language on her sales form. Who has the better argument now?

5. Buster buys a toaster from Selma's Appliance City. The contract of sale that he signs includes prominently on the front all of the language that we saw quoted in the immediately preceding examples. The first time Buster puts some plain white bread into the toaster and pushes down the handle the appliance bursts into flames. Before he can put out the fire Buster is seriously injured and most of his kitchen furniture is reduced to ashes. Buster brings suit arguing that the toaster was obviously unmerchantable. He claims damages both for his personal injury and for the harm caused to his property. Will the language in the contract of sale bar his recovery of any or all of his claimed damages?

6. Mr. Green owns and operates a private golf course. He contracts to buy a large amount of weedkiller for $835 from Statewide Chemical Providers, Incorporated. The contract of sale that he signs carries the following legend in bold type on the front:

> LIMITATION OF LIABILITY: THE EXCLUSIVE REMEDY OF BUYER AND THE LIMIT OF LIABILITY OF STATEWIDE CHEMICAL PROVIDERS, INCORPORATED FOR ANY AND ALL LOSSES, INJURIES OR DAMAGES RESULTING FROM THE USE OR HANDLING OF THIS PRODUCT SHALL BE REPAYMENT OF PURCHASE PRICE.

Green applies the weedkiller to the greens of his course with disastrous results. Many of the greens have to be totally recovered with new sod. In addition, because of the damage Green has to delay the opening of his course and he loses over a month's worth of income. Green sues Statewide for more than $36,000 in damages. Statewide contends that it should be liable for $835 but no more. Is this argument valid?

7. Ms. Doe owns and operates a pizza parlor. She contracts to buy a new pizza oven, which will replace her aging equipment, from Ovens of Brooklyn. The contract that she signs includes the following provisions prominently displayed:

   20.1 LIMITATION OF REMEDY: IN THE EVENT THAT ANY OVEN SOLD PURSUANT TO THIS AGREEMENT SHALL PROVE DEFECTIVE IN ANY WAY, SELLER AGREES TO REPAIR OR REPLACE THE PRODUCT AT THE BUYER'S PLACE OF BUSINESS FOR UP TO ONE YEAR AT NO CHARGE TO THE BUYER. SUCH REPAIR OR REPLACEMENT SHALL CONSTITUTE BUYER'S SOLE REMEDY FOR ANY BREACH OF WARRANTY.

   20.2 NO INCIDENTAL OR CONSEQUENTIAL DAMAGES: BUYER FURTHER AGREES THAT UNDER NO CIRCUMSTANCES SHALL IT HOLD SELLER LIABLE FOR ANY INCIDENTAL OR CONSEQUENTIAL DAMAGES RESULTING FROM ANY BREACH OF THIS AGREEMENT.

   The pizza oven delivered to Doe does not work correctly. Doe is forced to close up shop. Over the next two weeks Ovens working diligently is able to get a needed replacement part and makes the necessary repairs.

   (a) Doe's Pizza Parlor can reopen. Doe is willing to pay for the oven, but claims she has a right to subtract an amount equivalent to her two weeks of lost profits. The president of Ovens reminds her that she signed an agreement that included clause 20.2 quoted above. Does that clause effectively bar her from getting any lost profits, even if she can prove them with reasonable certainty?

   (b) Suppose instead that Ovens tries to fix the pizza oven over a period of several weeks, but its efforts are to no avail. Meanwhile, Doe's business remains shut. Eventually Oven's president agrees to send his employees over to Doe's to pick up the oven and that he will "void her purchase." Doe is willing, in fact anxious, to return the oven but claims that in addition the seller owes her a large amount for the profits she has lost over the long period when her pizza parlor has been closed and will remain closed until she can get another working pizza oven. The president points to clause 20.2 in the agreement that she signed. In this situation, does that clause act as a bar to her claim for lost profits?

8. Bart goes into Selma's Appliance City where he buys an expensive new radio receiver for his stereo system. The contract that he signs bears the following legend in double-sized red print directly over the spot where Bart is asked to and does put his signature:

   EXCLUSION OF WARRANTIES: BUYER HEREBY ACKNOWLEDGES THAT ANY AND ALL WARRANTIES, EXPRESS OR IMPLIED, INCLUDING THE IMPLIED WARRANTY OF MERCHANTABILITY, AND ANY WARRANTY OF FITNESS FOR A PARTICULAR PURPOSE ARE EXCLUDED FROM THIS CONTRACT AND SHALL NOT APPLY TO THE GOODS SOLD.

Bart takes the receiver home and hooks it up to his stereo. No matter how much he fiddles with it, he is unable to make the receiver work without a loud hum that totally overpowers any music (or public affairs broadcasting) he tunes to. He races back to Selma's and demands relief. She points to the language on the contract he signed and tells him to get out of her store. Does Bart have any remedy against Selma? Would your answer be any different if the problem with the receiver was not a loud hum but (like Buster's toaster in Example 5) that it had burst into flames causing damage to person and property?

Explanations

EXPLANATIONS

1. a. The attempted disclaimer of warranty will not be effective. It's always important to begin by setting out exactly the nature of the warranty being asserted. Billows claims a breach of an express warranty arising under §2-313(1)(b) and based on the description of the goods as "Colorfast, Washable Silk." The goods, Billows argues, were clearly not as warranted. Since Billows' argument relies on an express warranty, we look to §2-316(1). That section does not actually say that an express warranty can *never* be disclaimed, but the effect at least here is pretty much the same. Words argued to negate or limit an express warranty are "inoperative" to the extent that a construction of these words and the words creating the warranty as consistent "is unreasonable." There's no reasonable way, I would argue, to find consistent a seller's assertion that it warrants the goods to be washable and colorfast and at the same time disclaims all warranties to that effect. The expression of warranty wins out. Billows has an express warranty arising from the description of the goods.

   b. Billows' warranty claim is much less likely to succeed here. Silky points to the language in §2-316(1) that says, "Words or conduct relevant to the creation of an express warranty and words or conduct tending to negate or limit warranty shall be construed wherever reasonable as consistent with each other." That may well be the case here. An express warranty that a fabric, and particularly silk, is colorfast and washable can't reasonably be taken to mean that it won't lose any of its brilliance no matter how it's washed. Even without the limiting language in Silky's form, would Billows have been reasonable in expecting the product not to fade if he ran it through a process originally created to produce a trendy faded effect on jeans (such as "acid wash")? So the issue—a factual issue that we can't readily resolve without knowing more about what goes in the fabric industry—is whether it is "reasonable" to produce and sell fabric you characterize as "Colorfast, Washable" silk that needs to be washed with this level of care in order to hold its color. If so, then Silky's language is effective and Billows has no breach of warranty claim.

Another way of looking at this result from Silky's point of view is that the language does not really *disclaim* any express warranty but only further explicates it and must be taken into account in establishing the *extent* and *content* of the warranty. Any express warranty, especially one grounded in only a couple of brief words, is open to ambiguity. Section 2-316(1) prevents the out-and-out disclaimer or contradiction by words or conduct of any express warranty given by the seller. It does not interfere in appropriate cases with attempts by sellers to clarify or further explain what warranty they mean to be giving, as long as the meaning eventually arrived at is one that the "reasonable" buyer can be expected to appreciate and that cannot "reasonably" be said to take him or her by surprise.

c. This helps Billows' case, of course, but it still may not be enough. In particular, Billows' argument based on the salesperson's statement may fall victim to the parol evidence rule. Section 2-202 is explicitly referenced in §2-316(1), and Silky's lawyer would have to be a fool not to invoke it here. See also the first sentence of Comment 2. We will not revisit all the problems and issues that come up in application of §2-202 (for that, see Chapter 8). We know, however, there is a good likelihood that an oral statement that contradicts a record that is the final and complete agreement of the parties will not be given effect as part of the agreement of the parties.

2. a. Again we begin by getting straight in our own minds what warranty or warranties the buyer is trying to assert. Piper can argue with some force that the failure of the jars to hold liquid without leaking is a breach of the warranty of merchantability arising under §2-314 and that their tendency to discolor is a breach of a warranty of fitness for a particular purpose under §2-315. (This hypothetical is in fact based, if loosely, on the case of *Addis v. Bernardin, Inc.*, 597 P.2d 250 (Kan. 1979), which we saw in the last chapter as an intriguing example of the particular purpose warranty as it played out in a commercial setting.)

Whether or not Jars has effectively disclaimed either or both of these warranties by language in the agreement is to be tested by the criteria of §2-316(2). Read that subsection now, carefully, if you have not done so already.

First, note that to disclaim the warranty of merchantability arising under §2-314, the language must "mention merchantability." Here Jars' language does just that, so at least that criterion is met. What would be the result if the precise word *merchantability* had not been used? Almost assuredly on that fact alone a court would conclude that the warranty of merchantability was preserved. It's a magic word but it works, and there seems to be nothing that works as well. The courts have been exceptionally picky about what §2-316(2) requires in the way of a "mention" of merchantability, and it's hard to think of any other language or means of referring to *merchantability* that would do the trick other than use of those fifteen letters in that order.

The language that will suffice to disclaim the implied warranty of fitness, as you see from the last sentence of §2-316(2), can be much more general. Jars has probably met the language content requirement here, although wise counsel might want to spell out that the warranty of fitness for a particular purpose is also disclaimed.

Jars' problem here is not with the wording of the attempted disclaimer so much as with its failure to make this language "conspicuous." This is, as you see, a requirement if the language is to effectively disclaim either the warranty of merchantability or the implied warranty of fitness for a particular purpose. Curiously enough, the subsection does not make it absolutely mandatory that a disclaimer of merchantability be in a record, although it does do so for the disclaimer of the implied warranty of fitness. The warranty of merchantability can, in theory at least, be disclaimed by a clear statement that is entirely oral, as long as it mentions merchantability, though we can find no cases on point. Of course, a prudent seller could never feel comfortable relying on such an oral understanding.

On occasion we have characterized terms or language as "conspicuous," but we have not previously gone into what that term means when it is a statutory requirement. Because §2-316(2) requires that the disclaimer of the implied warranties must be "conspicuous," we will now examine the meaning of the term.

The definition of "conspicuous" was revised in the 2022 Amendments as part of the Amendments' goal of making the Code expressly applicable to electronic transactions. After all, in spite of the many examples that follow of written transactions, many of our purchases today are made electronically and the Code now reflects that by using the word "record." But, as explained in Chapter 2, many jurisdictions have not adopted the Amendments. However, this is less of a problem with the definition of *conspicuous* than it is with hybrid transactions. Because the language has been made more general, we should be able to apply the new rule as well as the old rule in our Examples without a difference in outcome.

The Amendments made two changes—one an addition and one a deletion. Amended §1-201(b)(10) added the italicized language to the definition:

> "Conspicuous", with reference to a term, means so written, displayed, or presented that, *based on the totality of the circumstances*, a reasonable person

> against which it is to operate ought to have noticed it. Whether a term is "conspicuous" or not is a decision for the court.

The added language indicates that the analysis must be on a case-by-case basis and the approach may vary depending on the context. For that reason, the Amendments also deleted a list of examples that were more applicable to language found in a written as opposed to an electronic record and that did not provide for context. The Official Comments added by the Amendments are very helpful in indicating the factors a court (and drafter) should look to when deciding whether language is conspicuous.

The general idea is of course the same in both the old and the new version. The Code is aware that, much of the time, a party enters into a contract without reading it. In requiring certain terms to be conspicuous, the Code is in effect saying, "We know you are not going to carefully read the entire agreement, but there are certain terms that we think are worthy of your attention, so at least read those." Of course, with many online contracts we don't even look at the Terms and Conditions we are agreeing to. For purposes of determining whether a term is conspicuous, that may not matter. The definition inquires whether a *reasonable person* ought to have noticed it. Whether the buyer actually noticed it or not should not matter.

Whether a term is conspicuous in any given situation is not always easy to determine. No precise objective test is available, and the courts tend to look not only at the size of type, its color, and its placement as part of the overall form, but also at any other unique aspects of the situation, including in some instances the sophistication of the party against whom the disclaimer is to operate. Thus it is perfectly possible to conclude that in a commercial context, where what is eventually signed is not a standard form but a long, involved document over which both parties and their attorneys have labored word by word, each and every clause is conspicuous even though it is set forth in a manner no different from the rest of the text. In contracts of adhesion, however, the courts insist on something like a "more than slight variation" from the surrounding text as well as prominent placement. Certainly if a court has reason to feel that a seller is just trying to squeak by with a minimal variation, particularly where a consumer buyer is concerned, it is unlikely to find the conspicuousness criterion met.

We explore this more in the following question. For the moment, we are faced with language in a preprinted form that is all in capital letters, to be sure, but which is otherwise in noncontrasting type and is on the back. I think that most courts would find, and find without much difficulty, that this term is not conspicuous.

b. Once it is on the front all in caps and printed in red ink (assuming that the rest of the form is in standard black), a provision should meet the test and be held conspicuous.
c. Courts have trouble with language on the back of forms and seem always on the ready to take advantage of the conspicuousness requirement of §2-316(2) to make their feelings known. On occasion, buyers have asked for a ruling that any disclaimer located on the reverse of a form is inconspicuous as a matter of law. The courts have not bowed to these requests, reasoning rightly that the location of the language is only one of the factors to be considered, but practically a term that is on the back of a preprinted form and not referred to anywhere on the front is unlikely to be held conspicuous.
d. While it's not an iron-clad cinch, this language on the front of the form located where it was and itself in bold red type probably saves the day for Jars the seller. To be safer, of course, Jars might want to consider putting the disclaimer language itself in bold red and on the front if at all possible.

One factor that has worked against seller in some similar situations is the implicit requirement that the *limiting* or *disclaiming* aspect of the provision, not just the provision in some general way, must be conspicuous and attention-calling. This notion is quite sensible in light of what §2-316(2) is all about. So, for example, a clause that is headed in big bold letters with something like "YOUR WARRANTY PROTECTION" but that contains a disclaimer of warranties in ordinary type would, as a matter of law, not be a conspicuous disclaimer. It is the unfavorable aspect of the language (the bad news) that must be conspicuous. See, for example, *Erpelding v. Skipperliner Industries, Inc.*, 2001 WL 640966 (D. Minn.). If Jars had referred to the clause on the back with the words "TERMS AND CONDITIONS ON REVERSE," it could easily have run afoul of this type of argument if the court were unsympathetic to Jars or the lawyer for Peter Piper particularly persuasive. Jars is probably safe, however, because it did use the word "LIMITATIONS" as well. Wouldn't this cause you to flip the form over and have a look—or later to curse yourself if you had not?

In *Hutton v. Deere & Co.*, 210 F.3d 389 (10th Cir. 2000), the purchaser had signed a two-page document. The front page included a paragraph headed "IMPORTANT WARRANTY NOTICE" informing the product purchaser that any express warranties were printed on the back of the sheet. It continued, "YOUR RIGHTS AND REMEDIES PERTAINING TO THIS PURCHASE ARE LIMITED AS INDICATED ON BOTH SIDES OF THIS PURCHASE ORDER. WHERE PERMITTED BY LAW, NO IMPLIED WARRANTY OF MERCHANTABILITY OR FITNESS IS MADE." Directly above the line provided for the buyer's signature was the following: "I (We) understand that my (our) rights in connection with this purchase are limited as set forth on both sides of this Purchase Order." The buyer was not a consumer but the operator of a commercial logging operation. The Tenth Circuit held that the disclaimer was "easily located and read" and consequently conspicuous. For a similar case, but here in the consumer context, in which prominent language on the front of the sales agreement directly above where the buyer signed her name, calling attention to unambiguous disclaimer language printed on a later page, was deemed by the court to make the disclaimer conspicuous, see *Cullen v. Premier Baths, Inc.*, 2012 WL 3638466 (N.D. Ill.).

e. When, if ever, Piper actually became aware of the term is immaterial. If the language on the form uses the appropriate language and is undeniably conspicuous then it has its intended effect. Look at Comments 3 and 4. Disclaimer is permitted. If seller can show the contract entered into meets the requirements of §2-316(2), there is no additional requirement that it prove the particular buyer actually *did* see the clause—it is a *reasonable person* test. There have been isolated cases, always in a consumer context as far as I know, in which the court seems to tack on the requirement of actual knowledge on the buyer's part, but you'll have to admit there is nothing in the section to support this idea, and it has had no widespread acceptance. If the drafters had wanted to put different criteria in this subsection, they were perfectly capable of doing so. Subsection 2-316(2) was intended to give the recipe by which sellers could effectively disclaim any or all of the implied warranties, and if an individual seller follows that recipe, he or she is entitled to the full benefit of what is cooked up.

Where does this leave Peter Piper other than with a firm determination never to deal with Worldwide Jars again and kicking himself for his own failure to be more careful in what he signs? Has he no other arguments? As we explore in the very last example, some buyers faced with a seemingly ironclad disclaimer under §2-316(2) have sought to invoke the doctrine of unconscionability. Whether a buyer should have much success with this argument is uncertain at best. In any event, recall that the doctrine of unconscionability tends to come into play almost exclusively where the party invoking it is a consumer or an otherwise downtrodden type. A businessman like Peter Piper, who is expected to sign commercial contracts day in and day out and who should know how to handle himself, will be very unlikely to get any help from the doctrine of unconscionability. To be unconscionable, a term has to be pretty bad. The fact that the Code permits disclaimers of warranty indicates that it is not in itself a bad thing—it just has to be done the right way.

There does remain one other avenue for Piper. If he can show that an *express* warranty was made, at least that the jars would hold pickles without leaking all over the place, then he could argue a breach of this express warranty, and the language of limitation would be irrelevant. Perhaps Jars' representative said something like, "Our jars will hold your pickles just right" during the course of the negotiation. But then you see Piper's problem: Will proof of this statement be allowed if a parol evidence challenge is mounted? If the court looks at the contract he signed with Jars as a final and complete statement of the parties' agreement (and it's likely that Jars has included a merger clause in the boilerplate somewhere), then Piper may be out of luck. Now for Piper to be successful he would have to show something on the form itself, some language or term, that created an express warranty. One argument is that just by describing the goods to be sold as "jars," an express warranty was given that each would be a jar (that is a type of container) and, as such, should contain things like pickles and their accompanying juices. Plato would probably agree that when you say "jar," you imply a certain amount of "jarness"—but how much?

f. The language of §2-316(2) and §1-201(b)(10) would seem to make it undeniable that a disclaimer must genuinely be conspicuous in order to be effective and that actual knowledge by the buyer of a hidden or obscure term should not make any difference. Most commentators and most courts would, I think, conclude as much. Hence Piper would not be bound by this term even though he *was* aware of it. There have been a few cases that dispute this result, holding or at least implying that an inconspicuous disclaimer can be effective if the seller proves actual knowledge on the buyer's part. See, for example, *Office Supply Co., Inc. v. Basic/Four Corp.*, 538 F. Supp. 776 (E.D. Wis. 1982). At first this conclusion may seem perfectly reasonable. After all, why should the buyer be relieved from a term that the seller could reasonably believe the buyer was aware of and by signing the unamended document implicitly agreeing to? What function is served by a strict rule that is centered entirely on what a reasonable person "ought to" notice? One argument that has been made against results like that in the *Office Supply* case is that it would encourage arguments by sellers, based on very little hard evidence and perhaps even made up out of thin air, that this particular buyer did see, or must have seen, or once admitted to having seen, what was in the finest of fine print. Beyond this, even if we were fully convinced by credible evidence that the buyer did see and appreciate what the seller was trying to do in the fine print, isn't the buyer entitled to rely on what does seem a fairly straightforward reading of the Code? We don't know what Piper was thinking when he signed the form knowing of the offending but inconspicuous clause in it. Perhaps while he was offended by the clause and Jars' attempt to limit its liability in such a drastic way, inside he was really chuckling to himself. The clause, he might have determined, was so obviously inconspicuous that all Jars was doing was deceiving itself. No court in the world would find this provision conspicuous and enforceable against him under §2-316(2). That being so, he could reasonably have concluded, why bother arguing over it? I think Piper should get the advantage of this reading of §2-316(2) and shouldn't have to play any other games. After all, as we said before, this subsection gives the seller an easy-to-follow recipe for disclaiming implied warranties. If the seller can't conform to a simple recipe, he or she deserves whatever half-baked results follow.

3. a. Piper has no claims again Simon for breach of any implied warranty by virtue of the "as is" language to which he agreed. See §2-316(3)(a) and Comments 6 and 7. An effective "as is" disclaimer deprives an aggrieved buyer of any chance of successfully invoking any implied warranties, no matter how faulty the goods may turn out to be. See *Castro v. Ernie's Auto*, 368 Mont. 414 (2012). In 2011, Lola Castro bought a used 1995 Cadillac DeVille from Ernie's on what was clearly an as-is basis. Castro drove the car off the lot, but it broke down after approximately 2.5 miles of driving. She attempted to return the car to the dealership and demanded her money back. Ernie's refused. Castro sued Ernie's, and the trial court awarded a directed verdict in favor of the seller. The Montana Supreme Court affirmed this ruling on appeal. For another example of the "as is" disclaimer in action, see *Pershing Pacific West, LLC v. Ferretti Group, USA, Inc.*, 2013 WL 275691 (S.D. Cal.).

Issues have arisen with respect to Article 2's treatment of this method of disclaimer, but none would seem to give Piper any workable arguments here. For one thing, what language other than *as is* itself comes within this subpart, that is, what language "in common understanding calls the buyer's attention to the exclusion of warranties and makes plain that there is no implied warranty"? The language of §2-316(3)(a) suggests "with all faults" and Comment 7 adds "as they stand." Beyond this it is hard to think of any other language, at least as a short term of art, that would work. The courts have understandably resisted finding that other phrases of a more ambiguous nature come under this provision. What if a seller states in big letters, "YOU DON'T GET ANY WARRANTIES. I MEAN IT! I MEAN IT! I MEAN IT!"? Most courts look at this as a disclaimer that fails under §2-316(2) because it omits the magic word "merchantability" rather than as one that succeeds under §2-316(3)(a) even though it is undoubtedly, in the words of that subsection, "language which in common understanding calls the buyer's attention to the exclusion of warranties and makes plain that there is no implied warranty." If the seller wants it to be as is, it's best to stick with *as is*.

A second issue is whether the language of *as is* or its equivalent must be conspicuous if it is to be effective. Section 2-316(3)(a) does not contain any such requirement. If the creators of Article 2 had wanted to make this an absolute necessity, they certainly would have known how to draft this subpart to get the desired effect. All they had to do is look to the subsection above for a model. On the other hand, what possible reason could they have for leaving out a requirement that the language be conspicuous? A majority of courts have concluded that this omission was just an oversight on the drafters' part, or if not an oversight, then an unfortunate dereliction of duty that the courts should feel free to correct and have required that such a general disclaimer under §2-316(3)(a) be conspicuous. See, for example, *Lumber Mutual Insurance Co. v. Clarklift of Detroit, Inc.*, 569 N.W.2d 681 (Mich. App. 1997). Note how the drafters of Article 2A wrote the equivalent rule in §2A-214(3)(a) and their Comment to that section, which seems to strongly imply without actually saying it, that they thought it prudent to correct a few glitches that have been recognized in the language of §2-316.

A final issue is more substantive. Is there any limit to the use a seller can make of an *as is* disclaimer? If not, then sellers are given a particularly powerful way of eliminating all implied warranties. A short sentence containing these two words placed conspicuously on the document (and to be sure the buyer's acceptance of that document) is all that stands between a seller and total freedom from liability based on any implied warranty. As a practical matter, the *as is* term isn't used all that often and rarely if ever in the case of new goods, but is this just some kind of transitory self-restraint on the part of people who sell goods, a self-restraint that they at any time could decide to abandon when the going got rough?

It's likely that there is some limit to when and where a general *as is* disclaimer is appropriate and can be found to work as the seller intended, although the limits haven't been tested very well at this point. There is a suggestion in a few cases, most notably in *Gindy Manufacturing Corp. v. Cardinale Trucking Corp.*, 268 A.2d 345 (N.J. Super. 1970), that an *as is* clause will not be effective if placed in a contract for the sale of new goods. Professors White and Summers opine in their well-respected treatise that this type of disclaimer might not be given effect even in the sale of used goods if the buyer is an ordinary consumer unaware of the special "commercial understanding" of this catchphrase recognized by more sophisticated business types. Some cases do seem to intimate as much. Textual support is found for each of these possible limitations in the introductory language of §2-316(3)(a), "unless circumstances indicate otherwise."

A number of years ago, the Federal Trade Commission looked into the practices of used-car dealers. The dealers made extensive use of the "AS IS" disclaimer, but the FTC discovered that they often misrepresented what it meant, telling buyers it meant something like the buyer didn't get any additional equipment with it or the dealer didn't wash the car before they sold it. The result was the "Used Car Rule," which you can find at 16 C.F.R. Part 455. It requires that the merchant seller of a used car place a disclosure form on the rear side window of the car. Among the required disclosures is a checkbox indicating either "AS IS — NO DEALER WARRANTY" or "DEALER WARRANTY." Language under the first box states: "The dealer does not provide a warranty for any repairs after sale." Language under the second box provides for the terms of the warranty.

If this disclaimer is effective against Piper in this situation, does he have any other recourse? Again, it would be important if he could show that there was some *express* warranty given that had been breached. Did the seller perhaps say, "It works just fine"? If so, is the writing such that this would be barred by the parol evidence rule? Here I do think it would be pretty hard to argue that a description found in the document created an express warranty that had been breached. True, something like "One Used Labelling Machine" does create a warranty that this machine is designed for and can eventually be made to serve this function, but does it necessarily imply to a reasonable person that the machine is ready to do so at once with no repairs? Two cases have concluded that a prominent "as is" disclaimer was effective to block any reliance by the buyer on claimed express warranties as well as on implied. In the first, the buyers bought a five-year-old pickup truck from a dealer. The truck was indisputably sold "as is." Within two days of the purchase, the buyer began to notice some problems with the truck when it was driven at high speed. One week later, the truck would not start at all. The buyer argued that the dealer's description of the truck as "in good condition" and that it "would not need repairs" created express warranties that had never effectively been disclaimed by the seller. The Texas Court of Appeals ruled that even assuming these statements did create express warranties they did not survive the purchase of the truck on an as-is basis:

> When a buyer agrees to purchase something "as is," he agrees to make his own appraisal of the bargain and to accept the risk that he may be wrong. In making his choice, a buyer "removes the possibility that the seller's conduct will cause him damage." [Buyer] acknowledged in a deposition that there was actual awareness that the "as is" clause was in the paperwork signed. When asked "Did you understand that you were buying the truck as is?" the response was, "In a way, I did."

Smith v. Radam, Inc., 51 S.W.3d 413 (Tex. App. 2001). In *Rawson v. Conover*, 20 P.3d 876 (Utah 2001), the Utah Supreme Court came to a similar result in a consumer-to-consumer sale of a used van, invoking in effect a parol-evidence-rule analysis (recall §2-316(1)) to exclude any express warranties purportedly made by the seller in the course of his sales pitch from the contract. The written agreement signed by the parties included the sentence, "No agreement, verbal [*sic*; shouldn't this have been "oral"?] or otherwise, not contained in writing in this agreement on this document will be recognized." It did not hurt the seller's case that the buyer had stated in a deposition that in the words of the court, "he did not consider any verbal [*sic*] statement made by [the seller] to be a warranty concerning the van." Contrast this result with that of *AAR International, Inc. v. Vacances Heliades S.A.*, 202 F. Supp. 2d 788 (N.D. Ill. 2002), where the lessees who had agreed to an "as is" lease *were* allowed to proceed on a breach of express warranty theory when the language creating the express warranties on which they sought to rely was *written into* the lease document itself, the same document that carried the "as is" clause.

b. Simon would argue that all implied warranties had been disclaimed under §2-316(3)(b), but this argument should fail. Apparently, Piper did not examine the machine before entering into the contract. Nor did he "refuse" to make an examination. Simon asked if Piper would like to try the machine, but he did not demand that he do so. See the second paragraph of Comment 8.

4. a. The television set given to Betty is not merchantable. As we'll discuss in the later chapters on so-called performance issues, she need not accept the set or if she has accepted it may revoke that acceptance. Eventually she *may* be able to get her money back (depending on a lot of things, including whether Selma has a right to cure and whether she does cure). For the moment, we are only concerned with whether Betty's rights are affected at all by the quoted language on the back of the form. While Selma as seller does have the right via §2-719(1)(a) to get a buyer's agreement to remedies "in addition to or in substitution for" those provided in Article 2, her attempt here will fail on at least one and maybe two counts. The first, easier point is that the language on the form says nothing about the "repair or replacement" feature being the buyer's *exclusive* remedy under the contract. According to §2-719(1)(b), resort to an additional or substitute remedy "is optional unless the remedy is expressly agreed to be exclusive, in which case it is the sole remedy." Selma's form says nothing about exclusivity and hence Betty has a right to repair or replacement but is not bound to that as her only available remedy. She can pursue any other option open to her under the provisions of Article 2, and this

would be true even if this exact language were reproduced in the biggest, boldest print on the front of the form.

b. Had Selma's form been more carefully drafted in what it said, the effectiveness of the clause would hinge on the other possible infirmity that we can point to here. I think we can assume that the language of limitation in fine print on the back of the form is not conspicuous as that term is used in the Code. The effect of this, however, is far from certain. Does language modifying remedies under §2-719 have to be conspicuous to be effective? The commentators are not in agreement on this, and those decisions we have are likewise divided. In *Insurance Co. of North America v. Automatic Sprinkler Corp.*, 423 N.E.2d 151 (Ohio 1981), the Supreme Court of Ohio held that conspicuousness was a prerequisite to an effective modification or limitation of remedy provision. The court commented that the two sections, §2-316 and §2-719, were to be read "*in pari materia*" (translating roughly as "pertaining to the same subject or manner") and concluded that "any other reading of §§2-719 and 2-316(4) would permit inconspicuous provisions excluding or limiting damage recovery to circumvent the protection for buyers in §2-316(2)." The Supreme Court of Virginia, on the other hand, rejected such an argument, stressing that Article 2 explicitly distinguished between modes of disclaiming warranties and limiting remedies in the event of breach and that this distinction had to be respected. *Flintkote Co. v. W.W. Wilkinson, Inc.*, 260 S.E.2d 229 (Va. 1979). The two sections do, as we can point out, display great deference one to the other. See §2-316(4). Then see the last sentence of Comment 3 to §2-719.

This issue was again raised in a case before a federal district court applying New York law to a commercial dispute. *American Dredging Co. v. Plaza Petroleum Inc.*, 799 F. Supp. 1335 (E.D.N.Y. 1992). The plaintiff argued that a limitation on consequential damages contained in a listing of "Terms and Conditions" incorporated by reference into a telex setting forth the contract between the parties was unenforceable as a matter of law as it was not conspicuous. The court found this argument without merit:

> Any limitation of remedy is governed by U.C.C. §2-719(3), not U.C.C. §2-316. The issues of disclaimer of warranty and of limitation of remedy are two distinct issues, governed by different requirements. [Citations omitted.] U.C.C. §2-719 provides that parties to a contract may agree to exclude consequential damages upon breach so long as such limitation is not "unconscionable." But, U.C.C. §2-719(3) does not require that the clause be "conspicuous."

The court went on to say that whether the limitation language was conspicuous was, however, a factor to be taken into account in the court's determination of whether the clause was unconscionable as a matter of law. (Recall that unconscionability, like conspicuousness, is expressly made a question for the court under Article 2.)

The court concluded in the *American Dredging* case that the language of limitation, coming as it did in a contract between two sophisticated parties each presumably with some bargaining power, was not unconscionable. To the same effect, see *Borden, Inc. v. Advent Ink Co.*, 701 A.2d 255 (Pa. Super. 1997). Were Betty the consumer buyer forced to make the argument of unconscionability, relying primarily on the placement of the provision in the small print on the reverse of Selma's prepared form and pointing to other indicia of unconscionable behavior by Selma, of course, she might be more successful. As we saw in general with respect to the unconscionability doctrine (in Chapter 9) and as we will soon discuss in the §2-719(3) context, consumer buyers are much more likely to get somewhere by arguing unconscionability than are commercial parties.

c. Under this set of facts, Selma should have the advantage of her limitation of remedy clause. She has solved the two potential problems with it by making it conspicuous (just in case that is a requirement) and expressly stating it to be the exclusive remedy of the buyer (which is undoubtedly required).

Does Betty have any argument that could potentially defeat this clause? It does not seem so. Once a clause falls within §2-719(1) there are only two ways for a buyer to get around it. Under §2-719(2) she might try to show that the remedy has or would "fail of its essential purpose." What does this mean? Section 2-719(2) starts in effect from the proposition that the parties have agreed to remedies in addition to or in substitution for those provided for in Article 2 and that *those* remedies *as of the time of agreement* are on their face a perfectly reasonable allocation of risks and rewards between two parties each looking out for his or her own interest. (We are *not* talking here about provisions that from their inception are inherently unfair and can be deemed to be unconscionable. This is the subject of the separate subsection (3), which will be discussed and compared shortly.) Look at Comment 1:

> Under this section parties are left free to shape their remedies to their particular requirements and reasonable agreements limiting or modifying remedies are to be given effect.

So we can assume that an exclusive "repair or replace" remedy provision is reasonable at the time of contracting. It would be hard to argue otherwise, as this particular type of modification of remedy is singled out for approval in §2-719(1)(a). There is nothing inherently unfair or improper about the seller's asking for the buyer's agreement to limit his or her potential remedies in this way, and if the buyer does agree this becomes an enforceable aspect of the contract between them.

It may turn out, however, that in some circumstances a clause that is fair and reasonable at the time of contracting fails to do the job intended for it by the parties. "Failure of essential purpose" under §2-719(2) is failure of the essential purpose *of the agreed-to exclusive remedy provision*. When that happens, the provision must be set aside. Note the language in Comment 1:

> [U]nder subsection (2), where an apparently fair and reasonable clause because of circumstances fails in its purpose or operates to deprive either party of the substantial value of the bargain, it must give way to the general remedy provisions of this Article.

Let's look at the exclusive remedy of repair or replacement of defective goods or parts. What is the "essential purpose" of this remedy? In *Clark v. International Harvester Co.*, 581 P.2d 784 (Idaho 1978), the court characterized the purpose of such a provision this way:

> The purpose of the exclusive repair or replacement remedy is to ensure that the purchaser receives a product which conforms to the express warranty [and any applicable implied warranty], i.e., that the product is free from defects, and if the product proves defective within the warranty period the seller is obligated to cure the defect within a reasonable time.

So the essential purpose of the provision in Betty's agreement with Selma is to ensure that Betty ends up with a new TV, working as it is supposed to, but recognizing that even a brand new set may take some reasonable adjustments to get it working just right. That being so, has the limited remedy failed of its essential purpose in our hypothetical? No. If Betty gives Selma the chance to repair and if Selma does so within a reasonably short period of time, Betty does have the benefit of her bargain. (Remember, her bargain included her agreeing that Selma would have the chance to make such repairs in lieu of being responsible for breach in other ways.) We will see a situation where Betty as buyer will be able to effectively argue that there has been a failure of essential purpose in the next question, but for the moment, the facts wouldn't support such an argument. And, as we now appreciate, whether there has been a failure of essential purpose under §2-719(2) must always be evaluated in light of the particular circumstances, what exactly has happened to the goods, *subsequent* to the contract's being entered into. The failure of essential purpose doctrine does not judge the clause in the abstract but rather how the clause has or will operate under a specific set of facts.

Contrast this to the unconscionability doctrine as it is invoked in §2-719(3). Whether a provision is unconscionable or not is in theory to be determined not in light of later events but as of the moment of contracting. Unconscionability is the second main line of attack a buyer may follow to get out from under a provision to which he or she has given assent and which expressly provides for an exclusive remedy in substitution for what would otherwise be available under Article 2. We have already explored in Chapter 9 the general doctrine of unconscionability as set forth in §2-302. You should now read §2-719(3) carefully to see how unconscionability works more particularly with regard to the matters we are here discussing. The concern of this subsection seems to be exclusively the possibility that a provision could limit or exclude the buyer's rights to consequential damages in an unconscionable way. In the hypothetical as we now have it, Betty has had no consequential damages nor is she seeking any relief of this nature. Whatever may be the effect of §2-719(3) on this clause once consequential damages do become an issue, it doesn't seem to apply to Betty here. We'll see an appropriate use of this subsection on behalf of one of Selma's customers as we move along, but unconscionability doesn't do anything for Betty under these circumstances.

For the moment, it seems fairly safe to say that Selma's clause will be effective under §2-719(1) and neither doctrine that could under appropriate facts allow the buyer to set aside or limit that clause is available to Betty. Betty is stuck with the exclusive remedy of repair or replacement of the TV set—as she did agree to in signing Selma's form.

d. Under these circumstances, Betty should be able to win with an argument that the exclusive remedy provision has now failed of its essential purpose. As the court continued in the *Clark* case quoted above:

> If . . . the seller is subsequently unable or unwilling to repair or replace a defective part within a reasonable time, the buyer is left with a defective product—not conforming to the warranty—and the limited remedy has not achieved its purpose. In such circumstances §2719(2) permits the buyer to pursue the other remedies provided by the UCC if the defect substantially affects the value of the buyer's bargain.

The Supreme Court of Alabama later applied the same analysis in *Miller v. Pettibone Corp.*, 693 So. 2d 1372 (Ala. 1997).

In other words, if Selma were permitted to take one more shot at repair and even if she were successful, Betty would not be left with the substantial benefit of her bargain. She paid for a new TV set. She would end up with a set that has already been patched up a number of times and seems incapable of functioning like a new set should. The repair or replace remedy has failed of its essential purpose. At some point, a buyer should be able to say, "Enough already." Incidentally, this is the function of "Lemon Laws" that have been enacted in every jurisdiction. Under those statutes, after a certain number of attempts at repair or a certain number of days in the shop, a car under warranty can be returned to the seller.

A provision limiting the buyer's remedies to repair or replacement of the goods sold can fail of its essential purpose in other ways as well. In *Alumaguard Corp. v. Road Safety Products Distributing, Inc.*, 2008 WL 2721152 (Ariz. App.), the seller contracted to provide aluminum piping needed by the buyer to construct and install handrails for a new ice hockey arena. It was clear to all that the materials had to be delivered well in advance of the arena's December 23, 2003 completion date. The seller was late in delivering some of the railing and the buyer had to hire three other entities to acquire and install temporary iron handrails between December 15 and December 22, 2003. The buyer brought suit against the seller for the damages, direct and consequential, caused it by the seller's delay. The seller responded by attempting to invoke an exclusive repair-or-replace remedy clause found in the contract between the two parties. The court concluded that the exclusive repair-or-replace remedy failed of its essential purpose under the circumstances—how could a later repair or replacement of the missing goods remedy a delay in their delivery—and that the aggrieved buyer was entitled to its full measure of damages.

Or consider a case decided by the Iowa Court of Appeals, *Midwest Hatchery & Poultry Farms, Inc. v. Doorenbos Poultry, Inc.*, 783 N.W.2d 56 (Iowa App. 2010). Doorenbos was a company that kept chickens for egg production and sold the eggs. It conducted its business at 2 barn facilities (one of which could house 112,000 birds and the other 134,000) in Sioux County, Iowa. Evidence presented at trial revealed that hens generally do not begin laying eggs until they are 17 or 18 weeks old. They continue producing until they are about 110 weeks old. The practice of Doorenbos Poultry had been to keep all chickens of a single age group through their productive life, and simultaneously replace those birds with new chickens that are 17 to 18 weeks old, a practice they used to maximize production and continue cash flow without interruption. In the fall of 2006, Doorenbos Poultry entered into a written contract with Midwest, a supplier of hens, to purchase 112,000 pullets (that is, young hens) at 18 weeks of age to be delivered on December 28, 2006. Over January 16, 17, and 18, 2007, Midwest delivered 115,581 pullets to Doorenbos. The buyer soon concluded the birds delivered were 13 to 14 weeks of age rather than 18 weeks. He testified he could not cancel the order and return the chickens because his former flock had already been removed from his building. He explained that the barns in which the chickens are kept do not have heating. Because the buildings in which the hens are housed maintain their temperature from the body heat of the birds, he believed the water lines in the barn would have frozen if he had not kept the pullets. Doorenbos sued Midwest for damages it suffered because the poultry it delivered was not of the age promised, meaning they didn't start producing eggs until some weeks after their delivery. Hatcheries, the defendant seller, countered by pointing to a provision in the parties' contract that limited the aggrieved buyer's option upon breach of warranty to either replacement of the pullets or refund of the purchase price it had paid. The trial court determined that the limited remedies provision failed of its essential purpose, allowing the buyer to collect monetary damages, and the appellate court affirmed:

> When it was notified of the breach, we agree that Midwest could have exercised its option under the contract, taken back the entire flock, and either replaced the chickens with eighteen week old pullets or refunded the entire purchase price. The record supports the conclusion that this did not happen because, as the district court noted, it was plainly impractical. . . . It would have been extremely inefficient for both parties to replace the pullets Midwest had delivered. The pullets that Doorenbos Poultry had in its barn would have had to have been rounded up, placed in cages, and loaded into trucks while more that 100,000 replacement birds were moved into the barn. As Scott Doorenbos testified, a simultaneous exchange would have been necessary because the birds provided the only source of heat for the barn. In addition, it does not appear that either party was interested in the option of removal and refund.

5. Selma's attempt to avoid consequential damages should fail here, certainly for the personal injury damages and possibly even for the other damages to Buster's property. Buster relies on §2-719(3) and the unconscionability doctrine. While clauses excluding consequential damages are not automatically and irretrievably unconscionable, "limitation of consequential damages for injury to the person in the case of consumer goods is prima facie unconscionable." It is true this is written as if Selma could overcome the presumption, but in all practicality the seller of consumer goods isn't going to have any luck doing so even if he or she has the gall to try. What about the damages to all the stuff in Buster's kitchen? Subsection (3) says that limitation of consequential damages "when the loss is commercial" is not prima facie unconscionable. As a matter of fact, in the general run of cases where both parties were reasonably powerful and supposedly sophisticated commercial entities, the exclusion of consequential commercial damages is upheld with no difficulty. Buster's situation is, of course, different. This portion of his loss was not to the person, but it wasn't "commercial loss" either. Unconscionability will have to be determined, as indeed it always must, by the court's review of all the facts, looking for evidence of what we have termed both *procedural unconscionability* and *substantive unconscionability*.

One case suggests that Buster may have a hard time collecting for the property damage caused by the toaster mishap, the loss of his kitchen furniture. In *NEC Technologies, Inc. v. Nelson*, 478 S.E.2d 769 (Ga. 1996), it was not a mere toaster that burst into flames causing property damage, but a 42-inch television set—at least according to the plaintiff's expert witness, whose version of the events was not shared by the local fire chief and fire marshal, both of whom "opined that the fire started from an electrical shortage unassociated with the television set." The owners brought suit against both the retailer from whom they had purchased the set and the manufacturer on a variety of theories including breach of the warranty of merchantability. In defending against the warranty claim, the seller pointed to a clause in the contract of sale that excluded all liability for incidental and consequential damages. The Supreme Court of Georgia held that even if the TV set was to blame for the fire, the limitation clause was effective to bar recovery on a breach of warranty theory for the resultant property damage. The clause was not per se unconscionable under §2-719(3) nor was the court willing to deem it unconscionable in the particular situation, given its finding that the evidence presented, even viewed in the light most favorable to the buyer, would not support an inference of either the procedural or substantive aspect of unconscionability.

Buster, whose purchase was limited to a simple toaster, might try to distinguish the *NEC Technologies* case by pointing out that the court in that case had made much of the fact that the record there reflected the ability of the buyers to actually bargain in a meaningful way over certain matters in the contract such as the amount they would be credited for the trade-in on their old 40-inch TV and the delivery arrangements. Buster seems to have taken the toaster and the language on Selma's form on a take-it-or-leave-it basis. Still his chances of collecting for the property damage, at least in Georgia, seem slim given that the Georgia Supreme Court concluded in *NEC Technologies*:

> There is nothing in the record to indicate that at the time the Nelsons executed the sales contract for their television set, they were not aware of the normal hazards associated with the use of any electrical appliance. A review of the record before the trial court reveals nothing to indicate that [the seller] had any knowledge that the particular design of the television set purchased by the Nelsons posed any greater danger than that represented by other products designed to utilize electricity in their operation. . . . [W]e cannot conclude under the circumstances in this case that the allocation of risk or property damage to the Nelsons was unconscionable. We recognize that to hold this exclusion of consequential property damages unconscionable could necessitate voiding as unconscionable such exclusions in the warranties of virtually every type of electrical appliance sold to a consumer, a result clearly contrary to [the Georgia legislature's adoption of] §2-719(3).

6. It's not clear who would win here. This question is based on the case of *Jim Dan, Inc. v. O. M. Scott & Sons Co.*, 785 F. Supp. 1196 (W.D. Pa. 1992). The buyer's recovery was limited in that case to return of the purchase price, $835. We are dealing here with a substituted remedy not of "repair or replace" but of "return of the good and repayment of the price." Such a substituted remedy is expressly contemplated by §2-719(1)(a). In *Jim Dan* the court first held that the language of this clause expressly stated return of the price to be the exclusive remedy and hence met the requirement of §2-719(1)(b). It then went on to hold that under the circumstances it had not failed of its essential purpose:

> [T]he clause does not fail of its essential purpose because . . . the clause does exactly what it was designed to do: limit the buyer's remedy to the purchase price of the product. [H]erbicides involve latent risks. In fact the herbicide industry often limits its liability to the purchase price of the product. Herbicide manufacturers limit damages because of the uncertainties inherent in the business and because decisions such as planting, cultivation, and harvesting are uniquely within the purchaser's control. Therefore, an herbicide manufacturer's decision to limit damages merely allocates risks among the parties, and [the seller's] exclusive remedy does not fail of its essential purpose. [Citations omitted.]

Nor was the clause unconscionable. As the court noted, "a commercial contract will rarely be found unconscionable." Appreciation of the commercial context favored the seller. Such limitations it turns out are common in the herbicide industry. (Recall §2-302(2).) The buyer was not inexperienced in making contracts or in purchasing pesticides, herbicides, and the like. While he had just purchased the golf course, he had previously owned a restaurant, a miniature golf course, and a driving range. Whether or not Jim Dan (as president of Jim Dan, Inc.) may have actually read the clause prior to applying the herbicide, the court concluded, §2-719(3) "should not be used to relieve [the buyer] of the misfortunes of its business practices."

See also *Bruce v. ICI Americas, Inc.*, 933 F. Supp. 781 (S.D. Iowa 1996), which comes to the same conclusion. But then see *Triple E, Inc. v. Hendrix & Dail, Inc.*, 543 S.E.2d 245 (S.C. App. 2001), in which the South Carolina Court of Appeals held that a farmer—a portion of whose tobacco crop was lost to the deadly "black shank" when a fungicide failed to perform as it was expressly warranted—was entitled to recover the value of his damaged crop and not just to the return of the cost of the ineffectual fungicide, even though the parties had contractually agreed to exclusion of consequential and incidental damages. This same line of thinking was adopted in *Nomo Agroindustrial SA v. Enza Zaden North America, Inc.*, 492 F. Supp. 2d 1175 (D. Ariz. 2007), and *Gibbs Patrick Farms, Inc. v. Syngenta Seeds, Inc.* (M.D. Ga.). A helpful compilation of the conflicting decisions on whether a limitation of remedies provision such as we have here is or is not unconscionable in the context of the agriculture chemical business is to be found in *DJ Coleman, Inc. v. Nufarm Americas, Inc.*, 693 F. Supp. 2d 1055 (D.N.D. 2010).

7. a. Clause 20.2 should bar Doe from getting anything for her lost profits. The limitation of remedy has not failed of its essential purpose. Doe would have to argue that the exclusion of consequential damages is unconscionable under §2-719(3). That subsection says that limitation of consequential damages "where the loss is commercial is not" prima facie unconscionable. So the matter of unconscionability must be reviewed taking into consideration the particular commercial context and the facts of the individual case. In just about every situation where a court has been confronted with such an argument, the decision has come down in favor of the exclusion. It has proved very hard, if not close to impossible, for a commercial buyer to prove an exclusion clause such as that in 20.2 unconscionable if its effect is to limit recovery for loss of property or other commercial loss. The commentators in general seem to approve of this run of decisions, reasoning that commercial parties should be and under the Code by and large are always free to allocate between themselves all manner of commercial risks.

   b. This question presents a much more difficult issue—in fact one on which the courts are dramatically split. Whether Doe can receive anything for what could be months of lost profits might depend primarily on what jurisdiction she finds herself in. The limited repair or replace remedy has clearly failed of its essential purpose. What is the effect of this, if any, on the companion exclusion of consequential damages provision? Doe as buyer argues that once the limited remedy fails, she is entitled to recover any and all of her damages without any limitation established in the agreement. In support she cites the full language of §2-719(2) emphasizing the concluding phrase: "Where circumstances cause an exclusive or limited remedy to fail of its essential purpose, *remedy may be had as provided in this Act.*" She points also to the concluding language of Comment 1 to the effect that when an apparently fair and reasonable clause fails of its essential purpose, "it must give way to the general remedy provisions of this Article." The general remedy provisions, and more specifically §2-714(3) and §2-715, allow the buyer to recover consequential damages in the event of a breach of warranty.

   The seller, Ovens of Brooklyn, argues that the two contract provisions 20.1 and 20.2 act *independently* of one another. Even if 20.1 is not enforceable having failed of its essential purpose, 20.2 still thwarts any attempt by Doe to recover consequential damages. After all, why should the buyer come out with *more* than she would have achieved had the limited remedy *not* failed of its essential purpose? Recall that in the previous question we found that she could not recover for loss of profits generally. Of course the buyer can argue that part of the price she paid for signing away her rights to consequential damages in 20.2 was the protection she got in 20.1. The limited repair or replace warranty assured her that "at least minimum adequate remedies" would be available and that there would be "at least a fair quantum of remedy for breach." See Comment 1. When that exclusive remedy failed, she would argue, all bets were off and the only fair thing to do would be to read 20.2 out of the contract as well.

As I mentioned, the courts have historically been split over just this issue. Some have ruled that when a limited remedy fails of its essential purpose then any exclusion of consequential damages found in the same agreement necessarily becomes unenforceable as a matter of law. Other courts have ruled just the opposite: The clauses these courts reason are independent. They hold that the failure of one is immaterial to how the other should be judged and that an independent exclusion of consequential damages for commercial loss will therefore survive. A third group of courts have articulated what they refer to as a case-by-case approach. Once the limited remedy fails, whether the exclusion of consequential damages provision should retain its effect is to be judged by a view to the overall "risk allocation package" that the parties entered into. Under this analysis, what factors are to be considered? In this hypothetical I purposefully made the two provisions separately numbered and set apart. More typically they occur together in the same clause or paragraph of the agreement, often as one run-on sentence. (See the language in Example 4c. Did it strike you as unusual at the time?) Should the way the two clauses were situated on the page affect whether the court considers them dependent or independent in the given case? Is such a "case-by-case" approach workable, or is it just a way of allowing the court to pick winners and losers with few if any guidelines?

If you would like to see a case or two that review this controversy, you may want to check out *Patapsco Designs, Inc. v. Dominion Wireless, Inc.*, 276 F. Supp. 2d 472 (D. Md. 2003), or *Razor v. Hyundai Motor America*, 854 N.E.2d 607 (Ill. 2006), *cert. denied* 549 U.S. 1181 (2007). In both of these cases, the courts concluded that the "independent" approach treating the two separate clauses—one for an exclusive remedy, even if it has failed of its essential purpose, and the other for limitation of consequential damages—as independent provisions each to be judged on its own terms has become, at least in recent years, the approach of the majority of courts.

An interesting variant on the problem was faced by the Colorado Court of Appeals. The written agreement signed by the buyers of a modular home contained a limitation of the buyer's remedial obligations to repair or replacement of defective parts. There was also a distinct clause under which the buyers agreed that under no circumstances would they have the right to return the unit once accepted and seek a refund, that is, to revoke acceptance. The court held that once the repair or replace remedy failed of its essential purpose, the buyers did have the right to revoke acceptance, whatever else the written agreement said:

> [T]he seller in its contract purported to limit buyers' remedy to repair of the modular home. However, as the record indicates, and the jury apparently determined, seller's repair remedy had failed to achieve its essential purpose—the value of the home remained substantially impaired. Accordingly, under these circumstances, buyers had the right to revoke acceptance notwithstanding the provision of the contract purporting to exclude that remedy.

Rose v. Colorado Factory Homes, 10 P.3d 680 (Colo. App. 2000).

8. Bart's predicament poses a final problem involving Article 2's treatment of disclaimers and limitations and a particularly difficult one at that. Bart signed the contract containing the clause at time of sale, so he has no argument that it is not part of the enforceable agreement. The clause itself is clearly worded as a disclaimer of warranty, so it must be judged by §2-316 criteria. And under §2-316(2) there seems no argument that it is not effective to disclaim all implied warranties. Selma has met that subsection's stringent requirements—the provision seems superconspicuous—and hence gets the result she intended.

   What is Bart to do? Perhaps as we've suggested before he can argue that the description of the goods as a "radio receiver" created an express warranty that there would be no hum, or that it wouldn't burst into flames, but this does seem to be stretching things a bit. A more appealing argument is to confront the situation head-on and argue that this clause cannot have effect because it is unconscionable. The issue—and it's one on which the commentators are split and that the courts rarely have confronted directly—is whether a disclaimer of warranty that meets the standards of §2-316 can nevertheless be deemed unconscionable under the Code and hence unenforceable.

   Some courts have suggested that a disclaimer could be unconscionable by virtue of the language of §2-719(3), where the effect of the disclaimer is the equivalent of denying all consequential damages. There are obvious problems with this conclusion, however. Section 2-719 governs provisions that seek to alter or limit remedies. For disclaimer of warranty the place to look is §2-316. The Code's basic structure says that the two types of provisions are to be treated distinctly. See Comment 2 to §2-316, which makes the drafters' intent abundantly clear. See also

Comment 3 to §2-719: "The seller in all cases is free to disclaim warranties in the manner provided in Section 2-316." So how can §2-719(3) be applied to what is undeniably a warranty disclaimer?

A different line of argument some courts apparently find appealing is that a warranty disclaimer can be held unconscionable under §2-302. After all, that section is expressed to pertain to "any clause of the contract." But §2-316 does not specifically refer back to §2-302, and an argument can be made that, being the more specific provision designed to deal with just such disclaimer clauses, it in effect preempts or supersedes the very open-ended §2-302. More to the point, the underlying philosophy of §2-316 is that a buyer is "protected from unexpected and unbargained language of disclaimer by denying effect to such language" through the mechanism of assuring the buyer's chance to see and appreciate any attempted disclaimer of implied warranty. Seller in this case has done everything §2-316(2) tells her she must do to protect the buyer from "surprise." She has followed the course laid out for her by the drafters. How then can the result be deemed unconscionable?

As a matter of practicality, were the radio receiver to be implicated in some dramatic personal injury, a court would be hard pressed (and probably wouldn't even try) to enforce the disclaimer as written. Perhaps one reason the courts have not had to treat this issue more often is that in many states separate consumer protection legislation renders ineffective any attempt to disclaim a basic level of warranty protection in a sale to a consumer purchaser. The question for us here then is whether, if a given state's legislature has chosen *not* to enact such protection, the court may and should read its adoption of the uniform provisions of Article 2 to fill in that gap.

CHAPTER 14

The "Privity" Puzzle

INTRODUCTION

In discussing warranty law in the preceding chapters, we always stuck close to home. By that I mean we focused exclusively on the two-party transaction and the two immediate parties to that transaction—Buyer and Seller. Seller warrants to Buyer. Buyer, if that warranty is not met, seeks some kind of relief from Seller. All well and good. The problems, however, start multiplying once we allow ourselves even to contemplate the fact that others may be involved. Seller may have bought either the goods themselves or some component part from another, and that person may have in turn bought from someone else even further up the line. The party who has bought may in turn sell the goods, but even if not, they can get passed on in some other way, such as a gift or a loan. Even if Buyer decides to hold on to the stuff for dear life, his or her use of the goods may affect the lives of a whole host of other people, especially if something goes haywire. A simple breach of a warranty arising out of a single sales transaction can leave an amazingly broad path of destruction.

You may have heard of the concept of *privity of contract* sometime in your prior studies. That may have happened in your Contracts course, or it may have been in Torts (where privity can take on the role of the all-purpose villain). Individuals are said to be in privity of contract if and only if they are actual parties to the same contract and each directly obligated one to the other by that contract. The age-old teaching is that no one can sue for breach of contract or claim contractual rights against another unless he or she can establish privity with that other party. In the days when this teaching was not only age-old but also still indisputably true, it made things relatively simple. A right or cause of action arising under warranty was thought to be the very paradigm of contractual obligation. That being so, and if traditional privity doctrine still held sway, the buyer and only the buyer had rights to assert a warranty claim. The buyer could assert that claim only against the buyer's immediate seller.

Today things are nowhere near this cut and dried. The citadel of privity, as the by-now classic metaphor goes, has been breached, shaken to its very foundations—a mere suggestion of its former self. The fact is, however, that chunks of that rubble still lay strewn over the field, and it's all too easy to trip over them. We live in a troubling and unsettled time as far as privity of contract is concerned, and no one can reasonably expect in a finite space to "clear up" or "solve" the privity puzzle. At best we may be able to select out some of the puzzle pieces and begin to examine how they might fit into the grander scheme of things.

The puzzle pieces on which we'll expend some energy are, not surprisingly given the scope of this book, those that go by the label of warranty and are governed by Article 2. Under the law as it now stands, however, many situations where we would be tempted to play with these pieces also invite investigation under other companion theories that come from the box marked "tort." Anyone representing a person hurt in some way by a product will naturally have to consider whether liability can be predicated under a negligence theory or via the burgeoning modern doctrine of strict products liability in tort. There's no way around the fact. These pieces don't fit neatly together. There are definite overlaps, or at least there definitely are large areas where two if not three of the concepts apply even if the exact outlines of these overlapping areas are anything *but* definite. The outstanding questions involve not just each doctrine in turn (warranty, negligence, and strict products liability), but also how each affects the reach of the other two. Trying to determine how the interplay works out in any one jurisdiction sometimes seems like a problem in N dimensions, with N being some number significantly larger than three. On top of this, developments in this area are nowhere near uniform across the states. In fact they often seem about as nonuniform as you can get. Any exploration of the field—and particularly one coming at the problem from the point of view of the normally *Uniform* Commercial Code—is bound to be unsettling.

My intention in this chapter, as you've undoubtedly gathered by now, is not to attempt an exhaustive or in-depth study. We will lay out some of the interesting problems that one would come across if one were to dare to fully enter into this exploration. To be fair, the drafters of Article 2 have in §2-318 set forth a trio of alternatives for the states, any one of which once adopted (or, as often has happened, adopted with some additional variations) does give definitive answers to *some* questions on how far the reach of warranty protection *minimally* extends in that jurisdiction. That's something. As we'll soon see, however, and as the drafters were only too keen to insist in their commentary, it's only a very limited part of the puzzle.

COMPARING AND CONTRASTING

The one thing we can say for certain about the relationship of warranty liability in contract as it relates to negligence and strict product liability in tort is a resounding negative: It is *not* true that, in any given factual situation, a potential plaintiff's case will necessarily fall into one and only one of the cubbyholes. Depending on the facts, of course, but also depending on the law of the jurisdiction, perhaps one, two, or all three theories may be advanced by an injured party with some hope of success. There are instances, of course, in which the courts in some states have ruled that one cause of action need not be extended to cover a particular set of circumstances just *because* those are covered, or more appropriately covered, by one of the other theories. But then there are instances where the logic is just the opposite. Some courts have reasoned that since the reach of these doctrines is a matter of sound public policy, there is no sense or justification for denying a suit on one theory when it would be allowed under another and where the two would, for all intents and purposes, seem to work to the same end. So the scope of one theory is extended just *because* of a desire to make it coextensive with the scope of another. No one has ever said the common law doesn't work in mysterious ways.

Make no mistake about it. The choice of which theory or theories a plaintiff is allowed to pursue can make a big difference. (You've had enough law study and badgering by the professorate to appreciate that.) Different causes of action call for proof of different essential elements and hinge on different material facts. A possible claim in negligence against a seller or manufacturer can be everything the plaintiff would wish, but then he or she will have to prove by competent evidence that there actually was negligence on the defendant's part. Breach of warranty and products liability in tort don't require proof of negligence. Each can be established as a matter of strict liability without regard to *how* the breach or defect arose. But then breach of warranty and products liability differ in many other respects. Products liability is premised on the product being sold by the defendant "in a defective condition unreasonably dangerous to the user or consumer or to his property," in the words of §402A of the Restatement (Second) of Torts. In comparison, goods need not be dangerous for a seller to be in breach of warranty (e.g., a perfectly well-made knife with a blue handle that was promised to have a red one). They need not even be "defective" as we ordinarily use that word (e.g., a diamond when a zircon was promised).

A claim in tort is usually subject to affirmative defenses such as assumption of risk and contributory or comparative negligence. The buyer's behavior may not come under the same scrutiny and with the same devastating effect if the suit is structured purely as a breach of warranty action. The same factors may, of course, come into play in determining what was the "ordinary use" to which the goods were to be put and whether the various criteria of §2-315 were met, but courts will not necessarily view these constraints as equivalent to the traditional tort principles referred to, as those historically have so often worked very harshly against potential plaintiffs.

What may be recovered under the various theories can differ as well. Actions for strict liability are generally restricted to those seeking recompense for physical injury to the person or to his or her property. Remedies for breach of warranty actions, as we will see in Chapter 27, can be sought for damage beyond personal injury or direct injury to the plaintiff's property. In warranty, the plaintiff may recover for the economic loss suffered with the decreased value of the product itself because it failed to live up to expectations. In addition, recovery may be had for consequential damages. For instance, if the buyer's business suffers loss of profits because of the breach, these may be recoverable under a warranty theory. There has been great debate (with no resolution in sight) whether the notion of products liability should be extended to protect affected individuals from such economic losses either direct (to the product itself) or consequential. Things are not all gloomy for the plaintiff forced to sue in tort, of course. Remember that a successful suit in tort may make available a whole measure of damages (including most particularly punitive damages) that are not provided for under Article 2.

There are what we might think of as procedural differences as well—aware as we always must be that what may be denominated a mere "procedural" point can, to a prospective plaintiff, spell the difference between ultimate success or ruin. For one thing, there's the statute of limitations. The statute of limitations for actions brought under Article 2 is found in §2-725. Each state will have adopted some other statute for actions in tort in general or for strict liability in particular. The length of the limitation may be greater or less than §2-725's four years, and may begin running at some different point in time. As you can imagine, a large percentage of the cases testing the limits of one theory or another and the potential for overlap arise as disputes over the relevant statute of limitations and how it is to be applied. Beyond the statute of limitation controversy, there is the question of notice. Section 2-607(3)(a) calls, as we will see in a subsequent chapter, for prompt notice by the buyer of any breach. If notice is not given within a reasonable time, the buyer is barred from any and all remedies under Article 2. There is in general no such draconian notice requirement governing strict liability actions. Finally, recall the complex scheme under Article 2 that allows for effective disclaimers of warranty and limitations of liability.

In a large number of cases, these will drastically reduce if not entirely eliminate the chance of success of a plaintiff claiming breach of warranty. Again we can only speak in general terms, as the law of products liability is anything but uniform across the board, but it can definitely be argued that a disclaimer or a limitation of remedy can have no effect whatsoever on any action brought under that theory.

And then there is *privity*. While the exact extent of *who* may sue *whom* under any state's version of products liability is certainly open to interpretation, revision, and a fair amount of questioning, privity per se has nothing to do with it. The rise of product liability in the United States can, to a large extent, be viewed as a growing conviction in the minds of commentators and courts that certain controversies would have been better dealt with if the word "privity" had never been invented. Compare this to *breach of warranty*, which is to this day and for better or worse still grounded in the law of contract. Historically, at least, it would have been absolutely essential for a plaintiff claiming breach of warranty to establish privity of contract with the party being sued. Privity of contract was no mere technicality. It was the linchpin—the very heart and soul of the action. As we will see in the examples and explanations of this chapter, Article 2 has relaxed this requirement to some degree. Still, matters of privity can't be ignored even in the most modern of warranty actions.

THE VERTICAL AND THE HORIZONTAL

To make it all the more interesting, privity comes in two types. For a long time now, commentators and courts have made the distinction for the purpose of analysis between *vertical privity* and *horizontal privity* concerns. Before we get into either of these varieties, let's start with the two parties who are in *direct privity* any way you look at it: Buyer and Seller. The simplest of diagrams does the trick:

Seller
||
Buyer

The double line represents a relationship of contract, a purchase and sale.

Vertical privity refers to the possibility that goods may be bought and sold more than once before they come into the hands of the ultimate buyer. Parties are said to be in vertical privity with the buyer if they are part of the chain of distribution that ends with the sale to the buyer. So, for instance, a manufacturer (Mfr.) may sell the goods to a distributor (Distr.) who then sells to Seller. (Since there are many sales going on, our original Seller is sometimes referred to as this particular Buyer's *immediate seller* with some hope that this will make things clear. Likewise, Buyer is referred to as this particular Seller's *immediate buyer.*) To add to the confusion, the manufacturer may have purchased a crucial part that later becomes the subject of dispute—and this could be anything from a jet engine to the tiniest screw—from another components manufacturer (Comp. Mfr.). Our vertical chain then looks like this:

Comp. Mfr.
||
Mfr.
||
Distr.
||
Seller
||
Buyer

The chain of course could be longer or it could be shorter; the main point here is that it is vertical. Should our friend Buyer be injured by a breach of warranty, she may seek to sue any or all above her in the chain of distribution.

As we have said, however, it is not only buyers themselves who may suffer harm when there is something wrong with a product. Issues of *horizontal privity* revolve around who other than the ultimate buyer may sue for injuries resulting from some fault with the product. In some instances, actual possession of the goods may be passed along (other than by sale) from Buyer to others. Buyer might give what she has purchased as a gift to a relative or loan it to a friend for his or her temporary use. So, for example, Buyer can purchase a car that is then given to a daughter on her successful graduation from law school. (We can all dream.) Or if that isn't in the cards, Buyer might at least allow it to be used by the offspring for an evening or two. Even if Buyer greedily keeps possession of the goods and makes use of them for herself, others can all too easily be affected when things go wrong. If the car breaks down and goes out of control with Buyer at the wheel, serious injury can come to anyone else she's invited along for the drive and even to the totally unrelated bystander who just happens to be in the way when the car comes crashing in his or her direction.

Our final diagram then looks something like this:

Comp. Mfr.
||
Mfr.
||
Distr.
||
Seller
||
Buyer——————————X

X is just about anyone who doesn't buy the product but is somehow affected by its use, and by the breach of warranty, after it gets into Buyer's hands. And of course we can't rest comfortably that there will be only one X involved. When troubles come, they often come in platoons. There could easily be a Y, a Z, and who knows how many others hanging about somewhere horizontally off to the side. Each of these parties when injured may claim some rights not only against Buyer for whatever she may have done to bring on or fail to prevent the injury, but also against Seller, based now on whatever warranty was part of the sale from Seller to Buyer. Or X, Y, and Z may try to turn the corner, taking on issues of both horizontal and vertical privity by suing, say, the Distributor who sold to Seller or the Manufacturer even further up the chain, but still grounding their actions in warranty theory.

We have come a long way quickly from what we now look back on fondly as the "simple" two-party transaction and disputes between mere buyers and sellers.

PRIVITY UNDER ARTICLE 2

Article 2 deals with the Sale of Goods, of which warranties are a big part. The drafters did not entirely duck the privity problem. Look at §2-318. When initially promulgated in 1962, the Code contained only a single version of this section: the one you now see labeled as "Alternative A." Apparently many state legislatures were uncomfortable with this language and sought to expand the scope of warranty protection beyond what the drafters had offered. In the hope of averting a flood of totally distinct, nonuniform versions of this section, the Permanent Editorial Board in 1966 came up with the trio of alternatives that you now see in the official version of the Code.

As it has turned out, the P.E.B.'s strategy was only mildly successful. The states have gone every which way on this. California and Texas have chosen simply to ignore §2-318 altogether and leave it out of their Article 2. These states' issues of privity, as they affect warranty actions, are presumably governed by another statute entirely or by a developing common law. Of the states that have adopted some version of §2-318, by far the greatest number have adopted Alternative A. Somewhere in the neighborhood of a half dozen have opted for Alternative B and a like number for Alternative C. In many of these instances, however, the alternative (whichever one it is) was adopted with variant language particular to the individual state. Even where states adopted identical versions of §2-318, significant differences can exist because, as we shall see, so much was left for further development by the courts. Interpretations can vary much from state to state.

The lesson is clear: Once the question comes down to the extent of warranty protection in any particular jurisdiction, some research is in order. Check out that jurisdiction's version of §2-318 and read it with an eye to catching any variations that state's legislature might have thought it wise to toss in. If you don't find any version of §2-318, or even if you do, check to see if there are any other statutes that may come into play. Research the case law of the jurisdiction to see how the courts have interpreted §2-318 and any other relevant enactment, as well as how they may have exercised their common law decision-making function to add to or subtract from what you see in the statute books. Finally, *and this is most important,* don't be too surprised if what you eventually end up with doesn't easily resolve itself into one comprehensible whole. When it comes to issues of privity, warranty, and related theories, many jurisdictions are currently in a state of flux. When questions such as these arise, you may well think, in the words of an old saying, "cursed to live in interesting times."

In analyzing the examples that follow, you will have to determine whether the suit being considered will be allowed or blocked by a lack of privity in a variety of situations. In each case, you should consider first of all whether the problem presented is one of vertical or horizontal privity. The traditional wisdom is that §2-318 was meant to address issues of *horizontal* privity only, leaving it to the individual jurisdictions' developing common law to sort out matters of vertical privity. See Comment 3. Certainly this is true for any state that has adopted Alternative A. Alternatives B and C leave room for argument that some vertical privity restrictions have been done away with along with allowing recovery by a broader class of horizontal plaintiffs (for lack of a better term). As you read the three alternatives and apply them to the examples that follow, even as you focus on horizontal privity issues, another question will emerge. Any of the three distinct versions says that the seller's warranty "extends" to people beyond his or her immediate buyer. A state's adoption of one or the other of these alternatives indisputably creates a *minimal* extension beyond the immediate parties—a legislatively defined floor, if you will. But does the particular version chosen serve as a *maximum* (i.e., a ceiling) as well? Some courts have reasoned as much, concluding that if it had been the intention of the legislature to weaken the requirement of horizontal privity still further, it could and would have done so by drafting §2-318 differently or by adopting another alternative. Other courts have not felt themselves constrained in this way. The language of §2-318, whatever version, says only that a warranty extends so far; it does not say it cannot extend further when sound public policy justifies the result. The drafters in Comment 3 invite the courts to continue on with the work of fashioning appropriate rules regarding vertical privity. There is no doubt about that. Might they not also be encouraging creative judging along the horizontal axis as well?

Examples

EXAMPLES

1. Buster is adding an enclosed outdoor pavilion to his restaurant, Buster's Beanery. He goes to Selma's Building Supply where he buys a glass door, manufactured by the Makedoor Corporation, of the size and type he needs. He installs the door himself. A few weeks later, during the first rainstorm following installation, it becomes apparent that the seal holding the glass in place is faulty. Water leaks through the door, flooding the pavilion room and ruining much of the furniture Buster has placed there. Buster realizes he must replace the door with one that doesn't leak as soon as possible. He goes back to Selma's, but he finds that store boarded up. Apparently Selma has gone out of the building-supply business. He quickly goes to another supplier where he gets a replacement door, which he installs.
   (a) Can Buster sue Makedoor for the cost of the replacement door? For the damage done to his furniture? For revenue loss during the time the pavilion room cannot be used due to the water damage?
   (b) Suppose instead that the problem with the door first becomes apparent not because of leakage but because the glass falls out as Buster is closing the door (gently) for the first time. The glass shatters and Buster is seriously cut. Can he sue Makedoor under a breach of warranty theory for his injuries?
   (c) Would your answer to either of the previous questions be any different if Buster could show that the reason he bought this particular

door from Selma was that he had seen an advertisement run by Makedoor for its "Super-Safe, Tight-Sealed" doors in a home and business improvement magazine?

2. Betty bought a large can of tuna from her local Shophere grocery store, which she used to make a number of tuna salad sandwiches. She left one sandwich at home to be eaten at lunch that day by her five-year-old daughter and another for the college student who had been given a room in Betty's home in exchange for helping her take care of her child. Betty took two other sandwiches to work. When she found herself not that hungry, she gave one of these away to a coworker who had forgotten his lunch. It turned out that the can of tuna was tainted and each of the people who ate a sandwich became seriously ill. Which, if any, of these people can sue Shophere on a breach of warranty theory?

3. Burns Construction Company employed Handy as a mechanic. One day while Handy was driving a bolt through a utility pole on his supervisor's directive, the head of the hammer that he was using shattered. Handy was hurt by a piece of flying metal. The hammer had been made by Cooper Industries. Can Handy sue Cooper on a breach of warranty theory?

4. Doe operates a pizza parlor in a shopping mall. She buys a pizza oven from the manufacturing firm Ovens of Brooklyn. Late one night soon after she buys it, the oven explodes with considerable force.
   (a) Jones, a passerby, is hurt by the flying debris. Can Jones sue Ovens on a breach of warranty theory?
   (b) The explosion of Doe's pizza oven is so forceful that it blows out the wall between her shop and that of her neighbor, Flicker, who runs a photography store. Fortunately, since it is late at night no one is in Flicker's store, but a good deal of damage is done to Flicker's equipment. Can Flicker sue Ovens on a breach of warranty theory? Would it make a difference if Flicker did not own the photo store as a sole entrepreneur but had instead sought financial backing from a number of others and incorporated as Flicker & Friends, Inc.?
   (c) Suppose that, in addition, Flicker could show that because of the explosion and the subsequent need for repair, his store had to be closed for something like two weeks, during which time he lost a considerable amount of photo-developing business that he can never recoup. During those weeks, even his most loyal customers went elsewhere to get their film developed. Could Flicker collect from Ovens for this loss of profit?
   (d) Just before the explosion at the shopping mall, Andrew had brought a large number of rolls of film into Flicker's store for developing.

These chronicled his recent trip to Outer Mongolia. All of the rolls of film were lost, apparently buried somewhere in the debris. Can Andrew sue Ovens for his loss under a breach of warranty theory with any hope of success?

(e) Would your answer to any of the previous questions involving the exploding pizza oven be any different if it turned out that Doe had purchased a used oven from Ovens of Brooklyn and that the contract she signed contained the statement "OVEN IS SOLD AS IS" in large bold type on the front?

(f) What would be the effect if instead of the "as is" provision, the contract had contained a conspicuous clause that read as follows:

> EXTENT OF WARRANTIES: SELLER AGREES TO BE LIABLE TO BUYER FOR ANY BREACH OF WARRANTY. BUYER AGREES THAT UNDER NO CIRCUMSTANCES SHALL SELLER BE HELD LIABLE HEREUNDER FOR ANY HARM CAUSED TO, OR FOR ANY INCIDENTAL OR CONSEQUENTIAL DAMAGES INCURRED BY, ANY THIRD PERSON OR PERSONS AS A RESULT OF ANY BREACH OF THIS AGREEMENT.

Explanations

1. a. This problem relates strictly to vertical privity. Makedoor made a sale to Selma, which presumably included a warranty that the door wouldn't leak like a sieve. Makedoor, however, did not sell directly to Buster. Can Buster sue Makedoor and, if so, for what?

We first ask whether §2-318 in any of its forms extends the right to sue for breach of warranty in spite of vertical privity problems as a matter of statutory dictate. The answer would appear to be a clear no. Most readers have taken it as an act of faith that this section simply doesn't speak to vertical privity. Possible relaxation of the privity requirement along the vertical axis has been intentionally left by the drafters and the legislatures to common law development by the courts or to a distinct enactment not part of the U.C.C. We note the language in Comment 3, which begins by referring to the first alternative's extension of warranty protection to some degree along the horizontal axis. It goes on:

> Beyond this, the section in this form is neutral and is not intended to enlarge or restrict the developing case law on whether the seller's warranties, given to his buyer who resells, extend to other persons in the distributive chain.

There is an argument to be made, however, that if a state's legislature has adopted either Alternative B or C (and some dozen states or so have done as much), then this has in effect cut down on the vertical privity problem. Can't Buster argue that he is a person "who may reasonably be expected to use, consume or be affected by" the door? Retailers like Selma buy doors by the dozens for the purpose of resale. But Makedoor has to know that eventually they'll be used one door at a time by individuals like Buster. Note that Alternative A contains the phrase "his [that is, the seller's] buyer," which is absent from either of the two other alternatives. And the language quoted above from Comment 3 says that the section *in the first alternative form* is neutral on vertical privity issues. While there is reason to believe that the drafters may not have intended as much, a court eager to extend warranty protection down the line of distribution may be excused for latching on to its legislature's adoption of either Alternative B or C as support (if not necessarily a statutory mandate) for that conclusion. Under our particular fact pattern, of course, Buster would gain nothing from this argument if his state had adopted only Alternative B. Section 2-318 even in that version extends warranty rights only to those seeking to recover for personal injury.

If Buster's jurisdiction has not adopted one of the more expansive versions of §2-318, or if the courts are not willing to read Alternative C so broadly, he is not necessarily out of luck. The courts in many states have concluded that, although §2-318 does not extend the right to sue to a situation such as his, adoption of that section was not intended to *restrict* the scope of warranty protection either. This much is clear from Comment 3. So it is up to the courts to decide the degree to which lack of vertical privity may stand in the way of a breach of warranty action. In many states, the answer to this question as it now stands is wrapped up in the type of injury sustained and the relief requested. If the ultimate buyer is suing for personal injury (as Buster will be in the next part of this example), it's probably true that most states would allow recovery on a breach of warranty theory. Once the injury is all of an economic sort, as it is here, the courts are more divided.

As an example of a case still holding the reins fairly tightly on vertical privity, see *Gregory v. Atrium Door & Window Co.*, 415 S.E.2d 574 (N.C. App. 1992), the case on which this question is loosely based. Doors manufactured by the defendant Atrium Door & Window were purchased by plaintiffs Mr. and Mrs. Gregory from a supplier, the W. R. Jones Co., for installation in their home. The doors quickly began to deteriorate. The Gregorys sued and were awarded a judgment against both the manufacturer and their immediate seller for breach of warranty. Atrium Door sought a reversal based on lack of privity. Atrium Door got its reversal. The court stated:

> Plaintiffs were in privity of contract with defendant-retailer W. R. Jones Company, from whom they had purchased the doors, but they were not in privity of contract with defendant-manufacturer Atrium Door and Window Company. . . .
>
> [O]utside exceptions created by [the North Carolina Products Liability Statute], the general rule is that privity is required to assert a claim for a breach of an implied warranty involving only economic loss. [Citations omitted.] The trial court's findings reflect that only economic loss resulted from the alleged breach in the form of malfunctioning and deteriorating doors, along with some water damage to flooring. There is no competent evidence of the privity between defendant Atrium and the plaintiffs required to support the trial court's findings and conclusion as to the alleged breach of these implied warranties. The judgment of the trial court is reversed.

The court concluded its opinion with the suggestion that perhaps the time had come for a reconsideration of "whether the privity requirement for implied warranties is still good policy." It appears that neither the legislature nor the Supreme Court of North Carolina acted on this recommendation.

In *American Dredging Co. v. Plaza Petroleum*, 799 F. Supp. 1335 (E.D.N.Y. 1992), the court noted:

> As for implied warranty claims, it is well settled in New York that a claim against a seller for economic loss for breach of an implied warranty of merchantability and/or implied warranty of fitness can be maintained only by those parties with whom the seller is in privity. If there is no seller-buyer relationship or sales contract between the parties, a cause of action based on breach of contract will not lie. [Citations omitted.]

See also *Falcon for Import and Trade Co. v. North Central Commodities, Inc.*, 2004 WL 224676 (D.N.D.), in which the district court judge—while making no secret of his "personal beliefs" that the plaintiff was right in characterizing the vertical privity requirement as "a dying concept" and "an antiquated notion in contractual warranty actions as well as in tort actions"—concluded that the decision simply to abolish the vertical privity requirement was one for the North Dakota Supreme Court, or presumably that state's legislature, and not for him. Kentucky is another state where the courts have steadfastly declined to extend warranty protection beyond what the legislature provided in its version of §2-318. See *Complex International Co., Ltd. v. Taylor*, 209 S.W.3d 462 (Ky. 2006) and *Capps v. The Bristol Bar and Grille, Inc.*, 2012 WL 1067908 (W.D. Ky.).

For an example of a state that has gone in the opposite direction, see the discussion of Pennsylvania law in *Israel Phoenix Assurance Co., Ltd. v. SMS Sutton, Inc.*, 787 F. Supp. 102 (W.D. Pa. 1992). SMS Sutton sold a replacement main cylinder for a hydraulic extrusion press to an Israeli company, KLIL Industries. The replacement cylinder, which had been manufactured by Hodgson Steel, Inc., later malfunctioned on several occasions, each of which temporarily shut down KLIL's plant. It eventually had to be replaced, causing another shutdown. The plaintiff insurance company provided coverage for KLIL's losses and in this action sued both Sutton and Hodgson Steel as KLIL's subrogee, claiming more than $800,000 in repair costs, replacement costs, and lost profits as damages. Hodgson sought a summary dismissal of that portion of the claim against it that relied on asserted breaches of implied warranties of merchantability and fitness for a particular purpose. Hodgson's request for summary judgment was denied. The federal district court concluded that privity of contract was not required to state a claim for breach of implied warranty under existing Pennsylvania case law and that this was true even where the claim was for purely economic losses of the type sustained here, including lost profits.

In *Hyundai Motor America, Inc. v. Goodin*, 822 N.E.2d 947 (Ind. 2005), the Indiana Supreme Court decided to further whittle away at what remained of the vertical privity requirement in that state. In an opinion that gives a good run-down of the various states that have limited or entirely abolished the vertical privity requirement in some or all warranty actions, it concluded that "Indiana law does not require vertical privity between a consumer and a manufacturer as a condition to a claim by the consumer against the manufacturer for breach of the manufacturer's implied warranty of merchantability." Note that even this result would not necessarily guarantee victory to Buster in our example should his case arise in Indiana. He bought the doors not as a consumer, but for his commercial enterprise.

These cases are cited merely as examples. Individual states may have leading cases on the area, but overall national trends are hard to come by. With only a little effort, you should be able to find jurisdictions that come down just about anywhere along the spectrum—or are still floating uncertainly in the void.

If, for whatever reason, Buster is barred from suing Makedoor, that does not leave him with no one to sue. He is in direct privity with Selma and can sue her. No doubt you see the potential problem with that course of action here: If Selma is still in the jurisdiction and available for suit, and if she shut down business not because she went bankrupt but only because she was tired of the rat race, then a suit is perfectly practical. But those are two big ifs. Just to conclude this analysis, if Selma can be found and made to pay damages to Buster, you should see that she will in turn have the right to go against Makedoor, who should make it up to her.

b. Buster may have more luck going against Makedoor on a breach of warranty theory once his injuries are of this type. For one thing, if his state has adopted Alternative B (not to mention C), we now have some argument that his suit has specific legislative sanction. Even if this is not so, many if not most state courts have ruled that as a matter of sound public policy, a breach of warranty action may be brought under these circumstances, whether it is expressly authorized by the Code or not. Note that the passages I quoted earlier from *Atrium Door & Window* and *American Dredging*, which would have worked against Buster if he suffered only economic loss, suggest that the same automatic bar would not necessarily apply where personal injury is involved.

c. Buster might collect in this situation even if he were only going for economic losses as in Example 1a. The difference here is that Buster can make some claim for having relied on an *express* warranty made by Makedoor. Some courts have said that this actually brings Buster into privity, or a kind of privity, with the manufacturer. Others conclude not that privity has been established, but that such advertising by the manufacturer—designed to bring in more business and intended to be seen by the ultimate buyer—in effect overcomes or renders moot whatever lack of privity there technically may be. Either way, the result is the same:The ultimate buyer can go directly against the manufacturer for breach of the express warranty. For an example, you might want to look at *Touchet Valley Grain Growers, Inc. v. Opp & Seibold General Construction, Inc.*, 831 P.2d 724 (Wash. 1992). The Washington Supreme Court went beyond the particular express warranties made to the ultimate buyer via advertising materials and its price book, and ruled that the buyer could sue on whatever *implied* warranties could be established based on the totality of the circumstances and the extent of the relationship—even if it wasn't privity of contract—between the manufacturer and the ultimate buyer, Touchet Valley. It stated:

> [W]e note that Truss-T [the manufacturer] knew Touchet Valley's identity, its purpose and its requirements for the grain storage building. Truss-T designed the building knowing the specifications were the purchaser's. As was its business practice, Truss-T delivered the components to Touchet Valley's construction site. And, when the first beams buckled . . . Truss-T joined Opp & Seibold [the intermediate seller] to attempt repairs. [Because of the] sum of this interaction, [Touchet Valley was] the intended beneficiary of Truss-T's implied warranties to Opp & Seibold. Those warranties assured the merchantability of Truss-T's fabricated building and their fitness for Touchet Valley's known particular purpose. Touchet Valley's warranty claims against Truss-T, based both on express and implied warranty claims, were reinstated.

Would the result of this case necessarily guarantee Buster the right to sue Makedoor for the breach of any warranty under the facts of his purchase? The situation in *Touchet Valley* was unusual and particularly favorable to the distant buyer, but other courts have gone even further and suggested that once a manufacturer advertises and sells its product by brand name in order to "make a market" for those goods, it implicitly extends at least the warranty of merchantability to anyone who buys the goods for their intended use no matter how far down the chain of distribution. As you can imagine, this type of analysis seems to go furthest when the breach of warranty results in personal injury and not just economic loss, but even that has been covered in some instances.

2. We turn with this question to problems of horizontal privity that *are* addressed by §2-318. Which of these various parties can sue depends, at least initially, on which Alternative Version of that section, or which non-uniform version drafted for a particular state, applies. Betty, of course, is in direct privity with the retailer and can sue no matter what. Her five-year-old's injuries are covered by any version of the section. Alternative A extends protection for personal injuries to "any natural person who is in the family or household of his buyer or who is a guest in his home if it is reasonable to expect that such a person may use, consume or be affected by the goods." Would this include the college student boarder/mother's helper? I think yes. Such a person is probably a member of Betty's "household." If not, maybe he or she counts as a "guest." Betty's coworker would not be automatically entitled to sue under Alternative A as he or she doesn't fit within the language.

   The coworker would, of course, have a much better case if either Alternative B or C were in force. He or she certainly counts as a "natural person" (as opposed to a "something" like a partnership, a trust, or a corporation), and you could argue just about anyone of the sandwich-eating type "may reasonably be expected to use, consume or be affected by" a tainted can of tuna.

   Even if Alternative A is applicable, the coworker may still be able to sue on the warranty of merchantability, if the courts in the particular jurisdiction take up his or her cause and choose to extend the reach of warranty protection *horizontally* beyond what is called for by the state's version of §2-318. Some courts have chosen to do so, concluding that §2-318 sets out only the minimal degree to which the bonds of horizontal privity have been relaxed in the jurisdiction and taking the drafters' Comments as inviting further extension by the courts along this axis as well as the vertical one. Other courts have not seen or have declined the invitation to fool around in the horizontal dimension, reasoning that the legislature's decision to adopt Alternative A instead of one of the other, more extensive alternatives speaks to the public policy of the state and is not to be circumvented or second-guessed by common law decision-making. See, for example, *Mugavero v. A-1 Auto Sales, Inc.*, 944 P.2d 151 (Idaho Ct. App. 1997).

3. Handy will not be able to sue Cooper if Alternative A is in force and the courts of his state have not extended protection beyond the legislative dictate. This was the result in *Bruns v. Cooper Industries, Inc.*, 605 N.E.2d 395 (Ohio Ct. App. 1992), on which this example is based. Ohio adopted Alternative A of §2-318. The employee did not fall within that version's scope, and as the court noted, "The Ohio General Assembly has declined the express opportunity to enlarge the seller's warranties under the Uniform Commercial Code to a buyer's employee." The employee could not sue the hammer manufacturer on a breach of warranty theory. Since he suffered physical injury, you may be thinking, that shouldn't make much of a difference. He could simply sue on a tort theory of negligence or products liability. Unfortunately for the employee, he was unable to demonstrate at trial the existence of any defect in the product at the time it left the manufacturer's possession. In fact, in his brief to the appellate court, he stipulated that there was no physical or chemical defect in the hammer at the time it left the defendant manufacturer's hands. Summary judgment in favor of the manufacturer on all counts was affirmed on appeal. Maybe this was just one of those accidents that just happen. Or maybe the real culprit was the plaintiff's employer, who gave him this hammer to undertake this particular task even though a warning placed on the hammer by the manufacturer (although it is unclear what this warning was originally supposed to have said and what difference it possibly could have made) had been obliterated over time. If this is so, then the employee would be barred from a suit against his employer by the workman's compensation statute. Maybe, after all is said and done, this *was* just one of those things that happen.

   Handy might well have a better time of it if his case came up in Illinois. That state's version of the Code includes Alternative A, but its courts have determined that warranty protection may also extend to an employee of the purchaser who is injured in the use of the goods "as long as the safety of the employee in the use of the goods was either explicitly or implicitly part of the basis of the bargain when the employer purchased the goods." See *Maldonado v. Creative Woodworking Concepts, Inc.*, 694 N.E.2d 1021 (Ill. App. 1998). The Illinois courts have, however, declined to extend this ruling to situations where the injured party was an employee not of the buyer, but of an independent contractor hired to transport the goods to the buyer's place of business or to use the goods once they had been delivered. See *Lukwinski v. Stone Container Corp.*, 726 N.E.2d 665 (Ill. App. 2000) and *Frank v. Edward Hines Lumber Co.*, 761 N.E.2d 1257 (Ill. App. 2001).

   Look at Alternative A once again. It shouldn't be hard for you to think up interesting hypotheticals that test the outer limits of that language. Be the law professor you've always wanted to be. Who exactly is in the "family" or "household" of the buyer? Who counts as a "guest in the home"? As a matter of fact, there seem to be very few cases where the courts have been called upon to explicate. In *Crews v. W.A. Brown & Son, Inc.*, 416 S.E.2d 924 (N.C. App. 1992), the North Carolina Court of Appeals was presented with an interesting problem: The Calvary Baptist Church purchased and installed a walk-in freezer that was expressly warranted to have a safety door of the type that could always be opened from the inside. Vicky Ann Buchanan Crews, a thirteen-year-old member of the congregation, was at the Church doing volunteer work when she thought she heard a noise coming from inside the freezer. She went inside to check. The freezer door closed behind her, and because of a malfunction in the safety release she was unable to get out. Ultimately she was rescued, but not before suffering severe frostbite to various parts of her body. The court held that under Alternative A, which had been adopted in North Carolina, neither Vicky Ann nor her mother could sue on a breach of warranty theory:

> Because a church does not have a "family" or a "household" in the ordinary meanings of those terms, Crews cannot be classified as a member of Church's "family" or "household" under N.C.G.S. §25-2-318. . . . Because a church is not a "home" within the ordinary meaning of that term, Church cannot be classified as a "home." Accordingly, because Crews was not in the buyer's "family" or "household," and because she was not a guest in the buyer's "home," N.C.G.S. §25-2-318 does not extend the coverage of Foodcraft's [the seller's] warranties to plaintiffs.

In *Denton v. Sam Blount, Inc.*, 669 So. 2d 951 (Ala. Civ. App. 1995), the Alabama Court of Civil Appeals applying North Carolina law held that a customer of a Wal-Mart store injured when he sat in a display patio chair could not proceed with a breach of warranty action against the company that had sold the chair to the retailer, as the customer was not to be considered a member of Wal-Mart's "household" or "family" or a guest in Wal-Mart's "home."

4. a. Jones would not have a claim under warranty law against the manufacturer-seller of the oven if the incident occurred in a state that had enacted Alternative A of §2-318, unless the courts of that state had independently extended the scope of warranty protection to a greater degree. If Alternative B or C governed, she would seem to have a good case.

   b. Flicker would not be able to sue under either Alternative A or B because he was not "injured in person" by the breach. While it may turn out that the courts in his jurisdiction have extended the reach of warranty beyond what is expressly provided for in either of those two versions, such extension is less likely in the case of injury other than personal injury. Under Alternative C, suit may be brought by anyone "who may reasonably be expected to . . . be affected by the goods and who is injured by breach of warranty." This version does not contain the limitation of the other two that injury be to the person, so Flicker should have a good shot at recovery under a warranty theory.

If Alternative C does apply, then the fact that the photo shop is really owned by a corporation will not make any difference. Note that Alternatives A and B speak in terms of "any natural person." Alternative C just says "any person." The omission was intentional. See §1-201(b)(27) for the Code's general definition of *person*. The Code does not define *natural* or *natural person*, but I think we get the point. So, for example, a limited partnership has been held not to be a "natural person." *S&R Associates, L.P., III v. Shell Oil Co.*, 725 A.2d 431 (Del. Sup. Ct. 1998).

c. Even if Flicker were fortunate enough to have Alternative C behind him, he might not be able to collect for this loss of profits. That alternative does not restrict claims to those for personal injury, and certainly direct injury to property is included, but the courts have not necessarily read even this version of §2-318 as far as to extend to what is referred to as "purely economic loss." If Flicker is fighting his battle under either of the other versions of §2-318, and hence having to convince the court to extend the reach of the warranty on its own volition, he would presumably have an even tougher time getting pure economic loss covered.

d. I doubt Andrew could recover from Ovens no matter what version of §2-318 is in place and regardless of how little the courts of the particular jurisdiction thought of traditional "lack of privity" arguments. This does seem to me to be stretching things just too far. But maybe I'm wrong, and you certainly are free to look for cases that would support Andrew's claim here. If you find any, you will, I assume, ask yourself the next question: If Andrew were a professional photographer who had taken these pictures on assignment for a magazine that had to delay publication or expend more money getting substitute pictures of Outer Mongolia, could the *magazine* sue Ovens of Brooklyn? And so on and so forth. It does make you somewhat nostalgic for the good old days of "no privity, no action," doesn't it?

In this regard, consider the result in *United Technologies Corp. v. Saren Engineering, Inc.*, 2002 WL 31319598 (Conn. Super.), in which the plaintiff suffered economic losses because of a problem that was discovered with an ammonia storage tank system newly installed in one of its manufacturing plants. The problem apparently could all be traced back to a single defective valve that had been used in the assembly of the system. The Superior Court of Connecticut held that the plaintiff could not proceed with a breach of warranty action against either the maker of the valve itself or an intermediate party through whom it had been obtained by the company that actually fabricated and installed the storage tank system, because the plaintiff admitted to not being in privity with either of these two parties. The court recognized that the privity requirement in some instances might leave a plaintiff without any remedy for its commercial losses:

> That result, however, is not grounds for extending the exception to the UCC privity requirement. "While it may seem that there should be a remedy for every wrong, that is an ideal limited perforce by the realities of the world. Every injury has ramifying consequences, like the ripplings of the water, without end. The problem of the law is to limit the legal consequences of wrongs to a controllable degree." [Quoting from *Waters v. Autuori*, 676 A.2d 357 (Conn. 1996).]

e. If Doe bought the oven "as is" and this disclaimer were effective, as it very well may be under §2-316(3)(a), this changes everything. See Comment 1 including the statement that, "To the extent that the contract of sale contains provisions under which warranties are excluded or modified, or remedies for breach are limited, such provisions are equally operative against beneficiaries of warranties under this section." Anyone who's been injured in this whole nasty mess must, if he, she, or it (remember the corporation) is suing on a breach of warranty theory, establish that such a warranty actually does exist as part of the contract between the seller and buyer. If the buyer agreed to take the goods without any or all warranties, this decision affects the rights not just of the buyer but of anyone who would sue through the buyer. See, for example, *Buettner v. R.W. Martin & Sons, Inc.*, 47 F.3d 116 (4th Cir. 1995) and *Theos & Sons, Inc. v. Mack Trucks, Inc.*, 729 N.E.2d 1113 (Mass. 2000).

f. This is not a general disclaimer of warranty or limitation of liability governed by either §2-316 or §2-719, but something else with which the drafters obviously had little patience. The last sentence of §2-318, in whatever version, would render this limitation invalid, at least to the extent that it might bar recovery for injuries to the person. Read Comment 1 in its entirety.

CHAPTER 15

The Magnuson-Moss Warranty Act

INTRODUCTION

The warranties of quality with which we have been concerned in the preceding chapters have all been firmly anchored in Article 2. The rules arise from the adoption by each individual state of that Article as part of its statutory law. There is yet one more piece to be added to the warranty law puzzle—a federal statute that may sometimes be invoked in those circumstances where consumer products prove to be defective. In 1975 the federal government enacted the Magnuson-Moss Warranty Act, 15 U.S.C. §2301 *et seq.* (the Act), with the objective of giving some greater level of warranty protection to buyers. Under the Act, the Federal Trade Commission (FTC) is given the authority to promulgate regulations in furtherance of the Act's objectives, and these regulations are to be found in 16 C.F.R. Parts 700–703. The regulations contain many helpful interpretations and are a great guide in the event you become lost in the text of the Act itself. See also the Businessperson's Guide to Federal Warranty Law at the FTC website.

Congress enacted the Act for numerous reasons: By requiring more uniform disclosure of warranty terms, the Act served to improve the adequacy of information available to consumers to prevent deception from manufacturers who would give certain warranties only to later disclaim them. The Act also encourages the use of dispute settlement procedures for quick and fair resolution of claims, and where such a procedure exists, the consumer is required to use it before bringing suit under Act. §2310(a)(3)(C). Congress also hoped to increase marketplace competition for warranties by requiring that warrantors designate their warranty as either "limited" or "full." In theory, consumers who could access the warranties before they made a purchase would compare those warranties and would of course opt for the best warranty. This would lead manufacturers to offer better warranties in order to win that competition. Did it work? We will let you be the judge.

It is important to stress the fact that there is nothing in the Act which mandates that any supplier provide a warranty along with its product. In fact, the Act expressly prohibits the FTC from imposing any such mandate in its role as chief enforcer of the Act. §2302(b)(2). The underlying philosophy is not to require written warranties of all suppliers. Rather, it is to ensure that when such warranties *are* given, they give the consumer purchaser the protection reasonably expected from those warranties. This may not be clear from an initial reading of the Act. Section 2304 is captioned "Federal minimum standards for warranties" and seems to establish those standards. However, §2303 states:

1. If the written warranty meets the Federal minimum standards for warranty set forth in section 2304 of this title, then it shall be conspicuously designated a "full (statement of duration) warranty".
2. If the written warranty does not meet the Federal minimum standards for warranty set forth in section 2304 of this title, then it shall be conspicuously designated a "limited warranty".

The Act does not define "conspicuously," but §700.6 of the accompanying Regulations states that that "[t]he designation or designations should appear clearly and conspicuously as a caption, or prominent title, clearly separated from the text of the warranty." It is therefore clear that the minimum standards apply only when a warrantor conspicuously designates the warranty as a "full warranty." Have you ever seen a product that is sold with a "full warranty"?

The interplay between the Article 2 warranties and the further consumer protection provided for in the Act is not always as clear as we might wish it to be, but we can start by focusing on how the two are distinct by asking a few questions:

- What is a written warranty?
- What products are covered?
- Who gives the warranty and to whom?
- Can the warranties be disclaimed or limited?
- What remedies are available?

WRITTEN WARRANTIES

The Act provides protection when a "warrantor warrants a consumer product to a consumer by means of a written warranty." See §§2303(a),

2302(a), 2304(a). You will note that the definition of a "written warranty" under the Act is different in significant ways from the express warranties provided under U.C.C. §2-313. Let's see if we can break down the definition of written warranty found at §2301(6):

A written warranty is:

1. ANY WRITTEN AFFIRMATION OF FACT OR WRITTEN PROMISE made in connection with the sale of a consumer product by a supplier to a buyer which relates to the nature of the material or workmanship and affirms or promises that such material or workmanship is defect free or will meet a specified level of performance over a period of time, OR

2. ANY UNDERTAKING IN WRITING in connection with the sale by a supplier of a consumer product to refund, repair, replace, or take other remedial action with respect to such product in the event that such product fails to meet the specifications set forth in the undertaking, **which written affirmation, promise, or undertaking becomes part of the basis of the bargain between a supplier and a buyer for purposes other than resale of such product.**

Analyzing this definition of a written warranty under the Act leaves us with several takeaways. The Act is similar to the U.C.C. in that they both typically require warranties to be part of the "basis of the bargain" to be enforceable. §2301(6)(b)); 16 C.F.R. §700.3(c). The nature of how the warranty is given is different—an express warranty under the U.C.C. can be oral, but a written warranty under the Act must be in writing. Samples or models can be the basis for an express warranty, but they are not warranties under the Act. In addition, the U.C.C. express warranties are affirmations of fact, but the Act is narrower in that it restricts coverage to two categories (the first of which has two parts). Firstly, the Act covers statements of quality and workmanship such as being "defect free" or guaranteeing a level of performance for a certain period of time. In *Skelton v. General Motors Corp.*, 660 F.2d 311 (7th Cir. 1981), GM distributed advertising materials depicting various models as having THM 350 transmissions. The cars actually had THM 200 transmissions. This would clearly be breach of a U.C.C. express warranty. But the court in *Skelton* found that Congress acted deliberately in not using the term "express warranty" from the U.C.C. when writing Magnuson-Moss, and thus Congress had not intended to cover the entire ambit of "affirmations of fact" such as the description of a transmission. Thus, a written warranty under the Act must contain either a "defect free" promise or a promise of quality or workmanship over a certain period of time. Secondly, the Act is broader in one way in that it explicitly covers remedial promises—promises to provide repair or replacement. Many authorities do not consider such statements to be warranties under the U.C.C. because they do not relate to the quality of the goods.

A key battle over the definition of "written warranty" frequently occurs with whether the promise of quality or workmanship meets a specified level *over a period of time*. Thus, many courts distinguish mere product descriptions (affirmations of fact sufficient for a U.C.C. express warranty) from the quality warranties under the Act by asking whether or not the warranty contains a duration. See 16 C.F.R. §700.3(a); *Bowling v. Johnson & Johnson*, 65 F. Supp. 3d 371 (S.D.N.Y. 2014) (food sell by date was not specified warranty duration but description, and thus not covered under the Act); *Kelleher v. Marvin Lumber & Cedar Co.*, 891 A.2d 477 (N.H. 2005) (sealer contained a written warranty because statement of "permanent" treatment was durational and thus was covered under the act). There may be some debate as to whether a promise to be "defect free" requires a duration, or if it is implied that "defect free" refers to the time of delivery. The latter theory would raise problems related to the discovery of latent defects. But the current body of Magnuson-Moss case law has few cases on such "defect-free" promises without a duration; still, a manufacturer wanting to make such a promise would be wise to add a temporal limitation to avoid uncertainty.

An additional durational problem arises with so-called "lifetime" warranties. Against whose lifetime is the warranty being measured? The FTC Businessperson's Guide outlines three possibilities using a lifetime warranty of a car muffler as an example. The warranty might be: 1) for the life of the car; 2) for the life of the original purchaser; or 3) for the life of the original purchaser so long as the purchaser still owns the car. See also 16 C.F.R. §239.4. Whatever the duration, under *Kelleher v. Marvin Lumber & Cedar Co.*, 891 A.2d 477 (N.H. 2005), a statement such as "permanent" may qualify as a guarantee of quality or workmanship for a definite period of time—thus a "lifetime warranty" may likely be covered under the Act.

CONSUMER PRODUCTS

U.C.C. warranties apply to all goods. But the Act only covers goods that are "consumer products." The Act defines "consumer products" as "products normally used for personal, family, or household purposes." Included within this subset are also goods which may be attached to real property, such as mobile homes, whether or not so attached. §2301(1). In interpreting what constitutes a consumer product under the Act, the courts have excluded goods like heart valves and firetrucks, reasoning that an average consumer would be unlikely to purchase these things in the ordinary course of life. See *Sylvania Township Board of Trustees v. Kovatch Mobile Equipment Corp.*, 878 F. Supp. 2d 857 (N.D. Ohio 2012). The regulations require that any disputes as to coverage should be resolved in favor of coverage. 16 C.F.R. §700.1. In addition to these requirements, the warranty content requirements of §2302 only apply to goods sold for over $5, and the designation of warranties as either full or limited starts at $10 under §2303(d). See also 16 C.F.R. §700.1(g).

Notice that the Act comes into play only if the item purchased is a consumer product, regardless of whether the particular purchaser is a consumer. So, for instance, a gasoline-powered lawnmower would likely be deemed a consumer product. The Act covers the item whether the buyer is a homeowner or someone engaged in the business of mowing other people's lawns for a living. On the other hand, suppose that a particularly wealthy individual purchases the type of walk-in refrigeration unit usually used only by restaurants, food stores, or butchers, to be incorporated into the truly over-the-top kitchen of a new palatial residence she is having built for herself. The unit would not be a consumer good and the Act would not be relevant to its sale. It is the nature of the goods being sold, not the situation of the buyer that determines whether the Act applies.

WARRANTORS AND SUPPLIERS

The Act covers "written warranties" given by "warrantors." Who is a "warrantor?" The term "warrantor" means any supplier (any person engaged in the business of making a consumer product directly or indirectly available to consumers) or a person who gives or offers to give a written warranty, or who is or may be obligated under an implied warranty. §2301. Thus, unlike the Code, the "remote manufacturer" who does not sell directly to the buyer is a warrantor. And a magazine is a warrantor if it stands behind its advertisers' products. A supplier becomes a warrantor by giving, in connection with the product it places into the stream of commerce, a "written warranty" of which the ultimate purchaser would presumably become aware and on which he or she could be expected to rely. There is some dispute as to whether a supplier may become a warrantor by merely placing a product with an implied warranty on the shelf. Additionally, §2310(d)(1) purports to provide relief for breaches of implied warranties standing alone in the absence of a "written warranty." However, courts have been reluctant to recognize an independent cause of action under the Act for breach of an implied warranty, reasoning that a primary purpose of the Act is to prevent consumers from being deceived by warranties, and such deception is most attributable to written warranties, not to implied warranties. See *Gross v. Shep Brown's Boat Basin*, 2000 WL 1480373 (D.N.H); *McNamara v. Nomeco Building Specialties*, 26 F. Supp. 2d 1168 (D. Minn. 1998).

In contrast, Article 2 warranties involve claims by the *buyer* of goods against the *seller* (usually the direct seller unless vertical privity requirement have been loosened by the state's case law). Thus, a manufacturer or a distributor may well find itself to have a warranty obligation under the Act to the ultimate buyer of the goods it makes or distributes. Lack of vertical privity will not protect a supplier who is otherwise obligated.

The kind of written warranty contemplated by the Act is the language of warranty often found in, say, the user's manual or setup instructions for some appliance or electronic device which comes packaged with a consumer product you buy from a typical retail outlet. You may, of course, get some express warranties of quality *from the retailer* along with the product, but that depends on what interactions you had with the retailer as "part of the basis of the bargain" you entered into at the time of sale.

But the written warranty in the box does not come from the retailer. It is language which comes from the *supplier*, typically the manufacturer of the product. If you later find that the product is not as warranted by the supplier, you must rely on this language in order to gain some measure of relief *from the supplier* under the Act. A common example of a written warranty governed by the Act is the one typically set forth in the owner's manual of a new automobile, which is provided by the automaker. The dealer that sells the car is free to disclaim all warranties and merely pass on the automaker's warranty to the buyer. See §2308(a).

FULL AND LIMITED DESIGNATION AND ADDITIONAL REQUIREMENTS

As we have noted, the Act does not require that any supplier make a written warranty. If it does, however, the Act requires that the written warranty meet certain standards.

One aspect of the Act, for example, sets forth requirements under which a potential consumer can become aware of the terms of any written warranty that may come "in the box" *prior to* making the decision to buy the product. This may be done by having the warranty terms on the outside of the box or, if that is not the case, by making the terms available for inspection at the retailer's premises. The careful consumer can then check out what warranty the supplier provided.

The supplier-warrantor must also "clearly and conspicuously" designate any written warranty it provides as either a "full" or a "limited" warranty under §2303 if the goods are above $10. If the warranty is designated as a "full warranty," it will have to meet the minimum standards set forth in §2304. Perhaps the most demanding of the requirements for a warranty designated a "full" warranty is that of §2304(a)(4): If the product or a component part of the product continues to contain a defect or malfunction "after a reasonable number of attempts by the warrantor" to remedy the situation, the warrantor must permit the consumer to "elect either a full refund for, or replacement without charge of," the product or defective part. Any written warranty that fails to comport with the minimum standards of §2404 will have to be labeled a "limited warranty," although again, it may be stated as a "limited [period of duration] warranty." It will probably not surprise you to learn that the great majority of written warranties given by suppliers are not designated as a "full warranty." They are "limited warranties" only and are clearly and conspicuously labeled as such.

DISCLAIMERS AND LIMITATIONS

Sections 2304 and 2308 of the Act provide some important rules regarding the extent to which a supplier that provides a written warranty can limit or disclaim any *implied warranties* which come with the product. Where do such "implied warranties" come from? Under the Act, "implied warranties" are meant to be those implied warranties arising "under State law . . . in connection with the sale by a supplier of a consumer product." The reference is, of course, to our old friends U.C.C. §§2-314 and 2-315, along with any other implied warranties that an individual state might have provided for.

It is important to appreciate that the Act itself does not provide for or create any implied warranties. Suppliers may not disclaim any already existing implied warranty under the Act. §2308(a). While a supplier under the Act may not disclaim any implied warranties, remember that written warranties are not required to be given; thus, a seller who does not give any written warranties may still disclaim the implied warranties.

Manufacturers may limit the implied warranties depending upon the designation of the warranty. Under §2304(a)(2), if a supplier's warranty is a *full* warranty, then the warrantor may not impose any limitation on the duration of any implied warranties which the consumer has available in connection with the product. This is true even though the full written warranty itself may be limited in duration if such a limitation is for no less than a reasonable period. See §§2302(b)(2), 2308(b). But under §2308(b), if the written warranty is a *limited* one, then the implied warranties *may* be limited in duration *to the duration* of the limited written warranty "if such limitation is conscionable and is set forth in clear and unmistakable language and prominently displayed on the face of the [written] warranty." Note that the concept of "duration" of a warranty of merchantability is alien to the U.C.C.—under the Code, goods are either merchantable or they are not, and duration has nothing to do with it.

Additionally, where the warranty is a *full* one under §2304(a)(3), the warrantor may not exclude or limit consequential damages for breach of that warranty, or for breach of any implied warranty which it had given under state law, "unless such exclusion or limitation conspicuously appears on the face of the warranty." We are aware, of course, that under §2-719(3), any attempt to limit consequential damages when there has been injury to the person in the case of consumer goods is prima facie unconscionable—and hence unenforceable—even if it is conspicuously displayed to the consumer buyer. It was not the intention of the drafters of the Act to override, under the doctrine of federal preemption, this rule of §2-719(3), which is in general more protective of consumers. Section 2311(b)(1) explicitly provides that nothing in the Act "shall invalidate or restrict any right or remedy of any consumer under State law or any other Federal law."

REMEDIES UNDER THE MAGNUSON-MOSS ACT

Section 2110(b) of the Act provides that the failure to comply with any portion of the Act or the regulations promulgated under it shall be a violation of the Federal Trade Commission Act. The United States Attorney General and the FTC are empowered to bring an action in federal district court to force compliance.

Additionally, a buyer who is damaged by a supplier's failure to comply with any written Magnuson-Moss warranty, or any implied warranty that such a supplier may have given (although likely only one accompanied by a written warranty), may bring a private cause of action for damages and "other legal and equitable relief." §2110(d). Before seeking such relief, if the warrantor has a dispute resolution procedure in place, the buyer is required to use it. §2310(a)(3)(C). If the buyer can proceed to suit, §2010(d)(1) permits the buyer to bring suit in either (a) any court of competent jurisdiction of any state or the District of Columbia, or (b) an appropriate federal district court.

But the right to a trial in federal court is limited by §2010(d)(3)(c) which requires that each individual claim be greater than $25, that the amount in controversy exceeds $50,000, and that there be at least a hundred class members if brought as a class action. Additionally, many courts have prevented plaintiffs from gaining federal jurisdiction through personal injury related consequential damages. These courts have reasoned that the purpose of the Act was to obviate the market from weak and deceptive warranties, but not to expand federal jurisdiction through recognizing federal personal injury claims. See *Lake v. Unilever U.S., Inc.*, 964 F. Supp. 2d 893 (N.D. Ill. 2013); *Washington v. Otasco, Inc.*, 603 F. Supp. 1295 (N.D. Miss. 1985); *Bush v. Am. Motors Sales Corp.*, 575 F. Supp. 1581 (D. Colo. 1984).

A consumer who prevails on a claim founded in the Act may be allowed by the court to recover "the aggregate amount of cost and expenses (including attorneys fees based on the actual time expended [by the attorney]) determined by the court to have been reasonably incurred by the plaintiff" in pursuing the cause of action. A plaintiff's costs, including attorney fees, are, of course, not normally recoverable in an action brought under the U.C.C. alone. Subpart §2010(d)(2) of the Act is of no small importance to a plaintiff who can legitimately pursue a claim *grounded in that Act*.

Examples

1. Joanna went to an upscale store to buy a loaf of her favorite bread, "WunderChleb." She particularly dislikes bread with added sugar. While at the store, she asked an employee whether the bread had any added sugar and the employee reassured her that the bread was sugar-free. When she went home and opened the bread's packaging, a no-sugar guarantee fell out. Were there any Magnuson-Moss warranties given, and if so, when?

2. Leon was ahead of schedule on his painting project and burning through supplies. He went to HouseWarehouse to buy some new brushes. He found some brushes for sale for $9.99 each. The packaging of the brush stated, "GUARANTEED TOP QUALITY 100%—2 INCH POLYESTER BRUSHES." What Magnuson-Moss warranties were given? Are there any issues with the prospective written warranty?

3. After many years of successful projects, Leon was loaded with cash and decided to buy his dream car, a 1976 Firebird for $20,000. Leon went to Karl's Classic Cars to buy the car. On the window was a notice with two boxes checked that stated "Full warranty" and "Limited warranty." In the description area was printed "1976 Firebird—Full Three-Year Warranty for All Parts Except Transmission—Lifetime Limited Transmission Warranty for 500 HTM transmission—SELLER HEREBY DISCLAIMS ALL IMPLIED WARRANTIES AND CONSEQUENTIAL DAMAGES." Leon took the car out for a spin but the transmission malfunctioned causing the car to crash into a building. Leon then spent a week in the hospital. As it turns out, the transmission was only a 300 HTM. What warranties were given under the Act, and were the disclaimers and modifications effective?

4. Leon now has a huge hospital bill of $20,000 to pay and has just received a demand letter from the building's owner. Desperate for money, Leon decides to pursue a claim for breach of warranty. In which courts can Leon sue and for what damages?

5. Trevor, a young successful lawyer and an avid golfer, decides to begin making his own golf clubs. Remembering his days in civil procedure he recalled that such clubs can be manufactured using a special metal shearing machine made by MacTire Manufacturer Corp. Trevor places

an order, and MacTire Manufacturer sends its machine to MacTire Sales Corp. MacTire Manufacturer warrants the machines' motor's quality as a limited warranty for two years repair and replacement, and limits all other implied warranties regarding the motor to two years. MacTire Manufacturer provides a full three-year warranty for the rest of the machine. MacTire Sales passes on the manufacturer's warranty but disclaims all implied warranties. After Trevor buys the machine, both the engine and a pulley break. Does Trevor have any claims under Magnuson-Moss?

6. Assume now that Trevor purchases for his business a shearing machine from HomeCrafts, which sells this particular machine mostly to home hobbyists. When it breaks down, HomeCrafts offers to service the machine and writes out a guarantee promising that the repair will last for a period of three years. If Trevor makes a claim under Magnuson-Moss, what result?

Explanations

1. Remember that Magnuson-Moss provides relief primarily for "written warranties" as defined in the Act. §2301(6). Thus, when Joanna asked the employee about the bread, the employee may have created an express warranty under U.C.C. §2-313, but did not create a "written warranty" as defined under the Act. But what about the guarantee in the bag? Typically to create a warranty under the Act, the warrantor must either promise that the product was defect free, guarantee quality or workmanship for a period of time, or promise remedial efforts such as repair or replace. None of these promises were made, so it is unlikely to be a written warranty under Magnuson-Moss. It may still meet the requirement of an express warranty under the U.C.C. Lastly, warranties are required to be a part of the basis of the bargain under both the Act and the Code, so there may be a question of whether the manufacturer's statement met that requirement as well since Joanna did not know about it until after she opened the package, and one does not typically expect additional terms to be included inside of bread packaging. §2301(6).

2. The sale does not meet the Act's requirements of a "written warranty" because there is no warranted duration of quality, promise of being defect free, or remedial promises. Further, the warranty regarding "top quality" may lack sufficient substance to be an affirmation of fact, and thus may not even be an express warranty under U.C.C. §2-313. However, the description as a two-inch polyester brush would likely suffice under the U.C.C. If there were a written warranty covered by the Act here, then there would be a question of whether the warranty would

extend to a commercial user. The Act covers the sale of consumer products — but the purchaser need not be a consumer. All that is required is a product normally used for personal, family, or household purposes. §2301(1). Many paint brushes are used for household purposes, and further, any question of the Act's scope regarding consumer products should be construed in favor of coverage. 16 C.F.R. §700.1. The fact that the sale is for less than $10 means that the warrantor would not be required to designate the product as having a "full" or "limited" warranty under §2303, but would still be subject to the other applicable provisions of the Act. For those curious, the sale price does not include tax for the purpose of Magnuson-Moss. 16 C.F.R. §700.1(d).

3. The Federal Trade Commission requires used car dealers to display a "Buyer's Guide" notice on the vehicle that indicates what warranties are given. See 16 C.F.R. §455.2. Here the seller gave both a full warranty and a limited warranty as shown by the notice. Note that it is acceptable under the Act for a warrantor to offer a mixture of full and limited warranties. §2305. Here, there was a full warranty given for parts other than the transmission, but here there was no breach of warranty for any of those parts. The lifetime warranty of the transmission will likely qualify as a written warranty under the Act because it could be regarded as a written affirmation regarding the quality and workmanship for a specific period of time or as a remedial undertaking under the Act. See *Kelleher v. Marvin Lumber & Cedar Co.*, 891 A.2d 477 (N.H. 2005). The facts here are similar to those of *Skelton v. General Motors Corp.*, 660 F.2d 311 (7th Cir. 1981) where a transmission was advertised as a 350 model but was in fact a 250. The court refused to expand the Act's definition of a written warranty to mere product descriptions, which would constitute express warranties under the U.C.C. Thus, the mere fact that the transmission was not the 500 model as promised will not create a cause of action regarding the mislabeled transmission under Magnuson-Moss, although it would likely be a breach of express warranty under the U.C.C. As to disclaimers, under the Act, "suppliers" cannot disclaim implied warranties if they give a "written warranty" — but otherwise suppliers can disclaim the implied warranties. Here the seller (a supplier who makes the goods directly or indirectly available) gave a written warranty regarding the transmission and thus cannot now disclaim the implied warranty. Under the full warranty, sellers cannot disclaim consequential damages unless the disclaimer appears on the face of the warranty, which it did. But the injury didn't arise out of a breach of the full warranty, but rather arose out of the limited transmission warranty. Under that breach, the consequential damages were likely effectively disclaimed. But U.C.C. §2-719(3) will likely apply here and bar the seller from disclaiming consequential damages for personal injury from consumer goods where the loss is not commercial.

4. As stated in the previous question, the consequential damages were likely effectively disclaimed. Thus, Leon will be unable to recover the consequential damages for the building's damage. Unable to claim the building's damages, the breach of warranty caused a maximum of $40,000 (medical expenses plus the loss of the car (although the car damage other than the transmission may arguably be consequential), which is insufficient to meet the required federal amount in controversy of $50,000 under the Act. Additionally, many jurisdictions do not allow personal injury claims to be brought under Magnuson-Moss, so Leon will likely have to file in a state court of a competent jurisdiction. Magnuson-Moss also allows buyers to recover attorneys' fees, but these would not be calculated in the amount in controversy.

5. Trevor got a limited warranty of repair and replacement of the engine plus a full warranty of all other parts, so this likely is a written warranty under §2301(6)(b). The main problem with Trevor's claim is that a metal shearing machine is one that is very unlikely to be used for personal, family, or household purposes; although golf may be a personal activity, manufacturing the golf clubs is likely not. Because these warranties are not covered under Magnuson-Moss, the seller may disclaim or limit the implied warranties under U.C.C. §2-316 and the manufacturer-warrantor would be able to disclaim them as well. But if the goods were covered under the Act, note that it is acceptable to have a mixture of full and limited warranties. §2305. If covered, MacTire Manufacturer would also be able to limit the duration of the implied warranty to that of the limited written warranty under §2308(b), and MacTire Sales still would be allowed to disclaim the implied warranty as the seller never made a written warranty under the Act. §2308(a).

6. Even though he is using the machine in his business, this machine is apparently primarily used for personal, family, or household services, so it is a "consumer product" under the Act. However, the Act applies primarily to the sale of consumer products; here we have a one-off repair. While the Act may apply to service contracts that provide services for a consumer product over a period—see §§2301(8) and 2305—this is a warranty of a single repair, which is not covered under Magnuson-Moss, and probably not under the U.C.C.

PART IV

Performance of the Contract

CHAPTER 16

Identification of Goods and the Seller's Tender

INTRODUCTION TO PERFORMANCE ISSUES

Everything up to this point has been ultimately directed toward answering the most elemental of questions: Have the parties entered into an enforceable contract for the sale of goods? If so, what are the terms of that contract? Now we will assume all that. We will assume that a prospective buyer and a willing seller have entered into an agreement of sale and that their agreement is enforceable under Article 2. Furthermore, we will assume that the terms of the contract are settled, unambiguous, and well understood by both of the parties.

This, however, is not the end of the story. Certainly it is not the end for the buyer and seller themselves, who are after all not interested in the contract for its beauty as an abstract legal device. Their needs are not met because, as good commercial lawyers, we are now able to recite in detail and with all the appropriate flourishes a listing of their manifold legal rights and responsibilities. Once the record is signed, the hands shaken, or the closing closed, the contracting parties are not unreasonably interested in actually *carrying out* the deal. It is not enough that they can file away the record or hang a picture of the ceremonial handshake on the office wall. Neither the buyer nor the seller can expect to get rich just by sitting back content in the knowledge that a deal has been made and waiting for the money to roll in. The buyer is interested in getting the goods and getting use out of them. The seller is quite naturally interested in getting paid the price. The parties have bargained for the *performance*, not merely the existence, of the contract.

Given that a contract exists and its terms are clear, who must do what, and how and when must it be done? The parties will have to plan and carry out their actions carefully. Each must avoid doing anything that will later leave room for interpretation by the other as a breach of the agreement. But neither can afford to play a purely defensive game. Both buyer and seller must be willing and able to make those moves that put the other under a return obligation. Otherwise the contract will ultimately be of no more value than a forgotten file or that memorial photograph hanging unnoticed on the wall.

The general obligations of the buyer and seller under the contract of sale are perfectly straightforward. Section 2-301 reads in its entirety as follows:

> The obligation of the seller is to transfer and deliver and that of the buyer is to accept and pay in accordance with the contract.

Obviously more detail is called for, and in fact, carrying out these general obligations can be a fairly intricate dance for the parties involved. This chapter and those that follow deal with various questions that arise as that dance proceeds to what is, in the vast majority of instances, its successful and satisfying conclusion. In those (we hope) rare instances where the music turns sour or someone treads on somebody else's toes, Article 2 will be there to step in—often to get the parties and the deal back in rhythm, to finish out the dance, or to at least set the ground rules for the unpleasant brawl that ensues.

The sections of Article 2 with which we are now concerned are often referred to in casebooks and other materials as the *TARR provisions.* We are dealing here with the important Code concepts of **T**ender, **A**cceptance, **R**ejection, and **R**evocation—the principal steps in this dance of performance. To be complete, we really should throw into this TARR an I for the opening move of Identification of the goods and a C for the all-important notion of Cure, which threads throughout much of the discussion. Each of these steps will be examined in turn and as they relate one to the other.

IDENTIFICATION

At the time the parties enter into a binding contract of sale, the subject of that sale will often be a particular unique item already in existence. It might very well be sitting right there in front of them. This need not necessarily be the case, however. The goods to be bought and sold may be part of a larger stock held at some distant point by the seller. Or they may not yet even be in existence: Article 2 clearly provides for the contract to sell *future goods.* See §2-105(2). At some time, of course, such future goods will have to come into existence. They may be produced specifically to fulfill the single contract, or they may just come off the assembly line and eventually be stored as part of a larger batch of goods. If the goods are held in bulk along with their brothers and sisters, there will then have to come a time when they are singled out as individuals. The buyer is expecting to get—and ultimately will get—some particular items, not just the abstract embodiment of goodliness.

The process or event in which an individual item or items become separated out from the whole world of other such articles and are designated as the particular goods "to which the contract refers" is called *identification of goods* under Article 2. Section 2-501 deals with identification and sets forth the rules for determining when identification has occurred. You can't really find a definition in this section, much as you might want to. As you can see, subsection (1) says in effect only that goods are identified to the contract giving the buyer "a special property interest and an insurable interest" in them "by identification." If this is a definition it's a perfectly circular one, and the section has been criticized on this basis. In practice, the lack of a precise definition isn't a very great problem for us. In fact, the whole notion of identification does not play as great a part in Article 2 performance problems as you initially might expect. Still, there are individual sections in Article 2 that make reference to and depend upon whether the goods have been identified. For instance, see §2-613 on Casualty to Identified Goods or §2-709(2) dealing with the seller's Action for the Price. The first few examples of this chapter will take you through the rules set out at the end of §2-501(1) for determining when identification has occurred.

Note initially that no one party is necessarily responsible for making identification happen. Identification to the extent we understand it is more an event than an activity. It may come about because of action by the seller or the buyer, or simply because the two are thinking along the same lines. Sometimes it just happens as nature takes its course. For example, in some instances, a newborn animal is identified to the contract for its sale at the moment of its birth—an event the timing of which neither the seller nor the buyer would claim to control.

TENDER AND ITS CONSEQUENCES

Tender, as that word is used in Article 2, can, like identification, be thought of as an event, but it also connotes an action and has the power of a verb. When we do use it as a noun to connote an event, there can be no doubt that (unlike identification) it is an event under the control of one of the two parties. Tender doesn't just happen. It is the seller's responsibility. Unless excused by the buyer's failure to make payment when all or part of the price is due before delivery (§2-511(1)), the seller takes the lead in the dance of performance by tendering goods in conformity with the terms of the contract. *What* exactly must be tendered, and *where* and *when* must tender take place? We have to assume that these matters are all covered by the contract of sale, either because of the explicit agreement of the parties, by applicable trade terms, or by virtue of some gap-filling provision of Article 2. (See particularly §§2-307 through 2-309, as covered in Chapter 9.)

Why does the seller tender? That's easy enough to appreciate. Presumably the seller wants the transaction to go through to its conclusion, and tender is the seller's way of moving the process forward and forcing the issue. Under Article 2, as in the common law, if both the seller and the buyer become uninterested in actually carrying through with the deal, then it just dies on the vine. The seller will not tender, the buyer will be relieved or at least not complain that this is so, and that will be the end of that. It is up to the parties, the buyer and seller, and not some abstract rule of law or outside authority, to prod the contract of sale along to some resolution or another.

To the seller, tender is crucial because of its consequences. Let's spell those out. It is important (for us and for the parties) to distinguish between tender that conforms to the terms of the contract and tender that is in some way nonconforming. Conforming tender puts the buyer on the spot. Look at the second sentence of §2-507(1). "Tender entitles the seller to acceptance of the goods and to payment according to the terms of the contract." Once the buyer has accepted, he or she will have to pay for the goods at the price contracted for (§2-607(1)). Should the buyer *fail* to accept a conforming tender, the seller has a host of remedies available under the Code. These are set forth starting at §2-703 and will be dealt with in a later chapter. For the moment, you can just assume that a wrongful rejection by the buyer gives the seller plenty of options to protect his or her interests.

What of a nonconforming tender? In that event, as we will see in more detail in the chapters to come, the buyer is in the catbird seat. For the moment, look at §2-601. With some exceptions to be discussed as we go along, the buyer may react to a tender that "fail[s] in any respect to conform to the contract" by doing just about what he or she wants, including rejecting the whole delivery.

Tender, conforming or otherwise, is the first step in the dance of performance.

THE PERFECT TENDER RULE AND THE CODE

As you are no doubt aware from your Contracts course, contracts for the sale of goods were historically governed by what became known as the *perfect tender rule*. What this meant was that the seller's tender had to be conforming in every respect—it had to be perfect—in order to trigger the buyer's obligation to take and pay for the goods. If the goods were in any way nonconforming (e.g., if there were too few items in the shipment or too many, if any warranty no matter how trivial was not met, or if the delivery was even one day too late or one day too early), the buyer could simply reject with no untoward consequences. And the buyer could usually get away with such a rejection even if the reason for not wanting the goods was in truth unrelated to the nonconformity relied upon to justify rejection.

Presumably you studied this result in Contracts, comparing it to the more flexible notion of *substantial performance* or *material breach* that holds sway in areas of contract law other than the sale of goods. At that time, you considered not only the history of the unyielding perfect tender rule for the sale of goods, but some of the arguments that could be made in its favor. Primarily there is the concern that the seller, given a right to insist upon acceptance of a "substantially" conforming tender, might be encouraged to cut corners, thereby foisting upon the buyer something quite different from what he or she was expecting. Beyond that, the common law courts were understandably reluctant to put the buyer in the uncomfortable position of having to determine at the very moment of delivery as the goods were sitting outside the door whether the seller's breach was "material" or not. A buyer who believed the breach to be material and rejected on that ground would always have to worry about later being second-guessed by a court. An incorrect application of the materiality standard (dare we say a wrong guess?) would find the buyer facing the full range of penalties for breach of contract.

I assume you also had occasion to consider the arguments that have been raised *against* the common law's perfect tender rule: principally, the concern that it gave the buyer the opportunity to get out of a deal on the merest pretext and, beyond that, the whole air of gamesmanship it lent to the performance of contracts for sale. Critics of the perfect tender rule tend to speak of the "rigid" or "formalistic" perfect tender rule, and you know they don't mean any of this as a compliment.

By the time work began on Article 2, criticism of the perfect tender rule had quite generally taken hold, and most commentators probably hoped and expected it not to survive the drafting of the Code. Such was not to be the case, however, as you should convince yourself by referring once again to §2-601. The buyer has the right to reject the whole should the tender of delivery "fail *in any respect* to conform to the contract." Perhaps you think you can eke out some flexibility for the seller by playing around with the word "conform," but look at the definition in §2-106(2). Goods are *conforming* "when they are in accordance with the contract," not when they are "substantially" or "materially" in accordance with the contract. The icing on the cake (for the buyer) is found in the opening sentence of Comment 2 to §2-106. However much one of the goals of the Article 2 drafters was to "modernize the law governing commercial transactions" §1-103(a)(1), in this one respect, they ended up retaining the most traditional (many would say archaic) of rules.

The language of Article 2 directly incorporates the perfect tender rule for the sale of goods. At the same time, there is every reason to believe that the perfect tender rule as it resides in Article 2 is but a shadow of its former self. Various other provisions of the Code, some of which we have already considered and some of which are yet to come, are generally seen as working together to virtually gut any "lack-of-perfect-tender"-style argument on which a buyer might try to insist. We can catalog the numerous provisions that work to mitigate the potentially harsh working of the perfect tender rule at this time. Don't worry about the details now. You may, however, want to return to this listing as a review after you have worked through all of Part IV on performance issues. For the moment, simply note the following:

- §1-304. A buyer's rejection must be made in good faith, which is defined in §1-201(b)(20). Recall or review the discussion of good faith in Chapter 9. Because good faith means "honesty in fact" in all jurisdictions, I take it that that means the real reason for the rejection of the goods must be the nonconformity and not, for example, an unfavorable shift in the market. And in those jurisdictions where good faith means "the observance of reasonable commercial standards of fair dealing," a reasonable buyer in the trade would not have rejected the goods.
- §2-605. A buyer may not later justify a rejection by pointing to defects on which he or she did not rely at the time of rejection. A buyer is foreclosed from later cooking up a good excuse for a wrongful rejection.
- Recall the significance given to trade usage, course of dealing, and course of performance by Article 2. (And see Chapter 7.) These trade terms actually become part of the agreement and, hence, the contract between the parties. If, in a given, trade buyers regularly give some leeway to sellers in judging compliance with the contract terms, that measure could also become part of any specific contract within the industry. For example, assume that Seller, a cloth manufacturer, contracted to deliver 10,000 yards of denim to a buyer in the business of making jeans. Assume furthermore that it is a trade usage in the sale of cloth to accept and pay at the contract rate for deliveries that are within 5 percent of the specified amount. Seller tenders 9,985 yards of denim. Seller can argue that this tender does "conform in every respect" with the contract. A contract stated to be for the sale of 10,000 yards of cloth puts upon Seller the obligation to deliver this amount plus or minus 5 percent. Buyer cannot reject even under the perfect tender rule.

- §2-504. As we will see in this chapter, some defects in the seller's manner of shipment will be grounds for buyer's rejection "only if material delay or loss ensues."
- §2-612. The perfect tender standard does not apply to so-called installment contracts. As we'll see in Chapter 21, such sales are governed under Article 2 by a rule of material breach.
- §2-608. Even if a buyer is given the right to reject for a nonmaterial breach under §2-601, if the buyer does accept and later tries to revoke his or her acceptance, a different standard will apply. See Chapter 19.
- §2-508. Finally, if the buyer does reject, the seller will have in many instances the important *right to cure*. We deal with this in Chapter 18.

All in all, it is difficult to conceive of a situation arising under the U.C.C. where the seller could unfairly or unreasonably fall victim to the buyer's capricious invocation of the perfect tender rule. With the adoption of Article 2, that rule remains on the books, but its spirit has been severely restrained if not entirely broken by the overall effect of the Code on matters of performance.

THE MEANS OF TENDER

If tender is an action on the seller's part, we need to inquire exactly what the seller must do to have tendered successfully and, by so doing, put the burden of response upon the buyer. The key sections here are §§2-503 and 2-504, which you should look over now. *One warning:* You will see various references in these sections and in others we confront in the next few chapters to things like documents of title, bills of lading, and warehouse receipts, negotiable and otherwise. If you have not yet encountered such documents of title, and particularly if you have not yet run into the concept of *negotiability* in your commercial law studies, you should not worry about picking up all the subtleties at the moment. For the time being, it is enough to think of such a document as something akin to the receipt you get when you take some clothing into the dry cleaners: It serves as evidence of the fact that you've turned the particular garment, be it a skirt or a pair of slacks, over to the cleaners, and beyond that, it stands as a kind of record of the service the cleaner is expected to provide. Typically it will note whether there is to be cleaning, pressing, or storage. Finally and most importantly, you will be expected to present the receipt at the cleaners if you want to get your clothing back. *Bills of lading* are documents of title given by commercial carriers when goods are delivered to them, and *warehouse receipts* are (as you might expect) documents given by commercial warehouses; they are indeed more complicated than this, but that's the basic idea and it will serve for the present.

Now back to the two basic sections on tender, §§2-503 and 2-504. As you can see, Article 2 itself does not dictate where tender must take place or in what manner. That is up to the parties. As §2-503(1) makes clear, "The manner, time and place for tender are determined by the agreement and by this Article," that is, by the parties' contract of sale, which is after all just the agreement as interpreted and amplified by the provisions of Article 2.

Tender may take place at the seller's place of business or residence, at the buyer's, or on some neutral territory. The mechanism by which tender is actually carried out is also up to the parties. In many instances, the contract will leave the exact method of tender up to the seller, in which case any means will suffice as long as the seller can be said to have suitably "[held] conforming goods at the buyer's disposition and give[n] the buyer any reasonable notification necessary to enable him to take delivery." At other times, the parties may have agreed on a single exclusive manner of tender (e.g., "Delivery by United Parcel Service to Buyer's business address on or before February 15"), in which case the seller will have to take the steps contemplated except in the rare circumstance where he or she is excused from doing so by unforeseen circumstances (see §2-614).

So the time, place, and manner of tender are up to the parties. There will be times when the seller tenders directly to the buyer in a face-to-face meeting at the point of sale. Other times, the seller will be expected to deliver to the buyer at some distant point by using its own personnel, such as when a department store makes deliveries with its own trucks and drivers. Or the buyer may send its own truck and crew around to pick up the goods from the seller's place of business. In other instances, the seller will ship to the buyer via some third-party commercial carrier, like a railroad or an air freight or trucking firm. Finally there will be the situation where the goods are held by the seller in some independent commercial warehouse. (By this we mean a warehouse other than one owned by the seller for the purpose of storing its own stuff. An independent warehouse is one operated by an unrelated party who runs a business storing things for a fee.) The parties might agree that the buyer will pick the goods up from this warehouse, or they could intend that the goods will become buyer's property even as they remain untouched and unmoved in the warehouse.

There obviously are any number of ways that a tender can take place, and hence a number of ways a seller's attempt at tender can go astray. The following examples, after an initial three on identification of goods and §2-501, all deal with when and whether a tender has taken place. They call for application of §§2-503 and 2-504.

Examples

1. Arnold Moneybucks goes into Stella's art gallery to view a show of recent works by a contemporary artist. He spots one small painting ("Black on Black"), which he decides to buy, and enters into a purchase and sale agreement with Stella. The agreement provides that Moneybucks will pick up the painting in a few weeks when the artist's showing is over.
   (a) At what point does identification of this painting to this contract occur?
   (b) Arnold then goes on to Bella's gallery, which is showing works by another artist. He sees a lithograph on the wall ("Author at the Keyboard") that he wants for his collection. Bella tells him that the artist has prepared a run of 100 copies of this lithograph, each of which she has in her possession and each of which she hopes to sell. Arnold contracts to buy one, which Bella agrees to deliver to him. When does identification occur in this sale?
   (c) Suppose instead that Bella has already sold the entire first run of the lithograph. She tells Arnold that the artist is preparing to make a second run of 50 additional copies, and Arnold contracts to buy one of these with delivery to be as soon as possible. When does identification occur?

2. In February, Farmer Jones contracts to sell to Agribuyer, Inc. his entire crop of spring wheat, which he expects to plant in late March and harvest during the summer. When does identification occur?

3. Meanwhile at the farm down the road, Farmer Smith does not contract to sell her crop prior to the growing season. When she harvests her wheat in July, she stores it in her silo. An agent of Agribuyer visits her farm and inspects the wheat in the silo. On behalf of his company, he contracts to buy 120,000 bushels of this wheat (about half of what is in the silo) to be delivered over the course of the next five months. When does identification occur under these circumstances?

4. Return now to the situation in Example 1. Stella telephones Arnold on a Friday to tell him that the show is ending on that day. She tells him that he can come into the gallery and pick up his painting.
   (a) Has Stella tendered to Arnold?
   (b) Suppose instead that Stella's contract with Arnold provides that she will deliver the painting to him. On Saturday she wraps the painting up, puts it into her delivery van, and drives to the address Arnold has given her. The address turns out to be Arnold's business office in a large office building. No one at the building is willing to accept delivery of the package on behalf of Arnold. Can Stella claim that

she has tendered as of this point? If not, what more must she do and how often must she do it?

(c) Assume that "Black on Black" is not a small painting but is in fact rather large. Assume further that Stella has agreed to deliver this monster canvas to Arnold's home, a quaint townhouse in a fashionable part of town. When Stella and her workers arrive with the painting, it soon becomes apparent that there is no way this painting can get through any of the doors into Arnold's house. Stella has to return the painting to her gallery where it now sits. Has she tendered?

5. Mazie's Department Store, located in Capitol City, contracts to buy six gross of sweaters from Knits Corporation. The contract provides that Knits will ship the sweaters from its manufacturing plant in Boston to Mazie's. Knits arranges for the sweaters to be picked up by Tony's Trucking Service. Tony picks up the cartons and agrees to deliver them to Mazie's, giving Knits a bill of lading covering the sweaters. Knits sends this bill of lading to Mazie along with a notation that she should expect to hear from Tony when the goods have arrived in Capitol City so that she can arrange for delivery to her store.

(a) At this point, has Knits fully performed its tender obligations? Would it affect your answer if you were to learn that the sweaters never arrive in Capitol City and are never delivered to Mazie's?

(b) Would your answer to the previous question change if Knits had turned over only five gross of sweaters to Tony's Trucking?

(c) What if Knits had shipped the full six gross of sweaters, but had simply placed the bill of lading in its own files and never told Mazie the shipment was coming?

6. Butterfield Foods, a preparer of frozen dinners, places a large order for freshly caught scrod with Seaside Fish Sellers, located in Boston. Seaside arranges for the fish to be picked up by Tony's Trucking and forwards the bill of lading along with a notification to Butterfield. Unfortunately, Seaside makes no special provision for shipment in a refrigerated truck. Has Seaside effectively tendered?

7. (You may want to skip this question and §2-503(4) until you have some familiarity with *negotiable* versus *nonnegotiable* documents of title. Or you may forge ahead—it really isn't that difficult.) When Sam moved from his large suburban home to a smaller apartment, he had to put his piano in storage in Willy's Warehouse. At the time of storage, he received a warehouse receipt from Willy and each month was billed a small storage fee. When it becomes apparent that he is never going to find room in his apartment for the piano, Sam contracts to sell it to Dave, who says that he is content that it should remain in the warehouse

for the time being. Sam gives Dave the warehouse receipt. Is this enough to constitute tender?

Explanations

1. a. Identification of the painting to the contract occurs at the time the contract is made. See §2-501(1)(a). In absence of any explicit agreement to the contrary, identification occurs "when the contract is made if it is for the sale of goods already existing and identified." Here again we seem to see *identification* defined, or at least characterized, in a way that relies on use of the word itself. This may be awkward, but there doesn't appear to be any problem here. The particular painting has been identified at the time of the contract of sale in the English language sense of the word. There is one and only one existing object that is being referred to by both the buyer and the seller as they conclude the deal.

   b. In this situation, identification cannot occur at the moment of contracting. We are told the item is in existence, but the particular lithograph (out of the 100) that is to be Arnold's has not yet been determined. Subpart (c) certainly doesn't apply. Technically, the particular lithograph that is to be Arnold's would be considered "future goods" because, while it is in existence, it hasn't yet been identified to the contract (see §2-105(2)). So under subpart (b) the single lithograph that will eventually hang on Arnold's wall would be identified when it is "shipped, marked or otherwise designated by the seller as the goods to which the contract refers." Of course, it's also possible that the moment of identification would be when one of the artworks is chosen in some manner that was "explicitly agreed to by the parties." And yet Arnold and Bella never talked about the language of identification. As Comment 3 tries to convey, such an agreement need not be explicitly hammered out nor be terribly precise. We have to look here at who will pick out which particular lithograph is going to be delivered to Arnold. If the contract explicitly or implicitly left this up to Bella, then identification would presumably occur when Bella makes the selection. This could be when she takes one lithograph off the pile, wraps it up, and puts Arnold's address on it. Identification could come earlier, for example, if she had immediately gone into her storeroom after concluding the deal with Arnold and put some kind of marker on one of the lithographs saying, "Sold to Moneybucks."

   In contrast, if the agreement between Bella and Arnold had been that he would sometime come by the gallery and pick out the particular lithograph that was to be his, then identification would occur when he actually made his selection.

Lithographs like this are traditionally numbered to show not only how many were made, but also what number in the run the particular item was. So, for example, if Arnold's turned out to be the 57th that was prepared by the artist, there would be a marking at the bottom reading 57/100. What if the custom in the sale of such lithographs is for a buyer to get the lowest number—that is, the earliest in the run that is still available? An argument could be made by Arnold that identification of that one particular item would take place immediately upon his contract with Bella. Note the concluding language in Comment 2 to the effect that "the general policy is to resolve all doubts in favor of identification." This has been read by commentators also to favor the earliest possible moment of identification for which an argument can be made.

c. In the absence of some other agreement, the moment of identification is now governed by subpart (b). At some point, Bella will receive the 50 additional prints. Identification occurs when one particular printed image is "shipped, marked or otherwise designated by [Bella] as the goods to which the contract refers."

What if Arnold had been able to convince Bella, who was able to convince the artist, to run off only one additional print especially for him? Once that one copy comes out of the press with Arnold's name associated with it, identification may have occurred. Again this is based on a policy favoring early identification. Certainly identification would have occurred by the time the one lithograph arrives in Bella's gallery, even if she is not yet aware of its arrival or made any plans to get it to Arnold.

2. Under subpart (c), identification occurs at the time Jones plants the wheat.

3. From what we have already discussed, particularly in answer to Example 1b, you might think that identification would occur in stages as individual shipments of wheat are taken out of the silo and loaded on trucks destined for Agribuyer. But look at Comment 5, which refers us to subpart (a), implying that identification would occur at the moment of contracting. According to the Comment, this hinges on the sale by Smith to Agribuyer of (in what is undoubtedly the clunkiest phrase you'll come across in your studies of Article 2) an "undivided share in an identified fungible bulk." What could this possibly mean? Well, the totality of the grain in Farmer Smith's silo is presumably an "identified fungible bulk," "identified" in that the parties are referring to a particular hoard of wheat and not just some amount of wheat of a certain type, and a "fungible bulk" because, well, that's what it is. See §1-201(b)(18) for the definition of *fungible*. *Bulk* is left to your imagination. I think what the drafters meant to be referring to is what I would call (with no great pride

of authorship) an *unsegregated* or *not yet isolated* share in an identified fungible bulk. That's what Agribuyer is contracting for, and presumably the drafters want identification to occur as soon as the contract is concluded in such a situation. But then why is this different from the unsegregated lithograph resting neatly in a pile with its 99 identical siblings?

The reasoning behind having a special rule for things like grain in an elevator or oil in a tank really has to do with some consequences of identification with which we are not now concerned. But in any event, is the result in Comment 5 justified in light of the language of §2-501? Look at §2-105(4), which seems to help although it's not clear how. Courts having to consider the question have followed the approach of Comment 5. See, for example, *Great Western Sugar Co. v. Pennant Products, Inc.*, 748 P.2d 1359 (Colo. Ct. App. 1987). Pennant contracted to buy 900,000 pounds of refined beet sugar from Great Western, deliveries to be made at Pennant's request during the fourth quarter of 1980. After Pennant received and paid for 371,500 pounds, it refused to take any more. Pennant was clearly in breach, but the question was one of damages. Great Western sued under §2-709(1)(b) providing for a seller's recovery of the price of "goods identified to the contract" that the seller is unable to resell with reasonable efforts. There was apparently a great sugar glut at the end of 1980 and sellers such as Great Western just couldn't move any of the stuff. Pennant claimed that an award under §2-709(1)(b) was not justified, as the remaining 528,500 pounds of sugar had never been identified to the contract. The Colorado Court of Appeals rejected this argument and followed the suggestion of Comment 5 to §2-501. The court put emphasis on the fact that "[w]ithout question, sugar is a fungible good," and that "at all time [Great Western's] inventory consisted of sufficient excess sugar to supply the remainder of its obligation" under the contract. For more on the same (arguably tedious) subject, see *Apex Oil Co. v. Belcher Co. of New York, Inc.*, 855 F.2d 997 (2d Cir. 1988).

4. a. Stella will argue that she has tendered. Section 2-503(1) requires that she "put and hold conforming goods at the buyer's disposition and give the buyer any notification reasonably necessary to enable him to take delivery." But what if her call was at the very end of the business day on Friday? Arnold could argue that tender requires that he have some chance to actually respond. Subpart (a) states that "tender must be at a reasonable hour." If Stella's gallery isn't open over the weekend, it may be that she can't be said to have effectively tendered until some time like the opening of business on Monday.

   But what does it matter if she's tendered on Friday or Monday as long as she has in fact tendered? Discussing tender in the abstract is distinctly unsatisfying. If Arnold does come by to pick up the painting within a reasonable time, the tender would extend through that time (see the latter part of subpart (a)), and that's all that matters. You have to think of some breakdown in the process in order to make the exact moment of tender relevant and, even then, it may not be crucial. For example, what if the painting were somehow damaged over the weekend through the fault of neither Arnold nor Stella? Who suffers the loss? Such "risk of loss" problems as they are called are dealt with in a separate part of Article 2 with which we deal in later chapters. (As a matter of fact, as you'll see in Chapter 23, the loss in this instance would be on Stella and the technical moment of tender would have nothing to do with it. In other risk of loss cases, however, the moment of tender is considerably more important.)

For a helpful case discussing what a seller must do to have tendered the goods short of actually delivering them and seeing things through to the point where the goods are in the possession of the buyer, see *Hansen-Mueller Co. v. Gau*, 838 N.W.2d 138 (Iowa App. 2013).

b. It's doubtful Stella's action on Saturday would constitute tender. Again we note the language in subpart (a) that "tender must be at a reasonable hour." Stella will have to make a delivery during normal business hours, or at least at some time when it would be reasonable to think that delivery would be accepted. Of course some buyers wouldn't want deliveries, particularly if they may be fairly disruptive, to come during regular business hours. Stella, if she's having any problems, can always contact Arnold and ask when he'd like (or at least tolerate) delivery. Presumably he has to be "reasonable" in what he will allow.
c. Yes. Her attempt at delivery constitutes tender. See §2-503(1)(b). For the operation of this language in a larger commercial setting, see *Camden Iron & Metal, Inc. v. Bomar Resources, Inc.*, 719 F. Supp. 297 (D.N.J. 1989). Camden contracted to sell 23,000 long tons of scrap metal to Bomar. The contract provided that Camden would be responsible for loading and securing the metal aboard a ship to be named by Bomar. Bomar sent a particular vessel, the *Kalli*, and asked that it be loaded with the metal. Witnesses for the plaintiff and defendant alike testified that the *Kalli* was unlike any other vessel they had ever seen. Among other problems, the type of hatches with which it was fitted would have made loading far more difficult and increased the possibility that loading it with the cargo would damage the vessel—damage for which seller Camden would have been potentially liable. As the court noted, "The number and size of the hatches on the *Kalli* materially changed not only the risks that Camden Iron could reasonably have foreseen with respect to damaging the vessel during loading, but the expense involved as well, for a slower loading rate means, ipso facto, a costlier steeve." When Bomar refused to consider getting another ship or agreeing to hold Camden harmless for damage that might be caused to the *Kalli* (which was soon to be scrapped anyway), it had in

effect prevented tender. Bomar was held to have breached the contract of sale and required to pay close to one-quarter of a million dollars in damages.

5. a. Yes, if we assume that the contract made with Tony's trucking is "reasonable with regard to the nature of the goods and other circumstances of the case." There's no reason to doubt that here. There has been an effective tender, *even if* the sweaters are somehow lost in transit.

The important thing to see in this question initially is that it is governed by §2-503(2), which will lead us to §2-504, and not by §2-503(3). What's the difference? Subsection (2) deals with what is referred to as a *shipment contract*. In such a contract, under the language of §2-504, the seller "is required or authorized to send the goods to the buyer and the contract does not require him to deliver them at a particular destination." That is, the seller is obligated to *send the goods off* properly but is not responsible for their actually *getting there*. But someone must be responsible for the goods eventually making their way to their intended destination. In the shipment contract, that responsibility is ultimately the carrier's. Here Knits is responsible to Mazie for getting the goods into the hands of a carrier and effectively arranging for their delivery. *Tony* is responsible to Mazie for carrying through with the delivery. (We'll deal with this type of problem in much more detail in the risk of loss materials of Chapter 24.)

In contrast to the shipment contract the parties can, if they so choose, put the responsibility for successful delivery on the seller by agreeing to a *destination contract*. The rules on tender are then governed by §2-503(3). It is easy to fall into the trap of thinking that just because the seller uses the buyer's address in making the arrangement with the carrier ("Deliver to 123 Main Street"), it has somehow turned into a destination contract. Indeed the seller will have to use the correct address to meet his or her tender obligation of making a suitable contract of carriage. But use of the destination in this situation is as an instruction to the carrier and not a legal commitment to the buyer. The difference between a shipment contract and a destination contract is like the difference between "I promise to send it to you at your correct address," and "I promise you'll get it." Read Comment 5 to §2-503. It's important to remember that under Article 2 the shipment contract is "regarded as the normal one." See *Windows, Inc. v. Jordan Panel Systems Corp.*, 177 F.3d 114 (2d Cir. 1999). Unless the circumstances indicate otherwise, we assume that the parties have entered into a shipment contract. (By way of analogy: Imagine that you told a friend, "I promise I'll call you at home this evening." Would you think you had somehow failed in your duty to your friend if you tried the number several times and always got a busy signal or no answer? How likely is it that you would ever promise more, such as "I promise we'll actually get to talk over the phone this evening"?)

If, as in this case, the parties have entered into a shipment contract, then whether the seller has effectively tendered is to be judged by the three criteria of §2-504. Knits seems to have met each of them here.

b. Knits cannot have effectively tendered if it has not put *conforming* goods into the hands of the carrier. Section 2-504 only uses the term "the goods," but it seems obvious that this has to mean goods conforming to the contract, in parallel to §2-503(1).

c. Here Knits does not tender because it has failed to meet its obligations under paragraphs (b) and (c) of §2-504. You can see why the buyer has a right to expect each of these actions by the seller. The buyer has to know the goods are on their way and by what mode of shipment. Otherwise how could the buyer know where and when to expect the goods and have the ability to get them from the carrier? While the idea of a receipt from the dry cleaner's that I advanced earlier in the text is only a rough approximation of the document of title such as a bill of lading, the approximation will work here. Imagine that a friend agreed to drop some clothes off for you at a dry cleaner so that you could pick them up later. This friend's actions are of little help to you and could even leave you not knowing where your favorite jacket or skirt was if your friend doesn't tell you which cleaning establishment had the garment and deliver over to you the receipt. You aren't going to be able to get your things back without at least showing the receipt to the cleaner. In most instances, it's the same with a bill of lading. The buyer is going to have to display the bill (and in fact will usually have to physically hand it over) to the carrier in order to take delivery.

If you are looking for a case on the importance of paragraph (c), check out *June G. Ashton Interiors v. Stark Carpet Corp.*, 491 N.E.2d 120 (Ill. App. 1986). Seller promised the buyer that the goods, in this case a shipment of carpeting, would be delivered to the point of pick-up by February 25. There was evidence that they were in that place, a carpet warehouse, by the 26th. Buyer went to the warehouse on the 28th and was willing to accept the carpet in spite of the late delivery. The goods could not be located. Even if they were there, the court said:

> Stark [the seller] had to make the goods physically available to Ashton [the buyer] at the destination so that she could take physical possession of them. This Stark failed to do. . . . Stark argues that its failure to locate the carpeting was due to Ashton's failure to provide proper tagging instructions which were necessary to locate the carpet. However it was Stark's duty to give Ashton any specific instructions which would be necessary for her to take delivery. Stark did not inform Ashton of

> the importance of the tagging numbers to locate the carpet. Even after Ashton telephoned Stark on February 28, Stark did not inform her of the procedures for locating the carpeting nor of the importance of the tagging identification numbers. Under these circumstances, Stark did not give Ashton the reasonable notice necessary to take delivery.

6. Seaside may not have effectively tendered. Section 2-504 requires that seller make "such a contract for their transportation as may be reasonable having regard to the nature of the goods and other circumstances of the case." If, as seems very likely, this shipment reasonably called for a refrigerator truck, then Seaside never tendered effectively. What if, perhaps because the fish were themselves packed in ice and the trip was to be quick, buyers and sellers similarly situated would feel comfortable with a nonrefrigerated shipment? Then, of course, Seaside has tendered in this instance.

   What if refrigeration would normally be used but the fact that Seaside failed to arrange for it here caused only minor damage to the shipment? Say only 5 percent of the scrod were at all affected by the heat. Look at the concluding language of §2-504: Failure to make a proper contract under (a), or failure to give proper notification under (c), "is a ground for rejection only if material delay or loss ensues." So if Seaside's failure to ship via a refrigerated truck causes some nonmaterial loss, what result? Butterfield would have to accept the shipment. It could of course, when making payment, rightfully withhold an amount for the damages it sustained. But that's very different from its having the right to reject the whole shipment. As I mentioned before, this concluding language in §2-504 is one instance where the Code cuts away from what was the very great leverage given the buyer by the traditional perfect tender rule.

   Note that the responsibility of the seller under a shipment contract to make a proper contract of carriage does not make the seller a guarantor of the carrier's service or that there will be no trouble along the way. The seller is required to make a reasonable contract of carriage, not a foolproof one. In *Cook Specialty Co. v. Schrlock*, 772 F. Supp. 1532 (E.D. Pa. 1991), the seller shipped the goods via R.T.L., also known as Randy's Truck Line, obtaining a certificate of insurance with a face amount of $100,000. The goods, which turned out to be worth something like $28,000, fell off the truck due to Randy's failure to properly secure them and were apparently rendered totally worthless. The buyer was only able to recover $5,000 from Randy, whose liability insurance was capped at this amount, and sued the seller for the difference. There was held to be no breach by the seller warranting such a recovery. The District Court concluded, "No inference fairly can be drawn from [§2-504] that seller has an obligation to investigate the amount and terms of insurance held by the carrier." Had, however, the buyer's opportunity to recover the full value of the goods from the trucking concern been thwarted not by the trucker's lack of sufficient insurance but rather due to the seller's failure to declare the proper value of the goods when arranging for their shipment, the result could have been different. See the last sentence to Comment 3.

7. Section 2-503(4) deals with goods that are "in the possession of a bailee and are to be delivered without being moved." That's our case here. The contract does not call for Sam to deliver it to Dave from the warehouse or for Dave to pick it up there. So what does §2-503(4) say? The correct analysis depends on whether the warehouse receipt is negotiable or not. If it is negotiable, tender of the receipt is tender of the goods. Here Dave has actually taken delivery of the receipt, so there clearly has been tender of the piano. While technically under the language of §2-503(4)(a) Sam could tender in this situation by "procuring acknowledgment" from Willy's Warehouse that Dave has the right to possession, Willy (for his own protection) would not give such an acknowledgment if he had issued a negotiable receipt, unless he was confident that the receipt had been effectively negotiated over to Dave.

   If the warehouse receipt is a nonnegotiable one, the situation is even easier. As you can see by the first part of subpart (b), tender of that receipt or a "record directing" Willy to deliver the piano to Dave will normally be enough unless Dave objects.

   That concludes our initial discussion of tender. Of course tender is important because of the reaction on the buyer's part that must follow. Which brings us to the next chapter.

CHAPTER 17

Acceptance or Rejection of Goods

THE BUYER MAKES A MOVE

Once the seller has tendered, the next move is up to the buyer. He or she must either accept the goods or reject them. There can be no middle ground, no Code-sanctioned hemming and hawing, and certainly no waiting around. As we will soon see, under Article 2 the seller has a right to expect some response to tender, and if the response isn't a rejection, it is by rule of law an acceptance. If the buyer doesn't make a choice within a reasonable time, the law will make one for him or her. So it is up to the buyer, not just in fairness to the seller but for the buyer's own sake, to examine the stuff and make a conscious decision about what to do.

It's important to emphasize at the outset that the buyer has to react to a tender *whether or not* it is conforming tender. If the tender conforms in every respect to the contract, then the buyer has a positive duty to accept the goods (see Comment 3 to §2-602), but this acceptance doesn't happen automatically. Nothing in Article 2 categorically precludes a buyer from rejecting perfectly conforming goods. It can be done. Of course it's a breach by the buyer to do so, but Article 2 is entirely prepared to deal with that eventuality. We deal with remedies in a later part of this book, but for the moment note the introductory phrasing of §2-703.

If seller's tender is nonconforming, the options rightfully open to the buyer are of course greater. But the choice is still up to the buyer, and the fact of a nonconforming tender doesn't eliminate the responsibility for making a decision. The law will not assume a rejection just because the goods aren't as promised. Look again at §2-601. Except in some circumstances with which we deal at other points, if the seller serves up goods that "fail in any respect to conform to the contract," the buyer may do one of a number of things. You shouldn't assume any more than the Code does that a buyer will always want to, or even be able to, reject nonconforming tender. Life is seldom so uncomplicated. Often the buyer will make the decision to accept long before any nonconformity becomes apparent. Even if the buyer *does* notice the problem straightaway at the moment of delivery, remember he or she has been expecting these goods and probably has made plans that hinge on having them available. The buyer may have no choice but to make do with what is at hand. There will be plenty of instances in which the buyer knowing of the nonconformity—and perhaps plenty mad about it—will still choose to accept the goods, using what can be had now and reserving the right to make a claim for damages later when things settle down. Note the subject of §2-714.

At present, we are not concerned with what remedies, principally money damages, a court may later dish out for this or that breach. We are still at the point where the goods have just arrived at the buyer's doorstep. The buyer *may* do one or the other, reject or accept. Each action has its consequences. Let's deal with them in turn.

THE CONSEQUENCES OF REJECTION

As we've already noted, a *wrongful* rejection—that is, a rejection not authorized by Article 2—is a breach and the buyer stands open to an action under the remedies provisions. What about a rejection that is not "wrongful"? Section 2-601 allows the buyer to reject a nonconforming tender in whole or in appropriate parts. Section 2-602 begins by setting out (with no great detail) the manner of rejection. Assume a *rightful* rejection—that is, one justified by the nature of the tender and that the buyer has carried out with exemplary style. What then? Section 2-602 goes on, along with §§2-603 and 2-604, to tell the buyer what may or must be done with any goods left in his or her possession. As the examples and explanations in this chapter will help you explore, there's really not much the buyer is obligated to do after a rightful rejection. A rightful rejection puts the ball back into the seller's court. In most instances, the seller is going to have to come and pick up the goods or arrange to get them back. As should be obvious, the seller will have no right to be paid anything for the goods, and is in fact open to a suit for damages. (As a signal ahead, be aware that the buyer's damages in the case of a rightful rejection are governed by §2-711.) As we will discuss in the chapter to follow, a seller faced with a rightful rejection may still have a right to try again under the notion of cure, but then again, he or she may not, and in any event, cure is not always easy. The buyer will have some minimal responsibility for protecting the goods after a rightful rejection, but the real pressure to deal with the situation is on the seller.

THE CONSEQUENCES OF ACCEPTANCE

Section 2-607 sets out the effects of an acceptance by the buyer. It is crucial to remember one thing: These consequences follow with respect to any goods the buyer actually does accept *whether or not* those goods conform to the contract, *whether or not* the buyer could have rejected them had he or she chosen to. The buyer, by accepting or by failing to effectively reject (which will turn out to be the same thing), has bought on to this bundle of consequences. Start with the most basic. Under §2-607(1), "The buyer must pay at the contract rate for any goods accepted." That's that. Nothing could be clearer.

Under subsection (2), one result of the act of acceptance is that the buyer has lost forever the opportunity to reject. This may seem obvious, but it's worth pausing over. Once goods are accepted, they are accepted. The buyer may, in appropriate circumstances, have the power later to revoke acceptance, but as we'll discover (in Chapter 19), the right of revocation will not necessarily be as clearcut and uncluttered as may have been the initial right to reject. The buyer who wants to make a clean rejection, taking advantage among other things of the perfect tender language of §2-601, had better do so when the time is ripe.

Skip for a moment to §2-607(4). "The burden is on the buyer to establish any breach with respect to goods accepted." While the section doesn't say so, as you may imagine, if goods are rejected, the burden will be on the seller to show that at the moment of tender, they conformed to the contract and usually in fact that they conformed "in every respect." You've had enough legal training to know how important a procedural point like this can be. Often the main reason the parties fight over whether the buyer can be tagged with having accepted the goods is just because of how significant the placement of this burden can be to the eventual outcome of litigation. We'll see at least one classic case of this in the examples and explanations, and you can easily imagine many others.

Finally in our rundown of the principal consequences of acceptance, we focus on §2-607(3)(a). This is an *extremely important* provision of Article 2. So important, in fact, that it deserves its own discussion.

NOTIFICATION OF BREACH UNDER §2-607(3)(a)

Section 2-607(3)(a) is short and to the point. Read it with all the drama you can muster:

> Where a tender has been accepted the buyer must within a reasonable time after he discovers or should have discovered any breach notify the seller of breach or be barred from any remedy.

The drafters were perfectly clear. The notification requirement applies to any breach and even more significantly lack of notification is a bar to any and every remedy.

As the first paragraph of Comment 4 says, a reason for requiring notification is to defeat what the drafters label "commercial bad faith." They are thinking here of the possibility under some prior law that a buyer could accept goods and make use of them but still, when time came around for payment, have the right to point to some previously undisclosed "problem" with the delivery in order to avoid paying or at least gain some leverage for knocking down the price from what had been agreed. There's no reason to allow, much less encourage, such behavior. But note that despite what the Comment says, the actual statutory language "designed to defeat commercial bad faith" makes no reference to the bad faith or the good faith of the buyer. It is all too easy for a perfectly honest buyer, even the "good faith consumer," to be deprived of any and all remedies by virtue of this provision. Of course, although the Comment on this subsection doesn't mention them, there are other reasons for putting even the buyer operating in perfectly good faith under an obligation to give timely notice as §2-607(3)(a) does. It's a simple matter of fairness to the seller. As one court summarized:

> The purpose of the notice requirement is to: (1) give the seller sufficient time to investigate the breach of warranty claims while the facts are still fresh; (2) foster settlement through negotiations; (3) allow the seller to avoid future defects; (4) allow the seller to minimize damages [including, we might add, by attempting to "cure" the defect as we will discuss in the next chapter]; and (5) protect the seller from stale claims.

Brookings Municipal Utilities, Inc. v. Amoco Chemical Co., 103 F. Supp. 2d 1169 (D.S.D. 2000).

The upshot of these concerns was §2-607(3)(a), which in such a draconian form was new to the law of sales when it was included in the Code. No one at the time seemed to doubt the basic wisdom and fairness of the provision. At the same time, the stakes are very high and the results can be harsh. The buyer who is found to have waited too long, or who has not given appropriate notice, loses the right to any remedy. Not surprisingly, it is fairly common for an action brought by a buyer against his or her seller to be met at the outset by a challenge under §2-607(3)(a). A successful argument by the seller under this provision throws the buyer out of court and puts an end to the whole matter.

The lesson from a counselling point of view should be apparent: Whenever a buyer experiences any problem with accepted goods, the seller should be notified as soon as possible and with as much specificity as possible about the problem. This notice should make clear that the buyer considers the problem to be a breach of the sales agreement and furthermore that he or she may have to pursue some remedy in light of what is now known about the goods.

From the litigation perspective, several issues can be and have been raised with respect to the application of §2-607(3)(a). First of all is the timeliness of notice. The buyer is given a "reasonable" amount of time. This is presumably a matter of fact in each case, but pity the poor buyer whose situation is not viewed sympathetically by the judge or jury, particularly since the clock started running not just when the breach was discovered but when it "should have been" discovered. See, for example, *Bev Smith, Inc. v. Atwell*, 836 N.W.2d 872 (Mich. App. 2013).

A second question is whether some sort of formal notification is still necessary where buyer can show that the seller should have known and perhaps in fact *did know* of the nonconformity of tender. The simplest situation is one where the seller delivers after the promised delivery date. The seller is as capable as anyone else of reading a calendar and has to know there's been a breach here. Is there any reason for insisting that the buyer give notice of the obvious? In one well-known case, a case involving no small amount of money, it was held that §2-607(3)(a) did in fact require notice in such a situation. In *Eastern Airlines, Inc. v. McDonnell Douglas Corp.*, 532 F.2d 957 (5th Cir. 1976), the court overturned a judgment for approximately $25 million because the question of notice under §2-607 had never been submitted to the jury. McDonnell Douglas sold airplanes to Eastern that were to be delivered on a set schedule. It began to fall behind in its deliveries. Eastern first indicated that it considered the seller to be in breach but later signaled by its actions that it was willing to accept the late deliveries. The appellate court held notice to be necessary, reasoning that the airline might by its actions have led McDonnell Douglas to believe that it did not intend to take legal action and that "[t]he purpose of the notice is to advise the seller that he must meet a claim for damages."

Other courts have been much more lenient than the Fifth Circuit was here, practically dispensing with the notice requirement when the seller must have known there was a problem. In 1996, however, the Illinois Supreme Court held that an automobile manufacturer's generalized knowledge based on newspaper and magazine reports and consumer group critiques that one of its car models was possibly unsafe did not relieve any particular buyer from complying with the prompt notice requirement of §2-607(3)(a), stating that, "even if a manufacturer is aware of problems with a particular product line, the notice requirement of §2-607 is satisfied only where the manufacturer is somehow apprised of the trouble with the particular product purchased by a particular buyer." *Connick v. Suzuki Motor Co.*, 675 N.E.2d 584 (Ill. 1996). The Illinois Appellate Court subsequently held, following the lead of *Connick*, that the requirement of a particularized notice as called for in §2-607 was not dispensed with, even when the auto manufacturer had itself issued a series of recall notices and press releases relating to a potential problem with one of its cars, the Audi 5000. *Perona v. Volkswagen of America, Inc.*, 684 N.E.2d 859 (Ill. App. 1997). The need for the requisite §2-607(3)(a) notice, even when the party to be notified did itself have knowledge of the defect in the goods delivered, has been reiterated in *Brookings Municipal Utilities*, quoted from earlier, and in *Drobnak v. Andersen Corporation*, 561 F.3d 778 (8th Cir. 2009). For all practical purposes, of course, there is no excuse for failing to give notice in any and every situation where it might conceivably be called for.

The *Eastern Airlines* case also brings out another problem with which the courts have had to wrestle. If notice is required under §2-607(3)(a), exactly how must that notice be given and what must it say? As to *notice* generally, see §1-202(a). Some sections of the Code require that notice be in a record, but §2-607(3)(a) does not, so it is fair to conclude that oral notice will suffice. (It's also fair to conclude that anyone who counsels a buyer that, as a practical matter, there's no reason to bother with notice in a record when oral notice has already been given is just asking for trouble.) But what exactly should the notice say? One court confronted with this problem offered a bit of review:

> Section 2-607(3)(a) does not prescribe any form for the required notice. The absence of specific guidelines has forced courts to develop standards for determining what constitutes adequate notice. Some courts have held that almost any complaint will satisfy the requirement. . . . The standard adopted by these courts is known as "the lenient standard of notification." Other courts require the buyer to notify the seller that the buyer considers the seller to be legally in breach. [Citing Eastern Airlines as an example.] The standard adopted by these courts is known as the "strict standard of notification."

Southeastern Steel Co. v. W.A. Hunt Construction Co., Inc., 390 S.E.2d 475 (S.C. 1990). So which is it to be? Some commentators view (and explicitly or implicitly criticize) the stricter standard as virtually requiring a record with the magic word "breach" contained somewhere therein. Which view would the drafters prefer? You can read the second paragraph of Comment 4 to §2-607, but it seems to want to have it both ways. It starts out in a very lenient tone, but closes with language that is less forgiving. In *Southeastern Steel*, the South Carolina Court of Appeals—which was not forced to choose since it concluded that the buyer hadn't given adequate notice under either standard—opined that the stricter standard appeared to be the majority view. (Later, in *U.S. v. Southern Contracting of Charleston, Inc.*, 862 F. Supp. 107 (D.S.C. 1994), the United States District Court, in a case applying South Carolina law, adopted the more lenient reading of the section's notice requirement.) Meanwhile, at about the same time as the South Carolina court was wrestling with the problem in *Southeastern Steel*, the Supreme Court of Ohio was declaring that state's rejection of the stricter view. See *Chemtrol Adhesives, Inc. v. American Manufacturers Mutual Insurance Co.*, 537 N.E.2d 624 (Ohio 1989). In *Arcor, Inc. v. Textron, Inc.*, 960 F.2d 710 (7th Cir. 1992), the Seventh Circuit concluded that, under Illinois law, the more lenient approach would suffice and furthermore that the buyer may be "deemed to have met the notice requirement when the seller has actual knowledge of the product's failure based on the seller's own observations." And yet, the Court of Appeals of Mississippi reviewing this particular issue in 2009 observed that "[b]y all accounts, the 'strict standard' is required by the majority of courts." *Peavey Electronics Corp. v. Baan USA, Inc.*, 10 So. 3d 945 (Miss. App. 2009).

A final problem under §2-607(3)(a) (or really a set of problems to which arguably not enough attention has been given) revolves around who has to give notice to whom. When it's a simple two-party transaction, a buyer and a seller, there's no real problem. Suppose, however, that a consumer buyer purchases some product from a retailer that had itself bought (perhaps indirectly through a distributor) from its manufacturer. The consumer is hurt because of some defect in the product and sues the manufacturer claiming a breach of warranty. Can that manufacturer defend under §2-607(3)(a) if timely notice had been given only to the retailer or the distributor? What if the consumer-plaintiff did in fact notify the manufacturer directly but later wants to sue the retailer, which had not initially been given notice? What if the plaintiff is not a buyer at all but some other party who is given the right to pursue a breach of warranty action under the state's particular version of §2-318? Could the manufacturer defend based on the fact that the buyer, not a party to the action, had not given adequate notice? Whatever you may think should be the answer to any of these questions, no clear resolution by the courts is yet in sight. About all that we can say with certainty at this point is that, as a matter of careful practice, a buyer or any prospective plaintiff is well advised to give notice to any and all to whom it might be of any interest whatsoever, practically or legally.

THE MODES OF ACCEPTANCE

As you can see from §2-606(1), the buyer may accept in one of three ways. An *overt acceptance*, in which the buyer "signifies" that he or she will take the goods is covered by subpart (a). Subpart (b) deals with what we might call the *acceptance by omission*. The buyer can also be held to have accepted under subpart (c) if he or she does "any act inconsistent with the seller's ownership" of the goods. Each of these modes of acceptance will be explored in the questions that follow.

You will need to refer to a number of Article 2 sections before going on to the examples and explanations. On the question of when and in what quantities or divisions a buyer may reject, see §2-601. Note also §2-606(2) and the definition of *commercial unit* in §2-105(6). The buyer's rights, if any, to inspect the goods before making a decision are governed by §§2-512 and 2-513. What constitutes acceptance is the subject of §2-606(1). The act of rejection is dealt with, albeit in a cursory fashion, in §2-602(1). Section 2-605 also has something to say on how a buyer who chooses to reject should seize the moment. The buyer's rights and responsibilities with respect to goods in its possession and rightfully rejected are laid out in §2-602(2), which refers you to §§2-603 and 2-604.

EXAMPLES

Examples

1. Mazie's Department Store contracts to buy six gross of sweaters from Knits Corporation. Of these, two gross are to be sized medium, two gross large, and the rest extra-large. (Mazie has found that no one seems to want this style of sweater in a "small.") The shipment arrives safe and sound in four large packing crates. Inside the cartons the sweaters are plastic-wrapped in bundles of two dozen each.
   (a) Mazie discovers that any one bundle contains six sweaters, each in the sizes small, medium, large, and extra-large. Mazie has her employees open each bundle. They put the small sweaters to one side of her storeroom. The other sweaters they arrange by color, putting some directly onto the shelves for sale and the rest in the storeroom. Has Mazie accepted? If so, *what* has she accepted?
   (b) Suppose instead that when Mazie opens the crates, she finds that one-fourth of the sweaters are small, but because the sweaters are grouped by size, all of these small sweaters are wrapped together in nine bundles. Her workers put these nine bundles, still wrapped in their plastic, to one side, and open up the bundles containing the rest of the sweaters. Under these facts, which sweaters, if any, have been accepted?

2. Bud sees an article about the latest model computer system, the PS/3, in a computer magazine. On January 12 he goes to Sue's Computer Depot. Sue does not have any of this model in her store yet, but is expecting a few shortly. She tells Bud she expects they will sell out quickly, but that

she is willing to let him buy one in advance. Bud contracts to buy a PS/3 from Sue. The contract calls for delivery to Bud by February 15. Payment is to be made by Bud in cash, one half by February 1 and the rest on delivery. By the end of January, Bud has begun to hear rumors that there is a particularly infuriating glitch in many of the PS/3's being shipped. Fortunately, it is fairly easy to test for whether a particular machine is subject to the problem. On January 31 Bud calls Sue, who tells him that her shipment of PS/3's has not yet arrived but is due any day. "By the way," she adds, "I haven't gotten your first payment." Bud replies that he has not sent it in and does not want to do so until he has had a chance to see the machine and check whether it is functioning properly. Sue says she wants that money now, and reminds him that there are plenty of other people who would like to buy one of the few models of the new machine.

(a) Does Bud have to make the February 1 payment? What could be the consequences if he does not? Would your answer be any different if Sue had told Bud when he called that the machines had in fact just arrived at her store and that she would be opening one up and customizing it to his specifications within the next few days?

(b) Assume that Bud does pay half the purchase price in cash to Sue on February 1 but does not get a chance to see, much less to try out, the machine. On February 5 she calls to tell him it is ready for him to pick up. He goes right over to the store. There he finds the machine in a box with his name on it. Sue demands the rest of the money. Bud refuses to give it to her unless he is given the chance to take it out of the box and test it. Sue refuses to let him unpack the machine in the store, and furthermore will not let him take it out of the store until she gets the rest of the price in cash. They are at loggerheads, standing there in the store with the boxed computer between them. The situation could get nasty. You come along, fortuitously carrying your copy of the U.C.C. How do you advise the two of them?

3. Barney buys a new DVD player from Selma's Stereo City. As one of Selma's clerks delivers over to him the player packed in a sealed box, he is asked to and does sign a record underneath a description of the item and the word "ACCEPTED." Later that day when he unpacks the player at his home, he immediately notices several large scratches on it. He takes it back to the store and tells Selma he wants his money back or replacement with an undamaged item. Can Selma refuse to take the damaged DVD player back based on the record Barney signed?

4. Joseph Sessa, a Philadelphia beer distributor, owned and raced standardbred horses as a hobby. He contracted to buy the horse "Tarport Conaway" from Gene Riegle, who had a farm in Ohio. Sessa sent Maloney,

a personal friend and a knowledgeable horseman, to Ohio to complete the transaction. On March 10 Maloney was given an unlimited opportunity to examine the horse. After observing the horse jogging, he proclaimed Tarport "a fine animal, good and sound." He delivered Sessa's check for the purchase price and arranged for Riegle to send the horse in a van to a designated raceway in Philadelphia. Tarport was picked up by the van on March 23. He arrived at the raceway at 4:30 A.M. the next day. By 8:00 A.M. he had been examined by a vet and was found to have tendinitis in both of his front legs. After this examination, Sessa called Riegle asking that he take the horse back and return the purchase price. Later, even after the tendinitis cleared up, Tarport was found to suffer from a thrombosis of the left and right iliac arteries, which provide the main blood supply to the hind limbs. On March 29 Sessa again called Riegle and demanded his money back. Was either of Sessa's calls an effective rejection?

5. Finkelstein contracted to buy the pacing horse "Red Carpet" from its owner Gerard Miron for $32,000. He took delivery at 3 P.M. on Monday at the seller's place of business without examining the horse and immediately had it transported to his own barn. The next morning, Finkelstein's trainer discovered that there had been an injury to one of the horse's legs. By 11:30 A.M. Tuesday, Finkelstein called Miron saying he rejected the horse because it was not as warranted. Assuming that a horse that is lame at the time of delivery would not be merchantable, did Finkelstein make an effective rejection?

6. Mr. Burns purchases a new Chevrolet from Sam's Autos. He picks the car up on February 1 and drives it off the lot. On February 4 he sets off on an extended cross-country trip that he has been planning for some time. About ten miles out of town, the car begins to stall and lurch. Soon it stops completely and will only make grinding noises. He pushes it into a gas station, where a mechanic tells him that the transmission on the car is "shot." He has the car towed back to his home, then he immediately calls Sam and tells him he rejects the auto as defective.
   (a) Is this an effective rejection?
   (b) Would it make any difference to your answer to the previous question if it were shown that on February 2 Burns had sent Sam a check for the full purchase price of the auto and the check had been received and deposited by Sam prior to his hearing from Burns on February 4?
   (c) How would you answer Example 6a if on February 3 Burns had taken the car to an auto customizing shop where he had it

decorated with elaborate flames running down the sides and snakes on the hood?

7. Seller contracts to deliver 1,000 "five-inch widgets" to Buyer "on or before March 1." A delivery of 980 widgets arrives at Buyer's plant on February 28. Buyer inspects the shipment.
   (a) On March 2 Buyer emails Seller, "I am not happy with the widgets you sent. Some go down to less than 4.8 inches. Please contact me." Has he effectively rejected the shipment?
   (b) On March 2 Buyer instead emails Seller, "I reject the widgets, as they do not meet the specifications for five-inch widgets." Seller later sues for the price, arguing that under industry standards the shipment does meet specifications. Her argument appears strong. Can Buyer now defend his rejection on the grounds that the shipment contained too few widgets?

8. Mrs. Bannin orders some drapes for her living room windows from Samantha's House of Window Treatment for a total price of $4,000. The drapes are delivered. The next day, Bannin buys and installs the necessary hardware and hangs the drapes. She immediately sees that they hang some five or six inches from the floor instead of the one inch she had planned. She measures the drapes and finds that they are not as long as were called for in her order.
   (a) She calls Samantha's. When her call is answered by a telephone answering machine, she leaves the message: "I am rejecting the draperies you sent as they are not the right length. Come and pick them up." She takes the drapes down and stores them in a closet. Does she have to do anything more to protect her rights in the situation? In particular, is it necessary for her to arrange somehow to return the drapes to Samantha?
   (b) Suppose that Samantha emails Bannin, telling her, "Have the drapes returned to me. When I get them, I'll send you a check for what I owe you." Is Bannin obligated to follow these instructions?
   (c) Suppose further that Bannin doesn't follow these instructions, but just keeps the drapes in the closet. Once again she calls Samantha and leaves a message indicating that the seller should pick up the drapes. Several months pass. Samantha is not heard from again. Bannin would like to use her limited closet space for other things. What should she do now?
   (d) Would your analysis of Mrs. Bannin's situation be any different if, instead of storing the drapes in her closet when she first telephoned her rejection, she had just left them hanging?

Explanations

1. a. Mazie has accepted under either §2-606(1)(b), by failing to reject in time, or §2-606(1)(c), by her act of putting some of the sweaters out for sale to her customers. We'll look at these methods of acceptance in more detail in questions to follow. For the moment, let's focus on exactly what she has accepted.

It appears that Mazie has accepted *all* 864 (that's six gross) of the sweaters *including the small ones*. Step back a bit and first note Mazie's options. What could she have done under §2-601 when the shipment she received was so obviously defective? It was up to her. She could have rejected the entire shipment, accepted it all, or she could have "accept[ed] any commercial unit or units and reject[ed] the rest." Note also §2-606(2), which states, "Acceptance of a part of any commercial unit is acceptance of that entire unit." Finally see Comment 2 to that section.

The question then becomes, "What is a *commercial unit* under the circumstances?" So we turn to the definition of that term in §2-105(6). It all depends on "commercial usage," of course, so we cannot be absolutely sure of anything without a thorough knowledge of the knitwear industry. It seems pretty safe to bet that, in sales by the manufacturer, no single one of the sweaters is a commercial unit on its own. We can test by asking the question, would Knits have accepted without comment an order for just one sweater, or 863 or 865 of them? Was its price given as an amount per sweater? Highly unlikely. More probably, it customarily deals in some standard multiple, either dozens or two dozens (which is suggested here by the packaging) or by the gross. In any event, under these facts, Mazie has broken into every commercial unit and has accepted them all. This doesn't leave her without a remedy, of course, but she has to pay at the contract rate for all of the stuff accepted—remember the prime directive of §2-607(1)—and will then have to show some actual damage that she can deduct by way of set-off.

It should be clear that while a single sweater is not a commercial unit for the sake of this transaction (a sale by a manufacturer to a retailer), the units can be different in different circumstances. It all depends on commercial usage and the realities of the situation. In any sale by Mazie to one of her retail customers, naturally, each individual sweater *would* be a commercial unit. In fact, one way of characterizing the business of retail sales is just this: The retailer's principal reason for being is its willingness to buy things in large commercial units, break up those units and then sell in smaller units, taking of course some measure of compensation for this service and the risks involved.

b. Mazie here has a good argument that although she has accepted the other sweaters, she has not accepted the small ones. This would depend on her showing that each and every bundle of two dozen was a commercial unit in and of itself. This seems quite possible. What if Knits could show that it usually and customarily dealt in larger units, such as crates of 216 each? (Six gross divided by four equals 216 equals nine bundles.) Then we'd have to inquire further. If the nine bundles she put aside all came out of one crate, she could argue that she has not accepted that crate, only the other three. If the nine bundles of small sweaters had been distributed among the four crates, then by accepting the other sweaters out of each of these crates, she's accepted them all.

So the final analysis of this question will depend on facts we don't have, both about how sales are customarily carried out in this industry and about what Mazie and her employees did here. A good exercise is to imagine yourself to be Mazie's attorney. What questions would you ask of her or of others to best represent her in the situation?

As you can see from these two questions, the issue of what makes for a commercial unit in any situation can be very important. There does not seem to have been much litigation on the point because, I would guess, commercial practice is sufficiently clear to the parties (and their attorneys once they've done a good job of investigation) in most instances. A few cases can be noted. In *Axion Corp. v. G.D.C. Leasing Corp.*, 269 N.E.2d 664 (Mass. 1971), the contract called for the sale of three valve-testing machines. The buyer acknowledged acceptance of two of the machines but claimed to have rejected the third. The seller argued that the second and third machines, "which were ordered together, delivered together, tested together, and complained of essentially as a unit," constituted a single commercial unit. The court found otherwise:

> The buyer here first ordered one machine separately. Later, after the second and third machines were ordered and delivered together, the seller took the third back separately to work on it. There is no evidence that there was a commercial usage to treat two machines as a single whole or that division of a pair of machines materially impaired their character or value, or that acceptance of one produced a material adverse effect on the other. In these circumstances, it could not be ruled as a matter of law that the two machines constituted a single commercial unit, or that one machine was not a commercial unit.

You can no doubt fool around with the facts here to create a clever hypothetical in which two machines, while physically separate, *do* constitute a single commercial unit. How about a washer/dryer combination bought for the home laundry room? Still probably not good enough. People certainly do consider and sometimes buy one or the other but not both. What about a computer that the maker will consider selling only in conjunction with its own brand of keyboard? Well, you can work out your own hypotheticals.

As one other valve-related example, in *Perkins Pipe & Steel Co., Inc. v. AcmeValve & Fitting Co.*, 276 N.E.2d 355 (Ill. App. 1971), the buyer had ordered a bunch of stuff: "two 14-inch steel flanges (the goods in issue), two 8-inch stainless steel flanges, two 6-inch PRV valves, one 6-inch steel flanged gate valve, and seven used valves. Apparently," the court concluded, "these were five commercial units of valves with the two steel flanges in issue constituting one such unit." The buyer was found to have made an effective rejection of these two valves, this one unit, even while accepting the rest. See also *Viking Packaging Technologies, Inc. v. Vassallo Foods, Inc.*, 804 N.W.2d 507 (Wis. App. 2011), in which it was held that a number of separate machines intended to work together as a complete "pasta packaging system" were to be considered as constituting a single commercial unit.

Getting away from valves, machinery, and the like, and moving on to animals, note *Texas Imports v. Allday*, 649 S.W.2d 730 (Tex. Ct. App. 1983). The buyer contracted to buy 49 head of cattle. It claimed to have accepted 27 of these cattle, which it found to be healthy, and rejected the remaining 22. The court held this to have been proper. Each cow was a commercial unit. This result seems clearly to be right when you consider that the contract called for 49 of the beasts. If they weren't commercial units one by one, we'd have to posit that the cattle industry deals in groups of seven or seven times seven. Barring a biblical injunction to this effect, I'd not assume it to be commercial custom.

Finally, consider the case of *Western Extralite Co. v. Safeco Insurance Co.*, 301 S.W.3d 527 (Mo. App. 2009). Western Extralite contracted to sell a large quantity of light fixtures to be installed in a new residence hall being built on the campus of the University of Missouri at Columbia. After the fixtures had been delivered and installed, the buyer discovered that the ballast transformers on a majority of the light fixtures were either defective or missing. The buyer replaced the ballasts on its own. When sued by Western Extralite for the contract price of the fixtures, the buyer attempted to argue that it had effectively rejected a portion of the ballasts supplied to it by Western Extralite under the contract. The court rejected this line of reasoning. After quoting the Code's definition of "commercial unit," the court went on to say:

> The smallest commercial unit at issue in this case was each individual light fixture, not each piece that was used in the assembly of that light fixture. Certainly the record reflects, and common sense dictates, that the removal of the ballast from the light fixture would impair its value and its use. The UCC does not allow for the rejection of an individual

> part of a commercial unit while accepting the rest. Indeed, "[a]cceptance of a part of any commercial unit is acceptance of that entire unit." [citing §2-606(2)]. By retaining the light fixtures and merely replacing a part in some of those fixtures, [The buyer] clearly accepted the fixtures.

2. a. Bud has to make the initial payment and has no right to withhold it pending an inspection. Bud contracted to pay a portion of the price before delivery and before inspection might be possible. Under §2-511(1), payment is a condition to Sue's duty to tender and complete delivery, so if he really wants the computer, he'd better send in that check. He gets no help from §2-512 because, at this point, there is no reason to think there is necessarily going to be a nonconformity, much less one that now "appears without inspection."

   Bud might want to consider using the insecurity mechanism of §2 609 (see Chapter 20), but it's not clear it would do much for him here. First of all, he'll have to show that on the basis of the rumors he has "reasonable grounds" for believing that the computer he's to get would be defective in this particular way. And if Sue is willing to tell him that she'll make sure he gets a good one, isn't that "adequate assurance" under the circumstances? If so, he's back in the position of having to send in his money before he has any right to delivery.

   If Sue has received her shipment of the new machines, Bud might be able to argue for a right to inspect prior to payment under §2-513(1) if he can show she has already *identified* a particular machine to the contract. But even then, is it "reasonable" to expect that he'd be allowed to come into her shop and play around with the computer before she herself has looked it over and satisfied herself that everything is in order and is ready to make a delivery? In some situations where terribly complex and highly specialized goods are being fabricated to a buyer's specifications, it might be in order for the buyer to make inspections during the course of the seller's manufacturing process, but it seems to me that Bud would be pushing this a bit far if he argued the right to do so here. Consumer buyers often do pay some money, if not all, up front and have to wait until delivery to test out the item.

   b. You advise the two that under §2-513(1), Bud has the right before payment or acceptance to inspect the machine "at any reasonable place and time and in any reasonable manner." So she certainly can't ask him to pay up in cash before he even opens the box. He has the right, at the very least, to be sure that there is a PS/3 in the box. See Comment 1. But does he have the right—right then and there—to take it out, plug it in, and take it for a test drive? Unless there is some special out-of-the-way place at Sue's Computer Depot for him to run through this drill, it doesn't seem to me "reasonable" for him to demand to do it at the store, clogging up her aisles. You may see it differently.

So what's the solution here, other than letting them duke it out? Well, it looks like one of the two will have to give a bit. You might suggest to Sue that she let him take the box out of the store (after a quick peek inside if he insists) in return for a personal check for the amount due. He might go for this as he can always stop payment if the machine turns out to be a dud when he gets to inspect it at home. Or you could suggest to him that he pay the cash, take it home, and really run it through its paces. If it isn't any good, he has all kinds of rights under the Code to reject it then. You could also help by investigating with the two of them, and in light of your own experience, what industry custom suggests here. If the two still can't work it out with all your help, you might just leave them to their own devices, asking as you leave why, if the matter is so important to them, they didn't initially take advantage of the opportunity clearly available under §2-513 to specify before the fact as part of the contract exactly when and how the buyer's inspection could take place.

For an interesting case dealing with the how, when, and where of the buyer's right of inspection in a contract for the sale and purchase of an airplane for $42,870.00, agreed to through the medium of an eBay auction, see *Smith v. Marquross*, 276 S.W.3d 926 (Tenn. App. 2008).

3. No. Barney has not "accepted" the goods under §2-606(1), so he has the right to reject under §2-601, and that's exactly what he's doing now. Selma could try to argue that there had been an acceptance under §2-606(1)(a), but you should see why this fails. Even if Selma had been willing to let him open up the box and try out the player right there in the store (and could therefore put up an argument that there had been a reasonable opportunity to inspect), it doesn't make sense to say that his signing as he did "signified" to Selma that "the goods are conforming or that he will take or retain them in spite of their nonconformity." His signature would presumably be evidence against him if he ever tried to claim he hadn't gotten receipt of the package, but that's about it. Remember that the acceptance that we are talking about here is not acceptance of an offer to contract or, as here, what we might call *acknowledgment of delivery.* Section 2-606 deals with *acceptance of the goods* as delivered and under the contract, which is quite a different matter. See Comment 1.

4. In *Sessa v. Riegle,* 427 F. Supp. 760 (E.D. Pa. 1977), the court held that there had been an acceptance under §2-606(1)(a):

> Sessa accepted Tarport Conaway through his agent Maloney on March 10, 1973. At that time, Maloney was permitted unlimited inspection and both Sessa [via a telephone conversation] and Maloney indicated that Sessa would take the horse.

Having accepted on March 10, any attempt to reject on a later date was doomed to failure (§2-607(2)). Did this mean that Sessa had to be satisfied with a lame horse? No, not necessarily. He would still have recourse (either the right to revoke his acceptance or to seek money damages) if the horse had not conformed to the contract—that is, had been unfit—at the time of seller's tender. Sessa's problem was that, having been found to have accepted, he bore the burden of showing the horse to have been injured or ill when it left Riegle's care. Remember §2-607(4). Apparently the type of problems involved can occur in a racehorse for a variety of reasons or simply out of the blue, and it is often difficult if not impossible to determine the cause of the problem much less when it occurred. In fact buyer Sessa offered expert medical testimony, but it was all, in the opinion of the court, nothing more than "conjecture." Sessa was found not to have met his burden of establishing by a preponderance of the evidence that either the tendinitis or the thrombosis was present in the horse on March 23.

5. Red Carpet figures in the well-known case of *Miron v. Yonkers Raceway, Inc.*, 400 F.2d 112 (2d Cir. 1968). Like the *Sessa* case discussed above, medical testimony was inconclusive on when and how the horse was hurt. So again the crucial issue became the applicability of §2-607(4) and whether the buyer or the seller had the burden of proof on this issue. Buyer had not overtly accepted under §2-606(1)(a), but Miron argued that Finkelstein had accepted by failing to reject after having had "a reasonable opportunity to inspect" Red Carpet. The time between delivery and the attempted rejection was very short (less than 24 hours), but the court held that an acceptance by omission *had* taken place:

> [W]hat is reasonable depends upon an evaluation of all the circumstances. . . . Finkelstein's own testimony showed that it is customary, when buying a racehorse, to have a veterinarian or trainer examine the horse's legs, and we agree [with the trial judge] that the existence of this custom is very important in determining whether there was a reasonable opportunity to inspect the horse. See Official Comment to UCC §1-204, para 2 [of the original version of Article 1]. We gather from the record that the reason it is customary to examine a racehorse's legs at the time of sale is that a splint bone is rather easily fractured (there was testimony that a fracture could result from the horse kicking itself), and although the judge made no specific findings as to this, we assume that is generally what he had in mind when he pointed out that "a live animal is more prone to rapid change in condition and to injury than is an inanimate object." As we have said, Finkelstein did not have the horse examined either at the place of sale or at his barn later the day of sale. He thus passed up a reasonable opportunity to inspect Red Carpet.

You may want to take the court's suggestion at this time and look at the language that is now to be found in §1-205 of the revised version of

Article 1. Notice that the custom shown appears to apply to immediate inspection only of the horse's legs. If there had turned out to be something else wrong with Red Carpet, such as a viral infection, the result could well have been different.

6. a. Sam will argue that Burns' attempted rejection came too late because by February 4 there had been a "reasonable opportunity to inspect" the car, bringing into play §2-606(1)(b). Burns will argue that with a complicated article like an automobile, a reasonable period for inspection would have to extend for some time, especially when the type of problem that eventually turns up is one that a typical consumer wouldn't be expected to find on a cursory examination.

   Those cases that we have do clearly establish the principle that, with an automobile, the period of inspection does not end, and the car is not accepted under §2-606(1)(b) just because it has been driven off the dealer's premises by the buyer. The most well-known case involves a very short time and a fairly big problem. In *Zabriskie Chevrolet, Inc. v. Smith*, 240 A.2d 195 (N.J. Super. 1968), problems with the buyer's new Chevrolet began to assert themselves within seven-tenths of a mile from the showroom. The buyer was barely able to get his new purchase (eventually travelling in first gear at something like five to ten miles per hour) all the way to his home, about two-and-a-half miles away. Once home, the buyer immediately called the distributorship and attempted to reject the car. Later in the course of litigation, the seller argued that the buyer had accepted the car by signing the contract and taking possession. The court did not buy this argument:

   > To the layman, the complicated mechanisms of today's automobiles are a complete mystery. To have the automobile inspected by someone with sufficient expertise to disassemble the vehicle in order to discover latent defects before the contract is signed, is assuredly impossible and highly impractical. . . . Consequently, the first few miles of driving become even more significant to the excited new car buyer. This is the buyer's first reasonable opportunity to enjoy his new vehicle to see if it conforms to what it was represented to be and whether he is getting what he bargained for. How long the buyer may drive the car under the guise of inspection of new goods is not an issue in the present case. It is clear that defendant discovered the nonconformity within 7/10 of a mile and minutes after leaving plaintiff's showroom. Certainly this is well within the ambit of "reasonable opportunity to inspect."

   So for Burns, it's all a matter of reasonable time—a question of fact—and we can't be certain of the result. I tend to think Burns would have the better time of it in front of any judge or jury. Most reasonable people, which has to include judges and jury members, would be understanding if a new car owner hadn't taken his new car out on the open road for a test drive for a few days. Other facts would also play a part: *Had* Burns in fact driven the car very much? Under what conditions? Earlier than the 4th? Had he then experienced anything that should have alerted him to transmission problems?

At the same time, it's probably true that if Burns tried to reject on this basis very much later, say two or three weeks after driving the car off the lot, he would have problems. This doesn't mean that he has to be content with a car with a messed-up transmission, but his argument under Article 2 will have to be based on something other than a straightforward rejection. As you'll see in a chapter to follow, he may still have the right to revoke his acceptance, which could give him the result he wants. But the route to revocation has its own complications, as you'll discover. At the very least, because the burden of proof will have shifted with acceptance, it will be up to Burns to satisfy the court that the transmission was defective on February 1 when tender was made. Contrast this to the rejection situation where Sam, if he wants to argue that Burns was wrongfully rejecting, would himself have to prove that the transmission was perfectly okay when the car was tendered. Given the mysteries of what goes on under the hood and of what can happen to a car over even a few days of hard driving, you can see the significance to Sam of examining as well as he can and rejecting if he is at all tempted to do so as soon as possible.

Just as the actual timing will be an important factor in any assessment of the factual issue, the nature of the defect will presumably be taken into account. Sam the seller's position here would be much stronger if Burns tried to reject on the 4th because he had only then discovered that the door to the glove compartment wouldn't open. What if Burns tried to reject on this basis but earlier on, say early on the morning of the 2nd? Sam might try to argue that Burns had had a reasonable opportunity to inspect, at least for defects of this nature, right there on the lot before he drove the car away "I told him. Look it over, it's just what you ordered." Should Sam win on this argument? I think not. As a practical matter, does the buyer of a new car go around checking each and every thing that could possibly go wrong, even those that don't require a skilled mechanic to investigate, before taking delivery of the car? (If Sam really did want to get some mileage out of an argument like this, he'd actually have to *demand* Burns make an inspection, and even then, his position might not be very strong. This is all a matter of §2-316(3)(b), which we met in Chapter 14.)

If Burns were allowed to reject for the faulty glove compartment door—thanks to the perfect tender rule of §2-601—that would not be the end of the story. We deal with the whole doctrine of cure, which may come to Sam the seller's assistance, in the next chapter.

b. Burns' sending in the check would probably not be in and of itself an acceptance. See Comment 3. Once again it's a question of fact. What really matters here is what the terms of payment had been and why Burns sent the check when he did. If the check constitutes acceptance, it would fall under §2-606(1)(a), and we have to inquire whether it "signifies" to Sam anything other than that Burns pays his bills on time. If, for example, the contract had called for payment one day after delivery, then this action couldn't be taken as an acceptance by the seller. If, on the other hand, in order to make the sale Sam had told Burns that he "shouldn't pay for it until you know it's the one you want," then it could be a whole other story.

c. Sam could hold Burns to have accepted by this flamboyant act under §2-606(1)(c). We normally don't take such liberties with other people's property. Examples of acts that have been held to trigger this provision are the buyer's actually reselling the goods to a third party or running them through its own manufacturing process. In *Mazur Brothers & Jaffe Fish Co., Inc.*, 3 U.C.C. 419 (Vet. Admin. Contract App. Bd. 1965), the seller had delivered a large order of raw shrimp on July 23. On the next day the buyer, a government hospital, cooked the shrimp only to notice an "unwholesome odor" and discoloration. It attempted to reject. The Veterans Administration Contract Appeals Board (which had jurisdiction over the case) ruled:

> Conversion of virtually the entire order of shrimp from a raw to a cooked state in preparation for service to patients far exceeded the testing necessary for inspection purposes. This alteration in the product rendered it incapable of return to [seller] in the condition in which it had been delivered, and in our opinion constituted an act of dominion inconsistent with [seller's] ownership.

As other examples of the buyer's taking actions with respect to the goods that precluded its later attempt to reject, see *Konitz v. Claver*, 954 P.2d 1138 (Mont. 1998) (buyer of timber accepted by processing the logs); *Weil v. Murray*, 161 F. Supp. 2d 250 (S.D.N.Y. 2001) (buyer of million-dollar painting accepted by having it cleaned and restored); *Fabrica de Tejidos Imperial, S.A. v. Brandon Apparel Group, Inc.*, 218 F. Supp. 2d 974 (N.D. Ill. 2002) (buyer of clothing items accepted by applying decoration to them and reselling to its own customers); and *Dan J. Sheehan Co. v. Ceramic Technics, Ltd.*, 605 S.E.2d 375 (Ga. App. 2004) (purchaser of ceramic tiles accepted by applying them to food court of retail mall under construction). Perhaps most interesting in this regard is *Design Plus Store Fixtures, Inc. v. Citro Corp.*, 508 S.E.2d 825 (N.C. App. 1998), where the North Carolina Court of Appeals affirmed a finding of the trial court that the buyer of a large quantity of retail display tables that did not conform with the contract specifications, and indeed eventually had to be totally replaced by the seller, had been accepted when they were donated to charity after replacement. The original defective tables, the trial court had found, still had salvage value and an effective rejection would have involved a return or allowing the seller to reclaim them.

If we do conclude that the decoration of the car absolutely bars a later rejection, can we go further on the seller's behalf and argue that even if it hadn't been so "improved," the fact that the car has been used for four days and driven a considerable number of miles is enough to allow him to invoke §2-606(1)(c) and claim an acceptance? In a word, no. If §2-606(1)(b) and the sections on inspection mean anything, we must conclude that the buyer's use of the goods as they are intended to be used during a period allowing for a reasonable opportunity to inspect cannot be considered action inconsistent with the seller's ownership. It is not inconsistent with the idea that Sam owns an automobile that he is allowing a (still potential) purchaser to drive around for a period of inspection and testing.

7. a. No. This is not an effective rejection. We can assume that this letter was sent within a reasonable time as called for by §2-602, but the problem is with what it *says*. The section requires a seasonable notification of rejection, which must actually let the seller know that the buyer is *rejecting* the goods, not just that he or she is unhappy with them or claims there is a breach. This letter would be sufficient for §2-607(3)(a) purposes, but that is another matter. A rejecting buyer does not just claim breach; he or she actually expects the seller to take the goods back. See, for example, *CMI Corp. v. Leemar Steel Co., Inc.*, 733 F.2d 1410 (10th Cir. 1984), holding that notification that the buyer had "a problem" with the goods was not sufficient to effect a rejection. To the same effect, see the case of *Ferraro v. Perry's Brick Co.*, 924 N.Y.S.2d 308 (Civ. Ct. N.Y.C. 2011), in which the court opined, "A buyer's mere complaint about the goods does not constitute a clear and unequivocal act of rejection."

b. Buyer has now given a notice of rejection that meets the requirements of §2-602. It turns out, however, that his action may be proven wrongful, as he did not have the right to reject on this basis. Section 2-605 does not allow him to then switch to justifying his rejection on the basis of a nonconformity that he didn't point to initially if that defect was "ascertainable by reasonable inspection" at the time and could have been cured by Seller if she had been notified of it. A delivery that contained too few widgets would seem to fit within this section. The policies behind this section are set forth in Comments 1 and 2.

What if, in addition to everything else, the shipment had arrived at Buyer's plant a few days late, say on March 4? He made no complaint at the time but tried to revoke solely on the claimed failure of the widgets to meet specifications. Later, when it looks like Seller will be able to show that the widgets were not too small, could Buyer rely on the lateness of delivery to justify his rejection? This was a nonconformity and under §2-601 he would have been able to reject on this basis. Under §2-605 it is also a defect that is easily ascertainable. Buyer knows when something is late as well as the next guy. But it seems that lateness is not a defect that could ever be cured (as we'll discuss in the chapter to follow), so §2-605(1)(a) doesn't apply. If Seller hadn't requested a record containing a full statement of Buyer's grounds for rejection, §2-605(1)(b) wouldn't apply either. So Buyer might be able to get somewhere with bringing up the late delivery even this far into the proceedings.

There may even be some reason for allowing him to do so. "If the shipment hadn't been late," he may argue, "I would have had more time to figure out how to make use of such stubby (albeit technically conforming) widgets. I didn't complain about those few days before, but now you can see how important they've become." If Seller believes that this argument is just so much hot air, and that the lateness never mattered to Buyer but is only being used by him now in a last ditch attempt to get out of buying some perfectly fine widgets, she can always call into question whether Buyer is acting consistent with his general obligation of good faith. Recall the important language in Article 1, §§1-304 and 1-201(b)(20).

8. a. Bannin has made an effective rejection and need do nothing more. The rejection met §2-602(1), as it was within a reasonable time and notice was reasonably given. (*Notice* under §1-202(a) does not require a record, and §2-602(1) itself speaks only in terms of notice, not notice in a record as is sometimes required in other sections of Article 2. So a call should be enough.) Once she has effectively rejected, she has very few obligations. Under §2-602(2)(b), she need only "hold [the goods] with reasonable care at the seller's disposition for a time sufficient to permit the seller to remove them." Storing them in a nice safe closet satisfies this responsibility. Of course she cannot simply throw the drapes out, donate them to charity, or leave them in a pile uncovered in her backyard.

Subpart (c) makes clear that she has no further obligation. Certainly she need not take the time and bother to send the drapes back. While the provisions of §2-602(2), which she is using as a guide, are expressly made subject to the provisions of the two sections that follow, neither makes a difference here nor need concern her. Section 2-603, which deals with a limited responsibility to do more, applies to a *merchant* buyer but Bannin is not a merchant. Section 2-604 just relates certain options that the rightfully rejecting buyer *may* choose to pursue. Nothing in that section is mandatory.

If Samantha, in response to Bannin's message, does come by and ask for the drapes back, must Bannin hand them over? Yes, *unless* she has already paid all or part of the price to Samantha. Until she is repaid this amount (plus any cost of inspection, care, and custody, which here would have to be zero), Bannin would have a security interest in the drapes under §2-711(3) and could refuse to give them up. If Samantha does come through with repayment, then this security interest lapses and Bannin would have to hand over the drapes. So the parties are back to square one—well, not exactly. Remember, rejection of nonconforming tender does not waive other rights of the buyer under the contract. Bannin may still have the right to money damages from Samantha for the seller's failure to meet her contract obligations.

b. Bannin need not follow these instructions. She can just repeat her demand to Samantha that she come and pick them up. As we've already discovered, no duty to follow such instructions is found in §2-602, and §2-603 doesn't apply because Bannin is not a merchant. Note that even a merchant buyer isn't under an absolute obligation to resell the merchandise on the seller's behalf or ship it back in the general case. The merchant buyer comes under such duties only when the seller itself "has no agent or place of business at the market of rejection," when the buyer has not yet paid for the goods, and (unless the goods are perishable or threaten to rapidly lose their value) when reasonable instructions are given by the seller. And even then, any duty to follow instructions and resell or reship is subject to any rights the buyer may have under §2-711(3) as a result of payments already made.
c. Under §2-604 (which the Comment tells us is *not* exclusively a merchant's section), it seems Bannin may, if she chooses, after a reasonable time has passed, either store the drapes under Samantha's name and at her expense, reship them to her, or resell them "for Samantha's account." If she did resell them (for what?) she could then subtract what she is owed (any payments made by her not yet refunded plus expenses of the sale) and send the residue on to Samantha.

Beyond following up on one of these options, could Bannin do something else? For instance, if she doesn't hear from Samantha after repeated attempts to contact her, can Bannin just throw the things in the trash or donate them to a local charity? You can make the argument that this would be all right. After all, §2-602(2)(b) only makes her responsible for holding the drapes at Samantha's disposition "for a time sufficient to permit the seller to remove them." Once that time has clearly passed, Bannin can argue she doesn't even have to "hold them with reasonable care." Responsibilities beyond this, she would argue, never applied to her since she is not a merchant. Section 2-604 protects her if she chooses to be nice and take one of the actions listed there, but it doesn't make any of them mandatory.

We might hesitate to advise Bannin she can just toss the drapes, however, because of the problems of what is referred to as improper *post-rejection use* or *exercise of dominion* under §2-602(2)(a), which we explore at some length in response to the next and final question. As a matter of prudence, if Bannin is thinking of ditching the drapes, she should make one final attempt to contact Samantha, in a record this time, warning her of what's in store if she doesn't respond. Better safe than sorry.

d. Mrs. Bannin should not have any problems if she leaves the drapes up for a few days, holding them "at the seller's disposition," but if she just keeps them up indefinitely it could be another story. Section 2-602(2)(a) says that "after rejection any exercise of ownership by the buyer with respect to any commercial unit is wrongful as against the seller." This section does not, of course, say what is the consequence of such "wrongful" behavior, but the courts have looked to §2-606(1)(c) and Comment 4 thereto. A rejection that is followed up by continued use of the goods can turn out to be an ineffective *attempt* to reject and hence an acceptance. Mrs. Bannin's hypothetical situation was inspired by the case of *George v. Fannin*, 588 N.E.2d 195 (Ohio App. 1990), in which Ms. Jennie Fannin was held to have "waived" her rejection and effectively accepted custom-made draperies by continuing to use them for approximately one year after she first complained of "shoddy" workmanship. Apparently they were still hanging in her home even after she had responded to the seller's suit for the purchase price and filed a counterclaim. The trial court had noted that in addition to "continuing to use [the drapes] despite their inadequacy and non-conformity," Ms. Fannin had not followed up her initial request that the drapes be fixed or taken back and never "request[ed] instructions from [the seller] regarding return of the rejected goods." Given the language of §2-602(2)(b) and (c), was the court right to give apparent weight to these factors?

So it certainly would be a good idea for our Mrs. Bannin to take the drapes down and store them if Samantha doesn't come to pick them up fairly soon. But what if she doesn't have any excess closet space to begin with? And what if, in anticipation of getting the new drapes, she had thrown away her old window treatment? Taking down the too-short drapes immediately would put her in blessed conformity with the Code, but would also leave her with totally bare windows and her neighbors peeking in. (We could suggest that she place a tag on the rejected drapes indicating something to the effect that they were hanging on her windows under protest, but would anyone other than a lawyer find this solution agreeable?)

It may be that the result in the *Fannin* case is more easily explained by the courts' belief that Ms. Fannin was being too persnickety or that by her actions she was actually trying to have her drapes and not pay for them too. In other cases, the courts have been more sympathetic to the consumer buyer who rejects but seems to have no choice but to continue making use of the goods for a time. Take *Garfinkel v. Lehman Floor Covering Co.*, 302 N.Y.S.2d 167 (Dist. Ct. Nassau Co. 1969), for example. On March 8 carpeting was installed in the buyer's home. Immediately he noticed an unsightly condition in the carpet and brought it to the seller's attention. Seller claimed to have fixed the problem, but the condition (unsightly "pressure bands") continued. On April 12 the buyer's attorney wrote to the seller rejecting the merchandise and demanding its removal. The seller did not remove the carpeting even after this, and a second certified mailing was made later in August. At the time of trial, the carpeting was still on the floor and still apparently looking pretty bad. Seller argued that this continued use barred what the court termed a "rescission" but which we would probably analyze as a flat-out rejection. The court contrasted the language and intention of §2-602 with the result under earlier law:

> The need for this provision of the Uniform Commercial Code has been apparent in this court for some time. Many cases were brought where a merchant delivered defective merchandise, bulky in character, expensive to transport and store. He then left the defective merchandise and refused to remove it. This placed the consumer in a dilemma. If the consumer removes and returns the goods, it is an expensive proposition. He is out of pocket money, in addition to the loss of the purchase price, in exchange for the gamble of recovering some of it by court action. On the other hand, if he retains the merchandise in his home, he loses [under prior law] the right to rescind the contract and the purchase money is gone. In return he has to seek the right to damages for which he will need expensive expert testimony.
>
> It is the opinion of the court that one of the beneficial purposes intended by the new commercial code was to put the burden on the merchant when the goods are defective and he is given proper notice of the defect. He delivered the goods and it is fair that he should remove them or let them remain at his peril.

This result under the circumstances seems unquestionably correct. What was the buyer supposed to do with all that carpet? Rip it up and leave it in large rolls in the living room? There are, however, other instances of post-rejection use that are more difficult to deal with. Sometimes the question whether to use the goods—even large and bulky goods—may seem more discretionary on the part of the rejecting buyer. A number of cases, not obviously consistent in outcome, have arisen in which the buyer has quickly and unequivocally rejected a car or a mobile home soon after delivery. In theory, it's clear what the buyer should do: Don't drive the car. Don't stay one more minute in the mobile home. Either can be parked somewhere safe and locked up tight. But what is the consumer purchaser supposed to do in such a situation? In almost every instance, a good deal of money (a stiff down payment if not the entire purchase price) is tied up in the goods. The buyer can't just go out and buy another car or trailer as if the first contract didn't exist, waiting until later to get his or her money back from the original seller. Does the rejecting car buyer have to keep taking taxis in order to avoid "waiving" his or her rejection? Does the mobile home buyer have to camp out in a hotel even if he or she has the money to do so? As I have said, there does not appear to be a consistent hard and fast rule on this. The courts tend to say that the buyer's "reasonable" use is okay, but more than this is not. In other words, each situation is going to be judged on its own merits, and we have to expect that other factors, not just the extent of the use, will come into play.

CHAPTER 18

Cure

AN INTRODUCTION TO CURE

Suppose the seller tenders. Suppose further that the buyer has a right to and does reject the goods, citing particular nonconformities in justification of this response. Is that the end of the matter? Maybe, but maybe not. For one thing, in many instances the buyer quite naturally looks to the seller to get things back on track, and the seller may be more than happy to oblige. The buyer still wants or needs the goods promised. He or she sensibly concludes that this particular seller is still either the only potential supplier of just what is wanted or, if not the only one, then at least the supplier best positioned to quickly and effectively fill the order. Plenty of times, a buyer's rightful rejection goes hand in hand with a request that the seller come back soon, but this time with goods conforming to the contract. The buyer still wants to play out this deal with this particular seller. If the seller can and will do so and both parties are eventually satisfied, then all well and good. If the buyer was in fact harmed in some way by the first nonconforming tender—perhaps through some additional but relatively minor expenses occasioned by the delay—then a bit of monetary damages subtracted from the purchase price can make it right.

The examples that we deal with in this chapter start from a different premise. Suppose that, following a rightful rejection, the buyer wants nothing more to do with this seller. He or she is either willing to do without the goods altogether or would prefer to procure them elsewhere. Has the seller nothing to say about this? To be more specific, can the seller claim some *right* to a second chance—that is, to a reasonable opportunity to come back to the buyer with a second tender of conforming goods? Or is the typical contract for purchase and sale so fragile a structure that one nonconforming tender automatically and forever puts an end to any obligation on the buyer's part?

In Code terminology, we ask whether the seller has a right to *cure*. One problem we will encounter is that the word "cure" is never defined in the Code, but at least preliminarily the concept is not that difficult to grasp. And there is some history to the term to which we can attend. The possibility of a seller's *right to cure* was not an entirely new innovation with the coming of Article 2. While there was no provision in the Uniform Sales Act similar to §§2-508, common law in many states had recognized that the seller had such a right at least to some extent. At the same time, it is clear that by including §2-508 and formulating it as they did, the drafters of Article 2 intended to make for a relatively robust and progressive law of cure that went beyond what the common law typically had provided.

Part of the reason for this attitude on the drafters' part has already been suggested. By preserving the perfect tender rule in the language of §2-601, Article 2 set up the possibility of the buyer's using that rule to wriggle out of a deal on the merest pretext or for the most minor infraction on the seller's part. One augmentation to the law of sales that the drafters could and did provide to counteract the potential harshness of the perfect tender rule was a clear articulation of the seller's right to cure in many instances. This returns some power to the hands of the seller to deal with sharp practice on the part of the buyer. One of the questions you should consider as you work through this material is whether cure as provided for in Article 2 pushes the balance too far in the opposite direction. Does the Code's treatment of cure put the buyer in the position of having to continue dealing with a breaching seller for a time beyond what is reasonable and fair? How likely is it under §2-508 that a buyer will eventually be made to accept, pay for, and live with goods with which he or she should not in all justice be saddled?

Your views on cure will depend very much on how you read and how you see the courts administering the provisions of §2-508. You should read that section now. There are some obvious issues that arise. Under what circumstances does the seller have the right to cure? What procedures does the seller have to go through to secure this right? Last but by no means least, what exactly does it mean to "cure" a defective tender? The answer to this last one—what precisely is cure other than a four-letter word?—is not at all obvious. You'll have a chance to explore these issues as you work through the following examples.

EXAMPLES

Examples

1. After testing at a hearing clinic, Mr. Riccardi is told that he would be helped by a hearing aid. The Model A-660 Acousticon is recommended to him. He goes to a store owned by Mr. Bartus where an ear mold is fitted to him and he orders the Model A-660, paying cash in advance. The contract provides for delivery by February 15. On February 2 Bartus calls Riccardi and tells him the hearing aid is ready. Riccardi immediately goes to the store, where he sees that the hearing aid is marked as an "Acousticon Model A-665." Bartus tells him that the Model A-660 has been "modified and improved" and that it is now the A-665. Riccardi rejects the hearing aid, saying that he wants only the Model A-660. Bartus says that he is willing to find and sell him a Model A-660 if that is what he really wants, and tells Riccardi that the Model A-660 could be ready by the following week. Riccardi objects. He tells Bartus, "Forget it. Just give me my money back."
   (a) Does Bartus have to return Riccardi's money immediately? If Bartus does tender a Model A-660 before February 15, what options does Riccardi have?
   (b) How would your analysis of the previous part differ if Bartus's initial tender of the Model A-665 had been on February 14 and, while he was willing to get Riccardi one of the older models, he could not promise it would be ready before February 21? What if Bartus could only suggest to Riccardi that he would do what he could to get a conforming Model A-660, but that he was not sure the model would still be available?
   (c) Suppose that instead of Riccardi's picking up the hearing aid, the parties had agreed that it would be delivered to his home. The Model A-665 is delivered on February 2. Riccardi, seeing that it is not what he ordered, sends it back to Bartus. On February 12 he gets a call from Bartus, who explains why he had sent the "new improved" A-665 and offering to immediately deliver either that model once again or a Model A-660 if Riccardi prefers. Either way, Riccardi can have delivery by February 15. Riccardi tells Bartus to forget about the whole thing. Bartus claims they still have a contract that he, Bartus, can fully honor. Does Riccardi have to accept and pay for some hearing aid from Bartus or else fear being held liable for a breach? Would it make a difference to your answer if Riccardi could show he had arranged to buy a hearing aid from some other store on February 10?

2. Bert, who is in need of a new refrigerator for his home, goes into Selma's Appliance City on a Thursday. There he contracts to buy a certain model,

the Cold Commander, in the color ivory. Selma agrees to deliver the refrigerator the following Tuesday.

(a) As Selma is bringing the boxed refrigerator into his house, Bert notices that the box says that the color is "avocado." Indeed the refrigerator in the box is a greenish avocado color, not at all the refreshing white that he had expected. Selma says, "It turned out that I didn't have any ivory in stock, but one will be coming in a couple of days. You can take the avocado now if you want, and I'll get you the ivory by next week." Bert says, "No way. Forget about it. I'll get my refrigerator someplace else." (As a matter of fact, that morning Bert had seen an ad for a special sale on the Cold Commander at another appliance store.) Selma says, "That's ridiculous. We have a deal. You'll get the ivory by next week. I'm holding you to this deal." Who has the better argument under the Code?

(b) Change the facts in the following way: The box in which the refrigerator was packaged was clearly labelled "ivory." When it was opened to reveal an avocado-colored machine, Selma was as surprised as Bert. Apparently there had been a mix-up at the manufacturer's factory. Selma is extremely apologetic and tells Bert she'll get him an ivory model "as soon as possible." Can Bert call the deal off under these circumstances?

3. Betty buys a color television set at Selma's Appliance City. She takes it home in her car. When she takes it out of its box and first turns it on at home, she is disturbed to find that no matter how she fiddles with the controls, there is a definite reddish tinge to all of the colors on the screen. She takes the set back to Selma's and asks for her money back.

(a) Selma refuses to refund Betty's money, but does offer to immediately give her a new set of identical make and manufacturer. Does Betty have to accept this offer?

(b) Instead of offering a new set, Selma says she will take the set into her repair shop and look at it. She says, "It probably just needs a minor adjustment. I'll fix it up and deliver it to you by the day after tomorrow." Betty would still prefer her money back, but can she insist on getting it?

(c) Suppose instead that Selma had said, "It looks like there's something wrong with the picture tube. But that can be replaced. Leave it here. I'll make the switch and get you back your set by the day after tomorrow." Does your answer to the question change?

(d) Assume that whatever Selma's initial diagnosis, Betty does leave the set for repair. It is returned to her with a note from Selma indicating that only the change of a minor part had been needed. Betty plugs the set in and turns it on. Now all of the colors have a *greenish* hue, which can't be eliminated. Betty lugs the set back to Selma who says, "I think I see the problem. One more adjustment should do it." She tells Betty to leave it with her for another repair. Can Betty insist on simply getting her money back *now?* Would your answer be any different if when Betty gets the set back after Selma's initial repair the color is just fine, but there seems to be something wrong with the sound? Selma offers to make this repair. If your answer in either instance is that Betty is legally obligated to let Selma make the additional repair, you can imagine the hypotheticals that would follow.

Explanations

1. a. This question is based on the well-known case of *Bartus v. Riccardi*, 284 N.Y.S.2d 222 (City Ct. Utica 1967), although I've tidied up the facts somewhat for our purposes. In the actual case, Riccardi wanted to reject the A-665 because of the sound quality and complained that it gave him a headache. But that doesn't matter. The issue here is not whether Riccardi has a right to reject—of course he does. He is under no obligation to accept something other than what he bargained for. The seller, Bartus, however, has the right to cure under §2-508(1). Here the time for performance has not yet expired, and Bartus immediately notifies Riccardi that he will make a conforming tender by February 15. Under §2-508(1), Riccardi must give Bartus a second chance to make a conforming tender before the promised delivery date. If Bartus does tender a good Model A-660 before February 15, Riccardi's options are no different from those of any buyer facing a conforming tender: accept or face the consequences of a wrongful rejection.

   b. Under these facts, Bartus is still probably within his rights if he insists on Riccardi's sticking to the deal and buying a Model A-660 from him, but the answer is not as clear-cut. Bartus will have to look to §2-508(2) for his right to cure. This subsection, granting the seller a right to cure even *beyond* the agreed delivery date, is an extension by the drafters beyond where most courts had been willing to take the common law notion of cure. Necessarily there are several criteria that the seller must meet if he or she is going to take advantage of this right. Reread this subsection carefully. First of all, in the instant case did Bartus tender the A-665 with "reasonable grounds to believe" that it would be acceptable to Riccardi? Comment 2 tells us that the purpose of this subsection is to avoid injustice to the seller by reason of a "surprise rejection by the buyer." Assume Bartus was indeed surprised that Riccardi wouldn't take the "new and improved" A-665. Does his surprise seem reasonable to you? It did to the court in the actual case, which stated:

> The model delivered to the defendant was a newer and improved version of the model that was actually ordered. Of course, the defendant is entitled to receive the model that he ordered even though it may be an older type. But, under the circumstances the plaintiff had reasonable grounds to believe that the newer model would be accepted by the defendant.

A second criterion is that the seller seasonably notify the buyer of his or her intention to cure. Bartus will have no trouble with that here.

Finally, under §2-508(2) Bartus must show that he offered to make a conforming tender within a "further reasonable time." Bartus had originally promised the hearing aid for February 15. Now Riccardi may have to wait until February 21. Is this extension beyond a "further reasonable time"? I'd argue no. Apparently in those days it took some time to calibrate a hearing aid for a buyer's particular needs. If Riccardi were to go to another supplier now and order an A-660, it would probably take at least that long for him to get it. Bartus seems to have a good case for the right to cure in this situation.

Notice that if Riccardi does have to accept tender of the Model A-660 on February 21, some days after he was promised it under the contract, and if he can show monetary damages arising from the lateness, he would have a valid claim against Bartus for breach of the contract of sale. The seller's right to cure does not mean that a later conforming tender is just as good as a perfect tender, only that it must be accepted by the buyer, who is then left with a claim for damages for any harm caused by the initial nonconformity of tender.

If Bartus, the seller, could not assure Riccardi, the buyer, that he would soon make a conforming tender but only that he would try to do so, this would not constitute a "seasonable notice" of the intention to cure. In *Allied Semi-Conductors Int'l, Ltd. v. Pulsar Components Int'l, Inc.*, 907 F. Supp. 618 (E.D.N.Y. 1995), the court held that an effective offer to cure requires more. In particular, the court held that for a seller to insist on its right to cure, it must demonstrate more than its "willingness to cure or [make] an offer to do so"; the willingness or offer is "insufficient in the absence of a present ability to deliver the goods." An interesting case focusing on what exactly a seller must do to cure is *Sinco, Inc. v. Metro-North Commuter R.R. Co.*, 133 F. Supp. 2d 308 (S.D.N.Y. 2001). Metro-North contracted with Sinco for the construction and installation of a "fall-protection system" that would ensure the safety of workers, many of whom would be performing their duties at great heights, during maintenance and renovation of Grand Central Terminal, both inside and out. During one of the first training sessions for Metro-North employees, a worker was examining one of the "sleeves," a crucial part of the system, when it fell apart in his hands. Other sleeves were found to be similarly defective. Training was, needless to say, immediately suspended. Sinco made various offers to make more sturdy sleeves in one way or another, but none of them was considered by the court to constitute sufficient cure. Taking its cue from the *Allied Semi-Conductors* case, it found:

> Sinco's bare offers of potentially curative performance were not enough. The contract called for reliable equipment to protect Metro-North's employees from grave injury or death, and Sinco's equipment had been shown to be unreliable. In order to effectuate a cure, Sinco was obliged to make a conforming tender—that is, to put a fall protection system and proof of its reliability at Metro-North's disposition, leaving it to Metro-North to accept the tender. In essence, Sinco had to take the initiative; it could not shift any part of its burden to Metro-North. It was not enough for Sinco merely to suggest possible solutions.

c. Bartus has seemingly lost his right to cure here by failing to seasonably notify Riccardi of his intention to supply him with the Model A-660. We don't know exactly when Bartus got the return of the Model A-665, but if he didn't try to contact Riccardi until February 12, it is probably too late. This would be true under the language of the section whether or not Riccardi had acted on the assumption that Bartus didn't care to cure. So Riccardi would not have to accept and pay for anything from Bartus, *and* if he has to pay more for a comparable hearing aid from the other store, he should be able to recover the difference in price from Bartus.

2. a. Bert has the better argument. This is clearly a defective tender and Selma has no right to cure under either subsection of §2-508. Subsection (1) is applicable only if the time for performance has not yet expired, and she isn't making any offer to cure by the end of the day on which delivery was promised. What about subsection (2)? Here Selma deliberately tendered a green refrigerator when she knew a white one was expected. There's just no way she can argue she had reason to believe that this would be acceptable. If this were to come out any other way, then a seller like Selma could in effect unilaterally extend the time for performance by making some lame tender and offering cure. That certainly isn't within the contemplation of §2-508. In *Central District Alarm, Inc. v. Hal-Tuc, Inc.*, 886 S.W.2d 210 (Mo. App. 1994), the contract for sale and installation of a video surveillance system specifically called for installation of a new Javelin VCR. When the seller's supplier failed to send the right piece, the seller installed the system with a used JVC brand VCR instead. When the buyer became aware that the equipment was not what was promised and insisted on its right to return the whole system—and when the seller eventually admitted to what it had done—the seller claimed that it had only installed the used model temporarily and offered to

replace it with a new Javelin VCR as soon as one became available. The seller considered this a good offer to cure, but the buyer and the court thought otherwise. There was nothing in the circumstances to indicate that the buyer had "reasonable grounds to believe that a used VCR would be acceptable," even on a temporary basis, "when a new one had been ordered."

It may be that Bert is, in our example, taking advantage of Selma's nonconforming delivery to get a better deal elsewhere, but that doesn't seem particularly unfair. If Selma wants to hold Bert to the deal the two of them struck, she's going to have to tender better than this.

b. This example is meant to explore an important question that still remains about the requirement in §2-508(2) that the "seller had reasonable grounds to believe [the tender] would be acceptable with or without money allowance." Does that include the situation we have here?

We begin with a bit of review. There are a variety of situations where this "reasonable grounds to believe" language becomes relevant. First, there is the case where the seller tenders something he or she knows to be different from what was promised but that he or she could reasonably expect would not be any less valuable or desirable in the eyes of the buyer. This is our Example 1b, where the seller tenders in all good faith a "new and improved" version of what was promised. It seems clear, and the court in the *Bartus* case concluded, that this meets the criterion.

A somewhat different situation is that where the seller tenders the goods knowing of some defect with which the buyer will probably be unhappy, but which the seller wouldn't expect to prompt a rejection because the defect doesn't appear that great or troublesome. If the seller is "reasonable" in this expectation that the buyer won't be a fanatic for details, then the drafters seem to think any rejection would be a "surprise rejection," in the words of Comment 2, and the seller should have the right to cure. That's the whole tenor of that Comment. Suppose, for example, that before making delivery Selma did check that the refrigerator was the right color, but she also saw that one of the shelves was bent slightly out of shape. Rather than call off the delivery, she takes the refrigerator to Bert's home and starts to bring it in. As she does so, she acknowledges the minor problem with one of the shelves but says she'll bring over a replacement the first thing the next day. True, §2-601 and its incorporation of the perfect tender rule would allow Bert to reject the entire refrigerator. But one of the purposes behind §2-508 in general is to move away from such a rigid and formalistic conception of the sales contract. If, as I think would be true in this slightly bent shelf example, Selma has the right to cure, then even if Bert can reject on this basis, it does him little good practically. Selma might have to take the refrigerator back with her out the door, but she will have the right to return with it (now with perfect shelves) the next day and expect an acceptance. Doesn't it just make sense to ask Bert to allow delivery now, even accepting the goods, and accept the cure the next day? (If for some reason the cure is not forthcoming, he can argue for relief under §2-608(1)(a), as we'll see in the next chapter.)

Of course this argument—that the seller would not reasonably expect the buyer to reject a nonconforming tender—only goes so far. It really only works for minor defects, those little annoyances of life with which we are apparently all expected to put up as reasonable men and women. As we saw in Example 2a, the seller cannot reasonably count on the buyer's accepting just about any old thing merely because it's been delivered to his or her door.

So much for review. What each of these previous situations had in common was that the seller was himself or herself *actually aware* of the nonconformity at the time of tender. In the hypothetical we must now confront, the seller is not herself aware of the nonconformity. Selma will argue for the right to cure under §2-508(2), saying that she had every reason to believe she was tendering just what the contract called for and what Bert expected. She understands Bert wanting to reject the refrigerator when it turns out to be the wrong color, and in fact she doesn't argue against his right to reject, but she claims that the rejection is as much a surprise to her as to anyone and that §2-508(2) gives her the right to cure. Bert argues that this case does not fall within the language of that subsection. How in heaven's name could Selma have "reasonable grounds to believe" he would accept a green refrigerator when he had contracted for a white one?

There has actually been a good deal of debate among the commentators as to whether §2-508(2) allows for cure in such a situation, where the seller apparently has no reason to know that what he or she is delivering is nonconforming in any way. Phrased another way, is cure beyond the contracted time of performance (which is the concern of §2-508(2)) limited to those cases where the seller had "reason to believe" that a particular nonconformity *of which the seller was aware* would not provoke a rejection? Put this way, I find it hard to see why §2-508(2) should be read so narrowly, but not all authorities have seen it this way. In particular, Professor Nordstrom in his treatise on Sales argues against allowing cure when the seller is unaware of the defect. Perhaps it's all in how favorably you look on the whole notion of cure and how easily you think it can get out of control and work oppression on the buyer.

What case law there is on the matter, I think it fair to say, is supportive of Selma's position and a broader reading of the subsection. Particularly important in this regard is the decision of the New York Court of Appeals in *T.W. Oil, Inc. v. Consolidated Edison*, 443 N.E.2d 932 (N.Y. 1982), which addressed the question directly:

> [W]e are asked . . . to decide whether a seller who, acting in good faith and without knowledge of any defect, tenders nonconforming goods to a buyer who properly rejects them, may avail itself of the cure provision of subdivision (2) of section 2-508 of the Uniform Commercial Code.

The facts were not in dispute. In January 1974, in the midst of a fuel shortage caused by an oil embargo of certain oil-producing nations, T.W. Oil bought for itself a cargo of fuel oil whose sulfur content was represented to be no higher than 1.0 percent. While the oil was still en route to the United States in the tanker *Khasmin*, T. W. Oil received a certificate from the refinery at which it had been processed stating that the sulfur content was in fact only .52 percent, better than was required. T. W. Oil contracted to sell this oil to Con Ed, a utility company, under a contract describing the oil as having a .5 percent sulfur content. (Both parties acknowledged a trade custom by which contracting parties rounded off specifications of sulfur content at, for instance, 1.0 percent, .5 percent, or .3 percent.) In the course of negotiations, T. W. Oil became aware that Con Ed was authorized to buy and burn oil with a sulfur content of up to 1.0 percent and would even mix oils containing more and less to stay within that figure. This contract with Con Ed called for delivery to take place between January 24 and January 30. The *Khasmin* discharged its oil into Con Ed's storage tanks on January 25. Independent testing reported a sulfur content of .92 percent. Con Ed seasonably and reasonably rejected the tender on February 14. The parties promptly entered into negotiation to adjust the price. By February 20 T. W. Oil had offered a price reduction "roughly responsive" (in the court's words) to the difference in sulfur content. Con Ed, however, although it could have used the oil, "rejected this proposition out of hand. It was insistent on paying no more than the latest prevailing price, which, in the volatile market that then existed, was some 25% below the level which prevailed when it agreed to buy the oil." The next day T. W. Oil offered to cure with a substitute shipment of conforming oil scheduled to arrive within a few days. This too was refused by Con Ed. T. W. Oil resold the oil from the *Khasmin* at a substantial loss. It sued for the difference and was awarded a judgment of $1,385,512.83. The Court of Appeals upheld this award against various challenges by Con Ed, including among others the argument that it was within its rights to refuse both of these offers to cure. The court, applying §2-508(2), found there to have been ample evidence supporting the trial court's determination that under the circumstances the seller had "reason to believe" the original tender would be acceptable. It had itself purchased the oil under a contract stating it to be .5 percent oil and had a refinery certificate reporting it to have a content within this trade description. Furthermore, the seller knew Con Ed could burn oil with a content up to 1.0 percent so that, with appropriate price adjustment, the *Khasmin* oil would have been suitable even when it did, to the surprise of both parties, have a content of .92 percent. The court considered, but was not at all sympathetic to, Con Ed's argument (following Professor Nordstrom) that the right to cure under subsection (2) is reserved for those cases where the seller *knowingly* makes a nonconforming tender that it has reason to believe will not be rejected. You can see how if this argument were to have been adopted for New York, the result in the instant case would have been to allow Con Ed's escape via the perfect tender route from an unfavorable bargain that (because of intervening changes in the market) it later regretted. The court's conclusion:

> [I]f seasonable notice be given, a seller [who does not himself have knowledge of any defect] may offer to cure the defect within a reasonable period beyond the time when the contract was to be performed so long as it acted in good faith and with a reasonable expectation that the original goods would be acceptable to the buyer.

Of course, even if you accept the *T.W. Oil* result, you can jiggle the facts around a bit to get some tougher questions. What if, in our hypothetical, it turned out that the previous day, Selma had experienced a similar problem with a mislabeled refrigerator that she had herself received in the same delivery from the same manufacturer? Would she be "reasonable" in delivering this one to Bert without first looking inside the box to make sure it was correctly labelled for color? What if the box was such that you could, albeit with some difficulty, get a look at the color of the item inside? Would she still fall within the protection of §2-508(2)?

3. a. Betty the buyer's story is loosely based on another well-known case, *Wilson v. Scampoli*, 228 A.2d 848 (D.C. Ct. App. 1967). (You can see that the controversy arose back in those olden days, still remembered by some of us, as color television was just being introduced, when television sets still had picture tubes and the user had to do a lot of fiddling with "color controls" or "settings" in the hope of getting a picture that was even minimally lifelike. Ask your parents. Or your grandparents.) The first question here is whether Selma has the right to cure at all. The answer would seem to be yes. Even assuming she has to rely on §2-508(2), the analysis of the previous question and

the result of *T.W. Oil* put Selma within that provision's reach. In fact the *Wilson* case, decided much earlier than *T.W. Oil*, assumed the same result with no discussion:

> A retail dealer would certainly expect and have reasonable grounds to believe that merchandise like color television sets, new and delivered as crated at the factory, would be acceptable as delivered and that, if defective in some way, he would have the right to substitute a conforming tender.

The real problem in this and the questions that follow is what exactly a seller may do to "cure." What can the seller insist the buyer take as a "conforming delivery"? We start with the easy (or at least the easiest) example. If seller is willing to immediately supply the buyer with identical factory-fresh goods, it's hard to imagine that this wouldn't be a good cure. At least this would be true with an ordinary TV set, where one direct-from-the-factory unit is assumed to be no better or worse than another. Compare this to the situation where the subject of the sale is one of a set of prints of a work ("Le Minotauromachie") by Picasso. In *David Tunick, Inc. v. Kornfeld*, 838 F. Supp. 848 (S.D.N.Y. 1993), the buyer contracted to buy a particular print of the work that the seller represented bore the master's signature. When the validity of the signature on the particular print was called into question, the seller offered to substitute a different print of the same work. Was this an effective offer to cure? Reviewing general reference works on art collection, the court took note that "two prints from a series produced by an artist each possess distinctive qualities that may impact their aesthetic and economic value" even when they are first produced, and that furthermore, "prints . . . are fragile and their value can be diminished by the manner in which they are treated over time." Thus, the court concluded, "each print is, by definition, unique," and hence, "there can be no exact substitute for a given print purchased by a collector." The court concluded that therefore, as a matter of law, when works of art such as this are involved, §2-508 does not "obligate a buyer to accept in lieu of a nonconforming print, a substitute print from the same series of prints."

Of course, as you will always be able to do when discussing cure even of your run-of-the-mill TV set, you can fairly easily add to the facts and create a hypo where the answer is not so clear-cut. What if Betty does accept this second set and finds the same "reddish tinge" when she takes it home? Can she now storm back into Selma's, drop this second set on the counter, and demand her money back? Or will she have to accept a third set and Selma's assurances that her string of bad luck is about to end? What if Selma offers her this third set but agrees to test it out in her store before sending Betty home with it? Would it make any difference to your answer if Betty had by this time read an article in a consumer magazine reporting that this model of color television set has been plagued with color problems? What if, when Betty took the second set home and turned it on, the color was just fine *but* there was some problem with the vertical hold that she couldn't clear up? My guess is that with your own experience as a consumer, you can easily think of any number of other possibilities and that in fact you were doing so as you worked through these questions.

What you begin to see (and perhaps worry about) is how easily the concept of the right to cure—perfectly understandable as a protection for sellers against harsh and unfair results—has the potential for turning on buyers. If the seller can get away with too much in the name of cure, the buyer may be forced to accept and pay for goods that are not at all as good as he or she contracted for or had the right to expect. The question becomes, of course, what is "too much" for the seller to assert in the name of cure.

As a matter of fact, in *Wilson* the court appeared to assume that substitution of a new set would have been good cure. The problem was that the buyer would have none of this—not even the seller's offer to take the set back for possible repair. On which see the example that follows.

b. Betty will probably have a tough time resisting this offer to cure. There is the possibility that only a "minor adjustment" will be made. Selma is offering to have it done promptly and is even offering to deliver it so that Betty doesn't have to make another trek to the store. In *Wilson* the court, having reviewed some earlier cases, declared:

> While these cases provide no mandate to require the buyer to accept patchwork goods or substantially repaired articles in lieu of flawless merchandise, they do indicate that minor repairs or reasonable adjustments are frequently the means by which an imperfect tender may be cured.

This language, or something quite like it, is found in a number of cases, and is a good summary of prevailing thought on the matter. Betty would run a big risk if she refused Selma's offer to make what might turn out to be a minor adjustment at this stage.

c. Even Betty would probably have to accept cure if it involved only a "minor repair." Once the necessary repair is more involved, she is most likely safe in refusing to accept Selma's offer. A leading case is *Zabriskie Chevrolet, Inc. v. Smith*, 240 A.2d 195 (N.J. Super. 1968), which we also saw in the previous chapter. Recall that Zabriski sold the Smiths a new 1966 Chevy, which began to stall, sputter, and wheeze less than a mile from the dealership. Soon it refused to go into "drive" at all.

Mrs. Smith and her husband were barely able to get it back to their house. The next day, the seller sent a wrecker to the Smiths' home and brought the Chevy back to his repair shop, where it was determined that the transmission was defective. He replaced it with a transmission from some other vehicle then on his showroom floor, and offered the auto up to the Smiths once again. They refused to take it and asserted their right to cancel the sale. The seller brought suit against Smith, but his action got nowhere. The court held (surprise?) that the auto as delivered to the Smiths was defective. Also, as we saw in the last chapter, the court held that they had not accepted the auto simply by driving it off the lot. What of Zabriskie's asserted offer to cure by letting the Smiths have the car with the replaced transmission? The court thought little of this argument as well. Acknowledging that the nature of what will suffice as cure is nowhere laid out in the Code and hence must be judged by the facts of each case, the court was quick to conclude that §2-508 does not "contemplate the tender of a new vehicle with a substituted transmission, not from the factory and of unknown lineage from another vehicle in [seller's] possession." Note also the language in *Wilson* that there is no obligation on the buyer's part to take "patchwork goods or substantially repaired articles."

Would it have mattered to the *Zabriskie* court if the seller had shown that the substituted transmission was in fact of the same quality or even better than the transmission originally in the Chevy? What if the seller had evidence to suggest that such a new transmission, especially when individually installed in a dealership's repair department, is actually more likely to be defect-free than a transmission that is installed as one of a great number running down a manufacturer's assembly line? It's at least possible that this is true. (We've all heard the assertion—although I don't know if it is correct—that a broken bone once healed is stronger than it had been before the break.) It's impossible to know of course whether any of this would have made the slightest difference to the result in *Zabriskie*, but consider the following language from the opinion:

> For a majority of people the purchase of a new car is a major investment, rationalized by the peace of mind that flows from its dependability and safety. Once their faith is shaken, the vehicle loses not only its real value in their eyes, but becomes an instrument whose integrity is substantially impaired and whose operation is fraught with apprehension. The attempted cure in the present case was ineffective.

This language became the origin of the *shaken faith doctrine* that is the focus of the next question.

d. We are entering the fringes of what is and what is not *cure* here. Each case necessarily will have to be decided on its own facts, and attempts at further explication tend to fall flat. Some commentators and cases have been taken to suggest that a seller can in any event have at most one chance to cure. If the second tender isn't "perfect," this reasoning goes, then that's it for the seller. It isn't that simple, however. Some goods are very complex, and a few minor adjustments might be perfectly understandable and to be expected before they work just right. Certainly there's nothing in §2-508 that limits the seller to one attempted cure. And in any event, would the rule apply to a single cure of any one defect as it appears or to one cure overall? Couldn't Selma here claim she did in fact successfully cure the "red tinge" problem? Now there's a second problem, a "greenish hue," which she's also willing to cure.

At the same time, even if the seller is willing and able to clear up every problem that crops up, eventually enough must be enough. Look again at the "shaken faith" language from *Zabriskie*. How would you feel about buying a new TV and having to have its color system and its sound system both repaired right at the outset? You could, of course, philosophize about broken bones once healed being all the stronger, but do people really react that way? Eventually the buyer expecting a brand new item is left feeling he or she is being asked to settle for "patched up" goods. The courts, often invoking the language we've seen in *Wilson* and *Zabriskie*, have on the shaken faith rationale allowed buyers eventually to reject repeated offers of cure, even if each attempt at cure is in itself successful.

On the other hand, not all courts are so quick to embrace the shaken faith doctrine. Recall *Sinco, Inc. v. Metro-North Commuter R.R. Co.*, discussed earlier, the case of the frighteningly defective safety gear intended for use by workers high atop Grand Central Station. Metro-North argued that the initial delivery of the defective equipment "was so severe a breach that it irremediably undermined [its] confidence in the fall-protection system, rendering futile any attempt at cure." Among other things, Metro-North's unions had "repeatedly expressed a complete lack of confidence in Sinco and its product" and that their members were not of a mind to use the system. If ever a situation called for application of the shaken faith notion, this would seem to be it, but the court held otherwise:

> If Sinco had timely tendered a cure, Metro-North would have been able to assess the reasons for the failure [of the initial tender] and the reliability of the cure. If, objectively, the cure was shown to be reliably safe, Metro-North would have been obligated to accept the cure, despite, perhaps, any lingering subjective misgivings of its employees.

As we have seen, however, Sinco was held not to have tendered a cure, so the employees never had to put their faith in a Sinco system. By the time the renovation work began, Metro-North had removed the Sinco installation and purchased an entirely different fall-protection system from another contractor—at a far greater price. The court sent the case to a magistrate judge for an investigation of the amount of damages owed to Metro-North.

Two other points about cure deserve noting before we exit this chapter. First of all, it has been suggested at times that only "minor" defects can be cured under §2-508. Besides the fact that there is no support in the language of the section for such a proposition, it turns out not to make much sense. Some major defects can be quite easily and successfully cured. A major appliance that is delivered in the wrong color can be quickly replaced by one in the right color and all is right with the world. Some "minor" defects seemingly never can be cured no matter how hard the seller tries. Most of us have had experience with a little grinding noise coming from "somewhere under the hood" that just can't be made to go away. We might as well face the fact. Cure is not a topic that lends itself to bright line rules, much as we might wish that were the case.

A second concluding point: One major question about cure has not been dealt with at all in this chapter. There is much controversy over whether the seller has a right to cure when the buyer is not rejecting the goods but is rather revoking his or her acceptance of them. Naturally enough this must wait for our discussion of revocation of acceptance, which not coincidentally happens to be the topic of the next chapter. We'll have to pick up on cure again at the end of that chapter.

CHAPTER 19

Revocation of Acceptance

AN INTRODUCTION TO REVOCATION

As we've already seen, the buyer's act of acceptance, if it occurs, is a watershed event in the performance of any sales contract. Not least among the consequences of acceptance is that the buyer may never thereafter reject the goods (§2-607(2)). Once you've accepted, even if you've accepted goods that subsequently turn out to be nothing like what was promised, you are forever barred from rejecting. So what is a buyer to do who has accepted goods only later to find out exactly how defective the stuff is that he or she now holds? One possibility is to look for monetary relief. The buyer will have to pay at the contract rate for the goods accepted, of course (§2-607(1)), but may be able to subtract from what is owed a significant amount for damages calculated on a breach of warranty theory. See §2-714 and the discussion in Chapter 27. Following this approach leaves the buyer owning and in possession of the goods, albeit having paid less for them than what had originally been called for under the contract. In many instances, keeping the goods at a reduced price may satisfy the buyer as much as he or she could be satisfied given the situation, but there obviously will be times when this result is not anything the buyer would choose to live with. In light of the deficiencies now apparent with the goods, the buyer has no use or desire for them whatsoever and wishes he or she had never accepted at all. Money damages may help a bit, but being told to keep and pay something—anything—for the defective goods is equivalent to rubbing salt in the buyer's wounds. Is there nothing else to be done?

Section 2-607(2) clearly states that the buyer's right to reject is lost forever at the moment of acceptance, but it also contains a tantalizing reference to the possibility that the buyer may, at least under certain conditions, later *revoke acceptance*. The reference is followed up in §2-608 with a full-blown treatment of the buyer's right to revoke acceptance in whole or in part. This chapter deals with that section and with that right. We will get into a series of examples plumbing the depths of §2-608 in short order, but first a couple of points.

The first question you might have is why this topic deserves a whole section of Article 2, and a whole chapter of this book, of its own. Might not a revocation of acceptance be just a rejection by another name? Article 2 says you can't reject after an acceptance, but you can revoke, so what's the difference? If there is one thing you will see in working through this material, it is that the Code drafters were not just playing with words; they definitely meant for there to be a marked difference in approach to and treatment of a rejection and a revocation. At least in theory, a buyer who accepts is meant to have a harder time justifying a revocation of acceptance than he or she would have had in carrying out a rejection at the first opportunity. This leads to the obvious question of why this should be. As you consider the questions and form your own analysis, you may come to some understanding of why the drafters thought it right to place additional hurdles in the way of the buyer attempting to revoke an acceptance. Without giving away too much of the game, I might initially note one thing: While not invariably true, typically goods that are the subject of an attempted revocation have been in the hands of the buyer for some time. They have seen service, often for a fairly long stretch, and are far from brand spanking new.

Before going on, let's also note how the situation stands if a buyer does first accept then revoke acceptance and is justified in doing so. What are the consequences, in law and in practice, of a rightful revocation? Almost certainly the goods are at that moment in the buyer's possession. Section 2-608(3) states, "A buyer who so revokes has the same rights and duties with regard to the goods involved as if he had rejected them." We have to refer back to §§2-602 through 2-604. The buyer is under a duty to hold the goods "with reasonable care at the seller's disposition." In some cases, of course, a merchant buyer may in addition be obligated to follow the seller's instructions about returning the goods or disposing of them for the seller's account. Most often, however, the buyer just holds on to them and waits for the seller to come and pick them up. When the seller does come around, is the buyer obligated to hand them over? That depends on the circumstances. If the buyer has made no payments to the seller, he or she must allow the seller to retake possession. But think of a situation in which a buyer has already paid for the goods. She wants to return them—she wants never to see them again—but she also wants to see her money returned. Does she have to let the goods go in exchange for the seller's *promise* to return her payments at some later date? Article 2 provides, in §2-711(3), that the buyer in this instance has a "security interest" in the goods for certain payments made and may "hold such goods" pending repayment by the seller. We do not treat in this book all the nuances of security interests, but it should be clear that this provision gives an aggrieved buyer some much needed leverage in order to get payments returned.

Say the buyer has chosen to revoke acceptance, the goods are back in the seller's possession, and the buyer has recovered any payments already made. Now at least have we come to the end of the whole sordid affair? No, not if the buyer is also claiming that some additional damage was caused to him or her because of the seller's failure to live up to the contract. The drafters introduced this new term, "revocation of acceptance," primarily to distinguish it from the more traditional concept of *rescission*. If the parties to a contract "rescind" their agreement, this is often taken to mean in effect that both renounce any and all rights under that agreement. The deal is undone. There is no longer any contract to enforce. Distinguish this from the case where the buyer has successfully revoked acceptance of goods under Article 2. The buyer has *not* waived and may still enforce any claim for damages to which he or she is entitled under the terms of the contract and the provisions of the Article. See Comment 1 to §2-608. To be fully vindicated, a buyer who has accepted what turn out to be nonconforming goods may, and often will, be perfectly reasonable in first revoking acceptance, getting his or her money back, and then following up with an action on the contract for an appropriate measure of damages. But we leave damages to another time. The questions here all focus on the revocation itself—whether it is permissible, how and when it is to be done, and so on. The answers to all of these are (supposedly) to be found in §2-608.

Examples

EXAMPLES

1. Alice buys a new car from Sam's Auto Sales. The contract calls for the car to be equipped with a special "racing package," which is intended to soup up the engine to a considerable degree. When Alice goes to pick up the car, she discovers that the special equipment has not been installed. There is simply the regular engine. Sam tells her the special package is "on order" and that he will be able to install it as soon as it arrives. Alice takes the car on that understanding. Several months later, she still hasn't heard from Sam, so she calls him. He tells her that he has since found out that the manufacturer no longer makes any kind of racing package for her model of car. Does she have the right to revoke her acceptance because of this?

2. Beth also buys a car from Sam. When she picks it up and drives it away, it appears from her inspection to be just what she ordered. Two weeks

later, she begins to notice that the car is riding much less smoothly. A mechanic tells her that the engine was never mounted properly and that it is beginning to work itself loose from the chassis. The shaking of the engine has already caused serious damage to the basic framework of the car, so that just tightening a few bolts will not solve the problem. Can Beth revoke her acceptance against Sam?

3. Carol is another buyer from Sam. She ordered a car with a dark blue interior. When she goes to pick it up, she discovers the car's interior is a pale blue. She says nothing and drives the car away. Two weeks later, she realizes that she really does not like the pale blue as much as the dark. She drives the car back to Sam's, where she insists that he take the car back and refund her money. Is Sam obligated to do as she demands?

4. Finally, we meet Diana, who also buys a car from Sam. Two days after picking the car up from the dealership, she runs over some glass and gets a flat tire. She opens up the covered well in the trunk where the manual tells her the spare tire is to be found. It turns out there is no spare tire in the space. Can she revoke on this basis?

5. Bailey, a lawyer who fancies himself something of an experienced world traveler, is searching for a new printer to go with his computer system. He goes to Sylvester's Computer City, where he looks at various printers and fiddles around with those on display. He looks at the Phaserjet 1000, which in his fiddling he discovers is even able to print the symbol for the Italian lira along with all kinds of other quirky characters. He buys the Phaserjet from Sylvester. Two days later, Sylvester delivers a Phaserjet 1000 fresh in a box from the factory to Bailey's home. Bailey sets the printer up and it works perfectly well. Several months later he is showing his new printer to a friend (who has suggested that he paid too much for what he got), when he tries to print out a document that includes the lira symbol. This symbol won't print out. He calls Sylvester to complain. Sylvester tells him that manufacturers sometimes make minor changes in a model after its introduction, and that this is what has happened here. The version of the Phaserjet 1000 that Bailey received was an upgrade from the original version on display and has "increased functionality" in all sorts of ways, including the ability to print out in all fonts the symbol for the unitary European currency unit, the euro. In fact, Sylvester tells Bailey, he is finding that the most recent version of the Phaserjet with its "enhanced character set" helps him sell this particular printer. Several computer magazines have commented favorably about this upgrade of the Phaserjet 1000. Apparently in the alteration, the lira, which is after all no longer a current form of currency, got lost in the shuffle. "But after all," Sylvester points out, "the lira is now ancient history and nothing that we find people seem to care about any more."

(a) On these facts can Bailey revoke his acceptance of the printer?

(b) Would your answer to the previous question be any different if Bailey was not a world-traveling member of the bar, but instead a writer on Italian economic history who had found in the past his work often referring to Italian lira and that he had purposefully checked out the model Phaserjet at Sylvester's for this symbol before making his decision on what to buy? Does it matter to your answer whether Sylvester knew of Bailey's special interest in the lira symbol at the time the sale was made?

6. Bill buys a mobile home from Trailer-O-Rama of Springfield. The unit, which the contract specifies be equipped with built-in heating and air-conditioning, is delivered to Bill's land and set in place in November. During the winter months, the heating unit works with no problems. In May, when the temperature first goes above 80 degrees, Bill turns on the air-conditioning. Air blows out, but it is not cold, or even cool.

(a) Bill immediately calls a mechanic to check the air conditioner. It turns out that there is no cooling system at all; behind the air-conditioning panel there is just a hollow space. Can Bill revoke his acceptance of the trailer?

(b) Suppose that instead of immediately calling in a mechanic in May, Bill does nothing. By the next day, it is cool again. When a heat wave strikes in June, he once again turns on the air conditioner. Again it blows only tepid air. Now he checks out the unit and for the first time discovers the lack of a cooling system. Could Bill revoke under this set of facts?

7. Return to the facts of Example 1. Alice buys a car from Sam that is to be equipped with a special racing package, but several months later, it becomes apparent he will never be able to provide this feature.

(a) Would it affect her ability to revoke if during the intervening months Alice had repainted the car a different color?

(b) Even if Alice had not repainted, could Sam argue against revocation by pointing to the fact that Alice has already subjected the car to several months of hard use? In fact the finish has already been noticeably affected and the tires are considerably worn.

(c) Assume that Alice does have the right to revoke her acceptance of the car. She sends Sam an email that says, "I am terribly upset that the car you've sold to me cannot be furnished as you promised! I expect you to make it up to me in some way." Has she effectively revoked?

(d) Now assume that Alice has a clear right to revoke and further that she does in fact give a clear and unequivocal notice of revocation. What does she do now? Can she continue to drive the car or must she immediately put it in storage?

(e) Assume that Alice does continue to drive the car for another two months before Sam is eventually convinced by his lawyer (who is learned in the Code) that he must acknowledge her right to revoke. He offers to take the car back. Alice, who paid cash up front, wants the full purchase price returned. Is Sam obligated to return to her all that she had paid?

8. Refer back to Example 5b. Bailey, the economic historian, rightly revokes acceptance of the Phaserjet printer because it cannot print out the symbol for the now defunct Italian lira. Soon after he receives the notice of revocation from Bailey, Sylvester makes the following offer: He will send an employee over to Bailey's home to replace a computer chip in the printer. The result will be a Phaserjet just like the one Bailey initially tried out in Sylvester's store. Must Bailey accept this offer, or can he simply ignore it, return the printer, and get his purchase price back?

Explanations

1. Yes, Alice has the right to revoke under §2-608(1)(a). Check that she meets all the criteria. As we saw in Chapter 17, an auto purchaser does not accept the car the minute it is driven off the lot, but in this case, enough time has passed to make it hard to argue Alice never accepted. I think we can assume that the absence of the special equipment is a substantial impairment of the value of the car to her. (Soon we'll see that "substantial impairment" isn't always so clear-cut, but here there seems no real question.) Finally, she accepted the car "on the reasonable assumption that its nonconformity would be cured and it has not been seasonably cured."

   So Alice has the *right* to revoke. *How* she must act if she wants to make an effective revocation is another matter, which we pick up again in Example 7. It's important to keep distinct in your mind the difference between a buyer *having the right* to revoke and his or her *actually having done so*. It's probably fair to assume that in most instances where buyers could legitimately revoke, they actually don't, but ask instead for some other form of relief—or just forget about the whole thing, living with the problem, grumbling to themselves, and getting that much more cynical about life.

2. Yes, Beth can revoke, here under §2-608(1)(b). She accepted the car without discovery of the nonconformity and, she'd argue, the acceptance was "reasonably induced . . . by the difficulty of discovery before acceptance." It may be true that a trained mechanic could have spotted the trouble even before he or she drove the car off Sam's lot, but I doubt many car buyers could or do make this thorough an inspection. This type of so-called latent defect is just what subpart (b) is meant to address.

Note also that even if the defect were something that *would* normally be spotted by a reasonable buyer making a reasonable inspection at the time of delivery, if the inspection is cut short by the seller's assurances, the buyer will not be barred from revocation. See Comment 3.

3. No. What Carol wants is to revoke her acceptance, and there is nothing in §2-608(1) that provides her the right to do this. She would have been perfectly within her rights to reject the car at the time of delivery because of the incorrect color, but now that she's accepted it, she isn't going to be able to undo the deed. (I'd say it's too late for her to reject on this basis even though only two weeks had intervened. Any arguments?) So she is going to have to pay for the car and pay at the contract price. Can she argue for a set-off because the car's interior was not the correct color? It's hard to see how, or if so, how it will amount to much in the way of money. This just points out once again how important it is for the buyer to take the acceptance/rejection decision seriously. Often there is no turning back. For a case that hinges on this point, that "revocation is unavailable for a nonconformity known to the buyer at the time of acceptance," see *Moore & Moore General Contractors, Inc. v. Basepoint, Inc.*, 485 S.E.2d 131 (Va. 1997).

4. This is a more difficult case. The question is whether the fact that a spare tire turns out to be missing from a new automobile "substantially impairs" the value of that car to Diana. While in the particular instance she can rightly be annoyed, it is doubtful that this slight defect is a "substantial" nonconformity. This language was put into §2-608(1) with the express purpose of tempering the potential severity of the perfect tender rule, which as we've seen, survives at least in form in §2-601 and is operative when the issue is the right to reject. The drafters wanted revocation to be possible when the defects that never get cured (subpart (a)) or later turn up (subpart (b)) are serious and materially affect the value of the goods to the purchaser. Once the goods have been accepted, minor defects are to be compensated for through monetary damages. So Diana isn't left without a remedy altogether. She can sue for the value of the tire and, presumably, her consequential damages of having to call a tow truck or whatever, but the lack of the tire does not give her the right to undo the deal and return the car.

   There are, as you might expect, a number of cases working over the "substantial impairment" standard, and they don't allow for distillation into a nice, neat rule. The easiest cases are those that find (or simply assume) the criterion has been met because there is found to be a major defect and it cannot easily be cured. See, for example, Beth's problem in Example 2. At the other extreme are those situations where the defect is minor (some would say trivial) and can quickly and effectively be cured, making the product as good as new. Such would seem to be Diana's case here, where the only nonconformity is the lack of a spare tire. The dealer can send over a spare tire of the type that was to come with the car—and that's that. At least one would think that revocation would not be available here. But consider *Colonial Dodge, Inc. v. Miller*, 362 N.W.2d 704 (Mich. 1985), the case that inspired this hypothetical. In April 1976, Mr. Miller ordered a new Dodge Royal Monaco station wagon equipped with a heavy-duty trailer package with extra-wide tires. He picked it up on May 28. The next day, his wife noticed that the new station wagon did not have a spare tire. Mr. Miller notified the dealership the next morning and insisted on having a spare tire. He was told none was then available. He immediately stopped payment on the checks he had tendered to pay for the vehicle and told the dealer that it could be picked up from in front of his home. It turned out that the tires were in short supply due to a labor strike. A tire did become available and was offered to Mr. Miller some months later. Meanwhile the car, which had been left sitting with only a temporary registration outside of Miller's home, had eventually been towed by the police to another dealership. Colonial Dodge sued for the purchase price of the car. The Michigan Court of Appeals determined that there had been a valid acceptance of the car and furthermore that there was no substantial impairment sufficient to justify a revocation of that acceptance. On further appeal (by now eight years have passed), the Michigan Supreme Court reversed. Because the parties had stipulated to the fact of an acceptance, the Supreme Court was left to decide on the revocation issue. It stated:

> In order to give effect to the statute, a buyer must show that the nonconformity has a special devaluing effect on him and that the buyer's assessment of it is factually correct. In this case, the defendant's concern with safety is evidenced by the fact that he ordered the special package which included special tires. The defendant's occupation demanded that he travel extensively, sometimes in excess of 150 miles per day on Detroit freeways, and often in the early morning hours. Mr. Miller testified that he was afraid of a tire going flat on a Detroit freeway at 3 A.M. Without a spare, he testified, he would be helpless until morning business hours. The dangers attendant upon a stranded motorist are common knowledge, and Mr. Miller's fears are not unreasonable. . . .
>
> We hold that under the circumstances the failure to include the spare tire as ordered constituted a substantial impairment in value to Mr. Miller, and that he could properly revoke his acceptance under the U.C.C.

Two members of the court offered separate dissents, which you may want to read. You can decide for yourself with whom you would have voted. Isn't the real problem here that Miller's better claim would have been that he never accepted the car in the first place, but that this argument somehow got stipulated away?

Another set of cases of which you should be aware involve a buyer's attempt to revoke where the defect initially may have seemed trivial but where repeated attempts to cure by the seller prove unsuccessful. In *Capitol Cadillac Olds, Inc. v. Roberts*, 813 S.W.2d 287 (Ky. 1991), for example, the Kentucky Supreme Court was confronted with the case of an Oldsmobile Calais that when stopped on a steep incline and put into park made an annoying "grinding noise." This problem was discovered by the buyers soon after they took possession. During the next six months, the car was repeatedly returned to the dealership for repair of this problem, but all efforts were unsuccessful. The court ruled that the question of substantial impairment was one best left to the trier of fact and that in the particular case, the persistence of the grinding noise, even if it was heard only in unusual circumstances, supported the jury's finding of a revocation. In reaching this conclusion, the court quoted with approval the following lines from that well-known New Jersey case we encountered in each of the last two chapters, *Zabriskie Chevrolet, Inc. v. Smith*, 240 A.2d 195 (N.J. Super. 1968):

> For a majority of people the purchase of a new car is a major investment, rationalized by the peace of mind that flows from its dependability and safety. Once their faith is shaken, the vehicle loses not only its real value in their eyes, but becomes an instrument whose integrity is substantially impaired and whose operation is fraught with apprehension.

Other courts have cited *Zabriskie* and invoked its shaken faith approach in the revocation context.

Even if the seller is able to cure each and every defect as it presents itself, and even if every defect is in and of itself not that significant, the cumulative effect can surely be a substantial impairment of the value of the goods to the perfectly reasonable buyer. After all, there comes a time, as one court has well noted, after which "enough is enough." *Rester v. Morrow*, 491 So. 2d 204 (Miss. 1986). In another case, a trial court judge in New York's Nassau County concluded that the seller of a restaurant computer system that was unable to get the system functioning properly after several months and more than 48 occasions on which the buyer had contacted it about problems had been given sufficient unsuccessful "*bytes* at the apple" to repair so as to justify the buyer's revocation. *The Inn Between, Inc. v. Remanco Metropolitan, Inc.*, 662 N.Y.S.2d 1011 (Dist. Ct. Nassau Co. 1997) (emphasis, and pun, in original).

5. a. This strikes me as a case where the admitted nonconformity — recall the printer should conform to the model under §2-313(1)(c) — does not "substantially impair" the printer's value to Bailey. You see the importance of the substantial impairment requirement. Bailey could have refused to accept this printer initially, but he doesn't have the

right to revoke now. You should consider, if you have not already done so, why the drafters thought it appropriate to make the standard for revocation different from that for rejection. As I suggested in the introductory material, because revocations generally come much further down the road and after the goods have been in use for some time, they will naturally tend to be much more like used goods, having suffered some amount of wear and tear associated with a period of regular use, than new goods. The right of revocation is reserved for the more egregious cases, and those where money damages are not likely to give satisfaction even to the most reasonable of buyers. Is there any value to be served by giving Bailey the right to back out of this purchase just because the printer can't print this one character? Not under these facts. This question is, of course, a set-up for the one that follows.

b. Revocation should be available here. Bailey will now emphasize that the defect in the printer, whatever may be its importance to others, "substantially impairs its value *to him*," which is the way the criterion is worded in §2-608(1). The drafters were concerned that incorporating a "substantiality" or "materiality" standard for revocation might work unfairly against some buyers, so they massaged it into giving us something quite novel, something we might be tempted to characterize as an *objective test subjectively applied* or perhaps a *subjective test to be exercised objectively*. Not surprisingly, there is no general consensus as to exactly how this wording is to be given effect, although the disagreements are probably more in shading than in the eventual result. The test seems to be something like whether a "reasonable person" *in the position of and having the particular needs of the buyer* would think the goods *substantially* impaired by the nonconformity. Got that? One court has set the inquiry as follows:

> Whether plaintiff [buyer] proved nonconformities sufficiently serious to justify revocation of acceptance is a two-step inquiry under the code. [T]he value of conforming goods to the plaintiff must first be determined. This is a subjective question in the sense that it calls for a consideration of the needs and circumstances of the plaintiff who seeks to revoke; not the needs and circumstances of the average buyer. The second inquiry is whether the nonconformity in fact substantially impairs the value of the goods to the buyer, having in mind his particular needs. This is an objective question in the sense that it calls for evidence of something more than plaintiff's assertion that the nonconformity impaired the value to him; it requires evidence from which it can be inferred that plaintiff 's needs were not met because of the nonconformity. In short the nonconformity must substantially impair the value of the goods to the plaintiff buyer. The existence of substantial impairment depends upon the facts and circumstances in each case.

Jorgensen v. Pressnall, 545 P.2d 1382 (Or. 1976). The *Jorgensen* approach has been adopted for Nevada by that state's supreme court in *Waddell v. L.V.R.V. Inc.*, 125 P.3d 1160 (Nev. 2006).

One authority refers to §2-608(1) as calling for a "personalized objective test." Call it what you will, it seems to help Bailey here. He does have a subjective, personalized reason for wanting the printer to have a particular feature and for being upset when he discovers that feature to be missing. And I think we all could agree that he is perfectly reasonable in feeling this way, given his situation. He could even bring forward "objective" proof of his individualized situation, such stuff as prior documents produced in the course of his scholarship that required the lira symbol for clarity and testimony of others supporting his assertion that he can expect to need this symbol in the future for use in his historical writings.

So if he is indeed a writer on economic history, Bailey has a very strong case for meeting the standard. This is not surprising, given that I was able to make up the facts to set out the issue. Not all cases will be so clear. What do you do with a case where you truly believe that the buyer thinks the value of the goods substantially impaired to him or her but this impression seems to you, as a reasonable person, to be based on a misapprehension on the buyer's part? Or how do you respond to the buyer who apparently has no special needs to which attention must be given but is able to satisfy you (with good, hard evidence) that he or she has been, is now, and always will be exceptionally picky about what he or she buys? In *Asciolla v. Manter Oldsmobile-Pontiac, Inc.*, 370 A.2d 270 (N.H. 1977), the court noted that in the case before it, "[t]he record indicate[d] that plaintiff was a particularly prudent and painstaking car buyer and that he had indeed once before refused to accept an automobile from the defendants which merely [?] had a dented fender which had been repaired." Would this buyer, should this buyer, be given a greater latitude in revocation than the ordinary Joe or Jane? The case itself does not actually address the question, since the car involved was among the more lemon-like in the literature and one with which just about anyone would be justifiably dissatisfied.

As to the issue of what Sylvester knew and when he knew it, Comment 2 makes it clear that, as far as the drafters were concerned, the seller's knowledge or lack of knowledge should play no part in the decision. Do you agree? I know of no case that picks up on the point.

6. a. Revocation would seem to be good here. The only issue is whether the attempted revocation took place "within a reasonable time after the buyer discovers or should have discovered the ground for it." See §2-608(2). Even though more than half a year has elapsed, I would

say yes, but the seller can argue that Bill "should have discovered" this defect earlier. This is, as are most questions under §2-608, a question of fact, but I wouldn't like to be representing Trailer-O-Rama at trial on this one. Perhaps persuasive counsel could convince a jury that a reasonable person makes more of an inspection and tries out all of the various features of a trailer soon after it is delivered. If Bill is "unreasonable," in that he is too trusting, he might be held to have lost the chance to revoke. He can still go against the seller for damages, of course, but will not be able to return the trailer.

b. Here Bill has probably lost his right to revoke because of delay in making the revocation. Still, it would be up to the trier of fact. Where an otherwise good case for revocation exists, the courts do not appear to be too strict with this timing requirement. In *Funk v. Montgomery AMC/Jeep/Renault*, 586 N.E.2d 1113 (Ohio App. 1990), Bev Funk was the buyer of a 1982 Renault who sought to revoke after experiencing problems with the car's air-conditioning for a second consecutive summer. The appellate court reversed a ruling of the trial judge that withheld the question of revocation from the jury on the ground that the attempt to revoke was untimely as a matter of law. What may eventually have made the difference (in this case as in many) is that the reasonable time that the buyer has to revoke is easily affected by how the seller reacts to initial complaints about the goods. As this court said, "the reasonable time requirement must include the time beyond which the seller is attempting to adjust, or cure, the problem." In another representative case, *Mercedes-Benz of North America, Inc. v. Norman Gershman's Things to Wear, Inc.*, 596 A.2d 1358 (Del. 1991), the Supreme Court of Delaware held that revocation could not be held to have been untimely as a matter of law even though it took place 18 months after delivery during which the buyer had put more than 12,600 miles on the car:

> Defendants acknowledge that the time for revocation may be extended "where the delay is prompted either by the seller's attempts to cure the defect, or where the delay was in reliance on the seller's continued assurances that the defect would be successfully repaired." . . . In such instances, revocations occurring two, three, and four years "after purchase and discovery of the nonconformity [have been found reasonable] depending on the number of promises to repair made, the length of time the repairs take, and the buyer's diligence in reporting problems." [Citations omitted.]

See also Comment 4. In our case, if Bill didn't make any initial complaint to the seller in May and just waited around until June, he will not be able to make this kind of "tolling" argument. Even if there is a significant tolling period during which the seller is fooling around and insisting that all will be well, eventually the buyer will have to conclude when enough is enough and make a move. No one is suggesting that the buyer can wait forever.

7. a. If Alice had taken this step, she would not be able to revoke. See §2-608(2) and the reference to "substantial change in the condition of the goods which is not caused by their own defects." (Notice, by the way, that this requirement would not bar revocation by Beth the buyer in Example 2. In her case, while there has been a substantial change in the condition of the car it is directly attributable to the car's own defects.)

   b. Sam would like to argue that, in this case as well, there has been a substantial change in the condition of the goods and he should not be required to take the car back following a revocation. Comment 6 does say that the seller should not be made to take return of goods that have "materially deteriorated except by reason of their own defect." A hard-driving woman like Alice can put a lot of miles on a car in a couple of months. Should the seller be able to get any mileage out of this argument? Obviously if it were to succeed, it could severely cut into the revocation right. At least when the buyer is a consumer and there has been only normal wear and tear for the period the goods have been in his or her hands, I have to doubt whether a court would let this stand in the way of a revocation. In a commercial context where the buyer has had long use of the goods and still could make use of them, but where their condition would make it virtually impossible for the seller to refurbish or resell them to anyone else, the argument has some appeal. Of course in such an instance, a court could and would probably avoid the issue altogether by rendering a decision that too much time had passed for a revocation.

   c. Alice's letter probably would be enough to satisfy §2-607(3)(a) (see Chapter 17), but would not be an effective notice of revocation as called for by §2-608(2). As to the mechanism of notice, refer once again to §1-202(d). Section 2-608(2) does not specifically call for a record, so oral notification would do. Alice's problem here is that the content of her email doesn't make clear she is revoking. See Comment 5. It is not enough that Alice let Sam know that she claims there has been a breach or that she wants some response from him. "While the [notice of revocation] need not be in any particular form and may be implied by conduct, it must inform the seller that the buyer does not want to keep the goods." *Allis-Chalmers Corp. v. Sygitowicz*, 571 P.2d 224 (Wash. App. 1977). See also *Mitcham v. First State Bank of Crossett, Arkansas*, 970 S.W.2d 267 (Ark. 1998), where the Supreme Court of Arkansas ruled that the buyer had not given an effective notice of revocation when he parked the malfunctioning piece of logging equipment in the front yard of his father's house alongside Highway 82 and hung a "lemon" sign on it. To be effective, Alice's communication should have made clear she did not want to keep the car. To be perfectly safe, she should have told him when and where and on what conditions he was expected to take return of the car.

d. Section 2-608(3) says that upon revocation the buyer "has the same rights and duties with regard to the goods as if he had rejected them." So we head back to §§2-602 through 2-604. Of particular importance is §2-602(2)(b). Alice is under a duty, subject to her rights under §2-711, to hold the car "with reasonable care at the seller's disposition for a time sufficient to permit the seller to remove [it]." So one thing she could do is just store it in a nice, safe place and wait for Sam to make a move. For a case in which the noble buyer actually did put the car in storage, even while continuing to pay insurance on it, see *King v. Taylor Chrysler-Plymouth, Inc.*, 457 N.W.2d 42 (Mich. App. 1990). But is it always realistic to ask the buyer to act this way? What is Alice supposed to do for transportation in the meantime? If she does continue to drive the car, Sam will also point to §2-602(2)(a) and argue that her use of the car after revocation is "wrongful" against him.

   In a large number of cases, the seller has argued that the buyer's "continued use" of the goods after a revocation in effect waived the revocation. (Be careful. You should distinguish this argument from what we discussed earlier in Example 7b, that prolonged use *prior to* an attempted revocation somehow makes the remedy of revocation unavailable. The issue here is *post-revocation* use.) Under some circumstances, you can imagine this argument of continued use being successful (e.g., if the buyer could have easily set the item aside and avoided having anything more to do with it, but instead kept using it, made no effort to look for an eventual replacement, and so on). But in the typical consumer case where it has come up, the courts have been sympathetic to the predicament in which the revoking buyer is found. Some courts have reasoned that the buyer who retains a security interest in the property under §2-711 is merely taking reasonable steps to protect the value of the property and that interest by, say, continuing to live in and maintain the trailer. Other times, the court will conclude that continued use by a consumer who has no financial means to immediately obtain a replacement is not "wrongful" at all, or if it is "wrongful," that this does not in and of itself bar a revocation but only gives the seller some rights to a set-off (as we'll discuss in the next part of this example). See, for example, *Liarikos v. Mello*, 639 N.E.2d 716 (Mass. 1994), or *Franklin v. Augusta Dodge, Inc.*, 652 S.E.2d 862 (Ga. App. 2007).

   Of course, not all continued use by a consumer will be considered reasonable and prevent a later finding that the consumer's attempted revocation has been rendered ineffective by that use. For instance, in *White v. Holiday Kamper & Boats*, 2008 WL 4155663 (D.S.C.), the Whites, who experienced a series of unresolved problems with an RV they had purchased, had their counsel send a letter to the seller declaring their decision to revoke their acceptance of the vehicle. Thereafter they put about 5,000 more miles on the RV. As the court noted:

> Since the purported revocation, Plaintiffs [who lived outside Knoxville, Tennessee] have lived in the RV for a period of time between selling and purchasing a new home in Tennessee, taken five or six trips to their daughter's home in Atlanta, Georgia, and driven to Jacksonville, Florida for a three-week trip. Further, since the beginning of the case at bar, Plaintiffs have taken a trip to Jacksonville, Florida, and then back through Atlanta, Georgia, that, in whole, lasted over one month.

In light of these facts, the district court held that the plaintiffs' continued use of the vehicle was enough to effectuate "reacceptance" of it and in consequence deprive the plaintiffs of the right to proceed on the theory of revocation of acceptance.

Initially the cases on "continued use" almost all involved a consumer buyer who had rightfully revoked acceptance of an automobile or a mobile home, big purchases of the sort that your average Joe or Jane can't just set aside in a closet or easily do without. More recently, however, an interesting new cluster of cases has begun to surface in keeping with the times in which we live. They involve purchases of expensive high-tech equipment by individual doctors or hospitals who then experience continuing problems with what they receive. For instance, in *Romy v. Picker International, Inc.*, 1992 WL 70403 (E.D. Pa.), aff'd 986 F.2d 1409 (3d Cir. 1993), Dr. Maurice Romy purchased a Magnetic Resonance Imaging (MRI) system from Picker to be used by his medical partnership. The MRI was delivered to Romy, who put it into use, but a new "rampability" option (something to do with hard-core and high-tech electronics, it would appear) that had been promised was never delivered. In fact it turned out that no maker of MRI equipment had as of the time of trial produced a "rampable" system for the commercial market. After a seven-day trial, the jury concluded Romy had legitimately revoked and awarded him damages of $2,130,905.00, representing the purchase price plus incidental damages. On appeal, the manufacturer argued that the doctor's continued use of the MRI after his having given notice of the nonconformity constituted a waiver of the right to revoke and barred him as a matter of law from that form of relief. The appellate court didn't buy the argument, stating:

> [A] court will annul a revocation and conclude that a reacceptance has occurred only where the buyer's actions with respect to the goods are

> deemed "unreasonable." . . . The record establishes that Romy's post-revocation use of the MRI was reasonable. The MRI was purchased for the use of Romy and his partnership, UDC, whose main function is the performance of magnetic imaging tests on patients. MRI equipment is vital to the operation of UDC's business, and without MRI equipment UDC would have had to cease virtually all of its business operations. Had Romy ceased using the Picker MRI system he would have failed to satisfy his duty to mitigate damages. Furthermore, since the MRI equipment had already been installed in UDC's offices, Romy could not easily remove and replace the MRI system. Therefore, the post-revocation use of the MRI was reasonable, and Romy did not waive his right to revoke acceptance of the MRI system.

In a similar vein is *Hospital Computer Systems, Inc. v. Staten Island Hospital*, 788 F. Supp. 1351 (D.N.J. 1992). The hospital purchased a custom computer billing and accounting software system from HCS. The system "went live" on January 1, 1986, after which there quickly emerged a series of problems that HCS kept trying to correct. By early 1987, an independent consultant hired by the hospital reported on his conclusion that there was just no way the system's problems could be fully remedied. On June 2, 1987, the hospital's president wrote HCS a letter stating among other things that the hospital had "decided to wipe the slate clean and try another vendorized system" and that it "would like to accomplish a reasonable and orderly transition from HCS to whatever our new system would be." For the next 18 months, the hospital continued to use the HCS system and make monthly payments under the contract. During the same time, and "unbeknown to HCS," it sought out and implemented a new system. The hospital stopped paying HCS when that new system became operational on February 1, 1989. The district court found that the hospital had effectively revoked in June 1987. Nor did its continued use of the system for 18 months thereafter constitute a waiver of the revocation. The court was urged by HCS to follow an earlier case, *Computerized Radiological Services v. Syntex Corp.*, 786 F.2d 72 (2d Cir. 1986), in which the Second Circuit had held a radiology group's continued use of a CAT scanner for 22 months following notice to have absolutely barred a revocation. Staten Island Hospital's situation, however, was found to be distinguishable. In *Computerized Radiological Services*, the Second Circuit had put emphasis on the fact that the buyer had failed to search for a replacement for a significant period of time after its attempted revocation. The hospital, on the other hand, it found:

> began almost immediately to search for a replacement system, and, considering the complexity of negotiating for, purchasing, and implementing a customized computer software system, its completion of these tasks within eighteen months could certainly be found by a jury to be reasonable.

This and other matters, the court concluded, were for the jury and would not be disposed of on summary judgment.

For a good discussion of the continued-use issue, here involving a farmer's purchase and use, over three harvest seasons, of an agricultural combine (which the court flat-out described as "a lemon"), see *Deere & Co. v. Johnson*, 271 F.3d 613 (5th Cir. 2001). The Fifth Circuit noted that while continued use of the goods after a revocation is typically not allowed, there are exceptions to this general rule. The court is to weigh the cost and availability of replacement by the buyer against the injury to the seller from the continued depreciation in the value of the goods as the buyer continues to use them. Significantly, the court stated:

> That simple depreciation alone usually does not constitute a substantial change in the condition of the good [which would bar revocation] is consistent with the doctrine of revocation of acceptance because the doctrine is meant to remedy a situation in which a latent defect arises. If simple depreciation of the non-conforming good was enough to nullify the revocation of acceptance, a buyer might not be able to revoke acceptance of a good with a latent defect.

Of course, it did not help the seller's argument in the particular situation that it continually refused to take return of the combine even when the buyer offered it. "How," asked the court:

> does one return a combine when the dealer refuses to take it back—park it, perhaps, illegally in their lot? We find unpersuasive the premise of Deere's argument: that a seller can refuse to accept the return of a non-conforming good, and then claim that the buyer nullified the revocation by not returning the goods in question.

e. The courts that have concluded that such post-revocation or continued use does not bar a revocation then go on to say that the seller should be able to recover from the buyer the "reasonable value" of that use. How is this value to be measured? If we were to take the difference in market values between a new automobile and one even only a few months old, the measure could be quite high and, it would seem, unfair to Alice. The cases that have had to consider the issue seem to settle on something like the fair market *rental* value of the goods for the period of time they were used by the buyer. But even then, if the seller has been holding on to the full purchase price for this period of time, and accumulating interest, is the calculation complete? In *Erling v. Homera, Inc.*, 298 N.W.2d 478 (N.D. 1980), a mobile home case, the Supreme Court of North Dakota remanded for "determination of the reasonable value of use of the home from the date of purchase to date of hearing on remand. The value of the use less interest at the rate of six percent per annum on the purchase price to the date of hearing on remand should be set off against the purchase price."

8. This question is an attempt to frame as clearly as possible an issue on which there is still unresolved debate: Does the seller have any right to cure following a revocation of acceptance? The answer is not obvious. Look at §2-508. This is the sole source in Article 2 of the right to cure and it speaks only of what follows a "rejection." If the drafters had wanted to provide for cure after a "revocation of acceptance," which is clearly a different animal under Article 2, they knew the words and could have included them in this section. There is some Latin maxim or other to the effect that when words are left out of a statute, we have to assume this was done intentionally. On the other hand, §2-608(3) says that the buyer who revokes has "the same rights *and duties* with regard to the goods as if he had rejected them." Arguably one of the duties of a rejecting buyer is the duty to allow for and accept cure. But then again §2-608(3) refers to "duties *with respect to the goods.*" Is the duty to cooperate with a possible cure such a duty, or were those five words meant to limit the revoking buyer's responsibilities to keeping and caring for the goods with reasonable care and sending them back to the seller in the rare instances where this is required by §2-603? In short, the language of Article 2 can be read as either repudiating or allowing for the notion of cure following revocation.

If the Code language is not determinative of the issue, that gives us all the more justification for deciding it on "policy" grounds. But again the matter isn't crystal clear. Some authorities focus on the policy inherent in Article 2 that encourages cure and that favors keeping the deal alive and whole if at all possible. They argue that there must be a right to cure after revocation, even if it doesn't allow the seller to string the buyer along forever. For example, see *North River Homes, Inc. v. Bosarge*, 594 So. 2d 1153 (Miss. 1992), another mobile home case, which lays out one approach to the problem that is followed in several states:

> Once a consumer has properly notified the seller of his or her intent to revoke acceptance, the seller has a right to cure the alleged defect. This right is not unlimited; that is, Mississippi law does not permit a seller "to postpone revocation in perpetuity by fixing everything that goes wrong" with the goods. "There comes a time when enough is enough"—when a consumer no longer must tolerate or endure the seller's repeated (though good faith) attempts to cure the defect. [Citations omitted.]

Other courts and authorities place greater stress on the policy allowing for revocation, but restricting it only to the more egregious situations where the buyer has been wronged in a significant way. They then conclude that if a situation is problematic enough to justify the buyer's revocation, then it is simply going too far to cut the seller some additional slack in the form of the right to cure. Even in the rejection situation there is legitimate reason to be concerned, as we discussed in the preceding chapter, that an overgenerous reading of the right to cure will overpower the innocent and hapless buyer. Allowing for cure following a fully justified revocation might be just that much worse. In *Gappelberg v. Landrum*, 666 S.W.2d 88 (Tex. 1984), the court reflecting this kind of reasoning stated unequivocally that "once a buyer has properly revoked acceptance of a product, the seller has neither the right to cure by repair or by replacement." The Court of Appeals of Michigan has stated that the text of Article 2 simply could not be read to allow the seller a right to cure after a revocation, commenting that this rule is in accord with the majority of jurisdictions that have considered the question. *Head v. Phillips Camper Sales & Rentals, Inc.*, 593 N.W.2d 595 (Mich. App. 1999). More recently, see the decisions of the Appeals Court of Massachusetts in *Kochanski v. Twin City Marine, Inc.*, 2010 WL 1265855 (Mass. App.), and *CB Aviation, LLC v. Hawker Beechcraft Corp.*, 2011 WL 5386365 (E.D. Pa.) (construing Kentucky law) which come to the same conclusion. And that, we are to take it, is that—at least in the majority of states. But I'm not so sure.

One reason for the lack of a consensus is that the issue is rarely if ever so neatly set out in the cases as it is in my hypotheticals, whatever a particular court might think. For one thing, in almost all of the cases that have been decided to date the seller *has* actually cured or attempted a cure (often time and time again) before the revocation is made or soon thereafter. But the cure doesn't make matters any better, and the goods continue in a ratty condition. So it is pretty easy to accept the argument, at least in such situations, that if all the criteria for a revocation are met, including "substantial impairment," then giving the seller yet another chance to cure isn't fair to the buyer. The seller has given it his or her best shot and this has been found wanting. Eventually, enough really is enough.

At the other extreme must be those situations where it quickly appears to all involved that cure is still possible and holds out a real chance of success. If this is the case, we have to believe that the buyer will almost invariably leap at the prospect—and the problem will rarely if ever appear in the reported cases. If the buyer were to refuse to allow for cure in such a situation, he or she might have difficulty sustaining this position should seller later be forced to bring an action for payment. The court could readily decide that there was after all the right to cure following revocation, but it wouldn't even have to make such a sweeping statement. The issue could be skirted entirely just by concluding that any defect that can easily and effectively be cured cannot by its nature "substantially impair the value" of the goods to this buyer or anyone else. So no revocation was possible in the first place. I'm afraid our friend Bailey the buyer, even if his case came up in Texas or Michigan and even in light of the language in the *Gappelberg* and *Head* cases, may have to accept Sylvester's offer and learn to live with his Phaserjet.

CHAPTER 20

Anticipatory Repudiation and Insecurity

WHEN TROUBLE PRECEDES PERFORMANCE

Look at the first sentence of Comment 1 to §2-609:

> This section rests on the recognition of the fact that the essential purpose of a contract between commercial men is actual performance and they do not bargain merely for a promise, or for a promise plus the right to win a lawsuit and that a continuing sense of reliance and security that the promised performance will be forthcoming when due, is an important feature of the bargain.

Truer words have never been written (even if the Comment drafter's syntax, punctuation, and lack of gender-neutral language leave something to be desired). The only question is why these words of wisdom appear here, in the commentary to this particular section. They would do just as well, it seems, in explanation of plenty of other sections or in some overall introduction to Article 2 in general. Perhaps, however, the point the drafters were trying to make is particularly relevant to the three sections starting with §2-609, which we are now going to examine.

Consider the following: If you have a contract with another and that other party actually breaches by not performing when and as due, it's not a pleasant situation. You're probably going to want to do something about it. And you probably have some idea, albeit vague, of what is to be done. You're the injured party. You've been wronged. At the very least you would think to call a lawyer and, together with that lawyer, look to the remedies provisions of Article 2. A breach is a dramatic event. It demands (or at least allows for) a response, and a response there may very well be. But what about when there's only been a *hint* of a breach or the slightest *suggestion* that one may be in the offing? Perhaps the other who promised you performance at some later date is now hemming and hawing and generally acting disagreeably. He or she may even be threatening to pull out of the deal altogether, offering up either no or merely the lamest of excuses. Still there's time before the grumbler's performance is due, and who knows what the future will bring? Maybe it's all an act or he or she is just having a bad day. Maybe he or she will have still another change of heart.

In this type of situation, is there anything to do besides wait and see what the morrow brings (getting your lawyer on the phone but keeping him or her on one very expensive hold)? As the drafters remind us in their Comment, a primary benefit of a contract for sale is the security for the future that it affords to each of the parties. Once that sense of security is threatened, what results is often worse than having no contract at all. If there is anything more worrisome than wondering if you will be able to make a contract on terms that meet your needs, it is having real reason to wonder whether things are going to go according to plan once you've made the desired contract. Sections 2-609 to 2-611 deal with two fundamental concepts that give a party experiencing genuine doubts about the other party's ability or willingness to perform when performance later becomes due something to do about the situation other than just wait and pray and agonize. It may be slightly awkward, but I suggest it is easier to deal with *anticipatory repudiation* as dealt with in §§2-610 and 2-611 and the *insecurity mechanism* of §2-609 in the reverse order from that in which they are given in Article 2. So we start with repudiation.

ANTICIPATORY REPUDIATION

Section 2-610 lays out the rights of a party, be it a buyer or a seller, when the other party to the contract of sale has repudiated prior to performance. The basic notion of anticipatory repudiation, and the possible responses available to the aggrieved party, should be familiar to you from your study of the common law of contracts. At least in theory, the situation is quite straightforward. One party informs the other that he or she is not going to do what was promised. There is a clear articulation that performance as provided for under the contract is no longer to be expected when due. No legitimate excuse is given. The repudiator has not merely hinted that performance may not be forthcoming when the time comes—it has said as much in no uncertain terms. Section 2-611 goes on to deal with the possibility of a retraction of a repudiation. The first examples in this chapter ask you to apply these two sections. The problems you will face should come as no surprise. Short of when a party uses some form of the verb "to repudiate" or cites these sections of the Code, how do we know a repudiation when we see or hear one? You'll find the line between a true repudiation, which triggers all kinds of consequences for each of the parties, and mere griping and whining isn't as clear as we might hope. Once we have determined that a repudiation has taken place, what *may* the other party do? Is there anything the nonrepudiating party *must* do? If a contracting party believes the other to have repudiated, but turns out to be mistaken in that belief, what harm is done? (The answer, potentially plenty.) Finally, how and when can a repudiator retract the repudiation, and where does this leave the parties?

INSECURITY AND DEMAND FOR ASSURANCE

Having dealt with the vagaries of repudiation, we will be in a better position to appreciate what is usually referred to as the *insecurity mechanism* provided for in §2-609. Life is not always as uncomplicated as we'd like it to be. The actions and words of others create impressions, but are these to be trusted? What precisely *did* that other person's statement mean? What exactly is going on here? Section 2-609 was meant to go beyond what was available under the common law to establish a means for dealing with (some of) the insecurities and ambiguities of commercial life.

It's important that you think of §2-609 in this way: It is about a process. Despite the first sentence in subsection (1), the value of this section isn't in some general hortatory principle. That first sentence is the one bit of language that really could be done away with without any noticeable effect. The importance of §2-609 to contracting parties is in what follows. The section sets forth a *mechanism*—a procedure that one or the other (or potentially both) of the parties to a sales contract can make use of to clarify the situation. The right conferred on a party by this section is the right to protection *by taking appropriate action*. But action under §2-609 must perforce be guided by that section, and as we will see, this Article 2 mechanism can be a trap for the unwary just as it can serve as a boon to the prudent and sober soul.

The later examples in this chapter will help you work through the various difficulties that come up when one party or the other seeks to take advantage of the §2-609 mechanism. You have by now had enough experience reading the Code that even as you first glance over this section, you will immediately sense where problems can arise. What constitutes "reasonable grounds for insecurity"? What must be done to make an effective demand under the section? If a response is forthcoming, how are we to judge if it gives "adequate assurance" of performance? If, as subsection (4) sets out, there is such a thing as a "justified demand" under this section, then we have to recognize that there can be unjustified demands as well. What consequence if any will there be for making an unjustified demand? Is there anything a party can do to protect against misapplication of §2-609 beyond being "reasonable" and following "commercial standards" in every little thing that he or she says and does?

A SPECIAL CASE: THE BUYER'S INSOLVENCY

While not dealt with in the examples and explanations of this chapter, we should at least note one other section in Article 2 that may be relevant in deciding what to do when trouble comes calling prior to performance. Section 2-702 gives the seller the right either to refuse delivery except for cash, to stop delivery entirely before it occurs, or even in some instances to reclaim goods already delivered in the event of a buyer's insolvency. The operative definition of *insolvency* is that given in §1-201(b)(23). The seller's rights in such a situation are, however, carefully circumscribed, and appropriate procedures have to be followed. See §2-705, for example, on stoppage in transit.

We will assume that insolvency of the buyer is not a factor in the following examples. The buyer could pay if he or she wanted to. But for some reason, or perhaps for no good reason, he or she is refusing to pay when due or otherwise threatening not to follow through on some obligation.

EXAMPLES

Examples

1. In January Belle, a clothing manufacturer, contracts to buy a large amount of woolen fabric from Serge's Material Mill. The contract specifies the price as $4 a yard, payable 30 days after Belle receives delivery. The date of delivery is given as March 15.
   (a) In February Belle receives an email from Serge that says, "I am sorry that I must rescind our agreement. I hope we can work together in the future." Is this a repudiation under §2-610? If so, what rights does Belle have as of receipt of the email?
   (b) Suppose that Serge's email instead had said, "I am sorry to inform you that delivery isn't going to be until the end of April at the earliest. I wanted to let you know as soon as possible. Other than that, everything's fine." How do you analyze this situation under §2-610? Would your answer be any different if Serge had said that, while he could no longer be sure of delivery by March 15, he could guarantee that the fabric would be delivered no later than March 17?
   (c) Suppose that Serge had written the following: "The fabric is all ready and you will be getting delivery on March 15 of just what you

ordered. However, I really can't let you have it for $4 a yard. I'll have to bill you at $4.15." He does not ask for any response from Belle. Is there any problem with Belle taking this as a repudiation and acting accordingly?

(d) What if instead, when Serge writes claiming that he will be owed the $4.15, he adds the statement that he will not ship the goods to Belle unless he hears from her acknowledging her duty to pay this increased price? He claims that the price rise is "in conformity with our contract in light of increased cost to me of materials and the custom in this industry of making adjustments in such circumstances." What is the situation here?

2. On Monday Larry agrees to sell Moe his used car, delivery to be made and payment tendered on Friday. On Wednesday Moe gets a visit from his friend Curley, who is driving the car, Larry's car! Curley tells Moe that he purchased it from Larry on Tuesday. Is Moe justified in saying there has been an anticipatory repudiation by Larry?

3. Just to make sure we don't suffer any illusions that only sellers can repudiate, let's flip the situation. Let us return to the Belle/Serge contract. Suppose that in February, Belle writes to Serge, "I am looking forward to receiving the order on March 15. It turns out that I won't be able to pay for it until May, but don't worry, you'll get your money. You know I'm good for it." What are Serge's options here?

4. In March Betrand, a maker of digital widgets, contracts to buy a large metal stamping machine to be specially manufactured to his order by Stamper Incorporated. The contract calls for delivery by October. On May 5, Betrand emails Stamper stating he no longer needs the machine and "rescinding" his order. Stamper reads the email on May 10.

(a) Stamper immediately stops the process of customizing the machine to Betrand's specifications. It simply sets the work aside. The president of the company emails back to Betrand, "You have a contract to buy the machine from us. We are readying it for you. Expect to hear from our lawyers." On May 31 Stamper receives another email from Betrand who says that he has reconsidered and is willing to take the machine. What is the status of the parties at this point? Is Stamper still obligated to deliver the machine in October?

(b) Would your answer to the previous question be any different if Stamper, instead of just putting the work aside, immediately sought and was able to find another buyer (albeit at a lesser price) for the machine? Prior to receipt of Betrand's email of May 31, it had begun configuring the machine to this new buyer's specifications and had instructed its attorney to begin a suit against Betrand for the difference in price.

5. Arnold Moneybucks enters into a contract to buy a painting from Stella's gallery, with delivery and payment to occur at the end of the gallery's current show. The day after signing the contract, Arnold calls Stella and says that he has decided against buying the painting. Stella responds, "I don't understand it. You were getting a great price. But if that's the way you feel, OK the deal is off." The conversation is at an end. A few minutes later, before Stella has even had the chance to remove the "SOLD" sign from the painting, Arnold again calls Stella saying that he has changed his mind once more. He will take the painting. Is Stella bound to sell it to him at the price originally agreed?

6. Sunny Toy Manufacturers (Mr. Sunny, President) enters into a contract to sell a large number of talking dolls to Bunny, the owner of a toy store. While Sunny normally does not sell on credit, at Bunny's urging, he agrees to do so in her case. The contract finally agreed upon specifies that payment is due within 90 days of delivery.
   (a) Prior to shipment, Sunny begins to regret that he ever extended credit to Bunny. He writes Bunny requesting that she agree to pay for the dolls upon receipt or in the alternative give a personal guarantee of payment. He gets no response to this request. Is he relieved under §2-609 from his obligation to ship the dolls at the time called for in the contract?
   (b) Would your answer to the previous question be any different if the reason Sunny wrote making this request was that at a recent toy-makers' convention he had heard reports from a couple of people that Bunny was in trouble financially and had not been paying her bills on time?
   (c) How would you respond to the Sunny/Bunny problem if the reason for Sunny's demand was that Bunny was in fact, at the time of the writing, overdue in a payment to Sunny on a separate contract for the sale of some toy trains? The trains had been delivered a few weeks after the two contracted for the dolls, but Bunny is refusing to pay for the trains, claiming that they were delivered with defective cabooses.

7. Betty, an industrialist, contracts to buy a large metal stamping machine from Stamper, Inc. Prior to delivery Betty hears from industry sources that others who have bought similar machines from Stamper are experiencing problems with them. Betty calls Stamper's headquarters and talks directly to the president of the firm. She tells him of her concerns. He replies, "I hear you. Let me check into this and get back to you." Four weeks pass and Betty has not heard a thing.
   (a) Would Betty be justified in writing an email to Stamper canceling the contract and threatening to hold them liable for damages if she is forced to pay more elsewhere for a stamping machine that meets her needs?

(b) Suppose instead that Betty writes to the company explaining her concerns. Within a week, she gets back an email from the president of Stamper that says, "You have nothing to worry about. I've checked into it and your machine is going to work just fine." That's it. She makes several calls trying to speak to the president, but she never gets through to him and he doesn't return her calls. Does Betty have a right to consider the contract at an end?

Explanations

1. a. Serge may think he's "rescinding" the agreement, but absent some special provision in the contract, he has no right to call a unilateral end to the deal. This is a repudiation by Serge. The Code does not define "repudiation," but note Comment 1 to §2-610, which tells us that anticipatory repudiation "centers upon an overt communication of intention or an action which renders performance impossible or demonstrates a clear intention not to continue with performance." In fact Serge's email is about as blatant a repudiation as you can imagine. One of the principal problems in this area, of course, is that parties rarely make their intentions known in such a pure, unadulterated fashion. Serge's flagrant repudiation, however, does allow us to explore the consequences. What are Belle's options once she's received this communication?

We should note at the outset that there is nothing to stop Belle, if she is so disposed, from letting Serge off the hook here. She could treat his email as a request that she agree to a *mutual* rescission of the agreement. If she does agree, then the rescission should be valid (see §2-209) and neither party would have any responsibility under the contract. It's doubtful that she's going to want to agree to this, however. More than likely she thinks herself aggrieved by Serge's action, so we must look to what she may do as the *aggrieved party* under §2-610. Under that section, she has several options. Subpart (a) says that she may just wait "for a commercially reasonable time" before she makes a move. Maybe Serge will, on his own, recognize the error of his ways and retract his repudiation. If she decides to wait she is under no affirmative obligation to tell him that's what she's doing as long as she is acting in good faith. See Comment 4. As a practical matter, of course, it makes a lot of sense for her to contact him, tell him what she thinks of the situation, and try to convince him to quit this foolishness.

While Belle may want to give Serge some time to reconsider and a second chance to do the right thing, there is no obligation on her part that she do so. Another possibility is for her immediately to take his email as signaling an end to their agreement and to spring into action. Under (b) she can resort to any remedy she would have for breach. In this case, §2-711 is the section cataloging buyers' remedies in general. We will deal with remedies in great detail in a later chapter, but for the moment, note that §2-711 allows for her to "cancel" in addition to pursuing other remedies. *Cancellation* is defined in §2-106(4). In other words, upon a repudiation, Belle could immediately declare that the whole deal was off and simultaneously retain her rights to pursue a remedy (typically an action for monetary damages) against Serge for any injury caused her.

Note also that under part (b), Belle does not have to decide to treat his repudiation as a breach immediately or forever lose the chance to do so. She can decide to wait a bit, and she can even tell Serge that she is willing to wait in the hopes that he will reconsider and perform, but when her patience wears thin, she may then choose to treat his behavior as a breach and resort to her formidable remedies.

Finally, note the provision in (c) that gives Belle, as the aggrieved party, the right to "suspend [her] own performance in response to the repudiation." (The reference to §2-704 isn't relevant here, as that would come into play only when a buyer repudiates, and even then only in a relatively small number of cases.) The right to suspend your own performance in the face of a repudiation doesn't seem to matter much here, but in other circumstances, it could make a great deal of difference. Suppose, for example, that in our situation, the contract called for Belle to make a prepayment of 20 percent of the price by March 1. If she doesn't make that payment, could Serge ever argue that *she* actually breached first and that he was therefore, somehow, let off the hook? Obviously the answer should be no. Once he repudiates, her obligation to pay by March 1 is suspended.

So it seems it's pretty much up to Belle to determine how she wants to handle the situation—with one possible exception. While §2-610 never says it in so many words, there's a good argument that the one thing Belle may *not* do is simply ignore the repudiation altogether and act as if it never happened. Suppose she just waits until March 15 without doing anything. She receives no delivery from Serge. She then goes out into the market on March 16 and buys a quantity of woolens to cover, but at a much higher price than the $4 a yard. Perhaps she suffers other losses as well. For instance, because even in the best of circumstances she will now not get delivery of the fabric until sometime after March 15, she may suffer decreased profits if her plant must remain idle for a time or if she has to pay overtime to her workers in order to meet her production schedule. Can she sue Serge, holding him responsible for all of these losses? Here, after all, there has been not merely a repudiation, but a breach about which she certainly has the right to complain. The problem for

Belle here, if she expects to recover every penny of her loss, is that §2-610 says she had the right upon getting the repudiation to wait "a commercially reasonable time" for performance. Depending on the circumstances, a court could easily conclude that waiting the whole way to the promised arrival date was waiting *beyond* a commercially reasonable time. What then? There is nothing in §2-610 to guide us (although you should look at the last sentence in Comment 1), but as we will see when we study buyers' remedies in more detail, there is a strong argument to be made that Belle would not be able to recover by way of damages the full difference in the cost of the fabric, much less the other consequential losses to her such as the amount spent on overtime. It will turn out (in Chapter 27) that this issue is among the most troubling and controversial in the area of remedies under Article 2, and not all authorities are in agreement about what should be the outcome. For the moment, it's sufficient for us to note that there is a fairly good argument to be made that Belle, the "aggrieved party" in this case, cannot just wait around forever. She must, after a "commercially reasonable" length of time, acknowledge that the repudiation is going to stick and that she is going to be the victim of a breach sometime in the future, then act accordingly in an effort to mitigate the damages she will suffer.

b. When Serge says that delivery is going to come six weeks late, he is repudiating. He is not disavowing the contract (in fact he says he's anxious to perform), but performance will not be as the contract provides. This is a repudiation. Belle may agree to a later delivery date, thus in effect concluding a modification, but she is under no obligation to do so. She may take any of the actions we allowed her in the previous example.

   What about the case when Serge tells her something like a month in advance to expect a delay of at most two days? Is this a repudiation? Well, yes, but under §2-610 it turns out we need to explore further. Belle's rights to suspend performance or to treat this as a breach are conditioned on the repudiation being such that the loss of those two days "will substantially impair the value of the contract" to her. Who's to say if two days late is substantial enough? If it is not, what about 10 days, or 20? Comment 3 refers us to how Article 2 deals with similar problems in installment contracts. We will examine this in the next chapter, which will be the better place to ponder over the subtleties of the "substantial impairment" standard. Surely it will come as no surprise if I tell you now that there will be no easy or clear-cut test for when impairment is substantial enough and when it isn't. In our case, Comment 3 asks us to consider whether "material inconvenience or injustice" will result if Belle is made to take the fabric on March 17, given that she can also expect to receive some measure of damages for the lateness. It seems unlikely that the two days are that big of a deal. If Belle does treat this not just as a repudiation but as a repudiation justifying her cancellation of the contract, she runs a terrific risk that a court will later judge that she has made a mountain out of a molehill. If that is the case, the court could conclude that her action in canceling for no sufficient reason was itself a repudiation on *her* part.

You can, of course, imagine situations where a statement by the seller that delivery will be a few days late would be enough to trigger all of the buyer's rights under §2-610. What's the use of Christmas trees delivered on December 26? Or consider the case of *Neptune Research & Development, Inc. v. Teknics Industrial Systems, Inc.*, 563 A.2d 465 (N.J. Super. 1989). The seller of a large specialized manufacturing machine (the Model RC-520 triple access Precision Vertical Machining Center) had originally agreed in April to a mid-June delivery date. Problems ensued and by late August, the machine still had not arrived. On August 29 a representative of the buyer visited the seller's place of business and saw the machine, which was almost completely assembled. Acting on behalf of the buyer, he agreed to take it, on the understanding that it would be ready to be picked up on September 5. On September 3, when the buyer called to make arrangements for the pickup, he was then told that the machine would be ready on September 9 or 10 at the earliest. At this point the buyer, "fed up" with the course of dealing and claiming to have lost all faith in the seller, canceled the contract. The buyer was held to have been within its rights in treating this final delay as a repudiation justifying cancellation. Normally, the court opined, a delay in delivery of a few days in a complex contract such as this would not be substantial at least where the contract did not make "time of the essence." In fact, the court suggests, the failure to make delivery in mid-June would not necessarily have been a material breach giving the buyer the right to cancel. But the judgment of substantiality has to be made taking into account all of the surrounding circumstances, and eventually enough is enough. The court concluded:

> Buyer had already waited a long time, seller had not been candid with buyer, and Sule [buyer's president] had good reason to believe that seller would not perform. In essence, the events of August 29 can be viewed as Sule giving seller "one last chance." Seller's failure to call buyer on September 3, as seller had promised to do, could only have deepened buyer's suspicion that seller was not going to perform. In light of these circumstances, [the seller's] unequivocal statement on September 4, that under no circumstances would the machine be ready by the promised delivery date, September 5, was a repudiation going to the essence of the contract.

We'll pick up on another aspect of the *Neptune* case a bit later on.

c. Serge will claim that he is not repudiating at all. He is continuing to promise his performance, which is the delivery of certain goods just as they were ordered and on the promised date. He is not, he would later claim, repudiating "with respect to any performance [for which he is responsible] not yet due." He finds support in Comment 2:

> Under the language of this section, a demand by one or both parties for more than the contract calls for in the way of counter-performance is not in itself a repudiation nor does it invalidate a plain expression of desire for future performance. However, when under a fair reading it amounts to a statement of intention not to perform except on conditions which go beyond the contract, it becomes a repudiation.

For an example of this Comment in operation, in the context of a contract for the purchase of some 10,000 barrels of methanol, see *Tradax Energy, Inc. v. Cedar Petrochemicals, Inc.*, 317 F. Supp. 2d 373 (S.D.N.Y. 2004).

In our hypothetical as now configured, Belle would seem to be taking a big risk by reading what Serge has said so far as a statement of his intention not to deliver. It would, of course, be different if he begins to make sounds with the clear implication that he isn't going to be shipping the stuff off unless and until he hears from her that she's willing to pay the greater amount. If she doesn't have grounds for taking his email as a repudiation, what she'll have to do is wait for the delivery, accept it, then refuse to pay any more than the $4 a yard. What will then happen? Belle has to know that Serge may then sue her for the extra money. She'll win, we assume, but it has to be pretty upsetting for her to have to accept some goods knowing that she's going to have to face a lawsuit (even a frivolous one) sometime down the road. If she would prefer to force the issue now, there should be some way she could take advantage of the §2-609 insecurity mechanism. You begin to see the importance of that section when repudiations, or possible repudiations, are not as clear-cut as they were in Example 1a.

d. It would be very hard, and certainly very risky, for Belle to treat this as a repudiation. Serge does not disavow any aspect of the contract. The problem comes, of course, if Belle disagrees that he has any right under their contract to a price in excess of $4 whatever the circumstances. But a disagreement about the terms of the contract, as long as Serge is acting in good faith, shouldn't be characterized as a repudiation. Serge's argument as to what the contract provides may be wrong, but he certainly isn't saying he is unwilling or unable to perform his obligations under that contract, whatever they turn out to be. At least that's how I would read the language from Comment 2 quoted above. It also seems to me to be the right result. It's a troubling case, to say the least, when the parties start wrangling even before performance over how to interpret their contract, but I hope that each of them would be wary about declaring the other to have "repudiated" when they recognize that there's an honest dispute. It would be a different matter if Serge's argument for an adjustment in the price was totally frivolous and made in bad faith. (Remember, we are helped here by a definition of good faith under §2-103(1)(b) for merchants that imports reasonable commercial standards.) Assuming good faith on the part of both parties, the situation here seems to be best summed up as one in which neither should yet be encouraged to raise the red flag of repudiation. The Code would encourage them to keep planning for performance according to schedule, assuming things can be worked out if only they keep talking to each other.

2. A repudiation can be found, according to Comment 1 as well as prior law, in "an action that renders performance impossible," which seems to be what we have here. Larry is not going to be able to deliver to Moe on Friday a car that is no longer his to sell. Of course, Larry could argue that it is not literally *impossible* for him to perform on Friday. He could, at least in theory, repurchase the car from Curley on Thursday. That doesn't seem a very convincing argument, and I see no good reason to countenance it here. There will be other situations, of course, when it will be far from clear whether a party's actions have actually disabled him or her from performing. Once again, if the other party is at all in doubt about whether to declare a repudiation, the sensible thing would be to go the §2-609 route.

   For an interesting case involving not just some old used car, but a very special one indeed, see *Hessler v. Crystal Lake Chrysler-Plymouth, Inc.*, 788 N.E.2d 405 (Ill. App. 2003). In February 1997, the Chrysler Corporation introduced a new "promotional" vehicle to be called the Plymouth Prowler, although at the time the company did not actually reveal whether it would manufacture or offer for sale any of the vehicles. David R. Hessler, obviously something of a Chrysler fan, was on the ball. He entered into a contract for one such vehicle (a two-door, V6, purple one at that) with the Crystal Lake Chrysler-Plymouth dealership on February 5, on the understanding that his deposit would be returned if no such vehicle was ever delivered to the dealership. Hessler believed, and by the time the case was finally resolved in 2003, the Appellate Court of Illinois eventually agreed, that Hessler was entitled to the first 1997 Prowler delivered to the dealership, if indeed any were delivered. On March 23 Crystal Lake entered into an agreement with one Salvatori Palandri, who it turned out was also promised the first 1997 Plymouth Prowler delivered to the dealership. Hessler kept on the prowl for a Prowler, eventually contacting 38 other Chrysler-Plymouth dealerships. In September he attended a "Chrysler customer appreciation event" at Great America and talked directly with a Chrysler representative, getting from him a list of dealerships that were slated to get delivery of Prowlers. Ultimately, on October 27, 1977, the Crystal Lake dealership delivered the one and only Prowler it received that year to Palandri. The appellate court determined that the dealership's contract in March to, in effect, sell the car already promised to Hessler to another "reasonably indicated to [Hessler] that [Crystal Lake] would not deliver to him a Prowler" under the agreement entered into in February, and was reasonably taken by Hessler as an anticipatory repudiation. Of course it didn't hurt Hessler's case that, by September, the owner of the dealership was responding to Hessler's anxious phone calls with statements that he would not sell Hessler the car even if he got one, giving as his reason the fact that Hessler had "gone behind his back" by contacting Chrysler directly.

3. This is a repudiation by Belle. Serge could decide it makes sense to treat her email as a request for a modification of their agreement and go along with the change. If he does not want to do this, Serge's options are all laid out in §2-610: He has the right to suspend performance (that is, he doesn't have to ship the fabric and won't be in breach when it fails to arrive by the 15th); he can immediately treat this as a breach and pursue his remedies as a seller under §2-703; he can wait for a "commercially reasonable time" and hope for a retraction, although after the end of a commercial reasonable time he may be obligated to treat the repudiation as a problem that is not going to go away and react to it as a breach, mitigating his damages as best he can.

4. a. The status of the parties at this point is that they have a contract for the purchase and sale of a machine. Although there has been a repudiation, there has never really been a breach. Under §2-611, the retraction of the repudiation "reinstates" the contract, "with due excuse and allowance to the aggrieved party for any delay occasioned by the repudiation." Stamper is obligated to deliver the machine, but the date of delivery is moved forward something like a month. Other than that, unless there are other consequences of the delay of which we are not aware, all other terms remain the same.
   b. If this were the case, Betrand would not be able to retract his repudiation as Stamper has "materially changed" its position because of the May 5 email (§2-611(1)). Stamper may, of course, decide it still wants to sell a machine to Betrand, but it is not obligated to do so and would have the flexibility of negotiating an entirely new contract if it chose. Or it could just tell Betrand to take a hike and keep its lawyer on the case.

5. No. Stella is not bound to the contract. Arnold has attempted a retraction of his repudiation and can rightly argue that Stella did not materially

change her position prior to the retraction. But §2-611 also states that the repudiator has no absolute right to retract if the aggrieved party has "canceled." Under §§2-610 and 2-703(f), Stella had the right to cancel immediately upon hearing the repudiation, and that seems to be what she did. The definition of *cancellation* in §2-106(4) doesn't actually say *how* you cancel, but Stella did say she was calling the whole thing off. Note also that §2-611(1) speaks of canceling or "otherwise indicating" that you consider the repudiation final. So an *indication*, not any particular formalism or any action taken in reliance, should be enough to frustrate a subsequent attempt by Arnold to retract.

There has actually been very little discussion about how and when a cancellation is executed. The *Neptune* case (remember the Model RC-520 triple access Precision Vertical Machining Center?) seems to be the first (in 1989) to confront the question. The law prior to the Code was unclear, but there was a plausible argument that a retraction was permissible at any time before the other party had suffered some change in position. The court in *Neptune* concluded that §2-611 was to the contrary, at least in the particular instance, commenting:

> [W]e assume that the drafters intentionally used the disjunctive: that is the breaching [don't they mean repudiating?] party loses the right to retract if the nonbreaching party materially changes his position or cancels. (Emphasis added.)

The court added to this careful (one might say obvious) reading of the section two other reasons for declining to give effect to the retraction despite the absence of any discernible prejudice against the nonrepudiating party. There is, they noted, a great value to certainty once the nonrepudiating party has had his or her say and means it to be final. In addition, the court said it could not ignore, in this instance, the repudiator's "less-than-exemplary conduct" throughout the course of the contract. Could Arnold Moneybucks distinguish *Neptune* and successfully argue that *his* retraction came in time and should be allowed to have effect? We will have to await further cases, if there are any, beyond *Neptune* exploring this issue, but in light of the "or" in §2-611(1), I don't see why the repudiator should have this argument. If Stella wants to uncancel her cancellation, I think that should be up to her and not forced on her by Arnold's latest change of heart.

6. a. No. Use of §2-609 is predicated on a party having "reasonable grounds for insecurity" about performance by the other. This is obviously not a precise requirement, and subsection (2) adds only a bit to our understanding. It should be clear, however, that "reasonable grounds" as that phrase is used here is meant to connote some *change*, or at least an objective reason to suspect change, in the probability that the other party will perform from what would have been true at the time

the agreement was entered into. Comment 1 speaks of "either the willingness or the ability of a party to perform materially declin[ing] between the time of contracting and the time of performance." It is not enough that a party like Sunny has second thoughts or himself revaluates the risks inherent in the sales agreement, finding greater reason to be edgy. In *Cole v. Melvin*, 441 F. Supp. 193 (D.S.C. 1977), the court made little of the seller's argument rooted in §2-609:

> The first requirement for application [of §2-609] is that "reasonable grounds for insecurity arise" with respect to the performance of one of the parties. Clearly, the drafters of the code did not intend that one party to a contract can go about demanding security for the performance of the other whenever he gets nervous about a contract. Some reason for demand for assurance must precede the demand. . . . After a search of the transcript, we have nothing . . . which even approaches being a factually established ground for insecurity. Obviously, something prompted Cole [the seller] to ask Melvin if he planned to perform. But, from everything in the record, it appears that Cole was prompted by purely subjective concerns which were not rooted in any objective facts that can now be legally equated with reasonable grounds for insecurity.

Note that if an argument such as Cole's—or Sunny's in our story—were to succeed, §2-609 would be transformed into a means for one party unilaterally to force a revision in the sales contract in his favor, getting some advantage that he hadn't thought it important (or possible) to insist on initially. That's not what the section is about.

Even if there has been some demonstrable change in circumstances, insecurity on a party's part does not always allow for use of the §2-609 mechanism. Subjective insecurity (which just about all of us are prone to on occasion, I have no doubt) is not enough; "reasonable grounds" for insecurity must be present. "Reasonableness" is always a tricky issue. In *By-Lo Oil Co., Inc. v. ParTech, Inc.*, 11 Fed. App'x 538 (6th Cir. 2001), the Sixth Circuit affirmed a determination by the district court that the plaintiff—owner and user of a software program necessary to the functioning of its business, distributed by ParTech, which was committed under the contract to give "continuing support to the user"—could not have had, in January of 1998, reasonable grounds for insecurity as to whether the computer would function properly after December 31, 1999. The court reasoned:

> [I]t is clear that as of January 7, 1998, By-Lo had no reasonable grounds to feel insecure [about the Y2K problem]. By-Lo does not complain about ParTech's previous service nor is there any indication that it was in a time pinch to obtain a new system if ParTech did not respond quickly. There is no indication that By-Lo had reason to believe that it would take a lengthy period of time to make any corrections ParTech required.

As it turned out, ParTech was able to give By-Lo a definitive answer to its concerns, and the new software to deal with the problem by December 1998. In the meantime, however, By-Lo had purchased an entirely new system, both software and hardware, from another company for $175,000. It argued that it was released from its obligations to ParTech by that firm's failure to respond definitively to its demand for assurance made in a letter sent on January 7, 1998. As we've seen, By-Lo had jumped the gun by attempting to invoke the §2-609 insecurity mechanism without reasonable grounds for doing so. Its contract with ParTech remained enforceable, its replacement of the ParTech system with another one notwithstanding.

If you're looking for a good case where such reasonable grounds unquestionably did exist, you could do no better than *Turntables, Inc. v. Gestetner*, 382 N.Y.S.2d 798 (App. Div. 1976). The court held that the seller had reasonable grounds to be concerned about the buyer's ability to pay, even if he had from the start agreed to a sale on credit and even though the buyer might not in fact have become insolvent as he feared. What warranted the seller's recourse to §2-609? The court stated:

> The buyer was in arrears in payment for goods already delivered; its "Fifth Avenue Showroom" turned out to be a telephone answering service; its Island Park factory turned out to be someone else's premises, to which the [buyer] did not have a key, and [buyer] did not lease space, had no employees, payroll machinery, or equipment therein; another supplier told [seller] it had been stuck with an unpaid bill of [buyer's]; [buyer] had a bad reputation for performance or payment, etc.

You get the idea. The seller refused to deliver. This nondelivery was held not to be a breach, as the buyer had refused following a written request to give any assurances whatsoever that it would be able to pay.

b. Comment 3 suggests this would be enough to allow for Sunny's use of the §2-609 mechanism. The Comment refers to an "apparently trustworthy source" of information that the other party is not performing his or her contracts. It would therefore be fair to inquire about the people from whom Sunny heard what he heard. But unless rumors of this type are known to be rarely based on anything, Sunny probably has the right to demand "adequate assurance of due performance." See *Clem Perrin Marine Towing, Inc. v. Panama Canal Co.*, 730 F.2d 186 (5th Cir. 1984), for a case that follows this line. What if the rumors are in fact unfounded? Isn't this unfair to Bunny? No, not if you remember that the idea is not that Sunny is automatically able to get out of the contract or unilaterally revise the agreement in his favor. What he *can* do is "demand assurance" from Bunny. If he does not get it within a reasonable time, not in excess of 30 days, he can treat the contract as repudiated by her.

Section 2-609(4) is really the crucial part of the section. The right to demand assurance under subsection (1) gives either party in an appropriate situation the opportunity to force the issue and seek clarification, leading perhaps to a clear-cut and definitive repudiation. The other party can, of course, always short circuit this result by giving adequate assurances if this is possible. If the rumors of her financial trouble are untrue, Bunny should be able to alleviate Sunny's fears by putting him in contact with her other creditors or getting some kind of clean bill of financial health from her bank.

So if Sunny is within his rights in making a demand in this instance, the issue becomes whether the particular demand he is making—that she either pay in cash or give a personal guarantee—is justified. He is not entitled to demand any and everything of her that would make him perfectly comfortable, only *adequate* assurance. Comment 4 goes into some length trying to elaborate what type of demand is justified. Necessarily, the question has to be addressed on a case-by-case basis. Is Bunny a businesswoman of "good repute" or a "known corner-cutter"? What does the application of commercial standards justify here?

You should take time to appreciate the consequences for Sunny if he has legitimate reason to make a demand under §2-609 but makes a demand that in substance is not "justified," perhaps because he demands too much or refuses to be assuaged by what a court later determines to be "reasonable" assurances. If Bunny does respond to his email in such a fashion and he, still insecure in his own mind but now not justifiably so, continues to refuse delivery of the dolls, *he* will be committing a breach or repudiation. Section 2-609 is meant to offer comfort for the contracting parties, but if either tries to push it too far or demands too much, it can end up blowing up in that party's face.

c. Does Sunny have reasonable grounds for insecurity in this situation? Under the common law, it was generally said that if parties had more than one contract with each other, each arrangement worked independently. The breach (or argued breach) of one had no effect on responsibilities under any other. The second paragraph to Comment 3 indicates that this isn't strictly true under this provision of Article 2. A ground for insecurity need *not* arise from or be directly related to the contract in question. (We've already seen that even rumors about how the buyer is treating his other creditors may be enough.) The next paragraph in the Comment specifically deals with the situation where the buyer is behind in his account with the seller on other contracts. So if Bunny is behind in payment to Sunny for other purchases and offers no good excuse, Sunny could make a demand for assurance that he will be paid for the dolls. And, what would be important to him, until he got such an assurance, he could also suspend his own performance. He would not have to continue preparing the dolls or ship them off until Bunny's account was cleared up or sufficient assurances of payment were arranged. In *Smyers v. QuartzWorks Corp.*, 880 F. Supp. 1425 (D. Kan. 1995), it was held that the manufacturer of a variety of devices used in the fabrication of quartz crystal resonators who had not been paid as promised on a contract for one product (a kind of quartz welder) had reasonable grounds for insecurity regarding the same buyer's performance of a distinct contract for a different product (a "goniometer").

The situation here is more complex, in that Bunny is arguing that Sunny has not been paid for the trains not because of any financial difficulty on her part, but because they were defective. Unless Sunny believes he can establish that Bunny is advancing this claim in bad faith, he would be risking a lot if he puts too much faith in the §2-609 mechanism here or pushes it too aggressively. The fact that she is not paying for goods that she in good faith believes to be defective is not a mark of a "cost-cutter" or of someone who is in any kind of financial difficulty. It's just standard, respectable business practice. The court presumably would be careful not to allow invocation of §2-609 to be used as a cudgel to force payment out of a buyer who has legitimate problems with delivered goods by legitimating the seller's threat to withhold unrelated merchandise as it becomes due.

7. a. Here, it is Betty the buyer who has reasonable grounds for insecurity. See the reference in Comment 3 to the buyer of precision parts who discovers that her seller "is making defective deliveries of such parts to other buyers with similar needs." A case in point is *Creusot-Loire International, Inc. v. Coppus Engineering Corp.*, 585 F. Supp. 45 (S.D.N.Y. 1983).

   The problem for Betty here is that she did not make a *written* demand for assurance—her demand was made over the telephone. There are a few cases where the courts have "waived" or "forgiven" a party's failure to put its demand in writing and given effect to a demand under §2-609 despite the fact that it was entirely oral. See *Atwood-Kellogg, Inc. v. Nickerson Farms*, 602 N.W.2d 749 (S.D. 1999). This may well be a good occasion to ask: What is the reason for the rule? It would seem that the purpose is to make sure the other party knows that something serious is going on—after all, if they don't respond to the demand, then they are the breaching party. In these cases, it seems there was no question that the demand was made, even if not in a formal writing, and that the party later held to have repudiated under §2-609(4) was well aware of the other's insecurity, the reasonable grounds for that insecurity, and what was being demanded in the way of assurance. The Washington Court of Appeals has declined to recognize an oral "demand" as sufficient, contrasting the situation before it with those rare cases in which "the courts found that the pattern of interaction between the parties made the demand for assurances sufficiently clear that no writing was necessary." *Alaska Pacific Trading Co. v. Eagon Forest Products, Inc.*, 933 P.2d 417 (Wash. App. 1997). It might be noted that the common law rule on demand for assurances, as found in Restatement (Second) of Contracts §251, does not require that the demand be in writing.

Good practice and common sense, of course, counsel that anyone seeking to use the insecurity mechanism put the demand in writing, make the writing as clear and precise as possible, date it, and get some proof that the other party received it. (Technically, notice does not require this last bit, see §1-202(a), but we're talking good practice and common sense here.) And recall that under the 2022 Amendments and UETA, a "record" is required rather than a writing.

b. Here Betty has reasonable grounds and has been careful enough to make a written demand. The question is whether she has received "adequate assurance." Are the president's words alone enough? I would argue not, at least not when coupled with his apparent refusal to give her any more information or even to speak with her. Perhaps she should be grateful for his silence. In *Smith-Scharff Paper Co. v. P. N. Hirsch & Co. Stores, Inc.*, 754 S.W.2d 928 (Mo. Ct. App. 1988), a demand for assurance was met with a torrent of words, not all of them friendly. When seller's justified written demand got no response, its president put in a call to the president of the buyer, about which he testified:

> I remember him yelling at me over the telephone, that I would have the audacity to question the integrity of their company, that they would honor all commitments, and, historically, they have bent over backwards to honor all of their commitments.

This, the court concluded, "was an unreasonable response to a simple request for assurance." Judgment for seller affirmed. See also *Koch Materials Co. v. Shore Slurry Seal, Inc.*, 205 F. Supp. 2d 324 (D.N.J. 2002), where a party's absolute refusal to give any information by way of reassurance seems to have been based solely on what the court characterized as his "I don't like lawyers" attitude.

In our hypothetical, what could the president of Stamper have done, and in the way of adequate assurance, what would Betty have the right to expect? The president should have responded in more detail about what problems they were experiencing, if any, with the product, whether there was reason to suspect that these problems might affect the machine being made for Betty, and if so, what corrective measures were being taken or quality controls instituted. The president could even have offered to let Betty come over and inspect the machinery as it was being fabricated. Certainly he should have returned her calls. The sort of assurances that are called for or that should serve to meet the §2-609 challenge are presumably as varied as the grounds for insecurity that can arise. There is no particular form that assurances must take, and a good business sense should serve as an adequate guide. A buyer or a seller who is justifiably asked to give adequate assurance—and who truly wants to and will be able to perform—should be able to find some way to assuage any reasonable fears of the other party.

CHAPTER 21

Installment Sales

THE INSTALLMENT CONTRACT UNDER ARTICLE 2

The term "installment contract" or "installment sale" is familiar from everyday use. For the purposes of analysis under Article 2, however, we defer to the definition in §2-612(1):

> An "installment contract" is one which requires or authorizes delivery of goods in separate lots to be separately accepted, even though the contract contains a clause "each delivery is a separate contract" or its equivalent.

Recall that the default rule in §2-307 is that the goods "must be tendered in a single delivery," so an installment contract reflects the parties' opting out of that rule. Note also that it is only the *delivery* that has to be in installments, payment can be all up front, all at the end, or anywhere in between and it will still be an installment contract.

The word "lot" is defined in §2-105(5) to mean:

> a parcel or a single article which is the subject matter of a separate sale or delivery, whether or not it is sufficient to perform the contract.

The word "parcel" is itself not terribly clear here. Although this definition of lot has never caused a whit of trouble, it might be better if expanded to include not only the parcel and the single article, but also something like "a collection of parcels or articles which taken together" are the subject matter of a separate sale or delivery.

In most instances, of course, we know a *lot* when we see one, and in fact there is rarely any great doubt whether a particular contract qualifies as an installment contract. Typically the seller is to make a series of separate deliveries over time and the buyer agrees to pay for each delivery according to some payment plan laid out in the agreement. The contract may call for delivery of specified lots on some predetermined schedule. So, for example, seller may be obligated to deliver 10,000 pounds of a given commodity by the first of the month for each and every month during a period of years. For its part, the buyer will be required to accept separately each of the monthly deliveries and pay for them, say by sending seller a check for $500 by the 15th of the following month. In some installment contracts, the exact quantities and dates of individual deliveries are not set out in advance. A construction contractor, for example, may contract to buy a total of 8,000 feet of a designated type of pipe from a supplier to be used in a particular building project. The contract will specify that the pipe is to be delivered to the construction site at such times and in such amounts (eventually aggregating to the 8,000 feet) as are called for by the contractor over the period of six months, during which construction is to take place. The contract will further provide that when a delivery is made, the contractor-buyer must pay for the pipe at a specified price per foot. Payment may be made due on delivery or within some specified period after delivery. Or the contract could call for payment, say, by the 15th of any month for all pipe delivered (no matter the number of deliveries) in the previous month. Any of these arrangements would clearly be an installment contract under §2-612(1), as each *requires* delivery in lots to be separately accepted.

In other circumstances, delivery in lots may not be explicitly called for in the contract, but may be anticipated nevertheless. As Comment 1 states, the definition in §2-612 is intended to cover, by its use of the word "authorized" in addition to "required," the possibility of a series of separate deliveries "tacitly authorized by the circumstances or by the option of either party." In this regard, look back to §2-307. Delivery in lots is *authorized* where "the circumstances give either party the right to make or demand delivery in lots" and furthermore the price, if it can, is to be "apportioned" among the lots. If you have any problem with this result, you may want to look at Comment 3 to §2-307 and to our treatment of that section in Chapter 9. (The treatment was brief, but then this section seems to give few people difficulty.) For present purposes, look at Comment 2 to §2-612. It is sufficient for finding an installment contract that the circumstances lend themselves to *delivery and acceptance* in distinct episodes. *Payment* by apportionment may be nice for one or both of the parties involved, but it is not a necessary condition for an installment contract.

Historically, some contracting parties have sought to avoid having their relationship characterized as an installment contract by inserting language in the agreement stating that each delivery is to be considered a separate contract or the like. Practically, of course, it's usually one of the two parties that sticks such language into the boilerplate for its own sinister purposes. As Comment 3 discusses, the definition of §2-612 makes abundantly clear that such "legalistic" language will not have any effect. The "singleness of the document and the negotiations" together with "the sense of the situation" are to control. You should not take from this Comment the idea that a contract must necessarily be evidenced by a single record if it is to be judged an installment contract. In *Cassidy Podell Lynch, Inc. v. Snydergeneral Corp.*, 994 F.2d 1131 (3d Cir. 1991), for example, the buyer contracted to obtain from the seller $350,000 worth of equipment—all of which it was to use to meet a single resale commitment. With the seller's blessing, the buyer entered 23 distinct purchase orders, the reason being that the seller had a self-imposed ceiling of $15,000 on any individual purchase order. Despite the multiplicity of papers, the court had no difficulty recognizing this as a single installment contract and applying §2-612 to the controversy between the parties. See also *Phoenix Color Corp. v. Krause America, Inc.*, 25 F. App'x 133 (4th Cir. 2001), in which the Fourth Circuit remarked that, "When something looks like an installment contract and walks like an installment contract, we find ourselves unable to conclude that it is not."

It has to be emphasized that the definition of installment contract is just that: a *definition*. There is no language in §2-612(1) that says that an installment contract is such-and-such "unless otherwise agreed" by the parties. Parties are not allowed to vary or contract out of a definition under the Code, even in the very freedom-of-contract-oriented Article 2. Nor may they simply ignore the consequences of that definition. As we will now note, Article 2 sets forth some special rules applicable to installment sales, and the buyer and the seller who have entered into what the Article deems to be an installment contract will have to play by those rules whether they would agree to them or not.

PLAYING BY THE RULES FOR INSTALLMENT SALES

Section 2-612, in subsections (2) and (3), sets forth the special rules that govern the performance of installment sales contracts. The questions that soon follow will explore the workings of these provisions. Read these subsections now. As you can see, the treatment of installment sales is different from the one-shot non-installment sale in that the perfect tender rule, as incorporated into §2-601, does not apply. The right to reject will now hinge on "substantial" nonconformity, which must mean something different than failure to conform "in any respect," the hallmark language of §2-601. (You should refer back to that section and note that it explicitly defers to §2-612 on the governance of installment contracts.) As you work through this material, you will want to consider what might have moved the drafters who otherwise felt committed to the perfect tender rule for sales to abandon that rule in the special circumstance of the installment sale. True, no one likes to take the perfect tender rule literally to begin with, but there may be more to the §2-612 result than just the drafters taking every opportunity they could to shoot holes in it. What makes installment sales different, and perhaps particularly unsuited to the perfect tender rule?

Examples

EXAMPLES

1. Birmingham Integrated Machines manufactures computers. One of the component parts of the machines it makes is a specific kind of On/Off switch. BIM contracts to buy a total of 600,000 switches (the #GH70) from Switcher International. The contract calls for the delivery of 50,000 switches no later than the 15th day of each month during the calendar year. BIM is to pay $2 per switch within ten days after delivery. On January 17, Switcher makes its first delivery to BIM. The shipment contains 49,000 of the #GH70 switches. Because it has been careful to keep an ample supply of switches in its own storeroom, BIM does not suffer any production problems on January 15 or 16. The BIM production manager says she does not anticipate needing more than 45,000 or 46,000 switches prior to the middle of February, as the beginning of the year is typically a period of slow production.
   (a) May BIM reject the January 17 shipment when it arrives?
   (b) Suppose that the delivery made on January 17 had contained only 40,000 of the switches. Could BIM have rejected in that case?
   (c) Suppose the January 17 shipment had contained 50,000 switches, but upon inspection it was found that they were all of the wrong type? The purchasing director calls up Switcher and is told that the seller will bring a full load of the correct model switches to BIM within the next two or three days. Could BIM have rejected?
   (d) Now suppose instead that Switcher made no delivery whatsoever on January 17. Instead it makes a conforming delivery of 50,000 switches on January 25. On January 21, the production manager had become concerned that she might have to shut down the entire production line for lack of On/Off switches. After consultation among the managers, the purchasing director arranged a contract to buy 50,000 of a similar switch (at $2.25 each) from another manufacturer, Mitch's Switches, which promised delivery of its product on

January 27. When the shipment from Switcher International arrives on January 25, is BIM obligated to accept it?

(e) The president of BIM is upset about what has happened and that he has even had to consider the prospect of shutting down production because of a failure in supply of such a rudimentary part. (Mitch has also indicated that he would be willing to supply the needed switches for only $1.90 apiece if he did not have to make delivery on short notice.) May the president simply email Switcher at the end of January saying that he is canceling their contract because of the lateness of the January delivery? If he did so, what would be the result?

(f) Suppose the President does not attempt to cancel the contract in January but only emails Switcher indicating his annoyance at what has happened. The delivery promised for February 15 does not arrive until February 20. Can BIM now cancel the contract and make other arrangements with Mitch? If not now, when?

2. Seller agrees to sell and Buyer to buy 1,000 large round blue buttons each month during the calendar year. Delivery is to be made by Seller no later than the tenth day of each month. On January 5, Seller makes a delivery that turns out to contain only 900 buttons. Buyer calls Seller to ask what has gone wrong. He doesn't yell; he simply points out the problem. Seller apologizes for the mistake and delivers the additional 100 buttons on January 7. On February 6 Buyer receives a shipment that contains 1,000 *small* round blue buttons. Again Buyer calls, and again Seller apologizes and makes a conforming delivery, now on February 8. In March the delivery arrives on the 7th. It contains the right number of large round buttons, but they are *yellow*. There follows another call, another apology, and another conforming delivery before the 10th of March. When a shipment of 1,000 large *square* blue buttons arrives on April 2, can Buyer reject this shipment? Can he cancel his contract with Seller and buy buttons elsewhere?

3. Buster the building contractor has been awarded a contract to construct an office building. He estimates that he will need something like 200,000 bricks to complete the work. He enters into a contract with Sarah's Building Supply that calls for her to deliver bricks (in commercial units of 10,000) to the job site as requested by Buster. Sarah will bill Buster at $1 apiece for any bricks delivered during a month at the end of that month, and she is to receive payment from Buster by the fifteenth day of the following month. Buster first calls for a load of 30,000 bricks in May. Sarah delivers the bricks and sends him a bill for $30,000 at the end of the month. She is asked to and does deliver a second load of 50,000 on June 5. By June 23, she still has not received any payment from Buster for the May bricks.

(a) He calls her and asks for another delivery. Must she make the delivery he is now requesting? Would Sarah be within her rights to cancel the contract at this time following up with a suit for the $80,000 now owed plus her lost profits on the bricks never delivered?

(b) What would be the consequence if Sarah immediately brought suit only for the $80,000 now owed her?

(c) Suppose that in fact Buster had sent Sarah a check for $30,000 on June 22. This check arrives at Sarah's on the 24th and clears with no problem. Meanwhile, after having been promised this payment, Sarah did deliver an additional 40,000 bricks in late June. She sends him a bill for $90,000 covering the two June deliveries. She receives a check from him on July 24. Sarah calls Buster and tells him that she is not happy with his lateness in payment and that she expects prompt payment in the future. He tells her it will never happen again. Sarah bills Buster for bricks delivered in July, but by August 16 has received no payment from him. Can Sarah cancel the contract now?

(d) Would your answer to the previous question be any different if Sarah had not complained to Buster at all about the late payments in June and July but simply deposited the checks as she received them?

4. Seller and Buyer have entered into a 20-month installment contract, starting with delivery in January, under which Buyer is to make payments by the twentieth day after receiving his monthly delivery. Seller makes the first ten deliveries and receives payment with no problem. After delivery in late November, Buyer calls Seller telling her that he is short of cash and "will not be able to make payment this month." Seller threatens not to make any future deliveries as long as Buyer is behind in his account. Buyer reacts, "You can't do that. If I don't get the stuff from you, it will ruin my business and just drive me deeper in the hole. I'm willing to agree that all future deliveries will be for cash. I might even be able to get you a guarantee from my bank that you'll be paid for those future deliveries. You'll just have to wait for the December payment. You'll get it eventually." Seller responds that she considers the contract at an end and will deliver no more stuff to Buyer. Is she within her rights to do this?

Explanations

1. a. No. BIM may not reject. Under §2-612(2), the buyer may reject an individual installment only if it is nonconforming and "the nonconformity substantially impairs the value of that installment." There are two nonconformities here, the late delivery and the short delivery, but there seems to be no way to argue that either "substantially impairs" the value of the January installment to BIM. A delivery short 1,000 out of the promised 50,000 units could obviously be substantially

deficient in many situations, but it doesn't look to be so here. If this were not an installment contract and the right to reject came under §2-601, the perfect tender rule would apply (at least in theory) and Switcher would have faced a legitimate rejection, even if BIM could not have shown and indeed would not have suffered any real hardship because of the sins of this delivery.

The obvious question is how we are to judge whether a nonconformity "substantially impairs the value of that installment." The equally obvious answer is that there is no set or easy way to make the call. You have presumably studied the doctrine of so-called material breach or substantial performance as it surfaced in the common law of contracts. You saw there that the measure of nonconformity or shortfall that triggers the rule is all a matter of degree and not subject to any bright-line test. If there isn't very much wrong at all with the tender, that's okay. (At least as far as meeting the performance *condition* and triggering the other party's duty to perform, everything is okay; the nonbreaching party can always seek damages for breach of the *promise* even for the most minute discrepancy.) If the tender is way off the mark, then that's another story. Too much is too much. The condition on the other party's performance has not been met.

The drafters of Article 2 and the courts applying §2-612 have not been able to do much with the "materiality" or "substantiality" concept. Look at the second paragraph to Comment 4. Does the drafters' list of factors on which the substantiality of a defect turns help? As a matter of fact, there has been virtually no litigation over the use of the phrase in subsection (2) of §2-612. Buyers, sellers, and judges seem to know a "nonconformity substantially impairing the value of an installment" when they see one. It will be another matter entirely when we again hit the substantiality measure in subsection (3).

b. Probably not. A shortfall of 10,000 switches *would* substantially impair the value of the installment to BIM because it would have to worry about running out of this vital component sometime in February, but it's more than likely that this is a nonconformity *that can be cured*. Under §2-612(2), the rule is clear. Even a substantially nonconforming tender must be accepted if the problem can be cured. Note in Comment 5 that not only must the buyer accept in this instance, provided the seller gives "adequate assurance of cure," but it also must be willing to suffer some reasonable minor outlay of time, money, and effort to make the cure a reality. What would be cure in this instance? One thing that Switcher could do would be to ship the additional 10,000 switches to BIM so that they got there within a couple of weeks. If BIM had a big enough reserve of switches to carry it through four weeks, it might even be enough for Switcher to promise that there would be 60,000 in the February delivery. In other instances, as the Comment suggests, the seller may cure simply by allowing a reduction in price to reflect the value of the nonconformity.

c. This is clearly a substantial nonconformity, but again it seems to be one that can be cured, and cure is being offered. So BIM cannot reject this shipment either. The only odd thing here is that under a literal reading of §2-612(2), BIM must actually "accept" this shipment even though it's entirely wrong stuff. What the subsection really means to say here is that the buyer need not either *reject* or *accept* in this situation, but has an obligation to *await the offered cure and then accept that* if it is conforming. It's a minor point of language, and not one that I've ever seen cause any true confusion in the real world.

   What if BIM does wait for a new shipment of the correct kind of switch and, when it comes in a few days, there is some problem with *that* delivery? Could BIM reject for an insubstantial nonconformity? Does it have to allow Switcher another chance to cure? We're quickly into the variety of problems that make the whole concept of cure both interesting and frustrating. (Recall Chapter 18.) One concern is that liberal employment of the cure principle, especially when coupled with a "substantial impairment" standard for rejection, can be so favorable to the seller as to put the buyer at a distinct disadvantage.

d. BIM may reject the shipment that arrives on January 25 under §2-612(2). Although we have no precise way of measuring these things, the lateness here seems unquestionably to have substantially impaired the value of the installment (or rather the value of BIM's having arranged to receive this installment on the 15th), and furthermore the lateness is not curable.

   One of the earliest cases on §2-612, and one of the better known, is *Graulich Caterer, Inc. v. Hans Holterbosch, Inc.*, 243 A.2d 253 (N.J. Super. 1968). Defendant Holterbosch, an American importer and distributor of Lowenbrau beer, was granted the franchise to operate the Lowenbrau Pavilion at the 1964 World's Fair. He entered into a contract with the plaintiff, a professional catering concern, for daily deliveries of platters of German food that were to be reheated using the then-novel "microwave cooking concept" and thereupon sold to the pavilion's patrons. Initial samples of the meals came out of the microwave in good condition and were apparently of high quality. Following a delayed and muddled opening of the Fair, the buyer first placed a firm order for meals for April 23. As the court explained:

> Upon delivery the members of defendant's organization were stunned by the product and complained immediately that the tendered units did not, in any way, match the contract samples. Rejecting this 955-unit installment as unacceptable, defendant described the food as "bland," unpresentable, tasteless and "just wasn't the type of food we could sell."

The court found that Holterbosch was within his rights in rejecting the April 23 delivery, "since the nonconformity of the tendered goods with the accepted sample was incurable, and thus substantially impaired the value of that installment." What happened next? You'll have to wait for a minute. As is often true when installment contracts are involved, the story didn't end there. We return to *Graulich* soon enough.

e. It is doubtful that BIM can cancel the entire contract because of the lateness of the first delivery even if it substantially impaired the value of *that installment* to the buyer. The test for whether there is a "breach of the whole" is found in §2-612(3). Does the "non-conformity or default with respect to one or more installments substantially impair[] the value of the whole contract" to BIM? While you could say it's anybody's guess once a standard of "substantiality" is to be applied, it seems to me highly unlikely that a problem with the first installment by itself would justify a buyer in treating this as a breach of the whole. Comment 5 isn't any great help here, but do note the first sentence: "Subsection (3) is designed to further the continuance of the contract in the absence of an overt cancellation."

   If the president of BIM did use the late January delivery (even if it were a very late one) to justify his cancellation as buyer, he runs a high risk that later, if Switcher claims it was ready, willing, and able to deliver properly from February on, his firm, BIM, will be found to have repudiated the agreement. It's all too easy for a court looking at things after the fact to be persuaded that the party to an installment contract who, in the heat of the moment, declared the other to be in breach of the whole acted rashly and was itself in breach. The president of BIM is going to have to tread carefully here.

f. After two successive late deliveries, BIM has a much stronger case that taken together there has been a breach of the whole. But who's to say? It's not even clear that BIM has grounds for rejecting this February shipment on the 20th. For that we have to go back to subsection (2). If they can't reject the individual installment under that provision, could they ever say that the cumulative effect was enough under (3)? It seems they should be able to, but there's no clear answer in the language of the section. Switcher can point to the fact that to its credit it came closer this time, being only five days late. Maybe it should be given a final chance to get it right in March and thereafter.

   If you do conclude that two late shipments are enough for the buyer to invoke §2-612(3), do they have to be sequential? Suppose the shipment is just fine in February, but then there is late delivery again in March. How do you rule?

   For one example of a two-strikes-you're-out result, I refer you back to *Graulich* (the case of the microwaved sauerbraten). To continue that story, after the first day's delivery (on April 23) was rejected as just not the type of food the buyer could serve, the buyer and seller conferred on how to make corrections. The court tells us what happened next:

> [A second delivery on April 24 was] likewise unacceptable. Of the 2520 units delivered, between 500 and 700 were distributed among the employees and patrons of the exhibit for a fast reaction. The complaints in response to the food were many and varied. Defendant, describing the sources of the unfavorable comment, stated that the sauerbraten was dry and the gravy, pasty and unpalatably "gooey," surrounded rather than enveloped the meat. The knockwurst platter suffered similarly, being dry and comparing unfavorably with the standards established by the samples. Generally, defendant complained that the food was simply not "German food" and as such was unacceptable for the Lowenbrau Pavilion.

Following the failure of this second delivery, the pavilion director quickly sprang into action, converting the microwave setup into a conventional kitchen using pot burners to successfully prepare food for the duration of the Fair. Peace and the reputation of good German cooking were restored. The court found that under the circumstances, the buyer had been justified not only in rejecting the second installment as it had the first, but also in canceling the contract altogether:

> The second unacceptable delivery and the failure of the plaintiff's additional curative efforts left the defendant in a position for one week without food. Time was critical. Plaintiff knew that platters of maximum quality were required on a daily installment basis. Because of defendant's immediate need for quality food and plaintiff's failure to cure, we find that the nonconformity of the second delivery, projected upon the circumstances of this case, "substantially impair[ed] the value of the whole contract [and resulted in] a breach of the whole."

The North Carolina Court of Appeals held that two nonconforming deliveries of custom-ordered retail display tables, those destined for stores in Oregon and Kansas, justified the buyer's treating the installment contract as having been breached as to the whole and refusing to take delivery of the third installment, intended for a store in New Mexico. As the court noted:

> Non-conformities in the Oregon and Kansas installments, individually and cumulatively, substantially impaired the contract as a whole. The tables of the first installments were impossible to assemble and were delivered late. The tables were not usable as delivered to Design [the buyer]. Citro [the seller] offered no cure of the defects and Design bore the expense of repairing the tables [in the first two installments] to meet a deadline known to both parties.

Design Plus Store Fixtures, Inc. v. Citro Corp., 508 S.E.2d 825 (N.C. App. 1998).

The results in these cases seem easy to live with, but it shouldn't be taken that two nonconforming deliveries, even two in a row, necessarily give the buyer the right to call the deal at an end. In other circumstances, the courts have called on the buyer to take a lot more grief without rendering the whole relationship asunder. In *Holiday Manufacturing Co. v. B.A.S.F. Systems, Inc.*, 380 F. Supp. 1096 (D. Neb. 1974), the buyer placed a long-term order for plastic cassettes (the type used in making audiocassettes) with the seller. The contract called for six million pieces in all. About one year after deliveries were to have begun—and after a long string of deliveries (some conforming and some not), notifications, reevaluations, redesigns, and corrections—the buyer attempted to cancel. Deliveries had been consistently late. The buyer could and did point to any number of instances of defects in quality. Was the cancellation justified? The court held that it was not. As to the lateness:

> There is no question that Holiday's cassette manufacturing project was behind schedule and that at no point during the existence of the contract was Holiday delivering five hundred thousand cassettes a month [as had been promised]. However, nowhere in either the correspondence between Holiday and B.A.S.F. or the inter-office correspondence of B.A.S.F. introduced at trial is there any indication whatsoever that B.A.S.F. was seriously concerned with Holiday's delivery delays. . . . The Court concludes that B.A.S.F.'s use of the Holiday sonic-welded cassette was a potentially very profitable business venture and that the delays which occurred in development of this relatively new product by a manufacturer unfamiliar with cassette production were liberally tolerated by B.A.S.F. Certainly B.A.S.F. cannot now be allowed to pursue this course of conduct concerning Holiday's failure to perform the contract on time [that is, continually urging them on to produce an acceptable product], and then be permitted to urge this nonperformance as a justification for canceling the contract.

What about the profusion of quality defects that had come up? The court considered each in turn, concluding that "the issue of whether these . . . substantially impaired the value of the cassette contract to B.A.S.F. is a close one." Looking at all of the evidence, however, the court concluded that B.A.S.F. as buyer was not justified in canceling the contract. Important to the court's determination was the fact that whatever defects (some very substantial in themselves) had been discovered were eventually cured by the manufacturer, even if new problems did then crop up. The court also noted that many months into the agreement, and not long before its attempted cancellation, B.A.S.F. had placed orders with Holiday for additional cassettes "virtually *identical*" (emphasis by the court) to those to be produced under the original contract. B.A.S.F. was held responsible for profits lost by Holiday.

You may want to read the *B.A.S.F.* case in its entirety to get the full flavor of what went on. It's a good example of how complicated and messy the situation can get in a long-term installment contract between two major commercial parties. Whether the decision itself is a good example of the application of §2-612(3) is a matter of opinion. Certainly the result can be questioned. Does the case represent an example of how the "substantiality" requirements of §2-612 could end up putting the buyer very much at the mercy of a seller who keeps pushing and trying and is never ready to give up, even if that seller never quite gets it right? Or is the decision defensible as reflecting an appropriate sensitivity on the part of the court to the fact that, in a contract of this nature, there are always going to be problems and the possibility of friction? In just about any installment sales agreement in a commercial setting, the buyer would, if it wished, be able to generate in time for litigation a list of horribles it has had to endure. Were the courts always to give the buyer the benefit of the doubt in such situations, the result might be to turn this species of installment agreement into one that was for all practical purposes at the option of the buyer, who could always drum up sufficient justification for declaring a "breach of the whole."

2. I believe this is an easy case, where the buyer should be able to cancel. Note the language in Comment 6 that reflects the (perfectly reasonable) idea that defects *cumulate* over time. Consider, however, the case of *Bodine Sewer, Inc. v. Eastern Illinois Precast, Inc.*, 493 N.E.2d 705 (Ill. App. 1986). The buyer was a construction contractor working on a sewer project. The seller made repeated deliveries of concrete pipe to the buyer's job site. There was no dispute that various installments were nonconforming. Nor did the parties dispute that all of these earlier defective deliveries were cured by the seller's later shipping conforming materials. When one more defective delivery arrived on April 24, the buyer attempted to get out of the contract altogether. Did it have the right to do so? The court said no. This nonconformity, like those before it, could be cured. As for the argument under §2-612(3):

> Where, as here, defective deliveries pursuant to an installment contract are consistently corrected, and the purchaser, during the time for the contract's performance, voices no concerns to the seller with respect to delays occasioned by the defective deliveries, the nonconforming deliveries do not substantially impair the value of the entire contract. [Citing B.A.S.F.]

Can this blanket statement possibly be true? If so, our button buyer may still have no grounds for cancellation. Should the result hinge on whether Buyer had yelled and threatened during these calls? Even if this series of events did not ever once actually cause him a delay, should he have to live with this situation a day longer? Does Buyer have to put Seller on actual notice that if you have ordered one type of button and you are constantly being delivered an entirely different type there is definitely something wrong?

The actual result in *Bodine Sewer* may be right for all we know. The main lesson I take from the case, however, is how futile (and possibly foolish) it is for a court to come up with general pronouncements when matters of materiality or substantiality of breach are involved. Notice, by the way, that the losing buyer in *Bodine Sewer* apparently tried to make an analogy with the shaken faith doctrine that comes up in connection with issues of cure. (See Chapter 18.) The court didn't seem to see the connection. Do you? If there is something to this idea, it may be undercut by language in Comment 6. You should be able to spot what language I am referring to. Is this part of the Comment justified by either the wording (such as it is) or the policies (such as you can imagine them to be) underlying §2-612(3)?

3. a. You can see we're now going through the same issues, but here with the *buyer* in breach. In theory, the analysis remains the same. Breach is breach and "substantiality" is, in practice if not in theory, to some extent in the mind of the beholder. One missing payment on the part of the buyer would presumably allow the seller to withhold future deliveries until things are cleared up. There is language to this effect in Comment 7. And see *Magic Valley Foods, Inc. v. Sun Valley Potatoes, Inc.*, 10 P.3d 734 (Idaho 2000). At the same time, it seems very unlikely that problems with one payment would automatically allow a seller to call in §2-612(3) and declare a breach of the whole.

   What if the payment was not entirely missing but only late? For example, suppose Buster's check had arrived on the 22nd. What if it isn't for the full amount? If Buster pays only $3,000 for the 30,000 bricks, that is presumably a substantial impairment of the value of this payment to Sarah, but what if his check is for $29,000? Does she have to continue delivering as if nothing is the matter? If so, what do you say to $28,000? And so on. Does it matter what his excuse is for the short payment? He could be disputing the quantity or quality of bricks delivered to him in May. Or he could be saying something equivalent to, "Don't think I'd ever be caught paying $1 per brick when it comes right down to it." How much should a court's application of §2-612 be affected by what it believes to be the parties' true motives? Or should all of this be left out of §2-612 analysis and instead disposed of under the separate rubric of good faith? Perhaps I should apologize for this long series of unanswered questions, but after all, I am a law professor. And under the circumstances, what would you have me say other than that these certainly are interesting and thought-provoking questions?

b. On one thing §2-612(3) is clear: If a party brings an action with respect only to past installments, the contract is reinstated. As Comment 6 explains, there was some question about this under prior law and the drafters wanted to settle it one way as opposed to the other.

c. The defects are certainly beginning to cumulate, and you may well conclude Sarah has sufficient grounds to consider the contract breached as to the whole. Of course, if she does declare a breach of the whole, she is taking some risk that she has jumped the gun. Would you be happy having to litigate her case if she did cancel when later it turned out that the August check had been in the mail and arrived on the 17th? If Buster has to go out and buy bricks for a lot more, he's going to seem awfully sympathetic after the fact. What could Sarah be counseled to do now to minimize her risk of being second-guessed (by a court!) in the future? On the insecurity mechanism of §2-609, see the prior chapter.

d. I hope you see how difficult it would be for Sarah to support any action based on a breach of the whole if she hadn't been complaining about the lateness all along the way. A court disposed to find for Buster would have any number of ways to reach a result favorable to him. Perhaps the parties established a course of performance (§1-303(a)) that allowed for payment later than the 15th of the month. The agreement may say that informal variation from what is laid out in the agreement is not to be effective, but we have to be aware of how cavalierly some courts are able to deal with what they consider mere boilerplate. Or perhaps there has been a waiver under §2-209. Neither course of performance nor waiver is free from ambiguity, but that is precisely why Sarah has so much to fear from them. If a court were to apply either of these two doctrines, it could rightly say of course that Sarah could reestablish the 15th as the absolute date for payment, but that she could only do so *prospectively* with notice to Buster and only with respect to payments not yet due. Any attempt on her part to cancel immediately under the circumstances would therefore have been unjustified.

A court, of course, would not even have to reach out to these other sections and concepts to find for Buster. It could conclude in a straightforward manner that the cumulative effect of the late payments was not such as "substantially impaired" the value of the contract to Sarah. After all, she was getting her money, and she wasn't even complaining. For a court that followed this route, much to the seller's dismay, see *Flood v. M.P. Clark, Inc.*, 319 F. Supp. 1043 (E.D. Pa. 1970).

4. Was Seller right to consider the contract breached as to the whole? I've set up the facts to highlight a bit of language in Comment 6 to which I alluded earlier:

> Whether the non-conformity in any given installment justifies cancellation as to the future depends, not on whether such non-conformity indicates an intent or likelihood that the future deliveries [or payments?] will also be defective, but whether the non-conformity substantially impairs the value of the whole contract. If only the seller's security in regard to future installments is impaired, he has the right to demand adequate assurances of proper future performance but has not an immediate right to cancel the entire contract.

If this is true, then Seller here, assuming that she can be adequately assured of future payments, has no right to cancel. Maybe this is right. After all, she's in no worse situation than if she had made a delivery under a one-shot contract and had to wait and/or sue for payment. But what if the amount owed on the one missing payment is a significant portion of the entire purchase price? What if the buyer is "asking" her to wait for more than one payment? Should Seller still have to continue delivering to Buyer as if nothing were wrong? If so, isn't the result that an installment buyer can always in essence extend himself credit at the seller's expense by acting as this buyer has? All the buyer would have to do is be sure not to overreach and to beg indulgence of the seller only for amounts small enough that it wouldn't be worth the seller's energy to sue or try some other drastic action. Meanwhile Seller would have to keep making deliveries.

In any event, it seems doubtful to me that in reality anyone or any court could keep this prospective/retrospective distinction that clearly in focus. Where issues of materiality of breach are concerned, maybe all we can say is that eventually enough is enough, and hope that our view of what is enough does not differ radically from that of the courts in their wisdom.

One further point to be explored is how §§2-612 and 2-609 interact. It should be clear how the latter may be used in service of someone stuck with an ambiguous situation under the former. But recall that the use of the §2-609 mechanism is always *optional* on the part of any party. In *Cherwell-Ralli, Inc. v. Rytman Grain Co., Inc.*, A.2d 984 (Conn. 1980), the buyer argued that the seller was not justified in terminating the contract in spite of repeated defaults on its part because it, the seller, had never invoked §2-609. There is no requirement, however, that the seller formally notify the buyer that it is insecure when in such a situation. After all, the buyer, who in the instant case had stopped payment on a check, should know perfectly well what could be going on in the seller's mind. As Ellen Peters, a well-respected U.C.C. professor and, later, a well-respected judge, opined in *Cherwell-Ralli*:

> If the buyer's conduct is sufficiently egregious, such conduct will, in and of itself, constitute substantial impairment of the value of the whole contract and a present breach of the contract as a whole.

For my money, the "sufficiently egregious" rule of thumb is about as good as any you're going to get on the workings of §2-612(3) in general—which makes it an appropriate, if not wholly satisfying, place to stop.

CHAPTER 22

Excuse of Performance

INTRODUCTION TO EXCUSE UNDER ARTICLE 2

As I noted at the very outset of this part of the book, when you get down to it, *performance* of the contract of sale is what the law of sales is all about. Abstract theories and legal constructs are all well and good, but what motivates the parties — the reason they have expended their considerable energies getting to that most blessed of legal states, that which we call contract — is that by entering into such an arrangement each has managed to extract from the other a binding commitment. The seller is legally bound to hand over the goods and to stand behind whatever he or she has sold. The buyer is required to take the goods and to pay for them. Should either fail to do what must be done, the other will have the support of the courts in extracting a remedy.

This focus on performance should not strike you as strange. As you saw in your study of the common law of contract, the duty to perform as promised is the very heart of contract law. All else is commentary. If contract is to have meaning, there can be no question that you are legally bound to do what you have contracted to do. But then as you also saw in your Contracts course, when push comes to shove (or rather, in light of an "unforeseeable change in circumstances"), you can sometimes find authority in the common law under which a contracting party will be let off the hook. The instances will have to be rare of course, but when performance is truly impossible (or at least can be said to be "impossible" as the contract lawyers will use that word), perhaps the law can cut the contractual obligor a little slack.

I am assuming that in your studies you had a chance to become acquainted with the doctrine of Impossibility of Performance, along with its near relatives Impracticability, Frustration of Purpose, and (the ever delightful) Failure of a Mutually Presupposed Condition. I will also assume that when you think back to this material, it is not without some discomfort. The instances in which the common law allows excuse of a party from his or her contractual obligation and the theory or theories on which these results are based, other than just doing it when it feels right, are impossible to pin down. No right-thinking person would characterize this as a question to which the common law of contract gives anything like an unambiguous answer. The answers purport to hinge on the determination of what is or is not "foreseeable," what the "essence of the contract" is as opposed to its mere "incidents," and so on. Modern theorists throw the discussion over into analysis of "risk allocation" and "minimization of transaction costs," but don't get much farther along. You yourself could be excused for concluding, as any number of learned and levelheaded commentators have concluded before you, that the common law of excuse from contract obligation in the event of unforeseen circumstances is about as big a muddle as one could hope to find in a whole lifetime of trying. You may even have seen the case in which, at the end of an opinion that is rightly considered one of the *better* attempts at applying the law of excuse to a contemporary contracts situation, Judge Mulligan of the Second Circuit Court of Appeals concluded as follows:

> Matters involving impossibility or impracticability of performance of contract are concededly vexing and difficult. One is even urged on the allocation of such risks to pray for the "wisdom of Solomon." [Citing Corbin on Contracts.] On the basis of all of the facts, the pertinent authority and further belief in the efficacy of prayer, we affirm.

American Trading and Production Corp. v. Shell International Marine Ltd., 453 F.2d 939 (2d Cir. 1972).

In the course of his opinion in the *American Trading* case, Judge Mulligan noted that the parties had cited the court to §2-615, but he declined to look into that section, reasoning rightly enough that the contract in question was not governed by the Code and that he had enough to deal with in applying the common law. Had he been tempted to follow this lead into the Code, it's doubtful the judge would have found there the answer to his prayers. Article 2 in §§2-613 to 2-615 addresses the problem and allows for either a total excuse or a modification of obligation in appropriate circumstances. What circumstances are these? Well, §§2-613 and 2-614 deal with some relatively concrete situations that may not be all that hard to figure out.

Section 2-615 is more general and arguably awe-inspiring. Certainly it can be the cause of a good deal more head scratching. The drafters have abandoned reference to "impossibility" and to anything as amorphous as the "essence" of the agreement. Their provision asks us to consider instead the measure of "impracticability" and ponder the "occurrence of a contingency the nonoccurrence of which was a basic assumption on which the contract was made." Could this be an answer to anyone's prayers?

The purpose of this chapter is not to rehearse all of the arguments you encountered, and the uneasiness you felt, in your study of the various doctrines of excuse under the common law. Our program is much less ambitious. It will be enough for us to see how these ideas work their way through the provisions of Article 2. You should now look over §§2-613 to 2-616. What is the relevance of these provisions to the questions below?

Examples

EXAMPLES

1. Arnold Moneybucks goes into Stella's art gallery, where he spots one small painting ("Black on Black") by a contemporary artist that he decides to buy. He enters into a purchase and sale agreement with Stella. The agreement provides that Stella will deliver the artwork to Arnold in a few weeks when the gallery's showing is over. The very next day, a fire (for which she is totally blameless) sweeps through Stella's gallery and totally destroys this painting along with many others by the artist. Needless to say, Stella does not deliver the painting to Arnold. Can he bring an action against Stella for her failure to perform?

2. On the same day on which he makes his contract with Stella, Arnold also visits Sheila's gallery in the same building, which is showing works by another artist. He sees a lithograph on the wall ("Author at the Keyboard") that he wants for his collection. Sheila tells him that the recently deceased artist had prepared a limited edition of 100 copies of this lithograph, each of which she has in her possession and each of which she hopes to sell. Arnold contracts to buy one, which Sheila agrees to deliver to him within a few days. Before she can do so, the fire (which isn't Sheila's fault either) also damages her gallery. Ninety of the 100 lithographs are destroyed.
   (a) Sheila reasons that each of the ten remaining ones will be worth quite a bit more than the original price she had placed on them and the price Arnold had agreed to pay. Is Sheila excused from delivering one of the ten surviving lithographs to Arnold for the original contract price?
   (b) Would your answer to the previous question be any different if Sheila could show that prior to the fire she had set aside one of the lithographs, marked it "Sold to Moneybucks," and prepared it for

delivery to Arnold—and that this particular piece was one of the 90 destroyed in the fire?

(c) If your answer to either of the two previous questions is that Sheila is still legally bound to perform by delivering one copy of the lithograph to Arnold, how would you deal with the additional fact that prior to the fire Sheila had entered into similar contracts on the same terms to sell one copy of "Author at the Keyboard" to each of 14 other individuals?

3. Farmer Jones has a crop of tomatoes growing on her land. A representative of Agribusiness, Inc. visits the land and inspects the tender young plants. Together with the farmer, this representative concludes that the crop should come in at approximately 100,000 pounds of tomatoes. Jones contracts to sell Agribusiness "the crop of California #5 Grade A tomatoes now growing on her land, anticipated to be approximately 50 tons" at $.55 per pound. In May an unexpected attack of tomato blight hits the area. Jones's farm is particularly hard hit and she is forced to plow under all of her crop. The market price of California #5 Grade A tomatoes soars to over one dollar a pound. Can Agribusiness sue Jones for its damages resulting from her failure to deliver tomatoes?

4. Suppose that Farmer Green, whose farm, Greenacres, is next to Jones's, contracted to sell all of his crop to Agribusiness, but in fact did so before he had even planted a crop. The contract signed in February by Green referred to "approximately 50 tons of California #5 Grade A tomatoes that Green intends to plant, grow and harvest upon his property, Greenacres, during that year's growing season." Green's crop is also totally destroyed by the blight. Does Agribusiness have any case against Green for nondelivery?

5. It turns out that Agribusiness contracted with various growers to buy a total of 50,000 tons of tomatoes when that year's tomato crop came in during the summer. On the basis of these contracts, it entered into a contract to supply Peter's Pizza Corporation with 1,000 tons of tomato paste, with delivery to be spread out over the first six months of the next year. In November, Agribusiness contacts Peter and tells him that it will have to "sharply curtail" its tomato paste deliveries to him "due to the severe shortfall in the California tomato crop occurring in this past growing year." Peter discovers that if he is forced to buy tomato paste elsewhere, the cost will be far higher than what he had agreed to with Agribusiness. If Peter does have to pay more for his paste and sues Agribusiness for the difference, does that firm have any defense based on the tomato blight? What other facts would you want to know before attempting an answer to this question?

6. Buster is building a home. He contracts to buy a large quantity of finished floor tile from Underfoot's Tile Company. The tile Buster selects is made from Pandonian Red marble, a rare material that is found (where else?) in the country of Pandonia. When Underfoot goes to purchase the marble that she will need to fill Buster's order, she discovers that a recent outbreak of civil unrest in Pandonia has greatly reduced the amount of marble coming out of the quarries in that troubled country. Pandonian Red marble is still available on the worldwide market, but at a much higher price. If Underfoot is forced to buy the marble to make Buster's tile at the current price, she can expect to make no profit and, in fact, to lose money on her contract with Buster. Is Underfoot excused from the contract under these circumstances?

7. In preparation for building his house, Buster also goes to Sarah's Building Supplies, where he looks over a large selection of sample doorknobs on display. He picks out one doorknob in a style he likes and contracts to buy a large number from Sarah. This particular knob is manufactured by Hardware Inc., a firm from which Sarah has regularly obtained supplies in the past. When she tries to contact Hardware to get the doorknobs to fill Buster's order, Sarah is stunned to discover that Hardware's main manufacturing plant has been severely damaged in a recent hurricane. There is no chance they will be able to produce any doorknobs in the foreseeable future, and all of their stock was destroyed. Sarah contacts other doorknob manufacturers, but none has a product at all like the one which Buster has selected. One firm does offer to make up some in the particular pattern, but says that because this would be a special order it would have to charge four to five times what Hardware had charged per doorknob.
   (a) Sarah contacts Buster and tells him this story. Is she excused from her contract of sale given what has happened? Would your answer be any different if the reason Hardware would not supply her with the knobs was not that a hurricane had ravaged its plant, but that it had just decided to discontinue that particular style of product since it had not been a big seller?
   (b) Suppose Buster makes the contract to buy, and Sarah is able to and does get the knobs from Hardware. However, just as Buster's house is nearing completion, a hurricane comes and blows everything that has been built so far down to the ground. The place is rubble. Buster, who had not purchased insurance, finds his plans in ruins. Sarah is ready, willing, and able to deliver the doorknobs. Is Buster obligated to take them and pay the price agreed?

8. Bozzo, who runs a construction business, enters into a contract to buy a large quantity of steel mesh needed for a specific building project from

Spang Industries, delivery to be made as called for during the years 2020 through 2022. Spang has no problem delivering what is called for during the first two years. When Bozzo calls for delivery in 2022, however, he is told that this will be impossible because the firm that makes the particular kind of mesh went out of business in late 2021. Bozzo discovers that this manufacturer had been threatening to shut down its operations as early as 2020 and that Spang had been aware of these threats. Bozzo is forced to complete the project with an alternate building technique that avoids the use of the mesh but which costs him more to accomplish. Bozzo sues Spang for his damages. Can the supply firm defend on the basis of §2-615?

9. Seller in Chicago contracts to manufacture and sell a quantity of widgets to Buyer, who is located in Smallville, Indiana. The contract calls for delivery to be made by rail. When manufacture is complete Seller contacts the railroad to arrange for shipment. It discovers that the railroad no longer runs trains to Smallville. Meanwhile Seller has discovered another buyer who is willing to pay much more for these widgets and who is willing to pick them up from Seller's Chicago plant. Can Seller simply ignore its original contract with Buyer? Suppose instead that Seller is more than willing to get the widgets off its hands and arranges for a trucking service to take them to Buyer in Smallville. Can Buyer refuse to take the goods because they did not come by rail?

Explanations

1. No. Stella is excused from performing under this contract by §2-613(a). The key is that this contract involved a distinct, already existing object—that is, delivery was required of "goods identified when the contract [was] made." Had there been no fire and Stella tried to deliver anything other than *this particular painting*, even another one with the same name ("Black on Black #2"), to Arnold, he could have rightfully considered this a nonconforming tender. On identification of goods generally, see Chapter 16, which not coincidentally uses this same fact pattern.

   So in this situation, Stella suffers the loss of the value of the painting itself as a piece of property. This is referred to as the "risk of loss" of the goods and is the subject of the next part of this book. Arnold, of course, would be complaining about the loss of the benefit of his bargain and the loss of a valuable contract interest. If many paintings by this artist have been suddenly destroyed, any one might now be much more valuable than it would have been just days before. But under §2-613, and given the important fact that Stella is in no way responsible for the fire, the contract is avoided, and Arnold will have to bear this loss himself. He cannot successfully sue Stella for nondelivery. In *Lane-Lott v. White*, 126 So.

3d 1016 (Miss. App. 2013), the contract called for delivery of a specifically identified pregnant quarter horse mare, Kcees. It turned out, however, that at the time of contracting, unbeknownst to either party, Kcees had already been, as the court put it, "misplaced:"

> While it is unclear whether Kcees had gone to that great pasture in the sky or was just in another earthly pasture at the time of the agreement, what is clear is that both parties were laboring under the misconception that the mare that had been impregnated was Kcees [instead of another mare that somehow had gotten involved in the proceedings and had been delivered to the aggrieved buyer]. Thus, the contract was void because at the time of formation neither party knew that an expecting Kcees *did not exist* (emphasis in original).

Notice how §2-613(b) would deal with the situation if the painting had not been totally destroyed in the fire but merely scorched. Arnold would then have had the right to inspect the painting and, at his option, avoid the contract or go through with it at a price reflecting a "due allowance" for the damage. How would this figure be arrived at? Presumably a disinterested appraiser could help out here.

2. a. Sheila would not be excused under §2-613 from delivering a copy of this lithograph. Here the contract does not call for goods "identified when the contract is made." Identification was to be by the seller and at some time *after* the contract was entered into. If Sheila is going to have any excuse, it will have to be under §2-615, and her argument there is nowhere near as straightforward. Look at Comment 4 to that section. Sheila could justifiably claim that delivery to Arnold will involve "increased cost" and that the economics of the situation have drastically changed, but has the fire "altered the essential nature" of what she has to do? I doubt she'd be relieved from her obligation in this situation, but like all impossibility (or as Article 2 would say, "impracticability") cases the answer is up for grabs.
   b. If Sheila can't make out an argument under §2-615 for "failure of a presupposed condition," then she's still out of luck. The answer under §2-613 remains the same. No avoidance of the contract. True, in this case, Sheila has identified the goods prior to their destruction, but the relevant criterion of this section is not whether the goods were identified at the time of casualty. What is important is whether the nature of the contract required goods that had to be identified at the time of the contract. That was not true in this particular contract, and that has not changed. Sheila should just identify another unsullied copy of the lithograph to her contract with Arnold and deliver that one under the terms of the original agreement.
   c. Now it seems as if Sheila should get some relief, but it's not clear what. Her argument of excuse, if any, would have to come under

§2-615. Subpart (b) supports the idea that while she would have to carry through as many contracts as possible (selling all of the ten remaining copies at the original price), she could be excused from her failure to perform on the five other contracts.

What would a "fair and reasonable allocation" look like in this instance? In the typical case where allocation of a lesser amount is called for, the seller is to deliver some quantity of a fungible good, and the buyer under any one contract can be allocated some percentage of what he or she had originally contracted to get. But I doubt anyone would want some chopped up portion of a lithograph. Sheila will have to decide on some way of determining who gets the remaining copies. Perhaps she should look at the order in which the contracts were entered into, or the order in which delivery was called for. Perhaps she should hold a lottery and pull names out of a hat.

If she does hold a lottery, would it be permissible for her to include in the drawing not only those 15 people who had, like Arnold, signed a contract for the lithograph before the fire struck, but also the name of her most steady and loyal customer, who had bought many works from her before and for whom she had been planning to hold back at least one copy of this lithograph? Look at the language of §2-615(b) and Comment 11. You can see that this language, as well as the procedural language in §2-615(c) and §2-616, is written more with the case of proportional allocation of fungible goods in mind. As a matter of fact, I know of no actual case where the court or a seller for that matter has had to come up with anything like allocation by lottery or on a first-come-first-served basis. Still, that would fit in with the general principle of §2-615(b), and it sure beats the Solomon-like judgment of cutting the lithographs into pieces.

It should be clear that the one thing Sheila *cannot* do is decide which buyers are to get the remaining copies by auctioning them off to the highest bidders. The fire should not be an excuse for a *greater* profit on any item than she had the right to under her contracts. See the case of *BRC Rubber & Plastics, Inc. v. Continental Carbon Co.*, 949 F. Supp. 2d 862 (N.D. Ind. 2013), in which a seller's argument that it was not in breach for failure to deliver to the buyer all that the contract called for based on §2-615 and its need to allocate what it had of the product in question among a number of customers was found wanting. "The record," the court reported, "contains a plethora of evidence that [the seller] did not allocate among its customers in a fair and reasonable manner, but rather, based on its own profit margins."

3. Farmer Jones should be excused from her failure to deliver. Because the crop was identified at the time of the contract and her obligation was to deliver this particular crop, §2-613 would seem to be all she needs.

4. Farmer Green should also have a defense to any suit brought by Agribusiness for nondelivery. His excuse will have to be based on §2-615. Looking at this section, there are three principal factors he'll have to establish. First, he will argue that delivery of the tomatoes has become "impracticable" due to the blight. Article 2 uses this term instead of "impossible," which was favored by the common law but which really never meant "impossible" in any event, just "way, way more expensive." See Comment 3.

   Green would then have to insist that the tomato blight was "a contingency the nonoccurrence of which was a basic assumption on which the contract was made." Here, the parties (if they had the stomach for it) could argue about how "foreseeable" such an occurrence was—the type of discussion you presumably saw in your earlier studies. No one knows exactly what this condition in §2-615 means, but it seems clear that the drafters at least thought a "local crop failure" caused by something like a disease or drought was enough to trigger the workings of the section. See Comment 4.

   Green would also have to show that under the contract, he did not "assume a greater obligation." It's possible to argue that Green *did* assume this obligation here. After all, he promised to deliver a crop of tomatoes and when it came time, he didn't do it. Courts have generally read this language more narrowly, looking for an express assumption by the contracting party of a *greater* obligation than is typical in the type of contract involved. Green shouldn't have trouble with this criterion unless there's something in the contract like, "Seller agrees to be responsible for delivery in event of tomato blight or other cause of crop failure."

   Of course, as in any case, whether any or every one of these three criteria have been met is a question of fact based on the particulars of the situation. As you discovered for the common law doctrine of impossibility, even if you review dozens of cases, it's hard to come away with any generalities other than that sometimes the defense works and sometimes it doesn't. Actually, the possibility of excusing the seller of farm products because of crop failure is, at least under the Code, one of the few exceptions where more can be said with some measure of confidence. Look at the first paragraph to Comment 9. Where the seller is a farmer "who has contracted to sell crops to be grown on designated land," he or she may be excused under this section. Of course this Comment is just the drafters' opinion, but the courts seem to follow this line with little or no exception. Unless there is some unusual factor here that we're not aware of, for example, if Green was somehow at fault for not protecting his crop from the dreaded tomato blight, he should be excused from performance under this contract.

   Imagine instead that the contract Green signs refers only to his obligation to sell "50 tons of California 5 Grade A tomatoes" at a set price and delivery date but makes no mention of his specific land. Green signs this contract assuming he'll grow this much of this type of tomatoes on Greenacres. He plants them, but his crop is wiped out by the blight. What result? Comment 9, by its reference to "designated land," suggests (although it doesn't actually say) that the result would now be different. The courts usually make this distinction and will not allow excuse simply because the seller was a farmer contracting to sell farm products that he or she contemplated growing him or herself. See, for example, *ConAgra, Inc. v. Bartlett Partnership*, 540 N.W.2d 333 (Neb. 1995) or *Clark v. Wallace County Cooperative Equity Exchange*, 986 P.2d 391 (Kan. App. 1999).

5. It is unclear whether Agribusiness has any possible defense here under §2-615. I think you have to start with the assumption that any argument for excuse isn't going to work, and that Agribusiness is going to have to answer in a suit for damages. Sellers make money by selling things others want and they take risks as part of their business. The buyer's interest was in buying. Should Peter have to worry about drought or pestilence in other parts of the country?

   Agribusiness, on the other hand, based its business decisions on its own dealings in the Sunshine State. It chose to contract to deliver tomato paste at a future date, and it failed to do so. Why shouldn't that be the end of the story? An operation like Agribusiness should know enough about the possibility of crop failures occurring at some kind of predictable rate, even if individual instances seem to strike at random, and should be able to do something to guard against being caught off guard with too few tomatoes. For one thing, perhaps it should have avoided contracting with suppliers all in one part of the country or in one growing area. Then again, there must be some situations, some crop failures that are so unexpected and so far-reaching that the entire market is thrown for a loop. Which is it here, and in any event, should that make any difference?

   While we professors make a big deal of it in your study of contracts, you should be aware that in general the courts have been unwilling to consider excuse under the doctrine of impossibility or its near relatives, and this reluctance appears to have continued under §2-615. See, for instance, *Leanin' Tree, Inc. v. Thiele Technologies, Inc.*, 43 F. App'x 318 (10th Cir. 2002).

   There are a few cases, however, that give Agribusiness some cause for hope in this particular situation. *Cliffstar Corp. v. Riverbend Products, Inc.*, 750 F. Supp. 81 (W.D.N.Y. 1990), is the case that inspired this hypothetical. Cliffstar ordered 3.2 million pounds of tomato paste (think of it) from Riverbend. All in all, Riverbend projected that it would produce something like 53 million pounds of paste during the season. Its field department contracted with growers in Arizona and California for 170,000 tons of raw tomatoes. By combining these firm contracts with plans to purchase additional tomatoes on the "spot" market, Riverbend planned to acquire sufficient tomatoes to meet its projections. Weather conditions in Arizona and California resulted in a crop shortage; the combined Arizona and California tomato harvest was about 8.45 percent less than early season estimates. However, the growers with whom Riverbend had contracted delivered only 95,000 to 100,000 tons of the 170,000 promised, or about 56 to 58 percent. Riverbend chose to allocate the paste it could produce among its customers. Cliffstar was told that it would be allocated only one million pounds of the stuff. Cliffstar demanded its full contract amount and, when that wasn't forthcoming, brought suit. Riverbend defended its actions and its failure to deliver the full 3.2 million pounds on the basis of §2-615. Cliffstar moved for a summary judgment claiming that there was no genuine issue as to material fact and that it was entitled to a judgment as a matter of law. The court refused to grant summary judgment, holding that there were genuine issues of material fact as to whether the crop shortage and the seller's response to it constituted grounds for excuse under the criteria applicable to a §2-615 argument.

So Agribusiness may be able to get to a jury to argue that the situation in which it found itself was "unforeseeable" and furthermore that this predicament could be said to have rendered its obligation to deliver the full 1,000 tons to Peter "impracticable," whatever that means. How will or should a jury respond? That's anyone's guess, but Agribusiness can also find some encouragement in the result of *Alimenta (U.S.A.), Inc. v. Gibbs Nathaniel (Canada) Ltd.*, 802 F.2d 1362 (11th Cir. 1986), in which the Eleventh Circuit affirmed a jury determination that found grounds for excuse in a similar situation involving devastation of the annual peanut crop through drought. But then of course each case will be judged on its own facts.

It's important to note here that even if Agribusiness can establish a good case of commercial impracticability, this does not relieve it from delivering any tomato paste whatsoever to Peter. Under §2-615(b), Agribusiness must "allocate production and deliveries among its customers." The seller is given some latitude in that it may, at its option, include in the allocation "regular customers not then under contract as well as his own requirements for future manufacture." Any allocation must, however, be "fair and reasonable." In *Cliffstar*, the tomato paste case, the plaintiff also challenged the allocation made to it by Riverbend. Cliffstar argued that any allocation had to treat it "equally," by which it presumably meant on a strictly pro rata basis. Apparently in making its allocation decisions, Riverbend had considered such factors as "customer loyalty, past performance, needs, the relationship between Riverbend and the customer, and Riverbend's projections of potential future sales to the customer." The federal district court concluded that, like everything else, the question of whether the seller had acted on a "fair and reasonable basis" was one to be decided on the facts by the jury. Implicit in its decision, however, was the conclusion that a strictly pro rata allocation is not required as a matter of law under §2-615. See also Comment 11.

Finally note the provisions in §2-615(c) and all of §2-616, which set up a procedure for the allocation process. For a case in which the adequacy of notice under §2-615 came into question, see *Red River Commodities, Inc. v. Eidsness*, 459 N.W.2d 805 (N.D. 1990).

6. Civil strife in Pandonia is presumably an unforeseeable occurrence, at least as far as §2-615 is concerned. It's unlikely, however, that Underfoot will have an excuse here. The marble is still available, albeit at a higher price. Note the beginning of Comment 4:

> Increased cost alone does not excuse performance unless the rise in cost is due to some unforeseen contingency which alters the essential nature of the performance. Neither is a rise or collapse in a market in itself a justification, for that is exactly the type of business risk which business contracts made at fixed prices are intended to cover.

In the case of *Rochester Gas and Electric Corp. v. Delta Star, Inc.*, 2009 WL 368508 (W.D.N.Y.), the defendant Delta Star contracted in June of 2005 to sell eight electrical transformers to the buyer, a public utility, for a set price that was to be "considered firm, unless otherwise noted." Delta Star later claimed, in November of 2005, that it was entitled to insist on receiving a greater price for the transformers because the demand for M3 core steel (the material out of which it was to manufacture them) began to outstrip supply and that, in fact, no M3 steel was to be had at any price since buyers in China and India were paying premiums above other markets for M4 steel. In a letter to the buyer, the defendant explained:

> Delta Star received notification from our sole electrical steel supplier, AK Steel, Butler, PA that they will not guarantee any core steel production as of December 7. Delta Star has relied upon this relationship for roughly forty years but now must quickly look to other suppliers. . . . Another factor that has definitely had an effect is the increase in distribution transformer demand due to the hurricanes hitting the gulf coast [referring to Hurricane Katrina].

Among its arguments, Delta Star pointed to §2-615. The federal district court, citing the Comment to this section quoted above and reviewing the New York courts' application of the section, ruled against the seller. It stated:

> [The seller's] allegation is that government-run companies in China are buying up the M3 steel causing the subsequent shortage in this country. However, as Delta Star pointed out in its letter to RG&E, a suitable replacement steel, M4, was available, albeit at a higher price. The March 2005

> magazine article presented as Appendix A to RG&E's memorandum of law in support of its application indicates, that from December 20, 2004, headlines showed that steel prices were increasing, dropping, rebounding, and dropping. . . . One of the suggestions contained in the article is the "need for clear bid documents specifying which party is to assume the risk of a change in material prices."

The court concluded:

> [N]o material issue of fact precludes summary judgment on [the] defense of commercial impracticability and failure of presupposed conditions. [Two of the seller's] affiants stated that M4 steel was available, albeit at a much higher price. "While it was also very difficult to obtain, ultimately Delta Star was able to secure a new supplier, albeit at a much higher price." [citing to one of these affidavits]. To paraphrase the Second Circuit, "[t]he mere fact that this undertaking may have become burdensome, as a result of subsequent, perhaps unanticipated, developments, does not operate to relieve [Delta Star] of [its] obligation." Canfield v. Reynolds, 631 F.2d 169, 177 (2d Cir.1980).

All of this seems pretty unforgiving. Has the "essential nature" of Underfoot's obligation been altered? You are as much of an expert on essentialness of nature as I am or anyone else is, but I tend to doubt §2-615 would provide relief here. In point of fact, the courts have been very reluctant to give any credence to the impossibility defense under §2-615 where the fundamental problem is just that a seller's own costs have gone up or because completion of the contract could only be done at a loss to the seller.

7. a. If §2-615 does offer any hope for a seller based solely on a change in cost, Sarah's case may be the one. Comment 4, which we began to quote in the analysis of the last question, concludes:

> [A] severe shortage of raw materials or of supplies due to a contingency such as war, embargo, local crop failure, unforeseen shutdown of major sources of supply or the like, which either causes a marked increase in cost or altogether prevents the seller from securing supplies necessary to his performance, is within the contemplation of this section.

Sarah's situation does seem to be "severe" and to involve not merely an increase in costs, but a "marked increase." I would even go so far as to say that it alters the "essential nature" of this agreement. Sarah contracted with the expectation she could directly obtain and then resell standard manufactured goods. If she were now held to perform, she'd be in the business of supplying specially manufactured doorknobs, which strikes me as of a different nature altogether. In some cases where the excuse was granted, the costs to seller do not simply rise to where a loss can be foreseen, but to some multiple of (4 or 5 times) what was originally contemplated.

I think that if excuse is available to Sarah in this instance, it would be the same whatever reason the manufacturing plant could or would no longer sell her the product (as long as it was not her fault). The unforeseen circumstance here is not the hurricane, but the total evaporation of the unique source of supply, which we have to assume comes as a total surprise to Sarah. See Comment 5. For a good review of the "failure of the sole source of supply" excuse—and how rarely the excuse will be available to a seller—see *Rockland Industries, Inc. v. E & E (U.S.) Inc.*, 991 F. Supp. 468 (D. Md. 1998), *modified*, 1 F. Supp. 2d 528.

b. Can Buster, a buyer, argue excuse based on the failure of a presupposed condition under §2-615? Look again at that section. It speaks only of a possible excuse for the seller. Doesn't this leave Buster out in the cold? Note, however, that Comment 9 to this section anticipates the possibility of excuse of buyer's performance. All the commentators and courts seem to assume that a buyer under the Code might have an argument based on what the common law referred to as frustration of purpose in the appropriate case. See, for example, *Power Engineering & Mfg., Ltd. v. Krug Int'l*, 501 N.W.2d 490 (Iowa 1993). If nothing else, Buster can cite the court to that old standby §1-103(b), which allows for supplementation by principles of law and equity not explicitly or implicitly displaced by the provisions of Article 2. While the doctrines of impossibility or frustration aren't specifically mentioned in that section, we are told the listing there is illustrative only, not exhaustive (Comment 4 to §1-103).

8. I included this question for two reasons. First of all, while the word "fault" nowhere appears in §2-615, it should be evident that for a seller to take advantage of this provision, he or she should be able to show that not only was the occurrence unforeseeable, but that it also could not have been averted through the reasonable care of the seller. Here, once it became aware of the problem, Sprang should have stocked up on the mesh or made some other arrangements to avoid this problem. Bozzo should win. Second, I wanted you to be aware that all the oddball names you run across in this volume (even where the seller is an "S" and the buyer a "B") are not solely the product of my fevered imagination. See *Frank B. Bozzo, Inc. v. Electric Weld Division of Fort Pitt Bridge Division of Spang Industries, Inc.*, 423 A.2d 702 (Pa. Super. 1980) (in which Bozzo did in fact collect from Spang Industries).

9. This question focuses us on the special provisions in §2-614 relating to the substitution of another *means* of performance. It should be clear that when delivery by rail becomes commercially impracticable, seller is still obligated to tender via a "commercially reasonable substitute" and buyer

is obligated to accept the widgets tendered in this manner. Without knowing more, it is impossible to say for certain whether delivery by truck meets this standard in this instance, but it seems fair to assume that it does unless and until one or the other party explains why this isn't so. See *Hansen-Mueller Co. v. Gau*, 838 N.W.2d 138 (Iowa App. 2013).

PART V

Risk of Loss

CHAPTER 23

Basic Treatment

INTRODUCTION TO RISK OF LOSS

What's true for people is also true for goods. The world is fraught with peril. Thieves will do what they are wont to do—make off with the goods. Clumsy handling can leave them seriously damaged or destroyed altogether. Fires, floods, hurricanes, and the like all take their toll. Sometimes goods simply disappear, leaving forever in doubt what exactly *did* happen to them.

When tragedies such as these occur, it is unfortunate but true that somebody, some legally recognized entity capable of owning property but therefore necessarily also capable of losing it, must suffer the loss. The goods are left worthless or worth less, and someone has either to suffer the loss personally or find another who is obligated to make good for the loss and then go against that person. The person who initially suffers the loss in value of the property is said to bear the *risk of loss* of the goods.

It is important to recognize from the outset that the party bearing the risk of any particular loss need not necessarily end up personally shouldering all of the dire financial consequences. He or she may be able to pass the loss on to another party. If the thief can be caught, the thief should pay. If someone like a carrier or a warehouse owner is legally responsible for the loss or damage, whether because of willful or negligent conduct, then the initial risk bearer will be able to go against that other party. Perhaps most important in many circumstances, the risk bearer may have insurance that covers the loss. That's what insurance is all about. The question of risk of loss, then, is who has to take the time and effort to pursue these other avenues—and who ultimately will be left holding the bag if, when all is said and done, the loss cannot be passed along.

In most situations, of course, the question of who bears the risk of loss of goods is easy to answer: The "owner" of the goods does, and in the vast majority of situations, it's not really open to dispute just who that owner is. When the goods are the subject of a contract of sale, however, and are then damaged somewhere along the route of delivery, both Seller and Buyer may find support in the facts for an argument that the risk of loss was on the other at the time of the catastrophic event. This chapter and the two that follow address the problems of risk of loss as between Seller and Buyer when the goods were the subject of a contract for sale at the time of the loss.

The significance of who, between Seller and Buyer, bears the risk is made abundantly clear by Article 2. Subsection 2-709(1) provides in part that Seller can recover from Buyer the price of any goods accepted but also "of any conforming goods lost or damaged within a commercially reasonable time after risk of their loss has passed to the buyer." Once the risk of loss has shifted to Buyer, Seller is entitled to payment of the price. If Buyer is to get any relief, it will have to be somewhere else. On the other hand, if at the time of damage or destruction the risk had not yet shifted to Buyer—if it had remained with Seller—then Buyer need not pay the price. Furthermore, unless his or her delivery obligation is excused under some other provision of the Code, Seller may face a successful action for breach if conforming goods are not tendered on time. Between buyers and sellers, let there be no doubt, the question of risk of loss is of more than academic interest.

Prior to the adoption of the Uniform Commercial Code, the question of who bore the risk of loss of goods was dominated by the notion of title. It was said that whoever had the "title" or "property" in the goods at the time of the unfortunate event would bear the risk. This might have made perfect sense, but what it didn't do was explain exactly how the question of title should be decided in a difficult case. The concept of title over property came to have a distinctly amorphous if not downright mystical quality. Adding to the confusion was the fact that this concept and this word, *title*, were invoked in other disputes not directly related to the risk of loss problem. It was said that those who actually understood where title would lie in a difficult situation constituted a very small club. Other commentators were convinced that there really was no way to find consistency or make sense out of the various decisions and that membership in this club, even if available, would be nothing to write home about.

The drafters of the Code made their main contribution to the area by eliminating any reference to title in considering risk of loss problems. Their approach, as we will see, deals with risk of loss directly and on its own terms. While there may be some questions left at the margins by the sections as they were eventually drafted, the general response has been very favorable. Article 2's treatment of risk of loss is among those areas where it has been most successful in establishing rules clear in their application and which generally achieve results in line with the drafters' articulated goals.

THE ARTICLE 2 APPROACH TO RISK OF LOSS

Before looking in detail at the particular sections that deal with risk of loss (§§2-509 and 2-510), it is worthwhile to note the basic philosophy behind Article 2's treatment of these problems. There is no need to guess. The first Comment to §2-509 states that "the underlying theory of these sections on the risk of loss is the adoption of the contractual approach rather than an arbitrary shifting of the risk with the 'property' in the goods." Language in the third Comment, which we will soon see and which the courts are fond of quoting, makes clear that the attempt in these sections is to place the risk on that party who is more likely at the moment of loss to have insurance on the goods. Of course this emphasis on the likelihood of insurance coverage, while admirably pragmatic, involves a kind of circularity. If the risk of loss is placed on the party most likely to have insurance coverage, at least if this approach is well-known to buyers and sellers and regularly followed by the courts, it will presumably lead to that party's actually getting insurance. You tend to insure against those risks you will have to bear.

This circularity, of course, can also be characterized as a glorious harmony between law and practice. More to our purposes, it does serve to emphasize the real reason behind any risk of loss rules. The law serves best when it encourages the parties to face up to the risks of loss before any loss occurs, if that is possible, and protect themselves with an appropriate measure of insurance. To the practicing attorney, the message is once again that counseling clients before disaster strikes, especially when the rules of the game are clear, is a lot easier than helping them to pick up the pieces afterwards. While the examples and explanations in this and the following chapters will mostly be worded as if the question is which party should bear the unbearable loss, remember that if this party has been attentive to his or her own welfare from the start, the real contest in most cases should be which party has to bear the much less onerous burden of having to file an insurance claim and cash the check that should be forthcoming.

Of the two risk of loss sections, §2-509 is undoubtedly the more important and we will concentrate on it first. Before doing so, however, note at least the heading of §2-510. If either seller or buyer is able to substantiate a claim that at the time of the loss the other was in breach, that section is the place to start analysis. We will deal with it as a distinct matter in Chapter 25. For the moment, assume that neither party is claiming the other was in breach at the time of the loss, or that if such a claim has been advanced, it has failed. How does the Code allocate the loss when there has been no breach?

The rules on risk of loss in the absence of breach are set out in §2-509. Like many Code sections, this one is best approached in an order other than that the subsections are written in. Read first §2-509(4). Whatever may be true about the general risk of loss rules arising out of the other parts of this section, the parties are always free—in fact we might say they are encouraged—to vary the results by "contrary agreement." What must the parties do to make such a special allocation of the risk? The courts have understandably been very strict on this. It would seem that the language relied upon will have to be fairly conspicuous and mention risk of loss specifically. So, for example, in *Hayward v. Postma*, 188 N.W.2d 31 (Mich. App. 1971), the court held that what it characterized as "boilerplate language" in a security agreement that spoke only of the buyer's obligation to keep the goods insured at all times was not enough. "Risk of loss," the court noted, "is nowhere mentioned" in the offered clause. In *Commonwealth Propane Co. v. Petrosol International, Inc.*, 818 F.2d 522 (6th Cir. 1987), the court held that a clause that referred only to when "title" to the goods would pass did not reallocate the risk of loss, reasoning quite correctly that the concept of title is no longer the key to risk of loss questions under the Code. See also *Berry v. Lucas*, 150 P.3d 424 (Or. App. 2006).

Contrast these cases to *Forest Nursery Co. v. I.W.S., Inc.*, 534 N.Y.S.2d 86 (Dist. Ct. Nassau Co. 1986), where the court found there *was* a sufficient expression of contrary intention. In that situation, the only documents that passed between the parties were the seller's invoices. These included the express provision, in italics, of "*No risk to Supplier,*" and a large legend at the top of the papers stating, "NOTICE: ALL SHIPMENTS TRAVEL AT RISK AND COST OF PURCHASER." Now that's making it clear. Perhaps the most significant application of §2-509(4) is found when the parties explicitly allocate risk of loss through the use in their agreement of so-called trade or delivery terms such as F.O.B., C.I.F., and the like. If these mean nothing to you now, that's perfectly understandable. They figure in the next chapter.

For the moment, we will assume that the parties have made no special agreement on risk of loss. Next look briefly at the introductory clauses *only* of subsections (1) and (2) of §2-509. Subsection (1) deals with the case where the goods are to be shipped by a carrier. The second subsection involves goods held by a bailee, which typically means a commercial warehouse, and which are to be delivered without being moved. In either instance, the seller is not personally handing over the goods. A third party, such as a shipping company, a common carrier, or a warehouse, is involved in the delivery. These cases deserve special attention and will be the subject of the chapter that follows.

So far, all we've done is eliminate a lot of situations. We aren't dealing with instances where there's been a breach of the sales contract, where the parties have made an explicit allocation of risk of loss, or where the delivery is to be carried out through a third party's actions. What's left? Section 2-509(3), which you should read now.

Examples

1. Sam's Autorama is a retail automobile dealership. On Friday morning, Sam sells a car to one Betty. He gives her the documents she will need to obtain insurance, a certificate of title, and plates for the car. She leaves, stating she'll pick up the car the following Monday. Over the weekend, the car is destroyed when a fire consumes Sam's business.
   (a) Must Betty pay for the car?
   (b) Would it make any difference to your answer if Betty had obtained a valid certificate of title under her state's title law on Friday afternoon?
   (c) What if you knew Betty had obtained insurance covering the car against all kinds of disasters, including fire, on Friday afternoon?

2. The Sparkle Store, a jewelry retailer, sells a bracelet to Mr. Burns. The store agrees to make some final adjustments to the bracelet and then to deliver it to his home. An employee of the store takes it to Burns' house. When he finds no one at home, he leaves the package containing the bracelet wedged between the screen door and the front door. The package is not there when Burns returns to his home at the end of the day. Must he pay The Sparkle Store for it? Would you think the result should be different if the employee had slipped the package through the mail slot in Burns' front door and it had been stolen by a thief who broke into the house before Burns got home?

3. Janice agrees to sell her old car to a friend, Tom. Tom gives her a check for the price and she offers him the keys. He tells her that he'll have to come around the following day to pick the car up. Before Tom comes to pick up the car on the following day, it is stolen from where it has been parked.
   (a) Who bears the risk of loss? Would it matter who had possession of the keys overnight?
   (b) Suppose instead that when Janice sold the car to Tom, they agreed that she would have it until the next day, and that Janice had said, "You can pick it up anytime tomorrow. The keys will be here for you." The car is stolen overnight. Who bears the risk? Would it make a difference if Tom had not come until two o'clock in the afternoon on the following day, and the car had been stolen sometime during that morning?
   (c) What if Tom had not paid for the car initially but had agreed to pay for it when he picked it up the next day? He never picks it up. A few weeks later the car is stolen from in front of Janice's house. Can Janice successfully sue Tom for the price?

4. Remember Sam from Example 1? As it happens, the fire at Sam's also consumed a trailer parked on the Autorama lot that Sam had been using as his temporary office. A few days before the fire, Sam had moved all of his belongings out of the trailer and into a new permanent office that had been built on the site. On Thursday, he had entered into a contract of sale for the trailer with one Bill, who had responded to a hand-lettered "FOR SALE" sign Sam had stuck in the window of the trailer. On Thursday, Bill had told Sam that it would take him a few days to come and pick up the trailer. Sam had said, "OK, whenever you want it, it's yours." Who, between Sam and Bill, bore the risk of loss of the trailer when it went up in flames over the weekend?

Explanations

EXPLANATIONS

1. a. No, Betty does not have to pay. Sam bears the risk of loss. Here Sam is clearly a merchant seller of automobiles. Section 2-509(3) says that the risk of such loss in the case of a merchant seller passes to the buyer only upon "receipt of the goods." *Receipt* is obviously the crucial concept here. The Definitional Cross References of the Code lead us to §2-103. We find in §2-103(1)(c) that *receipt* of goods means "taking physical possession of them." Betty has not taken physical possession of the car, so the risk of loss never passes to her.

   b. Whether or not Betty had "title" under her state's law regulating title to motor vehicles would not make a difference. *Receipt of the goods,* as that term is used in Article 2, is still the key. This simply emphasizes that the drafters did not want the concept of title to goods to control risk of loss questions under the Code as it had under earlier, and often more confusing, law.

   This same point is made in a different way in the case of *Hughes v. Al Green, Inc.*, 418 N.E.2d 1355 (Ohio 1981). In that case, Mrs. Hughes, after making a down payment, was allowed to take immediate possession on a Saturday of a car she bought from a dealership. It was agreed she would return it to the dealer the following Monday for the completion of certain new car preparations and the installation of a CB radio. Before leaving the dealership on Saturday, she signed a purchase contract and an application for certificate of title among other documents. On her way home, and obviously before she could have obtained legal title under the state's title law, she was involved in a collision. Was she obligated for the remainder of the purchase price? The court had no difficulty finding that she was. She had taken possession of the car, there had been receipt from the merchant seller, and hence the risk had passed to her. Ohio's certificate of title law was simply irrelevant for these purposes.

The Code's justification for the rule is found in Comment 3, which states:

> The underlying theory of this rule is that a merchant who is to make physical delivery at his own place of business continues meanwhile to control the goods and can be expected to insure his interest in them. The buyer, on the other hand, has no control of the goods and it is extremely unlikely that he will carry insurance on the goods not yet in his possession.

Which leads to consideration of our next hypothetical.

c. Even if Betty had insurance that would cover this loss, the risk of loss is still on Sam if she had not taken possession. The Code's justification for this rule is, according to Comment 3, based partially on who would be most likely to have insurance in the typical case, but the language of the Code makes clear that the result does not depend on who does or does not have insurance *in the particular case*. Similarly, the result would not be affected if for some reason Sam was not insured for the loss of this car. Presumably if Sam did want the risk to shift to Betty on Friday afternoon, and if she were willing to get insurance from that time on to cover the risk, the parties could have shifted the risk by explicit contrary agreement as provided for in §2-509(4). The fact that they happened to have insurance coverage, or in Sam's case failed to have it, would certainly not in and of itself constitute contrary agreement.

   An interesting case that tests the limits of this rule as to merchant sellers and that demonstrates how far out these limits run is *Ellis v. Bell Aerospace Corp.*, 315 F. Supp. 221 (D. Or. 1970). Ellis paid Bell Aerospace $102,110 for a new helicopter. The helicopter was ready for delivery in early February, and the contract provided that the buyer would deliver within ten days of its being ready. Ellis asked if he could take delivery later, in March. The seller told him that he didn't have the room to store the helicopter for that length of time and, with his acquiescence, made arrangements to have it stored at a local airport. The sales contract provided that Ellis was to receive several days of inflight instruction at the time of delivery. On March 11, he and his wife appeared at the Bell factory and attended ground school. Two days later, while on the first instructional flight with Ellis at the controls and an instructor aboard, the helicopter crashed. Ellis sued to recover the purchase price of the craft and won. The court reasoned that:

> Bell did not, at any time before the helicopter crashed, surrender to Ellis complete dominion and control over the helicopter. The helicopter remained, until it was destroyed, under the practical control of Bell. It

> would have continued to remain under Bell's control until Ellis had completed his full five hours of training, a matter of some two or three days.

Thus the risk of loss had not passed even though by the time of the crash, Ellis had obtained liability insurance covering the helicopter, had registered it in his name with the Federal Aviation Agency, and had agreed to have it stored at least temporarily with a third party.

2. Again we have the case of a merchant seller, only this time delivery by the merchant itself (not through some third-party carrier) is to be at some place other than its place of business. The rule is still the same. Did the buyer get receipt of the goods? When the package is simply left outside his door, it's pretty clear that he did not and that the risk of loss never passed. The fact that no one seems to know what happened to the bracelet is not important. Somehow it was lost and it is just this kind of loss that the merchant seller must bear until the buyer actually gains possession.

   When the package has actually been placed inside Mr. Burns' house, the argument for possession is of course stronger. I doubt, however, the result would be different. True, for a thief to get the bracelet he or she had to get inside the house and that put the bracelet at risk just like all of Mr. Burns' other possessions. But in this context, it seems that Mr. Burns would have to have been made aware that he had possession. Note the language in Comment 3 and the *Ellis* case, both quoted above, that emphasizes the consideration of whether actual "control" had gone from the seller to the buyer. It's possible Burns could have guarded against this loss if he at least knew he actually had the jewelry, perhaps by hiding it away where even this thief couldn't find it. If he didn't even know the property's location at the time, it's hard to say he has gotten receipt.

   The courts do seem to require that the buyer actually have possession in the sense of some chance to act on or to exercise dominion and control over the goods for risk to pass from the merchant seller. The mere fact that the seller has somehow gotten rid of them is not enough. In *Ron Mead T.V. & Appliance Corp. v. Legendary Homes, Inc.*, 746 P.2d 1163 (Okla. Ct. App. 1987), the seller, a retailer of household appliances, was to deliver appliances meant for installation in a new home to the construction site by 5:00 P.M. At 5:00, when the appliances had not been delivered, the buyer, a builder, closed the house and left for the day. Sometime between 5:00 and 6:30, the seller delivered the appliances. Finding no one there, the deliveryman put them in the unlocked garage. During the night, they were stolen. The Oklahoma Court of Appeals, affirming a finding for the buyer that it need not pay, quoted with approval the statement by the trial court that "[t]he act by the deliveryman of placing the goods in an unlocked garage, in a house under construction, and then locking the door did not give the Buyer the opportunity to take physical possession [of them]." In accord is *H & B Chevrolet-Cadillac, Inc. v. Boutell Driveaway, Inc.*, 1974 WL 21666 (Pa. Com. Pl.). There the after-hours delivery of an automobile did not effect receipt, where the car had been driven onto the retailer's lot and the keys slid under the showroom door. Obviously, the merchant seller has to meet a high standard if he or she wants to transfer the risk of loss onto the buyer.

3. a. Tom bears the risk. Janice is a nonmerchant seller, and the rules in that case are very different. Section 2-509(3) states that in the case of a seller who is not a merchant the risk passes to the buyer on "tender of delivery." When has this occurred? The crucial section here is §2-503 (as we dealt with earlier in Chapter 16). Subsection (4) deals with the case when the goods are in the hands of a bailee and are to be delivered without being moved. That certainly isn't the situation here. We'll deal with sale of goods held by a bailee in the following chapter. We can also put off for the moment the case where delivery is to be tendered through a third-party carrier, which is the concern in §§2-503(2), (3), and (5). That leaves the first subsection as our guiding text. Read it carefully.

   Janice was willing to let Tom have the car right away. She offered him the keys. This was tender to him of the car, so he bears the risk of loss from that time on. It really doesn't matter whether he took the keys then and there or left them with her overnight. Even if she kept the keys—if she had made it clear to him that he could have them and drive the car away anytime he wanted—she had made a tender.

   Although you may find this result hard to accept, remember the seller here is not a merchant or a professional seller and there's no reason to think she expects to take the risk any longer than she has to. One case makes the point quite well. *Schock v. Ronderos*, 394 N.W.2d 697 (N.D. 1986), involved the sale of a used mobile home by one nonmerchant to another. The buyer appeared at the sellers' property where the mobile home was located and paid the purchase price on a Friday. The buyer received a bill of sale and assurances from the sellers that title to the property would be delivered soon. He then prepared the mobile home for removal, including removal of the skirting around its foundation, certain "tie-downs," and the foundation blocks. The home was left sitting on its wheels. The buyer intended to take the mobile home off of the sellers' property the following Monday, and the sellers had no objection to its remaining on their property until that time. Later, on Friday evening, it was destroyed by high winds. The Supreme Court of North Dakota affirmed a denial of the buyer's claim for a return of his purchase price. The risk of loss had passed. This was so even though the trailer had apparently still been hooked up to electricity and natural gas connections on the sellers' property at the time of its destruction and some other personal property of the sellers (a piano and davenport) had still been aboard. The court found that tender had occurred, and the risk of loss had passed, as soon as the sellers acquiesced in the buyer's preparing the mobile home for removal. Had he wanted to take it away before Monday, the sellers were apparently willing and able to disconnect the utilities and remove their piano and davenport as soon as requested. The loss was on the buyer. In fact, the court affirmed a judgment of $3,080 on a counterclaim by the sellers for their expenses incurred in removing the mobile home (or presumably what was left of it) from their property!

b. Janice bears the risk if the car is stolen overnight. She is still a nonmerchant seller, but here she wasn't to tender delivery of the car until sometime on the following day. So when, exactly, would the risk have passed? It's hard to say exactly. Perhaps the moment is 9:00 A.M. of the next day. Perhaps a bit earlier. Reading §2-503(1) suggests it would be a matter of when Tom could have reasonably understood he had the right to come over, get the keys, and take the car without surprising (annoying?) Janice by his appearance at her door. So the crucial time is not when Tom comes to pick up the car but when he *could have* come to do so. If the car was stolen before that time, of course, the loss isn't his. For an interesting case in which an appellate court had to confront the question of exactly when tender in a nonmerchant seller situation did or was to occur—before or after a hailstorm severely damaged the vehicle being sold that was, at the time of the hailstorm, still parked in the seller's driveway—see *Capshaw v. Hickman*, 880 N.E.2d 118 (Ohio App. 2007). The seller contended that the fact of the car's still being parked in the driveway at the time of the hailstorm was nothing more than a "red herring." The appellate court found otherwise and remanded the case for further findings of fact on the timing of tender issue.

c. Janice would have a hard time collecting the price from Tom. Remember that §2-709 gives her a right to the price "of conforming goods lost or damaged *within a commercially reasonable time after* risk of their loss" has passed to her buyer. Once it should have become apparent to Janice that Tom didn't intend to pick up the car, and she had the opportunity to start protecting or insuring it as she had before, or even to start looking for someone else willing to buy the car, as she now has to accept the fact that Tom is not going to follow through with his contractual obligation to buy it, that length of time has presumably passed. The risk reverts to her. Janice can of course sue Tom, but only for the damage caused to her by his failure to buy the car—the lost contract interest, not the value of the car itself.

4. By now it is clear that if Sam is a merchant for the purposes of §2-509(3), the risk of loss of the trailer would not have passed at the time of the fire. If he is a nonmerchant, the risk would have passed. Which is it? Again we see the importance of the merchant classification in Article 2 and how the classification scheme depends not only on the particular seller's business, but also on the circumstances in which the question is being asked. We refer back to §2-104(1) and the second Comment to that section (as well as to Chapter 3). The Comment suggests the test here is whether Sam is a merchant under either the "practices" or the "goods" aspect of the definition. Is this so clear? Here, at least, the sale of cars and trailers may not seem so different. But what if the seller were in the business of selling something like flowers and houseplants, which are normally taken out of his or her establishment as soon as they are bought, and the particular sale involves a used air-conditioning unit that had already been disconnected and was ready to be taken away? This seems miles from the normal business of the seller, even if he or she is a merchant. It is not so clear that the courts would find such a situation to be covered by the merchant seller provision.

CHAPTER 24

Delivery Through Third Parties

WHEN THE GOODS GET SHIPPED

The situations governed by §2-509(3), as discussed in the previous chapter, all have one thing in common: Delivery of the goods is being made directly by Seller to Buyer. True, Seller's employees might be involved in dropping off the stuff, or Buyer's employees might be making a pickup, but because these employees qualify and are acting as agents for their employers, we're still talking about a straight handoff from one contracting party to another. There are other instances, we know, where delivery is not made directly. The contract may *require* Seller to ship the goods to Buyer via some particular third-party commercial carrier. Even if delivery in a particular manner is not required, it may be *authorized* under the agreement. Seller would be within his or her rights to make delivery via an independent third-party contractor — the kind that gets paid for moving stuff, big or small, from one place to another.

Section 2-509(1) sets forth the risk of loss rules where "the contract requires or authorizes the seller to ship the goods by carrier." Article 2 does not define the word "carrier" used in this subsection, but it is clear that it is to be taken as referring only to an independent third party that transports things from one place to another for profit. See Comment 2 to this section. If delivery is made on Seller's delivery van, or if Buyer sends its own truck around to get the goods, we are *not* in subsection (1). The delivery contemplated in §2-509(1) is made under a separate contract of carriage entered into with a commercial party "engaged in the business of transporting or forwarding goods," to quote from the definition of "bill of lading" in §1-201(b)(6). That document is the receipt issued by the shipper when it takes goods for shipment.

Look now at §2-509(1). How risk of loss is allocated is clearly governed by whether the particular case fits into subpart (a) or subpart (b). We are dealing here with the distinction between the *shipment contract*, which is the subject of subpart (a), and the *destination contract*, which comes under (b). You should recall this distinction from our discussion of tender in Chapter 16. The parties have entered into a *shipment contract*, when "the seller is required or authorized to send the goods to the buyer and the contract does not require him to deliver them at a particular destination" (§2-504). Seller is responsible for dispatching the goods properly on their way and meeting the other requirements of §2-504. He or she is *not* actually responsible for them getting where they are going. The *destination contract* is different; the Seller "is required to deliver at a particular destination" (§2-503(3)). He or she has an added layer of obligation and takes ultimate responsibility that the goods will get, if not literally into Buyer's hands, at least to that "particular destination" where Buyer is to take control of them. An important point of Code jurisprudence is found buried to some degree in Comment 5 to §2-503:

> [U]nder this Article the "shipment" contract is regarded as the normal one and the "destination" contract as the variant type. The seller is not obligated to deliver at a named destination and bear the concurrent risk of loss until arrival, unless he has specifically agreed so to deliver or the commercial understanding of the terms used by the parties contemplates such delivery.

If, as this Comment says and as the courts seem to have no trouble accepting, the shipment contract is the *normal* one under Article 2, then §2-509(1)(a) is the *normal* risk of loss rule when goods are delivered through a carrier, unless a specific agreement of the parties or the commercial understanding of the language they have used allocates the risk differently and throws the whole matter into subpart (b). See *Windows, Inc. v. Jordan Panel Systems Corp.*, 177 F.3d 114 (2d Cir. 1999), and *Wilson v. Brawn of California, Inc.*, 33 Cal. Rptr. 3d 769 (Cal. Ct. App. 2005).

As a matter of fact, commercial buyers and sellers often do allocate the risk explicitly in their agreements. They could do this by explicit use of the words "risk of loss" in conjunction with an agreed-to allocation of that risk, but often they do not. Historically the practice developed of allocating the risk of loss, along with the question of who would pay for the carrier's fee and other costs of carriage, as part of the price quotation. The agreement would say something like, "Price of $100 F.O.B. Boston." While this would seem to us laypersons as nothing more than a price quote with some other gibberish thrown in to make it look official, both parties as people engaged in the business would be expected to know from this term not only what the price was, but also who was to pay the freight and who would bear the risk of loss during shipment. As I say, the system could be Greek to most of us, but in point of fact, it worked very well for those concerned. Unfortunately, the courts occasionally got it wrong (see Comment 1 to §2-319), so the drafters thought it best to incorporate these so-called *delivery terms* directly into the statutory scheme. All of us are now made privy to the magical code, and courts kept from "unfortunate" error, just by looking at §§2-319 through 2-322. You should glance at these sections now. There is, to say the least, no reason for you to try and memorize what they say. The important thing is that you know these sections are there as part of Article 2 and that you can refer to them when the need arises. The need will arise, and you'll get sufficient practice in their use, in some of the examples that follow.

WHEN THE GOODS STAY PUT

Section §2-509(2) sets out the risk of loss rules where "the goods are held by a bailee to be delivered without being moved." Again, Article 2 does not define *bailee* directly, but it is meant to indicate "a person engaged in the business of storing goods for hire," to quote from the definition of "warehouse receipt" in §1-201(b)(42). Such a document is, not surprisingly, the receipt issued by a commercial warehouse when it takes in goods for storage. See also the definition of bailee in §7-102(a)(1). The idea behind §2-509(2) is that sometimes Seller will have put goods into storage with an independent commercial warehouse. (We are *not* talking about the case where they are being stored in Seller's own warehouse or where Seller delivers them directly to Buyer's warehouse.) To sell the goods, Seller simply agrees to transfer ownership to Buyer. The goods will stay where they are. If all goes well, the result, aside from Seller's having been paid the price, is that Buyer will now be the proud owner of the goods as they sit snugly in the warehouse. If something untoward happens to the goods in the midst of this transaction—some loss occurs through the fault of neither party—then the risk of loss is governed by subsection (2). Practically, of course, the underlying issue is which party is going to go against the warehouse (which not surprisingly has a duty to care for the goods (see §7-204)) to be made whole or, if the warehouse can prove it is not liable or has effectively limited its liability, must bear the consequence.

There have been a few cases where a merchant seller, seeking to avoid the unfavorable operation of §2-509(3), has argued that under the particular circumstances it had been transformed into a "bailee" by the time of the loss and hence could wedge itself into a more favorable result via §2-509(2).

Well-known in this regard is *Caudle v. Sherrard Motor Co.*, 525 S.W.2d 238 (Tex. Civ. App. 1975). In *Caudle*, as in the other cases that have had to deal with this argument, the court found against the seller. The courts have consistently reserved §2-509(2) for those situations where the goods have been put into the hands of a separate party engaged in the business of storing goods for hire, the commercial bailee. The seller who, as part of doing the deal, agrees to and does store the goods for a time on his or her premises doesn't qualify.

The examples and explanations ask you to apply the relevant subsections of §2-509. You'll find that this naturally leads you into other sections, particularly those that set up the criteria for tender (with which we dealt in Chapter 16) as well as those mentioned above that lay out the meaning of the various delivery terms. In answering these questions, you may assume, as you did in the previous chapter, that there has been no breach on either Seller's or Buyer's part. We'll deal with the consequences of breach on risk of loss in the chapter to follow.

Examples

EXAMPLES

1. Ben owns and operates an electronics store in Birmingham, Alabama. He regularly places orders with a large audio manufacturer, Stereo Supply, located in Sacramento. In need of some of Stereo's line of speakers, he sends that company a Purchase Order specifying that he wishes to buy five sets of speakers at the price set forth in the Stereo Supply catalog, which he keeps on hand. He receives back a copy of this Purchase Order initialed by someone in Stereo's sales department along with a note telling him that the speakers will be shipped to him via United Pick-Up Services ("UPS"), a well-known delivery service. Neither the catalog nor the Purchase Order makes any mention of the means or cost of shipment or of the risk of loss. Ben never receives the speakers, but some weeks later receives a bill for them. He calls up Stereo and is informed that the company had indeed, upon receiving his order, packaged the speakers and delivered them to UPS. That firm now acknowledges that the shipment apparently got lost somewhere in transit.
   (a) Assuming all this is true, does Ben have to pay the bill received from Stereo Supply?
   (b) Would your answer be different if Ben could show that his Purchase Order contained a space labelled "Ship To:" which he had filled in with his Birmingham address?
   (c) What if the Purchase Order had specified that "Seller shall pay freight"?
   (d) Suppose the Purchase Order had featured in large, bold print the language "NOTICE: ALL SHIPMENTS TRAVEL AT THE RISK AND COST OF SUPPLIER." Would this change your analysis?

(e) Finally, change the facts so that the speakers delivered by Stereo Supply to UPS were the wrong model and not the type ordered by Ben. What result here?

2. Mazie's Department Store, located in Capitol City, contracts to buy six gross of sweaters from Knits Incorporated, which is located in Boston. The price is agreed to as "$1,200/gross F.O.B. Boston." Knits delivers the sweaters to Tony's Trucking Service and arranges a contract for their delivery to Mazie. Knits receives a bill of lading from Tony's Trucking, which it immediately mails off to Mazie along with other details of the shipment. While en route, Tony's truck is sideswiped and falls off a cliff. Fortunately, no one is hurt, but all of the cargo is destroyed.
   (a) Who bears the risk of loss of the sweaters?
   (b) Would your answer be the same if Knits had never mailed off the bill of lading to Mazie nor otherwise informed her of the shipment?
   (c) How would you answer if instead the price term had read "$1,340/gross F.O.B. Capitol City"?
   (d) What if the price term had read "$1,340/gross C.I.F. Capitol City"?

3. Butterfield Foods, a preparer of frozen dinners, is located in Des Moines. It places a large order for freshly caught scrod with Seaside Fish Sellers in Boston. The contract is "F.O.B. Boston." Seaside delivers the fish to the Midwest and Atlantic Railroad and arranges for their shipment to the railyard in Des Moines. Butterfield is sent notice of this shipment and the bill of lading provided by the railroad. Unfortunately, Seaside neglects to arrange for shipment in refrigerated cars. The fish arrive in Des Moines in an awful state. Does Butterfield have to pay Seaside at the contract rate for the fish?

4. Seaside also makes a shipment by rail to a buyer in Omaha, this time remembering to pack the fish in ice and arrange for shipment in refrigerated railroad cars. The contract calls for payment "F.O.B. Boston." The fish are delivered to the railroad, which accepts them and furnishes a bill of lading. Notice of the shipment and the bill are sent forthwith to the buyer. The railroad expects to load the fish onto a train bound for Omaha the following day. Overnight, a hurricane hits the Boston area causing great damage to the railroad's yards and in particular the crates of fish. They are strewn all over the place. Obviously they have become worthless.
   (a) Who bore this risk?
   (b) Would your answer be any different if the price term of the contract had read "F.O.B. Cars Boston"?
   (c) Seaside makes a third contract to sell fish, this time to a buyer in Fargo, North Dakota. It packs the fish in ice and delivers them to the railroad. Again it makes an appropriate contract for shipment and forwards

the necessary documents. The shipment arrives in Fargo, where it is off-loaded from the railroad cars. Four days later, when Buyer arrives at the railroad yard to make a pick-up, she discovers that thieves have apparently broken into the railroad's facility in Fargo and made off with the fish. If the contract read "F.O.B. Fargo," who bore this risk? What if the contract had read "F.O.B. Buyer's Truck Fargo"?

5. Seller in Seaport, South Carolina, contracts to sell a large metal molding machine to Buyer in Baysville, New York. It is agreed that delivery will be "F.A.S. Gigantic." Seller delivers the machine, properly crated, to the Seaport Pier alongside the *Gigantic* and arranges with that ship's owner for delivery. Notice of this arrangement and the shipping company's bill of lading are mailed to Buyer. As the crate containing the machine is being loaded onto the ship, a winch breaks and the machine is dropped and severely damaged.
   (a) Who bears this risk of loss?
   (b) What if the contract documents had read "Ex-Ship Gigantic"?

6. Farmer Jones stores a large quantity of wheat at Walter's Wheat Warehouse. She receives a negotiable warehouse receipt from Walter. Jones goes into the big city and to the office of Agribusiness, Inc. A representative of that company agrees to buy all the wheat she has stored. Jones hands over the warehouse receipt. She goes home with a promise that Agribusiness will send her a check in payment within a week. She does not contact Walter. That night, Walter's Warehouse is hit by a tornado and all of the wheat is rendered worthless.
   (a) Who bears this loss? (For the purposes of this question and the two that follow, there is really no need for you to understand the difference between a "negotiable" warehouse receipt and a "non-negotiable" one. It is enough that you recognize that warehouse receipts come in two varieties, as in fact do bills of lading.)
   (b) Suppose instead that Jones had received a non-negotiable warehouse receipt from Walter and that she had not carried this document with her to the city. On Monday, she enters into a contract with Agribusiness and agrees to send it the non-negotiable receipt within three days. When she gets home, she immediately sends off the receipt. The receipt arrives in Agribusiness's offices with the Thursday afternoon mail. The tornado comes on Thursday night, wiping out the warehouse and along with it the wheat. Under these facts, who bears the risk of loss?
   (c) Suppose Jones could show that she stopped by Walter's after she mailed off the receipt and told him that "I've sold the wheat to Agribusiness," to which Walter replied, "Okay, I'll note that on my books." Walter makes the notation before the tornado hits. Who now bears the loss?

Explanations

1. a. Ben must pay for the speakers at the contract price because the risk of loss had passed to him prior to their disappearance. Since the contract is silent as to the risk of loss and no delivery term (like F.O.B. or C.I.F.) was used, the Code's assumption that this was a shipment contract controls. As the Comment to §2-503 that was quoted in the introductory text says, the shipment contract is the "normal" one, and there's nothing here to suggest that Ben and Stereo are acting abnormally. This being a shipment contract, we look to §2-509(1)(a). The risk passes to the buyer "when the goods are duly delivered to the carrier." To see what Stereo Supply has to do to "duly deliver to the carrier" and hence pass the risk on, we look to §2-504. Stereo Supply appears here to have met all three of the criteria (a) through (c).

   So the risk was on Ben at the time of the loss. He must pay the price. He may of course go against UPS for the loss he suffered, but it is his responsibility, not Stereo Supply's, to pursue the carrier and to prove it liable under some theory. Notice that this is true even though Stereo Supply and not Ben was the one to select the carrier. It is key to the seller's position here that the choice of UPS and the contract of carriage made with that firm were "reasonable having regard to the nature of the goods and the circumstances of the case." Barring any facts not given here, Stereo Supply appears to have lived up to this standard.

   b. The answer should still be the same. Ben bears the loss under this shipment contract. He could try to argue that the "Ship To:" language converted this into a destination contract, but it is doubtful this would succeed. The courts have generally followed the drafters' statement that the shipment contract is the normal one and, before they will find the contract not to be a standard shipment contract, they insist on there being very explicit language that unequivocally denotes a destination contract, such as a reference to risk of loss or use of a delivery term such as "F.O.B. destination." In particular, in the few instances in which they have been asked to find a destination contract based on language like that here ("Ship to" buyer's location), they have not responded favorably. After all, as the court pointed out in one such case, *Pestana v. Karinol Corp.*, 367 So. 2d 1096 (Fl. Dist. Ct. App. 1979), sellers who have entered into shipment contracts need to know where to send the stuff just as much as do sellers committed to destination contracts. Either type of agreement is going to have to include in its language the buyer's address, or where he or she wants the goods sent. As the court stated:

   > A "send to" or "ship to" term is a part of every contract involving the sale of goods where carriage is contemplated and has no significance in

determining whether the contract is a shipment or a destination contract for risk of loss purposes. . . . As such, the "send to" term contained in [the instant] contract cannot, without more, convert this into a destination contract.

c. Ben will still bear the risk. Cost of shipment and risk of loss are distinct aspects of any one contract and need not necessarily be allocated to the same party. This language tells us who is to bear the *cost* of the trip, but it does not refer specifically to the risk of loss. So as to risk of loss, the preference for a shipment contract, and an answer like that to Example 1a, still pertain. This is clearly in keeping with the drafters' intention. Reread Comment 5 to §2-503, but this time starting from the very beginning.

d. Here, finally, is a situation where Ben would not bear the risk of loss. The contract is no longer silent but expressly and unreservedly allocates the risk to the seller during shipment. The parties are always free to allocate the risk of loss as they choose by proper agreement (§2-509(4)), and that is what they have done here. Stereo Supply's only argument would be that it had never agreed to this term, but this shouldn't have much success as it actually initialed the document that conspicuously bore this legend.

   So, in this case, the parties have entered into a destination contract. We look, therefore, to §2-509(1)(b). There is no question that the goods were never tendered at the destination, so the risk of loss never passed from the seller. In some other cases, of course, the issue of tender will be closer. If so, we will have §2-503 to guide us. Review subsections (1) and (3) of that section.

e. Ben would not bear the risk of loss. The seller can, of course, shift the risk of loss under a shipment contract only by delivering *conforming* goods to the carrier. See *Graaff v. Bakker Brothers of Idaho, Inc.*, 934 P.2d 1228 (Wash. App. 1997).

2. a. Mazie bears the risk. Under §2-319(1), the term F.O.B. (which comes from "free on board" but which really "means" just what this section says it means, no more and no less) is not just a price term, but also a delivery term. Here we have "F.O.B. Boston." This is F.O.B. the place of shipment, so it marks out a shipment contract pursuant to §2-319(1)(a). See, for example, *NCIS, Inc. v. Bada Tek Co, Ltd.*, 2010 WL 2219186 (Ohio Com. Pl.). Assuming Knits met all of the criteria of §2-504 (and there's no reason here to doubt it), it bore the risk only until it "put the goods into the possession of the shipper." While the subsection does not explicitly say so, once the seller no longer bears the risk, it necessarily must fall, as between the two of them, on the buyer.

   b. The answer here is not perfectly clear. Knits did put the sweaters into the possession of the carrier. But §2-319(1)(a) also refers quite specifically to the seller's duties under §2-504, and we know these include what is required by subpart (c) of that section. Lastly, we note the concluding language of §2-504. It says that a seller's failure to carry out the obligation laid out in (c) is a *ground for rejection* only if "material delay or loss ensues." Is this relevant at all to a risk of loss problem where acceptance or rejection is hardly the issue? Should Mazie bear the risk unless she can show that material delay or loss was a direct result of her not being given notice in this instance? If so, she'd have to show, I suppose, that had she gotten the notice, she would have immediately insured these sweaters or that she would have called Tony and importuned him to be even more careful driving than he usually is. Even if the notice had been immediately sent off by Knits, however, it might not have arrived at Mazie's until after the accident had already happened. So Knits might even be able to affirmatively prove that the lack of notice could not have made a bit of difference in any way relating to this loss. If that is so, why could this failure on its part prevent the risk of loss from shifting to the buyer?

In *Rheinberg-Kellerei GmbH v. Vineyard Wine Co., Inc.*, 281 S.E.2d 425 (N.C. App. 1981), the parties entered into a shipment contract for the sale of some wine produced in Germany. The wine was delivered to a ship, the MS *Munchen*, on November 29. The first that the buyer learned about the shipment was on or about January 24. Meanwhile, the MS *Munchen* had been lost in the North Atlantic with all hands and cargo on board sometime between December 12 and 22. The trial court found that the risk had remained on the seller because of its failure to give "prompt notice" of the shipment to the buyer. This finding was upheld on appeal, where the court stated:

> The seller is burdened with special responsibilities under a shipment contract because of the nature of the risk of loss being transferred. . . . Where the buyer, upon shipment by seller, assumes the perils involved in carriage, he must have a reasonable opportunity to guard against these risks by independent arrangements with the carrier. The requirement of prompt notification by the seller, as used in [§2-504(c)], must be construed as taking into consideration the need of a buyer to be informed of the shipment in sufficient time for him to take action to protect himself from the risk of damage to or loss of the goods while in transit. . . . It would not be practical or desirable, however, for the courts to attempt to engraft onto [§2-504] of the U.C.C. a rigid definition of prompt notice. Given the myriad factual situations which arise in business dealings, and keeping in mind the commercial realities, whether the notification has been "prompt" within the meaning of the U.C.C. will have to be determined on a case-by-case basis, under all the circumstances.

This case suggests an answer to the problem we have been looking at—whether the prompt notice of shipment required under §2-504 is an absolute requirement for passage of the risk of loss off of the seller carrying out a shipment contract onto the buyer—but there is still room for doubt. After all, the court here stressed the buyer's need to have time to make arrangements to protect itself once it has the loss. And under the particular facts, it appears that had the seller given prompt notice, the buyer would have known that its wine was aboard the MS *Munchen* sometime before she went down. What if that good ship had gone down as soon as she left port, say on November 30? Even if the seller *had* given prompt notice, it is unlikely that the buyer would have received this notice until it was too late to matter. If that were the situation, should the seller be able to argue that its failure to give prompt notice was irrelevant to the risk of loss? As far as I can tell, no court has had to directly confront this question.

While it is not perfectly clear from these sections, I would argue that it is a better reading to say that for a seller to shift the loss under a shipment contract, it really has to meet the three criteria of §2-504 and take the consequences if it does not, even if its failure to take some step called for by that section does not contribute to the actual loss in any way or otherwise affect how the buyer could have protected itself. There is every reason for encouraging sellers to take their various responsibilities under §2-504 seriously, and making passage of the risk of loss dependent on them certainly is one good way to drive this point home.

c. This "F.O.B. destination" term created a delivery contract. See §2-319(1)(b). The risk remained on Knits until it tendered the goods in Capitol City "in the manner provided in this Article (§2-503)." The sweaters never made it to Capitol City, so they clearly were never tendered there. Knits bore the risk. Notice the price here is more per gross than it was in the shipment contract. That makes sense. Under this type of price term, not only has the seller agreed to take the risk of loss during transit, but it has also agreed to incur transportation costs as well. Naturally it will have to charge some more. And the buyer, who does not have to bear this risk or expense, is usually willing to pay the slightly greater price. (Of course the actual price in dollars and cents, no matter what the delivery term, is a matter of one-on-one negotiation and follows no logic outside of the law of supply and demand.)

d. Under §2-320(2), any C.I.F. term creates a shipment contract. See Comment 1. If Knits met all of the criteria of sections (a) through (e) the risk will have passed to Mazie. Here we have an interesting combination. It is a shipment contract, so the risk of loss is on buyer, but the seller agreed to obtain insurance to cover this risk and to bear the cost of this insurance as well as the freight to the stated destination. Of course, the price charged to the buyer will take into account these costs to seller. See subsection (1).

There is, as you can see, no magic to these various allocations of risks, responsibilities, and costs. It all comes down to each party's knowing what the other is talking about when they use these terms or symbols. Presumably they are able to deal with any allocation as long as it is clearly set out, or more importantly, select the one which best fits their situation at the time of contracting.

3. This is an "F.O.B. place of shipment" contract, and the risk of loss during transit would normally be on the buyer. The seller here, however, quite clearly did not meet its §2-504 obligations on shipment, which are referred to in §2-319(1)(a). You get to the same result by recognizing this is a shipment contract and hence is governed by §2-509(1)(a). The seller does not "duly deliver" to a carrier if it does not make an appropriate contract for carriage.

   Suppose Seaside did in fact arrange for shipment by refrigerated cars. Unfortunately, the refrigeration system on the cars failed somewhere along the line with the same unsettling results. It would seem that the risk had passed to the buyer Butterfield. That company would quite naturally try to sue the railroad for all the damage caused. Suppose, however, that the contract of carriage arranged for by Seaside contained a clause limiting the railroad's potential liability to a figure far below the value of the fish and that this clause was enforceable under law. Is Butterfield out of luck? No. Now it has another way of arguing that Seaside had never successfully passed the risk along. Look at the concluding sentence of Comment 3 to §2-504.

4. a. Butterfield bore the risk. Under §2-319(1)(a), it is sufficient for the risk to pass to buyer that the seller put the goods "in the possession of the carrier." That had been done here. See *Pagano v. Occidental Chemical Corp.*, 629 N.E.2d 569 (Ill. App. 1994).
   b. Under this term, the risk remained on Seaside. Look at §2-319(1)(c). The seller's risk continued until it had "loaded the goods on board." That had not happened yet.
   c. If the contract reads "F.O.B. Fargo," the question under §2-319(1)(b) would be whether the goods had been tendered in that city. We consult §2-503. If the buyer could have come and picked them up any time after they were off-loaded, there was tender and the risk had passed. The result would be otherwise, with the risk remaining on the seller, if the term had been "F.O.B. Buyer's Truck Fargo."

5. a. "F.A.S. Vessel" is explained by §2-319(2), which you can read and satisfy yourself that under these facts Buyer bore the risk of loss.

b. Under an "ex-ship" term, the risk does not pass to the buyer until "goods leave the ship's tackle or are otherwise properly unloaded" (§2-322(2)(b)). Hence, Seller bore the risk of loss.

6. a. Agribusiness bears the loss. This case is covered by §2-509(2) as the goods were held by a bailee, Walter's Warehouse, and were to be delivered without being moved. (Who would want to schlep all that wheat from one warehouse to another when the same effect can be had by handing over warehouse receipt?) The risk passed to the buyer under subpart (a) with its receipt of the negotiable document of title covering the goods.

b. The risk was probably still on Jones. Because the warehouse receipt is of the non-negotiable variety, subpart (a) is not applicable. Nor for the moment is (b). Under (c), the risk passes to Agribusiness upon its receipt of the non-negotiable document of title "as provided in (4)(b) of Section 2-503." Agribusiness did receive the document prior to the tornado and the loss of the wheat, but look at §2-503(4)(b). It tells us that "risk of loss . . . remains on the seller until the buyer has had a reasonable time to present the document. . . ." Agribusiness could certainly argue that a reasonable time had not passed here. What if the tornado came something like two or three days after the non-negotiable document had been received? The question gets trickier. We (and the parties) have to deal with the troublesome "R" word—*reasonableness*.

At the moment, you may not have a good handle on the difference between negotiable and non-negotiable documents of title, but you can see at least one reason why parties might prefer to deal in the former rather than the latter. Dealings in negotiable documents tend overall to be much more certain, crisp, and clean than are dealings in non-negotiable instruments. What we see here is just one example.

c. Jones would try to argue that the risk passed based not on §2-509(2)(c), but on subpart (b). Note the three subparts are joined with *or*, so risk will pass if any one of the conditions is met. Is Jones right that by the time the big wind struck, Walter had "acknowledged" Agribusiness's right to possession of the goods? This language in the section is imprecise to put it mildly, and we get no help from the Comments. In *Jason's Foods, Inc. v. Peter Eckrich & Sons, Inc.*, 774 F.2d 214 (7th Cir. 1985), the seller argued that risk passed under this provision when the bailee acknowledged to it, *to the seller*, that the goods had been transferred to the buyer's name and were now the buyer's property. The court, following the lead of several commentators, concluded otherwise. It held that subpart (b) requires an "acknowledgment" *to the buyer* for risk of loss to pass under this method. Of course, as the court itself recognized, this holding still leaves unanswered questions.

When exactly does the risk pass under §2-509(2)(b)? Is it when a form of acknowledgment is sent to the buyer by the bailee or when it is received by the buyer? What if the acknowledgment is lost in the mail? What if the buyer becomes aware of the transfer to its name through some other reliable source prior to the acknowledgment? Does the risk pass then? The court in *Jason's Foods* noted these questions but wisely left them for another day as they were not raised by the case before it. For a later case that follows the *Jason's Foods* approach, see *O.C.T. Equipment, Inc. v. Shepherd Machinery Co.*, 95 P.3d 197 (Okla. Civ. App. 2004).

CHAPTER 25

Delivery When There Has Been a Breach

INTRODUCTION

The two previous chapters dealt with risk of loss problems under §2-509. We assumed throughout that there had been no breach or repudiation by either party. Once a breach by either Seller or Buyer has been established, we no longer look to §2-509 for the risk of loss allocation rules but turn instead to §2-510. That much is clear. This section has, in fact, been the subject of a fair amount of academic criticism. As one court commented, "It is possible to conjure up a host of hypotheticals leading to seeming perverse results under §2-510. . . . The fact is, however," the court went on to say, "that those courts considering it have had little difficulty in applying it as written." *Jakowski v. Carole Chevrolet, Inc.*, 433 A.2d 841 (N.J. Super. 1981). In the questions that follow, I have tried to take a middle ground, exploring some of the questions left unresolved by the language of §2-510 without getting too academically perverse.

Examples

1. Mazie's Department Store, located in Capitol City, contracts to buy six gross (that's 864) of sweaters from Knits Incorporated, which is located in Boston. The price is agreed to as "$1,200/gross F.O.B. Boston." Knits delivers cartons containing 850 sweaters to Tony's Trucking Service and arranges a contract for their delivery to Mazie. Knits receives a bill of lading from Tony's Trucking, which it immediately mails off to Mazie along

with other details of the shipment. While en route, Tony's truck is caught in a flood. Many of the sweaters become waterlogged and their colors run. They arrive at Mazie's, but she declines to accept any of them.

(a) Who bears the risk of loss?

(b) Suppose instead that Knits had delivered the full six gross of sweaters to Tony's, but had failed to notify Mazie of the shipment. The first she knows of it is when the sweaters arrive in their sorry state at her store. She declines to accept any of them. Who bears the risk of loss?

(c) Finally, suppose that Knits had delivered 864 sweaters to Tony's Trucking and had, in addition, given the proper notice to Mazie. Tony drives through rough country and stormy weather, but there is no major flood and his truck is never swamped with water. When the sweaters arrive, Mazie examines them and finds that the colors have run on a good number of them. Tony insists that his truck had stayed watertight throughout the trip and that the sweaters must have been like that to begin with. Mazie telephones Knits and complains that they included in the shipment a number of defective items. She intends to reject the whole shipment. The delivery manager at Knits responds that his records indicate that his firm shipped six gross of sweaters, all of which met the contract specifications. He suggests that they must have gotten wet during shipment, whatever Tony may say. Assuming there is significant water damage to some of the sweaters, who bears this risk of loss?

2. Birmingham Integrated Machines, a computer manufacturer, contracts to buy 600,000 switches from Switcher International over the course of a year. Under the contract, Switcher is to ship by rail 50,000 switches no later than the tenth day of each month during 2015. The contract gives the prices as "$2 per switch F.O.B. Switcher Plant." Switcher delivers 49,000 switches to the railroad for delivery to BIM on January 8. It obtains a bill of lading and sends this bill with a notice of shipment to the buyer. The 49,000 switches are lost in a fire while en route. Who bears this risk of loss, Switcher or BIM?

3. Sam's Autorama is a retail automobile dealership. Sam contracts to sell a car to Betty. The contract provides that the car shall be treated with a special protective undercoating prior to delivery. Betty takes delivery of the car on Monday. On Tuesday she becomes aware that the car has not been given the undercoating as promised. She drives it back to Sam's. Sam acknowledges the problem and tells Betty to leave the car with him so that he can have the undercoating applied within a few days. Betty does leave the car with Sam.

(a) That night, before any work is done on it, the car is stolen from Sam's lot. Who bears the risk of loss for this theft?

(b) Suppose instead that Sam does apply the undercoating on Monday afternoon. He telephones Betty and tells her that she can pick her car up at any time. Betty says she will come over the next day. The car is stolen sometime late on Monday night. How does this affect your risk of loss analysis?

(c) Suppose that Betty had driven the car for two months prior to becoming aware that it had not been given the undercoating as promised. She returns the car to Sam, who agrees to remedy the defect, but before he can do anything, the car is stolen from his lot. Who bears the risk of loss in this situation? Assume that Betty had insured the car against theft from the moment she picked it up at the dealership and that her insurance would cover this loss.

(d) If Betty does collect on her insurance because of this theft, can her insurance company then bring suit against Sam for the amount it has had to pay out?

4. The wealthy Mr. Burns goes into the Sparkle Store, a jewelry retailer. He spots an emerald tie pin and admires the setting, but tells the owner he would like to buy such a pin only if it has a diamond in it. The owner of the store shows him a diamond, of which Burns approves. Burns signs a contract to buy the pin, with the emerald replaced by this diamond, for a price of $25,000. The storeowner agrees to have the pin ready within a week and to call Burns when he can take delivery. The owner puts the diamond in the pin and calls Burns, who tells him, "I've decided I don't want the pin after all. Sorry." The owner puts the pin in her safe, intending to return it to a display case the following day if she can't get Burns to change his mind. That night, it is part of a quantity of jewelry that is stolen.

(a) Can the owner make Burns pay the $25,000 for the pin?

(b) Would your analysis of the situation in the previous question be any different if the theft had come more than a month after Burns first refused to take delivery of the pin?

Explanations

1. a. The risk at the time of water damage was on Knits. Since this was an "F.O.B. place of shipment" contract, the risk for losses occurring in transit would normally be on the buyer, as we saw in the last chapter. Here, however, Mazie can point to §2-510(1). Note first that a seller bound to a shipment contract does not fulfill its obligations as set forth in §2-504 if the goods it puts into the hands of the carrier fail to conform to what is called for under the contract. *Graaff v. Bakker Bros. of Idaho, Inc.*, 934 P.2d 1228 (Wash. App. 1997). The tender failed to conform to the contract, which called for six gross (864) of sweaters.

Knits shipped only 850. For the buyer to avoid the risk of loss under §2-510(1), there need not simply be a nonconformity in tender, but a nonconformity such "as to give a right of rejection." Could Mazie have rejected even a perfectly undamaged delivery of 850 units? Barring any other information, we have to say yes under the perfect tender language of §2-601. Under §2-510(1), the risk remained on the seller, Knits, "until cure or acceptance." Cure isn't relevant here because the goods were damaged before the buyer had a chance to reject them. And Mazie refused to accept any of the sweaters, as she had the right to do. Knits bears all the loss and is going to have to look to Tony, Tony's insurance, or its own insurance for some relief.

b. Mazie would again argue under §2-510(1), but in this instance, that subsection doesn't apply. Why? Look again at the last sentence in §2-504. Knits' failure to give notification is "a ground for rejection only if material loss or delay ensues." Well, there was a subsequent loss, but it appears to be in no way tied to the lack of notice. Comment 6 to this section says that rejection by the buyer is "justified only when the seller's dereliction . . . in fact is followed by material delay or damage." I think what the drafters meant to say is that the seller's failure must at least, to some degree, have *contributed* to a subsequent delay or damage. If the shipment arrives at the same time and in the same condition it would have even if perfect notice had been sent, and there has been no additional burden on the buyer, then I don't think the buyer could ever reject on what then seems like a pure technicality. If that is so, then Knits' failure to give notice in this instance would not in and of itself have been a ground for rejection by Mazie. Now go back to §2-510(1). It does not apply in this case because the nonconformity of tender or delivery, such as it was, did not "give a right of rejection" to Mazie.

Following this line of reasoning, the situation is thrown back into §2-509(1)(a). Fortunately for Mazie, as we saw in the last chapter, there is at least one case that stands for the proposition that a seller's failure to give proper notice under §2-504 prevents the risk of loss from passing under a normal shipment contract. *Rheinberg-Kellerei GmbH v. Vineyard Wine Co. Inc.*, 281 S.E.2d 425 (N.C. App. 1981). So there is a good chance the risk will be found to have been on Knits, but it's an argument not under §2-510 but rather under §2-509. One argument that might work for Mazie is that had Mazie known that the goods had been shipped, and therefore the risk of loss had passed to her, she would have purchased insurance on them.

c. We really don't know who bears the risk of loss here. This question is designed to drive home the (fairly obvious) point that when a shipment arrives in poor shape, it is often very difficult if not impossible to tell exactly what has happened. And when and where the damage occurred is of more than intellectual interest. If the sweaters were in poor condition before they left Knits' plant, then Mazie need not accept them, obviously bears no responsibility for this damage (or even any other misfortune that happened to them along the way), and can refuse to pay a penny for them. She may even have a claim for substantial damages because of Knits' failure to perform on its contract. If, on the other hand, the sweaters were in good order when they left the plant but were damaged while in transit, then Mazie bears the risk of loss for this occurrence and must pay for them at the contract rate. Of course the issue here isn't just who has the bother of going against poor Tony, because if Tony has any argument that the sweaters were in bad shape to begin with, he may not have to pay anything. It all depends on *what* happened *when*, and that's something even the most careful reading of the Code won't answer for us.

2. Unless BIM can establish that the shipment of 49,000 switches when 50,000 were promised was a *substantial* nonconformity, it will bear the risk of loss. True the tender was defective, but now it has to be judged under §2-612(2). (See generally Chapter 21.) It may well be that the lack of even a fairly large number of units does not give the buyer the right under that subsection to reject the delivery. If that is so, BIM can't call in §2-510(1), as the nonconformity would not have given it a right to reject. Analyze the situation under §2-509 and you see BIM bears the risk of loss during shipment. Of course, if Switcher had shipped only, say, 25,000 switches, the substantial nonconformity would have given BIM as buyer the right to reject, §2-510(1) would apply, and the risk would have remained on the seller.

3. a. Sam bears the risk of loss. This question is based on the *Jakowski* case cited at the beginning of the chapter. The court first ruled that the seller never accepted the car merely by taking possession of it for such a short time. There had been no "reasonable opportunity to inspect" under §2-606. Since there was a clear nonconformity that gave the buyer the right to reject, §2-510(1) applied and the risk remained on the seller until cure or acceptance. The defect had not been cured at the time of the theft nor, of course, had the auto been accepted. The risk of loss remained on the seller.

   What would have been the result if Sam, after being told of the defect, had told Betty to bring the car in "early next week" for the undercoating and it then had been stolen from Betty's garage over the weekend? The analysis is still the same and Sam bears that risk even though the car was in Betty's possession at the time of the loss. You can see that this risk of loss allocation gives Sam every motivation to get the defect cured and the auto accepted by his buyer as soon as possible.

b. Sam now has an argument that the risk was on Betty at the time of the theft. Section 2-510(1) says the risk will remain on him until "cure or acceptance." He also can point to the last sentence of Comment 2, which says, "The seller's privilege of cure does not shift the risk, however, until the cure is *completed.*" He says cure had been effectively completed as of the close of business on Monday.

Sam's argument is very neat and tidy, but the result just doesn't make sense. Once the cure has been completed and a nondefective car is on Sam's lot waiting to be picked up by Betty, shouldn't the situation be just like that under §2-509(3)? Why should the seller be better off because it has taken him two tries to tender a conforming vehicle? If the analogy to §2-509(3) is right, then because Sam is a merchant, the risk would be on him until Betty took receipt—that is, physical possession, of the car. I know of no case where the facts are as I have posed them here, but I can't help believing the buyer would win on this one.

c. Betty bears the risk of loss. After a couple of months, it would be pretty hard for her to argue that she had never accepted the car. She could, of course, argue that this substantial nonconformity gave her the right to revoke acceptance. If she can and does rightfully revoke acceptance, the risk of loss is governed by §2-510(2). The buyer can treat the risk of loss as having rested on seller from the beginning only "to the extent of any deficiency of his [or her] effective insurance coverage." Betty has effective insurance coverage for this loss, so the risk that was transferred to her with her acceptance stays with her. Betty's insurance carrier pays for the loss.

d. No, her insurance company may not go against Sam. See the last part of Comment 3. Under this provision of Article 2, the risk *really was* on Betty at the time of the theft and not on Sam. Betty legally suffered the loss and her insurance made it up. Betty had no rights against Sam, so her insurance carrier does not have any either. If the carrier wants to be reimbursed for its outlay, it is going to have to go against the thief.

4. a. Burns would have to pay the Sparkle Store for the bauble, but only if this loss was not covered by the store's own insurance. Under §2-510(3):

> Where the buyer as to conforming goods already identified to the contract for sale repudiates or is otherwise in breach before risk of their loss has passed to him, the seller may to the extent of any deficiency in his effective insurance coverage treat the risk of loss as resting on the buyer for a commercially reasonable time.

Here the goods were identified and the buyer repudiated, so the subsection's rule governs. If Sparkle isn't insured for this loss, the risk will be on Burns for a "commercially reasonable time" following his repudiation. The discussion of the next question will delve more deeply into how that phrase should be applied in the situation, but it's doubtful that the time wouldn't run at least for a day or so. Of course this is a diamond, and a court might rule that for a merchant like this to leave such a valuable and thief-tempting object such as this uninsured for even one night was unreasonable. If, by the time of the theft, it had already been returned to the display case alongside all of the other stuff for sale, it could well be that a court would reason it should have as of that moment been insured just like the rest of her inventory of precious gems.

It's hard to imagine that the seller in this instance, the Sparkle Store, would not have effective insurance coverage for any and all jewelry on its premises regardless of their contract status, but there will be other circumstances where the seller's insurance will not cover and the repudiating buyer must bear the risk. An example that is often cited is *Multiplastics, Inc. v. Arch Industries, Inc.*, 348 A.2d 618 (Conn. 1974). Arch Industries contracted to buy 40,000 pounds of brown polystyrene pellets from Multiplastics, agreeing to accept delivery at the rate of 1,000 pounds per day after production of the pellets was complete. Multiplastics produced the pellets but Arch refused to issue release orders that would have signaled the seller to start delivery of the pellets, even after several requests that it do so. On August 18, Multiplastics sent Arch a letter stating that it had already held the pellets in storage for 40 days and that "we cannot warehouse these products indefinitely, and request that you send us shipping instructions." By August 20, with the help of several phone calls, the seller had gotten the buyer's agreement that it would soon issue the release orders, but in fact it never did so. On September 22, the Multiplastics plant, containing all of the pellets, was destroyed by fire. Its fire insurance did not cover the loss of the pellets. The court concluded that Arch, the buyer, had been in breach as of the date of the fire. Since it also concluded that a commercially reasonable time had not passed since the breach (see Example 4b), the risk of loss was on the buyer. Multiplastics was entitled to recover the contract price from Arch.

b. Even if the Sparkle Store did not have insurance covering this loss, it seems pretty clear that "a commercially reasonable time" would have passed and that under §2-510(3), it would have to bear this risk. I think it's likely that retail jewelers don't have diamonds hanging around their stores for months without insuring against their loss.

In the *Multiplastics* case, as I mentioned above, the court ruled that a commercially reasonable amount of time had not passed between the repudiation or breach, which it took as occurring on August 20, and the loss of the pellets in the fire of September 22. The court stated:

> The time limitation in [§2-510(3)] is designed to enable the seller to obtain the additional requisite insurance coverage. [T]he trial court found that the defendant repeatedly agreed to transmit delivery instructions and that the pellets were specifically made to fill the defendant's order. Under those circumstances, it was reasonable for the plaintiff to believe that the goods would soon be taken off its hands and so to forgo procuring the needed insurance.

This court suggests that the reason for the time limitation here is to give the seller a chance to get insurance coverage, at least once it becomes apparent that the goods won't be taken off its hands by this particular buyer. Another explanation for the limitation is that it encourages the seller to *try* to get the goods off of its hands by selling them to *someone* even if it isn't this buyer. There's no particularly good reason for the seller to hold on to the goods because this buyer won't take them. Better that he or she should get on with life and reintroduce the goods back into the stream of commerce with no undue delay. With specially manufactured brown polystyrene pellets, of course, there may be reason to hold on to the hope the buyer for whom they were produced will eventually agree to take them. With diamond jewelry, I'd say get it back on display as soon as possible. And again, once it is on display for sale to the general public, it would seem that the risk of its loss has reverted to the seller.

PART VI

Remedies

CHAPTER 26

Seller's Remedies

WHEN THE BUYER BREACHES

What can a seller do when the buyer breaches or repudiates the contract? The question of where to start looking for answers is easy enough. The drafters of Article 2 provide in §2-703 what they themselves characterize in a Comment as "an index section which gathers together in one convenient place all of the various remedies open to a seller for any breach by a buyer." After that kind of billing, it only makes sense for us to start out this chapter by quoting the section in its entirety:

> **§2-703. Seller's Remedies in General**
> Where the buyer wrongfully rejects or revokes acceptance of goods or fails to make a payment due on or before a delivery or repudiates with respect to a part or the whole, then with respect to any goods directly affected and, if the breach is of the whole contract (Section 2-612), then also with respect to the whole undelivered balance, the aggrieved seller may
>
> (a) withhold delivery of such goods;
> (b) stop delivery by any bailee as hereafter provided (Section 2-705);
> (c) proceed under the next section [§2-704] respecting goods still unidentified to the contract;
> (d) resell and recover damages as hereafter provided (Section 2-706);
> (e) recover damages for nonacceptance (Section 2-708) or in a proper case the price (Section 2-709);
> (f) cancel.

It's important to note that the section carries no requirement that the seller pick one and only one of these responses. As Comment 1 explains, "Whether the pursuit of one remedy bars another depends entirely on the facts of the individual case."

Indeed, just about everything depends on the facts of the individual case. What remedy (or remedies) will be at all desirable or of any interest to the seller, which one(s) will be available to him or her under Article 2, and just what result can be expected if any one remedial route is pursued, all depend on the state of things at the time of breach or repudiation and how the story develops as the parties react each to the other. For one thing, what is the condition of the goods at the moment of repudiation or breach? Are they even in existence? If so, have they been identified to the contract? If they do exist, they must exist somewhere. Where, in whose possession, are the goods? Are they held by the seller, the buyer, or some third party like a carrier or a warehouse? Then, of course, there's the question of payment. How much was the buyer supposed to pay and when? How much has been paid as of the time when seller decides to take remedial action? In this chapter, we will assume that an agreement between the parties created a valid contract enforceable against the buyer and that the buyer's subsequent actions amounted to a breach or a repudiation of that agreement. Beyond that, we have to be open to the full range of situations and possibilities.

To start, we should acknowledge that in some circumstances, the most understandable response is for a seller to do nothing. If the seller has not yet produced any goods under the contract or still has all of the goods that have been produced under its control, sometimes the easiest thing is just to take the repudiation or breach as the end of the story and go peddle the goods elsewhere. The options (a) and (f) of §2-703 quoted above support the seller if that is what it chooses to do. A buyer who has repudiated or breached cannot be heard to complain if the goods are not later delivered when, where, and as the contract initially called for. Look at the definition of *cancellation* in §2-106(4). The cancelling seller retains any additional remedies available under the Code, but there's no law that says it must pursue any of them.

Sometimes the best course is to forgive if not necessarily forget. As a practical matter, of course, an aggrieved seller may have other ways outside of recourse to the legal system, all perfectly legal in themselves, of responding to a buyer's breach. Seller may conclude that the breach is sufficiently egregious to warrant never dealing with this particular buyer again, or certainly not giving it any special favors in the future. Seller may even have a few choice words that he or she shares with others in the commercial community about how the buyer seems to do business. And would you want to be the buyer applying for membership to the business association or country club on whose board the aggrieved seller sits? There is good reason to believe, as you may have discussed in your Contracts course, that such "extra-judicial" sanctions can have a bigger part to play in how actual business parties think about breach than do the exact requirements of a legal regime like that laid out in Article 2. Remember, a buyer may breach a contract in good faith and for perfectly understandable reasons, even if they don't rise to the level of legal excuse. Sellers have been known to show a streak of human kindness and sympathy. On the other hand, a seller can be hopping mad but retain just enough objectivity to recognize that pursuing legal remedy in the particular situation would be fruitless or more trouble than it could possibly be worth. An aggrieved seller will choose between the various options open to it—taking into account a whole variety of factors. We'll stick with the legal ramifications of breach, however, which are more than enough for us to handle. One advantage of the Article 2 scheme is that it is fairly easy to calculate the likely recovery of the nonbreaching party; thus, the lawyer and client can have an intelligent discussion about the costs and benefits of pursuing legal action.

There follows a short textual review of two possibilities open to the seller under Article 2 that involve a kind of recapture of the goods, either of which is available only in a narrow range of circumstances. We then turn in the final introductory section and the examples and explanations to the core remedy of monetary damages. We ask, as the seller would no doubt ask us, what must be shown in order to recover a given measure of relief, and (not to beat around the bush) exactly *how much* money are we talking about here?

IF BUYER BECOMES INSOLVENT

Article 2 provides the seller with some limited protection in the event of the buyer's insolvency. Look at the definition of *insolvent* given in §1-201(b)(23). The buyer's business is going south. There is a good possibility that the seller, if it has sold on general unsecured credit, is never going to get paid, or at least not paid anything like the full purchase price for any goods delivered. When all the dust has settled, a general creditor may well get something like ten cents on the dollar, and should probably count itself fortunate if it gets that much. If the seller had the foresight and the bargaining position to sell on so-called secured credit, reserving what is characterized in Article 9 as a purchase-money security interest, and is careful to "perfect" that interest, then the chances of coming out of the situation more or less whole will be greatly improved. But this is all for your course in Secured Transactions, a separate and equally fascinating part of the Commercial Law curriculum. Absent a security interest, what the seller would like to do in such a situation, if it finds out about it in time, is to extricate itself from the whole mess by preventing delivery of the goods to the buyer or, if they have already been delivered, simply taking them back.

The buyer's insolvency, of course, is not in and of itself a breach, but it can be just as worrisome to the seller, if not more so. If the seller wants to be overly technical about things, it may be able to turn the events into a breach by invoking the insecurity mechanism of §2-609 and letting things ripen under that section into a repudiation. (See Chapter 20.) Practically, the smart thing is to move as soon as possible. Section 2-702 outlines the moves that the seller may take. Under §2-705(1), if the goods have not yet been delivered, the seller may upon discovering the buyer's insolvency "refuse delivery except for cash including payment for all goods theretofore delivered under the contract, and stop delivery under this Article." We'll deal with §2-705 and stoppage in transit in the following section.

What if the seller has *already* delivered the goods? Subsection 2-702(2) provides some chance that the seller may *reclaim* them, that is, actually take them back. This reclamation right is limited, as you can see. First of all, it applies only when the buyer "has received goods on credit while insolvent." If the buyer becomes insolvent even a short time after receipt of the goods, there is no reclamation right and the seller gets to stand in line with the other people owed cash, waiting for whatever payout eventually comes its way. Secondly, in order to invoke this right, the seller must make demand (except in the very unusual situation where the time limit is waived) within ten days of the buyer's receipt of the goods.

These express statutory criteria would seem stringent enough, but at least one court has added another layer of problem for the seller that hopes to exercise reclamation rights under this section. In *Tate Cheese Co., Inc. v. Crofton and Sons, Inc.*, 139 B.R. 567 (M.D. Fla. 1992), the court found that technical compliance with the two timing requirements was not enough under §2-702(2). In addition, the seller was responsible for vigorously following up on its reclamation demand and actually getting the stuff back. This decision was undoubtedly influenced by the nature of the goods involved. Tate Cheese Co., the seller, had delivered almost $11,000 worth of cheese to the buyer. As it turned out, the buyer was insolvent at the time of the delivery and the seller made a demand well within the ten days either to be paid immediately or for the return of the cheese. The buyer did not respond. Eight months later, the seller had done nothing more to get its cheese back. The bankruptcy court ruled that the time had long passed for the seller to be asserting its reclamation right. "Reclamation," the court stated, "is not a self-executing remedy. . . . It was incumbent on Tate to pursue the reclamation demand through appropriate judicial channels." Further, as the court pointed out:

> Diligent assertion of any reclamation right was particularly important in the instant case. It sought to reclaim cheese which is, of course, a perishable foodstuff. It is incomprehensible to the court that Tate made a written reclamation demand and then just sat on its rights for nearly eight months. . . . Had Tate

> been interested in regaining possession of the cheese, it should have sought judicial intervention rather than letting almost eight months elapse before pursuing reclamation of its perishable cheese. Tate is asking this court to establish a rule that a reclaiming seller can make a written reclamation demand and then wait for an unlimited period of time before enlisting judicial assistance in regaining possession of the reclamation goods. The court declines to do so under the circumstances of this case.

In *In re Waccamaw's Home Place*, 298 B.R. 233 (D. Del. 2003), another bankruptcy court cited with favor the *Tate Cheese* case and came to the same conclusion. The credit seller's right of reclamation begins with an appropriate demand for reclamation, but it doesn't end there; the seller must promptly and diligently follow up on that demand. See also *Paramount Home Entertainment, Inc. v. Circuit City Stores, Inc.*, 445 B.R. 521 (E.D. Va. 2010).

Section 2-702(2) provides reclamation rights only to the seller who has delivered goods on credit. What about the unpaid seller in a *cash* sale? Your first question, perfectly reasonably, is how a cash seller could even end up in this predicament. If the seller sells for cash and is careful enough to inspect the good old American greenbacks handed over at the moment of delivery, what could go wrong? The answer to this riddle has to do with the modern practice of using personal checks in so many situations. Under Article 2, payment by check is perfectly appropriate in the run-of-the-mill cash sale. See §2-511 and the Comments thereto. The unfortunate thing is that sometimes—brace yourself—checks bounce. And we're left with a cash seller who has delivered the goods and yet has not been paid.

While it is not spelled out in so many words in §2-507(2), this subsection is read in conjunction with §2-511 as giving the unpaid cash seller in such a situation a right to reclaim the goods. You see, in §2-507(2) we are told that the buyer's "right to retain" the goods is conditional upon its making the payment due. If the payment is by a check that is dishonored upon presentment at buyer's bank, the buyer has no right to retain the goods as against the seller. Therefore it must follow that the seller can reclaim them. The courts have recognized this reclamation right of the unpaid cash seller. Unfortunately, due in large part to the original language of Comment 3 to §2-507, many times the courts would then go on to import wholesale the requirement for demand within ten days of delivery, which we've seen as part of the statute in §2-702, into the unpaid cash seller situation. The fact that there was no ten-day limit set forth in §2-507 didn't seem to matter. The result was unfortunate, because in some instances the seller would not become aware that the check had been dishonored and that it wasn't going to be paid until sometime more than ten days after delivery. The upshot was, in some situations, to deny the unpaid seller any or all right to reclaim the goods for failure to meet a strict ten-day rule that was found nowhere in the relevant sections. This hardly seemed fair. In 1990, the Permanent Editorial

Board revised Comment 3 to §2-507 to state "There is no specific time limit for a cash seller to exercise the right of reclamation."

There has actually been a good deal of litigation in recent years involving the reclamation rights of someone who's sold to an insolvent buyer, but there's usually little dispute about whether the seller has such rights against the buyer. Rather, the cases have had to confront how this reclamation right stacks up against rights in the goods that are being asserted by other third parties, each of whom is anxious to get its hands on just about anything of value that the buyer holds as it sinks unceremoniously into bankruptcy. These may include people who claim to have bought the goods or a portion of them from the buyer. They think they should be able to just spirit the goods off and walk away from all the squabbling. Others who may legitimately claim an interest in the same bundle of goods include the trustee in bankruptcy, who is responsible for taking over control of the buyer's assets and using them to pay off debts in a prescribed way, and other creditors who may themselves assert a security interest in the goods that would, if found valid, arguably give them first dibs on the particular chunk of property. It can get to be quite a scene. These interesting issues of just how the seller's reclamation rights arising under Article 2 stack up against other rights asserted in the goods must necessarily wait until you study Article 9 in all of its rousing detail. You should expect the topic to be dealt with in your course on Secured Transactions.

STOPPAGE IN TRANSIT

As we saw in the prior section, a seller who is in the process of delivering goods to a buyer when it discovers the buyer to be insolvent has the right under §2-702(1) to stop delivery of the goods under §2-705. When you look at §2-705(1) you see that the right to stop delivery of goods in the possession of a carrier also extends to the seller who receives a repudiation from the buyer, or who does not receive a payment due before delivery, or who can assert any other right to withhold delivery as long as the seller is careful to stop delivery in "carload, truckload, planeload or larger shipments." (This last criterion was added in sympathy for the carriers. See Comment 1.) Subsection (2) gives a list of events that will serve to terminate the seller's power to stop delivery. Subsection (3) sets forth the procedure the seller must follow to exercise this option. If a seller has the right to and does properly stop the delivery in midstream, this is not the end of the story, of course. The goods are hung up somewhere and the seller is going to have to decide what to do with them and how to proceed further, if at all, against the buyer. As Comment 6 to this section points out, "After an effective stoppage under this section the seller's rights in the goods are the same as if he had never made a delivery." Seller's rights may be the same, but notice that its practical situation can be all the more trying: The goods are not directly in its possession, but are being held by some carrier or other bailee who is going to be more than anxious to drop them off somewhere, make delivery to someone, collect its fee, and be done with them.

WHEN SELLER GOES FOR THE MONEY

Whether or not the seller has been able to withhold delivery before it even gets started, stop delivery somewhere in transit, or even reclaim goods that were delivered right into the hands of the buyer, just keeping the buyer from possession is not necessarily enough of a remedy for the buyer's repudiation or breach. In many cases, it's going to take some amount of money, either voluntarily ceded by the buyer or extracted by judicial process, to make the seller whole. We now turn to the ways in which a seller may seek and be awarded monetary damages under the Code. Article 2 gives a variety of potential measures for seller's damages depending on the facts of the particular case. The first with which we'll deal is the possibility in a limited set of circumstances that the seller can recover the full contract price from the buyer under §2-709. At other times, the seller may resell the goods under §2-706 and, once it has done so, recover a "contract price minus resale price" differential under that section. If seller has no right to the contract price and if there has not been a §2-706 resale, we are next to look at §2-708(1) for the standard measure of damages. You'll recognize here the traditional "contract minus market" measure with which you no doubt dealt in your Contracts class. In some cases, as we will see, the seller can argue for a greater measure under the authority of §2-708(2). The seller may also sue for and receive incidental damages in the appropriate circumstances as measured by §2-710. We'll work our way through these sections in the examples and explanations.

Examples

EXAMPLES

1. Sparkle Plenty owns and operates a jewelry store. Bernie Bigbucks comes into the store and contracts to buy a large emerald ring that she has on display. The contract price is $12,000. It is agreed that Sparkle will have the ring delivered to Bernie's home the next day and that he will pay the full contract price within a week after that. Sparkle has one of her employees deliver the ring as agreed. She hears nothing for the next month, nor does she receive a check from Bernie.
   (a) Does she have a valid claim against him for the price of $12,000? Would it make any difference to your answer if it could be shown

that the emerald in the ring was not of the size that Sparkle had claimed it to be at the time of sale, but actually one-half carat smaller?

(b) Suppose instead that the day after the ring, which is in fact of the correct size, is delivered to Bernie, he calls Sparkle and says, "I have decided against buying the ring. It strikes me as a bit much and it doesn't look good with my new jeans. You can have one of your people come around and pick it up any time that is convenient for you." Would Sparkle be within her rights in just leaving the ring with Bernie and suing him for the full purchase price?

(c) Finally, suppose that the day after Sparkle had the ring delivered, she called Bernie to be sure that he had received and was happy with his purchase. He tells her, "Yes. I have the ring and love it. I'm wearing it right now. I doubt I'll ever take it off." Four days later, however, and before he has made any payment to her, he calls singing a different tune. "I find myself not at all happy with this purchase. I don't want the ring after all. Come and pick it up." In this situation would Sparkle have the right to sue for the price?

2. Meanwhile, in another part of town, Bernie Bigbucks goes to Sam the tailor and is fitted for a new suit that is to be made to his order. He picks out an expensive green plaid material. Sam is to be paid $1,000 for the completed suit.

   (a) Later that day, before Sam has begun work on the suit, Bernie calls and repudiates this agreement. If Sam sues Bernie for the $1,000 price, what would result?

   (b) Suppose instead that Bernie does not repudiate, but that Sam orders the fabric needed and completes initial work piecing together the suit. Bernie comes in for a fitting. He takes one look at himself in the mirror and says, "No, no, this won't do. I don't like the looks of this at all. Forget about it." He rushes out of the store, leaving Sam holding the uncompleted garment. Under these facts can Sam sue Bernie for the full purchase price with any hope of success? What should Sam do with the partially completed green plaid suit for the time being? Would he be within his rights in eventually giving it away to charity, ripping it apart for scraps, or wearing it himself?

3. In early February, Arnold Moneybucks contracts to buy an original oil painting ("The Virtues of Capitalism") for $1,700 from Stella's art gallery, Arnold's pickup and payment to come when the artist's showing at Stella's has closed at the end of the month. On February 15, Stella receives an email from Arnold saying that he no longer "agrees to take the painting."

   (a) Later that day, Stella sells the painting for $1,250 to another of her clients who had previously shown interest in this artist's work. Stella sues Arnold for the $450 difference. Does Article 2 make Arnold automatically pay this amount?

(b) Suppose instead that Stella had held on to the painting and included it with a group that she presented at auction in March. The painting goes for $1,125 at the auction. Stella sues Arnold for the $1,700 minus $1,125, or $575. What other facts would you want to know in order to determine whether she has the right to this amount?

(c) If the painting had instead fetched $1,800 at the art auction, would Arnold have any claim against Stella for $100? Does Arnold have any claim to the painting?

4. At the end of the salmon catching season, one large fishery, Salmons of Seattle, has on hand a great quantity of processed frozen salmon fillets. On August 1, it contracts to sell a large quantity of these fillets to Better Foods of Boise, Idaho, for a price of "$2 per pound F.O.B. Boise." Delivery is to be made by rail on or before August 21, and payment is to be made within 30 days of the buyer's receipt. On August 4, before the shipment has been delivered to the railroad, Better Foods contacts Salmons and repudiates the agreement. Additional facts that you may (or may not) need to answer this question follow:

Market price of fillets at Boise on August 1	$2.04
Market price at Seattle on August 1	$1.54
Market price at Boise on August 4	$1.92
Market price at Seattle on August 4	$1.40
Market price at Boise on August 21	$1.14
Market price at Seattle on August 21	$1.00
Cost of shipping from Seattle to Boise	$0.05

(a) If Salmons sues Better Foods claiming damages under §2-708(1), what amount should it receive?

(b) What if instead the price had been agreed to as "$1.98 F.O.B. Seattle"?

(c) Assume that the price was "$2 F.O.B. Boise" and that Better Foods did not repudiate but instead rejected the shipment for no good reason when it arrived in Boise on August 20. To what would Salmons of Seattle be entitled under §2-708(1)?

(d) Continuing on with the situation as in Example 4c, suppose that Better Foods could demonstrate that upon hearing of the rejection, Salmons had very quickly been able to arrange sale of the shipment to another buyer, Very Best of Boise, for $1.30 per pound and that Salmons' only additional cost for making this sale was an agency fee of $0.03 per pound. Should Salmons still be entitled to sue for and be awarded the amount you calculated in answer to Example 4c? Assuming Better Foods concedes its liability for breach of contract, what argument could it make that Salmons is due less under Article 2?

5. Hacker has a used personal computer, the B.I.M. PS/1, that she plans to replace with a newer model. She posts a "For Sale" notice on a bulletin board at her local laundromat describing the computer and stating an asking price of $400. The notice catches the eye of Billy, who comes to inspect the machine and offers her $350 for it. Hacker accepts this offer. Billy says he will come back the next week with the money. Hacker removes the notice from the laundromat. The following Monday, Billy calls and tells her he has not been able to come up with the money and that he will not be buying the computer. Hacker places a new notice on the bulletin board, again asking $400. A month later, Hacker is contacted by someone who has seen her notice and who offers to buy the machine for $350. If Hacker accepts this offer, what rights will she have against Billy? If Hacker doesn't accept this offer, what is her position?

6. Meanwhile, Hacker is looking for that new computer of her dreams. She sees a demonstration model of the brand new H.A.L. Super 2100 at Steve's Computer City. She contracts to buy a Super 2100 for $5,000, which Steve will deliver to her from the first shipment he gets of the new machines from the H.A.L. Corporation. When Steve gets this shipment, he immediately marks one of the boxes containing a single Super 2100 with the label "For Hacker." He contacts Hacker and tells her that the machine is ready for her to pay for and pick up. Hacker tells him that she has decided not to buy the Super 2100, but is instead looking to buy an even newer machine (the G.Z.K. Magnum Pro), which she hears will be coming out on the market soon. Steve takes the box he had marked for Hacker, removes the label, and puts it in his store room. Within two months he has sold this machine to another buyer (Headly) for $5,000.
   (a) If Steve sues Hacker for breach of her contract to purchase, to what measure of damages is he entitled under Article 2? Assume Steve paid the H.A.L. Corporation $3,200 for this machine. Furthermore, Steve's accountant tells him that based on his past year's business activity, his net profit—after taking into account general overhead costs (rent, advertising, salaries, taxes, and so on)—comes out as equal to approximately 10 percent of his total sales.
   (b) Would your answer to the previous question be any different if it were established that the H.A.L. Super 2100 is such a popular computer when it is first introduced that the manufacturer cannot keep up with nationwide demand and has to allocate only so many of the computers to each of its regular distributors? Steve is able to order and receive delivery of only 120 of the Super 2100's during the first year it is produced, all of which he quickly sells.
   (c) Assume instead that there is a plentiful supply of H.A.L. Super 2100 computers and that Steve can get delivery of as many as he wants. However, you also have the additional fact that Hacker ends up

contracting for and taking delivery of a G.Z.K. Magnum Pro from Steve, for which she pays $6,000. Does Steve have any right to substantial damages against Hacker under these facts? What more would you like to know?

7. Nobs Chemical Corporation is a company that buys and sells large quantities of industrial chemicals. It entered into a contract to buy all of its requirements of cumene (a chemical used as an additive to gasoline) from a Brazilian Supplier for the price of $400 per ton. It then went about looking for buyers of cumene in the United States. Nobs contracted to sell 1,000 tons of the chemical to the Koppers Company for delivery in the United States at a price of $540 per ton. Nobs expected to spend approximately $45 per ton transporting the chemical from Brazil to the buyer's place of business. Before Nobs actually purchased any cumene from its supplier for shipment to Koppers, that company repudiated, saying that it wanted none of the stuff. At the time of the breach, the market price of cumene in the United States had fallen to $265 per ton, and the price continued at this low level up to the time when delivery to Koppers would have been made. Nobs sues Koppers for $275,000 relying upon §2-708(1).
   (a) Can you see an argument for the defendant buyer that even assuming it was liable for breach, it should be liable for less than Nobs is claiming? Should this argument work?
   (b) Assume that in addition to the facts given above, the Nobs Chemical Corporation is able to show that because of Koppers's repudiation, it ended up buying only 3,000 tons of cumene from its Brazilian supplier instead of 4,000. Since the price under its supply contract was determined by its total orders during a calendar year, Nobs had been forced to pay an additional $25 a ton for each of the 3,000 tons it did buy from the supplier for delivery to another of its customers. Can Nobs recover this additional $75,000 ($25 times 3,000) from Koppers in its breach of contract suit?

Explanations

1. a. Sparkle has a good action for the price against Bernie under §2-709(1)(a).

   Having received delivery of the goods and not having given a notification of rejection after all this time, Bernie has accepted them. (Recall §2-606(1)(b) and the lengthy discussion of how acceptance occurs in Chapter 17.) As Comments 2 and 6 to §2-709 make clear, Article 2 treats the action for the price as an extraordinary remedy for the seller, something roughly analogous to specific performance for the buyer, not generally available but limited only to one of three situations. Note also the admonition in §2-703(e) that the seller can recover the price only "in the proper case." The one clearest case is that where the buyer has accepted the goods. (You will recall the prime directive of §2-607(1) that "The buyer must pay at the contract rate for any goods accepted.")

The second situation where the seller is allowed an action for the price is where the buyer fails to pay the price as it becomes due and conforming goods have been "lost or damaged within a commercially reasonable time after risk of their loss has passed to the buyer." Risk of loss, as you will remember, got a whole part of this book to itself (Part V) and will not be dealt with here. The third class of cases in which an action for the price may lie are those covered by §2-709(1)(b), which will come up soon enough in questions to follow.

If it were to be shown that the goods were nonconforming (that is, that the emerald was too small), it would *not* change the result—Sparkle could still sue for the price. A buyer is perfectly able to, and often does, accept nonconforming goods intentionally or otherwise. An action for the price lies for any goods accepted, whether they were conforming or nonconforming and whether they *could have been* rejected. If the goods are accepted, they must be paid for at the contract rate. Of course, if the ring tendered and accepted did turn out to be nonconforming, and if Bernie still has time to give notice of the nonconformity as required under §2-607(3)(a), then he could make a counterclaim for damages arising from this breach. Any damages proven by Bernie as an aggrieved buyer would be subtracted from what Sparkle is owed on the price, reducing the ultimate award to her (see §2-717), but they do not defeat the basic principle that she is entitled to be paid for the ring and paid according to the contract price.

b. No. Sparkle can decide not to retake possession of the ring, but she'd be a fool to do so, as she would not have an action for the price against Bernie. Here Bernie has attempted rejection, and it appears that his action meets the criteria of §2-602. The rejection may be *wrongful*, in that Bernie had no right to reject and hence by doing so has put himself in breach, but it procedurally fits the bill and hence is considered an *effective* rejection, meaning that it averts an acceptance. In the general case where the goods are effectively rejected and could be resold—and we have to believe this is so of an emerald ring—the seller has no right to sue for the price. See *Brandeis Machinery & Supply Co., LLC v. Capitol Crane Rental, Inc.*, 765 N.E.2d 173 (Ind. App. 2002). The aggrieved seller will have to take back the goods if they are not at the time of rejection in his or her possession and seek a monetary remedy against the buyer via one of the other routes we will explore later. See subsection (3). The justification that is usually given for this result (and which does seem to make a lot of sense) is that even if the seller is the aggrieved party, he or she is typically, as someone engaged in the sale of goods of this type, in a better position to make an effective and efficient resale than is the buyer.

c. The result here is open to dispute. Bernie initially accepted the goods (here under §2-606(1)(a)) and later attempted a revocation of acceptance (under §2-608). There's no doubt that the attempted revocation is not justified in the situation and is *wrongful*; the question is whether it is *effective* and actually works to "undo" the initial acceptance and all the results that flowed therefrom (including triggering the seller's right to an action for the price). As we saw in the discussion of the previous question, the Article 2 drafters plainly contemplated and allowed for a wrongful rejection that is nevertheless effective. But is there such a thing as a wrongful yet effective revocation of acceptance?

Bits and pieces of the Code and Comments can be read to support either side of this debate. Section 2-608(1) gives the conditions under which a buyer "may" revoke his or her acceptance, which suggests that there are times when he or she may not. Saying someone *may not* do something, however, is not the same as saying he or she *cannot*. But then §2-607(2) speaks to at least one circumstance in which the buyer actually "cannot" revoke. Returning to §2-709 itself, subsection (3) can be read as anticipating a case of wrongful revocation. It depends on what the word "wrongfully" qualifies: Is it just the immediately following "rejected," or is it the following phrase "rejected or revoke"? But then Comment 5 to the section says that accepted goods include "only goods as to which there has been no *justified* revocation of acceptance," which suggests that if there has been an attempted revocation that is unjustified or wrongful, then the goods remain accepted and an action for the price would still lie. All in all, the text of Article 2 and the Comments do not resolve the issue.

We can then ask what *policy* would favor. This all depends, of course, on the policy you want to focus on. Some have suggested that there should be room for an effective, albeit wrongful, rejection under Article 2, because there definitely is the possibility of an effective wrongful rejection, and the drafters seemed to favor a policy of treating rejections and revocations in a parallel fashion. Note, in this regard, §2-608(3). The wrongful revoker is no more or less a villain than the wrongful rejecter under this view and should be treated no more harshly. Is this persuasive?

Other policies can be teased out of Article 2 that may argue in the other direction. Recall (from Chapter 19) that the drafters made revocation under §2-608 a more difficult road for the buyer than rejection by adding a number of criteria. This suggests they had in mind at least some reason to treat the two possible behaviors (rejection and revocation) differently and, in particular, to discourage (or is that too strong a word?) revocations to some greater extent. If so, there would be no better way of cutting down on the number of wrongful revocations than by having a rule that tells the buyer that if his or her revocation turns out not to meet the substantive as well as procedural criteria of §2-608, it will simply be ineffective. You, as a wrongfully revoking buyer, will still be left with the goods and the obligation to pay the full price for them.

Finally, we can examine the policy behind the unquestioned result in the rejection situation (i.e., that even the wrongfully rejecting buyer is not subject to an action for the price) and see if it works equally well in the revocation case. A number of commentators have made the point that, while the facts in each case will differ, by and large the goods have been in the possession of buyer for a longer period where a revocation is being attempted. They're more like used goods than new goods. If withholding the action for the price in the case of an unjustified rejection is grounded on a belief that generally the seller continues to be in a better position to resell the goods than is the buyer, does the same hold true for goods that have been accepted but the buyer is at a later stage trying to revoke acceptance? It has been argued that this distinction is reason enough to allow the action for the price to the seller where the buyer unjustifiably revokes, even if it is clearly not available where the buyer unjustifiably rejects. Of course, in the particular question we are dealing with, this argument may not seem so persuasive. It's one thing to think of new and used goods being very much different and moving in distinct markets in the general context (does the typical hardware store deal in *used* tools and plumbing fixtures?), but it's not so clear that would be true in the case of fine jewelry and gems.

On the question of what the courts have done with the wrongfully revoking buyer and an action for the price, the answer is that few if any cases seem even to acknowledge the problem, much less confront it as squarely as a court would be bound to do if my hypothetical were actually before it. There is, as you will recall, a great deal of "play" for the court on whether what the parties are arguing about should even be analyzed as a rejection or a revocation. And even if the court decides to take it on as a revocation case, there is a good deal of latitude under §2-608 for determining whether, in any given situation, the revocation was in fact justified and was in fact carried out with procedural precision. Courts, as you are no doubt aware, sometimes get to work around or avoid problems in ways that your typical law student can't.

2. a. Sam has no action for the price here. There is no argument that the goods have been accepted or that the risk of loss on them had passed to Bernie, and hence there is nothing for Sam in §2-709(1)(a). Section 2-709(1)(b) requires that the goods be identified to the contract. That hasn't happened here. This exhausts the possibilities for a valid action for the price. Read Comment 6.

   Could Sam just order the fabric if he does not already have it on hand and make up the suit? He could then identify the suit to the contract when it was finished and bring an action for the price under §2-709(1)(b). No, not in this situation. To have any argument like this, the seller has to proceed under §2-704(2), which you should read now. I can't imagine that making up a green plaid suit to Bernie's measurements (no matter what his shape and size) would be an "exercise of reasonable commercial judgment for the purposes of avoiding loss."

   So, in this case, Sam cannot bring an action for the price. This does not mean, of course, that he has no remedy against Bernie, but it will have to come under another section. The other two sections that provide the seller with a route to money damages are §2-706 and §2-708. Section 2-706 doesn't apply to this case because there can be no resale of a suit that doesn't exist. So Sam will get his remedy under §2-708. How that remedy measures up is the matter of a number of questions later on.

   b. Sam may have an action for the price under §2-709(1)(b). Even if he does no more work on it, he shouldn't have trouble establishing that this particular assemblage of cloth has been identified to his contract with Bernie. Sam would then have to show either that he had been "unable after reasonable efforts" to resell the suit "at a reasonable price" or that "the circumstances reasonably indicate that such an effort would be unavailing."

   In a number of cases, the results hinged on the court's interpretation and application of this last phrase. It is fair to say that no clear-cut test has emerged. Results may individually strike us as correct, even if the reasoning seems to be on a case-by-case basis. Compare *Ultralite Container Corp. v. American President Lines, Ltd.*, 170 F.3d 784 (7th Cir. 1999), with *Data Documents, Inc. v. Pottawattamie County*, 604 N.W.2d 611 (Iowa 2000).

   In *Knitcraft Corp. v. Raleigh Limited, Inc.*, 943 N.E.2d 446 (Ind. App. 2011), the Court of Appeals of Indiana affirmed a judgment of the trial court that a breaching buyer—the contract being for the sale of a quantity of made-to-order garments—was not obligated to pay the seller the purchase price under §2-709(1)(b). The contract called for delivery of the garments between August 30, 2005, and October 15, 2005.

On May 16, 2005, more than three months prior to the first scheduled shipping date, but after the seller had started manufacturing the garments, the buyer attempted to "cancel" its order; this being so, even though the buyer had no right to cancel in this manner, the seller did not attempt to deliver the garments to the buyer. The evidence was that the manufacturer had not attempted to sell the clothing to another buyer but instead kept the garments until it eventually donated them to charity. As the court stated:

> The only evidence presented by Knitcraft [the seller] that any effort at resale would have been unavailing was testimony that the garments at issue were for the fall 2005 season and that the selling season for those garments would generally have been from January 5, 2005 through March 15, 2005. Hencier [the seller's sales rep] testified that the reason he made no attempt to resell the garments was because he presumed that after March 15, 2005, retailers already would have purchased all garments necessary for the fall 2005 season and already would have spent their entire budgets. When asked why Knitcraft did not attempt to sell the garments to "discount" stores such as T.J. Maxx or Marshalls, both Hencier and Bergin [seller's Vice President] stated that Knitcraft did not wish to hurt its reputation by allowing its garments to be sold at such stores. Again, the trial court was not persuaded by Knitcraft's presumptions and excuses. Instead, the trial court assessed the evidence and witness credibility and specifically concluded that it did not "find that the evidence presented reasonably indicates that such effort of finding another buyer would [have been] unavailing."

The appellate court determined that, given this evidence, the trial court's conclusion that the seller had failed to establish that any attempt to resell the goods to another buyer would be "unavailing" was unwarranted.

In our current hypothetical, maybe if the green plaid was green enough and plaid enough, Sam could convince a court that any effort to get anyone to even consider purchasing a suit like this would truly be unavailing. If Sam is in any doubt about being able to show this (and here I wouldn't be surprised if a court were skeptical that absolutely no one would be willing to take it off Sam's hands "at a reasonable price"), his better move would be to make some *reasonable* effort to resell it, even if it must be drastically retailored to fit the new buyer and the asking price reduced. If Sam does resell, he should be able to get any loss he suffers because of selling at a lesser price, including the extra incidental cost of the retailoring. If it can't be resold after reasonable efforts, Sam's case for the price is that much stronger. Notice that Sam's continued work on the suit in this situation would presumably be supported by §2-704(2), unlike in the previous question where no work had been done on it prior to the repudiation.

If Sam does bring an action for the price, what should he do with the partially completed suit? As we've just said, he'd be well-advised to keep it out in his showroom and continue making reasonable efforts to sell it to someone else. If he can't get himself to do this (for instance, if it is just so hideous that he is reasonably afraid that having it on display could hurt his business), he should still hold on to it if only in storage. See §2-709(2). The idea behind this subsection is presumably that if there is a judgment for the seller and the buyer is going to have to pay the full purchase price anyway, then he or she might decide he wants possession of the goods after all.

In the *Knitcraft* case, cited and quoted from above, the appellate court also noted:

> Here, Knitcraft neither held onto the goods for Raleigh [the buyer] nor resold the goods. Rather, Knitcraft donated the garments to a local charity. Knitcraft cannot now seek to recover the price of the goods pursuant to [§2-709], as Knitcraft has no proceeds to give to Raleigh and no goods to deliver to Raleigh in the event of a judgment in Knitcraft's favor. Accordingly, an action on the price pursuant to [§2-709] must fail.

Once the buyer has paid a judgment resulting from an action for the price, he or she has a right to the goods under the last sentence of subsection (2). Note, however, that in some instances the judgment may be even *greater* than the part of the purchase price that had gone unpaid. Under this section, the seller may recover the price "together with any incidental damages under" §2-710. Look at that section now. In most cases a seller's incidental damages suffered when the price is unpaid are, well, incidental. That would seem to be so in Sam's case. If he actually had to store the hideous green-plaid partially assembled outfit at some place other than his place of business, he could at least get his storage costs.

There are times, of course, when incidental damages do amount to something more. See *Commonwealth Edison Co. v. Allied Chemical Nuclear Products, Inc.*, 684 F. Supp. 1434 (N.D. Ill. 1988). Edison had entered into a contract with AGNS, an affiliate of Allied Chemical, under which that company would reprocess spent nuclear fuel for the utility. The court concluded that under the agreement, Edison was to be considered the seller and AGNS the buyer of the spent (but hardly harmless) nuclear fuel, which was to be taken for reprocessing from fuel assemblies that had been used in commercial nuclear power plants. AGNS refused to accept delivery of the spent fuel, nor did it make delivery itself of the called-for good, usable uranium and plutonium. Edison was forced to store the spent fuel at considerable expense. It sued AGNS under §2-709, asking for the price (the value of the good usable fuel it was to have received under the deal) along with its incidental expenses of storage. AGNS argued that the storage expenses should not have been allowed to Edison as an aggrieved seller, but the court disagreed. As District Judge Aspen noted:

> Although it truly boggles the mind to consider storage costs of 293 million dollars as "incidental," we find that these costs are indeed costs incurred by AGNS's alleged breach to provide [the usable fuel] and take . . . the irradiated [spent] fuel.

If Sam does succeed in getting a judgment in his action for the price and does collect on the judgment, he'll have to finish and then give up the suit if Bernie then wants it. If Bernie *still* doesn't want it, what then? I assume Sam can do pretty much what he wants, including tossing it away or giving it to charity. What if, after he has collected his judgment, Sam wears the strange outfit to a costume ball and (strangely enough) is deluged with offers to buy it? Perhaps green plaid is suddenly fashionable with the hip crowd. It seems he could sell the suit and keep the proceeds. Subsection 2-709(2) speaks only to proceeds of a resale "prior to the collection of the judgment." Is this right? I know of no case where something like this has happened and the buyer who's paid up later brings an action to get some part of his or her payment back.

3. a. Arnold may be made to pay the $1,250 difference between the contract price of $1,700 and the resale price of $1,250, but it's far from automatic that this will be so. Stella would sue for this difference invoking §2-706(1), but in order for her to succeed, she'd have to establish a number of factors. The resale must be made in good faith and in a commercially reasonable manner. In addition, under subsection (2), "every aspect of the sale including the method, manner, time, place and terms must be commercially reasonable." Finally under subsection (3), where the resale is at a private sale, as it was here, "the seller must give the buyer reasonable notification of his intention to resell." The Code nowhere defines a *private sale* (as opposed to a *public sale*), but Comment 4 indicates that a public sale is a sale at auction at which members of the general public may be present and in a position to bid on the goods, and a private sale is anything else. This does seem to be the distinction the drafters wished to make, and the one that is generally accepted.

   Will Stella be able to satisfy all these conditions? Even granting her the best of good faith, it may be hard. This will all depend on other facts we don't have, of course. The resale price does seem awfully low, and Stella may have a difficult time establishing that it was reasonable under the circumstances. She'd be in a better position, of course, if she could show that she'd made at least some effort to sell to others at a higher price.

We would have to know more facts, as well, to determine whether Stella met the notice requirement here. As to this, see the first paragraph of Comment 8 and take note of the definition of *notice* in §1-202(a). Subsection 2-706(3) requires only "reasonable notification," not "reasonable notification in a record," so the requisite notice can be oral. The question has come up in a few cases whether the notice requirement is in effect waived once the seller establishes that the breaching buyer had actually known, or should have known, that the seller was trying to resell, even if this information did not come from the seller directly. There is no clear answer to this. Some courts say that the notice requirement is clear enough from the section and must strictly be complied with if the seller is to sue under §2-706. See, for example, *Cook Composites, Inc. v. Westlake Styrene Corp.*, 15 S.W.3d 124 (Tex. App. 2000). (As we will see, the seller whose claim under this section is unavailing will still have an opportunity to collect under §2-708.) Other courts appear to be somewhat more flexible and, if they don't literally waive the notice requirement, are willing to find sufficient notice from the totality of the circumstances, not insisting upon proof of a single formal communication that was undeniably "notice" in a conventional sense.

If Stella is able to establish sufficient notice and the other prerequisites to her right to proceed under §2-706(1), she is then entitled in the words of that statute to:

> the difference between the resale price and the contract price together with any incidental damages allowed under the provisions of this Article (Section 2-710), but less expenses saved in consequence of the buyer's breach.

So the appropriate award under §2-706(1) would be calculated by first taking the $450 difference, then adjusting as necessary. If, for example, Arnold was to have picked up the painting from the gallery but the resale called for Stella to herself arrange and pay for delivery to the new buyer, this extra cost of shipment would be incidental damages for which she could also collect. If, on the other hand, her contract with Arnold had called for delivery of the painting in a certain type of frame, and the resale was of the painting unframed, there would be a certain amount of "expenses saved in consequence of [Arnold's] breach" and he would be entitled to a credit for this amount.

What is the situation if the facts do not support Stella's argument for recovery under §2-706—for example, if she hadn't given adequate notice? We deal with these after we consider the second type of resale, the public sale.

b. You can review §2-706(4) and its various subparts that set forth the numerous criteria for a public resale, which generally means a *sale at auction*. See as well Comment 9. If Stella's resale does meet all these conditions, again she can collect under §2-706(1) the contract price/resale price difference adjusted as before for incidental damages she may have suffered and subtracting expenses she may have saved.

If Stella's resale (either the private resale or the one at the auction) does not meet the tests laid out in §2-706(2) through (4), where does that leave her? The simple answer is that she will still have the right to sue under §2-708(1) for the difference between the contract price and the market value of the painting. The problem is, as you can no doubt imagine, that proof of market price can be very difficult, especially for something like artwork. Proof of resale price involves only bringing in a copy of the bill of sale covering the later resale. The price should be evident from that. Proof of market price of some particular goods at a particular time and place can involve estimation, differing expert opinions, and so on. The drafters tried to address these problems with §2-723, which you should look at, but they could only do so much. You see the trade-offs facing the aggrieved seller when the question is whether to pursue a remedy under §2-706 as opposed to §2-708. The amount of recovery should be more certain and more susceptible of proof if she goes the resale route. But in order to protect her rights under §2-706, she has to comply with a series of requirements, including generally a notice requirement, which can take time and effort and which can all too easily be messed up. A suit under §2-708 has no such preconditions. On the other hand, obtaining proof of market price high enough to give her the amount of recovery she thinks she deserves can be a nightmare.

You might reasonably be wondering at this juncture whether a seller who does resell but who, for one reason or another, does not meet the criteria for recovery under §2-706(1) and is hence forced to prove "market price" under §2-708(1) can at least use the resale price as evidence of that market price. The answer seems to be yes. See the *Cook Composites* case cited earlier. In such a situation, the actual resale price is evidence, but only evidence, of the market price. The buyer, of course, can be expected to bring in evidence that a correct market price for the goods would have been much higher than the resale price the seller actually received.

c. Arnold should have no claim against Stella for the additional $100 she made in the resale. See the first sentence of §2-706(6). There is the possibility that if Stella were to sue him for her incidental damages occasioned by the breach, he could argue this $100 as a setoff to those damages. The Code doesn't speak to this, neither authorizing it nor ruling it out. It seems reasonable to allow Bernie the setoff, but then Stella will have legal fees in bringing the action, which she is going to have to take care of without any payment from him. In any event, whether Stella's resale meets all the §2-706 preconditions or not, Arnold will have no claim in the painting as long as the eventual buyer bought in good faith. See §2-706(5).

4. a. Under §2-708(1), Salmons is entitled to "the difference between the market price at the time and place for tender and the unpaid contract price together with any incidental damages . . . but less expenses saved in consequence of the buyer's breach." We know the unpaid contract price here is $2 per pound. What was the time and place for tender under this contract? We can look at §2-503 generally as to tender, but once the parties have used a trade term such as F.O.B. to set the price, as Comment 1 to §2-708 reminds us, we have a series of special sections to which we can refer. Under §2-319(1)(b), when the parties have specified a price at "F.O.B. the place of destination," as they have here, the seller in effect tenders at that place, so the time and place of delivery would be in this instance August 21 in Boise. Thus, we use the given market price of $1.14 and the market price/unpaid contract price difference is $0.86 per pound.

   It remains to be considered whether the seller had any incidental damages or any expenses saved. The problem does not indicate that there were any incidental damages of the type provided for in §2-710. If Salmons did incur such charges, expenses, or commissions, it should speak up now and be prepared to prove them in a court of law. The situation does suggest that Salmons did save on one anticipated expense: the expense of shipping the frozen fillets to Boise. Under an F.O.B. Boise contract, Salmons was to bear the cost of shipment to Boise. So $0.05 per pound is to be subtracted from the damages owed Salmons by Better Foods. The final figure under these assumptions is $0.81 per pound.

   Notice that if the delivery were to have been made much later, say in August of the following year, and if Salmons brought suit right away, it is possible (even given the state of our court system) that the damages would have to be measured before the time of tender and, hence, before the market price could be known. What to do then? See §2-723(1). All of a sudden it seems our focus shifts back to August 4, the date of the repudiation. We'll spend some more time with this section, which can come into play when the breach is the buyer's or the seller's, in the next chapter.

   b. Under §2-319(1)(a), when the price is set "F.O.B. the place of shipment," the tender takes place when and where the goods are put into the possession of the carrier. So the place of tender is Seattle. It's not perfectly clear from the facts what was to be the time (the exact date) of tender, and indeed there may not have been an exact date in mind. The seller was to deliver the frozen fillets to the railroad in Seattle sometime during the middle of August, leaving enough time so they would arrive in Boise by August 21. If Salmons had already scheduled shipment, or if it had a set pattern of when it would ship on a contract such as this, this information would be helpful. Assuming for the moment that it would have shipped on August 4 or soon thereafter, Salmons is entitled to the difference between \$1.40 (the market price at the time and place of shipment) and the unpaid price of \$1.98, or \$0.58. Assuming the Seattle market price of frozen fish fillets dropped steadily during the month of August, as it appears it did (in other words, that frozen salmon fillets are not the subject of wild speculative market activity), this is the least Salmons can collect. If, for example, it could establish that it would have sent the shipment on its way significantly later in the month—say, August 17, when the price was something like \$1.05 in Seattle—and still made the delivery in time, we could advise Salmons to sue for the greater amount of \$1.98 minus \$1.05, or \$0.93 a pound.

Again we are assuming that Salmons has no incidental damages to speak of or to sue for. Furthermore, because in an F.O.B. shipment contract the seller does not bear the cost of shipping, but only the expense of "putting [the goods] into the possession of the carrier," Salmons avoided no transportation expense in the situation and nothing would be subtracted from the market price/unpaid contract price differential.

c. Subsection 2-708(1) treats this situation like that in Example 4a above as to the basic measure of damages. The market price/unpaid contract price difference is likewise \$0.86 per pound. In the case of a rejection in Boise, however, Salmons really had to pay the shipping expense, so this amount would not be subtracted from Salmons' damages.

d. As we said in answer to the previous question, Salmons, the injured seller, will claim damages at \$0.86 per pound under §2-708(1). Better Foods, however, will argue that an award in this amount would overcompensate Salmons. Salmons actually resold the goods for a price in excess of the market price, for \$1.30 per pound, and it had additional expenses of just \$0.03 per pound. If damages are measured as in §2-706(1), Salmons could recover (and Better Foods argues would be fully compensated by) just \$0.73 per pound (this being \$2.00 − \$1.30 + \$0.03). We're assuming for the purposes of this question that the fillets sold to Very Best are the very ones that would otherwise have been delivered to Better Foods, and that Salmons would not have made a sale to Very Best had there not been a breach by Better Foods.

The issue, which is one on which major Code commentators disagree most profoundly, is whether an aggrieved seller who actually does cover by reselling the subject goods to another at a price above the provable market price is entitled to no more than the damages it could get under §2-706. Or is the seller in all cases free to choose under which provision, §2-706 or §2-708(1), to proceed and is thus free to collect the market/contract differential even though it did resell?

The seller's right to collect under §2-708(1) in such a situation is found, it has been argued, in the language of these sections themselves. Subsection 2-708(1) says that the market/contract measure of damages is subject to subsection (2), which we'll get to in a while, and to the provisions of one other section (§2-723), but that's it. What it does *not* say is that the seller's damages may be measured this way only when the goods have not been resold. As a matter of fact, some language that could have been read as suggesting as much was actually excised from this subsection during the final phases of the drafting process, which culminated in an Article 2 that all the various interests could support. Note that §2-703(e) says that in the case of a buyer's breach, "the aggrieved seller may . . . recover damages for non-acceptance (Section 2-708) or *in a proper case* the price (Section 2-709)." Can't the placement of this italicized language be read as implying that the drafters didn't intend a seller's use of §2-708 to be limited only to "proper cases" or particular situations? Finally, look at Comment 1 to §2-703:

> This Article rejects any doctrine of election of remedy as a fundamental policy and thus the remedies are essentially cumulative in nature and include all of the available remedies for breach.

The contrary position—that the seller who resells the goods at a higher than market price is entitled to recover only the amount permitted under §2-706 and no more—cannot be so easily fashioned from statutory language. We can, however, look to other principles important to Code interpretation. It has been suggested that for the seller to ignore the resale in a situation like this, and to ask for damages measured under §2-708(1), shows a lack of good faith and hence runs afoul of §1-304. I find this hard to accept. It does seem to be stretching the concept of bad faith more than may be healthy. A more persuasive argument in favor of the buyer's position here can be based on the mitigation principle that is without a doubt firmly embedded in §1-305(a). Look at that subsection. See also the first Comment, which informs us:

> compensatory damages are limited to compensation. They do not include consequential or special damages, or penal damages; and the Uniform Commercial Code elsewhere makes it clear that damages must be minimized. [Citing among other sections §2-706.]

Those who hold the position that would allow Salmons to recover the \$0.86 per pound (under §2-708(1)) and not just the \$0.73 (under

§2-706) argue that an award including these extra few pennies need not necessarily be seen as overcompensation. Better Foods, after all, did breach, and the trouble and inconvenience that it presumably caused to Salmons of Seattle, which had to scramble to resell the fillets before something untoward happened to them, is sufficient justification for allowing the seller to seek and recover the larger amount. Otherwise the difficulties and the anxiety that the seller was made to suffer might not be sufficiently recognized in the final award. True, the seller can always sue for incidental damages in addition to the resale/contract difference under §2-706, but incidental damages are not always that easy to prove and evaluate in terms of dollars and cents. If all of the sales force at Salmons' Seattle office had to skip lunch one day, or even stay late into the night trying to find a new buyer for these goods, there will probably be no way of actually computing the cost to that company of all the hassle. So, the argument goes, to allow recovery of a little more under §2-708(1) is not undercutting any basic principle of the Code. Rather it is allowing a rough measure of "liquidated damages" for all the inconvenience caused to the seller. To do otherwise, to hold that the seller may recover no more than that to which it is entitled under the strict reading of §2-706, it might be said, would be a cramped and "illiberal" administration of remedies of the type the drafters sought to discourage (now citing §1-305(a) for the seller's purpose). The issue remains, to say the least, unresolved. For a decision by the Supreme Court of Oregon delving into the controversy in great detail and deciding what side has the better of the argument—at least in the state of Oregon—see *Peace River Seed Co-Operative, Ltd. v. Proseeds Marketing, Inc.*, 322 P.3d 531 (Or. 2014).

5. There is nothing tricky in this question. It's more of a review and a setup for the questions to follow. The simple answer is that Billy may have breached but it is unlikely that Hacker will be able to get anything out of him. Hacker may decide to sell now for $350, may keep looking for another buyer who's willing to pay more, or may just chuck the whole idea and keep the machine as a memento. In any event, she'll have no right to damages from Billy. Review the possibilities. If she brought an action for the price, she'd get nowhere. Section 2-709 allows for such an action only in a limited number of circumstances and none of those is present here. The goods have not been accepted, lost, or damaged. Resale was possible here, so §2-709(1)(b) is no help. If Hacker does resell and sues under §2-706, she'll have to prove that her resale met certain criteria, and even if she does, there seems to be no way she can show a positive measure of damages under that section. (We are assuming that the laundromat doesn't charge anything of significance for the right to post signs.) Finally, look at §2-708(1). There seems to be no way that

Hacker could show a market price below $350. It did take some time, but she has eventually been able to find another buyer at $350. The end result seems to be that Hacker should sell to this person and count herself lucky that she actually made the sale at the price she was anticipating. The difficulty, waste of time, and annoyance she has suffered because of Billy's breach are just things she'll have to live with.

In reality, a more difficult question would be what she should do if she is only able to find another buyer at a lower price, like $330. If she doesn't sell, she may only be hurting herself more, as the price of the thing erodes even further with each passing month. If she does sell for this figure, of course, she would be entitled to $20 under the Code. And just what lawyer would take her case? Even if she decided to go after Billy on her own through small claims court, the expenses of travelling to and from the courthouse would probably eat up anything she could hope to win. So much for Hacker as an aggrieved seller and potential plaintiff.

6. a. Now we have Hacker as a repudiating buyer and possible defendant. She will argue that while Steve may sue her for her actions, he, Steve, will be entitled to no damages—on the same analysis that was used against her, Hacker, in the previous question. Steve resold the machine, which was destined for Hacker, at the same price as she had contracted to pay. Ergo, Hacker will argue, Steve suffered no economic loss from the breach. He can try suing under §2-709, §2-706, or §2-708(1), but he'll recover nothing.

   Steve, however, will argue that his position as an aggrieved seller is different than hers was. He is what is generally referred to as a *lost-volume seller*. By this we mean that while the goods were resold, they were sold to someone who would have bought similar goods from him anyway. This resale was not made possible by the breach. Steve could have made a sale of a Super 2100 to Headly in any event. Steve is hurt in that the total number of sales he will make over the year is *one less* than it would have been if Hacker had not breached. Assuming that each sale means a bit of profit for the seller (which is, after all, the reason sellers are in business), Steve's profits for the year will be less than they would have been but for the breach. His situation is to be distinguished from that we considered in the previous question: Hacker had one old PS/1 to sell and she ended up selling it. Steve can sell as many of the Super 2100s as he can get willing customers coming through the door. The way Steve sees it, he has lost sales volume, lost some of the profit to which he was entitled, and is indeed worse off economically because of Hacker's breach.

   Steve finds his remedy in §2-708(2), which is written in a very broad manner but was clearly intended by the drafters to respond to the lost-volume problem. If the facts are as he says they are, Steve will be able to establish that the measure of damages provided in §2-708(1)—zero dollars here—"is inadequate" to put him "in as good a position as performance would have done." That being so, he is entitled to "the profit (including reasonable overhead)" he would have made from the sale. Look now at Comment 2. Steve's situation is that of a seller of "standard priced goods," so he argues he fits perfectly within subsection (2).

The question then becomes how exactly to measure "the profit (including reasonable overhead)" that he would have made from a completed sale of the Super 2100 to Hacker. No one is terribly happy with the drafters' use of this phrase. Anyone who has ever spent any time studying the principles of accountancy (or who has ever tried to make sense of what an accountant was trying to tell him or her) knows that what counts for "profit" or "reasonable overhead" in any given situation can be a field day for creative number-crunching. If the case involved significant sums, you can be sure that there will be more than one side to the exciting accounting story.

Take our situation, for example. Steve will argue that the profit he lost because of Hacker's breach is measured by the difference of the $3,200 he pays for each machine and the $5,000 he was to receive. He demands $1,800 to put him into the same economic position he would have been in but for the breach. Note that in Comment 2, the drafters say that normally when a lost-volume retailer sues, the measure would be "list price less cost to the dealer." Another way that Steve would get to this same figure would be to measure "profit (including reasonable overhead)" by the difference of the contract price of sale minus what were to have been his so-called "variable" or "direct" costs in connection with the sale.

Hacker would argue for a lesser amount. After all, Steve's own accountant figures that he makes only something like 10 percent profit on his overall sales. This, of course, takes into account the fact that he must not only buy the machines from his suppliers, but also must pay his salespeople, his rent, his advertising costs, and so on. Figuring all this in, he would make a profit of something like $500 on the sale of each H.A.L. Super 2100 during the year. That amount and no more, Hacker will argue, is enough to make up to him for his lost profits.

In this particular example, I think Steve has the stronger position. The section says he is allowed to include his "reasonable overhead" in his profit, whatever that means. As a practical matter, the sale of one computer more or less isn't going to change how much he spends on rent, salaries, and so on. The profit he would have made on one additional sale is more like $1,800. Another way of looking at this is that if his other overhead costs have to be covered by one fewer sale, then each and every other sale that he does carry through to conclusion is just that much less profitable. And all thanks to Hacker's breach.

The courts have shown themselves willing to consider the case of the lost-volume seller like our friend Steve here and to award damages under §2-708(2) pretty much as he would measure them, as contract price minus variable costs. See, for example, the well-known case of *Neri v. Retail Marine Corp.*, 285 N.E.2d 311 (N.Y. 1972), and *Kenco Homes, Inc. v. Williams*, 972 P.2d 125 (Wash. App. 1999), and *Jewish Federation of Greater Des Moines v. Cedar Forest Products Co.*, 796 N.W.2d 456 (Iowa App. 2003). If, however, the repudiated agreement covered what was to be a very large part of the seller's sales over a given period, so that once it fell through, he or she could be expected to economize and cut back on those various overhead items, a more sophisticated calculation of just what is and what is not lost profit "including reasonable overhead" resulting from the breach would be necessary. For a pair of cases giving particularly intricate and detailed analyses of exactly how much is to be awarded as damages to a lost-volume seller, you might want to look (at least if you just can't get enough of basic accounting principles) at *New England Dairies, Inc. v. Dairy Mart Convenience Stores, Inc.*, 2002 WL 229900 (D. Conn.), and *Stamtec, Inc. v. Anson Stamping Co., LLC*, 346 F.3d 651 (6th Cir. 2003).

In this example, we have focused on the problem of the lost-volume retailer or distributor. Notice that a manufacturer which contracts to fabricate the items it sells can also suffer a lost-volume problem and lost profits if a buyer breaches. According to Comment 2, the normal measure of damages in this instance would be "list price less manufacturing cost to the manufacturer." As you can imagine, the lost profits in such a situation are even more difficult to pin down and the parties' competing calculations even more subject to dispute.

b. The "lost-volume" recovery allowed to Steve in the previous problem was predicated, of course, on a showing that he was in fact a lost-volume seller. If, as we now posit, he would have been unable to sell more than 120 of the machines during the year, and if he did sell that many, he has no lost volume and the breach by Hacker didn't harm him. He has no rights under §2-708(2). He's back to recovering nothing from Hacker except perhaps a bit of incidental damages if those can be shown.

Similarly, for a manufacturer to qualify as a lost volume seller, it would have to establish that its production capacity would have allowed it to produce all of the goods it did sell over the relevant period and *in addition* the amount which it would have sold to the repudiating buyer. If its factory was working to full capacity for the whole time anyway, it suffered no loss of volume and could not proceed using §2-708(2). See *Razorback Concrete Co. v. Dement Construction Co., LLC*, 688 F.3d 346 (8th Cir. 2012).

c. Here is another situation where Hacker will be able to argue that Steve is not a lost-volume seller. He may have sold one fewer of one brand of machine because of Hacker's repudiation, but he made another sale (to her) that he otherwise would not have. It all depends on the facts. One thing we'd like to know is whether Steve had an unlimited supply of the Magnum Pro available to him. If not—if he could only have sold a given number because of a short supply of *that* new machine—then the profit he makes on his sale of one to Hacker is a profit he would have made anyway and can't be counted in Hacker's favor. We'd then be back to seeing whether Steve lost volume on the Super 2100. If Steve did have unlimited supplies of the two machines, then Hacker's argument that her breach only exchanged one sale for another on Steve's books and didn't cost him any profit has some power to it. Of course, we'd have to know what profit Steve was making on each Magnum Pro he sold. If it is less than $1,800 for some reason, he should at least be able to collect the difference in profits from Hacker.

7. a. This example is based on *Nobs Chemical, U.S.A., Inc. v. Koppers Co. Inc.*, 616 F.2d 212 (5th Cir. 1980). The first issue presented is whether the seller can elect to recover under §2-708(1) even when the buyer can argue that this would *overcompensate* compared to the measure in §2-708(2). Normally, as we've seen above, the idea behind subsection (2) is that a seller stands the chance of being undercompensated if it is relegated to the market/contract difference of subsection (1) in that it will not ultimately end up with the sum total of profit it had every reason to expect. The seller elects to proceed under subsection (2) because, in the words of that subsection, "the measure of damages provided in subsection (1) is inadequate to put the seller in as good a position as performance would have done." But what if, because of the circumstances, the measure of subsection (1) is *more than* adequate? Can the *buyer* now insist that the award be determined by the lost-profit formula of subsection (2)?

Look at the facts here. Nobs calculates its damages under subsection (1) as $275,000, which is just the $540 contract price minus $265 the market price at the time and place for tender multiplied out by the 1,000 tons. Koppers, however, argues that Nobs expected to make no more than $95,000 profit on the deal even if it had gone through exactly as planned. That firm was committed to buying all its requirements of cumene at $400 per ton. It would have to spend $45 per ton to get it delivered—all to receive the contract price of $540 per ton. You can check that ($540 – $400 – $45) times 1,000 is, sure enough, $95,000. Should Nobs receive substantially more in damages than it ever would have come up with had Koppers not repudiated? (You see why the facts work out as they do here, and why the situation will presumably not be that common. It all results from the seller's being committed to a requirements contract for all of the cumene in which it dealt so that it could not itself take advantage of the tumbling market prices of the stuff.)

So what should be the result under Article 2? Once again, we have a kind of dispute like we did in considering whether seller could ever be forced to use §2-708(1) when it would prefer the §2-706 measure (see Example 4d): a dispute between the language of the particular provisions of these sections (subsection (2) states pretty clearly that it's to be used only when the measure of subsection (1) is *inadequate* to get the seller what it wants) and the overriding principle of compensation as articulated in §1-305(a). Once again, as you might expect, a strong case can be made for the buyer's being able to restrict the seller to use of §2-708(2) "in those circumstances in which the defendant-buyer can show that §2-708(1) will overcompensate the plaintiff." The Fifth Circuit in *Nobs* adopted this approach; it determined that the lost profit of $95,000 was all that the seller could recover under the circumstances. The resolution of this issue in the buyer's favor in *Nobs* has generally—but not invariably—been followed in the few later cases presenting the same issue, and the commentators have been generally—but not uniformly—favorably disposed to the outcome. For two decisions, each of which gives a thoroughgoing review of the controversy, see *Purina Mills, L.L.C. v. Less*, 295 F. Supp. 2d 1017 (N.D. Iowa 2003), and *Westlake Petrochemicals, L.L.C. v. United Polychem, Inc.*, 688 F.3d 232 (5th Cir. 2012).

b. The second issue in *Nobs* was whether the aggrieved seller could recover the $75,000 loss suffered in this way. Why would there be any doubt? Well, how do we characterize this loss? It seems to be what we will call in the next chapter on buyer's remedies an example of "consequential damages" arising from the repudiation. The problem is that in all the sections we've seen providing for damages to the seller (§§2-706, 2-708, 2-709), there has been reference to something like "incidental damages allowed under the provisions of this Article (§2-710)." We look at §2-710 and, sure enough, it allows for the recovery of incidental damages characterized in a certain way. Compare this to §2-715, which applies to suits by an aggrieved buyer. The buyer is entitled to incidental damages and, in the appropriate case, consequential damages. Doesn't this make it perfectly clear that the drafters most certainly did *not* intend for consequential damages to be available to an aggrieved seller? These seem to have been left out intentionally.

In *Nobs* itself, the Fifth Circuit took the view that an aggrieved seller has no right to consequential, as opposed to incidental, damages under Article 2:

> We believe the trial court was correct in declining to award the plaintiffs the extra $75,000.00. Under UCC 2-708(2), in addition to profit, the seller may recover "incidental damages" and "due allowance for costs reasonably incurred." The code does not provide for recovery of consequential damages by a seller. [Citing §1-106(1).]

The Sixth Circuit Court of Appeals, in a case applying Michigan law, has come to the same conclusion. *Firwood Mfg. Co. Inc. v. General Tire, Inc.*, 96 F.3d 163 (6th Cir. 1996). The Eleventh Circuit upheld a district court's determination that Florida law does not allow for recovery of a seller's consequential damages. *Validsa, Inc. v. PDVSA Services, Inc.*, 424 F. App'x 862 (11th Cir. 2011).

CHAPTER 27

Buyer's Remedies

WHEN SELLER BREACHES

What can a buyer do when the seller has breached or repudiated? The question of where to start looking for answers is easy enough. The drafters provide in §2-711 an index or summary of the remedies available under Article 2 to the buyer who has been wronged, at least when the situation has not proceeded to the point of the buyer's accepting the goods. Before we even look at that section, however, it is well to remember what we have previously studied about the two so-called goods-related remedies that the buyer can and, in many cases, would be well advised to take advantage of in many situations. When the seller tenders goods that are not as promised, the buyer may reject them. (We gave rejection all the attention it so rightfully deserves in Chapter 17.) Even where the buyer accepts, if the goods are later discovered to be defective, there may be the possibility of revoking acceptance under §2-608 (as to which see Chapter 19). Avoiding acceptance is often by far the buyer's best line of defense. Recall, however, that rejection or revocation of the goods is not necessarily the end of the story for the aggrieved buyer. In the introductory text to the previous chapter, we explored briefly the possibility that in the event of a buyer's breach, the seller might choose for perfectly legitimate business or personal reasons not to pursue a legal remedy. Obviously the same is true for the buyer considering a claim against a seller. The buyer considering a legal remedy has the right to bring an action under the plan laid out in §2-711. Let's look at the first two subsections:

> (1) Where the seller fails to make delivery or repudiates or the buyer rightfully rejects or justifiably revokes acceptance then with respect to any goods involved, and with respect to the whole if the breach goes to the whole contract (Section 2-612), the buyer may cancel and whether or not he has done so may in addition to recovering so much of the price as has been paid
>
> (a) "cover" and have damages under the next section (Section 2-712) as to all the goods affected whether or not they have been identified to the contract; or
>
> (b) recover damages for non-delivery as provided in this Article (Section 2-713).
>
> (2) Where the seller fails to deliver or repudiates, the buyer may also
>
> (a) if the goods have been identified recover them as provided in this Article (Section 2-502); or
>
> (b) in a proper case obtain specific performance or replevy the goods as provided in this Article (Section 2-716).

The one case not covered by this scheme is an important one: that of the damages available to the buyer who has accepted the goods but later claims injury due to a nonconformity. That worthy topic gets a separate section all its own, §2-714, which we'll be taking a look at soon enough.

To get a good handle on what remedies will be available to a buyer in any situation, the key is first to get clearly in mind exactly what that situation is. As in the remedies for the seller (reviewed in the previous chapter), it's all going to depend on the facts of the individual case. Did the goods ever come into existence? If so, were they identified to the contract? Did the seller tender, and if so, what was the buyer's response? Were the tendered goods accepted or rejected, and if accepted, was that acceptance later "justifiably revoked"? When all the dust had settled, who ended up with the goods and where are they now? Finally, was any payment made by the buyer to the seller, and if so, how much? In this chapter, we are allowed to assume just a few things: (1) that an agreement between the parties created a valid contract enforceable against the seller, and (2) that the seller's subsequent actions amounted to a breach or a repudiation of that agreement. Beyond that, we have to be open to the full range of situations and possibilities.

IF THE SELLER IS INSOLVENT

Article 2 provides special relief in at least some situations where the buyer has not yet received or been shipped the goods but has paid all or a portion of the purchase price shortly before the seller becomes insolvent. The Code definition of when a party has become *insolvent* is given in §1-201(b)(23). The seller's business is in some kind of difficulty. The buyer has paid all or a part of the price and (while the seller's insolvency is not in and of itself a breach) there is the real possibility that the goods will never be shipped or delivered. An insolvent party's creditors will often have the power and the motivation to resist any moves by that party that lessen the amount of valuable stuff over which it has control. The creditors will not want to see goods leaving the seller's plant. From the point of view of the buyer, this has to be troubling. It has to wait around for further developments and, quite naturally, will be in doubt about whether the promised goods are going to be delivered on schedule. Just as important, even if the goods are never delivered, a seller that has been paid part of the purchase price may well not be in a position financially or legally to return any or all of that payment. The buyer stands a good chance of being left with neither the goods nor the money. What it *would* very likely end up with would be a contract claim against the seller for the amount of the payment and perhaps something more as damages of the type we'll talk about for the nondelivery of the goods. But the buyer will be an unsecured, general creditor for this amount. And we know how unlikely it is, should bankruptcy ensue, that a general creditor will ever see any significant portion of the money it is owed.

Section 2-502 provides the buyer with a right actually to pick up and take away promised goods in the possession of the seller if some payment has been made by buyer and either the goods are being bought as consumer goods and have not been delivered or, in any case, if the seller has "become[] insolvent within ten days after receipt of the first installment on their price." The buyer takes possession of the goods and extricates itself from the whole messy situation. There are significant conditions to this right of course. First of all, the goods must have already been identified to the contract under §2-501. In addition, the buyer must make and keep open a tender of the unpaid portion of the price. And, of course, this right of recovery only works in the commercial context if the seller has become insolvent within ten days of its receiving the initial payment. Should the buyer have not yet made a payment or if the insolvency occurs after this slender ten-day period, the buyer will have to go elsewhere for relief and may unavoidably end up entangled in the bankruptcy. We turn now to a brief rundown of the general remedies available to the buyer in the event of the seller's breach or repudiation before heading into the questions.

GOING FOR THE GOODS, GOING FOR THE CASH

As we'll explore in the examples and explanations, and as presented to us in the index §2-711, the aggrieved buyer will in some circumstances have the chance actually to obtain the goods through judicial process. The possibilities of an order for *specific performance*—a contractual remedy to which I trust you were introduced in Contracts—and of *replevy,* a property notion with which you may be less familiar, are covered by §2-716. If the buyer is not able to get the goods for one reason or another, or in the very likely situation that it doesn't want them (at least not from this seller) anymore, the remedies then take the form of money damages. The buyer may under §2-712 "cover" by buying the same or similar goods in substitution from someone else, then sue for the difference between what it paid for the goods and what it had expected to pay. Or the buyer can seek damages measured by a market price minus contract price formula under §2-713. If the buyer accepted tender of the goods, this does not, of course, impair its right to proceed against the seller for any damages suffered because the delivered goods are not as promised. See the concluding language of §2-607(2). The assessment of damages with respect to accepted goods is governed by §2-714. To each of the measures we will consider may be added so-called incidental or consequential damages as set forth in §2-715 if the facts allow.

One final point: If the buyer is entitled to some measure of money damages, how does it collect? When the buyer has paid the full purchase price and is left with no goods in hand, there is little to be done if the seller does not or cannot make voluntary amends but to bring a lawsuit, get a judgment, and enforce that judgment for all it is worth in any way possible. Sometimes, however, the buyer will have an easier road to recovery. In the event that the buyer has accepted the goods but not yet paid the full purchase price on them, any damages to which it is legally entitled may be deducted from what it has yet to pay under §2-717. If the buyer has rightfully rejected or justifiably revoked acceptance and the goods are in its possession, then §2-711(3) offers some help. The buyer has a security interest in the goods to the extent of any payment it has made or any expenses it has incurred in relation to its handling of the goods (not, however, for any other damages it may be claiming), so it need not release them back into the custody of the seller unless and until its payment has been returned and its expenses recompensed. Should this amount not be forthcoming, it may eventually resell the goods and try to get its money that way. As to any other damages it may have suffered, the buyer will have to proceed along other lines. See Comment 3 to §2-711.

We now bring all these sections (and a couple of others to which I'll direct you) to bear on our usual array of examples and explanations.

Examples

EXAMPLES

1. In early February, Arnold Moneybucks contracts to buy an original oil painting ("The Evils of Socialism") for $1,500 from Stella's art gallery. Arnold will pick up and pay for the painting when the artist's showing at Stella's has closed at the end of the month. On February 15 Arnold receives an email from Stella saying that she has decided against selling him the painting, that she has herself fallen in love with it, and that she will be keeping it in her private collection. Arnold realizes all the more

how much he himself is enamored of this work. Does he have the right to obtain a court order making Stella deliver the work to him?

2. Seller in Seattle contracts to deliver ten tons of noodles to Buyer in Boise. It is agreed that the goods will be shipped by rail under a nonnegotiable bill of lading consigning the goods to Seller's agent in Boise. When the shipment arrives in Boise, the railroad is to notify Buyer, who will then make payment to Seller's agent. This agent will then in turn produce a delivery order directed to the railroad authorizing delivery to Buyer. The goods arrive and Buyer is notified. Seller has instructed his agent, however, that the shipment not be turned over to Buyer but that, instead, it be put into storage in Boise for possible sale to another buyer at a higher price. Does Buyer have the right to get these noodles?

3. Buster contracted to buy a new refrigerator, the Penguin Deluxe, for \$1,000 plus a \$50 delivery fee from Selma's Appliance City. The refrigerator was to come in the Penguin appliance line's avocado color, which Buster had picked to blend in with his kitchen decor. Selma's delivery crew arrived at Buster's with a large box marked "Penguin Deluxe/Avocado," but when the box was opened, it turned out that the machine inside was a burnt orange color. Buster rejected the refrigerator on the spot and the delivery crew took it back to Selma's. Later that day, Selma called Buster to apologize for the error, which apparently resulted from some problem at the manufacturer's plant. Unfortunately, Selma explained to Buster, she doesn't have any of the refrigerators in the right color in stock and when she contacted the manufacturer, she was told that it no longer made the Penguin Deluxe in that color. "I'm sorry," Selma concludes, "but you're not going to be able to get what you want." That weekend, Buster goes to several of the town's other appliance stores. At the fourth store he visits, he finds they have one remaining Penguin Deluxe in the avocado color. He contracts to buy this machine (which this store will deliver free of charge) for \$1,200.
   (a) What rights does Buster have against Selma's Appliance City?
   (b) Would it make any difference to your answer if Selma could show that there was one appliance store in town that would have sold him just the refrigerator he wanted for only \$1,050?
   (c) How would you respond if it turned out that the refrigerator Buster eventually bought and had delivered was equipped with a special automatic ice-cube and crushed-ice feature that had not been included in the machine Buster originally contracted to buy from Selma?

4. Marinara Incorporated is a large producer of tomato sauces. It contracts with a garlic distributor, Cloves & Sons, for the delivery of 600 pounds of fresh #1 garlic at \$2 per pound, delivery to be made on April 1 to

Marinara's plant. On April 1, Cloves & Sons brings around several crates of garlic. Marinara's purchasing director discovers that the garlic in these crates is only of #2 quality, and isn't all that fresh. The purchasing director rejects the delivery. A month later, when Marinara's stock of garlic is running low, the purchasing director buys 600 pounds of #1 garlic from another distributor for the then-market price of $3.50 per pound. (The market price of garlic has been rising steadily since the end of the summer due to an unexpectedly poor garlic harvest.) Should Marinara Incorporated have any difficulty in collecting the $1.50 difference per pound from Cloves & Sons?

5. At the end of the salmon catching season, one large fishery, Salmons of Seattle, has on hand a great stock of processed frozen salmon and other fish fillets. On August 1, it contracts to sell a large quantity of salmon fillets to Better Foods, a food wholesaler in Boise, Idaho, for a price of "$2 per pound F.O.B. Boise." Delivery is to be made by railroad on or before August 21, and payment is to be made within 30 days of the buyer's receipt. On August 4, Salmons delivers some crates marked for Better Foods to the railroad with instructions that these be delivered to Boise, where that firm will take delivery. When a representative of Better Foods goes to the Boise railyard on August 21, she quickly discovers that the crates contain not salmon, but less valuable haddock fillets. She rejects the shipment. The following figures may (or may not) help you answer the questions.

Market price of fillets at Boise on August 1	$2.04
Market price at Seattle on August 1	$1.97
Market price at Boise on August 4	$2.16
Market price at Seattle on August 4	$2.09
Market price at Boise on August 21	$3.00
Market price at Seattle on August 21	$2.97
Cost of shipping from Seattle to Boise	$0.05

(a) If Better Foods seeks to recover damages based on §2-713, how much should it be awarded per pound?

(b) What would Better Foods be awarded if, instead, the price had been agreed to as "$1.98 F.O.B. Seattle"?

(c) Suppose that Salmons contracted for $1.98 F.O.B. Seattle, but never makes any shipment to Boise at all. Better Foods only becomes aware of this when its representative contacts the railroad on April 21 and asks when would be a convenient time to pick up the shipment she has been told to expect. She is told the railroad has not received any shipment from Salmons intended for Better Foods. She contacts Salmons, and that firm admits it never made the shipment. If Better Foods sues Salmons asking for recovery under §2-713, to how much is it entitled?

6. On May 1, Seller contracts to deliver wheat directly to Buyer's plant on or before December 15 for $1 per bushel. On June 1, Seller contacts Buyer and repudiates its contract. Buyer investigates the supply of wheat it has on hand and its anticipated needs, so it decides it can do without the wheat contracted for from Seller. In January, it sues Seller for damages under §2-713. It is able to show that the market price for such wheat in its vicinity on December 15 was $1.83 a bushel. Seller acknowledges that the market price of wheat had been steadily rising over the later part of the year, but points out that it was only $1.05 on June 1 when it had told Buyer not to expect delivery. What amount should Buyer be awarded under §2-713?

7. Marinara Incorporated, the tomato sauce manufacturer, contracts to buy a large amount of oregano from Herb, a spice and herb distributor, for $15 per pound. Delivery is to be made to Marinara's plant on or before May 15. By May 15, no shipment of oregano has arrived. The market price for oregano in the vicinity of Marinara's plant is $18 per pound. The Marinara purchasing director contacts a spice merchant who has been trying to attract the saucemaker's business and is willing to sell him the needed quantity of oregano for $17 per pound. The purchasing director makes the purchase on Marinara's behalf. Marinara's legal department then brings suit against Herb, claiming damages in the amount of $3 per pound under §2-713. Is Marinara entitled to this amount?

8. Barbara buys a watch, the Chronos Masterwork 660, from Sam's Jewelry Store. She pays $3,200 for the watch, which at the time of purchase, was marked with a prominent label as being "18 carat gold." A few months later, she shows it to a friend who is in the jewelry business who informs her that what she has gotten is not the 18-carat-gold version of the Masterwork, which in fact has been selling in most stores for $3,500, but only a gold-plated model. This model, the Masterwork 460, is a perfectly good watch, but can be had in the stores for something like $800.
   (a) If Barbara decides to keep the watch and to sue Sam for damages, to what amount is she entitled?
   (b) To what amount would she be entitled assuming all the facts remain the same except that the Masterwork 660 has been selling in most of the major stores for something like $2,800?

9. In January 2002, Rose bought a new Midas 500 automobile from Eden Autos, a Midas dealership, for the price of $47,000. Over the following three and one-half years, she drove it approximately 25,000 miles. During that period, she had to take it into the dealership for repairs 19 times. The dealership attempted each time to make the necessary repairs to Rose's satisfaction, but was never entirely successful. In June 2005, Rose decided that she could not stand driving the car anymore, and

she traded it in at another dealership for a Lodestar 330. The Lodestar dealership calculated her price for her newer car by including a "trade-in allowance" for the Midas 500 of $24,400. Rose then sued the Eden dealership claiming that the Midas had been defective from the day she received it and that she was entitled to damages. The dealership conceded that the auto may have been defective upon delivery, but argues that Rose suffered no damages on account of the defects as she eventually traded the Midas in for an amount that was its "fair market value" as of June 2005, even taking into account its condition. The dealership is prepared to offer the testimony of someone who has long been in the business of buying and selling such autos who is prepared to state that the $24,400 was indeed the fair market value of the trade-in.

(a) Given these facts, should Eden's argument that Rose is not entitled to any damages under §2-714(2) be successful?

(b) Add in the fact that Rose would be willing to testify that the new Midas, for which she had paid $47,000, was in her opinion (and in retrospect) not worth more than one-half that amount in 2002 considering all the difficulties she had with it. "If I had known then what I know now about this car," she would testify, "I would not have paid more than half price." How does that affect your evaluation of the dispute between Rose and Eden?

10. Dominic Doe buys a new pizza oven for his pizza parlor from Ovens of Brooklyn. The purchase price is $10,500. Soon after the oven is delivered, it becomes apparent that its temperature control is not functioning properly. Doe contacts the seller, but Ovens refuses to make repairs, claiming that the oven is just fine. Doe then calls Crafty, a repair person with whom he has had good experience in the past. Crafty tells him that the control clearly is faulty, but she is quickly able to find a control that will work in that brand of oven and installs it. The oven now works perfectly well, but Crafty tells Doe that because she has had to install a used part, there is no telling how long it will hold up and that "it's merely a patch-up job, though it should hold you for a while."

(a) Crafty charges Doe $1,200 for parts and labor. Doe brings suit against Ovens of Brooklyn. To how much is he entitled?

(b) Suppose instead that after Crafty installs the replacement control (still for $1,200), she tells Doe that she was able to find and install a brand new part and that in fact, "what you've got in there now is really much better than that control they had in there to begin with. When these ovens go, it's usually the temperature control that's the problem, so you can bet this oven's going to last you much longer with this new control." To how much is Doe entitled under these facts?

11. Buyer and Seller contract for the purchase and sale of 10,000 yards of carpeting. Buyer takes delivery of the carpeting at his store, but as soon as he inspects the first roll, it is immediately apparent that it is not what he ordered. Buyer calls Seller and rejects the goods. Seller says she will arrange to have this carpeting picked up and the correct carpeting delivered, but that this will necessarily take a few weeks. Having only limited floorspace, Buyer arranges to have the carpeting taken away and stored by a local warehouse, paying $200 for this service. Seller delivers the correct shipment to Buyer and collects the incorrect shipment from the warehouse. Seller accepts the second shipment as conforming with the contract in quality and amount, even though it has arrived some two weeks after the promised delivery date. Buyer now is to pay for the carpeting. What amount or amounts can he legitimately subtract from the purchase price under §2-717?

12. Assume that Dominic Doe, from Example 9 above, is able to show that because of the problem with the pizza oven, he has had to close down his shop for a period of four days, Thursday through Sunday. Normally he would not be open on Sunday, but as it happened, he had agreed to be open for a special private pizza party for which he was to receive $1,000. Does this information add to the amount to which he is entitled from Ovens of Brooklyn, and if so, by how much? What other information would you need to more fully evaluate the situation?

13. Bertha Moneybucks is considering the purchase of a large pleasure boat from Maryland Marine Sales. She is satisfied that the price quoted, $34,000, is a good one for the boat in question, but is very concerned that she won't get the boat in time for the prime boating season even though the seller is willing to promise delivery by May 1. In order to make the sale, the president of M.M.S. adds to the contract the following provision:

    > Seller promises to deliver the boat as provided for herein on or before May 1. In recognition of the distress and inconvenience which will be caused Buyer should delivery be delayed, it is agreed that the price to be paid by Buyer is to be reduced by $100 for each day delivery may be delayed beyond May 1.

    The boat is not delivered until June 15. Is Bertha entitled to deduct $4,500 from the purchase price of the boat? See §2-718(1).

14. Sam contracts to buy Dave's used car for $3,000. He gives Dave $800 as a down payment on the car. The next day, he calls Dave and tells him that the money he was counting on to complete the purchase would not be coming his way and he is going to have to back out of the deal.

Dave tells him, "That's all right. These things happen." Two weeks later, when Sam next sees Dave, he asks for his $800 back. Dave tells him that fortunately he was able to sell the car to someone else for $3,100, but that he has no intention of returning Sam's money to him. "I said it was all right, that I wasn't going to hold you to the deal or sue you or anything," explains Dave, "but you certainly can't expect to get your money back. After all, it was you who backed out. I was ready to sell to you." Sam decides not to get into a fight with Dave right there on the street, but now he is wondering: Is there any way he can legally recover his $800? Look at §2-718(2) and (3).

Explanations

1. Arnold will probably be able to get his hands on the artwork itself, but the question of whether he has *the right* to relief of this nature is more in doubt. First consider an argument by Arnold that he should be awarded specific performance of the contract under §2-716(1). I am assuming that you have studied the history and nature of this equitable remedy in Contracts. If so, surely you remember that while a court may exercise its equitable powers to give such relief, whether or not it does so is always discretionary on the court's part. That is in the nature of equity and specific performance. Note that §2-716(1) and (2) both carefully use the word *may* and not *must, shall, will*, or anything of the sort.

   Comment 1 to this section tells us:

   > The present section continues in general prior policy as to specific performance and injunction against breach. However, without intending to impair in any way the exercise of the court's sound discretion in the matter, this Article seeks to further a more liberal attitude than some courts have shown in connection with the specific performance of contracts of sale.

   You can see how the drafters sought to effectuate this "more liberal" approach in the language of the section itself. Notice that there is no mention of the traditional requirement that before the court will consider granting specific performance, it be established that "no adequate remedy at law" is available to the plaintiff. The section doesn't even require that the goods be in existence or identified to the contract. The only statutory requirement is that the goods be "unique" or that "other proper circumstances" be shown.

   In Arnold's case, it seems likely that he will prevail and be awarded specific performance as the artwork is "unique" in the most conventional sense in which equity would use this term. Note, however, in Comment 2 that the drafters hoped to be introducing along with this section (albeit through the Comments) a "new concept of what are 'unique' goods" for this purpose. "The test of uniqueness under this section must be made in terms of the total situation which characterizes the contract." Add to this the suggestion in §2-716(1) that specific performance may (and again we have to stress *may*) be granted in "other proper circumstances," and you have the go-ahead for some fairly creative use of the equitable power. Unfortunately, the drafters gave little indication about what this last phrase was meant to entail other than that "inability to cover is strong evidence" of such circumstances, whatever they may be. A critic could ask what this language in §2-716(1) adds other than to remind us that the court's discretion is always, well, within the discretion of the court.

It would be fair to say that, even under this new section, there has not been any wild expansion in the courts' willingness to grant specific performance when it comes to sale of goods. The traditional attitude that this is an exceptional remedy and one to be used sparingly and with discretion has suffered no fundamental rethinking. If the goods are not something pretty special but can be replaced through normal channels, the court is not going to be tempted into specific performance. However, a number of opinions have indeed taken the expanded and more liberal focus on "commercial feasibility of replacement" to heart as the drafters had hoped. Most notably, these have been where the seller and buyer have entered into a long-term relationship for the continuing supply of some type of fuel or other natural resource. In such a situation, the buyer could, of course, with enough time and energy and laying out enough money, make substitute arrangements to replace a supply that is abruptly cut off. It could then sue for whatever damage had been done. The courts recognize, however, that the disruption of the buyer's business, not to mention the inconvenience caused to others down the chain of distribution, could be enormous and at the same time difficult to evaluate with any certainty. Specific performance of the supply contract has been granted, although in most such cases, whether the court has done so by an expanded reading of "unique" or through reliance on the "other proper circumstances" language has been left unclear. For a triad of cases in each of which the buyer was granted specific performance in such a situation, see *International Casings Group, Inc. v. Premium Standard Farms, Inc.*, 358 F. Supp. 2d 863 (W.D. Mo. 2005), *Sherwin Alumina L.P. v. Aluchem, Inc.*, 512 F. Supp. 2d 957 (S.D. Tex. 2007), and *Almetals, Inc. v. Wickeder Westfalenstahl, GMBH*, 2008 WL 4791377 (E.D. Mich.).

Before we leave Arnold's dilemma, there is one more question: If, for some reason, Arnold were afraid that the court might in its discretion refuse to award him specific performance, could he invoke the right to replevin under §2-716(3) to reach the same outcome? Notice that if a case comes within the criteria of that subsection, replevin is a matter of right and not (as is true with specific performance) a discretionary remedy within the power of the court to grant or withhold. You may not be as familiar with replevin as you are with specific performance—at least it is much less likely that you would have spent time on it in Contracts. That's because under the common law, replevin is not a contractual notion or remedy at all, but a *property* concept. Traditionally, replevin is available if it is established that the defendant is wrongfully holding on to property that is rightfully the plaintiff's. The key to an action in replevin has always been the showing that the "title" to the goods in question rightfully resides in the plaintiff. The drafters of Article 2, of course, did everything they could to play down the whole notion of title as it might apply to the law of sales, so their provision on replevin makes no reference to that concept. Instead they require a showing that the goods have been identified to the contract and "cover is reasonably unavailable." See Comment 3, which says this about replevin and not much more. It would seem Arnold could avail himself of this provision, but then it's very unlikely that, given the strength of his argument for specific performance even under traditional doctrine, he would have to. There has been very little action whatsoever under §2-716(3), and it's hard to come up with any obvious situation, other than that of the following question, where its invocation would add much to an argument based on specific performance alone. Perhaps the amazing ability of the real world to come up with fact patterns even beyond the invention of law professors will eventually reveal a special part to play for subsection (3), but if so, only time will tell.

2. This is a situation of shipment under reservation under §2-505, and Buyer should be able to recover the noodles under replevin and §2-716(3). Buyer will, of course, have to pay the purchase price to get the noodles, which is what the language about "satisfaction of the [seller's] security interest in them" is all about. Here, at least, is one instance in which replevin would work for a buyer even though specific performance is highly unlikely. How unique can noodles be? Yet you can understand why Buyer would find it highly preferable simply to pay for and get this particular shipment of noodles rather than having to worry about cover, incidental expenses, proof of market price, or the like. Buyer is able to pay for the noodles, get the noodles, and get on with its business. Case closed.

3. a. Buster should be able to recover $150 from Selma. Under §2-712(1), he is entitled if he chooses to "cover:"

> by making in good faith and without unreasonable delay any reasonable purchase of or contract to purchase goods in substitution for those due from the seller.

   That's just what Buster did here. There certainly was no unreasonable delay and, under the circumstances, this seems like a reasonable purchase. Further, we have no cause to doubt Buster's good faith. See Comment 4.

The payoff for Buster comes in subsection (2), since he is entitled to recover as damages the difference between the cost of cover ($1,200) and the contract price ($1,000) together with any consequential or incidental damages "but less expenses saved in consequence of the seller's breach." Here he saved $50 by not having to pay for delivery under the substitute contract, so the final figure is $150 due and payable by Selma.

We are assuming that Buster had no consequential or incidental damages here. If there were any, he should come forward and prove them. Incidental damages under §2-715(1) could include any "commercially reasonable charges, expenses or commissions in connection with effecting cover." Unfortunately, if all that Buster suffered in order to effect cover was more than a little annoyance and a lost weekend spent touring the local appliance stores, it is unlikely he could get anything for this because no dollar figure attaches to his time and inconvenience. As to consequential damages, again we are told of nothing. If he did have such—say, for example, he was forced by the breach to go for a few days without a refrigerator at all and some frozen food had to be tossed out—then this amount should be added in as well, as long as it could be demonstrated that he had done all that he could have been reasonably expected to do to avoid this consequential loss. Note the last part of §2-715(2)(a).

b. Buster's recovery should not be affected by the fact that there was, somewhere in town, a store where he could have made cheaper cover. See Comment 2:

> The test of proper cover is whether at the time and place the buyer acted in good faith and in a reasonable manner, and it is immaterial that hindsight may later prove that the method of cover used was not the cheapest or most effective.

But what if Selma wanted to show that the place where the cheaper cover was available was the one big discount store in town that is generally known to have the lowest prices around? Could she argue that Buster's failure to even check at this store made for an unreasonable if not bad faith search for what he needed? Perhaps, but don't forget that Buster originally bought from Selma, so he might very well be able to demonstrate that, for one reason or another, he chooses not to shop at a place just because it's the cheapest. Even if Buster *had* been aware that there was a place where he could have covered more cheaply, that does not necessarily make his purchase at $1,200 from a store he trusts more or which he thought would give better service an unreasonable one.

A well-known and interesting case on the cover minus contract measure is *Laredo Hides Co., Inc. v. H & H Meat Products Co., Inc.*, 513 S.W.2d

210 (Tex. Civ. App. 1974), for it demonstrates how much leeway a court can allow a buyer doing its best to cover under difficult circumstances. The buyer sued for seller's breach of its agreement to sell all of its output of cattle hides during March to December 1972. Delivery was to be made at least twice a month. When the seller breached and eventually repudiated the agreement, the buyer was forced to go into the open market for hides and to make substitute purchases. The court awarded the buyer the cost of cover minus the contract price even though the cover purchases "had to be made periodically throughout 1972 since Laredo Hides had no storage facilities, and the hides would decompose if allowed to age," and even though the market price for hides was steadily increasing during the period in question. See also *Rockland Industries, Inc. v. E & E (U.S.) Inc.*, 991 F. Supp. 468 (D. Md. 1998), *as modified*, 1 F. Supp. 2d 528, and *Hessler v. Crystal Lake Chrysler-Plymouth, Inc.*, 788 N.E.2d 405 (Ill. App. 2003).

c. Selma will argue that by getting a better machine, Buster will receive a windfall if she is made to pay the full $150 previously calculated. Recall that under §1-305(a), the purpose of all of these remedy provisions is to compensate the plaintiff but no more. I doubt Selma's argument would get very far here. If it were to work, her breach would be, in effect, forcing Buster to pay for a feature that he never wanted and, for all we know, finds undesirable. Even if he comes to love the icemaker, I'd still let him keep it without worrying about a little too much in damages levied against Selma.

In some other situations, however, this factor—cover with goods of markedly better quality—might reasonably be taken into account in lessening the eventual damage award. Suppose the buyer is a commercial party that buys goods for resale (that is, a retailer or distributor). When it does not receive the ordered goods from the seller, it makes cover by buying the only available goods of that type, but ones that are of a higher quality. The buyer has no trouble selling these substituted goods and, in fact because of their quality, is able to get a higher price for them and make more of a profit than it had anticipated. Under those circumstances, it could well be argued by the breaching seller that the buyer's damages should be reduced by the amount of this increase in its resale profits. Running contrary to this conclusion, however, is the case of *KGM Harvesting Co. v. Fresh Network*, 42 Cal. Rptr. 2d 286 (Cal. Ct. App. 1995), which held that an aggrieved buyer of some lettuce was entitled to receive the full difference between the contract price and the price at which it covered, even though the buyer was able to pass along most of the additional expense suffered because of the breach onto other parties. Summarizing its decision, the California Court of Appeals concluded that when a buyer covers and is then awarded the difference between the cost of cover and the contract price, this "gives the buyer the benefit of his bargain. What the buyer chooses to do with that bargain is not relevant to the determination of damages under [§2-712]."

4. It's doubtful that Marinara is going to be able to collect the $1.50 per pound. The seller will argue that the purchase was made with unreasonable delay, especially considering what was going on in the volatile garlic market. Marinara will not be able to collect damages under §2-712. It will instead have to argue for damages based on §2-713, and it is likely that it will get far less under that section. We move on to how §2-713 works with the next explanation.

5. a. If the seller sues for recovery measured under §2-713, the two initial questions to be answered are as of what date and at what place is the market price to be determined. Subsection (1) tells us that we are to use the market price "at the time the buyer learned of the breach." That phrase will give us trouble in a different circumstance later on, but for the present, it seems clear that the date Better Foods learned of the breach was August 21. Subsection (2) says that "[m]arket price is to be determined as of the place for tender or, in the cases of rejection after arrival or revocation of acceptance, as of the place of arrival." Here we have a rejection after the goods have arrived in Boise, so the relevant market is Boise. The market price on August 21 in Boise was $3. The contract price was $2. Better Foods is entitled to damages to the tune of $1 per pound.

   Section 2-713 also provides, of course, for the aggrieved buyer's recovery of incidental or consequential damages as well as a deduction for any expenses saved by the buyer in consequence of the seller's breach. Here there are no incidental or consequential damages, or at least none that we know of. Did Better Foods save anything because of the breach? It appears not. This contract was F.O.B. Boise. Salmons of Seattle was to pay for the transportation and, we assume, has done so. So Better Foods was to incur no expense for transportation to begin with. Barring any additional facts of which we are not now aware, the $1.00 is all that Better Foods is entitled to under §2-713, and it's an amount that should make that buyer whole in an economic sense.

   b. The date when the buyer learned of the breach remains the same: August 21. The place of arrival, which is the relevant market because this was a shipment rejected, is still Boise. So we subtract the contract price of $1.98 from the market contract price of $3 and get $1.02. It appears that Better Foods will get more under this scenario, but wait: Better Foods has, under this price term, also taken upon itself the cost of transportation of $0.05 per pound. If it still must pay the carrier, then it can get a recovery of $1.02 per pound from Salmons, but it ends up with only a total of $0.97 in pocket. If, on the other hand, under the arrangement with the railroad, Better Foods is not liable for the shipping cost when it rejects the goods, then it is off the hook in that respect. But the §2-713 measure of damages must be decreased by the expenses saved in consequence of Salmon's breach. Better Foods would not have to pay the railroad anything but could only recover $0.97 from Salmons. All this is simply a result, as you can see, of the price of "$1.98 F.O.B. Seattle" actually being a less attractive price than "$2.00 F.O.B. Boise" when the cost of transportation between the two cities is $0.05 per pound.

c. The time that the buyer learned of the breach remains the same: August 21. What is the relevant market? Under §2-713(2), because this is not a case of rejection upon arrival or revocation of acceptance, the place to pick is the *place for tender*. Unfortunately, Article 2 nowhere specifies exactly where the place for tender is either in the general case or, more importantly for our purposes, in a shipment contract such as this. In a destination contract, it seems unavoidable that the place for tender is the actual destination. There's some greater question in a shipment contract. Looking at §§2-503(2) and 2-504 together, however, it seems fair to conclude that the drafters would want us to take the place where the goods are loaded on board and the seller completes its duties under the shipment contract as the place of tender in this situation.

So Better Foods' damages are to be measured initially as $2.97 minus $1.98 or $0.99 per pound. From this must be subtracted the $0.05 per pound transportation cost that the buyer will not have to pay because no stuff was ever shipped at all. Better Foods collects $0.94 per pound.

6. This example presents the problem of how to measure damages under §2-713 in light of an anticipatory repudiation. This issue has caused a great deal of controversy, and there is no general agreement by the authorities. The problem is that §2-713 says that the time at which market price is to be determined is "the time the buyer learned of the breach." That section also refers us to §2-723, which is supposed to help out but which really doesn't. Look at §2-723(1). It states a rule to be applied when the action based on repudiation comes to trial before the time for performance. So arguably it has no part to play in our particular hypo. If anything, it may be an evil influence. Notice that the drafters here use the phrase "when the aggrieved party learned *of the repudiation*." If nothing else, this reminds us that the drafters usually are careful to distinguish "breach" and "repudiation" to mean different events. A repudiation signals a breach may be in the offing, but it is not a breach in and of itself. It may be turned into a breach given the passage of time, or the nonrepudiating party may choose to treat it as a breach, but then it

also may be retracted so that no breach can ever be said to have occurred (§2-611). If a repudiation does ripen into a breach, typically the breach would come at least some time after the repudiation. But when? Is the nonrepudiating party ever *required* to treat the repudiation as the other party's last word on the subject and accept the repudiation as a breach? If so, that innocent victim could then be held to some obligation to take steps to mitigate prior to the initially promised date of performance. Look carefully at §2-610. It says that the nonrepudiating party *may* "for a commercially reasonable time await performance by the repudiating party." What it never says is that this party *must* do anything, and in particular, it never says what untoward consequences the nonrepudiating party will be made to face if, after the end of this "commercially reasonable time," it does nothing other than keep on waiting—waiting perhaps still in the hope that the repudiator will see the error of its ways, or waiting to bring a suit when it gets around to it, or when it thinks the circumstances will get it the biggest damage award.

We seem to have strayed very far from §2-713, but when we return to that section, we find a whole new level of problem in that section's directive that the time "when the buyer learned of the breach" be used to ascertain the correct market price. Since the adoption of Article 2, analysts have argued over at least three different readings that could be given this language in the repudiation case we have here. Let's take each in turn.

One suggestion is that Buyer's market damages should be measured with respect to the market value of wheat as of the time the buyer *learned of the repudiation*. At least the date in question would usually be easy to assess in most instances. In our case, the date would be June 1 and the damages would be $0.05 per bushel. The problem with this proposal is that the drafters refer in §2-713(1) to the time the buyer learned of the *breach*, and as we know, *breach* and *repudiation* are just not the same thing under Article 2, not just technically but as a matter of practice. There is no language in §2-713 that calls for or even really supports this result. And if this were the correct reading of §2-713, look what it would say to Buyer. You have just received a repudiation. The Code in §2-610 understands that you deserve some time to react. You may decide to cover, and even then, you may cover in one of a number of ways. If you do decide to cover, under §2-712 you can be sure that you will have a reasonable time to do so. If, however, it later turns out that you decide not to cover, you will be stuck with a remedy measured as of the moment this problem was first put before you. In a rising market as we have here, it almost seems as if it could cost you something if you don't cover. And you certainly will suffer if you do cover and a court later decides you took too long to do so. Perhaps the best thing for a buyer in this situation is to elect immediately to treat the repudiation as a breach and to cover as soon as possible. But this, as we've said, doesn't seem to square with what is said in §2-610(a). Besides which, it almost seems to penalize the buyer who is willing to cut the seller a little slack and give it some time to consider retracting its repudiation. It's hard to imagine that this is what the drafters would have intended. Professors White and Summers give this problem a good going-over in their treatise (§7-7) in spite of the fact that it involves making one's way through, in their words, "an impossible legal thicket" of Code sections. As to this approach—reading "learned of the breach" as equivalent to "learned of the repudiation"—they report, "Sad to say, most courts adopted this obvious, if pedestrian, interpretation of the 'learned of the breach' language." So much for approach number one.

A second candidate for the honors of "the time when the buyer learns of the breach" in this situation is equally easy to reckon. We take the actual date of delivery (the date, that is, when delivery had initially been promised but does not arrive) to do the market minus contract calculation. This is in fact how the problem was usually dealt with by the common law and how, in fact, it was handled by the Fourth Circuit in the case of *Hess Energy, Inc. v. Lightning Oil Co., Ltd.*, 338 F.3d 357 (4th Cir. 2003). In our hypothetical, that date would be December 15 and the measure of damages a whopping $0.83 per bushel. Technically this may be the easiest result to reconcile with the language of Article 2. Whatever is true of the repudiation, we reason, the breach doesn't actually occur until the date when delivery is not made as promised. So the buyer can't "learn of" the breach until that moment. Also, §2-723(1) is respected because that subsection is stated to apply only when an action is brought before the scheduled time for performance. But then we can have second thoughts. Why should Buyer here get the $0.83 per bushel in damages where it would have been entitled, under the clear mandate of §2-723(1), to only $0.05 if it had sued on December 1 instead of during the following January? What purpose would there be in the drafters' allowing for such an increase in damages principally because the suit was delayed?

Finally we come to the third and final contender: It has been argued that the appropriate time to set the market price on which the buyer can recover is the date, whatever it is, at the end of that "commercially reasonable time" given to the buyer to await performance under §2-610(a). One problem here, of course, is that we don't know exactly what that date is. The Code at other points refers to something being "commercially reasonable," but it seems particularly tricky to apply this language to judge when something *should have* happened when the whole problem is that nothing *did* happen. And what was supposed to happen anyway? Section 2-610, as we have noted before, says only that the buyer may await performance for such a length of time, but it doesn't say anything about

Buyer having to do anything once that time has run. Why can't Buyer just go on waiting and waiting if that is its considered choice? Comment 1 says that if the nonrepudiating party "awaits performance beyond a commercially reasonable time he cannot recover resulting damages which he should have avoided," but that seems to beg the question. If the buyer eventually decides never to purchase other goods in substitution—that is, not to cover—what does it mean to say that it shouldn't be entitled to resulting damages it could have avoided? In our case, should Buyer sue asking for the full $0.87, and if we argue (along with Seller) under this interpretation that this is somehow an inappropriate amount, what are we telling Buyer it should have done to avoid running up the damages that high? We certainly can't be saying it should have covered even when it had no desire to do so. Section 2-712 makes cover totally optional for the buyer. Perhaps all we end up saying is that Buyer could have avoided seeking damages of $0.87 per bushel by instructing its attorneys not to be so greedy and to ask instead for another, lower figure.

In spite of all the problems with reading §§2-712 and 2-610 together in this way, a number of commentators have concluded that this is indeed what the drafters would have preferred in this situation and what should be done. First we come to some conclusion about when a commercially reasonable party in Buyer's position would have realized that Seller in repudiating meant what it said and would not be changing its mind. We must settle on the date when such a reasonable buyer would wake up and smell the coffee so to speak and resign itself to the fact that it wasn't going to get any wheat from this Seller in December. Having come to rest on some date sometime after June 1 but presumably before December 15, we take the market value of wheat in Buyer's locale on that date and toss it into the §2-713 formula.

It may indeed be that this middle road is the one the drafters would have preferred in the situation. That turns out to be the conclusion of a number of commentators who have looked at the problem, and a goodly number of courts. See, for instance, the discussion in *Cosden Oil & Chemical Co. v. Karl O. Helm Aktiengellschaft*, 736 F.2d 1064 (5th Cir. 1984). It's only fair to point out, however, that the drafters didn't draft a statute that made it easy to reach this result. White and Summers conclude, following an exhaustive and detailed discussion of this conundrum, that the preferred interpretation is to stick with the common law result of measuring the damages as of the time set for delivery:

> Pre-Code common law, the Restatement (First) of Contracts, and the Uniform Sales Act all permitted the buyer in an anticipatory repudiation case to recover the contract-market differential at the date for performance. Before we permit the drafters to upset such uniform and firmly entrenched doctrine, we can rightfully ask for at least a sentence or two of comment and more explicit statutory language than "learned of the breach."

Perhaps the best we can do when all is said and done is to quote the court in the *Cosden Oil* case, which observed in a footnote: "The only area of unanimous agreement among those who have studied the Code provisions relevant to this problem is that they are not consistent, present problems in interpretation, and invite amendment." Amen to that.

7. This example presents a second of the great controversies involving application of §2-713: Is the buyer free to sue for the market minus contract measure of damages when it did in fact cover and covered at *below* the market price? Marinara argues for $3 per pound as the difference to which it is entitled under §2-713. Herb claims that because that company was able to buy the oregano it needed for $17, it was only damaged to the tune of $2 per pound and can be fully compensated by an award of that amount. What result?

   Again there is a difference of opinion among the experts. One side relies upon a strict reading of §2-713, which simply says that the aggrieved buyer is entitled to recover in this fashion. It doesn't say that the aggrieved buyer, in the event it should not cover, can get this much. Note also that §2-711 (the font of all wisdom about buyer's remedies) has a nice and simple *or* between subparts (1)(a) and (1)(b). Another argument for this position goes beyond the text. If the buyer makes many purchases of similar stuff over a period of time at a variety of prices, it may be possible for the breaching seller to point to just about any of these purchases, and in particular, one at a price near to or even lower than the contract price, and characterize it as the buyer's "cover" to replace what the seller didn't deliver. The seller, it is feared, might be able to wriggle its way out of paying damages for its breach just because the buyer had made other advantageous purchases of the same product sometime after seller's breach or repudiation. The problem might not seem so acute in the hypothetical we are considering, at least if we assume that Marinara usually buys only a given amount of oregano during any one year. If, however, the buyer is someone who regularly trades in goods and who will normally order as much as it can from whomever it can if the price is right, the potential for seller's abuse of a contrary interpretation is significantly greater. At least two cases support this interpretation: *TexPar Energy, Inc. v. Murphy Oil USA, Inc.*, 45 F.3d 1111 (7th Cir. 1995), and *Allied Semi-Conductors Int'l, Ltd. v. Pulsar Components Int'l, Inc.*, 907 F. Supp. 618 (E.D.N.Y. 1995).

   Those who would limit Marinara to $2 per pound here, and in general limit the buyer who covers to damages as measured by §2-712 even if (especially if) §2-713 would produce a heftier sum, point first of all to the general policy enunciated in §1-305(a) that Code remedies are to be applied for the purpose of giving the wronged party adequate compensation but, they would emphasize, no more than is necessary for this purpose. Note also the last Comment to §2-713:

> The present section provides a remedy which is completely alternative to cover under the preceding section and applies only when and to the extent that the buyer has not covered.

This is only a Comment, true, but shouldn't it be given some weight in deciding the issue? And to the argument that we saw earlier (that the breaching seller should not be given the option of deciding for the buyer which, if any, of its purchases of like goods served as cover), the response is that this is just a matter of proof with which the courts can and will deal should it become necessary. For one decision that followed this approach, denying the buyer the right to recover damages measured by §2-713 when it could not demonstrate that it had been damaged to a degree not fully compensated for by what was in effect the cover minus contract amount, see *NHF Hog Marketing, Inc. v. Pork-Martin, LLP*, 811 N.W.2d 116 (Minn. App. 2012).

8. a. Barbara has accepted the watch and paid for it at the contract rate. The question here is how much she can recover from the buyer for a very blatant breach of warranty. With respect to accepted goods, we look to §2-714. Before we do so, however, we want to remind ourselves once again about the importance of §2-607(3)(a). Now is as good a time as any to look at that subpart one more time. Having done so you are entitled to move on to §2-714(1):

> [The buyer of accepted goods] may recover as damages for any nonconformity of tender the loss resulting in the ordinary course of events from the seller's breach as are determined in any manner which is reasonable.

That's a very general statement. Read on to subsection (2):

> The measure of damages for breach of warranty is the difference at the time and place of acceptance between the value of the goods accepted and the value they would have had if they had been as warranted, unless special circumstances show proximate damages of a different amount.

This fits Barbara's situation exactly. The value of the watch she accepted was, at the time of sale, approximately $800. The value that the watch would have had if it had been as warranted was $3,500. Barbara is entitled to $2,700 in damages. Notice that at the time of purchase, Barbara had not only been expecting the higher quality watch, but also could reasonably have thought that she was getting a bargain, at something like $300 off the standard price. The $2,700 recovery, measured as it is by the true value of *what she was promised* and not by the purchase price, gets her the economic equivalent of everything she was promised including the benefit of her bargain.

In *Goodwin v. Durant Bank & Trust Co.*, 952 P.2d 41 (Okla. 1998), the buyer of a backhoe sought damages for an express breach of warranty that what he was to receive was a 1990 model. Instead it turned out he was delivered a 1987 unit. The Oklahoma Supreme Court had no difficulty in concluding that he was due damages measured by "the difference in value between a 1987 Case (model 580K) backhoe and a 1990 model of the same type and caliber equipment." Another interesting story is told in *JHC Ventures, L.P. v. Fast Trucking, Inc.*, 94 S.W.3d 762 (Tex. App. 2002). Fast Trucking, which used dump trucks to haul bulk materials such as sand, gravel, sludge, and the like, contracted to buy five new "Shape Shifter" trucks from their manufacturer. The Shape Shifters were unlike typical dump trucks in that they were built with a newly patented design that was touted for its "dual-dumping capabilities." They could dump their loads either from the rear, as would a normal dump truck, or could dump the stuff being hauled directly to the ground through a set of doors in the belly of the hopper. At least that's how they were supposed to work. The Shifters' belly dump doors could never be made to work properly—not just on these five machines but in general—and it turned out that the whole idea of creating such a revolutionary dump truck would have to wait to a later day. At trial, the buyer was awarded damages based on the §2-714(2) formula for the five trucks he bought that were not as warranted. What value would the trucks have had "if they had been as warranted"? It was hard to say exactly; no such truck had ever (successfully) been produced. The jury was allowed to conclude that this value was properly measured by the price that Fast Trucking had agreed to pay—given that it believed it was buying a truck with unique dual-dumping capabilities. And what was the value of the actual goods accepted? That was determined to be equivalent to the standard price of a like-sized regular single action back-dump-only truck. The difference between these values was upheld by the appellate court as a correct measure of the damages incurred by the buyer for the fact that the trucks did not, and in fact apparently could never, operate as warranted. The measure of damages was the value of the promise unfulfilled.

b. If the value of what she bought would have been $2,800 if it were as promised, then she is entitled to recover $2,000, which is just $2,800 minus the actual value of what she got ($800). She ends up with a total value of $2,800: $2,000 in cash and $800 in watch. Recall that she originally paid Sam $3,200. She still seems to come out behind by $400 and indeed she does, but the reason for this is that she initially made a *bad* bargain with Sam. She agreed to and did pay $3,200 for a watch worth only something like $2,800. Assuming he didn't put a gun to her head, Sam is not responsible for this loss. He *is* responsible in the contract, and by the measure of damages he will be made to pay, for her getting what she was promised by him, and that is $2,800 in value, however you slice it up.

9. a. This problem is based on *Rose v. Mercedes-Benz U.S.A., LLC,* 882 N.E.2d 112 (Ill. App. 2007). The Illinois Appellate Court determined that the buyer could recover damages "even when the [admittedly defective] vehicle had been traded in for its fair market value." This is so because buyer's potential damages under the contract minus market measure of §2-714(2) are to be measured as of *the time the car was sold to the buyer* and not some later time. The same conclusion was reached in *Shoop v. DaimlerChrysler Corp.,* 864 N.E.2d 785 (Ill. App. 2007), and *Mayberry v. Volkswagen of America, Inc.,* 692 N.W.2d 226 (Wis. 2005).

As the Wisconsin Supreme Court stated in *Mayberry*:

> We reject Volkswagen's claim that the "special circumstances" language in §402.714(2) prevents the plaintiff from maintaining her action by calculating damages based on the difference in market value and actual price at the time of resale. We hold that pursuant to §402.714(2), the appropriate method for measuring damages in this case is the difference between the warranted value of the vehicle in question and its actual value at the time and place of acceptance. When the plaintiff has established a prima facie case of damages under this standard, the "special circumstances" clause of §402.714(2) should not be construed so as to completely bar her breach of warranty claim simply because she used the defective product for a period of time and later resold it for more than its fair market value.

b. Unfortunately for the plaintiff in the *Rose* case, it was held that this proffered evidence—what the appellate court characterized as "lay person evidence regarding [her] subjective belief as to the diminished value of the subject vehicle at the time the vehicle was purchased"—should not have been admitted as evidence by the trial court. Although lay opinion evidence is not always to be excluded, a foundation must be laid for such evidence, and the necessary foundation had not been laid by the plaintiff in this case. It did not help, of course, that the plaintiff-buyer had testified that she had just "pulled a number out of the air" in coming up with the 50 percent figure. For another case where the court found such subjective "evaluation" by a disgruntled buyer insufficient to produce a question of fact for the jury of what the defective auto was worth at the time it was purchased, see *Hill v. Mercedes-Benz U.S.A., LLC.,* 619 S.E.2d 353 (Ga. App. 2005). Contrast these cases with the *Shoop* case cited in the prior (9a) part of this explanation. The buyer offered more than his own opinion as to the diminished value of the defective vehicle at the time of its delivery to him. As the court stated:

> Here, based on a visual inspection, a road test, and reviews of the Dakota's service history and technical service bulletins related to the Dakota, Thomas Walters opined that the truck's value was diminished by 35% at the time of purchase. Walters used the valuation guide of

> the Kelly Blue Book and his professional experience in estimating the Dakota's diminished value. Walters believed that the Dakota had these manufacturing defects at the time of sale. Plaintiff's second witness, Joseph Pennacchio, opined based on a review of the repair records that the value of the truck at the time of purchase was $22,300. Both of these witnesses were experienced in the inspection or appraisal of vehicles.

"Accordingly," the appellate court concluded, "the testimony of plaintiff's opinion witnesses created a genuine issue of material fact that the value of the Dakota was diminished at the time of the sale."

10. a. If Crafty had been able to repair the oven so that it was just as good as new, it would be fairly easy to say that the difference between the oven as promised and as delivered was $1,200. The courts have, in many instances, used the cost of repair as a measure of damages for nonconformity of accepted goods, and that seems an appropriate measure here. The cost of repair has been seen as an appropriate measure of damages under §2-714(2) even when there was no showing that the damages awarded would actually be used to make the repair. In *Fassi v. Auto Wholesalers of Hooksett*, 762 A.2d 1034 (N.H. 2000), the New Hampshire Supreme Court affirmed the award of the estimated cost of repair of a faulty transmission that amounted to a breach of warranty arising out of the sale of a used car. The defendant sellers argue that the estimated cost of repair should not have been awarded to the buyers since the trial court had not required the buyers actually use the damage award to repair the vehicle. The Supreme Court held this to be irrelevant; even if the buyers were to continue driving the car around with the faulty transmission—as was apparently possible if perhaps annoying—they were entitled to what they had bargained for in actuality or in damages.

    In our present hypothetical, the interesting issue is how to deal with the fact that the oven, even as repaired, is not as good as it was warranted to be by the seller. If Doe can establish by some credible evidence how much less the oven is worth as a patched-up job than it would be worth new and as warranted, he should be able to add this difference onto the cost of repair to get the full measure of his recovery. The value of the oven as warranted might not be that hard to establish. If nothing else, the purchase price of $10,500 would seem to be good evidence of that value. His difficulty will be in coming up with a figure for the value of the oven now as imperfectly repaired. Perhaps he can find a person who specializes in appraising used pizza ovens who would be willing to give it a shot.

    b. Here we have the even more interesting question of what to do under §2-714 where the nonconformity is repaired and the end result is a product *even better* than the buyer ever had a right to expect under the warranty. Doe argues for $1,200, the cost of repair, but now the oven manufacturer argues that some of that expense went into improving the oven, which will work to Doe's benefit, and that the heightened value of the oven should be subtracted from what it, as a breaching seller, has to pay in damages. What do you think of this? Perhaps if Ovens can come up with a very sound figure representing the increase in value over what Doe was first promised, it may get somewhere with this argument, but I can't say that I'm terribly concerned about Doe's being "overcompensated" in this way. Others would differ.

11. Buyer should be able to subtract the "loss resulting in the ordinary cost of events" due to Seller's late delivery "as determined in any manner which is reasonable." How exactly Buyer is going to put a figure on the effect of this delay is not at all clear, and maybe it will not be able to do so, but at least §2-714(1) leaves no doubt he is entitled to try. Note also the final part to Comment 1 to §1-305:

> [A purpose of subsection (a) is to] reject any doctrine that damages must be calculable with mathematical accuracy. Compensatory damages are often at best approximate: they have to be proved with whatever definiteness and accuracy the facts permit, but no more.

So good luck to Buyer as he tries to prove the damage caused to him by the two-week delay.

An interesting case to consider in connection with the damages that can be caused by late delivery is *Franklin Grain & Supply Co. v. Ingram*, 358 N.E.2d 922 (Ill. App. 1976). The defendant contracted to sell and apply fertilizer to the plaintiff farmer's crop. The fertilizer was applied after the time called for by the agreement, too late in fact to be of any benefit to the crops. When the seller sued for payment, the buyer counterclaimed for the damages caused by the delay. An award to the buyer for damages was upheld on appeal, the appellate court concluding:

> Though there is some uncertainty about evidence of loss of yield, complicated by many factors such as weather, date of fertilizing, and other matters, we cannot say that the trial court's decision that [buyer] had been damaged to the extent of five bushels per acre is against the manifest weight of the evidence. Testimony of adjoining and nearby farmers regarding their use or non-use of fertilizer and their yields furnished sufficient evidence to support the court's findings regarding damages.

Buyer should have no trouble getting reimbursed for the $200 paid to the local warehouse to hold on to the rejected goods. This would be a classic case of incidental damages under §2-715(1) to which he is entitled in addition to any other damage he may have suffered (§2-714(3)). For a case deciding what damages were to be awarded for the late delivery—two hours after the wedding ceremony was scheduled to start—of a set of eight bridesmaids dresses, see *Sagnia-Blythe v. Gamblin*, 611 N.Y.S.2d 1002 (Civ. Ct. N.Y.C. 1994).

Note in general that for the wronged buyer to recover for incidental damages under §2-715(1), only three criteria need be met. The expenses need to have been actually incurred, they must be "reasonable" in amount, and they must represent "expense incident to the delay or other breach."

12. Doe would claim his lost profits for the five-day period as consequential damages under §2-715(2). The criteria for award of consequential damages are more extensive than those we just saw for incidental damages under the same section. The damages need to have been actually suffered, of course, and they need to be reasonably certain of calculation. As to this last point, see Comment 4. There is also the requirement that they "result from the seller's breach"—that is, a causation element. Beyond that, there are two criteria in subpart (a), each of which should sound familiar to you. First of all, loss such as Doe is claiming here must result "from general or particular requirements and needs of which the seller at the time of contracting had reason to know." If this sounds like that old standby from Contracts, the rule of *Hadley v. Baxendale*, well that's just what it is. I won't repeat here all that I might about that doctrine, as you are no doubt perfectly familiar and comfortable with it. (Note in passing: Comment 2's pronouncement that the *tacit agreement test* that was offered up at one time as a refinement of *Hadley* has been explicitly rejected by the drafters of Article 2.) The final requirement is that the items claimed as consequential damages "could not [have been] reasonably prevented by cover or otherwise." Here we have the traditional mitigation principle of the common law incorporated into the Code.

    So it's not at all clear whether Doe can get any or all of his lost profits under the circumstances. Certainly the courts have shown themselves willing to accept loss profits caused by a seller's breach as includable consequential damages, but each of the criteria will have to be met. We would want to know, for starters, how much profit Doe makes on a typical day and how well he can back up this figure. It would also be important to know whether Ovens had any reason to know, at the time the contract was entered into, that he was going to be open that particular Sunday for the private party. Or would it be enough if Doe could show that Ovens was aware that he sometimes served private parties on Sundays? This is the kind of question, you'll remember, that made *Hadley v. Baxendale* so much fun. Also it will be important to explore whether Doe could have reasonably prevented this loss of profit "by cover or otherwise." It seems unlikely that cover would have been available quickly enough to make a difference, but maybe there was some other way Doe could have prevented or lessened his losses over these five days. It's all in the facts.

Two cases are interesting to compare in seeing how the criteria of §2-715(2)(a) are dealt with by the courts. In *Smith v. Russ*, 13 S.W.3d 920 (Ark. App. 2000), the defendants had sold the plaintiff for something like $1,000 a ten-year-old used car, which, it turned out, had been stolen. Eventually—after the buyer had been stopped by the police "for being in a stolen car" and both the buyer and the sellers spent some time in jail until the whole thing was sorted out and the car returned to its rightful owner—the buyer was left without a car. The sellers would not repay the buyer his purchase price or provide him with a replacement vehicle. The buyer, needless to say, sued, invoking, as you no doubt will have guessed, the warranty of title of §2-312. Among the damages claimed by the buyer and awarded to him by the jury was $10,395 representing "compensation for [the buyer's] lost tips and wages resulting from [his] lack of transportation with which to deliver pizzas and his consequent demotion from pizza delivery driver to cook." The Arkansas Appellate Court reversed this portion of the damage award. "[Buyer]," it noted, "never presented evidence that, at the time of contracting, [the sellers] had reason to know the particular needs" of the buyer as a pizza delivery guy.

In 2002, the Fifth Circuit was confronted with the lost profits issue in a more, shall we say, conventional setting. The plaintiff had purchased a large piece of industrial machinery, a "gas compressor train," from the defendant in 1990. Parts of the machine broke down, first in 1990, and again in 1993 and 1996. In each case, the seller eventually made repair, but the buyer suffered a period in which the amount of gas that it could compress, and hence of product that it could sell, was reduced by the malfunction. The buyer sued for the profits it claimed to have lost because of its decreased production. The court held its evidence was sufficient to support the jury's finding that the loss to the buyer because of the breach, and the consequential slow-down in the buyer's operation, would have been "reasonably foreseeable" to the seller at the time of sale. *Mississippi Chemical Corp. v. Dresser-Rand Co.*, 287 F.3d 359 (5th Cir. 2002).

See also *Federated Retail Holdings, Inc. v. Sanidown, Inc.*, 2010 WL 5298113 (S.D.N.Y.), in which the plaintiff-retailer was allowed to recover the lost profit damages it suffered when it found itself having to return to the defendant-seller nonconforming goods, leaving it without a stock of goods, which it established it otherwise could have sold to the public at a profit.

The range of items that can and have been considered as legitimate consequential damages is, not surprisingly, very broad. Where a breach of warranty results in injury to a person or property, §2-715(2)(b) makes extra sure that these things are included, the only criterion being that the injury was proximately caused by the breach. Consequential damages have been awarded when the buyer has lost profit from an anticipated resale or has been made to pay damages to or entered into a settlement with other third parties adversely affected by the goods. Consequential damages are where and as you find them. On the question of what effect is to be given a provision in the contract of sale purporting to limit or modify what the buyer can recover for consequential damages, see §2-719(3) and the discussion of that section in Chapter 13.

13. Yes, Bertha should be able to deduct the $100 for each day late. The language of this subsection of §2-718 will look familiar to you. It's the basic notion which you should have studied in Contracts: A liquidated damages clause is enforceable while what is characterized as a penalty clause is not. I hope you have secure in your mind how the courts, and here the Code, will make the distinction. See also Comment 1 to this section. Unless M.M.S. can make the argument that $100 a day is an "unreasonably large" amount, Bertha should have her boat, late but for a lesser price. This figure doesn't seem unreasonably large to me. Certainly if the boat were a day or two late, a subtraction of $100 or $200 wouldn't seem inappropriate. Maybe it's because I don't sell boats for a living.

14. This question is unique in this chapter because Sam, the buyer, is also the breacher. Certainly a man who's breached a contract can't go after the other fellow for contract damages, can he? No, he can't, but under §2-718(2), the drafters have allowed for the breaching (or, we have to assume, the repudiating) buyer's getting some measure of relief under the theory of restitution. Assuming there was no liquidated damage provision in the contract, Sam is entitled to any amount by which his payment exceeds the smaller of 20 percent of the value of the total performance (which in this case equals $600) or the flat sum of $500. So Sam has the right under this subsection to get $300 back. Dave has the right to keep $500 of the down payment as a kind of statutory liquidated damage sum. See Comment 2 and *Santos v. DeBellis*, 901 N.Y.S.2d 457 (N.Y. Sup. Ct. 2009). Notice that under subsection 2-718(3), even this $300 sum is subject to offset if Dave could show any damages resulting from Sam's breach. Assuming that Dave is not a lost-volume seller and given that he has sold the used car for more than the initial contract price, there probably will be no such offsetting damages. This raises one final point for consideration: What if Dave had resold for $2,400, thereby suffering damage of $600? A literal reading of §2-718

seems to unmistakably say that Sam should not get a penny of his down payment back. The amount to which he is entitled under subsection (2) is, as we have seen, only $300. Subtract $600 actual damages from that under subsection (3) and you see that Sam should consider himself lucky that he's not being asked to come up with even more money. But if the subtraction provided for in subsection (2) is intended to work as a kind of statutory liquidated damages provision, shouldn't it fall away once real damages have been proven? In other words, here Dave actually suffered $600 damage from the breach; if he got to keep that amount and had to return only $200 of the down payment, isn't he perfectly compensated? It seems likely that the drafters meant this to be the effect of these two subsections working in tandem. Unfortunately, that isn't what they wrote.

PART VII

Leases

CHAPTER 28

Lease or Sale?

AN EXPLOSION OF LEASES

Anyone who has ever rented a car or taken a canoe out for the day knows that goods, just as they can be bought and sold, can be the subject of a lease. What not everyone is aware of, however, is the extent to which transactions in goods of every kind are under current practice cast as leases. Histories of the subject inevitably (and rightly) refer to the explosive increase in the amount of equipment leasing since the Second World War and particularly in the later decades of the twentieth century. This phenomenon is evident not just in the consumer rental of things like automobiles and canoes, but also in the leasing of equipment by large industrial firms where in the past they might have entered into straight purchases and sales. For example, many airlines rent all or most of the planes that make up their fleets. Major manufacturers regularly enter into multimillion dollar leases for the massive pieces of industrial machinery that pound away in their factories.

What's behind this accelerating interest in the lease of goods? There are a number of explanations. Some have to do with the intricacies (to put it politely) of federal income tax law. Other considerations that encourage large corporations, their counsel, and their financial advisers to structure transactions as leases have meaning only to those who recognize and appreciate the subtleties of corporate accounting. Fortunately we do not have to delve into these matters. It is enough for us to acknowledge the importance of the lease of goods in the modern business environment.

ENTER ARTICLE 2A

Presumably most leases, either of the consumer or the commercial variety, work out splendidly, and all concerned find themselves perfectly contented. But if even a small percentage of these transactions end up in controversy, the lawyers and the courts will have plenty to do. What quickly became apparent with the mushrooming number of such disputes in the second half of the past century was that the common law did not have a particularly good handle on the variety and complexity of potential problems. Unlike real property leasing, where the common law had over centuries developed a respectably rich repertoire of doctrine, the lease of personal property had never been given much consistent attention by the courts. Issues of rights and responsibilities arising under the lease of goods involving huge pieces or bundles of property and large sums of money had to be decided under the relatively unexplored and often archaic territory of the so-called chattel mortgage or the common law "bailment for hire."

From our perspective, what was even more troubling was that the U.C.C. as initially written and adopted had no special provisions relevant to the lease of goods. True, §2-102, the scope provision of Article 2, can be quoted for the proposition that the "Article applies to *transactions* in goods," and a lease of goods is certainly a transaction. But because in every other respect Article 2 specifically addresses the sales transaction—e.g., the parties are referred to consistently as the "seller" and the "buyer"—it's hard to think that the drafters had leases in mind when they were doing their work. Zealous and inventive litigants would at times importune courts to apply bits and pieces of Article 2 to the lease situation, but the results were decidedly mixed. A whole cottage industry of cases, commentary, and various schools of thought and stylized "approaches" evolved in response to the question of whether the statutory rules of Article 2 were to be applied to the lease of goods, and if so, which ones, when, and to what extent.

Fortunately for us, the question of when and whether Article 2 could be applied to the lease of goods is now of only historical significance. As the practice of commercial leasing boomed and the courts struggled with the awkward working of Article 2 when the subject was leases, the A.B.A., A.L.I., and the U.L.C. were coming to a uniform conclusion: some change was needed in the uniform laws to take leases into account. Starting in the early 1980s, a number of special committees were established, drafts drafted, and meetings convened. All this activity culminated in a decision to go forward with an entirely new Article to be made part of the U.C.C.—the first new Article ever proposed!—to be squeezed in right after Article 2. Article 2A: Leases was initially promulgated in 1987, then quickly amended in 1990 in an effort to win passage in a number of key states. As of this writing, Article 2A is effective in all states except Louisiana. The 2022 U.C.C.

Amendments, discussed in Chapter 2, revised Article 2A to address electronic lease transactions.

WHEN IS A LEASE A LEASE?

An introduction to Article 2A is now in order. Look at §2A-102. The new Article "applies to any transaction, regardless of form, that creates a lease." For the definition of *lease*, see §2A-103(1)(j). What's of immediate importance here is what is said in the negative. A "sale" or "the creation of a security interest" is not a lease. Now go back and read at least the first two paragraphs of the Official Comment to §2A-102. Again, while the Comment is clear that Article 2A covers a wide diversity of leases, "sales and security interests are governed by other Articles of this Act." Sales we know are governed by Article 2. Creation and enforcement of security interests arising from agreement come under Article 9, which is the subject of a whole other area of commercial transactions (and a whole other book). If Article 2A is an article designed exclusively for and about leases, why all the talk about transactions that are *not* leases? The answer is that parties, for a variety of reasons having to do with tax and accounting considerations, will on occasion enter into an agreement that has the *form* of a lease but that is in *substance* a sale. Article 2A is intended to govern only the arrangement that we sometimes refer to as the *true lease*, which not only has the form of a lease, but also establishes a relationship that actually operates in the economic sense as a traditional lease of goods. Parties are not allowed to import wholesale the law of Article 2A into a transaction that is not a lease, even if both should wish it, simply by calling the parties "lessor" and "lessee" instead of "seller" and "buyer," and calling the consideration "rents due" instead of "payments."

To determine the correct Article of the U.C.C. to apply to a particular transaction, the true lease has to be distinguished from what is often called the *disguised sale*, but which must more fully be thought of as a "disguised sale with a security interest attached." To understand what all this is about, follow me through a simple (if admittedly farfetched) example: Suppose that Sue owns a special pass that will allow the holder to get into the movies free for the entire year of 2023. It is late 2022. Sue doesn't think she'll use the pass that much, but her friend Bob (an inveterate moviegoer) would love to have just such an item. Sue could sell the pass to Bob. If she sold it in December 2022 for the cash price of, say, $720, that would be a sale pure and simple. She would end up with the cash and Bob with the pass. The value of the pass as it may be affected for good or ill (for example, by a raising or lowering of the standard price of admission in their area) is now totally Bob's concern. Sue has no conceivable interest in the pass anymore, neither in the legal sense nor in the economic sense that she couldn't care less what value anyone else would ever put on it.

Now suppose that in late 2022 Bob does not have that kind of cash on him, but that he expects to come into funds early in the next year. If Sue is willing, they may enter into an agreement for the present sale of the pass to Bob on credit. In exchange for the pass, Bob agrees to pay the $720 on February 1. This is still a sale. Does Sue have any continuing interest in the value of the pass over time? No. Sue has traded her ownership interest in the pass for an interest in cash. What would happen if Bob cannot or does not pay when he is supposed to? Sue will then have a right to sue him for the price. Her action would have nothing to do with the pass per se—there is simply a debt owed to her. Even if Bob were to go bankrupt, Sue would have no special right simply to reclaim the pass. Bob's debt to her is what is called an *unsecured debt*. In any bankruptcy proceeding, she would be what is termed a *general creditor* (which is another way of saying, "pretty much out of luck").

To protect herself to a degree against the risk of Bob's nonpayment, Sue might ask that as part of the sale, Bob give her a *security interest* in the pass to secure this debt. Look at the first sentence *only* of §1-201(b)(35). This is the basic Code definition of a "security interest." In older days, before Article 9, we might have said he would give her a lien on his property or something called a "chattel mortgage." The idea is that Bob would give Sue an interest in some property of his (the pass) as collateral securing the payment of his obligation (the $720 he must pay her in February). Should Bob fail in his obligation to Sue, she could still bring a simple contract action on the debt, but she would also have the right to "go against" the collateral. That is, as a secured creditor, she could foreclose on that particular piece of the debtor's property, take it into her possession, then sell it to someone else and use the money from that sale to satisfy Bob's debt to her.

The important point for our purposes right now is that in this situation, there *still has been a sale* to Bob. Sue does retain an interest in the goods, but it is not an ownership interest, merely a secondary security interest. If over the course of 2023 the pass becomes much more valuable (say a lot of really fine films are coming out), she does not share in the bonanza. She can ask for no more than $720 from Bob. Even if Bob fails to pay and she repossesses the collateral, any value in the pass over and above the amount of the $720 still owed her would legally be Bob's, not hers. If the value of the pass should plummet, she is still owed her $720 and could, if she chose, sue on that debt ignoring the pass and its value entirely.

Change the facts just a bit. Suppose their agreement is that Bob will pay $180 on the last of each month January through April. Spreading out payment of the price in this way still results in an outright present sale of the pass—only, in this instance, the buyer has agreed to make and the seller agreed to accept payment through a series of four periodic payments. It is still a sale on credit with a reserved security interest in the seller, only now with a different credit term and payment schedule. Change the situation once again to where Bob will pay the full price but in twelve installments of $60 each at the end of each month in 2023. Again we have a present sale to be paid for through a series of periodic payments. From the time they enter into this agreement in late 2022, it is Bob, as the buyer, who would have to anticipate any gain or loss from the fluctuating value in movie passes over the coming year. Sue has effectively rid herself of any investment in movie-pass property.

Now imagine that Sue's lawyer suggests that they structure this last deal as a "lease." Bob's lawyer understands the (arcane) reasoning of this approach and doesn't object. The two sign a lease. Sue as lessor agrees to lease the pass for the term of twelve months starting in January 2023 to Bob for a "monthly rental payment" of $60. Bob agrees to make his rent payments and has no right to terminate the lease before the end of the year. The economic reality of what they have now done is, as you can see, no different from what we had when they entered into a sale with payment on a one-year payment by the month installment plan. Note that the lease probably contains language to the effect that if the lessee defaults in making payments, the lessor has the right to take the leased item back. This is the security interest part of the transaction. So even though the parties have called the transaction a lease, it is in fact a sale with reservation of a security interest. Of course at the end of the "lease" term, Sue as lessor would have the right to the return of the property, a right she would not have if she were the seller. But this right to the eventual return of the pass is meaningless. It's hard to imagine that Sue would even care if she never got it back. She'd probably tell Bob to toss it out when he is done with it. What is the value of a 2023 pass in January 2024? Its worth will only be the value of the paper on which it's written.

This hypothetical serves as a simple, if farfetched, example of a lease for a term exactly equal to what we would call the *full economic life* of the article. It is in just such situations, where the supposed lease term is chosen to extend at least through the full anticipated economic life of the collateral, that a "lease" is not a lease. Why isn't it a lease? Because the premise of a lease is that something of value is returned to the lessor at the end of the lease term. This is called the lessor's "reversionary interest."

Note that it would be perfectly possible for Sue and Bob to create a true lease covering this pass. If Bob were only going to be in town for the first half of 2023, he could lease the pass for the months of January through June at a rental of $60 per month. But we see here that at the end of the lease term, the item would still have economic life left in it. Six months of free movie-going remains. Sue would undoubtedly insist on its return on July 1. Beyond this, from the very beginning Sue would have known that the market value of movie passes for the second half of 2023 continued to be of direct economic importance to her. Now it is Bob who has no stake in the value of the property following the end of the lease term.

I've given an example where it should be easy to tell whether what purports to be a lease is one in reality. What makes this one so easy is that the item has such a defined and indisputable economic life—an unusual situation. More typically, the economic life of a piece of goods can only be *estimated* or *anticipated* at the time the agreement is entered into. Courts looking into the issue will rarely have such a clear-cut case before them.

To provide assistance for the real cases, the drafters of Article 2A also offered up to the states some rules for distinguishing between a true lease and a transaction that, while *in the form of* a lease, is really not one *in substance*. These rules are found in §1-203, a section helpfully captioned "Lease Distinguished From Security Interest." This section should be of some help as we work through the examples and explanations. Just a few points before we begin. First of all, note that §1-203(a) starts out with the injunction that whether a lease is created in fact "is determined by the facts of each case." That makes sense. Prior to the amendment of Article 1 in 1990, there wasn't much more said than this, leading courts to ferret out "the intent" of the parties to the transaction. If you look about halfway through the long Comment 2 to this section, you'll see a paragraph commencing with the rather understated observation that "[r]eference to the intent of the parties . . . has led to unfortunate results." Read that paragraph and note its conclusion that §1-203 "contains no reference to the parties' intent." What then replaces reference to intent? The Comment doesn't lay out the big picture as well as it might, but what follows makes clear that the focus is on the *economics* of the transaction, by which is meant the *business economics* of the transaction as it affects the parties. A true lease is distinguished, in a phrase you see recurring in the cases, by the true lessor's having by intention retained from the outset "an economically meaningful reversionary interest" in the property. This is explained to mean that at the time the transaction is entered into, each party, the lessor and the lessee, in making its business calculation as to the deal's worth and acceptability on the terms concluded, takes into account the fact that the goods will, at the end of the lease, be returned to the lessor, and furthermore that the goods as returned can reasonably be anticipated to have some economic value left to them at that time. Since the goods will ultimately arrive back into the hands of the lessor, it is the lessor who bears the risk that this "reversionary interest" will be more or less valuable, dependent on factors like future demand for this type of property, changing economic conditions, and so forth. The lessor truly retains what we think of as the ownership interest in the goods and hence has the ultimate stake in their value at the end of the day—meaning the end of the lease.

A diagram may come in handy at this point to bring together the various elements of the discussion and to focus us on the problem that we face:

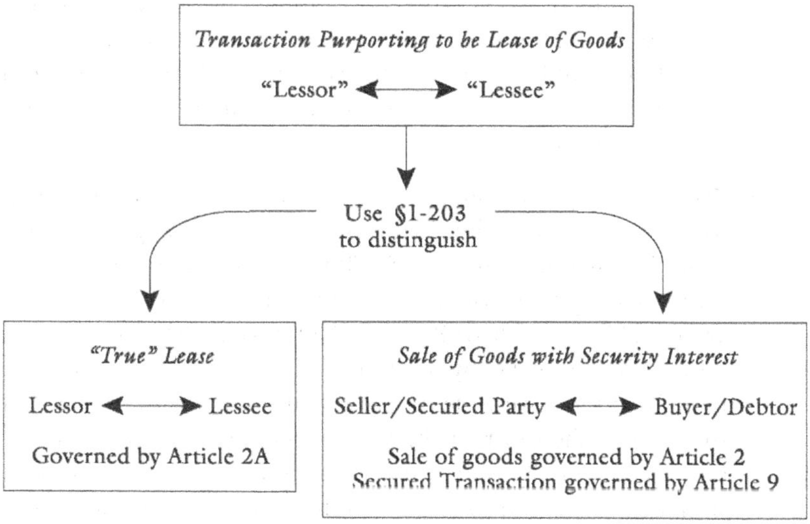

That's the big picture. To see how it is brought to life by the various snippets that come together in §1-203, we turn to some examples.

Examples

1. Professor Brock, exhausted after a hard year of dedicated law teaching, decides to take a vacation. He goes to Arrow Rent-a-Car and arranges for a month-long rental of a fairly new luxury sedan, for which he agrees to pay $1,000. Is the arrangement between Brock and Arrow a lease of the car?

2. Returning from his well-deserved vacation, Professor Brock decides that he is getting too old to continue commuting to his office by bicycle and that he really needs a gas-guzzling automobile of his own. He decides to lease, rather than buy, a car. He enters into an agreement with Smiling Sam of Sam's Autorama for a brand new Cadillac coupe. The agreement, denoted a "Lease" in all the documents, is to run for four years. Brock pays $616.26 at the time he picks up the car, which includes a "Security Deposit" of $300. He further agrees to pay $275.26 per month for each of the next 48 months. He agrees to return the vehicle to Smiling Sam "upon expiration of the agreement."
   (a) Does the transaction between the professor and Smiling Sam result in law in a true lease or something else?
   (b) Would your answer be any different if the agreement also included a provision that gave Brock the option of purchasing the Cadillac at the expiration of the four-year term for "$23,458.36 or 95 percent of

the value of the vehicle as determined by the National Auto Dealers Association Official Used Car Trade-In Guide, whichever is less"?

(c) How would you analyze the situation if the provision in the agreement *required* Brock to purchase the car after four years at the price so determined?

3. Tom Toner's Office Equipment has a thriving business catering primarily to the city's large legal community. Toner arranges for the purchase from their manufacturer, for $1,000 each, of several hundred of the latest model copying machines. He advertises widely that these machines are available "For Sale or Rent." Lydia Lawyer, whose practice is growing, needs an additional copy machine. Toner offers to sell her one of the new models and to have it delivered directly to her office for $2,450. Or, if she prefers, she can rent the same machine for $100 per month. Lydia decides to rent. She signs an agreement committing her to a minimum six-month term and to continuation of the lease thereafter on a month-to-month basis subject to her giving termination notice two weeks prior to the end of any month. Is this transaction a lease?

4. Barry Barmember, another lawyer just setting up his practice and in need of a copy machine, also responds to Toner's advertisement. He signs an agreement denoted a "Long-Term Office Equipment Lease," under which he agrees to "lease" one of the machines for $100 per month. The agreement provides that Barry will pay this amount for 60 months, at which time he will either return the machine to Toner or "at his option, purchase full title and right to the machine" for the sum of $10.
   (a) Is this transaction between Toner and Barry a lease or something else?
   (b) Would your answer be any different if the agreement signed did not contain any reference to what would happen at the end of the five-year period? All it said was that Barry was obligated to make monthly payments for 60 months and left it at that.
   (c) What if, instead, the agreement was drafted on the basis of a three-year "initial term" and a further obligation on the part of Barry to renew on the same terms and conditions for at least two additional years?

5. The Cinderblock Corporation has long been one of the area's largest construction contractors and, at any one time, may be involved in a variety of large building projects. While it owns some construction equipment of its own, when a particular project is undertaken, the project manager will determine if any special equipment is necessary for that job and for how long. When it is awarded the contract to construct a large downtown office park ("Moneybucks Plaza"), the manager of the project estimates that for the better part of two years, the work will require a specific type of 50-foot crane. With the approval of the president of

the corporation, Cinderblock's vice president for equipment and supply enters into a lease for the use of such a crane with a firm called Industrial Resources Incorporated. The transaction is characterized in the documentation as a lease for a term of two years. Cinderblock, which is to make monthly payments of $2,356.80 to Industrial Resources, is also obligated under the lease to carry adequate insurance covering the crane and its use during the two-year period and to assume all responsibility for its maintenance and repair. Do you see any reason, under the facts as you now know them, to doubt that this is a "true lease" of the crane by Cinderblock? How does it affect your view of the situation to learn that Industrial Resources operates out of a small suite of offices in a downtown office building, which, while it is well-equipped with a phone, a fax, and a number of file cabinets, is hardly the kind of place you could store a 50-foot crane, much less get it up the elevator?

Explanations

1. Yes, this is a lease of goods. I thought it worthwhile to begin with an example to leave no doubt that when you or I rent a car for a weekend out or a month in the country, it truly is a lease of goods under the Code and nothing else. To prove the point, look again at §1-203(a). The issue is to be decided by the facts of each case. Fine, we are always willing to consider the facts. Subsection 1-203(b) goes on, however, to set forth a set of four instances where we're told in no uncertain terms how to read the facts. If the lessee's obligation is for a term "not subject to termination by" that lessee *and* if at least one of the four criteria listed is established, then the transaction is to be deemed, on these facts alone, one creating a security interest and not a true lease at all. Subsection 1-203(b) sets out what the courts have begun to refer to as the "bright-line" test for determining whether the transaction created a security interest rather than a true lease. See, for example, *In re Sankey*, 307 B.R. 674 (D. Alaska 2004), which states, "Under this test, a security interest is conclusively found to exist if the lease [meaning, I assume, the transaction purporting to be a lease] is not subject to termination by the purported lessee and any one of the four enumerated conditions is found to exist."

   So we start by asking whether, in our particular instance, Professor Brock's obligation is to last through the term of what purports to be a lease and is not terminable at his will. The answer is yes. The term is one month, and Brock is given no option to shorten it at his pleasure. So the instant transaction has at least the potential for creating a security interest under the authority of §1-203(b). If, in another set of facts, the party denoted the "lessee" did have the right and power to terminate the "lease" at will, would this automatically rule out the possibility of a disguised sale with security interest? No, not unequivocally; it's just that the answer would not be definitively given by consideration of the four factors that immediately follow. Nor, for that matter, would we get much help from any distinct language in §1-203. We'd be thrown back to making the substantive determination based on "the facts of [the particular] case" as initially instructed. For the moment, however, Brock having committed himself irrevocably for a whole month, we can move on.

We now know that the transaction between Brock and Arrow, under the facts as given, must be considered to create a security interest if at least one of the factors in §1-203(b)(1)–(4) is found to exist. You should be able to convince yourself fairly easily that *none* of the factors fits the situation here. The term of the lease, one month, is pretty clearly less than the "remaining economic life" of the car. You don't have to go through any heavy economic calculation (no supply and demand curves or anything like that) to note that a fairly new luxury sedan can be expected to retain a nonnegligible economic value after one more month of use. It might be worth a little less on the used-car market, however that market is defined or its value estimated, but surely it's worth something. No one would give it up as worthless just because it had gone through one more month of wear and tear and was one month older. So the first factor isn't present.

The other factors—some of which we'll have to consider in later examples—all have to do with options or obligations on the part of the lessee, either to renew the lease or to purchase the goods, made part of the initial agreement. The simple rental agreement entered into by Brock and Arrow contains no such fancy stuff, so there's not much more to say than that none of those factors is present here.

None of the four factors being present, we cannot use the bright-line test as authoritative for calling this transaction anything other than a true lease. Does this mean that we have definitively established that it is a true lease? No, not exactly. You see that the language setting out this test says only that if this particular test is met—if the obligation is not terminable by the lessee and at least one of the four delineated factors is present—then a security interest has to be found. It says nothing about what the score is exactly if that particular test is not met. It certainly does *not* say that a security interest, as opposed to a true lease, must be found if *and only* if this test is satisfied. Nor does anything else in the following §1-203(c)–(e) give us something more on which to hang our hat.

With no "lease intended as security" having been established by the bright-line test, we are thrown back to the more general language of that relevant section, the invocation at its beginning of a "facts of each case" analysis. In and of itself, this wouldn't seem very helpful, but in the context of what we've already seen—from the history of this whole issue, the revision to Article 1 in 1990, and the official commentary to what is now §1-203 and to §2A-103(1)(j)—we are not exactly left in the dark. There should now be no doubt that in appraising the facts of any specific case, the fundamental principle, the prime directive if you will, to be remembered is that what distinguishes a true lease from another type of transaction disguising itself in a lease's clothing is that in a lease, the lessor retains an "economically meaningful reversionary interest" in the goods involved. As the court in the *Sankey* case, cited above, noted, if the bright-line test does not resolve the issue, it then becomes necessary "to examine all the facts to determine whether the economic realities of a particular transaction creates a security interest." This determination is commonly referred to by courts and commentators as the "economic realities" test.

The long and the short of it is that here Brock has leased a car. Is there any doubt that Arrow retains a reversionary interest in the car (that is, that it expects to get return of the car at the end of the month) or that this interest is "economically meaningful" to Arrow (that it is an interest of more than psychological or symbolic worth to the rental company)? If you have any doubt, just imagine what would happen if Brock never returned with the car after a month had passed. The good people at Arrow Rent-a-Car would, we can be sure, notice the absence of one of their vehicles and see it in their interest (not just psychologically) to chase down Brock and get their car back.

2. a. The facts and figures in this example come, with only minor tinkering on my part, from the case of *In re Paz*, 179 B.R. 743 (S.D. Ga. 1995). In this first part of the question, where Brock has committed himself only to a four-year lease of a new vehicle, the analysis is not really any different from the prior example. True, four years is a lot longer than a month, but it still doesn't cover the full "useful economic life" of an initially new automobile (and certainly not a new Caddy), so the situation is basically the same. You can think of it as a long-term lease, but it's a lease, in substance and not just in documentation, nevertheless.
   b. This part of the example, with Brock's having an option but not the obligation to purchase the car at the end of the initial four-year term, reflects the facts in the *Paz* case itself. Paz, the lessee, had gone into bankruptcy and was arguing (for reasons relevant to the law of bankruptcy that needn't concern us here) that the "lessor" was actually a secured party. The bankruptcy court, applying §1-203, concluded that the relationship was that of a true lease. The court first scrutinized the agreement and found no evidence that Paz as lessee had any right to terminate the lease prior to the expiration of its four-year term. It was then in the position of having to review each of the four factors, (1) through (4) of §1-203(b). It found none to be present. Because the vehicle was new at the beginning of the term, the court could not find that at the end of four years it would be devoid of economic

life, so (1) was not met. This is no different from our answer to the prior part of this example. Similarly, there was nothing in the lease that bound Paz to renew the lease for the remaining life of the vehicle or to eventually purchase the vehicle. So (2) was not met. Factor (3) could also be easily disposed of: "The lease was silent regarding renewal. Hence this factor is inapplicable."

The remaining factor, (4), deserves a bit more consideration. Paz did have the option (which is of course different than the obligation) to become the owner of the goods at the end of the four-year term. The issue then became whether this option was available to the lessee "for no additional consideration or nominal additional consideration." In order to get the car at the end of the four years, Paz would have had to part with $23,458.36 or 95 percent of its then trade-in value, whichever was less. The court, referring to the language in §1-203(d), concluded that whatever the exact figure might have been had Paz not gone bankrupt early in the relationship, the cost to him of exercising the option to buy would not have been "nominal."

The bankruptcy court, in citing to §1-203(d), makes the statement, "The Georgia Code provides that fair market value is not nominal." You could quibble by pointing out that the language of the agreement gave Paz the option of purchasing the vehicle for 95 percent, not 100 percent, of the *Official Used Car Trade-In Guide* evaluation, but it doesn't seem like a point very much worth pursuing here. Inclusion of the 5-percent reduction puts a little play in the price but doesn't suggest anything one would think of as a nominal figure. It probably just reflects the fact that "official trade-in" value of a used car may be normally somewhat higher than actual cash market value. A seller, trying to sell you a new car, will often inflate somewhat what he or she will "give you in trade-in" to conclude the sale of the new vehicle. Come back with the same used car and say you simply want to sell it to the dealer for cash, and you wouldn't be offered the same amount. What if the option-to-buy provision had been written in terms of "$23,458.36 or 9 percent of the value" as determined by the official guide? Then the situation, of course, would appear different. You could argue that however it was worded, the agreement in effect provided for nominal consideration and that, hence, the whole transaction was from its inception really a sale with the seller retaining a security interest. Of course, you'd also expect that the monthly payments that Paz would have had to make over the four-year term, prior to "buying" the car for a pittance, would have to have been that much higher for the seller to assure itself of making a respectable profit on the transaction.

Note that §1-203(d) basically speaks only of when additional consideration "is not nominal." As with much of §1-203, it speaks primarily in negatives. It doesn't say much about, and certainly never comes close to defining per se, what "nominal" additional consideration is. The introductory sentence of subsection (d) does state: "Additional consideration is nominal if it is less than the lessee's reasonably predictable cost of performing under the lease agreement if the option is not exercised." I take this sentence to mean that, in a case such as the one before us, we compare the lessee's cost of performance, meaning his return of the vehicle at the end of the term, with the cost to him of exercising the option. If the option price were set at the time of the initial transaction at $1, or even at a price so low that it would be "reasonably predictable" from the start that only a fool wouldn't take up the option, we can treat the additional consideration as nominal. Indeed, as one bankruptcy court judge noted, something like my suggested "only a fool" test has come to be widely adopted by the courts. As one court stated:

> The Economic Realities Test is also referred to in the case law as the "sensible person test," the "No Sensible Alternative But to Exercise the Option" Test, and the "No Lessee in its Right Mind Test."

In re WorldCom, Inc., 339 B.R. 56 (S.D.N.Y. 2006) (citations omitted).

So, for instance, if the option price in *Paz* had been set initially at a flat $500, say, and it would have been reasonably predictable that a four-year-old vehicle of this type would have been worth significantly more than this, then the consideration is nominal and what we're dealing with is not a true lease, but a sale. The buyer is to make monthly payments for four years, then one final payment—$500 in this situation—and the vehicle is his. In fact, the whole point of the U.C.C.'s substance-over-form approach here is that the sale was complete and the vehicle was his from the time the transaction was entered into. What the so-called "lessor" had during all that time was not ownership interest or "title" to the vehicle, but only a security interest securing the buyer's obligation to make the series and then the one final payment. Or, as we tend to say, the deal was such that it did not retain an "economically valuable reversionary interest" in the property itself.

Of course this is all spinning out further hypotheticals. In the facts as I gave them in part (b) of this example, and in the *Paz* case itself, the option price was not nominal and the transaction was a true lease. You certainly shouldn't get in the habit of assuming any long-term lease, either at the consumer or the commercial level, is likely to be just a disguised security interest. True leases are entered into by consumers like you and me, as well as by commercially sophisticated parties, all the time. The subject of the lease can be just about anything. See, for instance, *In re Harry & Larry Maronde Partnership*, 256 B.R.

913 (D. Neb. 2002), where Harry and his brother Larry, being hog farmers, had entered into an agreement with American Leasing, Inc. to expand their operation by leasing from American what turned out to be a total of 331 female swine. The lease was expected to run for at least four but no more than five litters. The lessees were to pay two isowean pigs (early weaned pigs less than 21 days old) to American, presumably per sow per litter. Evidence presented at trial indicated that there would be little or no economic life available in the sows *as breeding stock* at the end of the lease term, as more than four or five litters per female sow becomes too large. Or as the judge more daintily put it, "her size becomes a factor, as she is likely to outgrow the physical facilities and is more prone to cause mortality in the litter by accidentally laying on piglets." Such mature sows still had, however, economic value as animals held and eventually sold for slaughter. The arrangement between the Maronde brothers and American was a true lease of sows.

c. If Brock were obligated to make the purchase, whatever the price, this is no longer a lease but a "lease intended as security." It comes under §1-203(b)(2): Brock is obligated to continue paying on the "lease" during its term with no right on his part to terminate, and in addition he is "bound to become the owner of the goods." Hence, the transaction is a present sale of the Cadillac Coupe and in addition creates a security interest in favor of Arrow with the car as collateral, securing Brock's obligation to make the 48 monthly payments and the single final payment at the end.

3. Yes, this is a lease. While Lydia does not have the right to terminate the arrangement any time during the first six months, at the end of that time, the copier should still have plenty of viable "economic life." She has no obligation to renew, and while she has the right to do so on a month-to-month basis, the cost per month will never be "nominal." This seems like a lease, and it is. Notice how Toner definitely retains a meaningful reversionary interest in the particular copying machine he initially delivers to Lydia. He has to be aware from the outset that just about any time after six months, he will get notice from her that she no longer wants the machine. He would then be forced to pick it up and figure out how to continue making money off of it. This example, along with the one that follows, tracks pretty closely the Comment to the definition of *lease* in §2A-103(1)(j), which you may find helpful.

4. a. This is not a lease, but a sale with a security interest retained by the seller. It fits neatly under §1-203(b)(4): Barry has no right to terminate during the lease term of five years, then has the option to purchase the goods for "nominal additional consideration." From Barry's point of view, he is purchasing the machine for good but paying

for it in 60 installments. These installments presumably are calculated to reflect some kind of interest charge for the credit he is being advanced by Toner. But once he makes all the monthly payments (and comes up with the additional $10), the thing is his. Then consider it from Toner's angle. No economically meaningful reversionary interest here. The only way the copier is going to come back into Toner's possession is if Barry stops paying during the five years or doesn't want to fork over the $10 at the end of that time. Toner then may be forced to repossess, as could any seller who has retained a security interest in the goods sold on credit who isn't being paid the purchase price as agreed. But you (and Toner) have to assume that this would happen only if something were going wrong with the transaction, if Barry was finding it hard to pay his debts. Why else would he stop paying on something into which he has already sunk a good measure of his funds (building up what we can term in the broad sense "equity" in the machine) if after only a few more payments it would be entirely his?

b. It may not be as immediately obvious, but this should and presumably would be treated no differently from the prior situation and, hence, as a "lease intended as security." True, there is no right to purchase for a nominal consideration at the end of the term, but if we assume that all else is the same, don't "the facts of the case" lead to the same conclusion? Previously we saw that Toner was willing to part for all time with one of these copiers and would consider he has received an acceptable purchase price, if the recipient gave him in exchange a promise to pay $100 each month for the next five years—OK, and one additional token $10 bill at the end. Is it so different in the economic sense if all he gets is the same income stream with no promise of the $10?

Another way of looking at this for me is that the facts as presented in part (a) of this example indicate to us that once a machine such as this is five years old and has given five years of faithful service, it is virtually devoid of any further useful economic life as far as Toner is concerned. That doesn't mean that it won't make copies anymore, only that from the beginning he has evaluated the transaction on the assumption that, after that period of time, the machine would be sufficiently old and perhaps out of date that he really wouldn't have any use for it. Why else would he be willing to part with it for a paltry $10? If this is the case, of course, we assume that Toner has calculated the monthly payments of $100 taking into account that he has to wring all of its value to him out of the machine within those first five years. If, as we posited in (a), after that time he anticipates that he'd have no regrets having to part with it for $10, it seems that basically he'd be willing to part with it for nothing at all. He's sold the thing for five years' worth of payments of a specified sum. If that monthly sum is the same in this part of the example, if the product is identical and so on, then there's every reason to think that at the time of the transaction (here, the original term of the lease—the five years) was "equal to or greater than the remaining economic life of the goods." Hence, under the rules of §1-203, this too is a lease intended as security. The facts of this particular case allow us to conclude that from the very beginning, the economic nature of the transaction was a sale by Toner to Barry, which Barry would pay for over a five-year period. At the end of that time, the copier would be Barry's. In fact from the very date of the transaction the copier was Barry's, albeit one on which he had to make payments and one encumbered with a security interest held by Toner.

I would not want you to take from this example the conclusion that any time a purported lease is silent as to what is to happen at the end of the term it must be a sale with a disguised security interest. Far from it. Look, for instance, at the very first example of this chapter. The question becomes what the "expected economic life of the goods" is, and that would always be a question of fact for the particular case. In Example 1, we had no difficulty concluding that a new luxury sedan has an expected economic life of greater than one month, no matter how hard on it Professor Brock should turn out to be. The lessor would definitely be aggrieved, to put it mildly, should the vehicle not be returned. In the copier situation for this example, the particulars allow at least a fairly strong argument that Toner was working from the outset on the assumption that such a copier would have a useful economic life (as far as he was concerned) of approximately five years. At the end of that time, he anticipates, he really wouldn't want it back, presumably because he can conceive of no profitable use, as his business is run, for a five-year-old copier of this type. He knows that it simply isn't worth his while to have to deal with models this old or outmoded. If he hears that a potential client has on its hands a copier of this vintage, his reaction is most likely that here is someone ripe for a replacement with a new machine entirely.

This concept of "useful economic life" or "remaining economic life of the goods" is obviously important to the whole approach of Article 1's method for distinguishing a lease from a security interest, yet we're told nothing more than the invocation in §1-203(e), that it is something "to be determined with reference to the facts and circumstances at the time the transaction is entered into." I hope that is what I've been doing all along. Note that just because some goods are still in existence and being put to productive use by someone well beyond what was their anticipated "economic life" at the time of the initial transaction doesn't mean that there is something fishy going on or that someone made a mess of the initial evaluation. A lot of things can be perfectly fine and workable in the hands of their present owner without their having any kind of value to anyone else or any generalizable market value. Anyone who bought a brand new state-of-the-art computer printer anything like a decade ago knows what I'm talking about. If you have such a printer, it still may be serving you as well as it did on the day you bought it. Should you decide to buy a new printer, however, you're not going to get any trade-in value from it. You could try selling it for at least a little cash through an online ad or posting at the local laundromat, but good luck. Maybe, and only maybe, your favorite charity will take it off your hands, but even they may not find it worth their while. And forget trying to give it as a gift to one of your nieces or nephews; she or he will more than likely just ask what would make you think they'd want anything to do with "that old thing." In my experience, at least, old computer printers, as well as other computer components, often just get packed away in the rear of a closet or left out with the trash. They may still work perfectly well and have plenty of "useful life" left in them, but their "economic life" (except perhaps in the antique collector's world) is shot in an amazingly short amount of time.

For a good example of the economic realities test in operation, you may want to look at *In re Pillowtex, Inc.*, 349 F.3d 711 (3d Cir. 2003). In 1998, Duke Energy Royal entered into what was termed a Master Energy Services Agreement with Pillowtex, under which Duke agreed to install certain energy-savings equipment valued at $10.41 million in ten different Pillowtex facilities. Duke removed the existing equipment at these Pillowtex locations, then provided and installed the new equipment. In exchange, Pillowtex was to pay Duke on a monthly basis "one-twelfth of its annual energy savings" (really a set amount the parties had agreed to in advance) for the next eight years. Although the agreement was for an eight-year term, in it the parties stipulated that the "useful life" of the energy fixtures was some 20 to 25 years. The agreement further provided that at the end of the eight-year term, Duke had a series of options. One was to remove the new equipment it had installed and replace that equipment "with equipment comparable to" that originally in place. Another option Duke would have would be to "abandon the Equipment in place." When Pillowtex went into bankruptcy, Duke argued that this agreement was a true lease. The district court and later the Third Circuit found otherwise. As the circuit court noted:

> The economic realities of the particular transaction in this case belie any [plausible intent on Duke's part to take back possession of the equipment at the end of the 8 years rather than just abandon it]. Although the useful life of the lighting fixtures is 20-25 years, eclipsing

> the [agreement's] 8-year term, it would be unreasonable for Duke to incur the high costs necessary to repossess the fixtures: namely, the costs associated with removing, scrapping, and replacing the fixtures. Also, the uncontroverted evidence in this case establishes that there is little (if any) market value for used lighting fixtures. In short, it would have made no economic sense for Duke to spend large amounts of money to reclaim the fixtures, especially in the face of poor resale prospects.

The agreement was held not to be a true lease, but a sale on secured credit of the energy-saving equipment with the price to be paid over eight years. At the time the agreement was entered into, it would have been clear that the only economically realistic outcome at the end of the eight-year term would have been for Duke to have abandoned the equipment, giving Pillowtex full ownership.

c. If the facts are such that the copier has an "economic life" as determined at the time of the transaction of only five years, then this too would be a sale with a reserved security interest. This comes under §1-203(b)(2).

5. This seems clearly to be a lease. Even if the crane were getting pretty old as cranes go and perhaps destined for retirement from day-to-day service at the end of the two-year term, you'd have to assume it would have some nonnegligible value, as scrap metal if nothing else, when its time came to go wherever it is that old cranes go. Industrial Resources is not renting out disposable construction equipment or anything like that, and its intention from the inception of the deal to insist upon return of the crane at the end of the two years, its own reasonable perception of a valuable reversionary interest, can hardly be doubted.

So what's the problem? The problem is that prior to the revision of Article 1 in 1990, some courts, floundering around amidst the facts of individual cases, displayed a tendency to be distracted by certain aspects of lease transactions and make too much out of them. Seeing in one "factor" or another a seemingly clear indication of a sale and change of ownership, as opposed to a temporary change in possession as in a lease, and not having the benefit of §1-203 as we now have it, there were numerous examples of courts making bad or at least highly questionable calls. Part of this, to be fair, also stemmed from the earlier version of this section giving so very little guidance on how to deal with the characterization—true lease or security interest—issue, and unfortunate language in that version insinuating that the primary goal for the court was to ferret out the "intention of the parties" as to what manner of business arrangement they were creating. Not the least of the problems was that the reason this whole issue arises in the first place is that the parties themselves, even if you could read their minds, are not always that clear about why they are doing what they are doing and what they want the result to be. Or their intentions may be purposefully ambiguous, the transaction carried out in a way seeking to make it a lease for at least one purpose and not a lease for another.

Note the following language about halfway through the long Comment 2 to §1-203:

> Reference to the intent of the parties to create a lease or security interest led [prior to 1990] to unfortunate results. In discovering intent, courts relied upon factors that were thought to be more consistent with sales or loans than leases. Most of these criteria, however, are as applicable to true leases as to security interests. Examples include the provision of the typical net lease provisions, a purported lessor's lack of storage facilities or its character as a financing party rather than a dealer in goods. Accordingly, this section contains no reference to the parties' intent.

Not only was reference to the parties' intent removed from the section, but an additional paragraph consisting of language that is now to be found in §1-203(c) was added. Reading it, you see that again the section speaks in negatives, and nonconclusive ones at that: "A transaction in the form of a lease does not create a security interest *merely because*" this or that is to be done by one party or the other. You see now the genesis for this strange bit of statutory prose; it was intended to counter a series of individual cases that relied on one or another of these six factors almost to the exclusion of any other facts about the case to come to what the revisors call their "unfortunate results." The present language does not say that these factors may never be considered—only that the determination based on "the facts of the case" has to be made on the overall situation and, recall, with a focus on the "economics" of the relationship, not the "intent of the parties." It may help if you now read the three longer paragraphs of the Comment following the one I've just quoted.

Returning to Cinderblock and its 24-month lease of a crane, you see the particular relevance here of §1-203(c)(3). That the lease contains provisions calling on the lessee to provide insurance and take care of maintenance does not in and of itself give rise to the conclusion that the transaction creates a security interest. In fact, as the commentary suggests, it is fairly typical in what is often referred to as a "net lease." On the basis of all the facts, a court should hold this to be a lease.

I see no reason for the answer to change even when we introduce the fact that the lessor would have no obvious place to store the crane on its "return" at the end of the lease term. Apparently some decisions prior to the revision of this section took the "lessor's" lack of a storage facility as a strong and perhaps conclusive indication that it had no expectation of return of the goods. But this really doesn't follow. Why should Industrial Resources spend money on a great big barn of a storage facility when, at least if all is going according to plan, practically all of the equipment it owns will be leased out and, hence, at some construction site at any one time? When you think of it, even the typical rental car agency wouldn't have enough parking spaces if each and every one of its cars coincidentally were returned to its garage at the very same time. It counts on the fact that most of the cars are out there on the road most of the time. Is there any realistic expectation that Industrial Resources of our example would, at the end of the two years (or even earlier if the lessee fell too far behind in its monthly payments), tell Cinderblock just to keep the gosh darn thing and not bother returning it simply because it couldn't find a convenient place for the crane in its suite of offices within its filing cabinets? Presumably there are people right in that office suite whose principal responsibility and expertise is in arranging for the acquisition, disposal, relocation, and, when necessary, the short-term storage of all kinds of massive equipment, none of which would fit neatly next to the ferns or under the window. That's why they (the people, that is, not the ferns or the windows) earn the big bucks.

The other factors in §1-203(c) are all to the same effect. They're meant to undo some nasty business in a number of the earlier cases that, by stressing one aspect of the transaction or another, resulted in a true lease not being appreciated for what it was. The new version of the section wants all facts to go into the mix and the presence or absence of a "meaningful reversionary interest" in the lessor to be the key question.

One interesting situation that I did not put into the examples is the so-called full payout lease, at which §1-203(c)(1) is driving. In some instances, the type of goods and their scarcity, the general economic conditions, the relative bargaining positions of the parties, or probably a combination of all of these things, are such that the terms of the lease create (at least initially) the impression that by the time the lessee has made the final payment, it will have forked over as much as, or more than, if it had contracted to buy the thing outright in the first place. Some courts, reasoning from this fact alone, have in the past concluded that the transaction had to be a sale in disguise and not a true lease. Yet, it may still be true, even if "the present value [on which see §1-201(b)(28)] of the consideration the lessee is obligated to pay . . . is substantially equal to or greater than the fair market value of the goods at the time the lease is entered into," that the lease is not contemplated to run over the entire anticipated useful economic life of the goods. Some goods apparently can, due to inflation alone, appreciate in value even as the lessee is paying heavily for their use on a month-to-month or year-to-year basis. When the lease term is over, the lessor will certainly want them back, and will have agreed to a lease, a true lease, only on the clear understanding that it will get them back. Once again, it's all in the facts of the particular case. Section 1-203(c)(1) stands only for the proposition that, in the words of the Comment, "a full payout lease does not *per se* create a security interest."

CHAPTER 29

Provisions and Remedies in Lease Transactions

INTRODUCTION

Assume now that we have used the rule of §1-203 to determine that a transaction is a true lease. If so, it is governed by Article 2A. We will now examine some of the particular provisions of that Article. We have saved this discussion until after you have become familiar with the provisions of Article 2. This is because the drafters of Article 2A consciously used Article 2 as a model for the provisions of Article 2A. So you should have little trouble adapting your knowledge of sales law to lease law. If you look at the Official Comment to any provision of Article 2A, you will see a note on the Uniform Statutory Source, which is usually a section from Article 2. Below that, you will see notes on the Changes and Purposes of the section. These Comments often demonstrate how the provision differs from the Article 2 provision, often because of the way a lease differs from a sale. Or, as the Comments frequently state, they are changed "to reflect leasing practices and terminology."

Some provisions of Article 2A indicate changes in the law during the time between the promulgation of Article 2 in the 1960s and Article 2A in the 1980s. For example, in spite of increasing recognition of the law's need to protect consumers, Article 2 has only one rule that makes reference to consumers. Do you remember which one? It is §2-719(3), making the limitation of consequential damages for injury to the person prima facie unconscionable in the case of consumer goods. Article 2A, on the other hand, has some special rules for a "consumer lease," which it defines in

§2A-103(1)(e) as one entered into between "a lessor regularly engaged in the business of leasing" and one who enters the lease "primarily for a personal, family or household purpose." For example, §2A-106, limits the ability of the lessor to choose the applicable law or forum in a consumer lease. Recall that in Article 2, §2-302, the court limits the power of the court to find unconscionability in "the contract or any clause of the contract." But §2A-108 expands a court's power to find unconscionability to a lease or term that was induced by unconscionable conduct and to unconscionable conduct in the collection of a claim arising from a lease contract. Moreover, the court may award attorney's fees if the court finds unconscionability with respect to a consumer lease.

The provisions in Article 2A on contract formation are almost identical to those in Article 2—with one major exception. Section 2A-204 on the formation of lease contracts in general tracks §2-204 word for word. No doubt the drafters of Article 2A meant whatever jurisprudence of §2-204 there is to be followed when the transaction is a lease. There may be, however, one potential difference between the two sections in practice: The gap-filling provisions of Article 2, which can make up for a good measure of indefiniteness in many circumstances, were not carried over into Article 2A. This suggests, at least, that the measure of detail necessary to avoid failure for indefiniteness in negotiation for a lease may turn out to be somewhat greater, or at least different in some respects, than in the case of a sale. Like §2-204(1), §2A-204(1) specifies that an agreement can be established by "conduct by both parties which recognizes the existence of such a contract." And §§2A-205 and 2A-206 are analogous to those same provisions in Article 2. However, the good news is that Article 2A does not have a provision analogous to §2-207. See Huddleston, *Old Wine in New Bottles: UCC Article 2A—Leases*, 39 Ala. L. Rev. 615, 620 (1988): "To its credit, Article 2A does not contain any provision corresponding to section 2-207, the sales provision that has engendered much wasteful 'battle of the forms' litigation over contract formation." This tells you something about how much respect §2-207 gets in some quarters nowadays. Others are somewhat more charitable. Perhaps it is just that the lease agreement generally starts and ends with the lessor's version of the contract and the parties bargain out the details of price, quantity, and performance using that same form.

The analogous statute of frauds provision in §2A-201 (they even kept the number the same) shows a bit of modernizing by upping the threshold amount for the statute to kick in from $500 to $1,000. Clarifying something that probably should have been part of §2-201, the drafters of that provision in §2A-201(3) have made not only the quantity of goods leased, but also the lease term crucial to the record that evidences the oral lease. The definition of "merchant" in Article 2 is made applicable to Article 2A by §2A-103(3). Presumably it is to be interpreted in the same manner as it has been for the sales Article. While there are special "merchant rules" in Article 2A, the merchants' confirmation exception to the statute of frauds does not appear in §2A-201. The Comment to that section states that it was not included "as the number of such transactions involving leases, as opposed to sales, was thought to be small."

One important concept in Article 2A is the "finance lease." However, this concept makes sense only in the context of warranties in leases. The remainder of this chapter on leases will focus on warranties and remedies in lease transactions.

WARRANTIES IN THE LEASE OF GOODS

The discussion of warranties in Article 2 transactions in Chapters 10–15 focused on what will be expected, and what can be insisted upon, by the buyer of goods. The buyer expects to be getting good title to the property and that the goods will conform to certain standards of quality. People who lease goods will likewise have expectations that ought to be met. Lessees do not, of course, think they are getting title to the goods involved, but they do expect that the lessor is the owner of the goods (or at least rightfully holds them) and can legitimately lease them for a period of time to another. The lessee expects the right to use the goods without question and without interference from third parties. Beyond that, the lessee will necessarily have expectations, just as the buyer does, about the quality and characteristics of the goods, and will be depending on certain reasonable assumptions about what the goods are made of, how they will perform, how safe they are to use, and so on.

In other words, a lessee seems as deserving as the buyer of some measure of warranty protection. Do leased goods come complete with warranty, and if so, what are that warranty's bounds? There is no doubt that the common law recognized a measure of express and implied warranty protection for the lessee of personal property. However, while the fundamental principle of warranty covering leased goods may have been acknowledged, it had never been developed in any detail or in a systematic way, for the common law's treatment of personal property leases never progressed beyond a certain rudimentary and murky stage.

The addition of Article 2A to the Uniform Commercial Code has cleared things up considerably. That Article has its own set of warranty provisions that track, in many respects, those of Article 2 and that apply directly to warranty questions when the parties have entered into a lease of goods. We can review these sections now. In doing so, ignore for the moment any reference to the *finance lease*. This is an animal with which we'll deal in the next section and in the examples. For the moment, we are interested only in the straightforward two-party lease, in which the lessor has some property he or she is leasing to the lessee for some term. Of course, as we discussed in Chapter 28, we must assume that this term is shorter than the anticipated useful economic life of the goods. Otherwise, no matter how the parties have chosen to draft their transaction, they will not have entered into a "lease" for the purposes of the U.C.C. If the parties' deal is in reality a sale coupled with what the Comment to §2A-101 refers to as "a security interest disguised as a lease," then Article 2 governs all warranty questions as well as other sales aspects while Article 9 governs issues relating to the security interest aspect of the transaction.

As an example, we could think of Larry Lawyer and his rental of a copying machine for a year from an office supply firm. Or his rental of a car or a boat for the weekend. Now check out the following sections from Article 2A, which I've organized not numerically, but in the order of the warranty topics as we covered them in Chapters 10–14.

(1) *Warranties Against Interference and Infringement* (§2A-211). This section is modeled on §2-312 and the buyer's warranty of title, but with some obvious differences. The lessee does not expect to be getting an ownership interest in the goods or actual title. The Comment to this section reasserts that what was traditionally referred to as *the warranty of quiet possession* was abolished by Article 2 with respect to sales of goods, even if, as we saw in Chapter 10, something very much like it may remain in practice. Here, in the case of leases, the Code expressly retains this warranty of quiet possession. The basic idea is that the lessor warrants that "no person holding a claim or interest that arose from the act or omission of the lessor will be able to interfere with the lessee's use and enjoyment of the goods for the lease term." Note that the statement of when and how this warranty can be disclaimed, in terms analogous to §2-312(2), has been moved in Article 2A to the general provision on disclaimers and is found in §2A-214(4).

(2) *Express Warranties of Quality* (§2A-210). As you will notice and the Comment confirms, this section tracks virtually word for word §2-313. It has been revised only "to reflect leasing practices and terminology."

(3) *Implied Warranties of Quality* (§§2A-212 and 2A-213). Again, these track closely §2-314 on the Implied Warranty of Merchantability and §2-315 on the Implied Warranty of Fitness for a Particular Purpose.

(4) *Warranty Disclaimers* (§2A-214). Compare this to §2-316. It is basically parallel, with some minor changes. See the Comment to §2A-214. For example, any disclaimer of the warranty of merchantability must be in writing and conspicuous. It will not be effective if exclusively oral, which is at least theoretically possible under

§2-316. Exclusion by the use of "as is" or similar language must, under Article 2A, be in writing and conspicuous. This is nowhere stated in §2-316(3)(a), although it was probably intended. These changes in §2A-214 were made by the Article 2A drafters not so much because they felt that the rules for leases should be different from those governing sales, but to clear up what was thought to be some less than ideal drafting of §2-316. See Huddleston, *Old Wine in New Bottles: U.C.C. Article 2A Leases*, 39 Ala. L. Rev. 615, 658 (1988). Note that in jurisdictions that have adopted the 2022 U.C.C. Amendments, the terms "conspicuous" and "writing" in Article 2A would have the meanings used in §1-201 and in UETA. See Official Comment (g) to §2A-103 and the discussion in Chapter 6.

(5) *Modification of Remedies* (§2A-503). Here we have a pretty close copy of §2-719 with only minor variations. Certain "clarifications" of what is presumably the law under that Article 2 section have been expressly incorporated into §2A-503. See the Comments to §2A-503.

(6) *Third-Party Beneficiaries of Warranties* (§2A-216). The states are given basically the same choice of Alternatives as is found in §2-318.

THE "FINANCE LEASE" UNDER ARTICLE 2A

As you could not help noticing from your reading of Article 2A's warranty provisions, the drafters thought special recognition was appropriate for a distinct kind of transaction they refer to as the *finance lease*. What is a finance lease, and why do the rules change when that is what we are dealing with? Actually the drafters of Article 2A did not themselves first come up with the idea of the finance lease, nor did they coin the term, although as we will see, they did craft their own definition of the beast that, today in application of Article 2A, must necessarily be given its due.

The general setup of the finance lease is a creature of business necessity and the inventiveness of corporate and commercial lawyers. What makes it distinct is that a finance lease is a *three-party transaction*. Before we get to the finance lease itself, we have to think more generally about why and how a third party would come to be invited into a transaction we think of as a game for only two, the purpose of which is the acquisition of the use of goods by one from the other. Initially of course there are the two key players. Some company has or is willing to manufacture some particular item the use of which is desired by another. *A* may simply sell the goods to B. In this case, no third party need be involved, nor is Article 2A involved. This would be a straightforward sale from *A* to B governed by Article 2.

Suppose, however, that B (the entity wanting the goods) does not have the kind of cash on hand to pay the full purchase price right up front. *A*, the manufacturer, may agree to sell to B on credit, again making for a true Article 2 sale. Manufacturers, however, are not always in the position to extend credit on a single, large sale over what could be a period of many years. It is rare they would want to do this even if they could. Their business is making goods and selling them. They depend on large chunks of cash coming into their coffers each and every time some product is shipped out. Manufacturers don't want to get mixed up in the business of extending long-term credit. That is better left to financing institutions.

So here's where the third party comes in. It all has to do with money. This third party, C (no surprise), has plenty of cash on hand or can obtain it on very favorable credit terms, and is willing to lend it out to make the deal happen. In general terms, C's role is to provide B with financing. The financing party is an institution that makes its money by the business of extending credit and is only too happy to do so when the terms are right.

The most straightforward way C can become involved is if it lends the money directly to B. This allows B to make a cash purchase from *A*. The sale from *A* to B is again governed by Article 2. The loan from C to B is governed by the law of contracts and the specific provisions of the loan agreement. To protect itself against the possibility that B may one day be unable or unwilling to repay, C will typically demand that the item being purchased itself serve as collateral for this loan: C takes what is referred to as a *security interest* in whatever has been purchased with the money it advanced. This is meant to ensure that while the property itself will be in the hands of and can be used by B, should B fail to make loan payments to C in a timely fashion, C will be able to get its hands on the goods (foreclose) and recover its value that way. While the sale from *A* to B is governed by Article 2, the special relationship between B and C and the interest that C is intended to have in B's property is covered in Article 9. The law pertaining to Article 9 security interests is a topic for an entirely separate (and equally fascinating) part of your studies in commercial law. We needn't worry about it here. What's important for the time being is that if *A*, B, and C go this route, the lease form and Article 2A never come into play.

Another way for the parties to accomplish the same business result is for C itself to buy the goods from *A*. C then turns around and sells them to B, but now on credit terms B can handle. Legally now, of course, C is the seller of goods, but as you can imagine, it will not want to be stuck with all of the responsibilities a seller may have under Article 2, particularly the heavy burdens underlying the warranty provisions. The lawyers for C (the financing party) will make sure that B agrees to a binding waiver of just about any and all warranty rights it might otherwise have against C. B will agree to look solely to *A* (the original seller) for its recompense should there be anything wrong with the goods. Needless to say, an important part of the deal will be for *A* to sign something acknowledging and agreeing to take upon itself this accountability to B. Its willingness to do so is not a matter of charity—it wants to make the sale. This deal is structured differently, but the lease form and Article 2A are still nowhere to be seen. But we're getting warmer.

Yet another way that C's money can be used to facilitate B's acquisition from *A* is for C to buy the property outright from *A*, then *lease* it for a term to B. *A* gets its price for the sale of the goods immediately. B gets the use of the goods and pays over the period of use. Here, finally, we have the foundation for what has become known in the trade and in the legal lingo as the *finance lease*. The financing party is brought into the picture precisely to buy the goods just so it can rent them out to the ultimate lessee. The financing party is interested solely in financing and is neither the originator of the goods nor their ultimate user.

Much of the time, the finance lease is not a "lease" at all, if by the use of that word we mean (as we discussed in Chapter 28) an arrangement where the lessee obtains the right to use the property for some term of years *shorter* than the property's expected useful life. In a "true lease," remember, it is expected that the property will have some significant residual value after the term is over and the interest in that residual value continues to be held by the lessor. On the other hand, in what may be structured to appear a lease but is not a true lease, the stated lease term will cover what is expected to be the entire useful life of the item. Although the documents may read that the lessor will get the subject property back at the end of the lease, for all practical purposes, it is anticipated the goods will be worthless by that time. The lessor won't care about them. It plans to be fully compensated for the use of its money by the sum total of the rental over the term of the single lease. The documents may actually read that the lessee has the right to "buy" the goods at the end of the term for some nominal amount, but this just highlights how much of a sham lease we really have here.

Be careful. In the past, the commentators and the courts have often applied the term *finance lease* to a situation such as I've just laid out. The parties have in real economic terms simply done a sale from *A* to B with C providing the (secured) financing. Under the definitional scheme of the U.C.C., however, as made clear by §1-203, what we have here is *no lease at all!* Look again at the detailed language of that section and review Chapter 28 if you have any doubts. If the parties, whatever their arcane reasons and however they prepare the documents, have entered into such an arrangement where the "lessee" is in reality simply buying the goods on credit, then the transaction is not treated as a lease for purposes of the Code. Under the U.C.C., there are in effect two transactions: *A* (as seller) makes an Article 2 sale to B (as buyer). C gets what is referred to in the Comment to §1-203 as a "security interest disguised as a lease." This relationship between C (as lender and creditor) and B (as property owner and debtor) is governed by Article 9, *not* Article 2 and *not* Article 2A.

This point is important because for a transaction to be a *finance lease* under Article 2A as defined in §2A-103(1)(g), it must first and foremost be a lease under the Article 1 provision for distinguishing a lease from a security interest. This is apparent from the definition of *lease* in §2A-103(1)(j) and the Comments to both of these subsections. So it turns out that many of the transactions that, in the recent past and even today, may be called "finance leases" by the cognoscenti will really be disguised sales and will *not* be governed by the special provisions for finance leases under Article 2A! It's not clear how many Article 2A finance leases there actually *are* out there, tripartite deals in which the expected economic life of the leased property is distinctly longer than the lease term. Surely there are some, and that is enough of a reason to review the Article 2A treatment of this special case as we will do in a moment.

What then are the rules governing deals structured by the parties as finance leases but which do *not* meet the test of being true leases governed by Article 2A? The answer seems to be that parties who are sophisticated enough to enter into such an arrangement should be clever enough and have available the legal expertise to get for themselves *by individually bargained contract* results substantially similar to those laid out in Article 2A if that is what they do in fact desire. See the second paragraph of the Comment to §2A-103(1)(g): "Unless the lessor is comfortable that the transaction will qualify as a finance lease [under Article 2A], the lease agreement should include provisions giving the lessor the benefits created by the subset of rules applicable to the transaction that qualifies as a finance lease under this Article."

INTRODUCTION TO REMEDIES IN LEASE TRANSACTIONS

This explanation of the remedy provisions of Article 2A is abbreviated for two reasons. First of all, like most of Article 2A, the basic structure of the remedy provisions follows fairly closely that of Article 2. The remedies available to lessors and lessees under Article 2A are, by and large, meant to be analogous to those available to buyers and sellers under Article 2. Certainly the underlying philosophy is the same. See in Comment 2 to §2A-508 the reference to the goal of putting the lessee "in as good a position as if the lessor had fully performed the lease agreement" but no better and the parallel language characterizing lessor's remedies in Comment 4 to §2A-523.

Secondly, the drafters of Article 2A have been particularly generous with their Official Comments to these sections. There has in fact been criticism of what is said by some to be an attempt to "legislate by Comment," but the overall result has been to make the reader's task (and mine) that much easier. I will try to go through the list of available remedies, basically following the order in which we met the analogous provisions covering the sale of goods. In some instances, only a few words have been changed—the sole purpose being, in a phrase found repeatedly in the Comments to Article 2A, revision "to reflect leasing practices and terminology." Sometimes pieces of the puzzle have been moved around a bit, but the overall effect is basically the same. In those cases where the fact of a lease or traditional leasing practices called for a notably different approach or introduction of an entirely new level of complexity (as we'll see, for instance, with the concept of *present value*), we'll stop and note the difference.

There is one overriding difference between traditional practice in sales and that in lease transactions that seems to inform and run throughout these provisions. The drafters of Article 2A worked under the assumption that the parties to a lease transaction, at least a long-term commercial lease, were more likely than were the parties to a sale to include in the lease contract itself the remedies available in the event of a default. (Note from the outset this one semantic distinction: In sales, we tend to speak of a *breach*; in leases, it's a *default*.) Article 2, as we know, allows the parties, with some notable exceptions, to contract around its provisions or "otherwise agree" to just about anything they want. The same commitment to freedom of contract is apparent in Article 2A. The difference may come more in practice. In actual fact, lessors and lessees appear much more likely than sellers and buyers actually to take the opportunity in their contract documents to spell out what will happen in such-and-such an event. At least the drafters of Article 2A thought this was so and worked to accommodate this type of thing. See the "Damages" portion of the Comment to §2A-101 and Comment 1 to §2A-503.

One significant addition in Article 2A is seen right away in §2A-501, which introduces the Default provisions. Subsection (1) states that: "Whether the lessor or lessee is in default under a lease contract is determined by the lease agreement and this Article." This language has no precedent in Article 2. For sales, a breach occurs when a breach occurs and we know all about this from the Article itself. Leases, as we have just noted, are more likely to have express provisions drafted and agreed to by the parties—often very lengthy and prodigiously detailed—spelling out in no uncertain terms "the events of default." In this respect, the documents evidencing lease agreements often look more like security agreements drafted for the purpose of creating and making clear the parties' rights under an Article 9 security agreement. Note that the uniform statutory source for §2A-501 is not from Article 2 at all. Rather it is §9-601 of the original version of Article 9. If you have already studied Article 9, you will be able to appreciate this point. If you have not yet studied Secured Transactions, do not fear. The drafters of Article 2A decided, for better or worse, to model their work on Article 2 for the most part. See the "Statutory Analogue" discussion in Comment 1 to §2A-101. For our purposes, this decision was clearly for the better, as it allows us to review the Article 2A remedy provisions by tracking those we've already seen in studying Article 2.

One final pointer: The drafters stuck into Comments 3 through 5 of §2A-407 a pretty good synopsis of the special rules for finance leases. You might want to use those Comments to review. We now turn to remedies.

MODIFICATION OF REMEDY AND LIQUIDATION

Section 2A-503 governs the modification or impairment of rights and remedies under Article 2A. As you read through this provision, everything will seem more than vaguely familiar. Subsections (1) through (3) come directly from §2-719, the Article 2A drafters pausing only to rewrite to reflect lease terminology and to make explicit some things that they find implicit in the sales section. Subsection (4) is, as the Comment tells us, a revision of §2-701, but contains no change of great import.

We pass on to §2A-504, which should look even more familiar. Liquidation of damages is governed by rules borrowed from §2-718 with a touch of §2-719(2) thrown in. The drafters have, however, allowed for greater flexibility in some respects. Section 2A-504 covers the situation of a default (just as §2-718 deals with a breach) but also "any other act or omission." It allows for liquidation by the use of "a formula," not just "an amount." Liquidation under §2A-504 does not require proof of a situation in which there can be expected to be "difficulties of proof of loss" and "the inconvenience or nonfeasibility of otherwise obtaining an adequate remedy," as does §2-718(1). For other changes (indeed for a short course on the subject), see the Comment to this section.

LESSEE'S "GOODS RELATED" REMEDIES

We discussed the buyer's so-called goods-related remedies of rejection and revocation of acceptance, with the attendant issues of cure and all the rest, in an earlier part of the book in the context of performance of the contract for the sale of goods. Article 2A moves these topics from its Part 4 on Performance to Part 5 on Default. Otherwise the terminology and the treatment remain virtually identical. Section 2A-509 provides in its first subsection for the lessee's right to accept or reject the goods or to accept only some commercial units upon an improper delivery, just like §2-601. It even adopts the "fails in any respect" perfect tender language of that section. The procedure for rejection is found in §2A-509(2), which tracks §2-602(1).

The "installment lease contract" is defined in §2A-103(1)(i), which is a steal from §2-612(1). The provisions governing such a lease contract found in §2A-510 track the rest of §2-612 just as slavishly.

The general duties of any lessee with respect to rightfully rejected goods are listed in §2A-512, which has as its source parts of §§2-602 and 2-604. The special rules applicable to a merchant lessee upon rightful rejection are given in §2A-511, which follows §2-603 and one part of §2-706.

The doctrine of cure coming out of §2A-513 is the same, terminology aside, as cure in §2-508. Similarly, §2A-514 tracks §2-605, and §2A-515 on acceptance follows §2-606. Section 2A-516 on the effects of acceptance generally follows the similar section, §2-607, in Article 2. Some changes have been made to reflect the special situation of the finance lease, which was discussed earlier in this chapter, and the consumer lease, which is defined in §2A-103(1)(e). Neither special situation need detain us here.

You are no doubt beginning to get the picture of how Article 2A relates to Article 2. Imitation, after all, is the sincerest form of flattery—and, the drafters must have hoped, uniformity. To wrap up this section, we note that §2A-517 deals with revocation of acceptance. Here again we have no trouble divining the source for the general provisions. It is §2-608.

LESSOR'S REMEDIES

Look at §2A-523(1). The style, and quite a bit of the substance, should be familiar. This is an index provision, listing the remedies available to the lessor if the lessee "wrongfully rejects or revokes acceptance of the goods or fails to make a payment when due or repudiates with respect to a part of the whole." It is analogous to §2-703, which catalogs the seller's remedies in the event of a buyer's breach. Subsection (2) of §2A-523 gives the lessor's rights should it not exercise a right or obtain a remedy to which it is entitled under the first subsection. See Comment 19 for further explanation. Subsection (3) was necessary because a lessee may be in default of the lease contract in ways not enumerated in subsection (1). The lessee, for example, may be obligated under the terms of the lease to keep the goods in good repair or to have them protected by a given level of insurance coverage. These provisions are important to the lessor, who is expecting to get the goods back at the end of the lease term in decent condition. Should the lessee fail to meet its obligations under such a provision of the lease agreement, it will be a default, but not one of the sort that automatically triggers the provisions of subsection (1). The lessor will look to subsection (3) for its rights under the circumstances. See Comment 20.

In reviewing the various options open to the lessor under §2A-523(1) and the sections that follow, you should be able to make use of what you know about seller's remedies under Article 2 as we covered them in Chapter 26. If you want a bit more practice, the drafters of Article 2A have conveniently included discussion of a lengthy hypothetical in Comments 5 through 18 to this section. We'll move on to the sections themselves.

First we run into §2A-524 on the Lessor's Right to Identify Goods to the Lease Contract, which is nothing new. It comes directly from §2-704.

The next section, §2A-525, which deals with lessee's insolvency, does slow us down a bit. Subsection (1) is a revised version of §2-702, which deals with buyer's insolvency (see Chapter 26), but subsections (2) and (3) have no counterparts in Article 2. Their source is, in fact, Article 9—specifically §9-609. Here we *do* have a Code difference between Articles 2 and 2A that reflects an important practical distinction between sales and leases. When the seller sells goods, it parts with them forever. If it is not paid, it will have various means of trying to get some money out of the buyer, but it cannot simply take the goods back. If the seller is selling on credit and wants to have the right to come and retake the goods if it is not paid as it has been promised, it must look for a mechanism beyond the bounds of Article 2. The seller finds this mechanism in the *purchase-money security interest* allowed for and governed by Article 9. If—and it's a big if—the seller does secure for itself such a security interest, and if it protects that interest appropriately against other creditors, it will have the right under §9-609 to repossess the goods (which are now referred to also as the *collateral*) upon a default by the buyer. But in general, we should be clear the Article 2 seller has no such right.

The lessor under Article 2A is working under a different set of assumptions. Given that we are dealing with a true lease, which as you recall from Chapter 28, we must be if we are working within the scope of Article 2A, the lessor has from the very start always assumed that it would continue to be the owner of the goods. Further, it continues to assume that it will get the goods back at some time in the future. As long as the rent is paid, the lessee has the use of the goods. If the rent isn't paid, it is a fine old tradition in the law of leases, both of real property and of goods, that the lessor will be able to retake possession earlier than the end of the term. If you don't pay the rent on your house or apartment, you may eventually expect to be locked out with your stuff on the street. If you don't keep up with the rental payments on that car or that boat, you may find the lessor has taken it back to the lot or the showroom. Section 2A-525 reflects this facet of leasing. As the Comments elucidate, this section was included in Article 2A "to codify the lessor's common law right to protect the lessor's reversionary interest in the goods."

With that out of the way, we can look once again at §2A-523(1) and sketch out the parallels between the monetary relief afforded the lessor and those that are available to an aggrieved seller under Article 2. The aggrieved lessor may go after the lessee for cash in one of three ways: "In the proper case" it may bring an action for rent under §2A-529. If the lessor covers by disposing of the goods either through another substitute lease or through a sale, it may seek damages on a contract minus cover measure (§2A-527). Finally, it may seek damages under a contract minus market theory (§2A-528(1)), or, where the situation warrants, for lost profits (§2A-528(2)). All this is very much in keeping with the basic remedies for sellers under Article 2, with only a few changes worthy of note.

We saw in a previous chapter that the seller's action for the price is available in only a limited number of circumstances. So too for the lessor's action for the rent under §2A-529. In fact, it is even less likely to be available. Like the seller, the lessor can sue the lessee for the rent where the goods have been lost or damaged after the risk of loss has passed to the other party or where they cannot be disposed of in some way at a reasonable price. Unlike the seller, however, the lessor does not usually have a right to this type of relief just because the goods have been accepted. The lessor can sue for the rent only with respect to "goods accepted by the lessee and not repossessed by or tendered to the lessor." If the lessor has taken the goods back, or if the lessee is willing to let the lessor take them back, then the lessor is going to have to be the one to try to arrange some disposition of the goods that minimizes the damages the lessee can be made to pay. The reasoning behind this further narrowing of the right to collect directly the amount of the rent following a default is set forth in Comment 1.

Notice what the lessor can collect under this type of action should it be available. Section 2A-529 gives lessor the right to:

> (i) accrued and unpaid rent as of the date of entry of judgment in favor of the lessor, (ii) the present value as of the same date of the rent for the then remaining lease term of the lease agreement, and (iii) any incidental damages allowed under Section 2A-530, less expenses saved in consequence of the lessee's default.

The new concept here—new to the Code, that is, not to the world of finance—is that of *present value*. The idea is not difficult. Suppose a lessor was going to get rent of $100 a month, over time, for the remaining two years on the lease. A simple calculation tells us that the rent yet to come in is $2,400. But this calculation is *too* simple. It ignores the very basic principle that cash in hand today, which could be put in the bank and begin immediately earning interest, is inherently worth more than the same amount that is to be collected at some time in the future. Another way of looking at it is that if I had $2,400 today, I could place it in an interest-bearing account, take out $100 each month for the next two years, and still have some money in the account at the end of that period. Even a perfectly guaranteed income stream of $100 each month for the next 24 months is worth less than $2,400 today. There is some amount *less* than $2,400 that is the economic equivalent of the right to that income stream over that period of time *assuming* some particular rate of interest. This is the present value of that income stream, or those anticipated payments over time. Given a periodic payment amount, the number of periods and an assumed or agreed-upon interest rate, it is a matter of mathematics (more often now a matter of consulting an available table or cranking up a calculator) to find the equivalent present value.

You can see why the present value concept comes into play in remedies calculations once we are talking about leases. Typically the lessor is to get its money over time. If for some reason it is entitled to a judgment, that judgment is calculated as a lump sum. Our system doesn't traditionally award plaintiffs the right to receive bits and pieces of a judgment over time. So lease remedies must necessarily, if they are to be fair to the lessee and not overly compensate the lessor, take into account the present value concept. Hence the definition of *present value* for Article 2A purposes in §2A-103(1)(u):

> "Present value" means the amount as of a date certain of one or more sums payable in the future, discounted to the date certain. The discount is determined by the interest rate specified by the parties if the rate was not manifestly unreasonable at the time the transaction was entered into; otherwise, the discount is determined by a commercially reasonable rate that takes into account the facts and circumstances of each case at the time the transaction was entered into.

See also the Comment to this definition. Once you have the concept of present value firmly in place, there isn't that much that is new or challenging about the monetary remedies in Article 2A.

See, for example, the working of the cover minus contract measure in §2A-527(2). The basic calculation when the goods have been relet is the subtraction of the present value of what will be made by way of cover from the present value of the original lease. For the lessor to be entitled to this amount, the substitute or cover lease must be made "in good faith and in a commercially reasonable manner." Furthermore, the lessor must be able to establish that the new lease agreement is "substantially similar to the original lease agreement." The drafters of Article 2A recognized that this test of "substantial similarity" might be difficult in some instances. Unlike resales, where typically what the seller gives in the cover contract will be pretty much what it was to give to the breaching buyer, lease contracts may differ in many ways that can make direct comparison tricky. The drafters provided us with a lengthy set of Comments, Comments 4 to 7, on the substantial similarity issue. Note first of all, in Comment 4, that whether the new lease agreement is substantially similar to the original is to be decided on a case-by-case basis. Note further, as expressed in Comment 5, that even if there are significant differences between the two leases, this does not necessarily rule out recovery under this section:

> If the differences between the original lease and the new lease can be easily valued, it would be appropriate for a court to find that the new lease is substantially similar to the old lease, adjust the difference in the rent between the two leases to take account of the differences, and award damages under this section.

This Comment concludes with a helpful example that you may want to look at.

The third measure of damages to which a lessor may refer is the standard contract minus market value, here given in §2A-528. This is substantially the same as §2-708(1) at which we have looked, revised here to take into account the present value problem. (On the proof of market value see §2A-507.) Like its Article 2 precursor, §2A-528 has a second part that gives the lost-volume lessor the right to calculate its damages in a way analogous to the lost-volume seller's rights under §2-708(2). For an example dealing with the "lost-volume lessor," see *Collins Entertainment Corp. v. Coats and Coats Rental Amusement*, 629 S.E.2d 635 (S.C. 2006). Note that §2A-530 provides for the lessor's incidental damages in virtually the same language as we saw in §2-710 with regard to the seller.

Article 2A does provide for damages in one situation that Article 2 had no need to consider. Look at §2A-532. If the lessee returns the goods in a damaged condition or in worse shape than is permitted under the lease agreement, the lessor must necessarily have a right to recover for this injury, and it does.

LESSEE'S REMEDIES

Since we have already explored the concept of present value as it is used in Article 2A, as well as the notion of the "substantially similar" lease, there is nothing that should keep us from taking on the lessee's remedies under Article 2A at a particularly brisk pace. Section 2A-508 serves as an index. Subsection (3) is new (see Comment 4) and covers a default by the lessor that does not deprive the lessee of the goods and which is not so serious as to justify a rejection of the goods or a revocation of acceptance. For example, suppose the lessor has agreed in the lease to keep the leased goods in good repair or to provide regular tune-ups and it fails to do so. The lessee should be able to get this work done elsewhere and sue for the cost of this work.

We have already discussed the lessee's so-called goods-oriented remedies of §§2A-509 to 2A-517. Section 2A-518 provides for the lessee who does not get the goods or who has to reject them to "cover" in one form or another and sue for the difference between what it would have had to spend and what it must now pay on the substitute contract. Once again there is the criterion that the substituted agreement be "substantially similar" to the original lease and a set of Comments (3 to 7) that try to flesh out this concept. And once again the calculation of damages must take into account the present value aspect of this type of transaction.

An award of damages based on the market minus contract measure is provided for in §2A-519, again taking into account present values. Subsection 2A-519(4) gives the measure of damages if the lessee's complaint is a breach of warranty, in terms reminiscent of §2-714. Section 2A-520 sets out the concepts of incidental and consequential damages of the lessee in terms basically those of §2-715. Section 2A-521 on the lessee's limited rights actually to obtain withheld goods in an action for specific performance or under the right of replevin tracks §2-716. Finally, note the lessee's right to the goods on the lessor's insolvency under §2A-522.

Examples

EXAMPLES

1. Benny wants to open up business as a distributor of fresh fish to local stores and restaurants and realizes he will need a special type of refrigerated truck for his operation. He finds that just the type of truck he needs is manufactured by Acme Refrigerated Incorporated. Acme suggests a certain one of its models (the "Superchill") as having sufficient refrigeration power to keep the temperature in the storage compartment down to what Benny has indicated he will need (below 40 degrees Fahrenheit). Acme is willing to decorate a truck with Benny's logo and sell it to him, but Benny does not have the cash to pay for the expensive vehicle, and Acme will not extend him credit. Benny contacts the firm of Cartage Services, which carries on an extensive business selling, renting, and financing the purchase of commercial vehicles in his community. Cartage says it has no suitable refrigerated truck that it could rent to him. A deal is eventually arranged in which Acme will outfit a Superchill and paint it to Benny's specifications. Cartage contracts to buy this truck from Acme. Benny enters into a lease of the truck from Cartage at a monthly rental of $1,000 for a term of six years. Prior to signing this lease, Benny is given a copy of the contract of sale entered into by Acme and Cartage. Is the agreement between Benny and Cartage a lease governed by Article 2A? Review §2A-103(1)(j) and, more importantly, §1-203. It will help you to know that a truck such as the one involved can be expected to remain in usable condition for between 10 to 12 years. There is a regular market in six-year-old used trucks.

2. Is the agreement between Benny and Cartage a finance lease under Article 2A? See §2A-103(1)(g). Would your answer be different if you found out that as part of the agreement, Cartage agreed to be responsible for repairs on the truck if and when they became necessary?

3. Assuming this does qualify as a finance lease, what term does Article 2A use for Acme? How does it refer to the legal relationship between Acme and Cartage? Between Benny and Cartage? See the definitions in §§2A-103(1)(l), (x), and (y).

4. The truck is delivered to Benny and he accepts it. He uses it without complaint for a few months. Then the summer comes. He discovers that no matter how high he turns up the control on the refrigeration unit, the inside of the truck where the fish are kept gets warmer than 40 degrees. In addition, the windshield wipers don't work at all the first time he tries to turn them on. Does Benny have any rights against Cartage under his lease contract because of these problems? See §§2A-212 and 2A-213.

5. Does Benny have any remedy available against *anyone?* See §2A-209.

6. Can the lessee in Benny's position ever have any warranty rights against the finance lessor? If so, when? See §§2A-210 and 2A-211(1).

7. Even if, in the case as it stands, Benny has no warranty rights against Cartage, can he at least withhold his monthly rental payments until these defects are cleared up? See §2A-407.

8. Finally, suppose that Benny does bring suit against Acme. The manufacturer is able to point to a disclaimer of warranties conspicuously laid out in the contract of sale it entered into with Cartage. Can this disclaimer have any effect against Benny, who after all, was not a party to the sale agreement?

Explanations

1. This arrangement should easily meet the Article 1 test for being a true lease. We look, as that subsection tells us to, at the facts of the particular case. We may assume that Benny's obligation is for the full term of six years and not terminable by him, but none of the four factors in §1-203(b)(1)-(4) is present. The term of the lease is not "equal to or greater than the remaining economic life of the goods," Benny is not obligated to renew the lease or become the owner of the truck, nor has he any option whatsoever to become its owner.

2. This should be a finance lease under Article 2A. As you can see, there are three criteria. First of all, Benny was the one to select the truck. Cartage did not select the goods, nor did it manufacture or supply them. The principal role of the finance-lessor is to provide the funds. It is not involved with the product itself. Often the lessor is simply a financial institution, something like a bank, which wouldn't know the first thing

about trucks or the like, but the fact that, here, Cartage has more experience and may select or supply other trucks does not matter. See the Comment, which states that "[a] lessor who is a merchant with respect to goods of the kind subject to the lease may be a lessor under a finance lease."

The second criterion is that "the lessor acquires the goods or the right to possession and use of the goods in connection with the lease." The drafters acknowledge that this "in connection with" requirement will need some later fleshing out by the courts, but there is no doubt it is met by the facts here.

Finally, the lessee must have been given an opportunity to know certain key terms of the supply contract, some "advance notice" as it is said, prior to obligating itself under the lease. Here we are told that Benny was actually given a copy of the agreement between Acme and Cartage prior to his signing the lease, so condition (A) is met. The original version of Article 2A presented to the states in 1987 had the mechanism set forth in this (A) as the only way the advance notice could be given. Representatives of finance lessors objected. Among other things, it would have meant that for a finance lease to meet the Article 2A test, the lessee would have had to have seen *all* of the terms of the supply contract, including the price the lessor paid the supplier. Not all finance lessors were happy with that prospect. This accounts for the more limited notice mechanisms provided for in (B) through (D), which were added to the 1990 official version of Article 2A.

This would still be a finance lease under Article 2A even if Cartage did have the repair obligation. See the Comment. "[T]his definition does not restrict the lessor's function to the supply of funds. . . ." And later, "[t]he lessor is not prohibited from possession, maintenance or operation of the goods, as policy does not require such prohibition." If the three criteria of the definition are met, that is enough.

3. Nothing tricky here. Acme is the *supplier* and its arrangement with Cartage is the *supply contract*. The contract between Benny and Cartage is the *lease contract*.

4. Benny will not have rights against Cartage. Whatever rights he may have would have to be based on an implied warranty of one sort or another. The failure of the windshield wipers would be a breach of a warranty of merchantability. The truck is in this respect not "fit for the ordinary purposes." The fact that the refrigeration doesn't meet Benny's particular needs would be a failure of an implied warranty of fitness for a particular purpose. But both §§2A-212 and 2A-213 are clear: The lessor does not give these implied warranties in a finance lease. Benny's relief, as we see in the discussion of the next question, must lie elsewhere.

5. Benny can go against Acme, the supplier, for the breach of these warranties. This *pass through* under §2A-209(1) of the supplier's warranties (made part of the supply contract as a matter of Article 2 sales law) to the ultimate lessee in a finance lease is, in the language of Comment 1, "self-executing." All Benny need show is that the warranty of merchantability and an implied warranty of fitness for a particular purpose were warranties "in connection with or as part of the supply contract." Could he possibly run into trouble when he tries to show that the supply contract contained, by virtue of §2-315, an implied warranty that the storage compartment would cool down to below 40 degrees? After all, this seems to be a "particular purpose" of Benny's, not Cartage's. But I don't see how this could really be held against Benny. Don't forget, if this is an Article 2A finance lease, the assumption is that the goods were acquired "in connection with" this particular lease. So if Benny needed the fish to stay this cool and was renting a suitable truck from Cartage, it *was* the finance lessor's particular purpose to obtain a truck that would meet its particular lessee's particular requirements.

   Of course it would have been better for Benny to have insisted that anything this crucial to him be included as an express warranty in the supply contract. He has his right to advance notice of what's in this supply contract, at least as far as warranties are concerned, so he could check that he was getting the protection he needed. Do you see why the alternative mechanisms of §2A-103(1)(g)'s third criterion are written as they are?

6. The finance lessor can be stuck with warranty liability to its lessee, but it should be able to avoid any such problem by careful handling of the situation. Under §2A-210, the finance lessor *can* make express warranties. This section does not have the automatic exemption for the finance lessor of those creating the implied warranties of quality we just looked at. You can appreciate why the representatives of Cartage will be careful not to make any "affirmation of fact or promise" about the Superchill. That kind of talk they can and will leave to Acme and its representatives.

   Even less likely is that Cartage will have to worry about any warranties under §2A-211. Under subsection (2), the finance lessor is automatically protected from any liability "by way of infringement or the like." The finance lessor is not excluded from giving the warranty of quiet possession by subsection (1), but it would be liable only if the other's claim arose from its own act or omission. Cartage will, at the time of the deal, presumably ask for the appropriate back-up documentation to assure itself that Acme owns the truck and can rightfully sell it.

7. Benny has to keep making his payments. This is the so-called *hell-or-high-water provision* applicable to the finance lease. It is "so-called" because the

lessee is expected to continue sending in those rent checks come hell or high water. Virtually all finance lease arrangements that have been drafted in the past make this an explicit part of the lease agreement. (Remember, it is generally the financing institutions that do the principal drafting when they're lending the money. If you're borrowing money from a bank, you're going to have to live with the bank's forms.) Section 2A-407 is just intended to make this result "self-executing." Read the first Comment to this section. Look back to Comment 3 to §2A-209. It tells us that the irrevocable and independent obligation of the lessee is the price it pays for the pass through rights it gains against the supplier under that section.

For two straightforward if not terribly exciting examples of the power of §2A-407 to hold the lessee to its obligation to keep on paying no matter what, see *Wells Fargo Bank N.A. v. Brooks America Mortgage Corp.*, 419 F.3d 107 (2d Cir. 2005), and *Xerox Corp. v. Graphic Management Services, Inc.*, 959 F. Supp. 2d 311 (W.D.N.Y. 2013).

Notice that the self-executing hell-or-high-water clause is not made a part of any "consumer lease" via §2A-407. For the definition of *consumer lease*, see §2A-103(l)(e). What if the parties to a consumer finance lease draft their own hell-or-high-water clause? Is it enforceable as part of the actual explicit agreement of the parties? Or is it unenforceable as some kind of overreaching by the financing agent in a consumer transaction? The drafters of Article 2A tell us that this section does not address the issue. See Comment 6.

8. Benny will be stuck with whatever legal effect is given to the disclaimer in the supply contract, as governed by Article 2 principles. His rights against Acme arise from the workings of §2A-209, and that section is clear that whatever rights pass through to the lessee, pass through warts and all. See the last phrase of subsection (1) and Comment 1. Again we see the relevance of the advance notice criterion of §2A-103(1)(g)'s definition. If the lessee in the finance lease situation is to be stuck with the effective disclaimers and limitations negotiated by the supplier and agreed to by the lessor, he or she must have an opportunity to know about them before signing the lease.

Table of Statutes

Index